# The Twentieth-Century Performance Reader

*The Twentieth-Century Performance Reader* has been the key introductory text to all types of performance for over fifteen years. Extracts from over fifty practitioners, critics and theorists from the fields of dance, drama, music, theatre and live art form an essential sourcebook for students, researchers and practitioners.

This carefully revised third edition offers focus on contributions from the world of music, and also privileges the voices of practitioners themselves ahead of more theoretical writing. A bestseller since its original publication in 1996, this new edition has been expanded to include contributions from:

Bobby Baker; Joseph Beuys; Rustom Bharucha; Anne Teresa de Keersmaeker; Hanns Eisler; Karen Finley; Philip Glass; Guillermo Gómez-Peña; Matthew Goulish; Martha Graham; Wassily Kandinsky; Jacques Lecoq; Hans-Thies Lehmann; George Maciunas; Ariane Mnouchkine; Meredith Monk; Lloyd Newson; Carolee Schneemann; Gertrude Stein; Bill Viola.

Each extract is fully supplemented by a contextual summary, a biography of the writer, and suggestions for further reading. The volume's alphabetical structure invites the reader to compare and cross-reference major writings on all types of performance outside of the constraints and simplifications of genre, encouraging cross-disciplinary understandings.

All who engage with live, innovative performance, and the interplay of radical ideas, will find this collection invaluable.

**Teresa Brayshaw** is Director of Performing Arts at Leeds Metropolitan University. She teaches, directs and performs in a wide range of international performance contexts, and is co-editor of Training Grounds, located within the international journal *Theatre, Dance and Performance Training*.

**Noel Witts** is Emeritus Professor of Performing Arts at Leeds Metropolitan University, and was the founder and first Director of the Department of Performing Arts at De Montfort University. He has been a commentator on theatre for the BBC, has served as an Arts Council advisor for 20 years and has written widely on theatre, including most recently *Tadeusz Kantor* (Routledge). He was a founding member of the journal *Performance Research*.

# The
# Twentieth-Century
# Performance
# Reader

3rd edition

Edited by

Teresa Brayshaw
and
Noel Witts

Routledge
Taylor & Francis Group

LONDON AND NEW YORK

Third edition published 2014
by Routledge
2 Park Square, Milton Park, Abingdon, Oxon OX14 4RN

Simultaneously published in the USA and Canada by Routledge
711 Third Avenue, New York, NY 10017

*Routledge is an imprint of the Taylor & Francis Group, an informa business*

First edition published by Routledge 1996
Second edition published by Routledge 2002

*British Library Cataloguing in Publication Data*
A catalogue record for this book is available from the British Library

*Library of Congress Cataloguing in Publication Data*
The twentieth century performance reader / edited by Teresa Brayshaw and Noel Witts. — [3rd edition].
    pages cm
Includes bibliographical references and index.
1. Performing arts.  I. Brayshaw, Teresa.  II. Witts, Noel, 1937–
PN1584.T84 2013
791–dc23

2013003422

ISBN: 978-0-415-69664-7 (hbk)
ISBN: 978-0-415-69665-4 (pbk)
ISBN: 978-0-203-12523-6 (ebk)

Typeset in Bell Gothic
by Graphicraft Limited, Hong Kong

MIX
Paper from
responsible sources
FSC www.fsc.org   FSC® C013604

Printed and bound by CPI Group (UK) Ltd, Croydon, CR0 4YY

This edition is dedicated to all those readers who, over the years, have realised that performance is not something that can be defined precisely, but is a constellation of practices, many of which overlap and combine to produce new forms. This book simply suggests some of the twentieth-century artists who have contributed to the idea of performance as a shifting phenomenon that opens eyes to new worlds.

We would like to acknowledge the major contribution made to the first and second editions of this book by Michael Huxley, one of the first two joint editors.

# Contents

# CONTENTS

# CONTENTS

# CONTENTS

# Acknowledgements

Acknowledgements

WE NEED TO THANK a variety of people who have helped us by way of advice and expertise: Jonathan Pitches, Rachel Krische, Simon Murray, Neil Mackenzie, Constantin Chiriac, Richard Demarco, Claire MacDonald, Claire Hind, Alex Kelly, Oliver Bray, Gillian Dyson, Mark Flisher, Pete Brooks, Anna Fenemore, and many others.

But above all we wish to thank Talia Rodgers and Ben Piggott, of Routledge, who have borne with our delays, re-thinks, and general time-scale problems, with good humour and patience.

We gratefully acknowledge permission to publish extracts as follows:

'Interview' with Marina Abramovic from *Art into Theatre: Performance, Interviews and Documents*, by Nick Kay. Published by Routledge, 1996.

'The Speed of Change' (Interview with Laurie Anderson) from *Theaterschrift* 1(1). Reproduced by kind permission of Tom Stromberg.

'Actor, Space, Light, Painting' from *Adolphe Appia: Texts on Theatre*, published by Routledge, 1993.

'Theatre and Cruelty' from *Theatre and its Double* and *Twentieth Century Polish Theatre* © Calder Publications. Reprinted by permission of Alma Classics.

## ACKNOWLEDGEMENTS

Bobby Baker 'Diary Entries' from *Art, Not Chance: Nine Artists' Diaries*. Reproduced by kind permission of Bobby Baker.

'Words or Presence' from *The Floating Islands: Reflections with Odin Teatret*, by Eugenio Barba. Reproduced by kind permission of Eugenio Barba.

'Not How People Move but What Moves Them' from *Pina Bausch–Wuppertal Dance Theater, or, The Art of Training a Goldfish: Excursions into Dance*, edited by Norbert Servos. Reprinted by kind permission of Maria Schmidt.

'Acting Exercises: Notes for a Primary Lesson' from *The Life of the Theatre: The Relation of the Artist to the Struggle of the People*, by Julian Beck. Published by Limelight Editions, 1986. Reproduced by kind permission of Judith Malina.

'What is Epic Theater?' from *Illuminations*, by Walter Benjamin, © 1955 by Suhrkamp Verlag, Frankfurt a.M., English translation by Harry Zohn, copyright © 1968 and renewed 1996 by Houghton Mifflin Harcourt Publishing Company, reprinted by permission of Houghton Mifflin Harcourt Publishing Company. All rights reserved.

'Speech upon receiving an honorary doctorate degree' reprinted from *Joseph Bueys in America*, by Joseph Bueys. Available from Art Books International, an imprint of The Perseus Books Group. Copyright © 1997. Reproduced with permission.

'Notes on the Invention of Tradition' from *Theatre and the World: Performance and the Politics of Culture*, by Rustom Bharucha. Published by Routledge, 1993.

'The Theater as Discourse' from *The Theatre of the Oppressed*, by Augusto Boal, translated by Charles A. and Maria-Odilia Leal McBride, published by Pluto Press. Reproduced by permission of the publishers and of Theatre Communications Group.

'Short Description of a New Technique of Acting which Produces an Alienation Effect' from *Brecht on Theatre*, edited and translated by John Willett. Translation copyright © 1964, renewed 1992 by John Willett. Reprinted by permission of Hill and Wang, a division of Farrar, Straus and Giroux, LLC, and of Methuen Drama, an imprint of Bloomsbury Publishing PLC.

'Edited Transcript of an Interview with Trisha Brown' from *Contemporary Dance: An Anthology of Lectures, Interviews and Essays with Many of the Most Important Contemporary American Choreographers, Scholars and Critics*. Reproduced with permission from Abbeville Press.

'Four Statements on the Dance' from *Silence: 50th Anniversary Edition*, © 1961 by John Cage. Reprinted by permission of Wesleyan University Press.

'Current Trends' and 'The Director as Partly Actor' from *Copeau: Texts on Theatre*, edited and translated by John Rudlin and Norman H. Paul, first published by Routledge, 1990. Reproduced by permission of the publishers.

'The Actor and the Über-Marionette' from *On the Art of the Theatre*, by Edward Gordon Craig. Published by Routledge 2008.

'You have to love dancing to stick to it' from *Changes: Notes on Choreography*, by Merce Cunningham. Reproduced by kind permission of the Cunningham Trust.

Anne Teresa de Keersmaeker 'Interview' from *Dance Theatre Journal*, Vol. 9(1), Summer 1991. Reproduced by kind permission of David Hughes.

'The Dancer of the Future' from *The Art of Dance*, by Isadora Duncan. Published by Routledge.

'Some Remarks on the Situation of the Modern Composer', by Hans Eisler. Reproduced by permission of Daniel Pozner/The Stephanie Eisler Estate.

'On Performance Writing' from *Certain Fragments: Contemporary Performance and Forced Entertainment*, by Tim Etchells. Published by Routledge, 1999.

'Hello Mother' and 'It's My Body' reprinted from *A Different Kind of Intimacy: The Collected Writings of Karen Finley*, by Karen Finley. Available from Thunder's Mouth Press, an imprint of The Perseus Books Group. Copyright © 2000.

'How to Write a Play', by Richard Foreman from *Reverberation Machines: The Later Plays and Essays*. Reproduced with kind permission of the author.

Liner notes from the booklet from the Philip Glass album titled *Einstein on the Beach*, courtesy of Sony Music Entertainment.

'Performance Art from Futurism to the Present' from *Performance Art from Futurism to the Present*, by RoseLee Goldberg. © 1979 RoseLee Goldberg, reprinted by kind permission of Thames & Hudson Ltd, London.

'The Art of Camouflage' from *Dangerous Border Crossers: The Artist Talks Back*, by Guillermo Gómez-Peña. Published by Routledge, 2000.

'The Creature from the Black Lagoon' from *39 Microlectures: In Proximity of Performance*, by Matthew Goulish. Published by Routledge, 2000.

'Graham 1937', by Martha Graham, from *The Vision of Modern Dance*. Reproduced by kind permission of the Graham estate.

ACKNOWLEDGEMENTS

'Statement of Principles', by Jerzy Grotowski. Reproduced by kind permission of Mario Biagini and Thomas Richards.

'Of the Futility of the "Theatrical" in the Theater' © Alfred Jarry, 1985 from *Selected Works of Alfred Jarry*, Methuen Drama, an imprint of Bloomsbury Publishing.

'On Stage Composition' from *The Blaue Reiter Almanac*, edited by Wassily Kandinsky and Franz Marc. © 1974, reprinted by kind permission of Thames & Hudson Ltd, London.

'The Theatre of Death: A Manifesto', by Tadeusz Kantor, from *Twentieth Century Polish Theatre*, edited by Bohan Drozdowski. © 1980, reprinted by permission of Alma Classics Ltd.

'Interview with Elizabeth LeCompte' from *Art into Theatre: Performance, Interviews and Documents*, by Nick Kay. Published by Routledge, 1996.

'The Theatre of Gesture and Image' from *Theatre of Movement and Gesture*, by Jacques Lecoq, edited by David Bradby. Published by Routledge, 2006.

'Prologue to *Postdramatic Theatre*' from *Postdramatic Theatre* by Hans-Thies Lehmann. Published by Routledge, 2006.

'Robert Lepage in Discussion with Richard Eyre' reproduced from *Platform Papers 3: Robert Lepage*, published by the National Theatre, London, 1992, with permission.

'The Founding and Manifesto of Futurism' from *Marinetti: Selected Writings*, by F.T. Marinetti, edited by R.W. Flint, translated by R.W. Flint and Arthur A. Coppotelli. Translation copyright © 1972 by Farrar, Straus and Giroux, LLC. Reprinted by permission of Farrar, Straus and Giroux, LLC.

'First Attempts at a Stylized Theatre' © 1978, *Meyerhold on Theatre*, Methuen Drama, an imprint of Bloomsbury Publishing.

'Building up the Muscle of the Imagination' from *Collaborative Theatre: The Théâtre Du Soleil Sourcebook*, edited by David Williams. Published by Routledge, 1998.

'Process Notes on *Atlas*', pp. 171–174 from *Meredith Monk*, edited by Deborah Jowitt. © 1997 The Johns Hopkins University Press. Reprinted with permission of The Johns Hopkins University Press.

'19 Answers by Heiner Müller', reproduced by permission of Performing Arts Journal, New York.

'Lloyd Newson in Conversation with Jo Butterworth', reproduced by kind permission of Jo Butterworth.

'Epic Satire' © Erwin Piscator & H. Rorrison, 1980, from *The Political Theatre*, Methuen Drama, an imprint of Bloomsbury Publishing.

'A Quasi Survey of Some "Minimalist" Tendencies in the Quantitatively Minimal Dance Activity Midst the Plethora, or an Analysis of *Trio A*' from *Work 1961–73*, by Yvonne Rainer. Reproduced by kind permission of Yvonne Rainer.

'How Did Dada Begin?' from *Dada: Art and Anti-Art*, by Hans Richter, translated by David Britt. © 1965 Thames & Hudson. Reprinted by kind permission of Thames & Hudson Ltd, London.

'The Five Avant-Gardes or . . . or None?' from *The Future of Ritual: Writings on Culture and Performance*, by Richard Schechner. Published by Routledge, 1995.

'Man and Art Figure', pp. 17–32 from *The Theater of the Bauhaus* © 1961, by Oskar Schlemmer. Translated by Jerry Wensinger. Reprinted with permission of Wesleyan University Press.

'Meat Joy', pp. 61–62 from *Imaging Her Erotics: Essays, Interviews, Projects*, by Carolee Schneeman. © 2001 Massachusetts Institute of Technology. Reproduced by permission of the MIT Press.

'Theatre in African Traditional Cultures: Survival Patterns' © Wole Soyinka, 1993, from *Art, Dialogue and Outrage: Essays on Literature and Culture*, Methuen Drama, an imprint of Bloomsbury Publishing.

'Composition as Explanation' from *Look At Me, Here I Am*, by Gertrude Stein. Reproduced by permission of Peter Owen.

Stelarc 'Interview with Nicholas Zurbrugg' reproduced by kind permission of Anthony Zurbrugg.

'The Visionary Landscape of Perception' as published in *Reasons for Knocking at an Empty House: Writings 1973–1994*, in association with the Anthony d'Offay Gallery, London, 1995. Transcript of the original version presented in August, 1989, as part of a panel discussion at the 2nd Video Television Festival at Spiral Hill, Tokyo, and first published in *Delicate Technology*, eds. Video Gallery SCAN (Fujiko Nakaya) and I&S (Tokyo: Video Television Festival Organizing Committee, SCAN, 1989), 129–48. Also published as 'Perception, Technology, Imagination, and the Landscape', in *Enclitic* 11(3), July 1992, 57–60, and as 'Perception, technologie, imagination et paysage', in *Trafic 3*, Summer 1992, 77–82.

## ACKNOWLEDGEMENTS

Robert Wilson 'Interview' from Laurence Shyer, 'Robert Wilson: Current Projects', in *Theater*, Vol. 14, no. 3: 83–98. Copyright, 1983, Yale School of Drama/Yale Repertory Theatre. All rights reserved. Reprinted by permission of the publisher, Duke University Press. www.dukepress.edu

BOOK

# How to Use This Book

THIS BOOK CAN BE USED in many ways.
It contains extracts of conversations, scores, essays, notes, manifestos, proposals, perspectives and reflections from 59 key twentieth-century performance figures. These voices are presented in the book in alphabetical order.

The book can be:

- read from cover to cover or dipped into
- used to cross-reference other sources
- used as an introduction to key twentieth-century performance practitioners
- used to reflect upon those people, practices and provocations that we may already be partially familiar with
- used as a site of comparison and connection
- used as a source of inspiration for further reading, writing, making, creating and reflecting

There are, as one might expect, numerous themes and principles that emerge, when considering the book in its totality. When time is taken to absorb the information contained within the pages, certain connections and relationships become foregrounded. What follows are some insightful examples of thematic connections which have emerged for us as we have re-read the extracts and developed a deeper relationship with the material.

We hope that our readers, according to their reading and research styles, will find a similar degree of pleasure, and make their own

discoveries and insights as they mine the collection of performance-related material contained within the book.

## On methodology . . .

It takes a long time to find the vocabulary I'm looking for since I don't have an established system to work from. (De Keersmaeker)

Perhaps the hardest task facing us was the need to create a new collaborative model with an unusual division of labour specific to the project. We had to learn to trust each other's sensibilities and decisions. (Gómez-Peña)

I believe there are no techniques. There are methods, and every director has one, maybe an unconscious one. I believe I have one, but I do not know it. I love to listen, and I love to watch the actors – with a passion. I think that's already a way of assisting them. They know that I never tire of listening to them, of watching them, but how do I help them? I don't know. (Mnouchkine)

The process of making a piece is very much like a quest: you start out in the dark; you have a sense of the potential that opens out before you; there is a sense of danger because no one has gone this way before; you follow clues, listen to instincts, look for what is needed; soon, the way becomes apparent as more and more layers are added in and the piece takes on its own life. (Monk)

I only create when I have something to say, and the work is generally about issues that concern or affect my life at a given time. I'm interested in provoking myself, questioning my own and the performers' thoughts motivations and assumptions. (Newson)

It's so frustrating because I feel that the answers are already there in my mind but I don't know the questions to lead me to them. I imagine acting it out and then the scenes just evolve before my eyes. I imagine how exactly I will say the words and what my general demeanor will be. After I've worked out a section I stop and put it away until the next time it comes to the front of my mind. (Baker)

I try to look at things well, not to change them. That's not my job . . . I don't think the purpose of art is to make this a nicer, more civilized world. (Anderson)

Well I think we're all still holding back. It's quite natural because after all we want to be loved and liked. And I think there is something that holds you back somewhere. You think that there's this point and if you go beyond that then there's no exact telling where it will lead. (Bausch)

In a living theatre, we would each day approach the rehearsal putting yesterday's discoveries to the test, ready to believe the true play has once again escaped us. But the Deadly Theatre approaches the classics from the viewpoint that somewhere, someone has found out and defined how the play should be done. (Brook)

I think there's an important word that has lost its sense in the theatre, and that's the word 'playing'. It's become a profession, a very serious word, but the concept of playing has disappeared from the staging of shows. The only way you can attain these ideas is if you play. (Lepage)

The best participants have been persons not normally engaged in art or performance, but who are moved to take part in an activity that is at once meaningful to them in its ideas yet natural in its methods. (Kaprow)

If an actor of the old school wished to move the audience deeply, he would cry out, weep, groan, and beat his breast with his fists. Let the new actor express the highest point of tragedy just as the joy and grief of Mary were expressed: with outward repose, almost coldly, without shouting or lamentation. He can achieve profundity without recourse to exaggerated tremolo. (Meyerhold)

Except in struggle, there is no more beauty. No work without an aggressive character can be a masterpiece. Poetry must be conceived as a violent attack on unknown forces, to reduce and prostrate them before man. (Marinetti)

# On meaning . . .

That's not what I'm about. My meaning is the piece itself. I'm not going to now make meaning separately from that piece for you. Again it's not a thing where I'm withholding that — I don't have it. It only happens for me in the space. In the moment of the theatrical act. (LeCompte)

We are not, in these dances and music, saying something. We are simpleminded enough to think that if we are saying something we would use words. We are rather doing something. The meaning of what we do is determined by each one who sees and hears it. (Cage)

You know it's like being told stories when you were a child, or when kids tell stories. Very often there was no logical line in them, it's more the case of lots of different categories of things got thrown in together and you didn't worry if they didn't all fit together in a realistic sense. It's just that juxtaposition of different emotional layers that changes your perception. (De Keersmaeker)

I refuse to admit that the dance has limitations that prevent its acceptance and understanding – or that the intrinsic purity of the art itself need be touched. The reality of the dance is its truth to our inner life. Therein lies its power to move and communicate experience. (Graham)

The dancer's experience becomes the answer. The answer becomes the dance. The dance becomes the experience. The experience takes as long as it takes. It repeats and it rotates, and it repeats. The experience deserves 'respect' in the sense of the word's original Lain meaning 'to look twice'. For, as the great slow thinker Pina Bausch has said, 'We must look and look again'. (Goulish)

The result of choreography that goes beyond what the audience is familiar with is that you find out what you can do, what your own personal limitation edges are. In that arises the possibility of doing that which is not interesting to your audience, not up until now thought of as acceptable to an audience. (Brown)

But clarity is the lowest form of poetry, and language, like all else in our lives, is always changing. Our emotions are constantly being propelled by some new face in the sky, some new rocket to the moon, some new sound in the ear, but they are the same emotions. (Cunningham)

Our work delves into how individuals relate to one another, emotionally and intellectually, rather than being about movement or design patterns per se; exploring the individual's actions, and looking at how these in turn reflect political and social issues. (Newson)

And when we consider art forms from the point of view of survival strategies, the dynamics of cultural interaction with society become even more aesthetically challenging and fulfilling. (Soyinka)

Theatre must rediscover its true meaning in this spectacle of a temptation, where life stands to lose everything and the mind to gain everything. (Artaud)

NO! The experience shouldn't ADD to our baggage, that store of images that weighs us down and limits our clear view to the horizons. The art experience should rather (simply) ELIMINATE what keeps us moored to hypnotizing aspects of reality. (Foreman)

Theatre only has a meaning if it allows us to transcend our stereotyped vision, our conventional feelings and customs, our standards of judgement – not just for the sake of doing so, but so that we may experience what is real and, having already given up all daily escapes and pretences, in a state of complete defenselessness unveil, give, discover ourselves. (Grotowski)

This understanding of ritual, as a process applying to a great range of human activities rather than as something tethered to religion, is a very important development. (Schechner)

One of the original sources of all philosophy is the paradox of the hard and the soft: the body and the soul; the outer physical world and the world of thoughts and images within. This is one of the great mysteries of life, and the good thing about mysteries in the classic sense is that they don't have to be solved, only experienced. (Viola)

When the progression of a story with its internal logic no longer forms the centre, when composition is no longer experienced as an organizing quality but as an artificially imposed 'manufacture', as a mere sham of a logic of action that only serves clichés (something Adorno abhorred about the products of 'culture industry'), then theatre is confronted with the question of possibilities beyond drama, not necessarily beyond Modernity. (Lehmann)

## On audience . . .

I could only define the ideal viewer in negative terms. I just think people should stop making sense. (De Keersmaeker)

Audiences crave for something in the theatre that they can term 'better' than life and for this reason are open to confuse culture, or the trappings of culture, with something they do not know, but sense obscurely could exist – so, tragically, in elevating something bad into a success they are only cheating themselves. (Brook)

We are also inclined to forget that the printed play is not a finished piece of work until it is played on the stage by actors and brought to life by genuine human emotions; the same can be said of a musical score, it is not really a symphony until it is executed by an orchestra of musicians in a concert. (Stanislavski)

IT IS NECESSARY TO RECOVER THE PRIMEVAL FORCE OF THE SHOCK TAKING PLACE AT THE MOMENT WHEN OPPOSITE A MAN (THE VIEWER) THERE STOOD FOR THE FIRST TIME A MAN (THE ACTOR) DECEPTIVELY SIMILAR TO US YET AT THE SAME TIME INFINITELY FOREIGN, BEYOND AN IMPASSABLE BARRIER. (Kantor)

I mean – it's like the audience is *there*. They're the air that you breathe. The audience is the other part of the exploration process for theatre. There is no theatre without audience, so there is no life without breath. It's that essential. But it's an involuntary thing, breathing. And my awareness of the audience is almost always involuntary. Sometimes I'm conscious of it. (LeCompte)

Most audiences and critics want to be moved, knocked out. That is a sign of their illness, blindness, need to remain children. Most audiences want a perceivable, nameable content. That is, they want to be able to reduce the experience of the work to a gestalt of some sort that they can carry away from the theatre with them. (Foreman)

We say, 'They come here to relax, they don't want to think.' But it's not true. I believe in the intelligence of the audience, I believe that the audience wants to create. You have to give the audience food, not things that are already masticated and organized and painted. (Lepage)

## Towards definition . . .

Performance, like dreaming presents us with intersections. In a performance a performer is not a single entity. Instead of a unit, a performer is an identity in motion in a particular direction. (Goulish)

Perhaps our first subject was always this inadequacy of language. Its unsuitability for the job it has to do, its failure. And in this failure — by definition language is not and cannot express what it seeks to describe — an admission of the struggle in everyday life — to get blunt tools to do fine work, to carve out a life in, around, despite of and through what passes for culture in the late twentieth century. (Etchells)

In the software age we are beginning to model ourselves on information processing and not on machine construction. Limitations become merely local boundaries defined by lack of adequate translations and transformations. And just as the presence of human beings in a specific place over long periods of time creates a story, the electronic image landscape is beginning to create a layering of mental archeology. This is the world we are learning to inhabit as images become our tools. (Viola)

It does in fact have something to do with consciousness, with bodily consciousness, and the way we form things. But then it needn't have this kind of aesthetic form. It can have quite a different form and still be dance. (Bausch)

To understand dance for what it is, it is necessary we know from whence it comes and where it goes. It comes from the depths of man's inner nature, the unconscious, where memory dwells. As such it inhabits the dancer. It goes into the experience of man, the spectator, awakening similar memories. (Graham)

Each art has its own language, that is, its own methods. Each art is something complete in itself. Each art leads a life of its own. It is an empire in itself. (Kandinsky)

The only thing that is different from one time to another is what is seen and what is seen depends upon how everybody is doing everything. This makes the thing we are looking at very different and this makes what those describe it, it makes a composition, it confuses, it shows, it is, it looks, it likes it as it is, and this makes what is seen as it is seen. (Stein)

There is an anthropological determination of everybody's existence to be an artist in society. Then one can see that the rule of structure, the formulation and the forming and the sculpturing of the constitution of the future has to go through free individuals and has to come from the grass roots in cooperation of all people together. (Beuys)

Our intention is to affirm this life, not to bring order out of chaos nor to suggest improvements in creation, but simply to wake up to the very life we're living, which is so excellent once one gets one's mind and one's desires out of its way and lets it act of its own accord. (Cage)

Criticizing the course of a river means improving it, correcting it. Criticism of society is ultimately revolution; there you have criticism taken to its logical conclusion and playing an active part. A critical attitude of this type is an operative factor of productivity; it is deeply enjoyable as such, and if we commonly use the term 'arts' for enterprises that improve people's lives why should proper art remain aloof from arts of this sort? (Brecht)

The rallying cry must be – stop making objects that men can worship. Art shouldn't add new objects to the world to enslave men. It should begin the process of freeing men by calling into doubt the solidity of objects – and laying bare the fact that it is a web of relations that exists, only; that web held taut in each instance by the focal point of consciousness that is each separate individual consciousness. (Foreman)

I think the purpose of art is the free expression of the artist, whatever that might mean. (Anderson)

The performance might be a series of intimate gestures or large-scale visual theatre, lasting from a few minutes to many hours; it might be performed once only or repeated several times, with or without a prepared script, spontaneously improvised, or rehearsed over many months. (Goldberg)

Theatre means the collectively spent and used up lifetime in the collectively breathed air of that space in which the performing *and* the spectating take place . . . The theatre performance turns the behavior on stage and in the auditorium into a *joint text*, a 'text' even if there is no spoken dialogue on stage or between actors and audience. Therefore, the adequate description of theatre is bound to the reading of this total text. (Lehmann)

This act could be compared to an act of the most deeply rooted, genuine love between two human beings – this is just a comparison since we can only refer to this 'emergence from oneself' through analogy. This act, paradoxical and borderline, we call a total act. (Grotowski)

I have regularly challenged what is traditionally defined as dance. Issues rather than prettiness or aesthetics are important. (Newson)

At Judson, the performers looked at each other and the audience, they breathed audibly, ran out of breath, sweated, talked things over. They began behaving more like human beings, revealing what was thought of as deficiencies as well as their skills. (Brown)

But, and there's no question about it, the theatre is not supposed to represent psychology but *passions* – which is something totally different. (Mnouchkine)

Perhaps the theatre is not revolutionary in itself; but have no doubts, it is a rehearsal of revolution. (Boal)

I abhor a world which is regulated from the cradle to the grave. I prefer the dark to the dazzling light. Darkness is the best symbol for light. There is no way that one can understand the nature of light if one never observes deeply the darkness. A proper understanding of both requires that both their inherent natures be truly understood. (Hijikata)

## Artists' statements . . .

Whenever we work physically we find things that we never could find if we did nothing but think. All the time knowing that without living physically the powers of the mind diminish. (Beck)

Let us understand each other, however: it is not by killing oneself with exhaustion that one becomes creative. It is not on command, by forcing, that one opens oneself to others. Training is not a form of personal asceticism, a malevolent harshness against oneself, a persecution of the body. Training puts one's own intentions to the test, how far one is prepared to pay with one's own person for all that one believes and declares. (Barba)

I like the edges. Where you tip over the edges, I like the limits, working at the limits. Where you stay on and where you fall over or beneath it or off it. It's the notion of danger I think, of how much you can grasp. Of how happy you are to grasp things or to let them go. (De Keersmaeker)

Technology has always been part of the human trajectory. Technology is not an alien other. To be human is to be augmented, extended and enhanced by technology. Plugged-in, the body becomes a parasite sustained optically and stimulated electrically by an external and virtual nervous system. (Stelarc)

Indeed, no other artistic form of expression has such a boundless manifesto, since each performer makes his or her own definition in the very process and manner of execution. (Goldberg)

The task of art is to find what heretofore does not delight us, and make that part of some kind of composition in such a way that delight results. (Foreman)

To express what is the most moral, healthful and beautiful in art – this is the mission of the dancer, and to this I dedicate my life. (Duncan)

You have to love dancing to stick to it. it gives you nothing back, no manuscripts to store away, no paintings to show on walls and maybe hang in museums, no poems to be printed and sold, nothing but that simple fleeting moment when you feel alive. It is not for unsteady souls. (Cunningham)

The dancer of the future will be one whose body and soul have grown so harmoniously together that the natural language of the soul will have become the movement of the body. The dancer will not belong to a nation but to all humanity. (Duncan)

The dancer, through the butoh spirit, confronts the origin of his fears: a dance which crawls towards the bowels of the earth. I don't believe this is possible with European dance. (Hijikata)

While the arts do not create change, they register change . . . Dance need not change – it has only to stand revealed. (Graham)

Do away with the actor, and you do away with the means by which a debased stage-realism is produced and flourishes. No longer would there be a living figure to confuse us into connecting actuality and art; no longer a living figure in which the weakness and tremors of the flesh were perceptible. (Craig)

And what is there to see in an old picture except the laborious contortions of an artist throwing himself against the barriers that thwart his desire to express his dream completely? . . . Admiring an old picture is the same as pouring our sensibility into a funerary urn instead of hurling it far off, in violent spasms of action and creation. (Marinetti)

Hello Society –
No answer.

Hello America –
No answer. (Finley)

There is no point in filling our heads with a lot of new ideas and rushing on the stage to exploit them before we have learned the elementary rules. That kind of student will lose his head, he will either forget his science or think about it to the exclusion of everything else. Science can help art only when they support and complement each other. (Stanislavski)

Those who are creating the modern composition authentically are naturally only of importance when they are dead because by that time the modern composition having become past is classified and the description of it is classical. (Stein)

Let us hope for a dramatist who replaces or eliminates the director, and personally takes over the directing; rather than for professional directors who pretend to be dramatists. (Copeau)

I work with what they tell me, with what they feel is correct. It's very much a collaboration. I really like working with a dramaturg and I think they're underestimated – in terms of my work anyway. (Wilson)

How does the dream divide from the body; how does the body divide from the dream? I can't answer, but as a performer, I know that I have my own body and my own dreams, and the bodies of others and the dreams of others. In order to continue, I need them all. (Goulish)

This act could be compared to an act of the most deeply rooted, genuine love between two human beings – this is just a comparison since we can only refer to this 'emergence from oneself' through analogy. This act, paradoxical and borderline, we call a total act. (Grotowski)

We shall arrive, eventually, at what will simply be called the *House*: a sort of cathedral of the future, which in a vast, open and changeable space will welcome the most varied expressions of our social and artistic life, and will be the ideal place for dramatic art to flourish, *with or without spectators*. (Appia)

There should never be any soulless or feelingless words used on the stage. Words should no more be divorced from ideas there than from action. On the stage it is the part of the word to arouse all sorts of feelings, desires, thoughts, inner images, visual, auditory and other sensations in the actor, in those playing opposite him and through them together in the audience. (Stanislavski)

Hard for me to understand, having never much cared for punctuation.

I mean I'd rather say: Here are 26 letters:

a b c d e f g h i j k l m n o p q r s t u v w x y z

Now write a text for performance. (Etchells)

I have a real difficulty writing prose. I don't believe in literature as a work of art to be read. I don't believe in reading. I couldn't imagine writing a novel. Writing prose you are all alone. You can't hide yourself. (Müller)

Seen from this perspective, it might even be predicted that the situation will completely reverse itself: the stage designer will develop optical phenomena and will then seek out a poet who will give them their appropriate language through words and musical sounds. (Schlemmer)

The stage is still raised, but it no longer rises from an unfathomable depth; it has become a dais. The didactic play and epic theatre are attempts to sit down on a dais. (Benjamin)

And last, but not least, among the emblems of our time are the new potentials of technology and invention which we can use to create altogether new hypotheses and which can thus engender, or at least give promise of, the boldest fantasies. (Schlemmer)

# Noel Witts and Teresa Brayshaw

## INTRODUCTION: A CANON OF TWENTIETH-CENTURY PERFORMANCE

### PART 1: Noel Witts

This is the latest revised edition of this book, which was first published as long ago as 1996. The idea then, as now, was to allow readers to access key writings by twentieth-century performance practitioners that expressed their ideas about performance in their own words. The reader would be able to compare ideas, styles, key concerns across the wide field of performance, which included primarily theatre and dance artists, with one or two composers who we felt had made a major contribution to stage performance. In the second edition of the book, published in 2002, we wished to include the critical and theoretical perspectives on the field of performance that had been developed since 1996, and that edition contained a number of key theoretical writings. Since 2002 access to theory about performance has become much wider, and for this new edition we felt that the priority once again should go to writings by artists themselves, since some key figures who we omitted from the first and second editions should now join what we now perceive as being the 'canon' of performance in the twentieth century.

It has been encouraging to see the steady demand for this book, which is a unique collection of writings, from readers all over the world, a demand that reflects the perspective of many who see the ways in which previously discrete disciplines such as 'dance', 'drama', 'theatre' have merged and fed off each other in the last 20 years.

Consequently artists such as, for example, the UK company DV8, are crossing these boundaries in their work, while the visual artist Bill Viola now uses performative elements as key frameworks for his work. But there are also many ways in which historically visual artists have moved into, or used performance, many of whom we did not include in the two previous books. Artists such as Kandinsky, Beuys, the Fluxus movement, now seen as key, are once again present in the perspective of performance makers, and we felt the need to acknowledge this. We still include the major essay by RoseLee Goldberg, which was one of the first accounts of these phenomena, and we include other chroniclers such as Hans-Thies Lehmann. We also, from the perspective of 2011, felt the need to restore some figures who we had omitted from the second edition. All of this simply reflects our perception of the ways in which performance is now taught, studied and created, producing works of hybridity that some of the Western press, at least, finds difficult to deal with. Thus, for example, many of the London-based critics continue to see 'theatre' as being the traditional hierarchy of writer, director, actor, ignoring the less classifiable work of Forced Entertainment, Blast Theory, or Lone Twin.

As in the first edition we publish the writings in alphabetical order, thus allowing the reader to choose what is most relevant to his/her interests. But for those who wish to look at this material from an historical perspective we include the chronology at the back of the book, which enables this interest to be explored. We continue to point out what we see as the common interests and ideas that link many of these artists.

Looking back at the twentieth century it is notable how many of the major performance figures saw a need to write about their work, as if the ephemerality of performance needed some kind of written explanation, which would ensure that their ideas lived on for future generations. There are as differing voices in the writing as there are in the performance work created. Thus Stanislavski leaves a method with practical exercises in his books, while Tadeusz Kantor felt the need to write almost always in manifesto form, which often screams his disillusion. Yet Kantor's work, through the dissemination of his recorded legacy, has become of greater interest in recent years in educational and creative institutions. Figures such as Brecht, Artaud, Craig and Cage felt a need to leave behind essays, systems, manifestos, while others' views have to be accessed through interviews, where the perspective of the interviewer often controls the tone. In these cases we have had to choose carefully to give what we feel are the most important perspectives. It is interesting to chart the decline in writing about one's own performance concerns which has happened as the century progressed. In fact essay writers such as Tim Etchells of Forced Entertainment, and Matthew Goulish of Goat Island are now the exceptions. At the other end of the spectrum there is now much critical writing *about* all these figures, a collection of which would, and probably does, form another book.

One of the developments that helps us in 2012 is the increase in the availability of performance material via the internet. It is now possible to access the work of the Living Theatre, for example, via YouTube, which means that many of the ideas expressed in writing can now be seen in practice. Examples of dance works are easily seen, and the expansion of the DVD performance world means that even the most remote material can be seen in some recorded form. This throws up the question as to whether the writings or the documentation are most important, from which we conclude that writing often gives a reflective angle which can complement any documentation, so that, for example, Craig's often elliptical prose gives us a whole other perspective on the frustrations of his practice.

In earlier editions we felt a need to try to define and differentiate the field of 'performance' from other fields, as when we first published a book of performance writings we felt we needed to proselytise our view that many of the then divisions into visual art, drama, dance, theatre were becoming artificial as artists were crossing boundaries as a matter of course. We talked about performance as 'a contested space' which needed to be negotiated carefully. Since then the field of performance has been accepted, has broadened, the links with the visual arts have been made more obvious, the decline of the traditional categories made clearer, the old creative hierarchies broken down. Books with titles such as *Live: Art and Performance*[1], *Perform or Else*[2] or simply *Performance*[3] have validated our 1986 claims. But it is still interesting and encouraging that a book of 'performance' writings is still relevant; and that we are still providing a unique reading experience for practitioners, emerging artists, and the general reader.

## PART 2: Teresa Brayshaw

The first editions of this book have been used extensively by students, scholars and practitioners as a site of both reference and inspiration. In 1996, when the first edition was published, Mike Huxley and Noel Witts described the idea of this book as coming from a need to help the students on the BA (Hons.) Performing Arts course at the then Leicester Polytechnic to map out the multidisciplinary perspectives present in the field. Having been one of the students on that remarkable degree programme, back in the 1980s, I feel implicated in the reason for its creation. So, it is with a healthy degree of both reflection and gratitude that I, together with Noel Witts, undertook the revision and worked on the updated version we now present.

This revised edition of *The Twentieth-Century Performance Reader* has been updated and revised to include more of the key voices and figures who helped to shape the field of performance in the last century and as a result significantly impact upon the way we now understand the world and our place within it.

> In 1949 it was all very vague – nobody knew what Dada was, and nobody knew very much about Italian Futurism or Russian Futurism. I had to visit the artists themselves before I finally discovered the true art of the twentieth century.
>
> (Henri Chopin)[4]

So in the spirit of 'visiting the artists themselves' we present a revised collection of voices who articulate in diverse ways and in their own words what has been important in terms of making performance. It's a story of how key ideas and practices have found their way into mainstream practice.

When RoseLee Goldberg pointed out back in 1979 that, in dealing with performance history there is no use pretending to record every performer in the twentieth century, but instead to pursue the development of a sensibility, she was reminding us of the creative and playful possibilities available to us in our roles as editors and chroniclers.

> I believe that performance art is such a visceral art form that it allows for multiple points of entry — some are intellectual, but some are spiritual or emotional.
>
> (Guillermo Gómez-Peña)[5]

There is something about collecting together the thoughts, ideas, scores and strategies for performance making, which enables a level of reflective understanding of both the achievements of the contributors and a more informed realisation of the social and historical contexts in which they were working and living. The book becomes a kind of lens through which we are invited to (re)consider that which we may already know.

In our work at universities and festivals over the last 15 years, since this book was first published, we have seen a proliferation of degree programmes across Europe and America that focus in various ways upon performance. Music, Theatre, Dance, Live Art and Performance Studies students are increasingly encouraged to locate their investigations within interdisciplinary contexts. Training methodologies, performance and compositional strategies, audience responsibilities (expectations) and new technologies have called into question the means by which students of performance now orient themselves in relation to identifying a position in the field. Performance, as it is now constituted, has expanded rapidly over the last decade and with the massive increase in books on the subject as well as access to the internet, the sheer scale of information available to students, researchers and scholars can feel overwhelming.

In his book *Performance: a Critical Introduction*, Marvin Carlson observes that performance is 'an essentially contested concept'.[6] Nowhere is this more prevalent than in the range of performance study opportunities available in the UK where the number of university courses available to prospective students of theatre, dance and performance at both undergraduate and postgraduate levels has proliferated massively in the last 15 years.

Students can study Theatre with Law; Theatre with Tourism; Theatre with French, Spanish, German, Portuguese; Theatre with Theology, Sociology, Psychology; Theatre with International Politics; and even Theatre with Sport, Exercise Science and Criminology.

Or they can study various courses with the terms 'contemporary', 'art', 'theatre' and 'performance' in the title. Some of these courses involve varying degrees of the following practices – scenography, movement training, digital practices, autobiographical performance, live art, creative writing, dramaturgy, devising, physical theatre, sound art, performance art, body-based practices, performing in second life, critical writing, film making, event making, as well as activities with titles that people may be more familiar with – like acting, directing, writing, producing. In responding to developments in interdisciplinarity, student demand and technological developments, the academic and professional fields of performance have exploded.

This reader has been revised with all this in mind and can be used as both a temporary anchor to a lineage of practitioners who have been involved in asking questions about performance over the last 100 years, as well as a compass that can help to navigate direction within a stationary frame of reference.

The process of re-reading the material in the last two editions as well as the research undertaken for deciding which revisions to make is akin to the artistic practice of tracing. To trace means both to go over and to discover by investigation. When tracing paper is placed onto a picture, the picture is easily viewable through the tracing paper. Thus, it becomes easier to find edges in the picture and then to see shapes and discover form and content. Tracing is also an embodied process that enables us to directly connect in a 'hands on' way to the subject matter. It's a process of making visible. So we hope that the structure of the book, which continues to list practitioners in alphabetical order, rather than through any other categorisation, provides the good visibility needed to provide a clear and unobstructed view.

Performance is my strategy for becoming visible.

(Guillermo Gómez-Peña)[7]

## Which voices to include?

It's a fascinating part of the editorial process deciding which voices to include in this edition. And although this reader has never attempted to offer a comprehensive coverage of the whole history of twentieth-century performance, by virtue of a selection process, it does automatically exclude significant practitioners and innovators. We choose to focus though, on those voices which, for one reason or another, have made themselves heard to us, through our own research, our teaching and the insights we've gleaned from our students who have been collaborating with us through feeding back their reflections on the performance works they've encountered in live and documented forms.

The process of updating this reader has also involved the selection of practitioners who are currently still in the midst of creative processes and of developing methodologies and strategies for the realisation of their artistic endeavours and performance works. We also recognise the responsibility of comparing living artists, whose bodies of work have only really established over the last 20 years in the later part of the twentieth century (particularly when we have witnessed that development, sometimes at close quarters, e.g. Newson, Finley, Gómez-Peña, Baker, etc.), with those for whom we see much more of a clear impact from the earlier part of the century.

The more recent artists do not yet have the weight of history by which to assess longevity of impact – and so we are left partly imagining the legacy rather than remembering or tracing it.

## The vain attempt to categorise . . .

> It is no surprise that Performance has a baffling diversity. We might expect contradiction in a space such as this . . . a crowded contradictory space, written through with more histories than one can imagine.
>
> (Tim Etchells)[8]

> Many of the artists listed here might well find the categories of poet, composer, performance artist or filmmaker to be equally applicable to their work, or might prefer . . . dancer, choreographer, storyteller, public artist, or installation artist . . . or sound poet? or Fluxus artist? or painter? or composer? or typographer? or publisher? or theoretician?
>
> (Nicholas Zurbrugg)[9]

> Misinterpretation and mistranslation are essentially contemporary experiences.
>
> (Guillermo Gómez-Peña)[10]

> The history of Performance Art in the twentieth century is the history of a permissive, open-ended medium with endless variables.
>
> (RoseLee Goldberg)[11]

> Most performers talk about their work, what they do, what they value in it, and indeed much performance material has begun to be described as 'statement' or 'action', or 'a piece' or simply 'work', as if the performers themselves feel the need to de-categorise.
>
> (Huxley and Witts)[12]

The pedagogical dimension of the new material included in this revised edition is worthy of special mention since our intention is to provide an extended resource for students and the general reader. Many of the artists included in this book also hold posts at universities and academies, as professors, readers and research advisors as well as the more traditional role of visiting artist (Etchells, Finley, Gómez-Peña, etc.). The gradual shift within academia over the last decade towards a model that recognises both the creative process and pedagogy as viable sites for the development of new knowledge, has been achieved in part by a cultural redefinition of practice as research where artists, in some contexts, are seen as knowledge-holders who are expert in their field and should have that practice included in developing research agendas.

It's interesting to note, from our experience inside the academy, that the current concerns in emerging contemporary performance making revolve around the creation of new works for festivals and specific sites, contexts and audiences. Additionally there is a rise in the use of autobiographical material, one-to-one encounters, large-scale interactive encounters and events, new technology and a genuine attempt to connect with ideas of ecology and sustainability. In parallel we are seeing more and more dialogue between artists from the theatrical mainstream and artists from the independent sectors, and programmers and curators are forging new partnerships and new ways of working by actively profiling experimental practice. The experiments and risks taken by those artists in the last century, many of whom are cited in this book, are having an impact upon the current generation of creative practitioners. The contexts are different, the agendas appear less transparent, but there is real reason to be optimistic as we path-find our way into the next decade of the twenty-first century.

We have long considered whether we should, as in previous editions of this book, provide a general bibliography of performance. Whereas in previous editions it has been the book or article that has been the main research resource, now we have the vastly increased resources of the digital age. This would have meant adding to any booklist the many websites that now allow access to performance material of a variety of types. For this reason we have added some websites to the further reading sections following each chapter, in the hope that simply typing in an artist's name will bring up a variety of contemporary resources for further study. An increased book/website list would have taken up space that we judged would be better devoted to artists' writings. Source details for each of the 59 main texts can be found in their accompanying contextual summaries, along with further references specific to the individual artists or authors.

## Notes

1 Heathfield, A. (ed.) (2004) *Live: Art and Performance*, New York: Routledge.
2 McKenzie, J. (2001) *Perform or Else: From Discipline to Performance*, London and New York: Routledge.
3 Goldberg, R. (2004) *Performance: Live Art Since the 60s*, London and New York: Thames and Hudson.
4 Zurbrugg, N. (ed.) (2004) *Art, Performance, Media*, Minneapolis: University of Minnesota Press.
5 Thackara, T. (2011) 'Interview with Guillermo Gomez-Pena' in *Art Practical* 2.15.
6 Carlson cites Strine, Long and Hopkins from their 1990 survey article 'Research in Interpretation and Performance Studies: Trends, Issues, Priorities', who use W.B. Gallie's term 'essentially contested concept' in relation to performance. In Carlson (1996) *Performance: A Critical Introduction*, London and New York: Routledge.
7 http://www.hemisphericinstitute.org/artistprofiles/lpnostra/pocha_PerformanceChronology_2008_ENG.pdf
8 Etchells, T. (1997) 'Valuable Spaces: New Performance in the 1990s' in Childs, N. and Walwin, A. (eds) (1997) *A Split Second of Paradise: Live Art, Installation and Performance*, London: Rivers Oram Press.
9 Zurbrugg, N. (ed.) (2004) *Art, Performance, Media*, Minneapolis: University of Minnesota Press.

10  Thackara, T. (2011) 'Interview with Guillermo Gomez-Pena' in *Art Practical* 2.15.

11  Goldbery, R. (2011) *Performance Art: From Futurism to the Present,* London and New York: Thames and Hudson.

12  Huxley, M. and Witts, N. (eds) (2002) *The Twentieth-Century Performance Reader,* 2nd edition, London and New York: Routledge.

# Chapter 1

# Marina Abramovic

## INTERVIEW

*What was it that brought you to performance?*

It was very simple in a way. At the age of twelve I had already had an exhibition of work. Painting was very attractive to me. I know that I started painting the sky. First the clouds, then removing the clouds – just a kind of blue monochrome. At one point, looking at the sky, I saw the planes passing and leaving this white track, which was almost like a drawing. I was so impressed with this that I wanted to make a kind of concert. What I was interested in was that you could see the process – you could see things happening and dissolving all at the same time. So I went to the military base and asked for fifteen planes – and they sent me home. They asked – do you know how much this will cost?

Then, for some time, I did projects on paper, drawings of the sky, using fire, ice, and water. None of these projects were possible, basically because of the restrictions on things. Then I started shifting my interests to the idea of sound – like putting the sound of a bridge falling down every three minutes with an actual bridge. As you cross the bridge you hear the sound of the bridge breaking. This kind of shift. I realised a piece with one house in the middle of Belgrade. I placed speakers on a house and played the sound of the house falling down. This installation occurred for only one day – because everybody in the neighbourhood reacted very violently. It reminded them of the war and they removed it.

*What date was this?*

This was all around '68, '69, '70 to '71. I was interested in changing visual and acoustic information. My last one was in the

Cultural Centre in Belgrade. This was a place — a kind of hall — where people waited to go to the theatre, the cinema. They could have a coffee, sit, read a newspaper. It was a meeting place. I placed speakers there with the sound of an airport. It was a very cold, specific sound, telling all the passengers immediately to go to Gate 242 because the plane was leaving to Tokyo, Bangkok, and Hong Kong. I mean, at Belgrade there were only two gates at the time — and every few minutes there would be this information. So everybody waiting there became imaginary passengers, waiting for this trip. It was a way of going out. Yugoslavia during this time was really quite difficult. I was dealing with structures — socially, politically, culturally, you know, family. Everything was involved.

*Did the work put you into difficulty?*

Extremely. And that gives you a lot of energy later on. But its hard at the time, because you are rejected — to the point of questioning whether or not you should be put into a mental hospital.

After the sound work, there was a natural development toward work with the body. The effect on me from my first performance with the body was almost a state of shock. I had such a strong experience that I knew almost immediately it was the only way I could really deal with the public — because through it I could come to an ecstatic state. I could never reach this when I was just alone in the studio with my work.

*What was the first performance?*

The first performance with the body was *Rhythm 10* — the work with the knives. And — I don't know — the reality of the thing was a kind of immediate transmission of energy — the directness of the media and also the temporality, because it is only when you are there — the rest is just a memory. All this made such a strong impact. Painting, the illusional system, just didn't get to the point.

---

RHYTHM 10

The Content of the Action

1    I put a sheet of white paper on the floor
2    I put twenty knives of various sizes and shapes on the paper
3    I switch on the tape recorder
4    I varnish my left hand nails with blue nail varnish

The Action

I take a knife and stab it between two fingers of my left hand. Every time I cut myself I take another knife. When I have used all the knives (i.e.

---

change of all the rhythms), I switch on the tape-recorder reproducing the recorded sound of the Action. Then I switch on another tape-recorder.

The second part of the Action consists of repeating the game while listening to the recorded sound-rhythm of the knives. Following the rhythm of the knives' stabs I bring myself into the tempo of the previous rhythm, stabbing simultaneously with it.

I switch on the second tape recorder where the rhythm of the stabs has been doubled.

Marina Abramovic, *RHYTHM 10* (1973) (courtesy of the artist).

Also, theatre was an absolute enemy. It was something bad, it was something we should not deal with. It was artificial. All the qualities that performance had were unrehearsable. There was no repetition. It was new for me and the sense of reality was very strong. We refused the theatrical structure. The performances were always in an empty space with no lights, and even the video recording was one-to-one. I would ask for the camera to be put in one static position, and then left.

*Were you aware of performance work outside of Yugoslavia at this time?*
Not at the beginning. A few years later at Edinburgh I met Joseph Beuys for the first time, as well as Tadeusz Kantor and Hermann Nitsch. Then, it was like – there's a family, we were the same tribe. So it was very, very good.

*Were any particular performances by other artists important to the development of your work?*
I like Vito Acconci's work very much. He was one of the first to propose that the body is a place. His works are aggressive, but not in a physical way. It is more mentally. And from this came the whole idea of the body as a material, the body as a material through which you can transmit something. In sculpture it is the stone or clay or whatever, and here it is the body – make a drawing with the body, cut the body, open it, see what pain is, what the body is. Just exploring all the possibilities – the mental, physical limits, everything together. So Acconci began this kind of research.

After that, there was a very important event with Acconci, Dennis Oppenheim and Terry Fox in the seventies, when they performed in the same place [*Environmental Surfaces: Three Simultaneous Situational Enclosures*, Reese Palley Gallery, New York, January 1971]. Acconci turned around like a clock for one hour [*Second Hand*], Terry Fox was making bread from soap [*Celler*] – it was a kind of impossible, alchemical mystery. Oppenheim had a tarantula moving toward his face down a tube and he blew little balls of hair in its way, keeping it from biting his face [*Extended Armor*]. It was really good work. Then Chris Burden – very radical. Like the shot to his arm [*Shoot* (1971)], the crucifixion on the Volkswagen [*Trans-fixed* (1974)], the piece where he put electricity and water on the floor and left it up to the public to decide what would happen [*Prelude to 220, or 110* (1971)]. To me, they're very important pieces. Then with Gina Pane, the milk piece, when she drank milk and spat it out, irritating her system until she actually spat out a mixture of milk and blood – like the two liquids in the body [*Le Lait Chaud* (1972)]. Then Charlemagne Palestine and the *Body Music* [*Body Music I* (1973) *Body Music II* (1974)]. It was absolutely charismatic, shamanistic. Even now – and even though the tapes of this period are of such bad quality – they give you more energy than many live performances.

*What was it that brought you to the work with Ulay?*

It was very much to do with love. Also, I'd come to a point in my life when I was going very far in my performances. I was always considering – really – going to the point of playing Russian Roulette in the performance situation. I could see the chance that I'd kill myself, that I'd die. So it was, I suppose, also at that time a lucky solution. I just treated my body as if it was without limits. In my life there was a very strong male aspect. In all the performances there were a lot of strengths – the force, energy, or whatever. And meeting Ulay – at one point it went back to a female energy because he was the male. Then there was the idea of the hermaphrodite as the perfect human being, you know, who has both sexes and is self-sufficient. And of the two bodies coming into one. To me this was one step farther than just doing your own work. It was very important. Then, we absolutely stopped doing any of our own work and for twelve years we only did the work together. So when we finished our relationship, it was a big problem for me to go back to my own work, because I felt it was a regression. It was going back again.

---

### MARINA ABRAMOVIC AND ULAY

*How long will a performance of Nightsea Crossing be on any given day?*

U: By preference seven hours a day. We adopted a seven hour day because most institutions would be open for seven hours.

MA: 10.00 am until 5.00 pm. The seven hours was also important because we wanted to avoid people seeing the beginning and end. When they come to the gallery we are already there, like any other piece. And when they go at 5.00, the gallery is closed and the guard comes and tell us it's the end. The public only see one image.

U: Which is a motionless image. They do not see us sitting down or standing up. You see, the main interest is the process of being motionless for a long, long period of time. The fact of sitting on the chair is not as interesting as the process. After sitting for two, three or four hours, something happens. And that process is only possible for the audience or the spectator, again, if they are willing to sit too.

MA: I think the public wants to see a beginning and they want to see an end.

*Did you state that you would be sitting motionless for the duration of the performance?*

MA: No. So people are always waiting for something to happen. But when they finally come to realise that that's the reality of the thing, they start making contact with the piece itself. In *Nightsea Crossing*, after ten, fifteen, forty-eight hours, the whole space is charged with energy. And that energy affects you. To charge a space with energy needs a long time. After ten or twenty days the energy in the space becomes so dense from the repetition of the same thing that people get really affected. Something has changed — and it's not of the material world.

U: We never rehearse performances. In fact, the beginning of the perform-ance is when we enter our own physical and mental construction. It's the first time that we've experienced that — as it is for the spectator. And it is an experience that can go in very different directions. You see, we are very aware of the spectator, and we work with the spectator. We work for the spectator, through our consciousness. We don't sit and daydream, we are not in a trance. We just sit.

*Is it important that the spectator is aware of the context of the particular action they meet — that the performance is extended over 90 days and will occur in so many different places?*

MA: They can know this or not know this. It's not important. It's just the presence, the feeling for each of them. The idea of our sitting is that we're present in that moment with the mind and the body. What you see is exactly what is happening. And that is *the* reality. There are very few who can actually sit and just be without putting a story into the mind. In that moment, when you sit with the body *and* the mind, you manage to make contact with us, because you're taking the reality as it is without any projections. It's like *now*, it's *now*. And that's what the sitting is about. It's very difficult to be present, because your mind is thinking all the time, every second.

*What were the contexts out of which* Nightsea Crossing *arose?*

MA: The change in our work came when we went to Australia and lived in the desert. The heat was enormous, like 50, 55 degrees Celsius. Physically, you could not walk. We were in such circumstances that, actually, only our minds were functioning. And that completely opened another world to us. That connected straight into certain functions. It's almost physical, the mind. In our performance we had just reached the point where we could not go farther with the body, and now we have the whole other part of the mind.

*I'm interested in the use of objects and symbolism in the performance.*

MA: We are very impressed by the rituals of certain people, like the Aborigines, because they have a certain pattern of doing things, of using symbols in a way that they really function.

U: We have been trying to integrate certain symbols into our work. You see, the symbols natives use all have a very practical function. They're very practical. I think the symbols — the material, the colour, the shape, the placement of the symbol, and the approach to the symbol, has to be perfect. Then the symbol will be able to generate power. But only if it is perfect. If it is placed in the right time and the right place, and if the symbol itself consists of a certain kind of material and shape and form and colour. Then it can work. I mean, if you abuse a symbol it can bring harm.

MA: Yes, very much.

*In what way?*

U: I think, if you are exposed, if you are seriously busy with symbols and like to place them and like to give them function and you respect that function in a certain way, then you should be very serious about it. I have respect for symbols, because I have witnessed natives operating with symbols and how powerful a symbol can be.

MA: You see, the natives are completely connected with the earth's energy and the flow of nature. And from that they generate the whole thing. And in the simple way that we work, we work to be receptive to this.

U: I think that certain faculties which we call 'supernatural' in natives are faculties that are dormant in us —

MA: And for them they're natural.

U: For them it's a natural reality. It's a part of their daily existence.

MA: We feel, as performance artists, that we can't paint any more, because we really believe that objects are an obstacle. If you make an object, you put all your generating energy into the object. In the past, that was why many objects had this radiant energy, this power. But now, for many people the work is personal, because we don't really know the source, so the object simply becomes an obstacle. It's much more important to transform yourself first. Work on yourself. And afterwards you won't need the object to transmit the real idea – or whatever you want – the truth. You can do the work with just the power of your mind. You can transmit certain things, just directly, mind to mind. We don't have anything between us.

*And your work and relationship with Ulay ended at the culmination of the Chinese Wall walk.*

That was that. Saying goodbye.

*Was that conceived of as an ending?*

We wanted to have two separate experiences come together to make one work. But the problem was that it took eight years to get permissions from the Chinese Government and in this period our relationship changed completely. We were at the end of our relationship when the Chinese said yes. So the only way that we could do it was to end. It was like the perfect form for this scenario, for ending the relationship. It was dramatic and it was painful – everything together. And then, after this, the only way I could find things out was to create work which was actually directly to others.

*So has the way you consider the audience changed? Or the way you consider the work?*

The work. Now, the product that I give to the audience is for them to use. Before it was one-to-one, and now it's me and everybody else in relation. It is not closed.

*Does that take you back into installation work?*

No. I have two functions. One function – I'm always working with transformation. I have to transform something. So, the performance is one way of transforming work, in certain stages, psychologically, and going to another type of reality. Really, performance is to do with change and transformation. And some of those witnessing this could go with this. But the public always, until now, have had this role of being voyeurs, of not actually participating. They are always at a distance. But it is a time, now, especially at the end of the century, for the public to take a completely active part. So I'm building these kinds of objects. I don't call them sculptures, I call them transitory objects. They are almost like scenography, like a kind of floor, like a platform on which one can experience the quality of the material simply with the mind and the body, and go through this transformation.

*It always seemed to me that that opening up was implicit in* Nightsea Crossing *whereby, in watching, the viewer was participating – the viewer was actually doing what you, as the artists, were doing in the performance.*

Yes. Exactly. That's the seat of the thing. It's really interesting – but I want more from the public. Duchamp always said that to understand the work of art, the public has to be creative as well. We always forget this part. The public have to go with it. The more participation, the more energy there is, the farther I can go. The public's understanding is crucial. If all you have is distance, it is like an impasse.

---

MA: We are now engaged in the biggest project of our lives – which is the walk of the Chinese Wall. And the walk in China will deal with the exposure to the elements.

U: You know the concept?

*That you will walk towards each other, from each end of the wall, over a period of one year – photographed by satellite –*

U: And we will collect materials, using the oldest technique of copying reality, of imprinting. And satellite photography is the most advanced technology of documenting. So we will use this too.

MA: The Wall is 5,000 kilometres long, from the Gobi desert to the sea. So it is exactly between the elements of fire and water – one part of the Wall starts in the sea and one finishes in the desert. And the start of the wall is called the Dragon-Head and on the door to the wall is written 'The First Path on Earth' and on the other one is 'The Heroic Path to the Sky'. So Ulay will start at The Heroic Path to the Sky and I will start at The First Path on Earth and we will actually meet in the middle, going through the four seasons like four stages of life. The idea is that we are going to be exposed for one year to those forces. And with that will come a certain mental and physical transformation – through that walk. And that is the experience that we will give to the public afterwards. You see, you must work on your own change in order to give. And the walk is actually such a preparation – for that change.

U: I think it's very important that after the Chinese walk, we will be exposed again to an audience – an audience which will be invited for talks and discussions. I think the whole model of this relation between the

---

initiator – a person of particular experience – and an audience, the whole concept, is of a very special kind.

MA: We have been working a lot with the male and female principle – not just presenting our egos or our real relationship, but acting as a kind of example for the principle itself. So, you see, the Wall represents the female principle – the female as it is materialised at the Dragon-Line is water, while the male principle is represented as air. The Dragon-Head is the male and the Dragon-Tail is the female. So that, actually, I will be walking as a female on the male part, and Ulay will be a male walking on the female part of the Wall, and the coming together is the unifying of the principle of the mental and the spiritual.

*So, again, it's a taking on of a ritual function.*

MA: Yes. Not to be the 'I', but just to be part of the natural principle and to make that exchange. It's a de-personalisation. That's why they use masks in ritual – so that they leave the person behind and become *the* element.

U: I look for so much in art. But I think it's important to subtract.

MA: If you subtract you come to the point where you can really see the essence of the thing, where everything starts. You can see the roots of what you're doing. To me, the experience of Rothko paintings is really very, very strong. He really worked with essence.

U: Maybe not too many people have the courage to take away. It feels almost natural to all of us living in a time of a materialistic philosophy to add. We only have respect for goods, for cargo, for objects. I don't think too many people have the courage to renounce, because by subtracting you're making more space for other people. So I think by being very quiet, no action, that it is a good thing.

MA: And the Chinese Wall is, you know, it's a pioneering – it's just a very small step to count, maybe, in this lifetime, I don't know – but this is what we're trying to do.

U: You see, for non-English speaking people, as we are, the term 'perform-ance' exists only in the visual arts context. But I think, besides an art-work, 'performance' can indicate a great moment of behaviour or concentration. The point is, if you do the performance for an extended period of time, then its effect is much greater. Art is nothing but a vehicle. It has its limits. And often it is very limited. But still it may be – Kandinsky would say – a mighty agent. And I agree with that. In the earlier days, I approached art as

> the realisation of art. I was looking for a focus, and once I had a focus it would absorb me. There's a process in which you're totally involved, and then there's the product. Later on, though – actually it was in the desert – I started to become much more interested in the art of realisation. Rather than the realisation of art, the art of realisation.

So the time passes, and after all this time I find I'm fascinated by the theatre structure.

*How do you mean?*

I've made two theatre pieces. The first is called *Biography*. In it I play my life in the theatre, with all the performances I've done and video clips in one hour and twenty minutes. The second piece is called *Delusional*, which I play with 400 rats live on the stage.

*Biography* is the perfect structure – artist, performer, plays her own life. Why should I trust anybody else to play my own life? So in the piece I mix real performance art with the theatrical. It's a very interesting structure. Like the star that I cut with a razor blade, I cut one more time, in the theatre – and it's real. It's not fake blood, it's the real thing. The public is in total shock because they're so used to this symbolic language of the theatre. With the knife piece, *Rhythm 10*, I play it live, but I play it for five minutes, and I reach an incredible intensity. I have to shrink the performances in time and play one performance after another like a video clip, but with real intensity.

It took a great deal of courage for me to do this. When I played *Biography*, it was like a cleaning process, because I could not talk to Ulay at all for six years after we split. There was a lot of pain. And when I say goodbye to Ulay in this *Biography*, I really mean goodbye. It is a public statement too, that I have finished with this period of my life. And then I called him and I told him, you know. It's fine – but now he will come to Antwerp to see it.

Then there's the second piece, *Delusional*. This is another kind of cleaning process. This is to do with my time in Yugoslavia. The basic point of this piece was the notion of shame, shame of what's happening right now. I was thinking of what you don't show in public because you're ashamed – it's the most vulnerable and the most difficult and incredibly heavy kind of pressure on yourself, to show what you're ashamed of in front of the public. So the whole piece is about that. And I think those events are for me a kind of metaphor for the ending of this century, the rights over protecting territory – I mean it's really hell in our society.

*Looking at your performance, there seems always to have been a tremendous flow between your life and your work. The performance appears to be a kind of revelation of disciplines and experiences you're in any case engaged with.*

Yes. But every true artist is like that. I think that you have to come to a synthesis. You always have to start from yourself, but in the process the product that comes to the public has to be, kind of, transcendental and general. It has to become everybody else. But it starts with the personal, always. There is no other way. That's what you understand the best. You can't go from somebody else's problems. It's just not right. So the deeper you go into yourself, actually, the more universal you come out on the other side.

What happened to me was – I always wanted to leave. I had an obsession with travelling, in moving from place to place. Right now, I'm getting to the point where people say, well, where are you staying? And I can't tell. Every five or six days it is somewhere else. I have spent the last fifteen years like this, and I'm not going to change. That's the reality. I'm not fixed in one special place. And I think I keep with me all this Yugoslavia, you know, whatever this thing is, because you can't go away from those things. Wherever you go you bring these things and you add something else because of the interaction with other countries. Things change, and I'm not afraid of things changing. I absorb it into my work. I am going to Oxford next year, and I will give four lectures. Four different things. And the last one will be on art and travelling. Just this idea of the artist as a nomad, a modern nomad who doesn't belong to any nationality or any particular culture, but is a mixture of everything. And my main concept is the 'space in-between'. You know, the time when you leave one country – you've called everywhere, you take the plane, you go to the train station, to wherever. And then you go somewhere else. But before you arrive, that space in-between – that's the space where it is most intense. It's the space where you're open, where you're sensitive, vulnerable – and anything can happen. And another space I propose is the waiting space. We always consider waiting as losing time, but waiting is extremely important. It is where we need to put emphasis, because to wait is to deal with doing nothing. Doing nothing is exactly what it's all about. Cage says, we have to go to boredom, only through boredom can we come to another side. So the space in-between and the waiting space – that is where it happens.

■   ■   ■

## Source

Kaye, N. (1996) 'Marina Abramovic', *Art into Theatre*, Amsterdam: Harwood: 180–192.

## Marina Abramovic (1946–)

Marina Abramovic was born in Belgrade in 1946 to parents who were partisans in the Second World War. She trained at the Academy of Fine Arts in Belgrade from 1965 to 1970 and then studied as a postgraduate in Zagreb. She began presenting time-based work in Belgrade in the 1960s and in 1973 started teaching at the Academy of Fine Arts in Novi Sad, developing her work into performance and video. In Amsterdam in 1975 she met the German artist F. Uwe Laysiepen, known as Ulay, with whom she collaborated over twelve years, producing performances, videos and films shown widely in Europe and America. Most of these works presented both mental and physical intensity often developed to an extreme over extended periods of time. In 1976, for example in *Relation in Space* their two bodies crashed into each other over an hour at increasing speed; the following year found them for seventeen hours sitting back to back, their long hair tied together *(Relation in Time)*. The relationship ended in 1988 with *Lovers: Walk on the Great Wall*, where, having started at opposite ends of the Wall they finally met on a bridge in Shaanxi Province where they ended their long relationship.

Provocation is a constant characteristic of Abramovic's works, both in the political and the cultural sense, and she is therefore in a line of artists from the Futurists to Stelarc who have used deliberate provocation to persuade their audiences to reflect on issues. Abramovic's work owes something also to that of Joseph Beuys in its willingness to explore extremes, and its theatricality stems from the examination of everyday movement taken to the edge. There are times when there is a resemblance to some of the extreme movement of Pina Bausch in pieces such as *Café Müller (1978)*. Abramovic has said, 'I only learn from what I fear most', and this could be said to be at the core of the response she wants from audiences.

In this interview with Nick Kaye she talks about her performance history with some examples of the texts of her performances.

## Compare this interview with writings by the following authors in this reader

**Bausch** – who in a more tempered way uses action and movement to extremes in her dance/theatre pieces.
**Hijikata** – whose Butoh form also uses themes of cruelty, darkness and perversion
**Kaprow** – who may be said to be the father of the provocative happening
**Marinetti** – the futurist who wished art to provoke politically
**Stelarc** – another artist of extremes

## Further reading

Abramovic, M. (1994) *Biography*, Germany: Cantz Verlag.
Danto, A., Iles, C. and Biesenbach, K. (2010) *The Artist is Present*, New York: MOMA.
Goldberg, R. (1998) *Performance, Live Art Since the 60s*, London: Thames and Hudson.
Iles, C. (1996) 'An Interview with Marina Abramovic', *Performance Research*, Vol. 1 No. 2.
MacRitchie, L. (1996) 'Marina Abramovic: Exchanging Energies', *Performance Research*, Vol. 1 No. 2.
Richards, M. (2010) *Marina Abramovic*, London: Routledge.

# Chapter 2

# Laurie Anderson

## THE SPEED OF CHANGE

*After your 'Home of the Brave' tour you released a new record, 'Strange Angels.' A new performance 'Halcion Days' for Sevilla Expo '92 is in the pipeline. This performance will also be given later in Berlin (Hebbel-Theater) and Frankfurt (Theater am Turm). You have also started to give talks at a number of universities in America. Can you tell me more about this series of events?*

Instead of doing a music video for the album 'Strange Angels,' I chose to do a series of public service announcements about various political situations. During the last year I have been presenting a long talk entitled 'Voices From The Beyond' which is the most overtly political work I have ever done. I'm not even sure it's art anymore. It goes back and forth between story-telling and advocacy. So far I have given more than 20 such talks. A number of universities have invited me to talk to their students. During these events I don't sing and I don't show videos. All I do is project one slide and talk. The subjects I talk about deal with time going backwards. People believe in a kind of countdown ending in the year 2000. They all stare at the three zeros at the end of this number. I have more and more doubts directly connected with this countdown. Sometimes people need important signs because so many things have happened during the past two years. You have to realize that in the United States there are a lot of 'fundamentalists' who believe that in the year 2000 they will all be joining Jesus Christ. The holy city of Jerusalem, all the Americans flying out of their cars at midnight, as it were, to join Jesus

Christ straight off. Sixty million people in the United States are fascinated by the idea that at the end of this century God will come down to earth to drag all Christians away, to take them with him on the spot, whether they are busy telephoning or doing I don't know what. And even more people believe in hell and punishment.

*Well, all this sounds as though you are making tirades, which also has a negative ring to it.*

Yes, they are tirades, but I try to be realistic, not negative. However, it is interesting to see how people react to my talks. For example, I try and talk about the fact that ever since the Gulf War the United States has only had one news broadcasting service. What happened to ABC and all the other broadcasting stations? They have all been supplanted by CNN. The whole world is filtered for us by CNN.

*Have you been very preoccupied with the Gulf War and the discussions surrounding it?*

Yes. There have been so many arrangements with the American military. Just like in every war the military pursue a well-defined aim. Part of it consists in dictating to broadcasting stations how the war is to be reported, what language to use when and where. Therefore, the whole world has been listening to news broadcasts straight out of the Pentagon.

During the Gulf War it was almost impossible for anyone to object to policy or tactics. The war was presented of course as a drama, an advertisement, a show complete with super graphics and a thunderous patriotic soundtrack. It was already in post-production while it was still happening. Nobody complained for the same reason that moviegoers don't jump up during a movie and shout things like, 'Lousy plot!' If you complained you had to disguise it as yet another form of entertainment, like the musicians who got together to record 'Give Peace A Chance' and then announced that maybe they were for the war, maybe not, but they just felt like singing the song anyway. Now that the patriotic frenzy and the victory parades are history, the war can be discussed. It is now seen by many people as a cynical attempt to draw attention away from pressing economic problems. This does not mean that this kind of hysteria couldn't happen again. Far from it. As the hearings on sexual harassment proved, Americans love televised sex and power soap operas especially if they are happening in real time.

*That's where your tirades start?*

No, it's not that I beat people over the head saying: 'Look, didn't you realize, didn't you ask?' Actually I am a patriot. I believe that Americans are basically compassionate people.

*You are moving away from huge pop concerts and gigantic shows?*

Yes. At the moment I am working on a different level. That's why I'm more interested in working with small theatres and in small halls. At the universities I only project a single slide and talk and talk. People expect music and high-tech visuals. I think they're surprised that I'm asking them to think so much instead. As a storyteller, I find this really exhilarating. I can make lots of quick jump-cuts . . . move things around.

In Kurt Vonnegut's latest book one of the protagonists watches a video showing the Second World War backwards. To watch the Second World War forwards drives people to despair. But this character watches the film backwards. And backwards it is a vision of Utopia. An aircraft flies backwards, backwards over Germany. Bombs fly from the ground to the aircraft as if attracted by a magnet and then they return to America. The things I am working on have got this kind of dynamic. The speed of change. In another book I have read the author claims that terrorists are the only true artists. They are the only people capable of changing anything. Interesting theory.

*Do you now intend to change the world?*

I try to **look** at things well, not to change them. That's not my job. In the late '60s and early '70s I worked as a political cartoonist for a publication called 'The Street Wall Journal.' I also published pamphlets of my drawings – cartoons about men, women, and power – and handed them out on the street. At the same time, I was working as a sculptor and I saw this as quite separate from my political work.

Gradually politics and art coincided in a series of photo works such as 'Object/Objectivity' (in which I shot photographs of men who approached me – 'Hey, baby!' – on the street) and concerts such as a duet between the United States and Canada performed on the border. Much of my work has been about authority and reactions to authority.

*How do you now integrate your thoughts into your artwork?*

In America freedom of expression is being threatened. I think there is no point in making rules about whether artists should deal directly with these issues or use distance and filters. Both are certainly valid and it depends on the circumstances. In the last couple of years, the world has changed so quickly that it's impossible to absorb the shocks. At the same time, it's been very difficult for me to ignore them and I decided to use this information in performances, like thinking out loud. I didn't feel the need to translate them into songs or images. This would have been impossible. On the other hand, the most dangerous aspect of work that is political is the potential for advocacy and propaganda. I don't think that the purpose of art is to make this a nicer, more civilized world. I think the purpose of art is the free expression of the artist, whatever that might mean.

My idea of form is often an argument or a conversation so I don't have to abandon this dialectic to deal with the shifts between politics and art or between one political idea versus another. In fact, this form is deeply appropriate for the material.

In Vienna, not too long ago, I met the Czechoslovakian minister of Education and the Arts. And he made a suggestion. He had discovered some prehistoric wall-paintings in one of the caves in Czechoslovakia. He invited me to visit this cave and to transcribe these drawings into music. He suggested that I organize a concert in this cave. What makes it so special is the fact that the concert will have to take place in complete darkness because prehistoric men did the paintings in complete darkness. Yes, and I love this project.

*What is the situation like for artists in New York?*

For many artists it is impossible to survive the media offensive. Increasingly, avant-garde artists are being absorbed by it. New York is drained of money. We can't afford to show the new Robert Wilson piece. The avant-garde is the first to go.

*Are you an avant-garde artist?*

Fortunately, I don't have to think about this question. Why don't **you** tell people what I am? I don't even think that people want artists to be defined. But since I've been working on this new project I think that it has more to do with backwards than with forwards. Avant-garde has always been based on speed. And I'm interested in this theme.

*In America, there are a number of artists who use their success and the money they earn from commercial activities to help small theatre groups etc. Willem Dafoe, for example, the famous film actor, plays each night theatre for an audience of 99 people as a member of the Wooster Group.*

I think he's a good example. I really appreciate his loyalty to downtown theatre.

*You once said that art is for people who want to use it. Do you still believe that?*

Yes, I do. There is always a kind of search going on and of course this is expressed in the work of the artist.

*We have talked so much about politics and so little about your art. Now, be honest! If I ask you which you consider to be more important: form or content?*

Inseparable.

*(The interviewer was Tom Stromberg, New York, autumn 1991)*

■  ■  ■

## Source

Anderson, L. (1991, 1992) 'The Speed of Change: Interview with Tom Stromberg', *Theaterschrift* 1(1): 119–130.

## Laurie Anderson (1947–)

American multimedia performance artist. She has worked in many disciplines as performer, musician, singer, photographer, film maker, recording artist, and as a polemicist. Her early stage works included *United States Part I–IV* (1983), a seven-hour performance at the Brooklyn Academy Opera House. She reached a new, wider audience with *Home of the Brave*, which toured the world and was produced as a video of the same name, *The Nerve Bible* (1995) and *Songs and Stories from Moby Dick* (1999). She has recorded her work, including *Big Science* (1982), *United States Live* (1983), *Mister Heartbreak* (1984), *Home of the Brave* (1986), *Strange Angels* (1989) and most recently *Life on a String* (2001). Her music has been used for live dance – Trisha Brown's *Set and Reset* (1983) – and film – Spalding Gray's film *Monster in a Box* (1991).

Anderson's music and her performances embrace both live art and rock music, using the anti-theatrical understatement of the former and the full-blown stage theatricality of the latter to make memorable audio-visual statements. Her work is multi-referential and multilayered and there is a complexity of reference at the level of ideas. *O Superman* (1982) is dedicated to the French composer Massenet, and pastiches lines in his opera *Le Cid*. In *Strange Angels* (1989) she paraphrases Walter Benjamin's (1940) *Theses on the Philosophy of History* – 'history is an angel being blown backwards into the future'. Her most recent work has eschewed her signature use of technology for narrative and the use of traditional instruments.

In this interview she talks about the use of narrative as polemic. The presentation of her work has been simplified, recalling her earlier work, before her large-scale tours. She discusses her place as a US artist and how she uses her position as an artist to comment on her country.

## Compare this interview with writings by the following authors in this reader

**Benjamin** – on whom she draws, and to whom political comparison can be made
**Brown** – with whom she collaborated
**Foreman, Wilson and Lepage** – contemporary North American theatre artists who make visual theatre
**Schlemmer** – comparison with early visual theatre

## Further reading and listening

Anderson, L. (1982) 'Big Science', New York: Warner Bros.

Anderson, L. (1983) 'United States Live', New York: Warner Bros.

Anderson, L. (1989) 'Strange Angels', New York: Warner Bros.

Goldberg, R. (2000) *Laurie Anderson*, London: Thames and Hudson.

Goldberg, R. and Anderson, L. (2000) *Laurie Anderson*, New York: Harry N. Abrams Publishers.

Sayre, H.M. (1989) 'Three Performances', *The Object of Performance: The American Avant-Garde since 1970*, Chicago: University of Chicago Press: 145–155.

http://www.laurieanderson.com

# Chapter 3

# Adolphe Appia

## ACTOR, SPACE, LIGHT, PAINTING

Appia

T HE ART OF STAGE PRODUCTION is the art of projecting into Space what the original author was only able to project in Time. The temporal element is implicit within any text, with or without music . . . The first factor in staging is the interpreter: the actor himself. The actor carries the action. Without him there can be no action and hence no drama . . . The body is alive, mobile and plastic; it exists in three dimensions. Space and the objects used by the body must most carefully take this fact into account. The overall arrangement of the setting comes just after the actor in importance; it is through it that the actor makes contact with and assumes reality within the scenic space.

Thus we already have two essential elements: the actor and the spatial arrangement of the setting, which must conform to his plastic form and his three-dimensionality.

What else is there?

Light!

Light, just like the actor, must become active; and in order to grant to it the status of a medium of dramatic expression it must be placed in the service of . . . the actor who is above it in the production hierarchy, and in the service of the dramatic and plastic expression of the actor.

. . . Light has an almost miraculous flexibility . . . it can create shadows, make them living, and spread the harmony of their vibrations in space just as music does. In light we possess a most powerful means of expression through space, if this space is placed in the service of the actor.

So here we have our normal established hierarchy:

the *actor* presenting the drama;
*space* in three dimensions, in the service of the actor's plastic form;
*light* giving life to each.

But – as you have inferred, there is a but – what about painting? What do we understand about painting in terms of scenic art?

A collection of painted backcloths and flats arranged vertically on the stage, more or less parallel to one another, and extending upstage. These are covered with painted light, painted shadow, painted forms, objects and architecture; all of it, of course, on a flat surface since that is the nature of painting . . .

Our staging practice has reversed the hierarchical order: on the pretext of providing us with elements which are difficult or impossible to realize in solid form, it has developed painted décor to an absurd degree, and disgracefully subordinated the living body of the actor to it. Thus light illuminates the backcloths (which have to be seen), without a care for the actor, who endures the ultimate humiliation of moving between painted flats, standing on a horizontal floor.

All modern attempts at scenic reform touch upon this essential problem; namely, on how to give to light its fullest power, and through it, integral plastic value to the actor and the scenic space.

Our stage directors have, for a long time, sacrificed the physical and living presence of the actor to the dead illusion of painting. Under such a tyranny, it is obvious that the human body could never develop in any normal way its means of expression. This marvellous instrument, instead of sounding in freedom, exists only under severe constraints.

Everyone knows today that the return to the human body as an expressive element of the first rank is an idea that captures the mind, stimulates the imagination, and opens the way for experiments which may be diverse and no doubt of unequal value, but are all directed towards the same reform . . . Yet our contemporary productions have forced us into such a despicably passive state that we conceal it carefully in the darkness of the house. But now, with the current attempt by the human body to rediscover itself, our feeling almost leads to the beginning of fraternal collaboration; we wish that we were ourselves the body that we observe: the social instinct awakens within us, though in the past we coldly suppressed it, and the division separating the stage and the auditorium becomes simply a distressing barbarism arising from our selfishness.

We have arrived at the crucial point for dramatic reform . . . which must be boldly announced: the dramatic author will never liberate his vision so long as he believes it yoked by necessity to a barrier separating the action from the spectator . . . The inevitable conclusion is that the usual arrangement of our theatres must evolve gradually towards a more liberal conception of dramatic art . . .

We shall arrive, eventually, at what will simply be called the *House*: a sort of cathedral of the future, which in a vast, open and changeable space will welcome the most varied expressions of our social and artistic life, and will be the ideal place for dramatic art to flourish, *with or without spectators.*

■    ■    ■

## Source

Appia, A. (1919, 1954, 1993) 'Actor, Space, Light, Painting', *Adolphe Appia: Texts on Theatre*, ed. R.C. Beacham, London: Routledge: 114–115.[1]

## Adolphe Appia (1862–1928)

Swiss designer and philosopher of theatre; the first to write about theatre as a visual art form, where light and shadow, form and space, are as important, if not sometimes more so, than the physical performer. Apia's life was spent writing about, and experimenting with, the technical properties of light and shadow, primarily because of the profound influence of Richard Wagner's cycle of music dramas, *Der Ring Des Nibelungen* (The Ring of the Nibelung), for which he prepared detailed scenic and lighting scenarios which were summarily rejected by Wagner's family after the death of the composer in 1883. He wrote three books on theatre – *Music and the Stage* (1897), *The Staging of Wagnerian Drama* (1895), and *The Work of Living Art* (1921) – as well as numerous articles.

Appia's work has had a profound influence on modern stage design, and his stark blocks of shadow and light were instrumental in helping Wieland Wagner, Wagner's grandson, revive his grandfather's work at the theatre in Bayreuth following the profound and damaging embarrassments of the Nazi canonisation of the composer in the Second World War. Appia's collaboration with the Swiss choreographer Jaques-Dalcroze at Hellerau in the 1910s produced and initiated a whole new approach to movement and scenography, culminating in his production of Gluck's *Orpheus and Euridice* (1913).[2]

This essay represents a good summary of his thinking, concentrating as it does on principles of staging that emphasise the actor within the stage space.

## Compare this article with writings by the following authors in this reader

**Copeau** – a later admirer who also worked with Jaques-Dalcroze
**Craig** – similar concerns and explorations in England and Russia
**Foreman, Wilson and Lepage** – late twentieth-century examples of visual theatre
**Meyerhold** – a concern to see the actor within a scenic frame

**Piscator** – contemporary European view on the aesthetics of staging
**Schlemmer** – theatre spatial experiments at the Bauhaus

## Further reading

Beacham, R.C. (1987) *Adolphe Appia*, Cambridge: Cambridge University Press.
Brockett, O.G. and Findlay, R.R. (1973) *Century of Innovation*, Englewood Cliffs, N.J.: Prentice-Hall.
Volbach, W. (1968) *Adolphe Appia*, Middletown, Conn.: Wesleyan University Press.

## Notes

1    Beacham (1993: 239): 'This is excerpted from an untitled manuscript Appia prepared for presentation on 3 April 1919 at the Olympic Institute in Lausanne, accompanied by slides illustrating his designs. The conference was entitled "the future of drama and stage production"; the title "Actor, space, light, painting" was given to an abbreviated version of Appia's essay after his death.'
2    David Thomas, at Warwick University in 1991, produced a reconstruction of Appia's work.

# Chapter 4

# Antonin Artaud

## THEATRE AND CRUELTY

**W**E HAVE LOST THE IDEA of theatre. And in as much as theatre restricts itself to probing the intimacy of a few puppets, thereby transforming the audience into Peeping Toms, one understands why the elite have turned away from it or why the masses go to the cinema, music hall and circus to find violent gratification whose intention does not disappoint them.

Our sensibility has reached the point where we surely need theatre that wakes us up heart and nerves.

The damage wrought by psychological theatre, derived from Racine, has rendered us unaccustomed to the direct, violent action theatre must have. Cinema in its turn, murders us with reflected, filtered and projected images that no longer *connect* with our sensibility, and for ten years has maintained us and all our faculties in an intellectual stupor.

In the anguished, catastrophic times we live in, we feel an urgent need for theatre that is not overshadowed by events, but arouses deep echoes within us and predominates over our unsettled period.

Our longstanding habit of seeking diversions has made us forget the slightest idea of serious theatre which upsets all our preconceptions, inspiring us with fiery, magnetic imagery and finally reacting on us after the manner of unforgettable soul therapy.

Everything that acts is cruelty. Theatre must rebuild itself on a concept of this drastic action pushed to the limit.

Infused with the idea that the masses think with their senses first and foremost and that it is ridiculous to appeal primarily to

our understanding as we do in everyday psychological theatre, the Theatre of Cruelty proposes to resort to mass theatre, thereby rediscovering a little of the poetry in the ferment of great, agitated crowds hurled against one another, sensations only too rare nowadays, when masses of holiday crowds throng the streets.

If theatre wants to find itself needed once more, it must present everything in love, crime, war and madness.

Everyday love, personal ambition and daily worries are worthless except in relation to the kind of awful lyricism that exists in those Myths to which the great mass of men have consented.

This is why we will try to centre our show around famous personalities, horrible crimes and superhuman self-sacrifices, demonstrating that it can draw out the powers struggling within them, without resorting to the dead imagery of ancient Myths.

In a word, we believe there are living powers in what is called poetry, and that the picture of a crime presented in the right stage conditions is something infinitely more dangerous to the mind than if the same crime were committed in life.

We want to make theatre a believable reality inflicting this kind of tangible laceration, contained in all true feeling, on the heart and senses. In the same way as our dreams react on us and reality reacts on our dreams, so we believe ourselves able to associate mental pictures with dreams, effective in so far as they are projected with the required violence. And the audience will believe in the illusion of theatre on condition they really take it for a dream, nor for a servile imitation of reality. On condition it releases the magic freedom of daydreams, only recognisable when imprinted with terror and cruelty.

Hence this full scale invocation of cruelty and terror, its scope testing our entire vitality, confronting us with all our potential.

And in order to affect every facet of the spectator's sensibility, we advocate a revolving show, which instead of making stage and auditorium into two closed worlds without any possible communication between them, will extend its visual and oral outbursts over the whole mass of spectators.

Furthermore, leaving the field of analysable emotional feelings aside, we intend using the actor's lyricism to reveal external powers, and by this means to bring the whole of nature into the kind of theatre we would like to evoke.

However extensive a programme of this kind may be, it does not over-reach theatre itself, which all in all seems to us to be associated with ancient magic powers.

Practically speaking, we want to bring back the idea of total theatre, where theatre will recapture from cinema, music hall, the circus and life itself, those things that always belonged to it. This division between analytical theatre and a world of movement seems stupid to us. One cannot separate body and mind, nor the senses from the intellect, particularly in a field where the unendingly repeated jading of our organs calls for sudden shocks to revive our understanding.

Thus on the one hand we have the magnitude and scale of a show aimed at the whole anatomy, and on the other an intensive mustering of objects, gestures and signs used in a new spirit. The reduced role given to understanding leads to drastic curtailment of the script, while the active role given to dark poetic feeling necessitates tangible signs. Words mean little to the mind; expanded areas and objects speak out. New imagery speaks, even if composed in words. But spatial, thundering images replete with sound also speak, if we become versed in arranging a sufficient interjection of spatial areas furnished with silence and stillness.

We expect to stage a show based on these principles, where these direct active means are wholly used. Therefore such a show, unafraid of exploring the limits of our nervous sensibility, uses rhythm, sound, words, resounding with song, whose nature and startling combinations are part of an unrevealed technique.

Moreover, to speak clearly, the imagery in some paintings by Grunewald or Hieronymus Bosch gives us a good enough idea of what a show can be, where things in outside nature appear as temptations just as they would in a Saint's mind.

Theatre must rediscover its true meaning in this spectacle of a temptation, where life stands to lose everything and the mind to gain everything.

Besides we have put forward a programme which permits pure production, methods discovered on the spot to be organised around historic or cosmic themes familiar to all.

And we insist that the first Theatre of Cruelty show will hinge on these mass concerns, more urgent and disturbing than any personal ones.

We must find out whether sufficient production means, financial or otherwise, can be found in Paris, before the cataclysm occurs, to allow such theatre (which must remain because it is the future) to come to life. Or whether real blood is needed right now to reveal this cruelty.

■　■　■

## Source

Artaud, A. (1938, 1964, 1970) 'Theatre and Cruelty', *The Theatre and Its Double*, trans. V. Corti, London: Calder & Boyars: 64–67. Written in 1933, first published in 1938 in *Le Théâtre et son double* by Editions Gallimard and then in Antonin Artaud: *Œuvres Complètes, Tome IV* by Editions Gallimard (1964), from which text this 1970 English translation was made.[1]

## Antonin Artaud (1896–1948)

French actor and writer who, through his life experience, has had a profound influence on notions of theatre in our time. While not himself producing a tangible system he nevertheless, through the publication of the English translations of his collection of essays, *The Theatre and Its Double* (1958 and 1970), acted as a catalyst for generations of theatre makers by opening up new modes of perception. Artaud promoted a way of thinking which rejected logic and reason as 'the chains that bind us', and wanted the theatre, through its immediacy, to embrace the non-verbal elements of consciousness, and to arouse powerful therapeutic emotions in the audience. He wanted the theatre, through its power, to create a complete physical, mental and moral upheaval in the population, which would lead to enlarged and revolutionary perceptions, from which one can understand his attraction for the generation of the 1960s in Europe and the USA.

In this essay Artaud attacks psychological theatre, advocating instead a form of total theatre that will engage the spectator in creating his own power to change, not only himself, but also society as a whole. He thus, like many of the artists in this book, was constantly in conflict with established theatre forms, advocating instead the search for man's instinctive impulsive life. Much influenced by Freud's *Interpretation of Dreams*, Artaud's life became an emblem of man's search for consciousness, proposing in the process that the theatre abandon naturalistic set, space and language to create a new order.

## Compare this article with writings by the following authors in this reader

**Beck** – later, messianic claims for the purpose of theatre
**Brook** – who acknowledges him as an early influence
**Grotowski** – for a similar, contemporary, messianic role for theatre
**Hijikata** – for later Japanese celebrations of the irrational
**Jarry and Richter** – who wished theatre would stir audiences from their apathy
**Marinetti** – who wished to sweep away logic and embrace physicality and sensuality
**Soyinka** – a West African perspective on ritual
**Stanislavski** – a contemporary, contrasting view of theatre

## Further reading

Artaud, A. (1971) *Artaud on Theatre*, ed. C. Schumacher, London: Methuen.
Esslin, M. (1976) *Artaud*, London: Fontana/Collins.
Innes, C. (1993) *Avant Garde Theatre 1892–1992*, London: Routledge.

## Note

1    1938 edition published in *Collection Métamorphoses no. IV*. See also M.C. Richard's first English translation (1958), New York: Grove.

# Chapter 5

**Bobby Baker**

DIARY ENTRIES

BOBBY BAKER studied painting at St Martin's School of Art but has made her international reputation as a performance artist or 'live artist'. She performs solo and her work is intensely personal, comically and sometimes painfully drawn from her own experience. Her themes range from cooking, cleaning and parenthood to relationships with God. She also draws, creates postcards, devises websites and makes videos.

In the early summer of 2000 she was due to take part in a festival in East London, 'Art in Sacred Spaces', the inspiration of an Anglican priest. Churches, synagogues and mosques were the venues for performances and installations commissioned from a range of leading artists, reflecting a society of many faiths and none. Bobby Baker was invited to lead an otherwise ordinary morning service in her own distinctive way at her local church in North London.

A further five projects were in preparation as she was writing her diary. *Pull Yourself Together* was for Mental Health Week in April. Strapped to the back of a truck, she was driven around London shouting 'Pull yourself together!' at passers-by. *Box Story* is the fifth part of her ongoing series called 'Daily Life', jointly commissioned by the London International Festival of Theatre 2001 and the Melbourne Festival. *Expert Housework* – which soon changed its name – is a website where visitors encounter '40 remarkable actions gathered from daily life and shown in different rooms'. *The Meaning of Life* (also known as *Edible Outfits*) is another mental health project that may or may not see the light of day, and she also

becomes resident artist with *Time Out* as part of the national Year of the Artist scheme. *The Sermon* was to be delivered (preached?) on 28 May.

*21 January 2000*

Starting this diary is the most wonderful solution to my problems of making new work, the perfect displacement activity. I will write about how stuck I am and then I won't feel so guilty about doing nothing constructive. This period of six weeks with no other commitments to talk of seemed so precious but is slipping away with nothing resolved. It's so frustrating because I feel that the answers are already there in my mind but I don't know the questions to lead me to them. Resolving the questions is the answer! I lie on the bed and phone Jude to run ideas past her and then do the same with Charlotte (Judith Knight and Charlotte Aiken of ArtsAdmin consultancy). Both very encouraging, which provides temporary relief from anxiety. Decide that going to bed at 4.00 in the afternoon to listen to talking book is just not good enough. Must get up, do weekly shop, then *Fat Attack* video. Will try and resolve title for *Expert Housework* website whilst busy. Best ideas often come then. When have best ideas come? At every hour of day and night with no discernible pattern. Idea in car on way to supermarket for new title for website . . . *Housework House?*

*22 January*

Go to see Jo (Evans) and Will and the babies. Talking about *Expert Housework* (which I collaborated on with Jo) too anxiety-making. Discuss *The Meaning of Life* instead with huge excitement and enthusiasm (because it's in the future and therefore safer?). Thinking about its being focused exclusively on the mental health sector. Driving back, think about new title for this piece, but realise I can't do the title until I know more about the content. Do my best ideas come in the car? If so, will drive round London all day. Would enjoy that. Come to think of it, I thought up all of *Drawing on a Mother's Experience* whilst driving. Have put on a pound. Must do more Fat Attacking and drink less whisky.

*23 January*

Sunday. Bad day. Worried that I'm feeling so bleak about the world and life in general that any work I produce will be too profoundly dark to inflict on an unsuspecting public.

*25 January*

Bad day again. Impossible to work until I get to the studio and start drawing. Then my mind begins to function . . . just about. Thinking about title for website mostly and title for mental health project. Only come up with clichés. Then on the way back I think of a new title . . . *The Answer*. Quite like it . . . bit dull? Lying in bed at night reading *Roget's Thesaurus*, generally a great source of inspiration. Investigating the notion of perfection for *Expert Housework* rather than expertise which smacks too much of *Good Housekeeping*. Or what about competition? Prefer perfection but love idea of prizes, stardom.

*27 January*

Day out with American sister-in-law. Lunch, shopping for bras and make-up, Tate Gallery, dinner and film, not in order of preference. Feeling so high. Mind dwelling on bundle of problems all the time and rolling them around with relish. Then in the Tate read plaque next to sculpture of Pandora. Had overlooked Pandora connection with *Box Story* as I had been so intent on altar, coffin, death theme. 'In Greek myth, Pandora was the first mortal woman, created by Vulcan . . . he gave her the gifts of beauty, the power of song and eloquence. Zeus gave her a box containing every human ill and sent her to Earth. When she opened this box all the misfortunes that have since afflicted mankind flew out. The figure of Pandora, the original temptress, was often used in nineteenth-century art and literature as a vehicle for ambivalent feelings about women.' Love the bit about misfortune and the misogynistic slant. Sharpens my focus on what the stories will be about. *The Answer* too simplistic. Needs questions too or more perfect title. Neatly put that on list of problems to be solved. Productive day. Should go on outings all the time or become a taxi driver.

*29 January*

Struck down with despair. Struggling to think about projects but they all feel hopeless. Utter negativity. Will phone Jude on Monday to cancel everything except *Pull Yourself Together*, the only appropriate show in my current state of mind.

*30 January*

Great news! Jocelyn Pook has phoned to say she can compose the music for *Box Story*. Immediate celebration and change of mood. Would probably have scrapped the whole thing if she couldn't do it. Move straight onto *HouseWorkHouse* (definite new title approved by Jude).

*31 January*

Spend day drawing and reading thesaurus. Get nowhere except to make long lists of words appropriate to each project. Pol (Polona Baloh Brown, best friend, co-director and collaborator for ten years) asked me to do drawings for *Box Story* but can only draw fat me.

*2 February*

Andrew (husband) ill in bed so work in studio and look after him. Beautiful day. Bulbs sprouting everywhere. Spend morning on the net looking at colours. Why do most website designers ignore the fact that computer screens are essentially grey? Why the preponderance of beige when they look so dreadful together? Get strong ideas for colours I want us to use. Suddenly remember a whole bunch of faxes of film ideas I sent to a director three years ago. Wonder whether there's anything relevant to now. A pot of ideas! Most of it is directly related to *HouseWorkHouse*. So exciting. Obvious now that idea started as film but has transmuted into website. So many ideas forgotten about. Discover one entitled 'The Woman Who Mistook Her Mouth for a Pocket': perfect for *The Sermon*.

Mind explodes with new ideas. Can't stop laughing. Particularly like idea for pen clipped into mouth like pocket. Frantically look round house for pen that will fit lip. Can't find one. Dubious about going to stationer's to try out pens in mouth. Have to do Fat Attack exercises to calm myself down.

*9 February*
Consumed by all these titles, problems, questions. The problem is that there are too many problems. Resort to washing duvets to keep mind at bay.

*10 February*
Go to see Jo to talk about *HouseWorkHouse*. Tremendous help, huge improvement on yesterday. Just the process of explaining my ideas starts to clear the confusion. Everything seems to have come on quite a bit since we last spoke. That is what I'm missing at the moment. Normally I would be meeting Pol from time to time and talking things through. Can't wait for her to get back from Slovenia. I'm very excited about the mental health project. I'm listening to all the conversations round me in a constant search for a new title. It might pop out of someone's mouth and I mustn't miss it. Latest idea is *Shopping Trip*.

*11 February*
Meet Jocelyn Pook. Great talking about *Box Story*. Very positive about working with her. Discuss the way the music intertwines with the performance, a real collaboration rather than just tacking things together. She suggests the Hilliard Ensemble as a choir we might have. They want to work with her. Does it matter about them being men when I'd wanted a female choir? Odd how my mind starts to waver at the suggestion!

*13 February*
Ever since meeting Jocelyn I've been constantly thinking about stories for *Box Story*. Every story I hear, or memory I have, becomes a possible model. It's the theme I can't pin down. Keep on getting snatches of ideas, like one of putting a glass on my head and trying to pour wine into it while chatting to the audience. Also thinking of the story for *The Sermon*. I will be constantly putting things into my mouth (pocket) and taking them out, distorting my voice. Will the joke wear thin? The story is central in all these shows.

*20 February*
At Essex University for a two-week session with a group of MA Contemporary Theatre students. (Lots of driving involved.) Students are great but I am almost crazed with the desperate quest for solutions that is going on in my head. I can't stop searching but feel I'm getting nowhere. So glad Pol is back soon. Perhaps the problem is that I'm working on too many projects at once? Resolve to work on one thing at a time. This next week it will be *The Sermon*.

*21 February*

Yesterday's decision to concentrate on one thing at a time proved very successful. About an hour after taking that decision I sat down on the sofa and, almost in front of my eyes, a scenario for the sermon played itself through. I laughed with enjoyment especially at the bit where I climb into a towelling bag and take off my stained overall ready for washing. It was a huge relief after so much confusion and I must discipline myself to carry on with it. (A day later I'm not so sure I've got the nerve to undress in front of the congregation, even safely inside a bag, in the middle of a church service.)

*5 March*

Still constantly searching for a new title for the mental health project in every conversation. Drive myself half crazy listening to Radio 4 for a couple of hours and considering several thousand possibilities. Have also been considering the sermon in fits and starts. It's coming on quite well. I imagine acting it out and then the scenes just evolve before my eyes. I imagine how exactly I will say the words and what my general demeanour will be. After I've worked out a section I stop and put it away until the next time it comes to the front of my mind. I usually flag up a problem to be solved, put that away and hope for the best. I've decided not to worry about *Box Story* until I've talked to Pol.

*8 March*

Feeling fragile but working on the website helps. It's great with Deborah (Deborah May, film-maker and website designer) and Jo. The decision-making process is equitable. I have a way to go in understanding the technology but it's exciting. Search for a title increasingly compelling. Coped with a meeting yesterday by turning every phrase into a potential show.

*12 March*

Much better. Great week with the website. It's interesting how technology informs the creative decisions. Deborah has come up with a great solution for transferring my drawings of the house. Pol is back and we start work this week on *The Sermon* and *Box Story*. Feeling very positive about it all.

*19 March*

Slightly confusing week. Still so many conflicting ideas going on in my head. However, great breakthrough with the mental health project. Suddenly realise that the whole thing is becoming too epic. How about starting it as a research project, on a small scale? A whole series of activities based round an edible fashion parade then come to mind. Modest but manageable. Huge relief to get that one off my mind although I shall probably still go on searching for the perfect title as it's become such a habit. Pol back from Slovenia so have first working meeting with her for ages, which is also a relief and great pleasure. She likes the ideas for *The Sermon* very much but points out that I haven't got an ending. Am very worried about this. It is extremely difficult to know how to proceed in such a sensitive arena, i.e. a real church service. Pol very constructive, suggests working on one stage at a time. This week's work is to try and resolve what it is that I am trying to say. Rather daunting! Had a long talk about *Box Story*. She thinks that I'm worrying far too soon about the whole thing as we actually have ages to go, and she also points out that I am always confused and negative and think that this one is the worst ever! Also masses to sort out for the website and a workshop performance this next week. Have abandoned *Fat Attack* and resorted to the gym again due to boredom. Always think I'm going to resolve important problems while I'm exercising but never do.

*27 March*

Excellent week. Big leaps and bounds. Difficult meeting cancelled at last moment. I feel like I've been let out on bail. The result is a surge of new ideas. First the mental health project has become a fully fledged two-year plan entitled 'Edible Outfits' involving workshops, fashion parades, a book, a film and a website. Next, I've resolved a crucial element of *Box Story*. Deciding I can repeat the drawing idea from *Drawing on a Mother's Experience* I go through whole streams of ideas until I'm in a supermarket and see a collage of food on a package. One idea and image lead to another, and at one point I am leaving a meeting on my bike when I suddenly think of mapping. I am so excited that I nearly ride under a bus. Still finding it impossible to concentrate on the ending of *The Sermon*, ironically the most pressing problem.

*9 April*

Meeting with Pol about *Box Story* and *The Sermon*. She approves of new ideas, which is a relief, and while I am telling her all the different endings I've been thinking about the whole thing suddenly goes a stage further, culminating in a definite new image. She likes it as well so that seems to be that. Must get on with it but am quite caught up with preparing for *Pull Yourself Together*. New plan to give up dieting and spend time eating and exercising. Quite exhausting.

*16 April*

Sunday is my regular diary day, the only time I get a chance to reflect on things. Great time on Thursday when I had ideas for two new shows. Well, one was a bit over the top. I was driving along and saw three old ladies chatting on the corner of the street. I immediately thought of stationing three old ladies on the corner of every street in a given area (actually I thought of the whole country initially) so people could wander up to them and have a chat. There's a lot missing to the idea and the pragmatics are somewhat daunting. Never mind!

The other idea surfaced when I was Fat Attacking for the first time for ages and I'm so pleased with it that I can't write it down in case it gets spoiled, but it's a film, postcards, a book and a website – of course! Pol's set me the task of working on the sins I'm going to use in the sermon but it's an effort to focus on it. We both go to church this morning to consider the practicalities.

*1 May*

Weekend in Dorset. There's been a lot going on. *Pull Yourself Together* turned out to be a fabulous experience with great responses. Time-consuming though. Am definitely going to take on the *Time Out* Year of the Artist residency, although there is a worrying overload of the system. I've got to come up with something for the award ceremony on 5 June but think I'm going to develop an existing idea to do with symbolically eating the judges. Then I've got two or three months to think up a new idea for the rest of the residency. As usual, very excited when something is first proposed but panic when it dawns on me that I'm actually going to have to do it. My idea of bliss: to be expected to come up with endless new ideas but never to have to realise them. Is this true? Probably not, but it's a nice thought. The thought of raising money for *Edible Outfits* and *Box Story,* for instance, is so lowering. Went for a walk along the Dorset cliffs yesterday. Vertigo set in so I distracted myself by thinking about *The Sermon* instead.

*7 May*

Completely stuck. Can't get on with *The Sermon.* Unable to concentrate on *Box Story* or the *Time Out* project. Have resorted to hammock-swinging and water aerobics as displacement activities.

*14 May*

Glad to be back working on the sermon properly now with Pol. It will start with the pocket-as-mouth notion and an exploration of sermonising and lead on to the real subject – sin. It goes back to my original experience of church as a place where you are made to feel guilty. My text will be Jeremiah 2:22. 'For though thou wash thee with nitre, and take thee much soap, yet thine iniquity is marked before me, saith the Lord God.' I'm fascinated by the imagery of washing and stains – dirt and the unmentionable – and its connection to evil.

*29 May*

Find it impossible to write about the process of making the sermon while the intense phase is in progress, only partly due to being busy with it, preparing for the *Time Out* piece and writing the application for *Box Story.* It worries me that my idea is so transparently simple and yet I can't see any other way of structuring it given the extraordinary problems of performing during a real live act of worship. I have to contend with the existing congregation and their expectations (whatever those are) and the visiting public and their relationship to the piece as a work of art. Also possibly a great antipathy from the visiting public to the church, especially towards the sort of illiberal imagery I am playing with. It is like balancing on a knife-edge. I could never have done it without the good-humoured and generous compliance of the vicar, Dave Tomlinson, and Fraser Dyer, one of the church wardens, who is leading the service. When I describe the sermon and the sort of hymn I am looking for (I am choosing the hymns and all the texts for the service) Fraser comes up with one starting: 'There is a fountain filled with blood drawn from Emmanuel's veins.' General collapse in hysterical laughter. It is perfect imagery to set the scene – Gothic horror, serious side, how imbued with a sense of guilt we are, how to examine the roots of all that shame.

I'm reticent about coming up with personal sins, but this is blasted away in a great session with Pol. I suddenly remember an incident when I was driving down Holloway Road and, in a distracted moment, swerved onto the other side of the road and almost crashed into a car coming in the opposite direction. It swerved towards me at the same time. I was filled with rage and leaned out of the window waving two fingers at the driver. At that precise moment he leaned out and did the same to me. In a blinding flash we recognised each other . . . it was the vicar. We decide to use this story for the sin of rage and the rest of the examples follow on from there. A fine little bunch of confessions, each teetering dangerously close to the brink of embarrassing revelation, but to be delivered in such a way as to engage the congregation, spark off personal memories, tease their sensibilities, shock, amuse and entertain. We work on how to put it together so that each bunch of sins links to a particular stain so that while I am telling the stories I will rub different food-stuffs into my overall – ketchup, mint sauce, mustard. The stains/sins have to relax into each other in an intricate construction so as not to be cloying.

Once I am covered in sin there's a technical problem. I am to climb into the towelling beach-bag I've made in order to remove the stained overall in suburban decency. The bag has also been designed so I will resemble a priest in vestments. Then I am to emerge in a clean reconstituted overall later in the performance. The trouble is that the 'sins' rub off on the inside of the bag and will stain the pristine overall, destroying the final transforming image of cleansed absolution. Hasty consultation with the costume-maker gives us the idea of a lining which can be surreptitiously removed during the performance. I always get worried when technical hitches occur that the whole idea is flawed, that there should be a delicious simplicity to the construction of images. However, in the event it all works like a dream.

After taking off the overall I am to cut it into small pieces and put each piece in a different stain solution in a set of bowls on a table. I am building on an image of an overall impregnated with foodstuffs dried and encrusted – years of stubborn stains/sins to deal with. The problem is how to get from these soaking fragments to an overall reconstituted with hundreds of tiny, perfectly clean patchwork pieces all sewn together. We eventually decide that the washing image can be told as a story – that I can take people on a mental journey to my laundry room. I love those sections during a performance when you endeavour to conjure up a sensual image of an experience and then debunk the whole thing.

But how to tackle the next, crucial section, after the fragments have been got out of the washing machine and hung on the line in delightful, regimented order? How to indicate the range of possibilities of what happens next? I don't want to refer directly to divine intervention. I've already tackled absolution in the stain-slaying but I want it to go further, and be a reflection on a whole range of ideas to do with human frailty. Rather than prescribing a set of images I want the congregation to be able to take it in many different ways using religious or secular concepts, and to reflect on the divine in an un-bigoted way – a definite challenge. We discuss a range of possibilities but I just can't put it together, and then, one night just as my head is dropping onto the pillow, a single word comes into my mind, SILENCE. It turns out to be the pivotal moment in the sermon. I am to stand on the chancel steps and say: 'This is the moment when words simply fail,' and then stand in complete silence for a whole minute – a long time in a performance. I am to fold my hands in a devout way and gaze at the stained-glass windows, occasionally taking a peek at my watch to indicate my human frailty in needing to keep control of the time at such a solemn moment. Then it will be simple to turn back to the altar, remove the lining of the bag and put on the clean patchwork overall. At that moment the music is to start. I have a struggle choosing between religious and secular, taped or live organ music until I remember ABBA. The thought of dancing in an ungainly way up and down the nave in a scrappy overall just cracks me up. It debunks so much of the imagery and, hopefully, raises so many questions. I play *ABBA Gold* for hours before selecting 'Thank You For the Music'. I practise the gawky dancing on my own in the kitchen every night after several glasses of wine, roaring with laughter. I'm embarrassed to admit how much I revel in key moments of performance by myself.

On the day we are well organised. The congregation is welcomed with carefully prepared service sheets. Flowers are arranged. The organ is playing. With the church packed full, Dave, Fraser and I walk to our chairs from the vestry. The whole service has the solemnity and attention to detail we've worked so hard to establish. There are hymns, prayers, parish notices and finally the texts. First Jeremiah 2:19–26 (including the key verse) and then a reading from the Biotex Stain Removal packet with its references to blood and mud. Suddenly ripples of mirth pass through the congregation. And so I begin my sermon. It goes really well. I ad-lib a lot, which is always a good sign. Odd to hear roars of laughter during a church service. Several press photographers have sneaked in, against our wishes, and one bobs about in front of me taking pictures. After a withering comment from me he sits down for the rest of the sermon. The silence works particularly well. What especially pleases me is the poignancy of the event. I hadn't anticipated that. After my wild dancing I go quietly back to my seat. There is a silence again. I had wanted the service to continue as normal then, but after a pause loud whistles and applause break out. All very strange, given the context.

*1 May*
Very difficult to plunge into the *Time Out* piece immediately afterwards, and write the application for funding for *Box Story*. Sense of impending collapse.

*9 June*

*Time Out* piece goes well although there is a bit too much crisis management for comfort. The title is: 'To bring a sheep to consciousness we must eat it, therefore to bring the judges of the *Time Out* Eating and Drinking Awards to consciousness we should eat them.' The idea is to make 250 biscuit images of the judges and hand them out to participants in specially designed and printed boxes. It all goes pear-shaped when the biscuit dough refuses to work. Three batches crumble to pieces. I remix the dough and get it done at 2.00 on Saturday morning. My hands are swollen from the effort. Luckily Pol is there to help with packing them and the display panels but we only just get to the hotel where the event is being held in time on Monday morning. The show took place at 12.30 pm and the *Box Story* application is handed in by ArtsAdmin at 5.30 pm. Next time I'll try pacing myself . . .

*22 June*

Sitting on the beach at Paxos, reflecting. Wishing I'd worked harder at Fat Attacking. Can't stop thinking about *Box Story*. Every story I hear is a potential candidate for the show . . .

*The funding application was successful. The website was completed and can be found at www.bobbybakersdailylife.com.*

■  ■  ■

## Source

Allen, P. (ed.) (2001) *Art, Not Chance – Nine Artists' Diaries*, London: Calouste Gulbenkian Foundation.

## Bobby Baker (1950–)

British born performance artist Bobby Baker trained originally as a painter and art teacher at St Martin's School of Art and Goldsmiths College in London. Realising her interest lay primarily in making artworks, rather than teaching, Baker developed a series of paintings, installations and performances in which food and other edible materials were presented in various galleries and exhibitions across the UK. These included *An Edible Family in a Mobile Home* and *Meringue Ladies World Tour* (1976); *Elitist Jam* (1977); *Packed Lunch* (1979); *Drawing on a Mother's Experience* (1988). Baker evolved a series of performance lecture demonstrations including *Cook Dems* (1990), which toured extensively around theatres, recording studios and private houses.

Her *Daily Life* series included research projects, performances and shows that took place and toured to a variety of site specific environments including kitchens, schools, gardens and churches. Seminal works include *Kitchen Show* (1991); *How to Shop* (1993); *Take a Peek!* (1995); *Grown-Up School* (1999); *Box Story* (2001). In 2000 Baker created *Pull Yourself Together*, the first in a series of works addressing issues of mental health, which consisted of her being strapped to a car seat on the back of a truck and yelling out 'cheerful insults' at everyday audience members who happened to be passing by. Further live works on this theme included *How to Live* (2004) and *Give Peas a Chance* (2008) as well as a number of radio plays, photographs, essays and events that are documented in *Bobby Baker – Redeeming Features of Everyday Life* (2007), edited by Michele Barrett and Bobby Baker, and on her company's website Daily Life Ltd http://www.bobbybakersdailylife.com/MainMenu.html.

*Diary Drawings* (2009) is a currently touring exhibition of 158 drawings that address Baker's experience of day hospitals, acute psychiatric wards, breast cancer and recovery.

These diary entries document the everyday reality of living as Bobby Baker and enable us to get a sense of the range of projects she works on at any one time. The writing illuminates Baker's process of both thinking about and managing these multiple projects. The piece illuminates the anxieties and doubts associated with her work as a creator of multiple outputs as well as identifying the satisfaction that comes from finding solutions to problems and completing projects and collaborations. Written in real time over a six-month period in 2000, this text functions to demystify the artist and render the ordinary and the everyday as important elements in the working process.

## Compare this article with writings by the following authors in this reader

**Boal** – for addressing personal and political issues
**Finley** – for another autobiographical perspective
**Goulish** – for connections between multiple creative projects
**Kaprow** – for a perspective on art and the everyday
**Schneemann** – for moving between visual art and performance
**Viola** – a contemporary of Baker working in a range of media and gallery spaces

## Further reading

Baker, B. (2010) *Diary Drawings: Mental Illness and Me*, London: Profile Books Ltd.
Barrett, M. and Baker, B. (eds) (2007) *Redeeming Features of Daily Life*, London: Routledge.
Tushingham, D. (ed.) (1994) *Food for the Soul: A New Generation of British Theatremakers (Live)*, London: Methuen.
http://www.bobbybakersdailylife.com/MainMenu.html

# Chapter 6

# Eugenio Barba

## WORDS OR PRESENCE

TRAINING DOES NOT teach how to act, how to be clever, does not prepare one for creation. Training is a process of self-definition, a process of self-discipline which manifests itself indissolubly through physical reactions. It is not the exercise in itself that counts – for example, bending or somersaults – but the individual's justification for his own work, a justification which although perhaps banal or difficult to explain through words, is physiologically perceptible, evident to the observer. This approach, this personal justification decides the meaning of the training, the surpassing of the particular exercises which, in reality, are stereotyped gymnastic movements.

This inner necessity determines the quality of the energy which allows work without a pause, without noticing tiredness, continuing even when exhausted and at that very moment going forward without surrendering. This is the self-discipline of which I spoke.

Let us understand each other, however: it is not by killing oneself with exhaustion that one becomes creative. It is not on command, by forcing, that one opens oneself to others. Training is not a form of personal asceticism, a malevolent harshness against oneself, a persecution of the body. Training puts one's own intentions to the test, how far one is prepared to pay with one's own person for all that one believes and declares. It is the possibility of bridging the gap between intention and realization. This daily task, obstate, patient, often in darkness, sometimes even searching for a meaning for it, is a concrete factor in the transformation of the actor as a man and as a member of the group. This imperceptible daily transformation of one's own way of seeing, approaching and judging the problems of one's own existence and of that of others, this sifting of one's own prejudices, one's own doubts – not through gestures and grandiloquent phrases but through the silent daily activity – is reflected in one's work which finds new justifications, new reactions: thus one's north is displaced.

■

In the beginning, we had a programme of set exercises that we taught everybody and that everybody had to follow. These were exercises of every kind, taken from ballet, mime, pure gymnastics, Hatha-Yoga and acrobatics. We worked out a whole series of physical actions and called this 'biomechanics' after the term used by Meyerhold. We defined biomechanics as a very dynamic reaction to an external stimulus. The exercises were of an acrobatic nature and very violent. However, they had been transformed by our imaginations around what we thought to be the training of the oriental actor. Starting from this training as it existed in our fantasy, we wanted to achieve a rhythm of work that was intense yet had the same precision, the same economy of movement, the same suggestiveness and power that we attribute to the oriental actor. For us, biomechanics was not a technically exact and historical reconstruction of the exercises elaborated by Meyerhold, who had a particular aim in view: namely, the creation of a social *emploi* for the actor. We used this term to set in motion our imagination, to stimulate us. What could it be like, this biomechanics? We attempted to re-invent it, to rediscover it in our bodies according to our own justifications. It was the actors who, individually or in collaboration, worked out the map of this territory. Within it were also the 'battles', the fights, the exercises for the reflexes in which the actor must immediately adapt himself to a situation, think with his whole body, react with all of it.

■

In spite of my experience in oriental theatre, especially Indian Kathakali, I haven't drawn directly from it. I tried to make my actors imagine this theatre of colors and exoticism, acrobatics and religiosity, by appealing to their subjectivity and their fantasy.

Kathakali, like all oriental theatre, cannot be copied or transplanted. It can only serve as a stimulus, a point of departure. The actor in oriental theatre is immersed in a tradition that he must wholly respect. He is merely executing a role whose minutest detail has, as in a musical score, been elaborated by some master in a more or less distant past. As with a pianist or a classical ballet dancer, his evolution cannot be separated from virtuosity. In Western theatre, however, the actor is – or should be – a creator.

His clash with the text, through his own sensibility and his own historical experience, opens up a unique and personal universe to his spectators.

This essential difference also determines one's approach to the profession, the preparation, that which is now usually called training. Even today, the Kathakali or Kabuki actor begins his training at the same age as a European child who wishes to devote himself to ballet. The psychological and also physiological consequences are evident. It is meaningless to go to Japan or India and take exercises from Kabuki or Kathakali in order to adapt them passively to the European pedagogical tradition, in the hope that our actors, too might become 'virtuosi' like their oriental colleagues. Let me repeat, it is not the exercises in themselves that are decisive, but one's personal attitude, that inner necessity which incites and justifies on an emotional level and with a logic that will not allow itself to be trapped by words, the choice of one's own profession.

This attitude determines the creation of norms that become almost an artistic or ethical super-ego in the actor. Similar norms are also to be found in theatre forms based on a purely technical apprenticeship. Here the historical circumstances and the environmental conditions in which the theatre work evolves, influence the elaboration of these norms which are reflected in the technique. For example, the entire training of a young actor wishing to devote himself to Kabuki takes place in a rarefied atmosphere, without the possibility of contact with actors from other theatrical forms, either Noh or modern theatre, in a strict professional hierarchy petrified in family dynasties whose mentality contrasts with the efficient industrial vocation revealed by contemporary Japan.

The same applies to the Kathakali actor. While the Kabuki actor is owned by a large impresario firm which places him in various theatres, the Kathakali actor works on religious ground, the temple courtyard, dedicates his work and his performance to divinities, lives in a very modest way without the prospect ever of becoming a star like his Japanese colleague. These socio-historical circumstances, together with a particular professional tradition which still has great value and prestige for the young would-be actor, are decisive factors in the conception and elaboration of that expressiveness which is codified and so transformed into technique.

■

In the beginning of our activity we too believed in the 'myth of technique', something which it was possible to acquire, to possess, and which would have allowed the actor to master his own body, to become conscious of it. So, at this stage, we practised exercises to develop the dilation of the eyes in order to increase their expressiveness. They were exercises which I had taken from India while studying the training of Kathakali actors. The expressiveness of the eyes is essential in Kathakali and the control of their musculature demands several hours of hard training daily for many years. The different nuances each have a precise significance; the way of frowning, the direction of a glance, the degree of opening or closing the lids are codified by tradition and are in fact concepts and images which are immediately comprehensible to the spectator. Such control in a European actor would only restrain the organic reactions of the face and transform it into a lifeless mask.

Like a melting pot in which the most disparate metals fuse, so inside me at the outset I tried to blend together the most diverse influences, the impressions which for me had been the most fertile: oriental theatre, the experiments of the Great Reform, my personal experience from my stay in Poland and with Grotowski. I wanted to adapt all this to my ideal of technical perfection even in the part of the artistic work which we called composition, a word which had arrived in our theatre through the Russian and French terminology and Grotowski's interpretation of it. I believed that composition was the capacity of the actor to create signs, to consciously mould his own body into a deformation which was rich in suggestiveness and power of association: the body of the actor as a Rosetta stone and the spectator in the role of Champollion. The aim was on a conscious level, by cold calculation, to attain that which is warm and which obliges us to believe with all our senses. But I often felt this composition to be imposed, something external which functioned on a theatrical level but lacked the drilling force that could perforate the crust of all too obvious significations. The composition might be rich, striking, throwing the actor into relief, yet it was like a veil which hid from me something that I felt inside myself but which I didn't have the courage to face, to reveal to myself – or rather to reveal to others.

In the first period of our existence all the actors did the same exercises together in a common collective rhythm. Then we realized that the rhythm varied for each individual. Some have a faster vital rhythm, others a slower one. We began to talk about organic rhythm, not in the sense of a regular beat but of variation, pulsation like that of our heart as shown by a cardiogram. This perpetual variation, however minute, revealed the existence of a wave of organic reactions which engaged the entire body. Training could only be individual.

This faith in technique as a sort of magic power which could render the actor invulnerable, guided us also in the domain of the voice. At the start, we followed the practices of oriental theatre: straightforward imitations of certain timbres of the voice. Using Grotowski's terminology, we called the different tones of voice 'resonators'. In oriental theatre training, the young actor learns entire roles mechanically with all their vocal nuances, timbres, intonations, exclamations – a complete fabric of sounds perfected through tradition and which the actor must repeat precisely in order to gain the appreciation of a critical audience. We too began coldly to find a series of timbres, tones, intonations, and exercised them daily.

This period of calculated work, of pure 'technicity', seemed to confirm that the hypothesis of the actor-virtuoso was right. The effects produced were interesting. But during their work a few actors managed to reach the territory of their own 'vocal flora'. This opened up to stimuli that were striking in their suggestiveness, in their emotional charge, and were not based on logic or a certain intellectuality: enter the ghost of your father and you, Hamlet, cry out because you are afraid or because you are glad. And out comes a strangled, flat, impersonal, cliché of a cry.

So we discovered the value of personal images for engaging the voice, in order to attain one's individual sound universe. No more calculated effects or mechanically placed voice. Simply reactions, responses to the image which served as a stimulus. We began to talk of vocal actions. That which for us had once been a postulate – the voice as a physiological process – now became a tangible reality which engaged the entire organism and projected it in space. The voice was a prolongation of the body which, through space, hit, touched, caressed, encircled, pushed, searched far away or close by; an invisible hand which stretched out from the body to act in space or renounce action. And even this renunciation was spoken by the invisible hand. But in order that the voice might act, it must know *where* the point was toward which it was directed, *who* that point was and *why* it was addressing him.

From that moment I ceased to speak of resonators. The whole body of the actor resounded, the room resounded, as well as something inside me as I listened, provided the actor really addressed this point in space which, although invisible to my eyes, was concrete to him, perceptible to all his senses, present with physical features.

■

For a long time the 'myth of technique' nourished our work. Then gradually it brought me to a situation of doubt. I had to admit that the argument for technique was a rationalization, a pragmatic blackmail – if you do this, you obtain that – which I used to make the others accept my way of working, to give it a useful and logical justification. On a personal level – dimly, full of shadows – I felt that under the alibi of work which the others defined as theatre I was trying to annihilate the actor in my companion, wash him of the character, destroy the theatre in our relationship so that we might meet one another as men, as companions in arms who have no need to defend themselves, bound closer than brothers by the doubts and illusions of years passed patiently together: not the actor, not the character, but the companion of a long period of my life.

It was no longer a matter of teaching or learning something, of tracing a personal method, of discovering a new technique, of finding an original language, of demystifying oneself or others. Only of not being afraid of one another. Having the courage to approach one another until one becomes transparent and allowing glimpses of the well of one's own experience. From here stems that 'pudeur' which refuses the presence of strangers during the work. And when the time comes for others to be present – spectators – these are witnesses of this human situation that we continue to call theatre. Because we have no name for this new frontier beyond which there is little we can say to one another in a theatrical language, even if its phrases are said with perfection. Virtuosity does not lead to situations of new human relationships which are the decisive ferment for a reorientation, a new way of defining oneself vis-à-vis others and of overcoming the facile self-complacency.

Thus the training transformed itself into a process of self-definition, far removed from any utilitarian justification and guided by individual subjectivity. Everyone decides for himself on its meaning. Once again: the exterior forms of the exercises are of no importance. But self-discipline remains.

■

During training one often runs the risk of a sclerosis. This is caused either by the ingenuous attitude which leads one to believe that with training comes creativity, or by the lack of personal justification which brings about the repetition of exercises as gymnastics. We too have gone through similar periods. Then I succumbed to the temptation to explain, to come up with a sort of training philosophy, Ariadne's thread for my companions lost in the labyrinth of uncertainty. With great loyalty my companions tried to motivate their own work with my words, my explanations. But something was wrong, something didn't ring true, and in the end a sort of split became apparent between what they were doing and what they wanted to do or believed they were doing to satisfy me, to meet me. When I realized this, I gave up all explanation.

After working together many hours a day for many years, it is not my words but perhaps only my presence that can say something.

■   ■   ■

## Source

Barba, E. (1979) 'Words or Presence', *The Floating Islands: Reflections with Odin Teatret*, trans. J. Barba, F. Pardeilhan, J.C. Rodesch, S. Shapiro and J. Varley, Denmark: Thomsens Bogtrykheri 73–79. First published (1972) in *The Drama Review* 53.

## Eugenio Barba (1936–)

Born in southern Italy, emigrated to Norway in 1954. He is now, as a theatre director, theorist, and founder of Odin Teatret (1964), one of the century's major innovators and a focus for much contemporary experimental work. He studied in Poland with Jerzy Grotowski, and published the first book about him, *Towards a Poor Theatre* (1968). In 1966 Odin Teatret moved to Holstebro in Denmark, from where its fame spread as a performing company, and as a source for theatre training. Odin's performances range from the processional and celebratory to the intensely mythic and personal, and include *Kaspariana* (1967), *The Million* (1979), *Judith* (1987), and *The Castle of Holstebro* (1990), which have been performed across Europe. Barba is also a major and unique theorist of theatre practice, and in 1979 in Denmark founded ISTA (International School of Theatre Anthropology), a peripatetic meeting of theatre scholars and practitioners, with the aim of comparing both Eastern and Western methods of theatre practice. The major publication arising from this work has been *The Secret Art of the Performer* (1991), a dictionary of theatre anthropology.

This essay is from Barba's first Odin book and stresses his major and enduring theme, that the training of the performer is an individual and personal responsibility. Barba's work explores alternatives to psychological assumptions about performance, and with his use and examination of terms such as the performer's 'presence' or 'energy', provides a training philosophy, which is practised and studied in several European schools and universities as a major twentieth-century technique. Not to accept character as a unit of the measure of performance links him with many major practitioners featured in this book.

## Compare this article with writings by the following authors in this reader

**Boal** – a contemporary approach to theatre games and exercises
**Brecht** – an anti-psychological attitude to theatre
**Copeau** – another view of actor training
**Grotowski** – the roots of Barba's theory of performance energy
**Hijikata** – a contemporary Japanese approach
**Soyinka** – a West African perspective on ritual
**Stanislavski** – a parallel view of training

## Further reading

Barba, E. (2009) *On Directing and Dramaturgy*, London: Routledge.
Barba, E. and Savarese, N. (1991) *A Dictionary of Theatre Anthropology: The Secret Art of the Performer*, London: Routledge.
Turner, J. (2004) *Eugenio Barba*, London: Routledge.
Watson, I. (1995) *Towards a Third Theatre*, London: Routledge.
http://www.odinteatret.dk

## Pina Bausch

### NOT HOW PEOPLE MOVE
### BUT WHAT MOVES THEM

*Pina Bausch, when you left the Folkwang Dance Institute in 1973 and
came here to Wuppertal, you said that you were afraid of being devoured
by the machinery, the theater machinery that is. Do you still have that
feeling nowadays?*

Things are a lot different from what I had imagined they would be.
In those days, I thought it might not be possible to do anything
individual at all. I imagined the routine and the regulations and
all the rest of it. I thought that the theater would have to go on
running as usual. I was very afraid of that in those days.

*And what are you afraid of nowadays?*

At the moment . . . well, yes, perhaps I'm a little scared by the
situation I've got myself into, that I just don't have the time to say,
'Can't I just take off somewhere for two weeks?' I don't mean
holidays – well, yes, holidays then, simply to relax, to get away
from this pressure and this load for a moment. It just never
stops . . . Sometimes I wonder just how long I can take it . . . but
the problem takes care of itself usually. If things are giving you
pleasure, if they're fun – I mean work in general – then
one . . . what's the word again? . . . one regenerates on one's own.
That's nice in a way . . . yes, actually it has been great up until
now. Really, I'm surprised I have so much energy. Where else can
it come from?

*Could you say roughly how many hours you have to work in a week?*

One couldn't count it, because . . . well, one can't divide it. Actually . . . actually I'm always working. Every hour is a working hour and then again it's not. It depends what one means by the word.

*Is it a strain on you, the fact that audiences and critics now have such a tremendously high level of expectation?*

I don't know. Perhaps it has never really changed. Actually, the feeling has always been the same. There always comes a moment where one is so unsure about what one has done because one lacks the necessary distance — and then there's this fear which is always there anyhow and always has been. And it's absolutely no help at all saying, 'Yes, it's going to work. I've done other things before'. The fear remains the same.

*Would you say that this fear enters the pieces as a theme?*

No, I don't think so.

*Do you have themes? Specific themes? Or does this change?*

Well, I'd say they sort of move in a circle. It's always the same things or similar things. Actually the themes are always to do with man-woman relationships, the way we behave or our longing or our inability, only sometimes the color changes. I *have* noticed that. Nowadays I often find supposedly cheerful things a lot sadder. In some ways, I've changed a bit, too.

*You once said that basically you aren't interested in how people move, that you are more interested in what moves people. How does someone who holds that maxim come to be in dance theater?*

Well, why do we do it? Why do we dance in the first place? There is a great danger in the way things are developing at the moment and have been developing in the last few years. Everything has become routine and no one knows any longer why they're using these movements. All that's left is just a strange sort of vanity which is becoming more and more removed from actual people. And I believe that we ought to be getting closer to one another again.

*When you say 'we', you mean dance, choreography?*

Yes, and the dancers too.

*Where are you from and how did you first start to dance?*

My father ran a public house and initially I was taken along to a ballet school for children.

*That means you started off actually learning ballet as opposed to having seen it performed somewhere, which might have been a decisive experience for you?*

Yes, I had never seen any ballet before.

*And did you enjoy dancing right from the start?*

Well, I went along and I tried to do what the others were doing. Somehow I recall us having to lie on our stomachs and touch our heads with our legs, and then there was this woman who said, 'She's a real contortionist!' That sounds really stupid now, but somehow I was terribly pleased that somebody had praised me. When your father has a public house you're sort of always just tagging along; basically one is always on one's own. You have no family life either. I was always up till midnight or one o'clock, or sitting under a table somewhere in the public house. We never took our meals together either. That's why I never really had any. . . . My parents never had the time to look after me very much.

*Still, we're still a long way from this little girl actually making the decision that she wants to become a dancer.*

Oh, it was nothing like that at all. I simply went along and then they started taking me for small children's parts, the lift boy in some operetta or . . . oh, I don't know . . . the Moor in the harem who had to wave the fan, or a newspaper boy. Things like that. And I was always terribly scared.

*But you still had no plans to work in theater at that point?*

I didn't really think about it. That's probably something that just simply happened. I really was always very scared about doing anything, but I enjoyed it terribly. And by the time I was ready to leave school, which is when one really started to think, or had to think about what one was going to do, because one knew that school was over – by that time it was basically clear.

*And so you went straight from school to the Folkwang Dance Institute? Or was there a period in between?*

That's basically what I did. I went to the Folkwang School.

*And when did the dancer turn choreographer?*

In those days at the Folkwang School, they had a great interest in — what did they call it then? — in improvisation classes. Much more than nowadays. . . . But they weren't improvisation classes at all. We did a bit of composition work, worked on a few little dances and study pieces. Anyway, I was one of the more active students in this respect. But it wasn't until I returned from America and I found there was nothing really happening in the group I was in and I was feeling very dissatisfied as a dancer. . . . I would have liked to express myself in a totally different way, but we just didn't have the opportunity. We didn't have very much to do either. There was nothing new happening and actually it was frustration which made me think of maybe trying to do something for myself. But it wasn't because I wanted to choreograph. The sole reason was because I wanted to dance. Yes, the reason I wanted to do something for myself was because I simply wanted to dance.

*Something you just very briefly mentioned there: America. You studied dance for several years in New York. Was this episode in your life without any real significance or was it important for your development?*

I think it was very important. The mere fact of having lived in a city like that was very important to me. The people, the city — which to me embodies something of 'today' and where literally everything is mixed, be it nationality, interests, or fashionable things — all right next to one another. Somehow I find that incredibly important.

*But you wouldn't want to live there now?*

I relate very strongly to New York. You see, when I think about New York, I have this kind of feeling which is normally quite alien to me otherwise — it's a bit like it were home . . . homesickness in other words. It's very strange.

*One basically thinks of you as being a typical child of this countryside. Pina Bausch without the Bergisches Land or without the Ruhrgebiet, without Essen and Wuppertal — one somehow feels it wouldn't be possible. Could you imagine yourself, Pina Bausch, as ballet director at the Bavarian State Opera in Munich?*

If I were offered the chance, or if someone thought it right for me to go to one particular theater, be it in Munich or somewhere else, then really it's simply only a question of how strongly I feel that it's right for me to go. But I could only ever do the things I feel I must do, I think. If someone were to say, 'You can come and work here but you have to do this, this and this' — then I don't think I'd be able to.

*It would be impossible for you to do a traditional production of* The Sleeping Beauty, *for example?*

I wouldn't want to.

*You said that basically you live twenty-four hours a day for choreography and ballet . . .*

Well, I'm not so sure about choreography . . .

*Alright, but it occupies you around the clock, twice around the clock to be precise. How does this translate into practice? How do you approach a piece?*

I live from hand to mouth. That's the way it is. Yes, that's actually how it works too. . . . When we're working on a piece, I have absolutely no time to start thinking about the next piece – either that or I'm simply unable to divide my time. . . . It just isn't possible. I first have to finish the one I'm doing and then I go straight on to the next one. I can feel what I'm looking for but often I'm unable to say rationally just what it is. I cannot put it into words, perhaps I don't even want to put it into words sometimes. Sometimes you come across things quite by accident, something you read. But basically I do look for them.

*And where does the material come from, by and large?*

The material which appears on stage? Oh, that's a much later stage in the process. I always panic before I start on a piece. I really am very frightened of starting, of saying categorically, 'Alright, we're going to rehearse today.' And I shirk it. I keep pushing it away from me as long as I can and then I'll start on it around the corner, so to speak. Sometimes I might ask to see one of the dancers and I'll say, 'Could we maybe try something out?' Or I talk to them about it a bit. But basically I find it incredibly difficult taking the first step because . . . because I know they, the dancers, are then going to expect me to tell them what I want. And then I panic. I'm scared of having to tell them because what I have is often so vague. It's true, I know I can always say, 'Here I am – there are one or two particular things in my head at the moment,' and I might even find some kind of word to describe it and then I'll say, 'Right. Well, here's where we start from. Let's see where it takes us.' It's great that I'm even able to put this into words nowadays. Two years ago I couldn't. I just didn't have those kind of words. I found it so damned difficult because anything one said was suddenly . . . well, you were so pinned down. Then, all of a sudden, you would say something and hope that the other person would pick up the clue because what I meant was actually something else. Anything I said was just an aid to making myself understood. Sometimes it's just an idea or a thought. . . . I suddenly get the feeling that if I talk about it too much then I've dirtied it already. I can't say why that is. And then I always have this feeling that I must protect it. I must talk round it so that it remains untouched, at least to begin with. Basically I want the group to use their imagination. We're still not doing what we really want to do.

*And what do you really want to do?*

Well I think we're all still holding back. It's quite natural because after all we want to be loved and liked. And I think there is something that holds you back somewhere. You think that there's this point and if you go beyond that then there's no exact telling where it will lead.

*I always felt that this need to be loved was in fact something which made you want to produce, not something which held you back.*

Right, right . . . but then it's both. Because it's a process, you see. Wanting to be loved; that's definitely our motor. I don't know. It might be different if I were on my own, but there are always other people involved. I don't want to force people and say, 'Now you've got to do this.' What I'd like — and this was the actual aim — is to try and get somewhere as a group. I'd like the others in the group to feel that the things which occupy me are also of importance to them. Maybe that's something I can't do at the present because we haven't reached that stage as a group yet.

*You mentioned the word process. Process means development. You yourself have developed considerably. For example you've developed further and further away from the classical form of modern dance towards drama, although I know that this is only a very superficial description of the process. Do you have any idea where the process is leading you or where you yourself are going? Could you imagine retiring from dance completely and becoming a theater director, for example?*

That's possible. I don't know. I'm always trying. I keep desperately trying to dance. I'm always hoping I'm going to find new ways of relating to movement. I can't go on working in the previous way. It would be like repeating something, strange.

*Might it also be that movement simply no longer suffices for what you want to say — that you also require words?*

Words? I can't say exactly. But then again, on the contrary . . . it might be a movement. It is simply a question of when is it dance, when is it not. Where does it start? When do we call it dance? It does in fact have something to do with consciousness, with bodily consciousness, and the way we form things. But then it needn't have this kind of aesthetic form. It can have a quite different form and still be dance. Basically one wants to say something which cannot be said, so what one has done is to make a poem where one can feel what is meant. And so words, I find, are a means — a means to an end. But words are not the true aim.

*What would you describe the true aim as being? Communication, or is it art?*

I don't know. I don't know.

*(The interviewer was Jochen Schmidt, 1978)*

■   ■   ■

## Source

Bausch, P. and Schmidt, J. (1978, 1984) 'Not How People Move But What Moves Them', *Pina Bausch–Wuppertal Dance Theater, or The Art of Training a Goldfish*, trans. P. Stadie, ed. N. Servos, Köln: Ballett-Bühnen Verlag: 227–230.

## Pina Bausch (1940–2009)

German choreographer and director of Wuppertal Dance Theater. She began her career as a dancer after training first with Kurt Jooss at the Folkwang School in Essen and then in New York at the Juilliard School. From 1962 to 1968 she danced with the Folkwang Ballet, where she began her choreographic career. She became Director of Wuppertal Dance Theater for the 1973–74 season and has remained there. Her works for the company have included *Bluebeard* (1977), *Café Müller* (1978), and *1980 – A Piece by Pina Bausch* (1980), *Danzón* (1995 and *Wiesenland – A Piece by Pina Bausch* (2000). The company's repertory consists of a relatively small number of major pieces. Unlike others working in dance, she produces nearly all evening length works. The company has toured Europe, including the UK, in the Americas and extensively elsewhere.

Bausch's work is remarkable in both the scale and detail of her theatricality. She uses the smallest nuances of her dancers' attributes on stage and, at the same time, magnifies them into full-scale works that can last hours. Her dance theatre emphasises how people behave, presenting them in real time, as real people, yet writ large. The choreography appears deceptively simple, yet it is highly complex. The staging of her work has frequently transformed the stage area with hyperrealistic sets or with natural materials such as earth, water, turf and flowers.

She is credited by many as a founder of dance theatre and for redefining European dance in the late twentieth century. In her work Bausch presents 'people as they really are'. Servos likens her approach to Brecht's. *Tanztheater* is characteristically large scale (either theatrically or in length), presenting real people, real events and real emotions. The situations that explore the intimacies of life also reflect how it is socially constructed, especially through the analysis and portrayal of gender. These are facilitated by formal means that stress discontinuity, deconstruction and collage. Servos has characterised her work as a return to a 'language of the body' whilst Schmidt emphasises the 'renewal of the human image'.

Bausch is unquestionably the main figure in late twentieth-century German dance, her stature being comparable to that of Heiner Müller in theatre.

This interview is one of four with Jochen Schmidt and published in Servos's definitive study of her early works. It was conducted in November 1978, shortly before the première of *Kontakthof* (1978). She talks straightforwardly and frankly about aspects of her working method. Her observations are realistic, rather than codified, reflecting her attitude towards the making of her work.

## Compare this interview with writings by the following authors in this reader

**Brecht** – a comparable approach in theatre
**Brown, Cunningham and Rainer** – comparison with modern and postmodern American dance
**Kaprow** – for a durational use of everyday movement
**LeCompte** – another confrontational approach
**Lepage** – a theatrical contemporary
**Müller** – who acknowledges his admiration for her work
**Wilson** – the use of non-linear theatrical juxtapositions

## Further reading

*Ballett International* for the most extensive collection of articles and reviews on Bausch's work.
Climenhaga, R. (2009) *Pina Bausch*, London: Routledge.
Fernandes, C. (2001) *Pina Bausch and the Wuppertal Dance Theater: The Aesthetics of Repetition and Transformation*, New York: Peter Lang.
Servos, N. (ed.) (1984) *Pina Bausch–Wuppertal Dance Theater or The Art of Training a Goldfish*, trans. P. Stadie, Köln: Ballett-Bühnen Verlag.

# Chapter 8

Beck

## Julian Beck

### ACTING EXERCISES

**Acting Exercises:**

**Notes for a Primary Lesson (1)**

Not to submit to an acting lesson unless its graphic purpose is clear. The body, if not stimulated by an inspiring impetus, does not react with interest. The movements, consequently the expression, are empty because they are empty of meaning.

The Living Theatre works something like this: we find an idea that we want to express physically. Then we do what is necessary to realize it. If it requires special exercises, then we do them.

Whenever we work physically we find things that we never could find if we did nothing but think.

We have rarely been able to find sufficient time simply to exercise. There is hardly enough time to do the necessary. Emergency.

All the time knowing that without living physically the powers of the mind diminish.

Therefore we are always individually doing Yoga, as we go thru the day doing other things we check our breathing, our posture, our movement, regularly. And the body's awareness of what's around it, and the space.

To train the body to extend its ordinary capacities. To extend imagination and intellect. Exercise should not be used to train the body to express the banal. We want things not yet known to the controlled consciousness which is ruining us. If sensitivity is not heightened by the exercise, and only the banal is expressed, we remain what we are, frustrated, unfulfilled, crippled.

Aimless exercise reinforces the accessibility of the banal.

At the same time it is important to nourish the body with use. The body understands that; but exercise without objective confuses the mind.

■　■　■

## Source

Beck, J. (1972) 'Acting Exercises: Notes for a Primary Lesson (1)', *The Life of the Theatre: The Relation of the Artist to the Struggle of the People*, San Francisco: City Lights Books.

## Julian Beck (1925–85)

Performer and director. With Judith Malina he created the Living Theatre, whose view of theatre as a rite of purgation via contact with a collective of performers owed much to the ideas of both Artaud and Grotowski. Throughout the 1960s the Living Theatre became famous as New York and the USA's most revolutionary theatre company, creating large-scale and lengthy performance rituals, often based on archetypal subjects, such as *Frankenstein* (1965), or *Paradise Now* (1968).

In their performances character and plot were replaced by physical and collective imagery often demanding participation on the part of the audience, which was often gladly given. As in the work of Artaud and the Dadaists, the group presented the audience with a rejection of contemporary, war-torn civilisation – this was the period of the Vietnam War in America – in favour of individual spiritual change through the rites of theatre. The group – actors from all persuasions – often pursued their politics in performance to an extent that disturbed the authorities – the group's intention. In 1970 this culminated in a declaration to 'abandon theatre and . . . create circumstances which will lead to action'. The work included ceremonies of initiation and communion as a direct response to the 'machines' of a mechanistic and psychologically tortured outside world. The group became nomadic, moving from country to country for refuge.

'Acting Exercises' emphasises the attack on bourgeois values by proposing an essentially poetic approach to the world and to theatre, echoing the words of Artaud, a potent and compelling combination for the student generation of 1968, for whom the Living Theatre became representatives of a powerful artistic credo.

## Compare this article with writings by the following authors in this reader

**Artaud, Grotowski and Jarry** – messianic/revolutionary claims for theatre
**Boal** – a contemporary South American view of theatre as a force for change
**Brook** – a collective collaborative ethic
**Brown and Rainer** – contemporary, contrasting, response to the times
**Lepage** – an oppositional view of the function of performance
**Schechner** – North American theatre contemporary
**Stanislavski** – earlier, contrasting view of the actor's training

## Further reading

Bilder, E. and Malina, J. (1992) *Theaudric: Julian Beck's Last Notebooks*, Reading: Harwood.

Biner, P. (1972) *The Living Theatre*, New York: Avon Books.

The Living Theatre (1971) *Paradise Now*, New York: Random House.

Silvestro, C. (ed.) (1971) *The Living Book of the Living Theatre*, Greenwich, Conn.: New York Graphic Society.

# Chapter 9

# Walter Benjamin

## WHAT IS EPIC THEATER?

### The relaxed audience

'There is nothing more pleasant than to lie on a sofa and read a novel,' wrote a nineteenth-century narrator, indicating the great extent to which a work of fiction can relax the reader who is enjoying it. The common image of a man attending a theatrical performance is the opposite: one pictures a man who follows the action with every fiber of his being at rapt attention. The concept of the epic theater, originated by Brecht as the theoretician of his poetic practice, indicates above all that this theater desires an audience that is relaxed and follows the action without strain. This audience, to be sure, always appears as a collective, and this differentiates it from the reader, who is alone with his text. Also, this audience, being a collective, will usually feel impelled to react promptly. This reaction, according to Brecht, ought to be a well-considered and therefore a relaxed one – in short, the reaction of people who have an interest in the matter. Two objects are provided for this interest. The first is the action; it has to be such that the audience can keep a check on it at crucial places on the basis of its own experience. The second is the performance; it should be mounted artistically in a pellucid manner. (This manner of presentation is anything but artless; actually, it presupposes artistic sophistication and acumen on the part of the director.) Epic theater appeals to an interest group who 'do not think without reason.' Brecht does not lose sight of the masses, whose limited practice of thinking is probably described by this phrase. In the endeavor to interest the audience in the theater expertly, but definitely not by way of mere cultural involvement, a political will has prevailed.

## The plot

The epic theater purposes to 'deprive the stage of its sensation derived from subject matter.' Thus an old story will often do more for it than a new one. Brecht has considered the question of whether the incidents that are presented by the epic theater should not already be familiar. The theater would have the same relationship to the plot as a ballet teacher has to his pupil: his first task would be to loosen her joints to the greatest possible extent. This is how the Chinese theater actually proceeds. In his essay 'The Fourth Wall of China' (*Life and Letters Today*, Vol. XV, No. 6, 1936), Brecht states what he owes to this theater. If the theater is to cast about for familiar events, 'historical incidents would be the most suitable.' Their epic extension through the style of acting, the placards and captions, is intended to purge them of the sensational.

In this vein Brecht takes the life of Galileo as the subject of his latest play. Brecht presents Galileo primarily as a great teacher who not only teaches a new physics, but does so in a new way. In his hands, experiments are not only an achievement of science, but a tool of pedagogy as well. The main emphasis of this play is not on Galileo's recantation; rather, the truly epic process must be sought in what is evident from the labeling of the penultimate scene: '1633 to 1642. As a prisoner of the Inquisition, Galileo continues his scientific work until his death. He succeeds in smuggling his main works out of Italy.'

Epic theater is in league with the course of time in an entirely different way from that of the tragic theater. Because suspense belongs less to the outcome than to the individual events, this theater can cover the greatest spans of time. (The same is true of the earlier mystery plays. The dramaturgy of *Oedipus* or *The Wild Duck* constitutes the counterpole of epic dramaturgy.)

## The untragic hero

The French classical theater made room in the midst of the players for persons of rank, who had their armchairs on the open stage. To us this seems inappropriate. According to the concept of the 'dramatic element' with which we are familiar, it seemed inappropriate to attach to the action on the stage a nonparticipating third party as a dispassionate observer or 'thinker.' Yet Brecht often had something like that in mind. One can go even further and say that Brecht made an attempt to make the thinker, or even the wise man, the hero of the drama. From this very point of view one can define his theater as epic theater. This attempt is taken furthest in the character of Galy Gay, the packer. Galy Gay, the protagonist of the play *A Man's a Man*, is nothing but an exhibit of the contradictions which make up our society. It may not be too bold to regard the wise man in the Brechtian sense as the perfect showcase of its dialectics. In any case, Galy Gay is a wise man. Plato already recognized the undramatic quality of that most excellent man, the sage. In his Dialogues he took him to the threshold of the drama; in his *Phaidon*, to the threshold of the passion play. The medieval Christ, who also represented the wise man (we find this in the Early Fathers), is the untragic hero *par excellence*. But in the secular drama of the West, too, the search for the untragic hero has never ceased. In always new ways, and frequently in conflict with its theoreticians, this drama has differed from the authentic — that is, the Greek — form of tragedy. This important but poorly marked road, which may here serve as the image of a tradition, went via Roswitha and the mystery plays in the Middle Ages, via Gryphius and Calderón in the Baroque age; later we may trace it in Lenz and Grabbe, and finally in Strindberg. Scenes in Shakespeare are its roadside monuments, and Goethe crosses it in the second part of *Faust*. It is a European road, but a German one as well-provided that we may speak of a road and not of a secret smugglers' path by which the legacy of the medieval and the Baroque drama has reached us. It is this mule track, neglected and overgrown, which comes to light today in the dramas of Brecht.

## The interruption

Brecht differentiates his epic theater from the dramatic theater in the narrower sense, whose theory was formulated by Aristotle. Appropriately, Brecht introduces his art of the drama as non-Aristotelian, just as Riemann introduced a non-Euclidian geometry. This analogy may bring out the fact that it is not a matter of competition between the theatrical forms in question. Riemann eliminated the parallel postulate; Brecht's drama eliminated the Aristotelian catharsis, the purging of the emotions through empathy with the stirring fate of the hero.

The special character of the relaxed interest of the audience for which the performances of the epic theater are intended is the fact that hardly any appeal is made to the empathy of the spectators. Instead, the art of the epic theater consists in producing astonishment rather than empathy. To put it succinctly: instead of identifying with the characters, the audience should be educated to be astonished at the circumstances under which they function.

The task of the epic theater, according to Brecht, is not so much the development of actions as the representation of conditions. This presentation does not mean reproduction as the theoreticians of Naturalism understood it. Rather, the truly important thing is to discover the conditions of life. (One, might say just as well: to alienate [*verfremden*] them.) This discovery (alienation) of conditions takes place through the interruption of happenings. The most primitive example would be a family scene. Suddenly a stranger enters. The mother was just about to seize a bronze bust and hurl it at her daughter; the father was in the act of opening the window in order to call a policeman. At that moment the stranger appears in the doorway. This means that the stranger is confronted with the situation as with a startling picture: troubled faces, an open window, the furniture in disarray. But there are eyes to which even more ordinary scenes of middle-class life look almost equally startling.

## The quotable gesture

In one of his didactic poems on dramatic art Brecht says: 'The effect of every sentence was waited for and laid bare. And the waiting lasted until the crowd had carefully weighed our sentence.' In short, the play was interrupted. One can go even further and remember that interruption is one of the fundamental devices of all structuring. It goes far beyond the sphere of art. To give only one example, it is the basis of quotation. To quote a text involves the interruption of its context. It is therefore understandable that the epic theater, being based on interruption, is, in a specific sense, a quotable one. There is nothing special about the quotability of its texts. It is different with the gestures which fit into the course of the play.

'Making gestures quotable' is one of the substantial achievements of the epic theater. An actor must be able to space his gestures the way a typesetter produces spaced type. This effect may be achieved, for instance, by an actor's quoting his own gesture on the stage. Thus we saw in *Happy End* how Carola Neher, acting a sergeant in the Salvation Army, sang, by way of proselytizing, a song in a sailors' tavern that was more appropriate there than it would have been in a church, and then had to quote this song and act out the gestures before a council of the Salvation Army. Similarly, in *The Measure Taken* the party tribunal is given not only the report of the comrades, but also the acting out of some of the gestures of the comrade they are accusing. What is a device of the subtlest kind in the epic theater generally becomes an immediate purpose in the specific case of the didactic play. Epic theater is by definition a gestic theater. For the more frequently we interrupt someone in the act of acting, the more gestures result.

## The didactic play

In every instance, the epic theater is meant for the actors as much as for the spectators. The didactic play is a special case largely because it facilitates and suggests the interchange between audience and actors and vice versa through the extreme paucity of the mechanical equipment. Every spectator is enabled to become a participant. And it is indeed easier to play the 'teacher' than the 'hero.'

In the first version of *Lindberghflug* (Lindbergh's Flight), which appeared in a periodical, the flier was still presented as a hero. That version was intended as his glorification. The second version — and this is revealing — owes its origin to the fact that Brecht revised himself. What enthusiasm there was on both continents on the days following this flight! But this enthusiasm petered out as a mere sensation. In *The Flight of the Lindberghs* Brecht endeavors to refract the spectrum of the 'thrill' (*Erlebnis*) in order to derive from it the hues of 'experience' (*Erfahrung*) — the experience that could be obtained only from Lindbergh's effort, not from the excitement of the public, and which was to be conveyed to 'the Lindberghs.'

T.E. Lawrence, the author of *Seven Pillars of Wisdom*, wrote to Robert Graves when he joined the air force that such a step was for modern man what entering a monastery was for medieval man. In this remark we perceive the same tension that we find in *The Flight of the Lindberghs* and the later didactic plays. A clerical sternness is applied to instruction in a modern technique — here, that of aviation; later, that of the class struggle. This second application may be seen most fully in *Mother*. It was a particularly daring undertaking to keep a social drama free of the effects which empathy produces and which the audience was accustomed to. Brecht knew this and expressed it in an epistolary poem that he sent to a New York workingmen's theater when *Mother* was produced there. 'We have been asked: Will a worker understand this? Will he be able to do without his accustomed opiate, his mental participation in someone else's uprising, the rise of others; the illusion which whips him up for a few hours and leaves him all the more exhausted, filled with vague memories and even vaguer hopes?'

Like the pictures in a film, epic theater moves in spurts. Its basic form is that of the shock with which the single, well-defined situations of the play collide. The songs, the captions, the lifeless conventions set off one situation from another. This brings about intervals which, if anything, impair the illusion of the audience and paralyze its readiness for empathy. These intervals are reserved for the spectators' critical reaction — to the actions of the players and to the way in which they are presented. As to the manner of presentation, the actor's task in the epic theater is to demonstrate through his acting that he is cool and relaxed. He too has hardly any use for empathy. For this kind of acting the 'player' of the dramatic theater is not always fully prepared. Perhaps the most open-minded approach to epic theater is to think of it in terms of 'putting on a show.'

Brecht wrote: 'The actor must show his subject, and he must show himself. Of course, he shows his subject by showing himself, and he shows himself by showing his subject. Although the two coincide, they must not coincide in such a way that the difference between the two tasks disappears.' In other words: an actor should reserve for himself the possibility of stepping out of character artistically. At the proper moment he should insist on portraying a man who reflects about his part. It would be erroneous to think at such a moment of Romantic Irony, as employed by Tieck in his *Puss in Boots*. This irony has no didactic aim. Basically, it demonstrates only the philosophic sophistication of the author who, in writing his plays, always remembers that in the end the world may turn out to be a theater.

To what extent artistic and political interests coincide on the scene of epic theater will become manifest in the style of acting appropriate to this genre. A case in point is Brecht's cycle *The Private Life of the Master Race*. It is easy to see that if a German actor in exile were assigned the part of an SS man or a member of the People's Court, his feelings about it would be quite different from those of a devoted father and husband asked to portray Molière's Don Juan. For the former, empathy can hardly be regarded as an appropriate method, since he presumably cannot identify with the murderers of his fellow fighters. Another mode of performance, which calls for detachment, would in such cases be right and fitting and particularly successful. This is the epic stagecraft.

## Theater on a dais

The aims of the epic theater can be defined more easily in terms of the stage than of a new drama. Epic theater allows for a circumstance which has been too little noticed. It may be called the filling in of the orchestra pit. The abyss which separates the players from the audience as it does the dead from the living; the abyss whose silence in a play heightens the sublimity, whose resonance in an opera heightens the intoxication – this abyss, of all elements of the theater the one that bears the most indelible traces of its ritual origin, has steadily decreased in significance. The stage is still raised, but it no longer rises from an unfathomable depth; it has become a dais. The didactic play and the epic theater are attempts to sit down on a dais.

■　　■　　■

## Source

Benjamin, W. (1973) 'What is Epic Theater?', *Illuminations*, trans. H. Zohn, London: Fontana: 149–156. First published in 1939 in *Mass und Wert* 2; in 1955 in *Schriften* by Suhrkamp Verlag, Frankfurt-am-Main; first English translation 1968 and first published in Great Britain 1970.[1]

## Walter Benjamin (1892–1940)

German Marxist literary critic. He was a central figure, along with Adorno, Horkheimer and Marcuse, of the Frankfurt School, based on the Institute for Social Research that was founded in 1923. Benjamin and the early Frankfurt School were originators of Marxist critical theory, whereby cultural aspects of social change were acknowledged, as well as material ones. He had a considerable influence on the thinking of radical 1960s cultural movements.

Benjamin contributed a number of highly influential ideas to both the study of performance and its practice. Introduced to Brecht in the 1920s, they worked together, first in Germany and then during Benjamin's visits to Brecht in exile. They continued an extensive correspondence throughout the 1930s. Benjamin fled the Gestapo in 1940 and committed suicide whilst trying to cross into Spain. Benjamin's key contributions include the idea that the function of art in the twentieth century has changed from the ritual to the political,[2] and the idea that the author is not a special person but a producer[3] and therefore in a position to be on the side of the proletariat in the fight against capitalism and fascism. Benjamin writes about Brecht's work in many of his central political essays. In 'What is Epic Theater?', he praises Brecht's new form of theatre as one that corresponds to the new technology of the twentieth century. He goes on to describe precisely how this form of theatre differs from the old, bourgeois forms and how it therefore establishes a new and relevant relationship with its audience.

## Compare this article with writings by the following authors in this reader

Anderson — an oblique but telling acknowledgement of his ideas
Brecht — intellectual collaborator, correspondent and friend
Brook — a critique of the dead hand of bourgeois theatre
Cage — a contemporary, contrary view of the purpose of art
Soyinka — an intellectual stance that acknowledges West African roots

## Further reading

Benjamin, W. (1973a) *Illuminations,* trans. H. Zohn, London: Fontana.
Benjamin, W. (1973b) *Understanding Brecht*, trans. A. Bostock, London: NLB.
Friedlander, E. (2012) *Walter Benjamin: A Philosophical Portrait*, Cambridge, Mass.: Harvard University Press.
Leslie, E. (2007) *Walter Benjamin*, London: Reaktion Books.

## Notes

1    See also A. Bostock's translations in (1973b) *Understanding Brecht*: 1–22.
2    Described in his essay (1973a) 'The Work of Art in the Age of Mechanical Reproduction', *Illuminations*.
3    See (1973b) 'The Author as Producer', *Understanding Brecht*.

# Chapter 10

## Joseph Beuys

SPEECH UPON RECEIVING
AN HONORARY DOCTORATE
DEGREE FROM THE NOVA
SCOTIA COLLEGE OF ART AND
DESIGN, HALIFAX 1976

**D**EAR FRIENDS, DEAR PRESIDENT, dear members of the staff, dear students, and dear parents of the students and dear all other people who are here now present with their self-conscious "I." I endeavor not to throw the dollop of fat on the table, the dollop, the complexity of the whole differentiated theory as is existent and developed in my work during the last ten years almost, as the theory of sculpture, as the "Energy Plan of the Western Man," as the "Warmth Ferry," as the "Sun State" and as the totalization of the idea of art. I stress the point after my greeting words to all of you who are present with your self-conscious "I" because already now I am standing on the basis of the problem of how an enlarged understanding of art could work and could break through the borders of isolation which the present culture stands in, isolated from or against all other fields of society, such as the whole democratic energy field, the economic energy field.

Here I am standing now in the language problem and in the basic problem of the inspired speaker, since I stress being present with the self-conscious "I." As a starting point when I come to the desk here I invent my beginning as only a normal living being, as only a natural person. But already in being interested to speak to you, to the audience, to the people, to the receiver, since I can speak with sense; then I speak already not only as a natural person but I also speak as an engaged person. In this manner I am not only describing as a natural person can describe but I am also describing and determining a "me." I speak already as an interested ego, and I am more interested in the receiver.

I'm here standing in the field of relations and communications. In this field already appears the whole ability of the people working together in communication, bringing together all different abilities in experiences of life with results of research, with results of investigation. This field contains already an indefinite number of different problems. It is, it appears as, a kind of addition, an endless addition of all problems contained already in the problem of cultural doings. But to go on with this being interested, to go on to stress the element of relationship and communication as a democratic love process in language, I must bore or drill deeper to the thought level of the self-conscious "I" because only this position in consciousness can find a united substance with the ability to metamorphize the conditions in the society, which are no other things than a collection of sometimes already dead things or old things and which therefore work like an illness in society and work like a cancer, especially in the process of creating freedom. I cannot understand the idea of creativity where it is not related to the self-conscious "I" which stands in the field of inner freedom.

From this basic position there is a point in the world where everybody can change the world through his free individuality. When he observes and when he comes to a clear observation of facts he can work through these means. Now he stands in the culture and looks at other fields in the society and then he can see what is contained in the theory of an enlarged understanding of art growing and working through all power fields of the society. I would only stress this point, where there appears freedom in culture, where the outcome through active doings by free individuals with their self-conscious "I" is an amelioration, a bettering of the position of men in having consciousness of the whole problem, since now they are looking not only at the artist's problems but everybody's needs. There is also the question of equality in law in the society and the whole democratic power field. The idea of creativity is now flowing in this field, and one sees that creativity, these signs of freedom, and this declaration of art, which are related to a principle: the possibility to mold the world, to design the world, to sculpture the world, are not restricted to the problems of the artist. There is an anthropological determination of everybody's existence to be an artist in the society. Then one can see that the rule of structure, the formulation and the forming and the sculpturing of the constitution of the future has to go through free individuals and has to come from the grass roots in cooperation with all people together. Then one can see from this enlarged understanding of art that the battery of abilities, and therefore this society, which can be called an ability-society, could work and transform the whole power field of brotherhood, or the social field, or the until-now-called economical field. I say "until now," since this traditional idea of economy is still restricted by convention in the same way that traditional art is restricted.

But in enlarging this understanding of art, we are in the process of the totalization of the idea of art. We see that the totalization of art is now no longer related to the activities of artists and specialists in their insulated, isolated field of so-called cultural freedom. In reality this field is not free, it is only a free place where you can do what you want without rules and without responsibility. We can see that a totalized idea of art would ameliorate the possibilities in this field too. We see that the economical ideas are to be molded and sculptured according to this idea of totalized freedom, and that the totalized understanding of art totalizes the understanding of economy. No longer can the idea of production and enterprise be restricted in a field where only a physical production operates. All productions are now invested with the idea of a new anthropological declaration of human individual freedom and the enterprise which results from freedom. This is to declare that a spiritual being has therefore firstly the need for spiritual goods. By having these spiritual goods in a positive quality and by sculpturing the freedom field and the free field of cultural doings, the people will see that they have a need to organize only secondly all other needs, i.e., physical needs.

But the most important thing is to organize, and now appears the idea of organization as the idea of sculpture, as the idea of design, as the idea of molding and sculpturing the society. To regulate these processes, to have the means to regulate and to care for a structure in law necessitates a constitution. A law appears as a sculptural good of the people. It means it has to be done by the people. Therefore it now becomes a problem of basic questions. It will not be the practice of the future that only a minority with a special interest have the full political power to sculpture or to induce laws. And you will find that this law structure could work in the power field of economics, that there would be a law for the money, because the money is the most important sculpture as a regulating means of all creative processes. Since money regulates in all fields, in all the bloodstream of the society, it therefore has to have the character of a bloodstream. It has therefore to be described as a law-money, a bill of rights, while now it is only standing in a money-economics. The character of this money-economics will be metamorphized and will form an ability-society or spiritual-society.

I can only speak briefly and cannot expand on the whole score of complexities of such a view on the possibilities in society; I will only say that this stress on the free self-conscious "I" is not easy, is not comfortable. It asks for a lot of toughness, strong effort and continuous work. And therefore I will close this short speech, in which is implied my cordial thanks for what I received before, with the idea that there are only existing two possibilities, compulsion or making a sacrifice. In this sacrifice is implied the work of mankind in the future. Once more, only two alternatives exist, compulsion or sacrifice. In this way, in conclusion, I look back to the vision of John Milton, *Paradise Lost* and *Paradise Regained*.

■   ■   ■

## Source

Beuys, J. (1990) 'Speech upon receiving an honorary doctorate degree' (1976), New York: Four Walks and Windows.

## Joseph Beuys (1921–1986)

Beuys was born into a Catholic family in northwestern Germany and though he was primarily a sculptor he is important as being one of the major visual artists of the twentieth century to offer an expanded notion of art, which included performance, installation, debate and public discussion. He created performances of 'actions', the two most famous of which are *How to explain pictures to a Dead Hare* (1965), and *I like America and America likes me*, which took place in New York in 1974. Beuys spent three days in a gallery space with a wild coyote from the desert, and flew in and out of the United States without once touching American soil. He was met at the airport, covered in felt – a symbolic material for him – loaded into an ambulance and driven directly to the gallery. He explained 'I wanted to isolate myself, insulate myself, see nothing of America other than the coyote'. At that time America was heavily engaged in the war in Vietnam, which Beuys vehemently opposed, and he saw his work as an artist as a direct challenge to the domination of American art.

Many of Beuys' works involve images and materials that have an extra-artistic meaning. He identified with the plants and wildlife where he lived, and incorporated certain animals in his work. 'The figures of the horse, the stag, the swan, and the hare constantly come and go: figures which pass freely from one level of existence to another, which represent the incarnation of the soul.' Beuys was also one of the founders of the Green Party, and since his death his work is now seen as a major link with other artists who saw their work in a political context. He used materials such as fat, with its puzzling flexibility, and felt, which can absorb other objects, and which for Beuys became a symbol of warmth.

In 1971 Beuys founded the Organisation for Direct Democracy through Referendum, and also helped establish the Free International University, which aimed to evolve the creative spirit outside the confines of academia. In the 1970s he was brought to the Edinburgh Festival by Richard Demarco, where as part of the exhibition 'Strategy: get arts' he ran seminars, discussions and workshops which were hailed as one of the key demonstrations of the power of the artist.

Beuys' artworks and performances were not concerned with entertainment: they are a demonstration of the environmental and ideological concerns of which his work *7000 Oaks*, begun in 1982, is one of the final examples of art attempting to generate an 'ecological wakening' for mankind.

His speech accepting an honorary degree encapsulates the totality of his thinking.

Compare this article with writings by the following artists in this reader

**Abramovic** – a performance artist of extremes
**Brecht** – another German activist
**Cage** – an American shifter of perceptions
**Maciunas** – a movement of the erosion of boundaries

## Further reading

Tisdall, C. (1979) *Joseph Beuys*, London: Thames and Hudson.
Schirmer, L. (1996) *The Essential Joseph Beuys*, London: Thames and Hudson.
Thompson, C. (2011) *Felt: Fluxus, Joseph Beuys, and the Dalai Lama*, University of Minnesota Press.
Mesch, C. and Michely, V. (eds) (2007) *Joseph Beuys: The Reader*, MIT Press.

# Chapter 11

# Rustom Bharucha

## NOTES ON THE INVENTION
## OF TRADITION

ET ME SHARE some thoughts with you on that worn-out, inexhaustible subject – tradition. Instead of attempting to define it in a pan-Indian context, I would like to situate it within its multiple uses in the contemporary Indian theatre. To what extent has 'tradition' (which originates from the Latin word – *tradere* – to 'hand over' or 'deliver') been used in the context of 'handing down knowledge' or 'passing on a doctrine?' And to what extent has it been 'invented' (to use Eric Hobsbawm's valuable term) in response to larger political, economic and social factors?

As I demonstrate in this essay, tradition can be invented in any number of ways, even though we may not be aware of it. The most conspicuous of 'inventions' are 'fabrications', such as the Republic Day Parade, where the diverse cultures of India are 'unified' through a carefully choreographed spectacle. In recent years, this kind of 'invention' has become increasingly virtuosic as is evident in the Festivals of India and the Utsavs of New Delhi. Here, through a conglomeration of effects, which could include songs, dances, tableaux, symbols, floats, fireworks, informal minglings between 'native' performers and 'foreign' spectators, selling of Indian food and other 'indigenous' activities, an atmosphere is constructed whereby 'the Indian tradition' is affirmed, not necessarily as people in India would understand it, but as our government would like to represent it to the world.

In this essay, I will not deal with this ubiquitous phenomenon but focus instead on the more seemingly 'creative' inventions of tradition that have been implemented by our own artists, directors and 'experts' in the Indian theatre. Much of the discussion will focus on the *discourse* of theatre, in which concepts of the 'folk' and the 'theatre of roots' will be examined as inventions of the urban intelligentsia. More often than not, when people 'invent' tradition ('authentic' or 'spurious', through acts of 'cultural preservation' or 'subversion'), they unavoidably imply that they are no longer in touch with its immediacies. Yet an illusion is often maintained whereby the 'invention' is placed within the mainstream of tradition itself.

## Mediations of technology

At a very basic level, one could say that 'inventions' develop from an urge to 'find out or produce something new'. They are not 'discoveries' of things which already exist but need to be 'exposed', 'made known'. Inventions uphold a different sense of the unknown. Instead of 'exposure', they are concerned with *making* new artefacts. Very often, these artefacts emerge through the mediations of a new technology and machinery that precipitate an alteration of forms. In the following section let us examine some of these mediations through the intervention and assimilation of 'foreign' structures of representation.

It is well known that our tradition has always provided us with a surfeit of narratives in the theatre. Our 'professional theatre' in the late nineteenth century scored some of its most spectacular successes with theatrical renderings from the *Mahabharata* and the *Ramayana*. That all-Indian phenomenon, the Parsee theatre, funded and administered by the Parsees, but acted, directed, designed and most important, seen by a wide range of communities all over India, invariably had a stock of 'traditional' plays. Invariably, they were mythological in content, providing a direct stimulus to the religious blockbusters of the early Indian cinema.

The point to be stressed here is that our 'tradition' had already been mediated by the colonial machinery of the nineteenth-century theatre, the conventions and stage tricks derived from the pantomimes and historical extravaganzas of the English Victorian stage. However, it should also be emphasized that these derivations had been thoroughly 'Indianized' through music, song, colour, pathos, melodrama and the histrionic delivery of lines that are intrinsically a part of the popular theatrical tradition in India.

At a very elemental level, 'tradition' in the nineteenth-century commercial theatre meant 'spectacle'. It provided audiences with new possibilities of adoring gods and mythological heroes in kinetic, technicolour settings. In its importation of theatre technology, there were trapdoors that facilitated supernatural ascents and descents, a 'fly system' that enabled *apsaras* to float rather precariously into the wings and, at a later stage, the novelties of the revolving stage, cloud machines and the cyclorama.

So alluring were these derivations of an essentially foreign theatre tradition, and so widespread their influence, that even today one can trace their remnants in a number of 'traditional' performances. In Yakshagana, for instance, or of what remains of it, traces of the popular Gubbi theatre tradition still linger in painted backdrops and histrionic acting styles that are anathema to the purists. I have even seen a Krishnalila performance in a village where a very belligerent female impersonator upstaged Krishna in a sequinned costume and a wig that looked like relics from *Shirin Farhad*.

At one level, these commercial interventions are 'perversions', but nonetheless, they have been absorbed within traditional performance structures in deference to 'popular taste'. It needs to be emphasized that the clear-cut distinctions between 'popular culture' (which is the category in which 'company theatre' or 'Parsee theatre' could be placed) and 'folk culture' (to which Yakshagana ostensibly belongs), cannot be regarded as absolute or mutually exclusive. Nor can we assume that it is 'folk forms' which invariably influence popular entertainment, because they happen to be older and 'rooted' in the cultural psyche of the people. Very often, it is the other way around, when, for example, the 'perversions' of commercial Bengali theatre, notably cabaret, have directly influenced the 'folk' theatre tradition of Jatra.

In fact, if there is one 'indigenous' source of influence that has played a fertile role in promoting new genres, it would not be the 'folk theatre' (which is struggling to hold on to its identity), but the 'company theatre' tradition, which no longer exists, but whose idiom has been absorbed in the commercial Hindi cinema, and more recently, in the representation of myth on Doordarshan serials. If one had to trace the origins of mass appeal embedded in Ramanand Sagar's *Ramayana*, one would have to turn to its use of Parsee theatre conventions, which are barely recognizable, yet perceptible, submerged under layers of conventions from other traditions. Apart from the obvious influence of mythological films, there are traces of science fiction, advertising, high tech, cartoons and even through some convoluted process of unconscious assimilation, the visuals of Monty Python.

Whatever one may think of its artistic merits, one cannot deny that Sagar's *Ramayana* has been sufficiently convincing to millions of people to serve as a source of *darshan*. What may seem bizarre and mindlessly eclectic has been intensely familiar to the masses. The eternal fiction of the *Ramayana* has not merely survived its 'invention' on the idiot box, it may even have stimulated a form of Hindu revivalism, whose manipulative possibilities by fundamentalists and politicians need not be stressed. One can despair about the absence of historicity in representations like Sagar's *Ramayana*, but they also reveal very decisively that people are prepared to accept new 'inventions' of tradition so long as their faith in dominant myths is substantiated and enriched.

In this regard, in reflecting on the mediation of new technologies to project myths, what needs to be stressed is not so much the technology itself, but how it is viewed. The *Ramayana* has been seen within the proscenium framework of the Parsee theatre tradition, which in turn has been miniaturized on the two-dimensional rectangular television screen. It has also been seen for many years in numerous stagings of the Ramlila held in many parts of India, most notably in

Ramnagar, where the *lila* extends over the entire town for a month. The fact that the *Ramayana* has survived its diverse 'inventions' testifies not only to the innate richness of the epic and its deep significance to most Indians, but it also reveals the phenomenal viewing capacities of the Indian spectators, who are capable of seeing the illusion of an image with or without its technological mediation. Sometimes, if they feel inclined, they may focus only on the technology, such as a 'special effect' in the Ramayana serial, and applaud its sheer virtuosity. But at other moments, all that matters to them is the 'vision' that they alone see, which is precipitated by the representation, and yet detached from it.

*Darshan* is capable of subverting technology. Even if an Indian spectator may not be fully conscious of his seeing capacities, there is nothing quite like his ability to see God within an actor's frame. Nor can one underrate his capacity to tune in and out of an image. While avant-garde circles in America and Europe may cultivate the faculty of 'selective inattention', it seems to me that this comes very naturally to our spectators. Particularly in our rural and *mofussil* audiences, one finds an almost collective concentration and dispersal of energies. One moment could be totally rapt, as the spectators see a divine presence on stage. This could be followed by a very candid, and frequently, critical response to the representation on the level of pure theatricality. At still other moments, the play could be seen in a state of collective somnolence. But then, at just the appropriate moment in the narrative, everyone could be awake and totally absorbed in the action on stage.

I dwell on this enormously flexible seeing process because it may be one of the contributing factors to our 'invention' of tradition. Certainly, it would be wrong to say that it is only 'artists' who are capable of invention. What seems more pertinent (though harder to substantiate) is that there is a collusion between the artist and the people regarding the nature and limits of invention. At this point in time, one can say that technology has not yet coopted the 'visionary' possibilities of seeing assumed by our spectators in their viewing of myths. But in time to come, as these performances get increasingly commodified and the onslaught of the media becomes more fierce, it will be critical to see how the viewing capacities of our spectators will be altered. Will they still be able to see what they choose to see and are willed to see, or will they be numbed into total passivity? Will the 'inventions' of tradition on the media create new myths, or will they simply reduce myth to the level of commercials?

## Environmental changes

Apart from the mediation of technology in determining 'inventions' of tradition, there are more practical matters that affect the changes in 'traditional forms'. A year ago, I attended a Ramlila performance in the village of Amaur near Kanpur to find a permanent Ravana made out of stone. I could scarcely conceal my disappointment that the principle of burning the demon-god, so essential for the celebration of the *lila*, had been ignored for economic reasons. 'It is too expensive to burn Ravana every year', I was told. 'After all, this is a small village, not Ramnagar.' Only later did I realize that Ravana had been burned, but symbolically, through his headgear and weapon, which were made out of paper and wood. The rest of his body remained indomitably cast in stone, but nonetheless, he had already been 'burned'.

These paradoxes of faith reveal the acute consciousness of our people, both to everyday matters of survival and the endurance of faith. For them, it is not a matter of 'using' tradition (as it is for us in the so-called contemporary theatre); it is a question of *living* tradition and making the necessary adjustments to keep it going. If a traditional performance dies, then maybe it was meant to, because it could no longer be sustained either economically or socially.

About the worst attitude to tradition is to incarcerate it within an immutable form that ostensibly never changes. If tradition lives today, it is because it has always changed in the course of its history. How it changes within its own performative and cultural context is frequently undocumented and even forgotten, because the change occurs slowly, organically, in deference to the larger needs of its community.

It is only in recent years through interventions like tourism, film document-ation and interculturalism that the changes in 'traditional' performances have become at once more visible and swift. It could also be that we have developed a new awareness, a post-colonial consciousness, of what was previously taken for granted. In this context, I believe that one must differentiate between those changes which are intrinsic to growth of a traditional performance, and those which are imposed on it through external intervention, though I must acknowledge that it is sometimes difficult to differentiate between them.

When I hear, for instance, of how a Theyyam performer has of his own accord incorporated a flashing electric bulb into his headgear to enhance his sense of the demoniac, this seems like a perfectly valid response to electricity, an intervention in the rural performer's world. The change in the costume is intrinsic insofar as it comes from the performer's response to his changing environment. On the other hand, can I deny that I am disturbed to see neon lights in a *koothambalam*, where, ideally, the *koodiyattam* performer should be watched in the glow of the *vilakku*, his eyes illuminated by the fire in the lamp? The problem with this use of electricity is that it does not seem to bother the performers themselves. It is my 'aesthetic' sense that is jarred, revealing my own 'taste' and cultural conditioning.

Still more problematic is the transportation of a traditional performance from its own environment to a proscenium-bound, air-conditioned theatre in New Delhi or a *mela* in Paris. This environmental change alters the very context of the performance. In some extravaganzas, the performers are merely 'slotted' into a spectacle over which they have no control. Reduced to exotica, they resemble spots of colour without mind, body or soul.

How does one accept these changes in performances resulting from altered environments?

1    In the case of the Theyyam performer, one cannot but appreciate the sheer ingenuity of the performer in incorporating a historical change (electricity) within the framework of his costume. Here one senses an organic relationship between the environment and the performer.

2    In the case of the neon lights in the *koothambalam*, one can accept these lights as useful even though they fail to enhance the energy of the performance. At best, one could say that the performer learns to accept them, and then forget them, not unlike classical singers who have adjusted to the sound of the harmonium. In the long run, the use of 'conveniences' like neon lights and harmoniums is, perhaps, best accepted as a compromise – useful, but not particularly creative.

3    In the case of the altered environments provided by proscenium theatres and spectacles, it is difficult to accept their impositions on the choices of the performers. Inadequate exposure to these spaces, and more specifically, to the power relationships embodied in them, create an imbalance between what the performers are ready to give and what is expected of them from a foreign clientele.

In such spaces, the performers invariably fail to represent themselves. Rather, they are represented by the environments themselves, and by all the values – political, social, commercial – embodied in them. This does not mean that traditional performers should not perform in these 'alien' spaces, but new mechanisms and relationships need to be explored whereby performers have more time and power to control their representations.

## Inventing the 'folk'

Expertise plays an important role in determining categories in which 'tradition' can be placed. One such category is the 'folk', which received an official sanction at the First Drama Seminar organized by the Sangeet Natak Akademi in 1956. Inaugurated by Dr S. Radhakrishnan, who was then the Vice-President of India, the Seminar was part of a series that was intended to serve as a cultural counterpart to Nehru's Five-Year Plans. The intention of the Akademi was to hold 'one seminar every four years for each of the arts of dance, drama, music, and film'.

Predictably, in the immediate wave of post-Independence nationalism, there was a definite drive among the participants to uphold the 'Indianness' of Indian culture. Some of our most prominent artists and cultural figures, including Mulk Raj Anand, Kamaladevi Chattopadhyay, Balraj Sahni, Sombhu Mitra and V. Raghavan, pondered a wide spectrum of immediate problems. They included the ownership of theatres, censorship laws, the Dramatic Performances Control Act, entertainment tax and almost as a secondary issue, the state of 'folk drama'.

One should remember that 'folk theatre' had not yet become fashionable and that the models of 'professionalism' in theatre continued to be European.

Nonetheless, there was a fervent attempt in the Seminar to confront 'traditional' sources for the rejuvenation of our theatre. The most animated discussion in this regard was the one relating to *bhavai*, where the conflicting views of the participants reveal some of the deeply entrenched premises and problems under-lying the urban construction and use of 'folk theatre' in India today.

First of all, it becomes very clear from the discussion on *bhavai* (as from the Seminar in general) that the Indian theatre had already become regionalized, with 'experts' representing each state. The 'folk drama' as a category had also been regionalized. No attempt was made in the Seminar to situate the concept of the 'folk' in a larger historical perspective to see, for instance, how 'folk forms' became vehicles for contemporary political content during the IPTA days, thereby revealing the innate urban assumption that the 'folk' is not contemporary. Like a vessel, it has to be 'filled' with new ideas and political content. Instead of questioning such assumptions, the participants of the Seminar seemed to accept totally the validity of 'folk drama' as an adequate category in which to confront the specificities of rural cultures in India.

Before proceeding with the discussion on *bhavai*, I believe it would be useful to reflect on the morphology of the term 'folk' in the Indian theatre. Since the participants in the Seminar did not question their use of this deceptively simple term, it is necessary for us to do so here.

It is not clear when the term 'folk' entered the vocabulary of the Indian theatre worker. Certainly, it became popular during the IPTA movement when urban artists were compelled to discover their 'roots' in rural cultures. What needs to be emphasized is that the 'folk' has become an established category in the Indian theatre today. Actors and directors use it freely without questioning its obvious, yet diffused links to the word 'people'. Nor is it assumed to be a 'foreign' word, any more so than 'tradition', which is used more readily than the Indian equivalents of *parampara* or *sampradaya*.

Even in the academic world of folklore studies, it is significant that Indian equivalents for 'folklore' have been established only in recent years (Claus and Korom 1988, p. 32), The diffused use of the term 'folk' in Indian contexts could be related to the fact that our established culture refused to accept it as a respectable object of study. As late as 1932 the Indian folklorist, Sarat Chandra Roy, had lamented the fact that 'folklore' had not received the attention in India that 'tradition' was beginning to receive in discussions conducted by the Indian Science Congress, the Oriental Conference, and the Bombay Historical Congress (ibid., p. 31). Four years later, in 1936, when Dr Chelnat Achyudia Menon published *Ballads of North Malabar*, we are told that it was the first book of its kind in Kerala that 'raised the subject in public estimation' by 'persuading' the 'educated Malyalee' that folk studies had a 'place in the cultural life of the country' (Raghavan 1945, p. ii).

In the context of the class and caste consciousness of the educated Indians, it is not surprising that the 'folk' were associated not just with 'people', but 'common people'. Perhaps 'peasant' was one of the closest associations with the word 'folk' in its early history. Countering this history of prejudice, the IPTA movement glorified the 'folk' in the context of the freedom struggle. The 'folk' became emblematic of our 'lost heritage' and 'authentic history' that we were determined to reclaim from the British.

Along with the patriotic aura surrounding the 'folk' in IPTA, there is also an inner tension underlying this word with specific reference to 'people'. In the initial phase of the IPTA movement, when it was only too easy for artists with vastly different economic and political backgrounds to subsume their differences under the immediate pressures and lure of patriotism, one could say that the 'folk' and the 'people' embraced each other's needs. But there was also an unspoken assumption that it was the 'folk' who performed for the 'people', not the other way around. We don't speak of the 'folk' watching a 'people's performance', it is 'people' who watch a 'folk performance'.

Unavoidably, it was 'people' who were viewed in a more corporal light; they were 'flesh-and-blood' figures who constitute the 'mass'. The 'folk', on the other hand, were inextricably linked to *forms – burrakatha, tamasha, nautanki*. Even today, I would argue that in the nebulous vocabulary of the Indian theatre artist, and his even vaguer social consciousness of his means of production, the 'folk' has been disembodied from the needs of the 'people'. Quite literally, it has become a nomenclature for a wide range of supposedly non-urban performance traditions, that are primarily enjoyed by urban audiences.

Significantly, for those IPTA artists with a more politically active ideology (inevitably Marxist), who favoured a realist intervention in the arts modelled on Bijon Bhattacharya's *Nabanna*, it was the rhetoric of 'the people' that dominated over the 'folk'. Not surprisingly, this group can be most strongly identified with the Bengal front of the IPTA movement. If it is not too much of a witticism, I should emphasize that after Independence, the 'people' stayed on in West Bengal, while the 'folk' eventually gravitated in the direction of New Delhi, which is the centre for all folk-related activities, including the handicrafts and the cottage industries. This is the centre where tradition is 'invented', 'manufactured', and 'exported' with an increasingly efficient and centralized system. It is also the centre where definitions of 'Indian culture' are made and disseminated.

To return to the Drama seminar in New Delhi, one notes that 'folk drama' was defined not so much through an analysis of the term (which was taken for granted), but through a debate as to how one should intervene in 'folk culture'. The underlying thrust of Dina Gandhi's address on *bhavai*, which provided the source of the debate on 'folk drama', was not 'Why should we intervene?' but rather, 'We must intervene now. How do we go about it?' Part of the problem with her suggestions, as with most urban recommendations for the 'folk arts', is that she assumed an empathy with the folk artists, and then proceeded to represent them as if she were speaking on their behalf. In the process, her own use of these 'folk forms' became confused with their 'indigenous' state of being, which she lamented was in a state of decay, if not total extinction.

From Gandhi's address, it becomes obvious that her concern was not only for the 'folk form' and its 'extraordinary life-force', but for its artists, who were going to be 'wiped off due to neglect, unemployment, and actual starvation' ('Discussion on *Bhavai*', p. 114). Instead of confronting this crisis through active involvement, however, Gandhi recommended 'researches and studies' which could confirm that *bhavai* had 'a definite contribution to make to our culture' (ibid.). In retrospect, this priority given to research is problematic since it almost seems like a precondition before the *bhavai* artists can be 'saved'. Gandhi seems oblivious of the ironies involved in conflating the economic necessities of the *bhavai* performers with the need to develop their artistic potential. For her, the 'sacred duty' of 'emancipating' the folk artists could come about only through the organization of a research centre, a training school for the traditional performers, and a careful study of *bhavai* texts, so that 'spurious interpolations can be eliminated' (ibid.).

Countering Gandhi's advocacy of intervention, the extremely sophisticated and westernized Alkazi then spoke up in the Seminar for the people. 'We want to educate the Bhavai artists', he said. 'But we do not for a moment consider that the nearer they reach us, the quicker would they discard the arts of their forefathers' (ibid., p. 120). Then also, in response to the 'so-called crudities and vulgarities' entering the *bhavai* form, he asked: 'Should we be so prude and puritanic as to evaluate every art in the light of our own moral code?' (ibid., pp. 120–1). More prosaically, he affirmed that 'we should not poke our noses in this affair because we do not really know what would exactly be good for this form and for its exponents' (ibid., p. 121). The job should be left to anthropologists.

Though, predictably, there was a resistance to this suggestion – an anthropological intervention is scarcely less 'neutral' than an artistic one – the debate between Gandhi and Alkazi does resonate even today, despite a sense of *déjà vu*. We have heard their positions before in other post-Independence contexts, and we continue to hear them even now. While Alkazi seemed to accept the inherent distance, culturally and socially, between the 'urban' and the 'folk' artist, thereby upholding his innate elitism, Gandhi wanted to bridge the gap in some meaningful way. Yet, this 'bridging' could scarcely be seen as altruistic. As Balraj Sahni pointed out, with reference to Gandhi's production of *Mena Gurjari*, which 'contemporized' the folk form (notably by eliminating the male impersonation of women), these experiments in folk drama were a valuable source of growth for 'our own [urban] theatre'. All Gandhi wanted to do, according to Sahni, was to 'revitalize her own art', and to retain as much of *bhavai's* 'indigenous' qualities as 'a sophisticated audience would be able to appreciate' (ibid., p. 122).

This is about the most honest statement that one could hope to find about the urban use of folk forms. Let us acknowledge that this 'use' is more useful to the urban artist than to the 'folk' who inspired the creation. 'Folk drama' is essentially an urban construct that cannot claim to be entirely 'indigenous' (and therefore, 'authentic'). It is a simulation of the 'folk form', sufficiently 'indigenous' (yet not entirely *desi*) to win the approval of urban audiences. The clientele of 'folk drama' is not the 'folk', but city people who need to be reminded of their 'roots and native places' from which they are irrevocably displaced. . . .

## Beginnings

There are two images from our mythological tradition that seem relevant to this discussion, or rather, my need to intervene in its history. At one level, the images are quite unrelated, separated by narrative and time – one is from the *Mahabharata*, the other from the Punjabi legend of Puran Bhagat. And yet, at a subterranean level, these images are united through their advocacy of what I must call 'violence'. Today, we could do with some of this 'violence' in our suffocatingly safe theatre.

In the *Mahabharata*, there is that memorable moment when Yudhisthira receives permission from Bhishma to kill him. The 'father' legitimizes his own death at the hands of his 'son'. Violence receives a paternalistic, if not divine sanction. It is now Yudhisthira's *dharma* to kill Bhishma.

There is a different kind of violence in the story of Puran Bhagat, which does not involve killing, but rather, a rejection of the father and whatever he represents – family, kingdom, state, authority, love. After being incarcerated in a dungeon for the first twelve years of his life, then exiled, and later imprisoned, Puran Bhagat goes through many trials and humiliations before he acquires the self-realization of a *yogi*. In the final episode, when his father begs him to take over the kingdom, Puran rejects the offer: 'If you cannot govern your kingdom, let it go to the dogs. . . . I will have none of you and your belongings. I am a *yogi*. I must go' (Gill 1986, p. 146). And he *leaves* without any attempt to reconcile differences or to affirm traditional ties.

In Puran's exit, one finds a paradigm of rejection. I do not believe that there is a single artist in the Indian theatre today who is prepared to 'reject' tradition as resolutely as Puran turns away from his father and inheritance. Perhaps, this is a totally unfair demand on my part. Maybe our artists are still too close to 'tradition' (or whatever they make of it) to dissociate themselves from its hold in order to pursue their own journeys in theatre.

At the same time, they do not believe that they have the right to 'kill' tradition with as much respect and fervour as Yudhisthira kills Bhishma. Perhaps, they have not yet received the inner sanction to fulfil this necessary task. It is safer, therefore, for them to fold their hands and deify tradition, perpetuating deference and cowardice.

Unable to 'reject' or 'kill' (which, in artistic terms, would involve a subversion of the 'traditional form'), our theatre artists remain in limbo. They don't know how to free themselves from tradition or live with it without compromising on their own truth. In the meantime, they 'invent' tradition not so much from an inner necessity, but in deference to larger cultural and political factors that favour a sanctification or dressing-up of the past.

It is time to end this facile use of our tradition. Instead of bothering with the minutiae of hand-held curtains, masks, make-believe *poorvarangas*, and stirring exits and entrances to throbbing drums, we need to ask ourselves some crucial questions: *What is our sacrifice in theatre today? Who are we performing for in the absence of gods? How can we transform ourselves through theatre? What are we celebrating on stage?*

I ask these questions not because I have the answers, but because they seem necessary to begin a confrontation with tradition that could transcend its 'inventions' in our theatre today.

## References

Awasthi, Suresh (1985), 'In Defence of the "Theatre of Roots"', *Sangeet Natak*, Nos. 77–8.

Bhatt, Haridasa (n.d.), 'Theatre for all – Folk Performing Arts of Karnataka', typewritten manuscript.

Claus, Peter and Korom, Frank (1988), 'Folk, Folklore, and Folkoristics', *Folkoristics and Indian Folklore*, Haywatrd: WRC Consulting, April 1988.

Eliot, T.S. (1969), 'Tradition and the Individual Talent', *The Sacred Wood*, London: Methuen.

Gill, Harjeet Singh (1986), 'The Human Condition in Puran Bhagat', *The Word and the World*, New Delhi: Sage Publications.

Kambar, Chandrasekhar (n.d.), 'Yakshagana As I See', typewritten manuscript.

Kapur, Anuradha (1988), 'Thinking about Tradition: The Ramlila at Ramnagar', *Journal of Arts and Ideas*, No. 16.

Raghavan, M.D. (1945), *Folk Plays and Dances of Kerala*, Trichur: Mangalodyam Press.

Rea, Kenneth (1978), 'The Tradition and the Innovation', in *Theatre in India: The Old and the New, Theatre Quarterly*, Vol. VIII, No. 31, Autumn 1978.

Williams, Raymond (1981), *Culture*, Glasgow: Fontana Press.

—— (1985), *Keywords*, London: Flamingo Books.

All references to the First Drama Seminar organized by the Sangeet Natak Akademi, including 'Discussion on *Bhavai*', are taken from a printed documentation of the entire Seminar, which unfortunately does not identify either the publisher or the date of publication.

■  ■  ■

## Source

Bharucha, R. (1993) 'Notes on the Invention of Tradition', *Theatre and the World*, London: Routledge: 192–200, 208–210.

# Rustom Bharucha (1946–)

Writer, director and dramaturg, who lives and works in India. Bharucha's writings include those from the period when he was working in New York (1981–84) and subsequently in India. Of his theatre projects, the most renowned is *Request Concert* (1986–88), with Franz Xaver Kroetz, which was seen in India, Indonesia, Korea, Germany and Japan.

In his book *Theatre and the World* Bharucha analyses and takes issue with many Western ideas of interculturalism, beginning historically with Craig, Artaud and Grotowski. He writes extensively on more recent intercultural projects in the theatre and in writing. He gives a detailed analysis of Schechner and of Peter Brook's *Mahabharata* from this perspective. He is critical of Western artists and theorists who either simply appropriate other cultures or suggest that culture is a matter of choice.

This essay, in contrast, explores ideas of the development of an indigenous cultural tradition. He says that much of what passes for 'tradition' in Indian theatre has in fact been mediated by imperialism. Hence the need to invent tradition in the new age of technology. His view seems in sharp contrast to European and African ideas of tradition.

## Compare this article with writings by the following authors in this reader

**Artaud, Craig and Grotowski** – who, in *Theatre and the World*, he identifies as early 'interculturalists'

**Brook** – a different view on the idea of tradition, with whom Bharucha takes issue

**Hijikata** – a contrasting, Japanese view of the use of tradition in contemporary times

**Schechner** – a contrasting stance on tradition and on intercultural experiment

**Soyinka** – a different stance on tradition, and also, elsewhere, on interculturalism

## Further reading

Bharucha, R. (1993) *Theatre and the World*, London: Routledge.

Bharucha, R. (2000) *The Politics of Cultural Practice*, London: Athlone Press.

# Chapter 12

# Augusto Boal

## THE THEATER AS DISCOURSE

G EORGE IKISHAWA used to say that the bourgeois theater is the finished theater. The bourgeoisie already knows what the world is like, *their* world, and is able to present images of this complete, finished world. The bourgeoisie presents the spectacle. On the other hand, the proletariat and the oppressed classes do not know yet what their world will be like; consequently their theater will be the rehearsal, not the finished spectacle. This is quite true, though it is equally true that the theater can present images of transition.

I have been able to observe the truth of this view during all my activities in the people's theater of so many and such different countries of Latin America. Popular audiences are interested in experimenting, in rehearsing, and they abhor the 'closed' spectacles. In those cases they try to enter into a dialogue with the actors, to interrupt the action, to ask for explanations without waiting politely for the end of the play. Contrary to the bourgeois code of manners, the people's code allows and encourages the spectator to ask questions, to dialogue, to participate.

All the methods that I have discussed are forms of a rehearsal-theater, and not a spectacle-theater. One knows how these experiments will begin but not how they will end, because the spectator is freed from his chains, finally acts, and becomes a protagonist. Because they respond to the real needs of a popular audience they are practiced with success and joy.

But nothing in this prohibits a popular audience from practicing also more 'finished' forms of theater. In Peru many forms previously developed in other countries, especially Brazil and Argentina, were also utilized and with great success. Some of these forms were:

*1    Newspaper theater:* It was initially developed by the Nucleus Group of the Arena Theater of Sao Paulo, of which I was the artistic director until forced to

leave Brazil.[1] It consists of several simple techniques for transforming daily news items, or any other non-dramatic material, into
theatrical performances.

(a) Simple reading: the news item is read detaching it from the
context of the newspaper, from the format which makes it
false or tendentious.

(b) Crossed reading: two news items are read in crossed (alternating) form, one throwing light on the other, explaining it,
giving it a new dimension.

(c) Complementary reading: data and information generally omitted
by the newspapers of the ruling classes are added to the
news.

(d) Rhythmical reading: as a musical commentary, the news is
read to the rhythm of the samba, tango, Gregorian chant,
etc., so that the rhythm functions as a critical 'filter' of the
news, revealing its true content which is obscured in the
newspaper.

(e) Parallel action: the actors mime parallel actions while the
news is read, showing the context in which the reported
event really occurred; one hears the news and sees something
else that complements it visually.

(f) Improvisation: the news is improvised on stage to exploit all
its variants and possibilities.

(g) Historical: data or scenes showing the same event in other
historical moments, in other countries, or in other social
systems, are added to the news.

(h) Reinforcement: the news is read or sung with the aid or
accompaniment of slides, jingles, songs, or publicity materials.

(i) Concretion of the abstract: that which the news often hides in
its purely abstract information is made concrete on the stage:
torture, hunger, unemployment, etc., are shown concretely,
using graphic images, real or symbolic.

(j) Text out of context: the news is presented out of the context
in which it was published; for example, an actor gives the
speech about austerity previously delivered by the Minister of
Economics while he devours an enormous dinner: the real
truth behind the minister's words becomes demystified – he
wants austerity for the people but not for himself.

2    *Invisible theater:* It consists of the presentation of a scene in an
environment other than the theater, before people who are not
spectators. The place can be a restaurant, a sidewalk, a market,
a train, a line of people, etc. The people who witness the scene

are those who are there by chance. During the spectacle, these people must not have the slightest idea that it is a 'spectacle,' for this would make them 'spectators.'

The invisible theater calls for the detailed preparation of a skit with a complete text or a simple script; but it is necessary to rehearse the scene sufficiently so that the actors are able to incorporate into their acting and their actions the intervention of the spectators. During the rehearsal it is also necessary to include every imaginable intervention from the spectators; these possibilities will form a kind of optional text.

The invisible theater erupts in a location chosen as a place where the public congregates. All the people who are near become involved in the eruption and the effects of it last long after the skit is ended.

A small example shows how the invisible theater works. In the enormous restaurant of a hotel in Chiclayo, where the literacy agents of ALFIN were staying, together with 400 other people, the 'actors' sit at separate tables. The waiters start to serve. The 'protagonist' in a more or less loud voice (to attract the attention of other diners, but not in a too obvious way) informs the waiter that he cannot go on eating the food served in that hotel, because in his opinion it is too bad. The waiter does not like the remark but tells the customer that he can choose something *à la carte*, which he may like better. The actor chooses a dish called 'Barbecue a la pauper.' The waiter points out that it will cost him 70 *soles*, to which the actor answers, always in a reasonably loud voice, that there is no problem. Minutes later the waiter brings him the barbecue, the protagonist eats it rapidly and gets ready to get up and leave the restaurant, when the waiter brings the bill. The actor shows a worried expression and tells the people at the next table that his barbecue was much better than the food they are eating, but the pity is that one has pay for it. . . .

'I'm going to pay for it; don't have any doubts. I ate the "barbecue a la pauper" and I'm going to pay for it. But there is a problem: I'm broke.'

'And how are you going to pay?' asks the indignant waiter. 'You knew the price before ordering the barbecue. And now, how are you going to pay for it?'

The diners nearby are, of course, closely following the dialogue – much more attentively than they would if they were witnessing the scene on a stage. The actor continues:

'Don't worry, because I *am* going to pay you. But since I'm broke I will pay you with labor-power.'

'With what?' asks the waiter, astonished. 'What kind of power?'

'With labor-power, just as I said. I am broke but I can rent you my labor-power. So I'll work doing something for as long as it's necessary to pay for my "barbecue a la pauper," which, to tell the truth, was really delicious – much better than the food you serve to those poor souls. . . .'

By this time some of the customers intervene and make remarks among themselves at their tables, about the price of food, the quality of the service in the hotel, etc. The waiter calls the headwaiter to decide the matter. The actor explains again to the latter the business of renting his labor-power and adds:

'And besides, there is another problem: I'll rent my labor-power but the truth is that I don't know how to do anything, or very little. You will have to give me a very simple job to do. For example, I can take out the hotel's garbage. What's the salary of the garbage man who works for you?'

The headwaiter does not want to give any information about salaries, but a second actor at another table is already prepared and explains that he and the garbage man have gotten to be friends and that the latter has told him his salary: seven *soles* per hour. The two actors make some calculations and the 'protagonist' exclaims:

'How is this possible! If I work as a garbage man I'll have to work ten hours to pay for this barbecue that it took me ten minutes to eat? It can't be! Either you increase the salary of the garbage man or reduce the price of the barbecue! . . . But I can do something more specialized; for example, I can take care of the hotel gardens, which are so beautiful, so well cared for. One can see that a very talented person is in charge of the gardens. How much does the gardener of this hotel make? I'll work as a gardener! How many hours work in the garden are necessary to pay for the "barbecue a la pauper"?'

A third actor, at another table, explains his friendship with the gardener who is an immigrant from the same village as he; for this reason he knows that the gardener makes ten *soles* per hour. Again the 'protagonist' becomes indignant:

'How is this possible? So the man who takes care of these beautiful gardens, who spends his days out there exposed to the wind, the rain, and the sun, has to work seven long hours to be able to eat the barbecue in ten minutes? How can this be, Mr. Headwaiter? Explain it to me!'

The headwaiter is already in despair; he dashes back and forth, gives orders to the waiters in a loud voice to divert the attention of the other customers, alternately laughs and becomes serious, while the restaurant is transformed into a public forum. The 'protagonist' asks the waiter how much he is paid to serve the barbecue and offers to replace him for the necessary number of hours. Another actor, originally from a small village in the interior, gets up and declares that nobody in his village makes 70 *soles* per day; therefore nobody in his village can eat the 'barbecue a la pauper.' (The sincerity of this actor, who was, besides, telling the truth, moved those who were near his table.)

Finally, to conclude the scene, another actor intervenes with the following proposition:

'Friends, it looks as if we are against the waiter and the headwaiter and this does not make sense. They are our brothers. They work like us, and they are not to blame for the prices charged here. I suggest we take up a collection. We at this table are going to ask you to contribute whatever you can; one *sol*, two *soles*, five *soles*, whatever you can afford. And with that money we are going to pay for the barbecue. And be generous, because what is left over will go as a tip for the waiter, who is our brother and a working man.'

Immediately those who are with him at the table start collecting money to pay the bill. Some customers willingly give one or two *soles*. Others furiously comment:

'He says that the food we're eating is junk, and now he wants us to pay for his barbecue! . . . And am I going to eat this junk? Hell no! I wouldn't give him a peanut, so he'll learn a lesson! Let him wash dishes. . . .'

The collection reached 100 *soles* and the discussion went on through the night. It is always very important that the actors do not reveal themselves to be actors! On this rests the *invisible* nature of this form of theater. And it is precisely this invisible quality that will make the spectator act freely and fully, as if he were living a real situation — and, after all, it is a real situation!

It is necessary to emphasize that the invisible theater is not the same thing as a 'happening,' or the so-called 'guerrilla theater.' In the latter we are clearly talking about 'theater,' and therefore the wall that separates actors from spectators immediately arises, reducing the spectator to impotence: a spectator is always less than a man! In the invisible theater the theatrical rituals are abolished; only the theater exists, without its old, worn-out patterns. The theatrical energy is completely liberated, and the impact produced by this free theater is much more powerful and longer lasting.

Several presentations of invisible theater were made in different locations in Peru. Particularly interesting is what happened at the Carmen Market, in the *barrio* of Comas, some 14 kilometers away from downtown Lima. Two actresses were protagonists in a scene enacted at a vegetable stand. One of them, who was pretending to be illiterate, insisted that the vendor was cheating her, taking advantage of the fact that she did not know how to read; the other actress checked the figures, finding them to be correct, and advised the 'illiterate' one to register in one of ALFIN's literacy courses. After some discussion about the best age to start one's studies, about what to study and with whom, the first actress kept on insisting that she was too old for those things. It was then that a little old woman, leaning on her cane, very indignantly shouted:

'My dears, that's not true! For learning and making love one is never too old!'

Everyone witnessing the scene broke into laughter at the old woman's amorous outburst, and the actresses were unable to continue the scene.

*3   Photo-romance:* In many Latin-American countries there is a genuine epidemic of photo-romances, sub-literature on the lowest imaginable level, which further-more always serves as a vehicle for the ruling classes' ideology. The technique here consists in reading to the participants the general lines in the plot of a photo-romance without telling them the source of this plot. The participants are asked to act out the story. Finally, the acted-out story is compared to the story as it is told in the photo-romance, and the differences are discussed.

For example: a rather stupid story taken from Corín Tellado, the worst author of this brutalizing genre, started like this:

A woman is waiting for her husband in the company of another woman who is helping her with the housework. . . .

The participants acted according to their customs: a woman at home expecting her husband will naturally be preparing the meal; the one helping her is a neighbor, who comes to chat about various things; the husband comes home tired after a long day's work; the house is a one-room shack, etc., etc. In Corín Tellado, on the contrary, the woman is dressed in a long evening gown, with pearl necklaces, etc.; the woman who is helping her is a black maid who says no more than 'Yes, ma'am'; 'The dinner is served, ma'am'; 'Very well, ma'am'; 'Here comes Mr. X, ma'am'; and nothing else. The house is a marble palace; the husband comes home after a day's work in his factory, where he had an argument with the workers because they, 'not understanding the crisis we are all living through, wanted an increase in salaries . . .,'and continuing in this vein.

This particular story was sheer trash, but at the same time it served as a magnificent example of ideological insight. The well-dressed woman received a letter from an unknown woman, went to visit her, and discovered her to be a former mistress of her husband; the mistress stated that the husband had left her because he wanted to marry the factory owner's daughter, that is, the well-dressed woman. To top it all, the mistress exclaimed:

'Yes, he betrayed me, deceived me. But I forgive him because, after all, he has always been very ambitious, and he knew very well that with me he could not climb very high. On the other hand, with you he can go very far indeed!'

That is to say, the former mistress forgave her lover because he had in the highest degree that capitalistic eagerness to possess everything. The desire to be a factory owner is presented as something so noble that even a few betrayals on the way up are to be forgiven. . . .

And the young wife, not to be outdone, pretends to be ill so that he will have to remain at her side, and so that, as a result of this trick, he will finally fall in love with her. What an ideology! This love story is crowned with a happy ending rotten to the core. Of course the story, when told without the dialogues and acted out by peasants, takes on an entirely different meaning. When at the end of the performance, the participants are told the origin of the plot they have just acted out, they experience a shock. And this must be understood: when they read Corín Tellado they immediately assume the passive role of 'spectators'; but if they first of all have to act out a story themselves, afterwards, when they do read Corín Tellado's version, they will no longer assume a passive, expectant attitude, but instead a critical, comparative one. They will look at the lady's house, and compare it to their own, at the husband's or wife's attitudes and compare them with those of their own spouses, etc. And they will be prepared to detect the poison infiltrating the pages of those photo-stories, or the comics and other forms of cultural and ideological domination.

I was overjoyed when, months after the experiments with the educators, back in Lima, I was informed that the residents of several *barrios* were using that same technique to analyze television programs, an endless source of poison directed against the people.

4   *Breaking of repression:* The dominant classes crush the dominated ones through repression; the old crush the young through repression; certain races subjugate certain others through repression. Never through a cordial understanding, through an honest interchange of ideas, through criticism and autocriticism. No. The ruling classes, the old, the 'superior' races, or the masculine sex, have their sets of values and impose them by force, by unilateral violence, upon the oppressed classes, the young, the races they consider inferior, or women.

The capitalist does not ask the working man if he agrees that the capital should belong to one and the labor to another; he simply places an armed policeman at the factory door and that is that – private property is decreed.

The dominated class, race, sex, or age group suffers the most constant, daily, and omnipresent repression. The ideology becomes concrete in the figure of the dominated person. The proletariat is exploited through the domination that is exerted on all proletarians. Sociology becomes psychology. There is not an oppression by the masculine sex in general of the feminine sex in general: what exists is the concrete oppression that men (individuals) direct against women (individuals).

The technique of breaking repression consists in asking a participant to remember a particular moment when he felt especially repressed, accepted that repression, and began to act in a manner contrary to his own desires. That moment must have a deep personal meaning: I, a proletarian, am oppressed; we proletarians are oppressed; therefore the proletariat is oppressed. It is necessary to pass from the particular to the general, not vice versa, and to deal with something that has happened to someone in particular, but which at the same time is typical of what happens to others.

The person who tells the story also chooses from among the rest of the participants all the other characters who will participate in the reconstruction of the incident. Then, after receiving the information and directions provided by the protagonist, the participants and the protagonist act out the incident just as it happened in reality – recreating the same scene, the same circumstances, and the same original feelings.

Once the 'reproduction' of the actual event is over, the protagonist is asked to repeat the scene, but this time without accepting the repression, fighting to impose his will, his ideas, his wishes. The other participants are urged to maintain the repression as in the first performance. The clash that results helps to measure the possibility one often has to resist and yet fails to do so; it helps to measure the true strength of the enemy. It also gives the protagonist the opportunity of trying once more and carrying out, in fiction, what he had not been able to do in reality. But we have already seen that this is not cathartic: the fact of having rehearsed a resistance to oppression will prepare him to resist effectively in a future reality, when the occasion presents itself once more.

On the other hand, it is necessary to take care that the generic nature of the particular case under study be understood. In this type of theatrical experiment the particular instance must serve as the point of departure, but it is indispensable to reach the general. The process to be realized, during the actual performance or afterward during the discussion, is one that ascends from the *phenomenon* toward the *law*; from the phenomena presented in the plot toward the social laws that govern those phenomena. The spectator-participants must come out of this experience enriched with the knowledge of those laws, obtained through analysis of the phenomena.

5   *Myth theater:* It is simply a question of discovering the obvious behind the myth: to logically tell a story, revealing its evident truths.

In a place called Motupe there was a hill, almost a mountain, with a narrow road that led through the trees to the top; halfway to the top stood a cross. One could go as far as that cross: to go beyond it was dangerous; it inspired fear, and the few who had tried had never returned. It was believed that some sanguinary ghosts inhabited the top of the mountain. But the story is also told of a brave young man who armed himself and climbed to the top, where he found the 'ghosts.' They were in reality some Americans who owned a gold mine located precisely on the top of that mountain.

Another legend is that of the lagoon of Cheken. It is said that there was no water there and that all the peasants, having to travel for several kilometers to get a glass of water, were dying of thirst. Today a lagoon exists there, the property of a local landowner. How did that lagoon spring up and how did it become the property of one man? The legend explains it. When there was still no water, on a day of intense heat all the villagers were lamenting and praying to God to grant them even a tiny stream of water. But God did not have pity on that arid village. At midnight of the same day, however, a man dressed in a long black poncho and riding a black horse arrived and addressed the landowner, who was then only a poor peasant like the others:

'I will give a lagoon for all of you, but *you*, friend, must give me your most precious possession.'

The poor man, very distressed, moaned:

'But I have nothing; I am very poor. We all here suffer from the lack of water, live in miserable shacks, suffer from the most terrible hunger. We have nothing precious, not even our lives. And myself in particular, my only precious possession is my three daughters, nothing else.'

'And of the three,' responded the stranger, 'the oldest is the most beautiful. I will give you a lagoon filled with the freshest water of all Peru; but in exchange you will give me your oldest daughter so that I may marry her.'

The future landlord thought for a long while, cried a lot, and asked his frightened eldest daughter if she would accept such an unusual marriage proposal. The obedient daughter expressed herself in this way:

'If it is for the salvation of all, so that the thirst and hunger of all the peasants will come to an end, if it is so that you may have a lagoon with the freshest water of all Peru, if it is so that that lagoon will belong to you alone and bring you personal prosperity and riches — for you will be able to sell this wonderful water to the peasants, who will find it cheaper to buy from you than to travel so many kilometers — if it is for all this, tell the gentleman in the black poncho, astride his black horse, that I will go with him, even if in my heart I am suspicious of his true identity and of the places he will take me.'

Happy and contented, and of course somewhat tearful, the kind father went to inform the man in black of the decision, meanwhile asking the daughter to make some little signs showing the price of a liter of water, in order to expedite the work. The man in black undressed the girl, for he did not want to take anything from that house besides the girl herself, and placed her on his horse, which set off at a gallop toward a great depression in the plains. Then an enormous explosion was heard, and a large cloud of smoke remained in the very place where the horse, horseman, and naked girl had disappeared. From the huge hole that had been made in the ground, a spring started to flow and formed the lagoon with the freshest water of all Peru.

This myth no doubt hides a truth: the landlord took possession of what did not belong to him. If formerly the noblemen attributed to God the granting of their property and rights, today explanations no less magical are still used. In this case, the property of the lagoon was explained by the loss of the eldest daughter, the landlord's most precious possession — a transaction took place! And serving as a reminder of that, the legend said that on the nights of the new moon one could hear the girl singing at the bottom of the lagoon, still naked and combing her long hair with a beautiful golden comb. . . . Yes, the truth is that for the landlord the lagoon was like gold.

The myths told by the people should be studied and analyzed and their hidden truths revealed. In this task the theater can be extraordinarily useful.

6 *Analytical theater:* A story is told by one of the participants and immediately the actors improvise it. Afterward each character is broken down into all his social roles and the participants are asked to choose a physical object to symbolize each role. For example, a policeman killed a chicken thief. The policeman is analyzed:

(a)  he is a worker because he rents his labor-power; symbol: a pair of overalls;
(b)  he is a bourgeois because he protects private property and values it more than human life; symbol: a necktie, or a top hat, etc.;
(c)  he is a repressive agent because he is a policeman; symbol: a revolver.

This is continued until the participants have analyzed all his roles: head of a family (symbol: the wallet, for example), member of a fraternal order, etc., etc. It is important that the symbols be chosen by the participants present and that they not be imposed 'from above.' For a particular community the symbol for the head of the family might be a wallet, because he is the person who controls the household finances, and in this way controls the family. For another community this symbol may not communicate anything, that is, it may not be a symbol; then an armchair may be chosen. . . .

Having analyzed the character, or characters (it is advisable to limit this operation to the central characters only, for the sake of simplicity and clarity), a fresh attempt to tell the story is made, but taking away some of the symbols from each character, and consequently some social roles as well. Would the story be exactly the same if:

(a)    the policeman did not have the top hat or the necktie?
(b)    the robber had a top hat or necktie?
(c)    the robber had a revolver?
(d)    the policeman and the robber both had the same symbol for the fraternal order?

The participants are asked to make varying combinations and the proposed combinations must be performed by the actors and criticized by all those present. In this way they will realize that human actions are not the exclusive and primordial result of individual psychology: almost always, through the individual speaks his class!

7    *Rituals and masks:* The relations of production (infrastructure) determine the culture of a society (superstructure).

Sometimes the infrastructure changes but the superstructure for a while remains the same. In Brazil the landlords would not allow the peasants to look them in the face while talking with them: this would mean lack of respect. The peasants were accustomed to talking with the landlords only while staring at the ground and murmuring: 'yes, sir; yes, sir; yes, sir.' When the government decreed an agrarian reform (before 1964, date of the fascist *coup d'état*) its emissaries went to the fields to tell the peasants that now they could become landowners. The peasants, staring at the ground, murmured: 'yes, friend; yes, friend; yes, friend.' A feudalistic culture had totally permeated their lives. The relationships of the peasant with the landlord were entirely different from those with the agent of the Institute of Agrarian Reform, but the ritual remained unchanged.

This particular technique of a people's theater ('Rituals and masks') consists precisely in revealing the superstructures, the rituals which reify all human relationships, and the masks of behavior that those rituals impose on each person according to the roles he plays in society and the rituals he must perform.

A very simple example: a man goes to a priest to confess his sins. How will he do it? Of course, he will kneel, confess his sins, hear the penitence, cross himself, and leave. But do all men confess always in the same way before all priests? Who is the man, and who is the priest?

In this case we need two versatile actors to stage the same confession four times:

First scene: the priest and the parishioner are landlords;
Second scene: the priest is a landlord and the parishioner is a peasant;
Third scene: the priest is a peasant and the parishioner is a landlord;
Fourth scene: the priest and the parishioner are peasants.

The ritual is the same in each instance, but the different social masks will cause the four scenes to be different also.

This is an extraordinarily rich technique which has countless variants: the same ritual changing masks; the same ritual performed by people of one social class, and later by people of another class; exchange of masks within the same ritual; etc., etc.

## Conclusion: 'Spectator,' a Bad Word!

Yes, this is without a doubt the conclusion: 'Spectator' is a bad word! The spectator is less than a man and it is necessary to humanize him, to restore to him his capacity of action in all its fullness. He too must be a subject, an actor on an equal plane with those generally accepted as actors, who must also be spectators. All these experiments of a people's theater have the same objective – the liberation of the spectator, on whom the theater has imposed finished visions of the world. And since those responsible for theatrical performances are in general people who belong directly or indirectly to the ruling classes, obviously their finished images will be reflections of themselves. The spectators in the people's theater (i.e., the people themselves) cannot go on being the passive victims of those images.

As we have seen in the first essay of this book, the poetics of Aristotle is the *poetics of oppression*: the world is known, perfect or about to be perfected, and all its values are imposed on the spectators, who passively delegate power to the characters to act and think in their place. In so doing the spectators purge themselves of their tragic flaw – that is, of something capable of changing society. A catharsis of the revolutionary impetus is produced! Dramatic action substitutes for real action.

Brecht's poetics is that of the enlightened vanguard: the world is revealed as subject to change, and the change starts in the theater itself, for the spectator does not delegate power to the characters to think in his place, although he continues to delegate power to them to act in his place. The experience is revealing on the level of consciousness, but not globally on the level of the action. Dramatic action throws light upon real action. The spectacle is a preparation for action.

The *poetics of the oppressed* is essentially the poetics of liberation: the spectator no longer delegates power to the characters either to think or to act in his place. The spectator frees himself; he thinks and acts for himself! Theater is action!

Perhaps the theater is not revolutionary in itself; but have no doubts, it is a rehearsal of revolution!

**Note**

1 Under the author's leadership the Arena Theater developed into one of Brazil's – indeed, one of Latin America's – most outstanding theaters. After 1964, when military rule was established in that country, Boal's work continued, though hampered by censorship and other restrictions imposed by the government. His outspoken position against the authoritarian regime led to his imprisonment and torture in 1971. Released after three months and acquitted of all charges, he was nevertheless compelled to leave Brazil in order to insure the safety of himself and his family. After political circumstances also forced him to leave Buenes Aires, Argentina, he took up residence in Portugal.

■  ■  ■

**Source**

Boal, A. (1974, 1979) 'Poetics of the Oppressed: Fourth Stage: The Theatre as Discourse', *Theatre of the Oppressed,* trans. C.A. and M.O.L. McBride, London: Pluto: 142–156. Originally published as *Teatro de Oprimido.*

## Augusto Boal (1934–2009)

Brazilian director and political activist turned politician, who developed a series of theatrical strategies to effect change in the lives of individuals on a personal, social, and political level. His work has become a system known as Theatre of the Oppressed, which makes use of a composite series of games and exercises, published as *Games for Actors and Non-Actors* (1992). Boal began to develop his thinking while director of the Arena Theatre in São Paolo (1956–71). He moved to Argentina in 1971, where he devised the techniques of invisible theatre as a way to stimulate debate on current political issues. Invited to participate in a Peruvian literacy campaign in 1973, he developed image theatre, which promotes physical expression over the spoken word. Boal's work has been influential among theatre practitioners in Europe as an alternative means of training and of restoring theatre to a meaningful role in society outside theatres; a democratic forum for potential change in people's lives. The rainbow of desire is the name given to a new series of exercises which examine individual and internalised oppressions in more detail, and which places the work more in the field of psychotherapy. Boal was a Member of Parliament of Rio de Janiero's Workers

Party (PT), where he developed his most recent theatre form – the legislative theatre – which involves using theatre techniques to enable communities to propose laws.

This section from Boal's first book describes in some detail strategies used among the poor and dispossessed of Peru in 1973. It proposes theatre as a universal language, which explains its attraction for Western directors and actors looking for a renewed role for theatre in the second half of the twentieth century.

## Compare this article with writings by the following authors in this reader

**Barba** – contemporary approach to theatre games and exercises
**Beck** – a contemporary North American view of theatre
**Brecht** – another, European, political role for theatre to which Boal refers
**Brown** – comparison with a dancer working with non-theatrical processes and spaces
**Grotowski and Stanislavski** – acting exercises
**Kaprow** – for performance as intervention in life
**Rainer** – whose work in a North American context stressed the democracy of the body

## Further reading

Babbage, F. (2004) *Augusto Boal*, London: Routledge.
Boal, A. (1992) *Games for Actors and Non-Actors*, trans. A. Jackson, London: Routledge.
Boal, A. (1995) *The Rainbow of Desire*, trans. A. Jackson, London: Routledge.
Boal, A. (2001) *Hamlet and the Baker's Son*, London: Routledge
Schutzman, M. and Cohen-Cruz, J. (eds) (1993) *Playing Boal*, London: Routledge.

# Chapter 13

# Bertolt Brecht

## SHORT DESCRIPTION OF A NEW TECHNIQUE OF ACTING WHICH PRODUCES AN ALIENATION EFFECT

W HAT FOLLOWS REPRESENTS an attempt to describe a technique of acting which was applied in certain theatres (1) with a view to taking the incidents portrayed and alienating them from the spectator. The aim of this technique, known as the alienation effect, was to make the spectator adopt an attitude of inquiry and criticism in his approach to the incident. The means were artistic.

The first condition for the A-effect's application to this end is that stage and auditorium must be purged of everything 'magical' and that no 'hypnotic tensions' should be set up. This ruled out any attempt to make the stage convey the flavour of a particular place (a room at evening, a road in the autumn), or to create atmosphere by relaxing the tempo of the conversation. The audience was not 'worked up' by a display of temperament or 'swept away' by acting with tauntened muscles; in short, no attempt was made to put it in a trance and give it the illusion of watching an ordinary unrehearsed event. As will be seen presently, the audience's tendency to plunge into such illusions has to be checked by specific artistic means (3).

The first condition for the achievement of the A-effect is that the actor must invest what he has to show with a definite gest of showing. It is of course necessary to drop the assumption that there is a fourth wall cutting the audience off from the stage and the consequent illusion that the stage action is taking place in reality and without an audience. That being so, it is possible for the actor in principle to address the audience direct.

It is well known that contact between audience and stage is normally made on the basis of empathy. Conventional actors devote their efforts so exclusively to bringing about this psychological operation that they may be said to see it as the principal aim of their art (5). Our introductory remarks will already have made it clear that the technique which produces an A-effect is the exact opposite of that which aims at empathy. The actor applying it is bound not to try to bring about the empathy operation.

Yet in his efforts to reproduce particular characters and show their beha-viour he need not renounce the means of empathy entirely. He uses these means just as any normal person with no particular acting talent would use them if he wanted to portray someone else, i.e. show how he behaves. This showing of other people's behaviour happens time and again in ordinary life (witnesses of an accident demonstrating to newcomers how the victim behaved, a facetious person imitating a friend's walk, etc.), without those involved making the least effort to subject their spectators to an illusion. At the same time they do feel their way into their characters' skins with a view to acquiring their characteristics.

As has already been said, the actor too will make use of this psychological operation. But whereas the usual practice in acting is to execute it during the actual performance, in the hope of stimulating the spectator into a similar opera-tion, he will achieve it only at an earlier stage, at some time during rehearsals.

To safeguard against an unduly 'impulsive', frictionless and un-critical creation of characters and incidents, more reading rehearsals can be held than usual. The actor should refrain from living himself into the part prematurely in any way, and should go on functioning as long as possible as a reader (which does not mean a reader-aloud). An important step is memorizing one's first impressions.

When reading his part the actor's attitude should be one of a man who is astounded and contradicts. Not only the occurrence of the incidents, as he reads about them, but the conduct of the man he is playing, as he experiences it, must be weighed up by him and their peculiarities understood; none can be taken as given, as something that 'was bound to turn out that way', that was 'only to be expected from a character like that'. Before memorizing the words he must memorize what he felt astounded at and where he felt impelled to contradict. For these are dynamic forces that he must preserve in creating his performance.

When he appears on the stage, besides what he actually is doing he will at all essential points discover, specify, imply what he is not doing; that is to say he will act in such a way that the alternative emerges as clearly as possible, that his acting allows the other possibilities to be inferred and only represents one out of the possible variants. He will say for instance 'You'll pay for that', and not say 'I forgive you'. He detests his children; it is not the case that he loves them. He moves down stage left and not up stage right. Whatever he doesn't do must be contained and conserved in what he does. In this way every sentence and every gesture signifies a decision; the character remains under observation and is tested. The technical term for this procedure is 'fixing the "not . . . but"'.

The actor does not allow himself to become completely transformed on the stage into the character he is portraying. He is not Lear, Harpagon, Schweik; he shows them. He reproduces their remarks as authentically as he can; he puts forward their way of behaving to the best of his abilities and knowledge of men; but he never tries to persuade himself (and thereby others) that this amounts to a complete transformation. Actors will know what it means if I say that a typical kind of acting without this complete transformation takes place when a producer or colleague shows one how to play a particular passage. It is not his own part, so he is not completely transformed; he underlines the technical aspect and retains the attitude of someone just making suggestions.

Once the idea of total transformation is abandoned the actor speaks his part not as if he were improvising it himself but like a quotation (7). At the same time he obviously has to render all the quotation's overtones, the remark's full human and concrete shape; similarly the gesture he makes must have the full substance of a human gesture even though it now represents a copy.

Given this absence of total transformation in the acting there are three aids which may help to alienate the actions and remarks of the characters being portrayed:

1    Transposition into the third person.
2    Transposition into the past.
3    Speaking the stage directions out loud.

Using the third person and the past tense allows the actor to adopt the right attitude of detachment. In addition he will look for stage directions and remarks that comment on his lines, and speak them aloud at rehearsal ('He stood up and exclaimed angrily, not having eaten: . . .', or 'He had never been told so before, and didn't know if it was true or not', or 'He smiled, and said with forced nonchalance: . . .'). Speaking the stage directions out loud in the third person results in a clash between two tones of voice, alienating the second of them, the text proper. This style of acting is further alienated by taking place on the stage after having already been outlined and announced in words. Transposing it into the past gives the speaker a standpoint from which he can look back at his sentence. The sentence too is thereby alienated without the speaker adopting an unreal point of view; unlike the spectator, he has read the play right through and is better placed to judge the sentence in accordance with the ending, with its consequences, than the former, who knows less and is more of a stranger to the sentence.

This composite process leads to an alienation of the text in the rehearsals which generally persists in the performance too (9). The directness of the relationship with the audience allows and indeed forces the actual speech delivery to be varied in accordance with the greater or smaller significance attaching to the sentences. Take the case of witnesses addressing a court. The underlinings, the characters' insistence on their remarks, must be developed as a piece of effective virtuosity. If the actor turns to the audience it must be a whole-hearted turn rather than the asides and soliloquizing technique of the old-fashioned theatre. To get the full A-effect from the poetic medium the actor should start at rehearsal by paraphrasing the verse's content in vulgar prose, possibly accompanying this by the gestures designed for the verse. A daring and beautiful handling of verbal media will alienate the text. (Prose can be alienated by translation into the actor's native dialect.)

Gesture will be dealt with below, but it can at once be said that everything to do with the emotions has to be externalized; that is to say, it must be developed into a gesture. The actor has to find a sensibly perceptible outward expression for his character's emotions, preferably some action that gives away what is going on inside him. The emotion in question must be brought out, must lose all its restrictions so that it can be treated on a big scale. Special elegance, power and grace of gesture bring about the A-effect.

A masterly use of gesture can be seen in Chinese acting. The Chinese actor achieves the A-effect by being seen to observe his own movements.

Whatever the actor offers in the way of gesture, verse structure, etc., must be finished and bear the hallmarks of something rehearsed and rounded-off. The impression to be given is one of ease, which is at the same time one of difficulties overcome. The actor must make it possible for the audience to take his own art, his mastery of technique, lightly too. He puts an incident before the spectator with perfection and as he thinks it really happened or might have happened. He does not conceal the fact that he has rehearsed it, any more than an acrobat conceals his training, and he emphasizes that it is his own (actor's) account, view, version of the incident.

Because he doesn't identify himself with him he can pick a definite attitude to adopt towards the character whom he portrays, can show what he thinks of him and invite the spectator, who is likewise not asked to identify himself, to criticize the character portrayed.

The attitude which he adopts is a socially critical one. In his exposition of the incidents and in his characterization of the person he tries to bring out those features which comes within society's sphere. In this way his performance becomes a discussion (about social conditions) with the audience he is addressing. He prompts the spectator to justify or abolish these conditions according to what class he belongs to (13).

The object of the A-effect is to alienate the social gest underlying every incident. By social gest is meant the mimetic and gestural expression of the social relationships prevailing between people of a given period (14).

It helps to formulate the incident for society, and to put it across in such a way that society is given the key, if titles are thought up for the scenes. These titles must have a historical quality.

This brings us to a crucial technical device: historicization.

The actor must play the incidents as historical ones. Historical incidents are unique, transitory incidents associated with particular periods. The conduct of the persons involved in them is not fixed and 'universally human'; it includes elements that have been or may be overtaken by the course of history, and is subject to criticism from the immediately following period's point of view. The conduct of those born before us is alienated [*Entfremdet*] from us by an incessant evolution.

It is up to the actor to treat present-day events and modes of behaviour with the same detachment as the historian adopts with regard to those of the past. He must alienate these characters and incidents from us.

Characters and incidents from ordinary life, from our immediate surroundings, being familiar, strike us as more or less natural. Alienating them helps to make them seem remarkable to us. Science has carefully developed a technique of getting irritated with the everyday, 'self-evident', universally accepted occurrence, and there is no reason why this infinitely useful attitude should not be taken over by art (17). It is an attitude which arose in science as a result of the growth in human productive powers. In art the same motive applies.

As for the emotions, the experimental use of the A-effect in the epic theatre's German productions indicated that this way of acting too can stimulate them, though possibly a different class of emotion is involved from those of the orthodox theatre (18). A critical attitude on the audience's part is a thoroughly artistic one (19). Nor does the actual practice of the A-effect seem anything like so unnatural as its description. Of course it is a way of acting that has nothing to do with stylization as commonly practised. The main advantage of the epic theatre with its A-effect, intended purely to show the world in such a way that it becomes manageable, is precisely its quality of being natural and earthly, its humour and its renunciation of all the mystical elements that have stuck to the orthodox theatre from the old days.

# Appendix: selected notes

1   *Edward II* after Marlowe (Munich Kammerspiele).
    *Trommeln in der Nacht* (Deutsches Theater, Berlin).
    *The Threepenny Opera* (Theater am Schiffbauerdamm, Berlin).
    *Die Pioniere von Ingolstadt* (Theater am Schiffbauerdamm).
    *Aufstieg und Fall der Stadt Mahagonny*, opera (Aufricht's Kurfürstendammtheater, Berlin).
    *Mann ist Mann* (Staatstheater, Berlin).
    *Die Massnahme* (Grosses Schauspielhaus, Berlin).
    *The Adventures of the Good Soldier Schweik* (Piscator's Theater am Nollendorfplatz, Berlin).
    *Die Plattköpfe und die Spitzköpfe* (Riddersalen, Copenhagen).
    *Señora Carrar's Rifles* (Copenhagen, Paris).
    *Furcht und Elend des Dritten Reiches* (Paris).

3    E.g. such mechanical means as very brilliant illumination of the stage (since a half-lit stage plus a completely darkened auditorium makes the spectator less level-headed by preventing him from observing his neighbour and in turn hiding him from his neighbour's eyes) and also *making visible the sources of light.*

## Making visible the sources of light

There is a point in showing the lighting apparatus openly, as it is one of the means of preventing an unwanted element of illusion; it scarcely disturbs the necessary concentration. If we light the actors and their performance in such a way that the lights themselves are within the spectator's field of vision we destroy part of his illusion of being present at a spontaneous, transitory, authentic, unrehearsed event. He sees that arrangements have been made to show something; something is being repeated here under special conditions, for instance in a very brilliant light. Displaying the actual lights is meant to be a counter to the old-fashioned theatre's efforts to hide them. No one would expect the lighting to be hidden at a sporting event, a boxing match for instance. Whatever the points of difference between the modern theatre's presentations and those of a sporting promoter, they do not include the same concealment of the sources of light as the old theatre found necessary.

(Brecht: 'Der Bühnenbau des epischen Theaters')

5    Cf. these remarks by Poul Reumert, the best-known Danish actor:

. . . If I feel I am *dying*, and if I *really* feel it, then so does everybody else; if I act as though I had a dagger in my hand, and am entirely filled by the one idea of killing the child, then everybody shudders. . . . The whole business is a matter of mental activity being communicated by emotions, or the other way round if you prefer it: a feeling so strong as to be an obsession, which is translated into thoughts. If it comes off it is the most infectious thing in the world; anything external is then a matter of complete indifference. . . .

And Rapaport, 'The Work of the Actor', *Theater Workshop*, October 1936:

. . . On the stage the actor is surrounded entirely by fictions. . . . The actor must be able to regard all this as though it were true, as though he were convinced that all that surrounds him on the stage is a living reality and, along with himself, he must convince the audience as well. This is the central feature of our method of work on the part. . . . Take any object, a cap for example; lay it on the table or on the floor and try to regard it as though it were a rat; make believe that it is a rat, and not a cap. . . . Picture what sort of a rat it is; what size, colour? . . . We thus commit ourselves to believe quite naïvely that the object before us is something other than it is and, at the same time, learn to compel the audience to believe. . . .

This might be thought to be a course of instruction for conjurers, but in fact it is a course of acting, supposedly according to Stanislavsky's method. One wonders if a technique that equips an actor to make the audience see rats where there aren't any can really be all that suitable for disseminating the truth. Given enough alcohol it doesn't take acting to persuade almost anybody that he is seeing rats: pink ones.

## 7 *Quotation*

Standing in a free and direct relationship to it, the actor allows his character to speak and move; he presents a report. He does not have to make us forget that the text isn't spontaneous, but has been memorized, is a fixed quantity; the fact doesn't matter, as we anyway assume that the report is not about himself but about others. His attitude would be the same if he were simply speaking from his own memory. [ . . . ]

8    The epic actor has to accumulate far more material than has been the case till now. What he has to represent is no longer himself as king, himself as scholar, himself as gravedigger, etc., but just kings, scholars, gravediggers, which means that he has to look around him in the world of reality. Again, he has to learn how to imitate: something that is discouraged in modern acting on the ground that it destroys his individuality.

9    The theatre can create the corresponding A-effect in the performance in a number of ways. The Munich production of *Edward II* for the first time had titles preceding the scenes, announcing the contents. The Berlin production of *The Threepenny Opera* had the titles of the songs projected while they were sung. The Berlin production of *Mann ist Mann* had the actors' figures projected on big screens during the action.

13    Another thing that makes for freedom in the actor's relationship with his audience is that he does not treat it as an undifferentiated mass. He doesn't boil it down to a shapeless dumpling in the stockpot of the emotions. He does not address himself to everybody alike; he allows the existing divisions within the audience to continue, in fact he widens them. He has friends and enemies in the audience; he is friendly to the one group and hostile to the other. He takes sides, not necessarily with his character but if not with it then against it. (At least, that is his basic attitude, though it too must be variable and change according to what the character may say at different stages. There may, however, also be points at

which everything is in the balance and the actor must withhold judgment, though this again must be expressly shown in his acting.)

14   If King Lear (in Act I, scene 1) tears up a map when he divides his kingdom between his daughters, then the act of division is alienated. Not only does it draw our attention to his kingdom, but by treating the kingdom so plainly as his own private property he throws some light on the basis of the feudal idea of the family. In *Julius Caesar* the tyrant's murder by Brutus is alienated if during one of his monologues accusing Caesar of tyrannical motives he himself maltreats a slave waiting on him. Weigel as *Maria Stuart* suddenly took the crucifix hanging round her neck and used it coquettishly as a fan, to give herself air. (See too Brecht: 'Übungsstücke für Schauspieler' in *Versuche II*, p. 107.)

## 17   The A-effect as a procedure in everyday life

The achievement of the A-effect constitutes something utterly ordinary, recurrent; it is just as widely-practised way of drawing one's own or someone else's attention to a thing, and it can be seen in education as also in business conferences of one sort or another. The A-effect consists in turning the object of which one is to be made aware, to which one's attention is to be drawn, from something ordinary, familiar, immediately accessible, into something peculiar, striking and unexpected. What is obvious is in a certain sense made incomprehensible, but this is only in order that it may then be made all the easier to comprehend. Before familiarity can turn into awareness the familiar must be stripped of its inconspicuousness; we must give up assuming that the object in question needs no explanation. However frequently recurrent, modest, vulgar it may be it will now be labelled as something unusual.

A common use of the A-effect is when someone says: 'Have you ever really looked carefully at your watch?' The questioner knows that I've looked at it often enough, and now his question deprives me of the sight which I've grown used to and which accordingly has nothing more to say to me. I used to look at it to see the time, and now when he asks me in this importunate way I realize that I have given up seeing the watch itself with an astonished eye; and it is in many ways an astonishing piece of machinery. Similarly it is an alienation effect of the simplest sort if a business discussion starts off with the sentence: 'Have you ever thought what happens to the waste from your factory which is pumped into the river twenty-four hours a day?' This waste wasn't just swept down the river unobserved; it was carefully channelled into the river; men and machines have worked on it; the river has changed colour, the waste has flowed away most conspicuously, but just as waste. It was superfluous to the process of manufacture, and now it is to become material for manufacture; our eye turns to it with interest. The asking of the question has alienated it, and intentionally so. The very simplest sentences that apply in the A-effect are those with 'Not . . . But': (He didn't say 'come in' but 'keep moving'. He was not pleased but amazed). They include an expectation which is justified by experience but, in the event, disappointed. One might have thought that . . . but one oughtn't to have thought it. There was not just one possibility but two; both are introduced, then the second one is alienated, then the first as well. To see one's mother as a man's wife one needs an A-effect; this is provided, for instance, when one acquires a stepfather. If one sees one's teacher hounded by the bailiffs an A-effect occurs: one is jerked out of a relationship in which the teacher seems big into one where he seems small. An alienation of the motor-car takes place if after driving a modern car for a long while we drive an old model T Ford. Suddenly we hear explosions once more; the motor works on the principle of explosion. We start feeling amazed that such a vehicle, indeed any vehicle not drawn by animal-power, can move; in short, we understand cars, by looking at them as something strange, new, as a triumph of engineering and to that extent something unnatural. Nature, which certainly, embraces the motor-car, is suddenly imbued with an element of unnaturalness, and from now on this is an indelible part of the concept of nature.

The expression 'in fact' can likewise certify or alienate. (He wasn't in fact at home; he said he would be, but we didn't believe him and had a look; or again, we didn't think it possible for him not to be at home, but it was a fact.) The term 'actually' is just as conducive to alienation. ('I don't actually agree'.) Similarly the Eskimo definition 'A car is a wingless aircraft that crawls along the ground' is a way of alienating the car.

In a sense the alienation effect itself has been alienated by the above explanation; we have taken a common, recurrent, universally-practised operation and tried to draw attention to it by illuminating its peculiarity. But we have achieved the effect only with those people who have truly ('in fact') grasped that it does 'not' result from every representation 'but' from certain ones: only 'actually' is it familiar.

## 18  About rational and emotional points of view

The rejection of empathy is not the result of a rejection of the emotions, nor does it lead to such. The crude aesthetic thesis that emotions can only be stimulated by means of empathy is wrong. None the less a non-aristotelian dramaturgy has to apply a cautious criticism to the emotions which it aims at and incorporates. Certain artistic tendencies like the provocative behaviour of Futurists and Dadaists and the icing-up of music point to a crisis of the emotions. Already in the closing years of the Weimar Republic the postwar German drama took a decisively rationalistic turn. Fascism's grotesque emphasizing of the emotions, together perhaps with the no less important threat to the rational element in Marxist aesthetics, led us to lay particular stress on the rational. Nevertheless there are many contemporary works of art where one can speak of a decline in emotional effectiveness due to their isolation from reason, or its revival thanks to a stronger rationalist message. This will surprise no one who has not got a completely conventional idea of the emotions.

The emotions always have a quite definite class basis; the form they take at any time is historical, restricted and limited in specific ways. The emotions are in no sense universally human and timeless.

The linking of particular emotions with particular interests is not unduly difficult so long as one simply looks for the interests corresponding to the emotional effects of works of art. Anyone can see the colonial adventures of the Second Empire looming behind Delacroix's paintings and Rimbaud's 'Bateau Ivre'.

If one compares the 'Bateau Ivre' say, with Kipling's 'Ballad of East and West', one can see the difference between French mid-nineteenth century colonialism and British colonialism at the beginning of the twentieth. It is less easy to explain the effect that such poems have on ourselves, as Marx already noticed. Apparently emotions accompanying social progress will long survive in the human mind as emotions linked with interests, and in the case of works of art will do so more strongly than might have been expected, given that in the meantime contrary interests will have made themselves felt. Every step forward means the end of the previous step forward, because that is where it starts and goes on from. At the same time it makes use of this previous step, which in a sense survives in men's consciousness as a step forward, just as it survives in its effects in real life. This involves a most interesting type of generalization, a continual process of abstraction. Whenever the works of art handed down to us allow us to share the emotions of other men, of men of a bygone period, different social classes, etc., we have to conclude that we are partaking in interests which really were universally human. These men now dead represented the interests of classes that gave a lead to progress. It is a very different matter when Fascism today conjures up on the grandest scale emotions which for most of the people who succumb to them are not determined by interest.

## 19  Is the critical attitude an inartistic one?

An old tradition leads people to treat a critical attitude as a predominantly negative one. Many see the difference between the scientific and artistic attitudes as lying precisely in their attitude to criticism. People cannot conceive of contradiction and detachment as being part of artistic appreciation. Of course such appreciation normally includes a higher level, which appreciates critically, but the criticism here only applies to matters of technique; it is quite a different matter from being required to observe not a representation of the world but the world itself in a critical, contradictory, detached manner.

To introduce this critical attitude into art, the negative element which it doubtless includes must be shown from its positive side: this criticism of world is active, practical, positive. Criticizing the course of a river means improving it, correcting it. Criticism of society is ultimately revolution; there you have criticism taken to its logical conclusion and playing an active part. A critical attitude of this type is an operative factor of productivity; it is deeply enjoyable as such, and if we commonly use the term 'arts' for enterprises that improve people's lives why should art proper remain aloof from arts of this sort?

['Kurze Beschreibung einer neuen Technik der Schauspielkunst, die einen Verfremdungseffekt hervorbringt', from *Versuche* II, 1951, less notes 2, 4, 6, 10, 11, 15, 16 and part of 7]

■  ■  ■

## Source

Brecht, B. (1940, 1964) 'Short Description of a New Technique of Acting which Produces an Alienation Effect', *Brecht on Theatre: The Development of an Aesthetic*, trans. and ed. J. Willett, New York: Hill & Wang: 136–147.

## Bertolt Brecht (1898–1956)

German dramatist, poet and theatre director. Brecht worked as assistant to the great German director, Max Reinhardt, before establishing himself as a writer-director in the 1920s. He collaborated extensively with three composers – Kurt Weill, Hanns Eisler and Paul Dessau – on works that have changed the ways in which theatre can be of use in changing an audience's perception of society. In his major works, *The Threepenny Opera* (1928), *The Caucasian Chalk Circle* (1945) and *Mother Courage* (1949), as well as in his more overtly political experiments such as *The Mother* (1932), he pioneered new techniques of both acting and staging, as well as of using music with text.

Brecht wanted actors to evolve a 'Verfremdunseffekt', which has been misleadingly translated as 'alienation'. The German means simply 'to make strange', and the technique he describes is intended to make an audience attend to the contradictions in society that his plays present, with greater concentration.

After going into exile in Europe at the start of the Second World War, Brecht went to America, where he was eventually called to trial for his alleged communist sympathies. After returning to the new state of East Germany at the end of the war, he established his own company, the Berliner Ensemble, to perform his plays. Over the period of six years before his early death in 1956, he developed one of the greatest acting ensembles of Europe, which was to have a profound effect on much subsequent theatre performance. His major concern is clear – that of the role of the actor in the twentieth century. Modern times, according to Brecht, demand new techniques – theatrical as well as industrial – and his attempt to revolutionise theatre is one of the most significant contributions to both theory and practice.

Compare this article with writings by the following authors in this reader

**Barba** – a later anti-psychological attitude to theatre
**Benjamin** – friend and comrade, developed a Marxist theoretical approach
**Boal** – another, South American, political role for theatre
**Copeau, Grotowski and Stanislavski** – different European approaches to actor training
**Etchells** – for a postmodern view by a writer/director
**Foreman and Wilson** – comparisons with later directors/scenographers
**LeCompte** – a later non-psychological approach
**Meyerhold and Piscator** – contemporary, European views of political theatre
**Müller** – a later German director

## Further reading

Esslin, M. (1964) *Brecht: A Choice of Evils*, London: Methuen.
Fuegi, J. (1995) *The Life and Lies of Bertolt Brecht*, London: HarperCollins.
Mumford, M. (2009) *Bertolt Brecht*, London: Routledge.
Thomson, P. and Sachs, G. (eds) (1994) *Cambridge Companion to Brecht*, Cambridge: Cambridge University Press.
Volker, K. (1979) *Brecht: A Biography*, London: Marion Boyars.

# Chapter 14

# Peter Brook

## THE DEADLY THEATRE

I CAN TAKE ANY EMPTY SPACE and call it a bare stage. A man walks across this empty space whilst someone else is watching him, and this is all that is needed for an act of theatre to be engaged. Yet when we talk about theatre this is not quite what we mean. Red curtains, spotlights, blank verse, laughter, darkness, these are all confusedly superimposed in a messy image covered by one all-purpose word. We talk of the cinema killing the theatre, and in that phrase we refer to the theatre as it was when the cinema was born, a theatre of box office, foyer, tip-up seats, footlights, scene changes, intervals, music, as though the theatre was by very definition these and little more.

I will try to split the word four ways and distinguish four different meanings – and so will talk about a Deadly Theatre, a Holy Theatre, a Rough Theatre and an Immediate Theatre. Sometimes these four theatres really exist, standing side by side, in the West End of London, or in New York off Times Square. Sometimes they are hundreds of miles apart, the Holy in Warsaw and the Rough in Prague, and sometimes they are metaphoric: two of them mixing together within one evening, within one act. Sometimes within one single moment, the four of them, Holy, Rough, Immediate and Deadly intertwine.

The Deadly Theatre can at first sight be taken for granted, because it means bad theatre. As this is the form of theatre we see most often, and as it is most closely linked to the despised, much-attacked commercial theatre it might seem a waste of time to criticize it further. But it is only if we see that deadliness is

deceptive and can appear anywhere, that we will become aware of the size of the problem.

The condition of the Deadly Theatre at least is fairly obvious. All through the world theatre audiences are dwindling. There are occasional new movements, good new writers and so on, but as a whole, the theatre not only fails to elevate or instruct, it hardly even entertains. The theatre has often been called a whore, meaning its art is impure, but today this is true in another sense – whores take the money and then go short on the pleasure. The Broadway crisis, the Paris crisis, the West End crisis are the same: we do not need the ticket agents to tell us that the theatre has become a deadly business and the public is smelling it out. In fact, were the public ever really to demand the true entertainment it talks about so often, we would almost all be hard put to know where to begin. A true theatre of joy is non-existent and it is not just the trivial comedy and the bad musical that fail to give us our money's worth – the Deadly Theatre finds its deadly way into grand opera and tragedy, into the plays of Molière and the plays of Brecht. Of course nowhere does the Deadly Theatre install itself so securely, so comfortably and so slyly as in the works of William Shakespeare. The Deadly Theatre takes easily to Shakespeare. We see his plays done by good actors in what seems like the proper way – they look lively and colourful, there is music and everyone is all dressed up, just as they are supposed to be in the best of classical theatres. Yet secretly we find it excruciatingly boring – and in our hearts we either blame Shakespeare, or theatre as such, or even ourselves. To make matters worse there is always a deadly spectator, who for special reasons enjoys a lack of intensity and even a lack of entertainment, such as the scholar who emerges from routine performances of the classics smiling because nothing has distracted him from trying over and confirming his pet theories to himself, whilst reciting his favourite lines under his breath. In his heart he sincerely wants a theatre that is nobler-than-life and he confuses a sort of intellectual satisfaction with the true experience for which he craves. Unfortunately, he lends the weight of his authority to dullness and so the Deadly Theatre goes on its way.

Anyone who watches the real successes as they appear each year will see a very curious phenomenon. We expect the so-called hit to be livelier, faster, brighter than the flop – but this is not always the case. Almost every season in most theatre-loving towns, there is one great success that defies these rules; one play that succeeds not despite but because of dullness. After all, one associates culture with a certain sense of duty, historical costumes and long speeches with the sensation of being bored; so, conversely, just the right degree of boringness is a reassuring guarantee of a worthwhile event. Of course, the dosage is so subtle that it is impossible to establish the exact formula – too much and the audience is driven out of its seats, too little and it may find the theme too disagreeably intense. However, mediocre authors seem to feel their way unerringly to the perfect mixture – and they perpetuate the Deadly Theatre with dull successes, universally praised. Audiences crave for something in the theatre that they can term 'better' than life and for this reason are open to confuse culture, or the trappings of culture, with something they do not know, but sense obscurely could exist – so, tragically, in elevating something bad into a success they are only cheating themselves.

If we talk of deadly, let us note that the difference between life and death, so crystal clear in man, is somewhat veiled in other fields. A doctor can tell at once between the trace of life and the useless bag of bones that life has left; but we are less practised in observing how an idea, an attitude or a form can pass from the lively to the moribund. It is difficult to define but a child can smell it out. Let me give an example. In France there are two deadly ways of playing classical tragedy. One is traditional, and this involves using a special voice, a special manner, a noble look and an elevated musical delivery. The other way is no more than a half-hearted version of the same thing. Imperial gestures and royal values are fast disappearing from everyday life, so each new generation finds the grand manner more and more hollow, more and more meaningless. This leads the young actor to an angry and impatient search for what he calls truth. He wants to play his verse more realistically, to get it to sound like honest-to-God real speech, but he finds that the formality of the writing is so rigid that it resists this treatment. He is forced to an uneasy compromise that is neither refreshing, like ordinary talk, nor defiantly histrionic, like what we call ham. So his acting is weak and because ham is strong, it is remembered with a certain nostalgia. Inevitably, someone calls for tragedy to be played once again 'the way it is written'. This is fair enough, but unfortunately all the printed word can tell us is what was written on paper, not how it was once brought to life. There are no records, no tapes – only experts, but not one of them, of course, has firsthand knowledge. The real antiques have all gone – only some imitations have survived, in the shape of traditional actors, who continue to play in a traditional way, drawing their inspiration not from real sources, but from imaginary ones, such as the memory of the sound an older actor once made – a sound that in turn was a memory of a predecessor's way.

I once saw a rehearsal at the Comédie Française – a very young actor stood in front of a very old one and spoke and mimed the role with him like a reflection in a glass. This must not be confused with the great tradition, say, of the Noh actors passing knowledge orally from father to son. There it is meaning that is communicated – and meaning never belongs to the past. It can be checked in each man's own present experience. But to imitate the externals of acting only perpetuates manner – a manner hard to relate to anything at all.

Again with Shakespeare we hear or read the same advice – 'Play what is written'. But what is written? Certain ciphers on paper. Shakespeare's words are records of the words that he wanted to be spoken, words issuing as sounds from people's mouths, with pitch, pause, rhythm and gesture as part of their meaning. A word does not start as a word – it is an end product which begins as an impulse, stimulated by attitude and behaviour which dictates the need for expression. This process occurs inside the dramatist; it is repeated inside the actor. Both may only be conscious of the words, but both for the author and then for the actor the word is a small visible portion of a gigantic unseen formation. Some writers attempt to nail down their meaning and intentions in stage directions and explanations, yet we cannot help being struck by the fact that the best dramatists explain themselves the least. They recognize that further indications will most probably be useless. They recognize that the only way to find the true path to the speaking of a word is through a process that parallels the original creative one. This can neither be by-passed nor simplified. Unfortunately, the moment a lover speaks, or a king utters, we rush to give them a label: the lover is 'romantic', the king is 'noble' — and before we know it we are speaking of romantic love and kingly nobility or princeliness as though they are things we can hold in our hand and expect the actors to observe. But these are not substances and they do not exist. If we search for them, the best we can do is to make guesswork reconstructions from books and paintings. If you ask an actor to play in a 'romantic style' he will valiantly have a go, thinking he knows what you mean. What actually can he draw on? Hunch, imagination and a scrap book of theatrical memories, all of which will give him a vague 'romanticness' that he will mix up with a disguised imitation of whatever older actor he happens to admire. If he digs into his own experiences the result may not marry with the text; if he just plays what he thinks is the text, it will be imitative and conventional. Either way the result is a compromise: at most times unconvincing.

It is vain to pretend that the words we apply to classical plays like 'musical', 'poetic', 'larger than life', 'noble', 'heroic', 'romantic', have any absolute meaning. They are the reflections of a critical attitude of a particular period, and to attempt to build a performance today to conform to these canons is the most certain road to deadly theatre — deadly theatre of a respectability that makes it pass as living truth.

Once, when giving a lecture on this theme, I was able to put it to a practical test. By luck, there was a woman in the audience who had neither read nor seen *King Lear*. I gave her Goneril's first speech and asked her to recite it as best she could for whatever values she found in it. She read it very simply — and the speech itself emerged full of eloquence and charm. I then explained that it was supposed to be the speech of a wicked woman and suggested her reading every word for hypocrisy. She tried to do so, and the audience saw what a hard unnatural wrestling with the simple music of the words was involved when she sought to act to a definition:

> Sir, I love you more than words can wield the matter;
> Dearer than eyesight, space, and liberty;
> Beyond that can be valued, rich or rare;
> No less than life, with grace, health, beauty, honour;
> As much as child e'er loved, or father found;
> A love that makes breath poor, and speech unable;
> Beyond all manner of so much I love you.

Anyone can try this for himself. Taste it on the tongue. The words are those of a lady of style and breeding accustomed to expressing herself in public, someone with ease and social aplomb. As for clues to her character, only the façade is presented and this, we see, is elegant and attractive. Yet if one thinks of the performances where Goneril speaks these first lines as a macabre villainess, and looks at the speech again, one is at a loss to know what suggests this – other than preconceptions of Shakespeare's moral attitudes. In fact, if Goneril in her first appearance does not play a 'monster', but merely what her given words suggest, then all the balance of the play changes – and in the subsequent scenes her villainy and Lear's martyrdom are neither as crude nor as simplified as they might appear. Of course, by the end of the play we learn that Goneril's actions make her what we call a monster – but a real monster, both complex and compelling.

In a living theatre, we would each day approach the rehearsal putting yesterday's discoveries to the test, ready to believe that the true play has once again escaped us. But the Deadly Theatre approaches the classics from the viewpoint that somewhere, someone has found out and defined how the play should be done.

■  ■  ■

## Source

Brook, P. (1968, 1990) 'The Deadly Theatre', *The Empty Space*, Harmondsworth: Penguin: 1–17. First published (1968) by McGibbon & Kee.

## Peter Brook (1925–)

European theatre director, who studied at Oxford, and established himself by directing relatively conventional Shakespearean productions, alongside opera at London's Covent Garden. Notable productions included *Titus Andronicus* (1955, with Laurence Olivier), *King Lear* (1962, with Paul Scofield), and *Oedipus* (1968). In the early 1960s he read Artaud's *Theatre and Its Double*, newly available in English translation, and staged his famous 1964 Theatre of Cruelty Season, which included Artaud's *Spurt of Blood*. There followed a series of productions which have now achieved the status of classics – Peter Weiss's *Marat/Sade* (1964), *US* (1966), and *A Midsummer Night's Dream* (1970). In 1970 Brook left the UK to found the International Centre for Performance Research in Paris, with the help of a million-dollar grant from the Ford Foundation. This international company of performers, whose 'disunity is their unity', went on to develop *Orghast at Persepolis* (1971), played in the classical ruins in Iran, *The Ik* (1975), and others, culminating in a performance of the Indian epic *Mahabharata* (1985), which toured the world. A more recent piece of theatrical research has been *The Man Who* (1993), based on the neurological discoveries of Oliver Sacks.

Brook's restless eclecticism has meant that he cannot easily be classified, but he shares with the Polish director Grotowski a continual search for some form of universal understanding based on theatre. In spite of criticism from some non-Western sources he remains the major British director of our time, and one of the few whose work is always an occasion for celebration, and a source of inspiration to others. This essay introduces his concept of deadly theatre, or the theatre of which we see most, against which all Brook's variety is juxtaposed.

## Compare this article with writings by the following authors in this reader

Artaud – an early inspiration, for a search for universal meaning
Beck – North American notion of collective collaboration
Benjamin – another critique of the dead hand of bourgeois theatre
Copeau – for an earlier French notion of the responsibilities of theatre
Grotowski – a contemporary explorer of theatre whom Brook acknowledged as unique
Meyerhold – for the concerns of a Russian director/precursor
Schechner – for another, North America, view of intercultural experiment

## Further reading

Croydon, M. (2003) *Conversations with Peter Brook 1970–2000*, London: Faber.
Reeves, G. and Hunt, A. (1993) *Peter Brook*, Cambridge: Cambridge University Press.
Selbourne, D. (1982) *The Making of A Midsummer Night's Dream*, London: Methuen.
Williams, D. (1988) *Peter Brook, a Theatrical Casebook*, London: Methuen.
Williams, D. (ed.) (1991) *Peter Brook and the Mahabharata*, London: Routledge.

# Chapter 15

# Trisha Brown

## TRISHA BROWN:
## AN INTERVIEW

**M**Y DANCE TRAINING began in Aberdeen, Washington, when I studied with a teacher, Marion Hageage, whose background was primarily musical. I studied acrobatics – that was my long suit – tap, ballet and jazz dance. I was in my early teens at this time and my class was at the end of the day when the instructor was tired and, sharing her privacy with me, would dance around in a slow jazzy manner punctuated with meaningful silences and high kicks. I tagged along as fast as I could go, memorizing the outflow. These dances, which could best be categorized as Hollywood style dance routines, were performed in local recitals and hospitals. Later I attended Mills College and became a dance major by the end of the first year. The training incorporated Martha Graham technique and Louis Horst composition which culminated in a senior recital. I also spent a couple of summers at Connecticut College studying with Louis Horst, José Limón and Merce Cunningham. Doris Humphrey was there also, but I was not advanced enough to be in her classes. After graduation from Mills College I went to Reed College to teach and started the dance department. I stayed there two years, but exhausted conventional teaching methods after the first few months and then became involved with improvisational teaching. During this period I began developing my own dance vocabulary.

In the summer of 1959, I joined Simone Forti, Yvonne Rainer and other dancers at Anna Halprin's six week workshop in Marin County, California. Anna was working with the choreographic idea of task, such as sweeping with a broom – an ordinary action,

organized by an ordinary activity and performed as if you were not performing but off alone somewhere, sweeping up. There was also experimentation with sound – verbalization and singing as a material, and beyond that, defined or wide open improvisations night and day by very talented people. Improvisation has been a rich and continuous involvement for me. If you stand back and think about what you are going to do before you do it, there is likely to be a strenuous editing process that stymies the action. On the other hand, if you set yourself loose in an improvisational form, you have to make solutions very quickly and you learn how to. That is the excitement of improvisation. If, however, you just turn the lights out and go gah-gah in circles, that would be therapy or catharsis or your happy hour, but if in the beginning you set a structure and decide to deal with X, Y and Z materials in a certain way, nail it down even further and say you can only walk forward, you cannot use your voice or you have to do 195 gestures before you hit the wall at the other end of the room, that is an improvisation within set boundaries. That is the principle, for example, behind jazz. The musicians may improvise but they have a limitation in the structure just as improvisation in dance does. This is what I would call structured improvisation because it locates you in time and place with content. The workshop was invaluable because Anna Halprin has a rampant imagination and puts a high priority on originality and self-exposition.

Six months or a year later I had pretty much burned up everything on the West Coast and Simone Forti urged me to come to New York. When I got there I continued to improvise with Simone and Dick Levine, and began taking Robert Dunn's class at Merce Cunningham's studio. Robert Dunn was applying the Cagian concepts of chance and indeterminacy to dance. One of Bob's most important contributions was the method of analysis of the work shown. After presenting a dance, each choreographer was asked, 'How did you make that dance?' The students were inventing forms rather than using the traditional theme and development or narrative, and the discussion that followed applied nonevaluative criticism to the movement itself and the choreographic structure as well as investigating the disparity between the two simultaneous experiences, what the artist was making and what the audience saw. This procedure illuminated the interworkings of the dances and minimized value judgements of the choreographer, which for me meant permission, permission to go ahead and do what I wanted to do or had to do – to try out an idea of borderline acceptability. I remember his giving an assignment to make a three-minute dance and that was the whole assignment. This assignment was totally nonspecific except for duration, and the ambiguity provoked days of sorting through possibilities trying to figure out what time meant, was 60 seconds the only difference between three minutes and four minutes, how do you stop something, why, what relation does time have to movement, and on and on. Dick Levine taught himself to cry and did so for the full time period while I held a stopwatch instructed by him to shout just before the time elapsed, 'Stop it! Stop it! Cut it out!' both of us ending at exactly three minutes. That dance is a good example of the practice of substituting one medium, in this case acting/crying, to solve a dance problem.

I definitely do want my audiences to understand my work although I have done my share of dances that were difficult for the general public. In the 1960's, my audiences were small but consistent and knowledgeable. We grew up together. Now my audiences are larger, informed through literature and aware that some dance is not entertainment.

There was improvisation in 1969 where I asked the audience to yell 'yellowbelly' which means 'coward' in Aberdeen, Washington; I performed the piece twice. The first time they were very sweet about it so I stopped and I asked them to yell in a nasty way and they did. They started jeering and yelling. I was improvising and absolutely frozen and I have not any idea what I did, although I had a few amorphous possibilities prepared. When I stopped, they really jeered at me, so I started up again and finally we both stopped. It was terrifying because it was confronting the performer's fear that you will get up before an audience and forget what you are doing. The point was to set up precisely that situation and it certainly tested both me and the audience. The second time I performed it in Rome and had them yell in Italian. It was a more sophisticated audience and they just would not yell. When they sat back and refused to yell, I refused to move. Then when someone would yell, I would start and stop moving when they stopped yelling. It was the most amazing relationship until they got very angry and all began to yell. Then I performed my dance which was an improvisation, for this time I had absolutely nothing prepared, nothing at all. I started spinning and continued until I was totally dizzy, then I stopped and tried to do a beautiful articulate dance, but without any success. That relationship to the audience was certainly rough and symbiotic.

The first performance of *Accumulation* (1971) was four and a half minutes long and accompanied by the Grateful Dead's *Uncle John's Band*. Movement one, rotation of the fist with the thumb extended, was begun and repeated seven or eight times. Movement two was added and one and two were repeated eight times. Then movement three was added and one, two and three were repeated, eventually bringing into play the entire body. At first the additions were in numerical sequence but later movements got wedged in between earlier additions and the piece grew in several directions, expanding rather than lengthening. The second performance was in silence and 55 minutes long. I worked in performance to keep the separateness and clarity of each move against the blurring effect of relentless repetition. What went through my mind was, 'This is all there is.' By then another move would be active and 'This is all there is.' The tempo was mainly constant but fluctuated in relation to biological changes of temperature, fatigue and second winds. Since I did not use music, these delicate changes in time could occur. Both the dance and its structure were visible and bare-bone simple. None of the movements had any significance beyond what they were. And I never felt more alive, more expressive or more exposed in performance.

The result of choreography that goes beyond what the audience is familiar with is that you find out what you can do, what your own personal limitation edges are. In that arises the possibility of doing that which is not interesting to your audience, not up until now thought of as acceptable to an audience. There is also a question of tension in the relationships between an audience and a performer. In dances of this sort it seems that you are stretching or pushing or rather raising the level of tension considerably. In *Primary Accumulation* (1972) a supine solo figure systematically accumulates 30 moves in eighteen minutes. The figure rotates 45 degrees each on the last two moves, making a 90 degree turn with the completion of the phrase. The phrase is repeated until a 360 degree turn is achieved, revealing all sides of the dance/dancer in the last two minutes of the dance.

This object-like dance became the material for other dances. In *Group Primary Accumulation*, four dancers placed equidistant from each other in a line from downstage to upstage perform the piece in unison. After the 360 degree turn, two movers enter and transport the performers to new positions that relate to the physical space and also to each other. The movement unavoidably changed in an unconscious theme and variations as the dancers were carried, stacked, stood and separated.

Two dancers lying side by side eighteen inches apart performed *Split Solo*. All of the movements of *Primary Accumulation* that occur on the right side of the body were done by the person on the right and all the movements on the left side of the body by the person on the left. The dance went in and out of looking like one huge fat person or two people having one dance, shifting their roles of doing and waiting. The final version of *Group Primary Accumulation* was for four dancers on four rafts on a lake. The dance/dancers were set free to drift and spin in a continuously changing spatial relationship and inaccurate unison.

My involvement with Judson Memorial Church came out of Dunn's classes and the compositions we were making. Judson was the only place to perform then and that is how it began. The first piece that I showed at Judson was called *Trillium*, a structured improvisation of very high energy movements involving a curious timing and with dumb silences like stopping dead in your tracks. It was a kinesthetic piece, a serial composition where I involved myself in one movement after another accompanied by a tape by Simone Forti. In thinking of the opening section of *Trillium*, I am reminded of working in a studio on a movement exploration of transversing the three positions sitting, standing and lying. I broke those actions down into their basic mechanical structure, finding the places of rest, power, momentum and peculiarity. I went over and over the material, eventually accelerating and mixing it up to the degree that lying down was done in the air.

In *Rulegame 5* (1964) there were seven rows of masking tape laid down in an area approximately 21 feet by 21 feet. Five performers proceed along the above prescribed path, changing height in equal amounts, from highest (erect) on row one to lowest (prone) on row seven. The performers may pass other performers parallel to themselves only if the relationship of high, middle and low is correct, and if not, they speak to each other and make the proper adjustments. The scheme served as a structure for movement and language improvisation, but could have been performed as a task if the element of time had been dictated.

There is a performance quality that appears in improvisation that did not in memorized dance as it was known up to that date. If you are improvising with a structure your senses are heightened; you are using your wits, thinking, everything is working at once to find the best solution to a given problem under pressure of a viewing audience. In contrast, at that time, modern dancers glazed over their eyes, knuckling down behind that glaze to concentrate and deliver their best performance – an understandable habit but unfortunately resulting in the robot-look. At Judson, the performers looked at each other and the audience, they breathed audibly, ran out of breath, sweated, talked things over. They began behaving more like human beings, revealing what was thought of as deficiencies as well as their skills.

Another piece I made at this time, *A String*, was composed of three parts. To make the third section titled *Inside* (1966), I stood facing a wall in my studio at a distance of about twelve feet and, beginning at the extreme left, I read the wall as a score while moving across the room to the far right. Any question that arose about the speed, shape, duration or quality of a move was determined by the visual information on the wall. An odd distribution of actions and gestures emanated from the architectural collection of alcove, door, peeling paint and pipes. After finishing the first wall, I repositioned myself in the same way for the second wall and repeated the procedure for the third and fourth. Therefore, in performance, I moved along the edge of the room, facing out, on the knee caps of the audience, who were placed in a rectangular seating formation duplicating the interior of my studio. I was marking the edge of the space, leaving the center of the room empty, the movement concretely specific to me, abstract to the audience. And I looked at them. I added the problem of looking at the audience, not 'with meaning,' but with eyes open and seeing.

In these early works, I used trained dancers as well as non-trained dancers. My own style of movement in, say, *Trillium* was too personal and difficult to teach to others and therefore remained solo material. In group pieces centering around tasks, I used untrained dancers – ordinary people who were well aligned and physically alert. Some trained dancers, in an effort to appear bigger than life and project across those footlights, puffed themselves up with tension and a dramatic delivery which stylized the movement, making it impossible for them to do an ordinary activity like walking. I am using trained dancers now because my work has become technically so demanding that a non-dancer could not do it.

Ordinary movement includes climbing, falling, leaning and balancing. In *Planes* (1968), the first of a series of dances that came to be known as equipment pieces, I built a thirteen foot by eighteen foot wall with holes cut out at equal intervals across its surface which functioned as hand and footholds, enabling three dancers to continuously turn, spin and climb in slow motion and all directions while appearing to be free-falling. The audience's perspective was altered. The back wall of the stage became like the floor of the auditorium.

I continued to find or construct the environment as well as the dance. *Man Walking Down the Side of a Building* was exactly like the title – seven stories. A natural activity under the stress of an unnatural setting. Gravity reneged. Vast scale. Clear order. You start at the top, walk straight down, stop at the bottom. All those soupy questions that arise in the process of selecting abstract movement according to the modern dance tradition – what, when, where and how – are solved in collaboration between choreographer and place. If you eliminate all those eccentric possibilities that the choreographic imagination can conjure and just have a person walk down an aisle, then you see the movement as the activity. The paradox of one action working against another is very interesting to me, and is illustrated by *Walking Down the Side of a Building* where you have gravity working one way on the body and my intention to have a naturally walking person working in another way.

*Floor of the Forest* (1969) was performed in a twelve foot by fourteen foot pipe frame across which were tied ropes densely threaded with clothes – sleeves were woven beneath pant legs forming a solid rectangular surface. The frame was suspended horizontally at eye level in the center of an empty room. Two people dressed and undressed their way through it. It was done as naturally as it could be done. A normally vertical activity performed horizontally and reshaped by the vertical pull of gravity. It was strenuous. Great strain and effort to support the body weight while negotiating buttons and zippers. We rested at times and when we rested hanging down, an article of clothing became a hammock. The audience ducked down to see the performers suspended or climbing below the frame or stretched upward to see the activity above. They had to choose which part of the dance to look at. The second time *Floor of the Forest* was performed (1969), the frame was suspended overhead and a full-scale rummage sale took place below. The audience trying on clothes below is added to the horizontal dressing and undressing of the performers above. The audience had to choose between looking up at the dance or down at a bargain or drop back to the outside edge of the room in order to take it all in. The clothes were familiar to me, I had collected them from friends. The piece, therefore, continues to this day through my seeing or being told of one of those bargains.

Pure movement is a movement that has no other connotations. It is not functional or pantomimic. Mechanical body actions like bending, straightening or rotating would qualify as pure movement providing the context was neutral. I use pure movements, a kind of breakdown of the body's capabilities. I also use quirky, personal gestures, things that have specific meaning to me but probably appear abstract to others. I may perform an everyday gesture so that the audience does not know whether I have stopped dancing or not and, carrying that irony further, I seek to disrupt their expectations by setting up an action to travel left and then cut right at the last moment unless I imagine they have caught on to me, in which case I might stand still. I make plays on movement, like rhyming or echoing an earlier gesture in another part of the body at a later time and perhaps out of kilter. I turn phrases upside down, reverse them or suggest an action and then not complete it, or else overstate it altogether. I make radical changes in a mundane way. I use weight, balance, momentum and physical actions like falling, pushing, etc. I say things to my company like, 'Toss your knees over there,' or, 'Start the phrase and then on the second count start it again,' or 'Do it and get off it.' I put all these movements together without transitions. I do not promote the next movement with a preceding transition and, therefore, I do not build up to something. If I do build up, I might end it with another buildup. I often return to a neutral standing position between moves; it is for me a way of measuring where I have been and where I am going. An even pulse (without musical accompaniment) does the same thing with time. A pulse brackets a unit of time that can be measured, divided, filled up completely or partially. If I am beginning to sound like a bricklayer with a sense of humour, you are beginning to understand my work.

I was thinking of *Locus* (1975) while talking about movement. *Locus* is organized around 27 points located on an imaginary cube of space slightly larger than the standing figure in a stride position. The points were correlated to the alphabet and a written statement, 1 being A, 2, B.

| T | R | I | S | H | A | | B | R | O | W | N | |
|---|---|---|---|---|---|---|---|---|---|---|---|---|
| 20 | 18 | 9 | 19 | 8 | 1 | 27 | 2 | 18 | 15 | 23 | 14 | 27 |

| W | A | S | | B | O | R | N | | I | N |
|---|---|---|---|---|---|---|---|---|---|---|
| 23 | 1 | 19 | 27 | 2 | 15 | 18 | 14 | 27 | 9 | 14 |

I made four sections each three minutes long that move through, touch, look at, jump over, or do something about each point in the series, either one point at a time or clustered. There is spatial repetition, but not gestural. The dance does not observe front, it revolves. The cube base is multiplied to form a grid of five units wide and four deep. There are opportunities to move from one cube base to another without distorting the movement. By exercising these options, we travel. The choices of facing, placing and section are made in performance by the four performers. This describes the structure of the dance – you have to fill it in with the kinds of movement mentioned before.

The most recent accumulation entitled *Pyramid* (1975) also has a score. It is based on nine ascending and descending time units of nine counts in five measures. 1, 2, 3, 2, 1. The first fifteen measures are accumulated. When sixteen is added, one is dropped; add seventeen, drop two . . . ; we continue this process up to 30 at which point we de-accumulate by dropping sixteen, return to 30, drop seventeen, return to 30, etc. until the piece erases itself. The four performers made their own movement. At this moment, I am working on a piece *Solo Olos* in which I am making a natural progression of non-functional movement. By natural progression I mean that movement B will be the simplest most obvious next move after A; C after B. When the sequence passes through a neutral position, there will be more than one obvious next move generating B1, B2 and more – an intersection of several directions. The progression and its alternatives will be executed forward and backward, and wherever possible to the left and right. The dancers will work side by side, back up, rejoin, wait, branch off, overlap, bunch, delay or pass in performance.

■   ■   ■

## Source

Brown, T. and Livet, A. (1978) 'Trisha Brown: Edited Transcript of an Interview with Trisha Brown', *Contemporary Dance*, ed. A. Livet, New York: Abbeville: 44–54.

## Trisha Brown (1936–)

American dancer and choreographer. She studied with Anna Halprin (1959), then with Robert Dunn at Merce Cunningham's New York Studio (1960). She was a founder member of Judson Dance Theatre (1962–66) and then of the Grand Union. She established the Trisha Brown Company in 1970. Her choreography spans a huge range of improvisational and compositional means. In the early 1960s she explored various improvisational structures in *Trillium* (1962), *Rulegame 5* (1964) and *Yellowbelly* (1969). From 1968 she made a number of Equipment Pieces where her dancers were denied a 'natural' relationship with gravity by the intervention of various ropes, pullies and mechanical devices: *Rummage Sale* (1971), *Floor of the Forest* (1971) and, in particular, *Man Walking Down the Side of a Building* (1969). The last consisted precisely of what its title suggested. During the early 1970s she made a number of analytical dance pieces, notably the series based on accumulation as a process, including *Accumulation* (1971), *Group Accumulation* (1973), and culminating in *Accumulation with Talking plus Water Motor* (1978). Brown extended her investigations of choreographic method in collaboration with many visual artists and musicians, dating back to early explorations at Judson. Notable amongst these multifaceted theatre works have been *Glacial Decoy* (1979) with Robert Rauschenberg, *Son of Gone Fishing* (1981) with Donald Judd and Robert Ashley, and *Set and Reset* (1983) with Robert Rauschenberg and Laurie Anderson. Rauschenberg contributed visual presentations again for *Astral Convertible* (1989) and *Foray Forêt* (1990).

Since 1995 Brown has made a number of works, which have challenged and redefined the relationship of dance to music. Her *M.O.* (1995) is a working of J.S. Bach's 'Musical Offering.' Her setting of the dance to the music develops the compositional strategies in her previous work to present a dense, sophisticated postmodern restatement of the Baroque. In 1998 she staged Monteverdi's opera *L'Orfeo* for the Theatre Royale de la Monaie, Brussels. In 1999 she collaborated with jazz composer Dave Douglas for *El Trilogy – Five Part Weather Invention, Rapture to Leon James, Groove and Countermove*.

This edited transcript details key points in her career to 1978. It is especially valuable for its lucid description of her experiments into choreographic process. It details precisely what strategies she set up, and why she made the choices of process that she did. It shows her concern for herself as a performer, for performance and for her audience. Her description of the performance quality given by structured improvisation is exemplary, as is her description of her use of 'movement'.

## Compare this interview with writings by the following authors in this reader

**Anderson** – collaborated on the music for *Set and Reset*
**Bausch** – a contrasting European approach to dance making
**Beck** – a theatre contemporary with a different approach to the same times
**Boal** – comparison with a director working with non-theatrical processes and spaces
**Cage** – a musician working with concerns for structure and process
**Hijikata** – an antithetical approach to the body
**Rainer** – also at Judson, but whose strategies, although about process, were different.

## Further reading

Banes, S. (1987) 'Gravity and Levity', *Terpsichore in Sneakers: Post-Modern Dance*, 2nd edition, Middletown: Conn.: Wesleyan University Press.
Brunel, C., Brown, T. and Delahaye, G. (1987) *Trisha Brown*, Paris: Editions Bougé.
Eleey, P. (ed.) (2008) *Trisha Brown: So That the Audience Does Not Know Whether I Have Stopped Dancing*, Minneaoplis: Walker Art Centre.
Sayre, H.M. (1989) 'Tracing Dance: Collaboration and the New Gesamtkunstwerk', *The Object of Performance: The American Avant-Garde Since 1970*, Chicago: University of Chicago Press: 101–144.
http://www.trishabrowncompany.org

# Chapter 16

# John Cage

## FOUR STATEMENTS ON THE DANCE

*This article was part of a series*, Percussion Music and Its Relation to the Modern Dance, *that appeared in* Dance Observer *in 1939. It was written in Seattle where I had organized a concert-giving percussion ensemble.*

### Goal: New Music, New Dance

Percussion music is revolution. Sound and rhythm have too long been submissive to the restrictions of nineteenth-century music. Today we are fighting for their emancipation. Tomorrow, with electronic music in our ears, we will hear freedom.

Instead of giving us new sounds, the nineteenth-century composers have given us endless arrangements of the old sounds. We have turned on radios and always known when we were tuned to a symphony. The sound has always been the same, and there has not been even a hint of curiosity as to the possibilities of rhythm. For interesting rhythms we have listened to jazz.

At the present stage of revolution, a healthy lawlessness is warranted. Experiment must necessarily be carried on by hitting anything – tin pans, rice bowls, iron pipes – anything we can lay our hands on. Not only hitting, but rubbing, smashing, making sound in every possible way. In short, we must explore the materials of music. What we can't do ourselves will be done by machines and electrical instruments which we will invent.

The conscientious objectors to modern music will, of course, attempt everything in the way of counterrevolution. Musicians will not admit that we are making music; they will say that we are interested in superficial effects, or, at most, are imitating Oriental or primitive music. New and original sounds will be labeled as 'noise.' But our common answer to every criticism must be to continue working and listening, making music with its materials, sound and rhythm, disregarding the cumbersome, top-heavy structure of musical prohibitions.

These prohibitions removed, the choreographer will be quick to realize a great advantage to the modern dance: the simultaneous composition of both dance and music. The materials of dance, already including rhythm, require only the addition of sound to become a rich, complete vocabulary. The dancer should be better equipped than the musician to use this vocabulary, for more of the materials are already at his command. Some dancers have made steps in this direction by making simple percussion accompaniments. Their use of percussion, unfortunately, has not been constructive. They have followed the rhythm of their own dance movement, accentuated it and punctuated it with percussion, but they have not given the sound its own and special part in the whole composition. They have made the music identical with the dance but not cooperative with it. Whatever method is used in composing the materials of the dance can be extended to the organization of the musical materials. The form of the music-dance composition should be a necessary working together of all materials used. The music will then be more than an accompaniment; it will be an integral part of the dance.

. . . . . . . . . . . . . . . . . . . . . . . . . . . . . . . .

When I was growing up in California there were two things that everyone assumed were good for you. There were, of course, others – spinach and oatmeal, for instance – but right now I'm thinking of sunshine and orange juice. When we lived at Ocean Park, I was sent out every morning to the beach where I spent the day building rolly-coasters in the sand, complicated downhill tracks with tunnels and inclines upon which I rolled a small hard rubber ball. Every day toward noon I fainted because the sun was too much for me. When I fainted I didn't fall down, but I couldn't see; there were flocks of black spots wherever I looked. I soon learned to find my way in that blindness to a hamburger stand where I'd ask for something to eat. Sitting in the shade, I'd come to. It took me much longer, about thirty-five years in fact, to learn that orange juice was not good for me either.

Before studying Zen, men are men and mountains are mountains. While studying Zen, things become confused. After studying Zen, men are men and mountains are mountains. After telling this, Dr. Suzuki was asked, 'What is the difference between before and after?' He said, 'No difference, only the feet are a little bit off the ground.'

*The following piece was printed in* Dance Observer *in 1944.*

## Grace and Clarity

The strength that comes from firmly established art practices is not present in the modern dance today. Insecure, not having any clear direction, the modern dancer is willing to compromise and to accept influences from other more rooted art manners, enabling one to remark that certain dancers are either borrowing from or selling themselves to Broadway, others are learning from folk and Oriental arts, and many are either introducing into their work elements of the ballet, or, in an all-out effort, devoting themselves to it. Confronted with its history, its former power, its present insecurity, the realization is unavoidable that the strength the modern dance once had was not impersonal but was intimately connected with and ultimately dependent on the personalities and even the actual physical bodies of the individuals who imparted it.

The techniques of the modern dance were once orthodox. It did not enter a dancer's mind that they might be altered. To add to them was the sole privilege of the originators.

Intensive summer courses were the scenes of the new dispensations, reverently transmitted by the master-students. When the fanatically followed leaders began, and when they continued, to desert their own teachings (adapting chiefly balletish movements to their own rapidly-growing-less-rigorous techniques), a general and profound insecurity fell over the modern dance.

Where any strength now exists in the modern dance, it is, as before, in isolated personalities and physiques. In the case of the young, this is unfortunate; for, no matter how impressive and revelatory their expressed outlooks on life are, they are overshadowed, in the minds of audiences, and often, understandably, in the dancers' own minds, by the more familiar, more respected, and more mature older personalities.

Personality is a flimsy thing on which to build an art. (This does not mean that it should not enter into an art, for, indeed, that is what is meant by the word *style*.) And the ballet is obviously not built on such an ephemeron, for, if it were, it would not at present thrive as it does, almost devoid of interesting personalities and certainly without the contribution of any individual's message or attitude toward life.

That the ballet *has* something seems reasonable to assume. That what it has is what the modern dance needs is here expressed as an opinion.

It is seriously to be doubted whether *tour jeté, entrechat six,* or *sur les pointes* (in general) are needed in the modern dance. Even the prettiness and fanciness of these movements would not seem to be requisite. Also, it is not true that the basis of the ballet lies in glittering costumes and sets, for many of the better ballets appear year after year in drab, weather-beaten accoutrements.

Ballets like *Les Sylphides, Swan Lake,* almost any *Pas de Deux* or *Quatre,* and currently, the exceptional *Danses Concertantes* have a strength and validity quite beyond and separate from the movements involved, whether or not they are done with style (expressed personality), the ornamented condition of the stage, quality of costumery, sound of the music, or any other particularities, including those of content. Nor does the secret lie in that mysterious quantity, form. (The forms of the ballet are mostly dull; symmetry is maintained practically without question.)

Good or bad, with or without meaning, well dressed or not, the ballet is always clear in its rhythmic structure. Phrases begin and end in such a way that *anyone* in the audience knows when they begin and end, and breathes accordingly. It may seem at first thought that rhythmic structure is not of primary importance. However, a dance, a poem, a piece of music (any of the time arts) occupies a length of time, and the manner in which this length of time is divided first into large parts and then into phrases (or built up from phrases to form eventual larger parts) is the work's very life structure. The ballet is in possession of a tradition of clarity of its rhythmic structure. Essential devices for bringing this about have been handed down generation after generation. These particular devices, again, are not to be borrowed from the ballet: they are private to it. But the function they fulfill is not private; it is, on the contrary, universal.

Oriental dancing, for instance, is clear in its phraseology. It has its own devices for obtaining it. Hot jazz is never unclear rhythmically. The poems of Gerard Manley Hopkins, with all their departure from tradition, enable the reader to breathe with them. The modern dance, on the other hand, is rarely clear.

When a modern dancer has followed music that was clear in its phrase structure, the dance has had a tendency to be clear. The widespread habit of choreographing the dance first, and obtaining music for it later, is not in itself here criticized. But the fact that modern choreographers have been concerned with things other than clarity of rhythmic structure has made the appearance of it, when the dance-first-music-later method was used, both accidental and isolated. This has led to a disregard of rhythmic structure even in the case of dancing to music already written, for, in a work like Martha Graham's *Deaths and Entrances,* an audience can know where it is in relation to the action only through repeated seeings and the belying action of memory. On the other hand, Martha Graham and Louis Horst together were able to make magnificently clear and moving works like their *Frontier,* which works, however, stand alarmingly alone in the history of the modern dance.

The will to compromise, mentioned above, and the admirable humility implied in the willingness to learn from other art manners is adolescent, but it is much closer to maturity than the childish blind following of leaders that was characteristic of the modern dance several years ago. If, in receiving influences from the outside, the modern dance is satisfied with copying, or adapting to itself, surface particularities (techniques, movements, devices of any kind), it will die before it reaches maturity; if, on the other hand, the common denominator of the completely developed time arts, the secret of art life, is discovered by the modern dance, Terpsichore will have a new and rich source of worshippers.

With clarity of rhythmic structure, *grace* forms a duality. Together they have a relation like that of body and soul. Clarity is cold, mathematical, inhuman, but basic and earthy. Grace is warm, incalculable, human, opposed to clarity, and like the air. Grace is not here used to mean prettiness; it is used to mean the play with and against the clarity of the rhythmic structure. The two are always present together in the best works of the time arts, endlessly, and life-givingly, opposed to each other.

'In the finest specimens of versification, there seems to be a perpetual conflict between the law of the verse and the freedom of the language, and each is incessantly, though insignificantly, violated for the purpose of giving effect to the other. The best poet is not he whose verses are the most easily scanned, and whose phraseology is the commonest in its materials, and the most direct in its arrangement; but rather he whose language combines the greatest imaginative accuracy with the most elaborate and sensible metrical organisation, and who, in his verse, preserves everywhere the living sense of the metre, not so much by unvarying obedience to, as by innumerable small departures from, its *modulus*.' (Coventry Patmore, *Prefatory Study on English Metrical Law*, 1879, pp. 12–13.)

The 'perpetual conflict' between clarity and grace is what makes hot jazz hot. The best performers continually anticipate or delay the phrase beginnings and endings. They also, in their performances, treat the beat or pulse, and indeed, the measure, with grace: putting more or fewer icti within the measure's limits than are expected (similar alterations of pitch and timbre are also customary), contracting or extending the duration of the unit. This, not syncopation, is what pleases the hep-cats.

Hindu music and dancing are replete with grace. This is possible because the rhythmic structure in Hindu time arts is highly systematized, has been so for many ages, and every Hindu who enjoys listening to music or looking at the dance is familiar with the laws of tala. Players, dancers, and audience enjoy hearing and seeing the laws of the rhythmic structure now observed and now ignored.

This is what occurs in a beautifully performed classic or neo-classic ballet. And it is what enables one to experience pleasure in such a performance, despite the fact that such works are relatively meaningless in our modern society. That one should, today, have to see *Swan Lake* or something equally empty of contemporary meaning in order to experience the pleasure of observing clarity and grace in the dance, is, on its face, lamentable. Modern society needs, as usual, and now desperately needs, a strong modern dance.

The opinion expressed here is that clarity of rhythmic structure with grace are essential to the time arts, that together they constitute an aesthetic (that is, they lie under and beneath, over and above, physical and personal particularities), and that they rarely occur in the modern dance; that the latter has no aesthetic (its strength having been and being the personal property of its originators and best exponents), that, in order for it to become strong and useful in society, mature in itself, the modern dance must clarify its rhythmic structure, then enliven it with grace, and so get itself a theory, the common, universal one about what is beautiful in a time art.

. . . . . . . . . . . . . . . . . . . . . . . . . . . . . . . . . . . . . . . . . .

In Zen they say: If something is boring after two minutes, try it for four. If still boring, try it for eight, sixteen, thirty-two, and so on. Eventually one discovers that it's not boring at all but very interesting.

At the New School once I was substituting for Henry Cowell, teaching a class in Oriental music. I had told him I didn't know anything about the subject. He said, 'That's all right. Just go where the records are. Take one out. Play it and then discuss it with the class.' Well, I took out the first record. It was an LP of a Buddhist service. It began with a short microtonal chant with sliding tones, then soon settled into a single loud reiterated percussive beat. This noise continued relentlessly for about fifteen minutes with no perceptible variation. A lady got up and screamed, and then yelled, 'Take it off. I can't bear it any longer.' I took it off. A man in the class then said angrily, 'Why'd you take it off? I was just getting interested.'

During a counterpoint class at U.C.L.A., Schoenberg sent everybody to the blackboard. We were to solve a particular problem he had given and to turn around when finished so that he could check on the correctness of the solution. I did as directed. He said, 'That's good. Now find another solution.' I did. He said, 'Another.' Again I found one. Again he said, 'Another.' And so on. Finally, I said, 'There are no more solutions.' He said, 'What is the principle underlying all of the solutions?'

I went to a concert upstairs in Town Hall. The composer whose works were being performed had provided program notes. One of these notes was to the effect that there is too much pain in the world. After the concert I was walking along with the composer and he was telling me how the performances had not been quite up to snuff. So I said, 'Well, I enjoyed the music, but I didn't agree with that program note about there being too much pain in the world.' He said, 'What? Don't you think there's enough?' I said, 'I think there's just the right amount.'

*Many of my performances with Merce Cunningham and Dance Company are given in academic situations. Now and then the director of the concert series asks for an introductory talk. The following remarks were written for audiences in St. Louis and at Principia College in the autumn of 1956. Then a few months later, in January 1957, they appeared in* Dance Observer.

## In This Day . . .

In this day of TV-darkened homes, a live performance has become something of a rarity, so much so that Aaron Copland recently said a concert is a thing of the past. Nevertheless, I would like to say a few words regarding the new direction taken by our company of dancers and musicians.

Though some of the dances and music are easily enjoyed, others are perplexing to certain people, for they do not unfold along conventional lines. For one thing, there is an independence of the music and dance, which, if one closely observes, is present also in the seemingly usual works. This independence follows from Mr. Cunningham's faith, which I share, that the support of the dance is not to be found in the music but in the dancer himself, on his own two legs, that is, and occasionally on a single one.

Likewise the music sometimes consists of single sounds or groups of sounds which are not supported by harmonies but resound within a space of silence. From this independence of music and dance a rhythm results which is not that of horses' hoofs or other regular beats but which reminds us of a multiplicity of events in time and space — stars, for instance, in the sky, or activities on earth viewed from the air.

We are not, in these dances and music, saying something. We are simpleminded enough to think that if we were saying something we would use words. We are rather doing something. The meaning of what we do is determined by each one who sees and hears it. At a recent performance of ours at Cornell College in Iowa, a student turned to a teacher and said, 'What does it mean?' The teacher's reply was, 'Relax, there are no symbols here to confuse you. Enjoy yourself!' I may add there are no stories and no psychological problems. There is simply an activity of movement, sound, and light. The costumes are all simple in order that you may see the movement.

The movement is the movement of the body. It is here that Mr. Cunningham focuses his choreographic attention, not on the facial muscles. In daily life people customarily observe faces and hand gestures, translating what they see into psychological terms. Here, however, we are in the presence of a dance which utilizes the entire body, requiring for its enjoyment the use of your faculty of kinesthetic sympathy. It is this faculty we employ when, seeing the flight of birds, we ourselves, by identification, fly up, glide, and soar.

The activity of movement, sound, and light, we believe, is expressive, but what it expresses is determined by each one of you — who is right, as Pirandello's title has it, if he thinks he is.

The novelty of our work derives therefore from our having moved away from simply private human concerns towards the world of nature and society of which all of us are a part. Our intention is to affirm this life, not to bring order out of chaos nor to suggest improvements in creation, but simply to wake up to the very life we're living, which is so excellent once one gets one's mind and one's desires out of its way and lets it act of its own accord.

. . . . . . . . . . . . . . . . . . . . . . . . . . . . . . . . . . . . . . . . . . . . . .

When Vera Williams first noticed that I was interested in wild mushrooms, she told her children not to touch any of them because they were all deadly poisonous. A few days later she bought a steak at Martino's and decided to serve it smothered with mushrooms, When she started to cook the mushrooms, the children all stopped whatever they were doing and watched her attentively. When she served dinner, they all burst into tears.

One day I went to the dentist. Over the radio they said it was the hottest day of the year. However, I was wearing a jacket, because going to a doctor has always struck me as a somewhat formal occasion. In the midst of his work, Dr. Heyman stopped and said, 'Why don't you take your jacket off?' I said, 'I have a hole in my shirt and that's why I have my jacket on.' He said, 'Well, I have a hole in my sock, and, if you like, I'll take my shoes off.'

*This piece appeared in* Dance Magazine, *November 1957. The two pages were given me in dummy form by the editors. The number of words was given by chance operations. Imperfections in the sheets of paper upon which I worked gave the position in space of the fragments of text. That position is different in this printing, for it is the result of working on two other sheets of paper, of another size and having their own differently placed imperfections.*

## 2 Pages, 122 Words on Music and Dance

To obtain the value
of a sound, a movement,
measure from zero. (Pay
attention to what it is,
just as it is.)

A bird flies.

# FOUR STATEMENTS ON THE DANCE

Slavery is abolished.

the woods

A sound has no legs to stand on.

The world is teeming: anything
can happen.

movement

sound

| Points in | | Activities which are different |
| time, in | love | happen in a time which is a space: |
| space | mirth | are each central, original. |
| | the heroic | |
| | wonder | |
| The emotions | tranquillity | are in the audience. |
| | fear | |
| | anger | The telephone rings. |
| | sorrow | |
| | disgust | Each person is in the best seat. |

Is there a glass of water?           War begins at any moment.

Each now is the time, the space.

lights

inaction?

Are eyes open?

Where the bird flies, fly.                    ears?

■  ■  ■

## Source

Cage, J. (1961, 1973) 'Four Statements on the Dance', *Silence*, Middletown, Conn.:
    Wesleyan University Press: 87–97.
'Goal: New Music, New Dance', first published in 1939 in *Dance Observer* as part of
    a series, 'Percussion Music and Its Relation to Modern Dance'.
'Grace and Clarity', first published in 1944 in *Dance Observer*.
'In This Day . . .', written in 1956 and published in 1957 in *Dance Observer*.
'2 Pages, 122 Words on Music and Dance', first published in *Dance Magazine*,
    November 1957.

## John Cage (1912–93)

A composer and philosopher who used music as both a philosophic and an aesthetic
medium, and who saw in performance a mode of enlarging our political as well as our
aural horizons. His work spans the period from 1938 to 1993, during which time he
worked extensively with the American dancer and choreographer Merce Cunningham.
He was musical director of the Cunningham Company from 1944, and their collaborations have provided some of the most stimulating formalist dance of the twentieth
century.

Much of Cage's music investigates the medium, and questions assumptions about
what is or what is not acceptable. His most famous composition, *4′33″* (1952), offers
the listener a silent piano around which the ambient sounds provide the music, which
is thus shaped by the individual listener. In 1946 he wrote *Theatre Piece*, which allows
the performers to write their own scenario within prescribed time limits, using the
notions of chance, which Cage took from the Chinese. He was also much influenced by
the Dada artists, and by his friendship with Marcel Duchamp.

The first of the four statements was written on the US West Coast in 1939, after
he had studied with another American composer, Henry Cowell. The others, in 1944,
1956 and 1957 give a twenty-year span of his ideas on dance. It could be said that
Cage's radical questioning of musical language parallels Beckett's reduction of the
play text, and that his explorations into the process of music making may be usefully
compared to Brecht's contemporaneous quest for a new acting technique. Cage wrote
and delivered lectures for a large part of his life, and in many of them used similar
rhythmical structures to those of his musical compositions. His unstated connections
between seemingly disparate ideas reflect his lifelong interest in Zen Buddhism; an
interest which led to connections between music and dance, and between the visual and
performing arts, which influenced generations of performing artists. His writing is
lucid, simple and often startling. By making surprising connections he forces us to
contemplate the obvious in a new light.

## Compare this article with writings by the following authors in this reader

**Benjamin** – for a different, contemporary, European perspective on art and its purpose
**Brown** – a dancer working with similar concerns for structure and processes
**Cunningham** – his major artistic collaborator
**Foreman** – a contemporary American theatre innovator
**Kaprow** – a contemporary destabiliser of norms
**Rainer** – a later manifesto on dance
**Schechner** – interest in non-Western forms

## Further reading

Cage, J. (1968) *A Year from Monday*, Middletown, Conn.: Wesleyan University Press.
Kostelanetz, R. (ed.) (1970) *John Cage*, New York: Praeger.
Nichols, D. (ed.) (2002) *The Cambridge Companion to John Cage*, Cambridge University Press.
Robinson, J. (ed.) (2011) *John Cage*, Cambridge, Mass.: London MIT Press.
Silverman, K. (2010) *Begin Again: A Biography of John Cage*, New York: Alfred A. Knopf.

# Chapter 17

# Jacques Copeau

## CURRENT TRENDS/
## THE DIRECTOR
## AS PARTLY ACTOR

## Current trends

Direction has played so prominent a part in the work of the contemporary theatre; it has aroused so much curiosity; it has given rise to so much research, effort and striving; and it has helped shed light on so many basic problems that it has often – and wrongly – been considered an art in itself. Some have asserted that the director possesses universal talents, ranging from those of the actor to those of the creative writer, and including those of the painter and composer. As a matter of fact, that is a portrait of the ideal director. But this ideal has turned the head of more than one director.

In the cinema as in the theatre, there is a conflict between technicians and writers for the realisation of unity under the guidance of a master-creator. As cinema techniques develop and improve, and as the cinema establishes its own traditions, the director tends increasingly to take the place of the writer. But that place was left vacant; for one cannot really say that up to now we have had masters of the cinema. We usually say that the dramatist is the master in the theatre, and fundamentally, of course, every-thing does depend on the creative writer. Thus far there has been no split between creator and realiser: there is a perfect unity in simplicity. But an increasing simplicity in the means of realisation will bring about a division of labour. The unity thus lost will be found again only in exceptional cases.

In principle there is no reason why a first-rate dramatist, with rich experience in the theatre, should not also be a first-rate director, quite capable of directing his plays admirably. Up to a certain point, his experience as a director may usefully influence his concepts of drama. But it must be acknowledged that in our day the playwright is usually a master who has let slip the instrument of his mastery. This has come about for many reasons not all of which are his fault. He writes for the stage; yet the stage may repel him or baffle him. He finds it indispensable to get help from a method of interpretation. So he turns to the specialist in this method: the director.

Hence the director is the playwright's right-hand man, or substitute in the matter of producing the play. His work is based on an agreement, a kind of contract which he is able to sign because of his insight and to which he is bound because of his sincerity. But trouble arises the moment he makes use of some of his professional skills to distort the playwright's work, to introduce into the fabric of that work his own ideas, intentions, fantasies and doctrines.

Technical competence, profound understanding and genuine enthusiasm can and should develop in the director a second inspiration, which is released when he makes contact with another's work. To this extent he participates in creation. He is also a critic and often better able than the playwright himself to discern errors in playwrighting.

It is easy to understand why a gifted director is tempted to conceal the playwright's lack of skill by means of his own technical resources. Admittedly too he becomes impatient when certain masterpieces are said to be unplayable; so he toys with the idea of revising them or removing the difficulties in them. It need not surprise us, therefore, if he proceeds boldly to the very source of creation and convinces himself that he can shape the entire process.

It is true that creating a dramatic work in words and actually mounting it on stage with live actors are but two phases of one and the same operation. And it is also true that all great dramatists, from Aeschylus to Shakespeare, from Aristophanes to Molière, and from Racine to Ibsen, have been directors. We could cite many others of lesser genius – Voltaire, Diderot, etc. – who had original ideas about directing. The fusion of dramatist and director, however, is in a *descending* line; it is difficult to see how this order could be reversed.

Let us hope for a dramatist who replaces or eliminates the director, and personally takes over the directing; rather than for professional directors who pretend to be dramatists. (No matter how experienced a craftsman he may be, he is immediately too much the professional.) But since we lack great dramatists who stage their own plays personally and with authority, the great director shows his mettle only when he confronts a written masterpiece, particularly when that masterpiece is considered unplayable. Because he believes in it, he understands it; and because he has insight and respects it, he wrests its secret from it.

Does not perfection in directing arise from the friendly conflict between a great creator and his great interpreter? Whenever this salutary conflict is avoided; whenever the technician of the theatre, freed from restraints, visualises things like an actor, and only in terms of the acting, his production thins out and dries up. It resembles that of the musical virtuoso who composes solely for his own instrument. He obtains perfection without depth, without nuances, without mystery. An added dimension is lacking. And artistic creation suffers a mortal blow.

## The director as partly actor

I am not quite an actor. He who is 100 per cent actor cannot live away from the stage. I am doing very well without having set foot on it for several years. There is a type of actor whose ignorance of other arts and techniques does not bother him at all, but my curiosity for these things is almost infinite. The true actor enters into his role and becomes its prisoner, unable to leave it. I have known some actors whose faculty for persistent metamorphosis was something hallucinating; Zacconi, for example. I believe that my own dominant faculty is that of dual personality, for however important my role, my ears and eyes could not avoid being aware of my partners. One day, when I was playing Alcestis in *The Misanthrope*, the actor who was playing Oronte came on stage with one of his shoelaces untied. Immediately, my eyes became so fixed on those laces that my unfortunate comrade forgot his lines. In this presence of mind, this sang-froid, this refusal to forget oneself, there is the sign of a personality that objects to following the basic law of dramatic interpretation. It is like a leak in the actor's painfully worked-out system of creating an illusion for himself, his confederates and for the spectators. This is a problem that has always been and probably always will be subject to much controversy.

The first difficulty for an actor is to get the idea of the role he intends to take on. The second is to find the means to enter into it. I may add that there is a third difficulty, perhaps the greatest of all, and that is to come out of it once we have entered. Some actors are very skilful in sketching out their role, but not only do they make no progress during rehearsals, on the contrary, to the extent that they exert themselves, one could say that they forget it, that their role escapes them, and the wild efforts they make to recapture it are useless. It is rather common to see an actor lost in his role.

The art of helping the actor, of showing him his way and clearing it for him, is perhaps the most pleasant and successful one I have ever practised. It is a delicate art that requires an actor, but not too much of a one. The instructions must be slight, for the slighter they are, the more effective they become. One must know the man or woman being instructed well, and one must treat them tactfully. It is also important that they know you well, that they like you and have confidence in you. This is relatively easy when working with the same ones. With my Vieux Colombier company, rehearsals were a kind of game. According to my mood, or theirs, I knew how to shake them up, lecture to them or encourage them. I also knew how to protect them from authors, for authors are always in a hurry. Either they try to stir the actors up with flattery, or they discourage them by asking them at the outset to do things they cannot do, things that they must be allowed the pleasure of discovering for themselves. Perhaps they won't find them until the twentieth rehearsal or even until they face the public. The director's primary quality is patience. One cannot imagine how much is needed for certain inner states, the simplest movements or the most elementary gestures to mature in an actor. The second quality of a director is discretion. One must never take the place of the author under the pretext of helping the actor. It is enough to call forth or engender in him certain feelings, to point out certain actions which express them, but without doing them, for there are things which are not fully or really expressed except through his own means and temperament, his own personality. That is why I said that a good director should be part actor, but not completely. He is there to smooth the way that leads to the role and to brush away the undergrowth. But once reaching a certain point, it is advisable to leave the actor alone to penetrate his role. In any case, a time always comes when the director can do no more for the actor. That has often been my experience. [ . . . ]

The role of the director then, both his duty and his privilege, is to be present everywhere and yet be invisible, without oppressing the actor's personality nor offending the author's intention, and to use his genius only to serve both. All his effort is directed to composing and building a perfectly coherent and proportional object, solid and harmonious, like those tiny cathedrals in the hands of the kneeling donor in the old altar-pieces.

[From: 'Souvenirs pour la radio', May/June 1945 op. cit., published in *Notes sur le Métier de Comédien*, M. Brient, 1955, pp. 41–4; and in *Registres I*, pp. 195–6]

■　　■　　■


## Source

Rudlin, J. and Norman H. Paul (1990) *Copeau: Texts on Theatre*, London: Routledge: 124–126, 129–131.


## Jacques Copeau (1879–1949)

French actor, writer, director and teacher. Copeau was a contemporary of Appia, Craig and Stanislavski. Like them, he sought a totally new approach to the theatre, where the performer was restored to their rightful place. He began his early writing for the theatre as critic, reviewer and playwright. In 1913 he founded his Vieux Colombier Theatre in Paris, announcing its debut with a manifesto – 'An Attempt at Dramatic Renovation'. For some years Copeau worked with the company and the school attached to it. In this time he tried to find ways to return theatre performance to the performer. He became more convinced that the problem with theatre lay in the training for it. It was his belief that the actor had to be trained as a whole, not in part. Thus there was a need for a full education rather than mere training.

In pursuit of these ideals, Copeau left mainstream theatre activity in 1924, took some of his actors with him and formed a group, 'Les Copiaus', in Morteuil in Burgundy, where he originally came from. The group toured local villages and later more widely in Europe. During this time he developed his education of the actor by working with this group of actors. They performed occasionally; when they did it was the performers who were more and more the focus, rather than the text. In this, Copeau pioneered and anticipated the greater changes of the latter part of the century.

Copeau's approach to performance gave greater emphasis to the corporeal, to its physicality. His actor education placed great emphasis on this, both at Vieux Colombier and with 'Les Copiaus'. One of his most ardent followers in 1924 was Etienne Decroux. It was Decroux who developed Copeau's work as mime and helped found the modern and subsequently postmodern mime as a rejuvenated art form.

## Compare this article with writings by the following authors in this reader

**Beck** – a later, contrasting approach to acting
**Craig** – a contemporary view on theatre
**Stanislavski** – a contemporary approach to acting
**Meyerhold** – a contemporary approach to acting

## Further reading

Evans, M. (2006) *Jacques Copeau*, London: Routledge.
Leabhart, T. (1989) *Modern and Post-Modern Mime*, London: Macmillan.
Rudlin, J. (1986) *Jacques Copeau*, Cambridge: Cambridge University Press.

# Chapter 18

# Edward Gordon Craig

## THE ACTOR AND
## THE ÜBER-MARIONETTE

NAPOLEON is reported to have said: 'In life there is much that is unworthy which in art should be omitted; much of doubt and vacillation; and all should disappear in the representation of the hero. *We should see him as a statue in which the weakness and the tremors of the flesh are no longer perceptible.*' And not only Napoleon, but Ben Jonson, Lessing, Edmund Scherer, Hans Christian Andersen, Lamb, Goethe, George Sand, Coleridge, Anatole France, Ruskin, Pater,[1] and I suppose all the intelligent men and women of Europe — one does not speak of Asia, for even the unintelligent in Asia fail to comprehend photographs while understanding art as a simple and clear manifestation — have protested against this *reproduction* of Nature, and with it photographic and weak actuality. They have protested against all this, and the theatrical managers have argued against them energetically, and so we look for the truth to emerge in due time. It is a reasonable conclusion. Do away with the real tree, do away with the reality of delivery, do away with the reality of action, and you tend towards the doing away with the actor. This is what must come to pass in time, and I like to see the managers supporting the idea already. Do away with the actor, and you do away with the means by which a debased stage-realism is produced and flourishes. No longer would there be a living figure to confuse us into connecting actuality and art; no longer a living figure in which the weakness and tremors of the flesh were perceptible.[2]

The actor must go, and in his place comes the inanimate figure — the Über-marionette we may call him, until he has won for himself a better name. Much has been written about the puppet, or marionette. There are some excellent volumes upon him, and he has also inspired several works of art. To-day in his least happy period many people come to regard him as rather a superior doll — and to think he has developed from the doll. This is incorrect. He is a descendant of the stone images of the old temples — he is to-day a rather degenerate form of a god. Always the close friend of children, he still knows how to select and attract his devotees.

When any one designs a puppet on paper, he draws a stiff and comic-looking thing. Such a one has not even perceived what is contained in the idea which we now call the marionette. He mistakes gravity of face and calmness of body for blank stupidity and angular deformity. Yet even modern puppets are extraordinary things. The applause may thunder or dribble, their hearts beat no faster, no slower, their signals do not grow hurried or confused; and, though drenched in a torrent of bouquets and love, the face of the leading lady remains as solemn, as beautiful and as remote as ever. There is something more than a flash of genius in the marionette, and there is something in him more than the flashiness of displayed personality. The marionette appears to me to be the last echo of some noble and beautiful art of a past civilization. But as with all art which has passed into fat or vulgar hands, the puppet has become a reproach. All puppets are now but low comedians.

They imitate the comedians of the larger and fuller blooded stage. They enter only to fall on their back. They drink only to reel, and make love only to raise a laugh. They have forgotten the counsel of their mother the Sphinx. Their bodies have lost their grave grace, they have become stiff. Their eyes have lost that infinite subtlety of seeming to see; now they only stare. They display and jingle their wires and are cocksure in their wooden wisdom. They have failed to remember that their art should carry on it the same stamp of reserve that we see at times on the work of other artists, and that the highest art is that which conceals the craft and forgets the craftsman. Am I mistaken, or is it not the old Greek Traveller of 800 B.C. who, describing a visit to the temple-theatre in Thebes, tells us that he was won to their beauty by their 'noble artificiality'? 'Coming into the House of Visions I saw afar off the fair brown Queen seated upon her throne – her tomb – for both it seemed to me. I sank back upon my couch and watched her symbolic movements. With so much ease did her rhythms alter as with her movements they passed from limb to limb; with such a show of calm did she unloose for us the thoughts of her breast; so gravely and so beautifully did she linger on the statement of her sorrow, that with us it seemed as if no sorrow could harm her; no distortion of body or feature allowed us to dream that she was conquered; the passion and the pain were continually being caught by her hands, held gently, and viewed calmly. Her arms and hands seemed at one moment like a thin warm fountain of water which rose, then broke and fell with all those sweet pale fingers like spray into her lap. It would have been as a revelation of art to us had I not already seen that the same spirit dwelt in the other examples of the art of these Egyptians. This 'Art of Showing and Veiling,' as they call it, is so great a spiritual force in the land that it plays the larger part in their religion. We may learn from it somewhat of the power and the grace of courage, for it is impossible to witness a performance without a sense of physical and spiritual refreshment.' This in 800 B.C. And who knows whether the puppet shall not once again become the faithful medium for the beautiful thoughts of the artist. May we not look forward with hope to that day which shall bring back to us once more the figure, or symbolic creature, made also by the cunning of the artist, so that we can gain once more the 'noble artificiality' which the old writer speaks of? Then shall we no longer be under the cruel influence of the emotional confessions of weakness which are nightly witnessed by the people and which in their turn create in the beholders the very weaknesses which are exhibited. To that end we must study to remake these images — no longer content with a puppet, we must create an über-marionette. The über-marionette will not compete with life — rather will it go beyond it. Its ideal will not be the flesh and blood but rather the body in trance — it will aim to clothe itself with a death-like beauty while exhaling a living spirit. Several times in the course of this essay has a word or two about Death found its way on to the paper — called there by the incessant clamouring of 'Life! Life! Life!' which the realists keep up. And this might be easily mistaken for an affectation, especially by those who have no sympathy or delight in the power and the mysterious joyousness which is in all passionless works of art. If the famous Rubens and the celebrated Raphael made none but passionate and exuberant statements, there were many artists before them and since to whom moderation in their art was the most precious of all their aims, and these more than all others exhibit the true masculine manner. The other flamboyant or drooping artists whose works and names catch the eye of today do not so much speak like men as bawl like animals, or lisp like women.

The wise, the moderate masters, strong because of the laws to which they swore to remain ever faithful — their names unknown for the most part — a fine family — the creators of the great and tiny gods of the East and the West, the guardians of those larger times: these all bent their thoughts forward towards the unknown, searching for sights and sounds in that peaceful and joyous country, that they might raise a figure of stone or sing a verse, investing it with that same peace and joy seen from afar, so as to balance all the grief and turmoil here.

In America we can picture these brothers of that family of masters, living in their superb ancient cities, colossal cities, which I ever think of as able to be moved in a single day; cities of spacious tents of silk and canopies of gold under which dwelt their gods; dwellings which contained all the requirements of the most fastidious; those moving cities which, as they travelled from height to plain, over rivers and down valleys, seemed like some vast advancing army of peace. And in each city not one or two men called 'artists' whom the rest of the city looked upon as ne'er-do-well idlers, but many men chosen by the community because of their higher powers of perception — artists. For that is what the title of artist means: one who perceives more than his fellows, and who records more than he has seen. And not the least among those artists was the artist of the ceremonies, the creator of the visions, the minister whose duty it was to celebrate their guiding spirit — the spirit of Motion.

In Asia, too, the forgotten masters of the temples and all that those temples contained have permeated every thought, every mark, in their work with this sense of calm motion resembling death — glorifying and greeting it. In Africa (which some of us think we are but now to civilize) this spirit dwelt, the essence of the perfect civilization. There, too, dwelt the great masters, not individuals obsessed with the idea of each asserting his personality as if it were a valuable and mighty thing, but content because of a kind of holy patience to move their brains and their fingers only in that direction permitted by the law — in the service of the simple truths.

How stern the law was, and how little the artist of that day permitted himself to make an exhibition of his personal feelings, can be discovered by looking at any example of Egyptian art. Look at any limb ever carved by the Egyptians, search into all those carved eyes, they will deny you until the crack of doom. Their attitude is so silent that it is death-like. Yet tenderness is there, and charm is there; prettiness is even there side by side with the force; and love bathes each single work; but gush, emotion, swaggering personality of the artist? — not one single breath of it. Fierce doubts of hope? — not one hint of such a thing. Strenuous determination? — not a sign of it has escaped the artist; none of these confessions — stupidities. Nor pride, nor fear, nor the comic, nor any indication that the artist's mind or hand was for the thousandth part of a moment out of the command of the laws which ruled him. How superb! This it is to be a great artist; and the amount of emotional outpourings of today and of yesterday are no signs of supreme intelligence, that is to say, are no signs of supreme art. To Europe came this spirit, hovered over Greece, could hardly be driven out of Italy, but finally fled, leaving a little stream of tears — pearls — before us. And we, having crushed most of them, munching them along with the acorns of our food, have gone farther and fared worse, and have prostrated ourselves before the so-called 'great masters,' and have worshipped these dangerous and flamboyant personalities. On an evil day we thought in our ignorance that it was us they were sent to draw; that it was our thoughts they were sent to express; that it was something to do with us that they were putting into their architecture, their music. And so it was we came to demand that we should be able to recognize ourselves in all that they put hand to; that is to say, in their architecture, in their sculpture, in their music, in their painting, and in their poetry we were to figure — and we also reminded them to invite us with the familiar words: 'Come as you are.'

The artists after many centuries have given in, that which we asked them for they have supplied. And so it came about that when this ignorance had driven off the fair spirit which once controlled the mind and hand of the artist, a dark spirit took its place; the happy-go-lucky hooligan in the seat of the law — that is to say, a stupid spirit reigning; and everybody began to shout about Renaissance! while all the time the painters, musicians, sculptors, architects, vied one with the other to supply the demand — that all these things should be so made that all people could recognize them as having something to do with themselves.

Up sprang portraits with flushed faces, eyes which bulged, mouths which leered, fingers itching to come out of their frames, wrists which exposed the pulse; all the colours higgledy-piggledy; all the lines in hubbub, like the ravings of lunacy. Form breaks into panic; the calm and cool whisper of life in trance which once had breathed out such an ineffable hope is heated, fired into a blaze and destroyed, and in its place – *realism*, the blunt statement of life, something everybody misunderstands while recognizing. And all far from the purpose of art: for its purpose is not to reflect the actual facts of this life, because it is not the custom of the artist to walk behind things, having won it as his privilege to walk in front of them – to lead. Rather should life reflect the likeness of the spirit, for it was the spirit which first chose the artist to chronicle its beauty.[3] And in that picture, if the form be that of the living, on account of its beauty and tenderness, the colour for it must be sought from that unknown land of the imagination, and what is that but the land where dwells that which we call Death? So it is not lightly and flippantly that I speak of puppets and their power to retain the beautiful and remote expressions in form and face even when subjected to a patter of praise, a torrent of applause. There are persons who have made a jest of these puppets. 'Puppet' is a term of contempt, though there still remain some who find beauty in these little figures, degenerate though they have become.

To speak of a puppet with most men and women is to cause them to giggle. They think at once of the wires; they think of the stiff hands and the jerky movements; they tell me it is 'a funny little doll.' But let me tell them a few things about these puppets. Let me again repeat that they are the descendants of a great and noble family of Images, images which were indeed made 'in the likeness of God'; and that many centuries ago these figures had a rhythmical movement and not a jerky one; had no need for wires to support them, nor did they speak through the nose of the hidden manipulator. [Poor Punch, I mean no slight to you! You stand alone, dignified in your despair, as you look back across the centuries with painted tears still wet upon your ancient cheeks, and you seem to cry out appealingly to your dog: 'Sister Anne, Sister Anne, is *nobody* coming?' And then with that superb bravado of yours, you turn the force of our laughter (and my tears) upon yourself with the heartrending shriek of 'Oh my nose! Oh my nose! Oh my nose!'] Did you think, ladies and gentlemen, that these puppets were always little things of but a foot high?

Indeed, no! The puppet had once a more generous form than yourselves.

Do you think that he kicked his feet about on a little platform six feet square, made to resemble a little old-fashioned theatre, so that his head almost touched the top of the proscenium? and do you think that he always lived in a little house where the door and windows were as small as a doll's house, with painted windowblinds parted in the centre, and where the flowers of his little garden had courageous petals as big as his head? Try and dispel this idea altogether from your minds, and let me tell you something of his habitation.

In Asia lay his first kingdom. On the banks of the Ganges they built him his home, a vast palace springing from column to column into the air and pouring from column to column down again into the water. Surrounded by gardens spread warm and rich with flowers and cooled by fountains; gardens into which no sounds entered, in which hardly anything stirred. Only in the cool and private chambers of this palace the swift minds of his attendants stirred incessantly. Something they were making which should become him, something to honour the spirit which had given him birth. And then, one day, the ceremony.

In this ceremony he took part; a celebration once more in praise of the Creation; the old thanksgiving, the hurrah for existence, and with it the sterner hurrah for the privilege of the existence to come, which is veiled by the word Death. And during this ceremony there appeared before the eyes of the brown worshippers the symbols of all things on earth and in Nirvana. The symbol of the beautiful tree, the symbol of the hills, the symbols of those rich ores which the hills contained; the symbol of the cloud, of the wind, and of all swift moving things; the symbol of the quickest of moving things, of thought, of remembrance; the symbol of the animal, the symbol of Buddha and of Man – and here he comes, the figure, the puppet at whom you all laugh so much. You laugh at him to-day because none but his weaknesses are left to him, He reflects these from you; but you would not have laughed had you seen him in his prime, in that age when he was called upon to be the symbol of man in the great ceremony, and, stepping forward, was the beautiful figure of our heart's delight. If we should laugh at and insult the memory of the puppet, we should be laughing at the fall that we have brought about in ourselves – laughing at the beliefs and images we have broken. A few centuries later, and we find his home a little the worse for wear. From a temple, it has become, I will not say a theatre, but something between a temple and a theatre, and he is losing his health in it. Something is in the air; his doctors tell him he must be careful. 'And what am I to fear most?' he asks them. They answer him: 'Fear most the vanity of men.' He thinks: 'But that is what I myself have always taught, that we who celebrated in joy this our existence, should have this one great fear. Is it possible that I, one who has ever revealed this truth, should be one to lose sight of it and should myself be one of the first to fall? Clearly some subtle attack is to be made on me. I will keep my eyes upon the heavens.' And he dismisses his doctors and ponders upon it.

And now let me tell you who it was that came to disturb the calm air which surrounded this curiously perfect thing. It is on record that somewhat later he took up his abode on the Far Eastern coast, and there came two women to look upon him. And at the ceremony to which they came he glowed with such earthly splendour and yet such unearthly simplicity, that though he proved an inspiration to the thousand nine hundred and ninety-eight souls who participated in the festival, an inspiration which cleared the mind even as it intoxicated, yet to these two women it proved an intoxication only. He did not see them, his eyes were fixed on the heavens; but he charged them full of a desire too great to be quenched; the desire to stand as the direct symbol of the divinity in man. No sooner thought than done; and arraying themselves as best they could in garments ('like his' they thought), moving with gestures ('like his' they said) and being able to cause wonderment in the minds of the beholders ('even as he does' they cried), they built themselves a temple ('like his,' 'like his'), and supplied the demand of the vulgar, the whole thing a poor parody.

This is on record. It is the first record in the East of the actor. The actor springs from the foolish vanity of two women who were not strong enough to look upon the symbol of godhead without desiring to tamper with it; and the parody proved profitable. In fifty or a hundred years places for such parodies were to be found in all parts of the land.

Weeds, they say, grow quickly, and that wilderness of weeds, the modern theatre, soon sprang up. The figure of the divine puppet attracted fewer and fewer lovers, and the women were quite the latest thing. With the fading of the puppet and the advance of these women who exhibited themselves on the stage in his place, came that darker spirit which is called Chaos, and in its wake the triumph of the riotous personality. Do you see, then, what has made me love and learn to value that which to-day we call the 'puppet' and to detest that which we call 'life' in art? I pray earnestly for the return of the image – the über-marionette to the Theatre; and when he comes again and is but seen, he will be loved so well that once more will it be possible for the people to return to their ancient joy in ceremonies – once more will Creation be celebrated – homage rendered to existence – and divine and happy intercession made to Death.

Florence: March 1907

## Notes

1    Of sculpture Pater writes: 'Its white light, purged from the angry, bloodlike stains of action and passion, reveals, not what is accidental in man, but the god in him, as opposed to man's restless movement.' Again: 'The base of all artistic genius is the power of conceiving humanity in a new, striking, rejoicing way, of putting a happy world of its own construction in place of the meaner world of common days, of generating around itself an atmosphere with a novel power of refraction, selecting, transforming, recombining the images it transmits, according to the choice of the imaginative intellect.' And again: 'All that is accidental, all that distracts the simple effect upon us of the supreme types of humanity, all traces in them of the commonnness of the world, it gradually purges away.'

2    From another point of view, and one not lightly to be either overlooked or discussed, Cardinal Manning, the Englishman, is particularly emphatic when he speaks of the actor's business as necessitating 'the prostitution of a body purified by baptism.'

3    'All forms are perfect in the poet's mind: but these are not abstracted or compounded from Nature; they are from Imagination.' – William Blake.

■    ■    ■

## Source

Craig, E.G. (1911, 1956) 'The Actor and the Über-Marionette', *On the Art of the Theatre*, New York: Theatre Arts Books: 80–94. Written in 1907, first published in 1911.

## Edward Gordon Craig (1872–1966)

British theatre designer, actor and visionary, who became the first British theatre artist to write a book of theatre theory. Craig's life was full of unresolved schemes for designs and performances, though he did manage to create a short-lived theatre school in Florence in 1913. However, his collaboration with Stanislavski on *Hamlet* (1912), which is well documented, has become a case study in the problems of international collaboration. On the whole Craig was rejected by the British theatre establishment, and was taken up in great measure by the French and the Russians. His ideas bear much resemblance to those of Adolphe Appia, whom he met on one occasion. Together their thinking can be said to have influenced generations of European theatre directors. Craig died in France in 1966.

*On the Art of the Theatre* was published in 1911, and was described by its author as a 'dream put into words'. In it he discusses the nature of theatre as a collaborative art, but yet one where the visual must predominate, and where the performers need to be directed by a master figure who controls what the audience see. Like Meyerhold in Russia, he denied the psychology of traditional Western theatre, and in particular that of naturalism. For Craig a performance was a total kinaesthetic marriage of sound, shape, light and movement. He saw the Western actor as a fallible, unreliable source, and in this extract he suggests that recourse to non-Western forms might produce the kind of precise visual and aural result that he sought.

His notorious theory of the Über-Marionette masks a passionate desire to question the role of the actor in the totality of the performance. If the theatre of the future is to move beyond the natural, then the actor needs to lose his personality, and as in certain forms of Asian theatre, take on the attributes of a puppet.

## Compare this article with writings by the following authors in this reader

**Appia** – parallel design aesthetics
**Duncan** – an extensive artistic and personal relationship
**Foreman and Wilson** – later ideas on visual theatre
**Kantor** – a later admirer
**Meyerhold** – a similar insistence on the performer's discipline
**Schlemmer** – a later, European, visual aesthetic
**Stanislavski** – the Hamlet collaboration

## Further reading

Bablet, D. (1962, 1966) *The Theatre of Edward Gordon Craig*, trans. D. Woodward, London: Heinemann.

Innes, C. (1983) *Edward Gordon Craig*, Cambridge: Cambridge University Press.

Rood, A. (ed.) (1977, 1978) *Gordon Craig on Movement and Dance*, London: Dance Books.

Senelick, L. (1982) *Gordon Craig's Moscow Hamlet*, London: Greenwood Press.

# Chapter 19

## Merce Cunningham

## YOU HAVE TO LOVE DANCING
## TO STICK TO IT

you have to love dancing to stick to it. it gives you nothing back, no manuscripts to store away, no paintings to show on walls and maybe hang in museums, no poems to be printed and sold, nothing but that single fleeting moment when you feel alive. it is not for unsteady souls.

and though it appeals through the eye to the mind, the mind instantly reject its meaning unless the meaning is betrayed immediately by the action. the mind is not convinced by kinetics.

alone, the meaning must be clear, or the language familiar and readily accessible.

the kinesthetic sense is a separate and fortunate behavior. it allows the experience of dancing to be part of all of us.

but clarity is the lowest form of poetry, and language, like all else in our lives, is always changing. our emotions are constantly being propelled by some new face in the sky, some new rocket to the moon, some new sound in the ear, but they are the same emotions.

you do not separate the human being from the actions he does, or the actions which surround him, but you can see what it is like to break these actions up in different ways, to allow the passion, and it is passion, to appear for each person in his own way.

it is hard for many people to accept that dancing has nothing in common with music other than the element of time and division of time. the mind can say how beautiful as the music hints at, or strikes out with color.

you have to love dancing to stick to it. it gives you
nothing back, no manuscripts to store away, no paintings
to show on walls and maybe hang in museums, no poems to
be printed and sold, nothing but that single fleeting
moment when you feel alive. it is not for unsteady souls.

and though it appeals through the eye
to the mind, the mind instantly reject
its meaning unless the meaning is
betrayed immediately by the action.
the mind is not convinced by kinetics

the kinesthetic sense is a separate and fortunate
behavior. it allows the experience of dancing to
be part of all of us.

alone, the meaning must be clear, or
the language familiar and readily
accessible.

but clarity is the lowest form of
poetry, and language, like all else
in our lives, is always changing.
our emotions are constantly being propelled by some new
face in the sky, some new rocket to the moon, some new
sound in the ear, but they are the same emotions.

you do not
separate
the human be
from the
actions he
does, or
the actions
which surround him,
round him,
but you can
see what it
is like to
break these
actions up
in differ-
ent ways, to
allow the
passion, and
it is pass
sion, to ap-
pear for each
person in his
own way.

it is hard for many people to
accept that dancing has nothing
in common with music other than
the element of time and division
of time. the mind can say how
beautiful as the music hints at,
or strikes out with color.

but the other extreme can be seen
& heard in the musical accompany
ments to the movements of the
wild animals in the Disney films.
it robs them of their instinctual
rhythms, and leaves them as caricatures. ture, it is a man-made
arrangment, but what isn't?

the sense of human emotion that a
dance can give is governed by familiarity with the language, and the
elements that act with the language;
here those would be music, costume,

Original page from *Changes: Notes on Choreography*

but the other extreme can be seen and heard in the music accompanying the movements of the wild animals in the Disney films. it robs them of their instinctual rhythms, and leaves them as caricatures. [s]ure, it is a man-made arrangement, but what isn't?

the sense of human emotion that a dance can give is governed by familiarity with the language, and the elements that act with the language; here those would be music, costume,

■    ■    ■

## Source

Cunningham, M. (1968) 'you have to love dancing to stick to it', *Changes: Notes on Choreography*, New York: Something Else.


## Merce Cunningham (1919–2009)

American dancer and choreographer. He danced with Martha Graham (1939–45), and presented his first programme of solo works in 1944. He worked extensively with John Cage, especially in ventures at Black Mountain College. In 1952 he formed the Merce Cunningham Dance Company for whom he has choreographed ever since. He first began using chance operations in his choreography in 1951 for *16 Dances for Soloist and Company of Three*. Chance subsequently became a central part of his making processes. In 1964 he presented the first of his *Events* where dances and parts of dances from his repertoire were recombined into a choreographic collage. His stage work includes *Rainforest* (1968), *Walkaround Time* (1968) that pays homage to Duchamp, and *Duets* (1980). Cunningham has produced extensive repertory for television and video including *Westbeth* (1975), *Blue Studio: Five Segments* (1975), *Fractions I and II* (1978), and *Points in Space* (1989). He has collaborated with many musicians and artists, particularly John Cage, with whom he worked extensively to establish his particular relationship between dance and music; also David Tudor, Robert Rauschenberg, Frank Stella, Andy Warhol, Jasper Johns, Charles Atlas.

Most recently Cunningham pioneered the use of new technologies for dance. He used the software *Lifeforms* to choreograph works such as *CRWDSPCR* (1993). His *Biped* (1999) was a collaboration with visual artists Paul Kaiser and Shelley Eshkar. They used motion capture technology and a 3D figure, BIPED, in 'Character Studio' software to produce an animation that was projected on a fine gauze in front of the live dancers. As with Cunningham's earlier collaborations the animation, the live dance, and, here, the sublime music of Gavin Bryars, coexisted in time and space without predetermined relationship.

Cunningham's work is celebrated for the emphasis it places on dancing for its own sake. Critics and historians have variously spoken of the formalism of his work, its modernism and its invention. He consistently made dance that stands on its own with the other arts and which speaks for itself: 'My work is without literary reference or without psychological determination in any way. The music does not support the dance in any conventional way. The music is made separately from the dance. What you have in my work is the dancing itself'.[1]

This extract is a series of observations on dancing. Although brief, they draw attention to many of Cunningham's main ideas. They emphasise that he was a dancer himself and that many of his concerns were to do with the transitory nature of dance.

## Compare this article with writings by the following authors in this reader

**Bausch** – alternative, European, contemporary view of dance and theatre
**Brown and Rainer** – who later developed choreography in a more postmodern way, but who also stress the centrality of the dancer
**Cage** – his main musical collaborator, for relationship between music and dance
**Meyerhold** – an earlier precedent for alternative theatrical staging
**Richter** – Dada as historical antecedent for many of Cunningham's ideas
**Schlemmer** – Bauhaus antecedents
**Wilson** – later formal theatre explorations

## Further reading

Cage, J., Cunningham, M., Johns, J. and Sontag, S. (1979, 1990) *Dancers on a Plane*, London: Thames & Hudson.
Copeland, R. (2004) *Merce Cunningham: The Modernising of Modern Dance*, London: Routledge.
Cunningham, M. (1985) *The Dancer and the Dance: Conversations with Jacqueline Lesschaeve*, New York: Marion Boyars.
Cunningham, M. (1994) 'Four Events that have Led to Large Discoveries' in Harris (1997): p. 276.
Harris, Melissa. (ed.) (1997) *Merce Cunningham: Fifty Years*, New York: Aperture.
Klosty, J. (1975) *Merce Cunningham*, New York: Dutton.
http://www.mercecunningham.org

## Note

1   Cunningham, M. and Witts, D. (1980) Interview with Merce Cunningham, in *Merce Cunningham and Dance Company Programme*, Everyman Theatre, Liverpool, 25–28 June, p. 1.

# Chapter 20

# Anne Teresa de Keersmaeker

## INTERVIEW

### Legs

*When I got off the train at Brussels Central, the first thing I saw was an enormous advertising poster for stockings. It read: Legs are beautiful, legs are fun. A good omen, perhaps, for my meeting with Belgian choreographer, Anne Teresa de Keersmaeker.*

I asked her in what part of the dancer's body she was interested, as a choreographer.

Anne Teresa de Keersmaeker: I don't work like that. Developing a vocabulary is a constant evolution. My work process is very much more technical. I don't work with images. I often take existing movement phrases from old pieces and reshape them. For example, I will take a movement phrase, concentrate it in the hands, and try giving it a different feel. It takes a long time to find the vocabulary I'm looking for since I don't have an established system to work from. There may be some kind of distinctive hallmark, but neither architecturally, nor formally is there an established system in the same way as there is in classical ballet. People like Forsythe alter ballet, add new layers to it, but underneath there's always a recognisable classical ballet vocabulary. Although I think the vocabulary I use has specific qualities or energies, I have to start from scratch for each piece.

My vocabulary is always going through an evolution which, though not a principle, I find really exciting. It is sometimes good to have a point of departure. Let me give you an example: The very first movements in *Stella*, the disorder movements as I call them,

come from a sleeping scene between a man and a woman in *Ottone Ottone*. It was a scene where the couples were doing very slow ground movements together. That was the first molecule. And then from that first layer we went on to work with the music and then find other little molecules which expressed the energy as well as the architecture of the musical cells. It's a repetitive piece which builds up in melodic phrases.

The costumes also come from *Ottone Ottone*, and the set came from *Bartok Annotations*: I needed colour at the back, so I said let's put that up. It then turned out that the place where we premiered the piece had a totally white stage, and we needed a set. So then we thought let's turn the *Bartok* set around and paint it white. It wasn't purpose-built. It was one of those unpremeditated things that just grew out of the material we had to hand.

## Layers and loads

*I met Anne Teresa de Keersmaeker in Le Greenwich, a rather bohemian chess cafe in Brussels, our conversation punctuated by the occasional slap of palms on timers. Here was another apt link with Stella, where the box set from Bartok Annotations encloses the three upper sides of the stage, with a forest of metronomes along the downstage apron. The stage becomes a board of play; the dancers have their set places on the margins of the board, and move in strictly defined ways into and out of the central open space or arena of play.*

**DH: I have a problem with the way in which you talk about the emotional content of your work, the emotional loads and layers, of psychology. It must be said that there is a strong emotional charge to the piece. These isolated women seeming to cry out for contact and companionship in a world where their texts and trajectories and repetitive actions lock them into islands. It seems to me that you create this effect by your strategic use of space. So when I see *Stella* it's as much about that formal, spatial thing. The spatial composition and fragmenting composition.**

ATdeK: It's a composition too. Construction and deconstruction are linked. Space, volume, structure and trajectories in space are very important to my work, both choreographically and dramatically. They're important in the construction and in the emotional building. *Stella* is very much a piece about the solitary writing of these five women. They mark their own space, their own spots, and their own trajectories within the space. And it's about the crossing of this space. Not necessarily the immediate act of crossing – it could be about where someone originally came from, where they come back, and where trajectories cross. You can load up a space emotionally just by stepping into it and out again. If somebody comes to the same spot five times and another person then approaches it, the spot is still somehow charged with the original presence. Even when empty, the space is loaded and there is some kind of direct confrontation. This kind of thing happens in real life too, though that isn't particularly significant to the piece.

# Ligeti

*The metronomes downstage provide the instrumentation for Ligeti's Symphonic Poem for
100 Metronomes, which involves the metronomes, wound to different tensions, being set off
at the same time. They tick seemingly at random for some minutes before falling into step
with one another, and finally, tick out of phase again. Only one remains playing and that
eventually winds down. Whilst the Symphonic Poem is playing, Carlotta Sagna performs a
delicate and minimal task upstage, becoming almost invisible. I thought it an extraordinarily audacious piece of theatre.*

ATdeK: I find it a bit strange that you should call it audacious. It's only
audacious because we are living in times when there is no patience for that sort
of thing. We live in a world where we're so far away from nature. When you
look at nature, you see things taking the time they need. When I go into my
garden and spring is getting nearer, things are just taking their time even if you
want them to go quicker. But no, things take their own time and it's beautiful.
That's its strength. I have difficulty with that too. Things taking their time. We
all do. Not with the Ligeti but in general.

There are so many masterpieces in art and music, the last string quartets of
Beethoven, for example, which, in my opinion, are amongst the most brilliant
bits of musical writing. But 85% of people would say they prefer hotshot pop
songs. Now I like those pop songs too, but there are really a lot of people who
can't listen to Beethoven any more because their ears are spoilt. That's the
cultural environment we're living in. But it isn't just a question of the relationship
to time, it's also about pleasing. People like to be pleased. When they get back
in the evening they don't like to be disturbed because their lives are already so
hectic. They don't want to have to deal with doubts, they want to have fun, they
want to lose themselves in things. People want affirmation. People's sense of
perception has got flattened so much.

**DH: *Stella* is certainly a shattering work. It shatters the compo-
sure of the watcher. The sense of self, of affirmation. It's like the
cohesion and unity of character. Aristotelian unities are broken down
in *Stella*. There's no unity of character, place, anything. You don't get
your sense of character reaffirmed at *Stella*, right?**

ATdeK: *Stella* is not the first thing to shatter character, to splinter things up.
If you speak about the Wooster Group, if you speak about Pina Bausch's work,
also if you speak about the Italian Futurists. It's not something particularly
innovative about *Stella*. It's a scandal to still have to adhere to this Western need
for a rational comprehension of those things. In painting they've been going
through this kind of thing for such a long time that it's an accepted thing today.
I don't know why people have such problems with these things when we're
dealing with theatre.

**DH: Perhaps its because we identify so immediately with the
bodies of the dancers and expect rational human behaviour. What we
get is all the ingredients of character, but splintered up: text off in**

one place, emotions changing like costume, obsessions, madness, incoherence. Perhaps its easier to accept that splintering when it's in art or literature, when it's more removed from an immediate recognition, and physical identification.

ATdeK: It's strange for me because of the way I relate to the different elements in the show, personally. I've always had a very close relationship to music, for example. Music always gave the initial framework to the pieces I made. I see all the elements as things in themselves at first, but when I work on a piece I don't continue to see them in that way. When you make a composition you have sound, you have space, you have volumes, you have colours, you have flesh and you put those things together. The metronomes become, in the piece, as much theatre and dance as what the dancers do and say.

The reference in *Stella* to Ligeti is quite important. Like him, I'm not interested in mathematics for its own sake. I'm only interested in the way that it can free up emotional and poetical processes which are what help me in the way I build and construct the piece.

The metronome piece is very clearly mathematical, but it is also visually very engaging. It's a very dry example, but it makes you think and feel in time, and you can imagine all kinds of images with it. If you think of the last string quartets of Beethoven, or the fourth string quartet of Bartok or the fugues of Bach or the Flemish Polyphonists, mathematical construction, building, in all of those things is very important. But what comes out of it is an emotional load, although you can shift the emphases of the emotions.

The text is very much linked to the dance and the movement. It's not separated. In a sense the text becomes a kind of music because it is danced to, and in a sense the metronomes become a kind of dance – because it's visual, it's movement. Carlotta puts a melodic line over the metronomes which is a way of dividing time. That, of course, is what the metronomes are doing. But Carlotta's dance also has a very strong imaginative and emotional resonance because she's almost naked. The meaning, though, is different in everybody's head.

I find it important to put on the metronomes the kind of focus that forces people to pay attention to them. It's very important that what she's doing makes you look and listen to the metronomes, otherwise there's no sense in putting them there. When I make dances I want the dancers to make people listen to the music. Sometimes it's the reverse, but I find it important that people come out and that they've really listened to the music. 95% of the people who see my shows would never have listened to that music, would never have had the chance to enjoy it and would never have got to know it.

More and more I find it a problem to work with taped music. After the experience of doing the Reich and the Bartok with live and recorded music, I find it so wrong to work with recordings. Doing shows with live musicians costs such a lot. But that's the way it ought to be. I find it very funny. People sometimes excuse themselves after performances, for finding that they were looking at the musicians, not the dancers. But all I have to say is "Great. That's what I want."

**DH: The classic image of your work is the strong, unison dancing of groups of female dancers, but things have moved quite a way from that, haven't they?**

ATdeK: The main breaking point for me came with *Ottone Ottone*. So *Stella* isn't such a break. And it comes from working with Jean Luc Ducourt, too. All through the making of Stella he had a very big influence. It's been quite painful at moments, but also quite fertile. He has a totally different way of working. His imagination is totally different from mine. It's a motor where two are working together and one provokes the other. He has done quite a lot of the work with Fumiyo Ikeda. But I would do work and he would look and give hints about the direction in which it should go. Then I'd work some more and he'd look again. It's building together, which is totally different to the way I worked before, when I was generally alone in my head with the dancers. He's also one of the strongest performers I've ever worked with.

**DH: How far has *Stella* moved on beyond *Ottone Ottone*?**

ATdeK: *Ottone Ottone* was for sixteen dancers and had a narrative that was based looseley on the story of the opera, the *Coronation of Popeia*. The challenge for me in *Ottone, Ottone* was how to tell the story without really telling it. It's not necessary to spend energy saying the same thing twice. It's redundant to have the dancing be a kind of mimetic illustration of what's set in the music. It's OK for a boarding school but I don't want anything to do with it. I think the best thing I can say is that in *Ottone Ottone* I was working with character but really bumping into the notion of character. And it was very much about writing choreographically on the individuals. The choreography for the earlier pieces was about group and unison writing. It's not so much unison any more. I'm desperately trying to break out of that.

## Linearity, Logic and Landscape

**DH: How would you define the cultural landscape of your ideal viewer?**

ATdeK: I think I could only define the ideal viewer in negative terms. I just think people should stop making sense. If you want to grasp a linear, logical narrative understanding of all the events happening on stage, then you get in trouble as a performer. And you're in trouble as a spectator too I think, because that's not what *Stella's* about. Now this doesn't mean that the mind is not supposed to work in this kind of performance. It isn't to say that you mustn't feel things as a spectator, but I like it when a performance makes you think of lots of things, not just what's actually happening on stage. I like the edges. Where you tip over the edges, I like the limits, working at the limits. Where you stay on and where you fall over or beneath it or off it. It's the notion of danger I think, of how much you can grasp. Of how happy you are to grasp things or to let them go.

You know it's like being told stories when you were a child, or when kids tell stories. Very often there was no logical line in them, it's more the case that lots of different categories of things got thrown in together and you didn't worry if they didn't all fit together in a realistic sense. It's just that juxtaposition of different emotional layers that changes your perception.

Closed systems aren't really very credible any more, in mathematics and biology and the other sciences. If people get frustrated from the first moment because they don't understand the Japanese speech that Fumiyo makes, if they get stuck on that, they're lost. My advice would be not to stick to questions like tell me why or what, because there are so many whys and so many whats. The piece was not made in such a way that its easy to answer the why's and the what's and that's made clear in the performance. It's funny, people come up to me and say in that scene I felt this or I thought that, was that right? I find that so strange, and I say please think that and feel that. In the way I make it I'm not thinking of one thing, I think of a thousand things.

**DH: Surely the problem comes here because the form is relatively unusual, to strict dance audiences at least, and so perhaps they think that you have an idea that they haven't been able to decode, to translate, to reconstruct?**

ATdeK: It's the Westernized narrowed mind.

**DH: *Stella* broadens the mind?**

ATdeK: It broadens the heart too, I hope. Although I'm not as interested in the heart and the emotions per se, but in how they can be used theatrically. How does the image change if you put another image over it or another emotional layer over it? And it doesn't matter if it's sad or happy, pain or joy, that's all secondary, I'm mainly interested in how it changes from that to that. With everything. And even this process I don't want to grasp at every point intellectually. And that's a very strange way of talking about it, because in the way I construct a piece I work very cerebrally. At the same time the material I take is very emotional, with an almost melodramatic edge on it. I think it's very important in dealing with emotions to put something very opposite to it. Otherwise it gets so like marmalade. Just sentimental and tacky.

■　■　■

## Source

Interview with David Hughes, *Dance Theatre Journal*, Vol. 9(1), Summer 1991.

## Anne Teresa de Keersmaeker (1960–)

One of the key European choreographers, Anne Teresa de Keersmaeker studied the flute at school, then studied from 1978–1980 at the MUDRA school in Brussels, and after at the Tisch School of the Arts at New York University. In 1982 she came to prominence as a choreographer with *Fase*, to music by Steve Reich, which was shown at the Avignon Festival that year. Since then she has created a series of astonishing choreographic works often dealing with the relationship between music and movement, many of which have been performed by her Rosas company, which she founded in 1983. *Rosas danst Rosas* (1983) to music by Thierry de Mey, has been performed worldwide; she has staged work by Heiner Müller as well as working with contemporary composers such as Reich, Ligeti and Terry Riley. Her piece *Achterland* (1990) is set to live violin music by Ysaÿe and Ligeti, and explores one of her basic interests – the relationship of performers to theatre and other spaces. In 1995 de Keersmaeker established an international school for contemporary dance in Brussels; in 1997 she collaborated with the Wooster Group on a series of solos, while in 1998 she directed Bartok's *Bluebeard's Castle* at La Monnaie, Brussels. In 1999 she created *I Said I*, a piece for performers, stage scenery, and a live DJ. She is now seen as the next great European woman choreographer after Pina Bausch, and has won numerous international awards for her work.

In this interview she discusses *Stella* (1990), a piece for five women to music by Ligeti. The title refers both to Goethe's play of the same name and to a character from Tennessee Williams's play *A Streetcar Named Desire*, from which some of the textual material of the piece is derived. *Ottone, Ottone* is a piece from 1988 which was based on Monteverdi's opera *L'incoronazione di Poppea*.

## Compare this interview with writings by the following authors in this reader

**Bausch** – another European choreographer
**Brown** – a senior American choreographer
**LeCompte** – director of the Wooster group
**Newson** – a UK contemporary choreographer

## Further reading

Bremser, M. and Sanders, L. (2011) *Fifty Contemporary Choreographers,* London: Routledge.

Grau, A. and Jordan, S. (2000) *Europe Dancing: Perspectives on Theatre, Dance, and Cultural Identity*, London: Routledge.

# Chapter 21

# Isadora Duncan

## THE DANCER OF THE FUTURE

THE MOVEMENT OF WAVES, of winds, of the earth is ever in the same lasting harmony. We do not stand on the beach and inquire of the ocean what was its movement in the past and what will be its movement in the future. We realize that the movement peculiar to its nature is eternal to its nature. The movement of the free animals and birds remains always in correspondence to their nature, the necessities and wants of that nature, and its correspondence to the earth nature. It is only when you put free animals under false restrictions that they lose the power of moving in harmony with nature, and adopt a movement expressive of the restrictions placed about them.

So it has been with civilized man. The movements of the savage, who lived in freedom in constant touch with Nature, were unrestricted, natural and beautiful. Only the movements of the naked body can be perfectly natural. Man, arrived at the end of civilization, will have to return to nakedness, not to the unconscious nakedness of the savage, but to the conscious and acknowledged nakedness of the mature Man, whose body will be the harmonious expression of his spiritual being.

And the movements of this Man will be natural and beautiful like those of the free animals.

The movement of the universe concentrating in an individual becomes what is termed the will; for example, the movement of the earth, being the concentration of surrounding forces, gives to the earth its individuality, its will of movement. So creatures of the earth, receiving in turn these concentrating forces in their different relations, as transmitted to them through their ancestors and to those by the earth, in themselves evolve the movement of individuals which is termed the will.

The dance should simply be, then, the natural gravitation of this will of the individual, which in the end is no more nor less than a human translation of the gravitation of the universe.

The school of the ballet of today, vainly striving against the natural laws of gravitation or the natural will of the individual, and working in discord in its form and movement with the form and movement of nature, produces a sterile movement which gives no birth to future movements, but dies as it is made.

The expression of the modern school of ballet, wherein each action is an end, and no movement, pose or rhythm is successive or can be made to evolve succeeding action, is an expression of degeneration, of living death. All the movements of our modern ballet school are sterile movements because they are unnatural: their purpose is to create the delusion that the law of gravitation does not exist for them.

The primary or fundamental movements of the new school of the dance must have within them the seeds from which will evolve all other movements, each in turn to give birth to others in unending sequence of still higher and greater expression, thoughts and ideas.

To those who nevertheless still enjoy the movements, for historical or choreographic or whatever other reasons, to those I answer: They see no farther than the skirts and tricots. But look — under the skirts, under the tricots are dancing deformed muscles. Look still farther — underneath the muscles are deformed bones. A deformed skeleton is dancing before you. This deformation through incorrect dress and incorrect movement is the result of the training necessary to the ballet.

The ballet condemns itself by enforcing the deformation of the beautiful woman's body! No historical, no choreographic reasons can prevail against that!

It is the mission of all art to express the highest and most beautiful ideals of man. What ideal does the ballet express?

No, the dance was once the most noble of all arts; and it shall be again. From the great depth to which it has fallen, it shall be raised. The dancer of the future shall attain so great a height that all other arts shall be helped thereby.

To express what is the most moral, healthful and beautiful in art — this is the mission of the dancer, and to this I dedicate my life.

These flowers before me contain the dream of a dance, it could be named 'The light falling on white flowers.' A dance that would be a subtle translation of the light and the whiteness. So pure, so strong, that people would say: it is a soul we see moving, a soul that has reached the light and found the whiteness. We are glad it should move so. Through its human medium we have a satisfying sense of movement, of light and glad things. Through this human medium, the movement of all nature runs also through us, is transmitted to us from the dancer. We feel the movement of light intermingled with the thought of whiteness. It is a prayer, this dance; each movement reaches in long undulations to the heavens and becomes a part of the eternal rhythm of the spheres.

To find those primary movements for the human body from which shall evolve the movements of the future dance in ever-varying, natural, unending sequences, that is the duty of the new dancer of today.

As an example of this, we might take the pose of the Hermes of the Greeks. He is represented as flying on the wind. If the artist had pleased to pose his foot in a vertical position, he might have done so, as the God, flying on the wind, is not touching the earth; but realizing that no movement is true unless suggesting sequence of movements, the sculptor placed the Hermes with the ball of his foot resting on the wind, giving the movement an eternal quality.

In the same way I might make an example of each pose and gesture in the thousands of figures we have left to us on the Greek vases and bas-reliefs; there is not one which in its movement does not presuppose another movement.

This is because the Greeks were the greatest students of the laws of nature, wherein all is the expression of unending, ever-increasing evolution, wherein are no ends and no stops.

Such movements will always have to depend on and correspond to the form that is moving. The movements of a beetle correspond to its form. So do those of the horse. Even so the movements of the human body must correspond to its form. The dances of no two persons should be alike.

People have thought that so long as one danced in rhythm, the form and design did not matter; but no, one must perfectly correspond to the other. The Greeks understood this very well. There is a statuette that shows a dancing cupid. It is a child's dance. The movements of the plump little feet and arms are perfectly suited to its form. The sole of the foot rests flat on the ground, a position which might be ugly in a more developed person, but is natural in a child trying to keep its balance. One of the legs is half raised; if it were outstretched it would irritate us, because the movement would be unnatural. There is also a statue of a satyr in a dance that is quite different from that of the cupid. His movements are those of a ripe and muscular man. They are in perfect harmony with the structure of his body.

The Greeks in all their painting, sculpture, architecture, literature, dance and tragedy evolved their movements from the movement of nature, as we plainly see expressed in all representations of the Greek gods, who, being no other than the representatives of natural forces, are always designed in a pose expressing the concentration and evolution of these forces. This is why the art of the Greeks is not a national or characteristic art but has been and will be the art of all humanity for all time.

Therefore dancing naked upon the earth I naturally fall into Greek positions, for Greek positions are only earth positions.

The noblest in art is the nude. This truth is recognized by all, and followed by painters, sculptors and poets; only the dancer has forgotten it, who should most remember it, as the instrument of her art is the human body itself.

Man's first conception of beauty is gained from the form and symmetry of the human body. The new school of the dance should begin with that movement which is in harmony with and will develop the highest form of the human body.

I intend to work for this dance of the future. I do not know whether I have the necessary qualities: I may have neither genius nor talent nor temperament. But I know that I have a Will; and will and energy sometimes prove greater than either genius or talent or temperament. . . .

My intention is, in due time, to found a school, to build a theatre where a hundred little girls shall be trained in my art, which they, in their turn, will better. In this school I shall not teach the children to imitate my movements, but to make their own. I shall not force them to study certain definite movements; I shall help them to develop those movements which are natural to them. Whosoever sees the movements of an untaught little child cannot deny that its movements are beautiful. They are beautiful because they are natural to the child. Even so the movements of the human body may be beautiful in every stage of development so long as they are in harmony with that stage and degree of maturity which the body has attained. There will always be movements which are the perfect expression of that individual body and that individual soul; so we must not force it to make movements which are not natural to it but which belong to a school. An intelligent child must be astonished to find that in the ballet school it is taught movements contrary to all those movements which it would make of its own accord.

This may seem a question of little importance, a question of differing opinions on the ballet and the new dance. But it is a great question. It is not only a question of true art, it is a question of race, of the development of the female sex to beauty and health, of the return to the original strength and to natural movements of woman's body. It is a question of the development of perfect mothers and the birth of healthy and beautiful children. The dancing school of the future is to develop and to show the ideal form of woman. It will be, as it were, a museum of the living beauty of the period.

Travellers coming into a country and seeing the dancers should find in them that country's ideal of the beauty of form and movement. But strangers who today come to any country, and there see the dancers of the ballet school, would get a strange notion indeed of the ideal of beauty in that country. More than this, dancing like any art of any time should reflect the highest point the spirit of mankind has reached in that special period. Does anybody think that the present day ballet school expresses this?

Why are its positions in such contrast to the beautiful positions of the antique sculptures which we preserve in our museums and which are constantly presented to us as perfect models of ideal beauty? Or have our museums been founded only out of historical and archaeological interest, and not for the sake of the beauty of the objects which they contain?

The ideal of beauty of the human body cannot change with fashion but only with evolution. Remember the story of the beautiful sculpture of a Roman girl which was discovered under the reign of Pope Innocent VIII, and which by its beauty created such a sensation that the men thronged to see it and made pilgrimages to it as to a holy shrine, so that the Pope, troubled by the movement which it originated, finally had it buried again.

And here I want to avoid a misunderstanding that might easily arise. From what I have said you might conclude that my intention is to return to the dances of the old Greeks, or that I think that the dance of the future will be a revival of the antique dances or even of those of the primitive tribes. No, the dance of the future will be a new movement, a consequence of the entire evolution which mankind has passed through. To return to the dances of the Greeks would be as impossible as it is unnecessary. We are not Greeks and therefore cannot dance Greek dances.

But the dance of the future will have to become again a high religious art as it was with the Greeks. For art which is not religious is not art, is mere merchandise.

The dancer of the future will be one whose body and soul have grown so harmoniously together that the natural language of that soul will have become the movement of the body. The dancer will not belong to a nation but to all humanity. She will dance not in the form of nymph, nor fairy, nor coquette, but in the form of woman in her greatest and purest expression. She will realize the mission of woman's body and the holiness of all its parts. She will dance the changing life of nature, showing how each part is transformed into the other. From all parts of her body shall shine radiant intelligence, bringing to the world the message of the thoughts and aspirations of thousands of women. She shall dance the freedom of woman. . . .

■　■　■

## Source

Duncan, I. (1928) 'The Dancer of the Future', *The Art of the Dance*, New York: Theatre Arts Books. Written c. 1902 and first published 1928.

## Isadora Duncan (1878–1927)

American dancer and choreographer. She was born in the USA but spent most of her professional life in Europe (1899–1927), where she gained a reputation as one of the foremost dancers of the age. She performed mainly as a solo dancer but also with children trained at the many schools that she set up from 1904 onwards. Her repertoire was extensive and she toured some of her works for two decades.[1] These included *Brahms Waltzes* (1905), *Fifth Symphony* (1915) to Beethoven, *Marseillaise* (1915), and *Marche Slave* (1917).

Duncan performed throughout Europe, visiting most major cities, especially Paris, London, St Petersburg (1905) and Berlin. She returned to the USA in 1909, 1911, 1917 and 1922 but was not always well received, first, because of her private reputation, later, after 1917, because of her political affiliation. She was fêted by many major artists of the period, including Rodin and Edward Gordon Craig, with whom she had a personal and artistic relationship. In 1921 she was invited to establish a school in Moscow by Lenin's newly formed Soviet government. She became a Soviet citizen. She returned to Paris in 1927 where she gave her last concert at the age of 49; she died, prematurely, in a car accident in Nice in the same year.

It is evident from the extensive accounts of her dancing that Duncan was a re- markable performer who heralded the freedom and the political concern that later modern dancers would emulate. The evidence provided by contemporary critics makes it quite clear that it was her dancing that gained her a reputation as one of the most talked-about women in Europe. We are fortunate that Duncan committed her ideas to paper too.

In this early extract she surveys the dancer's position at the turn of the century and finds ballet wanting. Some of the writing now seems fanciful, but the rest contains the essentials of the ideas that became the foundations for the new modern dance. She looks to a new way of moving 'to find those primary movements for the human body from which shall evolve the movements of the future dance . . .' for the dancer of the future who 'shall dance the freedom of woman'.

## Compare this article with writings by the following authors in this reader

**Craig** – artistic collaborator and father of her first child
**Marinetti** – another view of the promise of the new century
**Piscator** – a contemporary theatre approach
**Stanislavski** – whom she met in St Petersburg, a great admirer of her work

## Further reading

Daly, A. (2002) *Done into Dance: Isadora Duncan in America*, Middletown, Conn.: Wesleyan University Press.
Duncan, I. (1928) *The Art of the Dance*, New York: Theatre Arts Books.
Kurth, P. (2002) *Isadora Duncan: A Sensational Life*, London: Back Bay Books.
Magriel, P. (ed.) (1948) *Isadora Duncan*, London: A & C Black.
http://www.isadoraduncan.net

## Note

1    Layson, J. (1983) 'Isadora Duncan: A Preliminary Analysis of her Work', *Dance Research*, 1, 1: 39–49, lists at least 223 dances.

# Chapter 22

# Hanns Eisler

## SOME REMARKS ON THE SITUATION
## OF THE MODERN COMPOSER

WHEN MEDICAL SCIENCE was not yet able to diagnose the cause of serious diseases, such as tuberculosis, beri-beri, or diseases of the blood, patients were in a sorry plight. These diseases were considered to be matters of chance, misfortunes for which there was little alleviation, or it was believed the sick were possessed and should be exorcised by prayer. When modern science and technology discovered new methods of diagnosis and new apparatus, it became known that these diseases were not personal disasters, but were caused by microbes and if recognized in time, were curable. Those were the great days of chemotherapy. The latest scientific research has produced a still more interesting result. It has been ascertained that a large number of these diseases, such as tuberculosis and beri-beri, are the result of social conditions, and many of them will disappear entirely when social conditions are changed. What a colossal development of human knowledge – disease, as fate, incurable; disease, caused by bacteria, curable. Disease, caused by social conditions, which are changeable, curable.

If we modern composers were able to apply some of this objectivity, common sense and knowledge to our own field, we would be more successful. But that requires a scientific approach instead of the noncommitted futile natterings about art. This is urgently necessary, since the crisis in modern music is sharpening, while barbarism in music is on the increase.

The people have become musical illiterates, despite technical progress in music. It is high time for contemporary composers to see reason and alter their attitude. In order to contend successfully with this state of anarchy and barbarism a new type of composer, teacher and musician is needed. I would appeal above all, to the modern composer, for as the producers of music, they are the most important. If we wish to create a new type of composer, then we must first challenge the old type wherever we find him. This can only be done with scientific methods, objectively and fairly; therefore it is necessary to raise the practice and theory of music to the level of contemporary thought. Unfortunately, it is true to say that at a time when new methods of working and reasoning have already been introduced in industry, medicine, chemistry, physics, sociology and political economy, wholly antiquated methods are still applied in the theory and practice of music. The so-called modern composer is mainly to blame for this state of affairs. We shall have to find a new definition for the word 'modern.' After all, it should be possible to determine what, for our time, is progressive or retrogressive in music.

The crisis in music has been caused by the general crisis in society. In music it appears concretely in the technique of composing. This, in turn, has contributed to the complete isolation of modern music from social life. The modern composer has meanwhile become a parasite, supported by wealthy patrons out of personal interests, and no longer carries out any rational work in society. Consequently, the composer's profession still has something of the subservient character of the seventeenth century. He can no longer maintain himself from his compositions, which is already suspect, but for example, has to hang around the salons in order to be seen. That is particularly detrimental to young composers for they are thus cut off from the realities of life. This seclusion leads to most modern works having nothing to say about the most urgent issues of the day. Some modern composers are only concerned with themselves. (So let them!) Others have form and technique problems. (It's a fine thing to contemplate technique, so why disturb them?) Lastly, there are the so-called lyrical temperaments, exquisitely sensitive and profound, who know definitely spring will come and the moon will shine when the nights are light. (That's a boost for Hollywood.) Now modern composers are of the opinion that 'absolute music,' more accurately music without words, cannot express anything definite at all, and certainly nothing about 'the urgent issues of our day.' Music without words, they say, cannot achieve this nor is it the purpose of music. (The purpose of music is only to be found in music itself. Music for music's sake.)

But we know from history that so-called absolute music reached the highest point of expression in one particular period. Beethoven's symphonies were the music of the struggle of the young bourgeoisie against decaying feudalism. We also know from history that instrumental music was not always predominant. In the fifteenth and sixteenth centuries instrumental music played a subordinate role to vocal music. Instrumental music and the concert (as the organized form of musical life) are not eternal, but historical forms. They arose and developed within capitalist society and they enter a crisis when capitalist society enters a crisis. In 1750 the Mannheim Symphonic School was new and revolutionary. In 1810 it embodied the highest musical expression of the period. By 1890 what was left was pedestrian naturalism à la Richard Strauss, or the artificial, sentimental *Weltanschauung* music of Gustav Mahler. By 1933 there were no longer any achievements of significance in this sphere and it is quite impossible to define the purpose of a symphony. So a really progressive composer will have to realize that this is a completely archaic art form, which should no longer be employed. Why continue the useless? We are witnessing a new blossoming and predominance of vocal music following the instrumental era of the nineteenth century. Instrumental music will play an increasingly subordinate and insignificant role in music. A solution to the music crisis emanating from purely instrumental music can't be found. The experiences of the last twenty years demonstrate this quite clearly. Modern composers have tried almost everything and the result is complete anarchy. The composer today depends only on his own personal recipe and his own taste. If this would guarantee a high musical culture, then there would be nothing against it. But since it inherently helps to produce barbarism and decay it is harmful. There were periods of great styles in the history of music, which were generally considered obligatory. As everybody knows it is often not easy to distinguish between an early Beethoven, Haydn or Mozart, without an exact analysis. Certain cadences were generally accepted as well as certain formal methods, such as the employment of additional musical elements in the transition, or as the development or the recapitulation. Despite all these generally accepted elements of form, the composers were not uniform; each possessed individuality.

Modern music will only exist when there is a new modern style which is obligatory for all and useful to society. At a time when modern music no longer has a public but is only promoted privately a composer can do as he likes. He can compose like Czerny and with a few false basses write a '*Book of Exercises for* non-*Dexterity.*' He can copy Brahms with the twelve tone technique or sit on top of the piano declaring he is expressing his innermost soul. Since these three methods are as useless as they are unsalable the difference is minute. We find the same sort of anarchy in aesthetics. Today there are no aesthetic standards in music, for the difference between beautiful and ugly has become a matter of personal taste and experience. A modern type of composer must take note of that. The terms 'beautiful' or 'not beautiful' which played such an important role fifty years ago are out of date. They no longer say anything about the value and therefore must be replaced by the new 'useful' and 'useless.' Many fellow musicians believe the only criterion is good or bad music. That sounds quite reasonable. Unfortunately, however, it is difficult today to agree on what is good and what is bad music. Some composers consider Stravinsky primitive, others consider Schönberg obsolete. There are a number of very talented modern composers, whose composing is technically bad from a certain point of view. Careless part writing, lack of artistry in the form, inability in the counterpoint. Yet there are others who will defend these composers, maintaining they intended to so write and it was not done out of ignorance, but to achieve certain 'effects.' Unfortunately, the terms 'good' and 'bad' alone are no longer adequate as criteria, nor yet the terms 'modern' and 'old-fashioned.' But when we combine these criteria with the new criteria of 'useful' and 'useless' we will make better headway, especially if we go one step further and ask 'useful for whom?' Technical standards among modern composers are bad, though generally not yet admitted. Among the best of them we often find only mannerisms instead of originality, style imitation instead of style, superficial tricks in place of fundamental technical workmanship. Anyone looking at what you might call a polyphonic work of a talented young composer would find little counterpoint, merely an imitation of it, or the use of certain counterpoint mannerisms. So today the terms 'good' and 'bad' must be applied with the greatest of care and in any case only in connection with 'useful' or 'useless.'

The new type of composer will also have to learn that the crisis in modern music has been brought about mainly by the growth in technical devices. The radio, gramophone records and sound film have created a completely new situation. The concert compared with sound film is just as old-fashioned as the mailcoach compared with the airplane. Sound film and radio are destroying the old forms of music listening for there is a big difference between listening to a symphony at a concert or on the radio. There is a glaring contradiction between classical music and the modern means of production. Take a simple experiment – if you turn on the radio in a car driving along the street of a big city then you will realize that classical music does not fit the modern way of life. It requires a passive listener who is easily affected and who can shut off his thinking. The technique of composing classical music is dependent on this and arose because of it. If listened to over the radio or in a film many of the formal devices seem antiquated. For instance, the principle of recapitulation, of the development, indeed the whole sonata form itself. Sound film is making the masses unaccustomed to listening to music in the abstract but accustomed to seeing pictures of real life while they hear music. So a more realistic type of listener is arising in contrast to the old idealist concert-goer. This is a very interesting process. It is not altered by the fact that the film industry is helping to produce a barbaric condition in culture and that it is a political and moral device for blunting the intellect of the masses. Whether film will become a wonderful art form for mankind or a sordid commodity is a question of power, that is to say, a political question and not an aesthetic-cultural one. The sound film will also decisively change the state of instrumental music. The first experiments have been made to produce music synthetically on the film sound track. The sound chart of the composer's score is copied onto the film track. It sounds adventurous, but it has already been done. It is known how the tone A looks graphically on the film track and this graphic sign can be changed back again into music. The manual labor of the musician is thus replaced by the machine; this will lead to a complete revolutionizing of techniques of composing. But this means the composer can make himself absolutely independent of the inadequacies of the instruments and musicians. The conductor, the virtuoso and the instrumentalist will become superfluous. The result will be a still greater mass poverty among musicians, if the present form of society is not changed by then. It will not take too long, if we think of the short time that it took for the sound film to develop. Music-making by man will then have a new function, it will be for the music-lover and the amateur. (Just as the train, the car and the plane have not made walking or rambling disappear.) Great music will be put directly by the composer onto the apparatus; with the help of technicians, but no longer of 'artists.' (There will no longer be problems about the tempi or the rendering.) These are the material fundamentals and prerequisites for a new style in music.

It is not possible in such a brief exposition to enlarge on such problems systematically. They can only be touched on, so to speak. Nevertheless, from what has already been stated it is clear along what lines the new type of modern composer should think in order to arrive at a new musical practice. What are our main difficulties? Certain social situations have produced certain musical forms, that is, they produce a certain musical diction. If the material productive forces of a society develop at a quicker speed than the music, then music will lag behind and a contradiction will arise between it and society. With modern composers it is as though they find themselves in an airtight room, where there is no possibility of solving even the smallest technical problem. (All these struggles for a new technique and new aesthetics expire without showing any result. There are no victors any more, only the vanquished.)

Even if modern composers were of one mind at least on some questions, another type of man with a rough voice and hard hands would appear, bang on the table and demand, 'For whose benefit?' And that is the main question.

In order to check the decay of music and to find a new technique, a new style and thus a new circle of listeners, the modern composer will have to leave his airtight room and find his place in society. It is not a question of sentimentality and kindheartedness but a question of music.

The modern composer must change *from a parasite into a fighter*. In the interests of music we must ask ourselves: What social attitude is the most useful? Once we have realized that the present form of society has produced musical barbarism, then we must try to change it. However, that is a very difficult matter, not easily achieved. We cannot conduct such struggles alone, but must form an alliance with those sections of the people who suffer under this order of society and who are combating it. That is an alliance of the progressive intellectuals, scholars, doctors, engineers, artists and the working class. The composer must understand once and for all that this alliance alone will provide the guarantee of bringing order into the chaos in music. This path is long and difficult, but in the interests of music it must be taken. It is also a question of character for there is a difference between a weakling, a futile dreamer (and whoever is futile is also harmful), or a modern man, a realist, who thinks and fights for his cause. In these times of mankind's great battles for a new world musicians should not desert the field. Let us join the struggle on the side of truth against falsehood. Then we will best serve our cause, the cause of modern music.

■    ■    ■

## Source

Eisler, H. (1935, 1978) 'Some Remarks on the Situation of the Modern Composer', *Hanns Eisler: A Rebel in Music*, trans. M. Meyer, ed. M. Grabs, Berlin: Seven Seas Books: 106–113.[1]

## Hanns Eisler (1892–1962)

Born in Leipzig and studied composition under Schoenberg and Webern, winning prizes for his early work. He became a committed Marxist, and was involved in some of the revolutionary activities of the German communist party in the 1920s. He wrote choral works and marching songs that became popular with left-wing groups throughout Europe, many of them in the minor key, which Eisler thought was more threatening or dangerously energetic.

In the 1930s he met Bertolt Brecht, with whom he formed a lifelong friendship, composing together at least two theatre works that have been seen as masterpieces – *Die Massnähme* (*The Measures Taken*) (1930), and *Die Mütter* (*The Mother*) (1932), from the novel by Maxim Gorky. Both works display a distinct theatrical relationship between words and music, and are pioneering in that these elements have an equal expressive weight, as well as being both memorable and powerfully uplifting. After Hitler came to power in Germany, Eisler's music was banned, and he moved to Hollywood, returning after the Second World War to the German Democratic Republic to work with Brecht once again within the new socialist state, with works including *The Mother* (1951) with Brecht's wife Helene Weigel in the title role. From 1948 to 1961 he wrote scores for seventeen plays, his view being that good theatre must also incorporate music that can both serve and elevate the performance as a major signifier of meaning, hence his inclusion in this book.

Eisler's essay on the modern composer demands new thinking and new compositional techniques to serve what he sees as the new anti-bourgeois era. Ironically it is only in the late twentieth century that Eisler's call for a new modern style has seen composers such as Adams, Glass, Bryars and Smith producing music that has bridged the gap between the classes, generations and countries.

## Compare this article with writings by the following authors in this reader

**Benjamin** – a fellow Marxist in Germany in the 1930s
**Brecht** – his main collaborator
**Cage** – on music and performance
**Glass** – another, later, theatre composer
**Müller** – a later German playwright

## Further reading

Betz, A. (1976, 1982) *Hanns Eisler Political Musician*, trans. B. Hopkins, Cambridge: Cambridge University Press.
Willett, J. (1968) *The Theatre of Bertolt Brecht*, London: Methuen.

## Note

1   *Einiges über die Lage des modernen Komponisten*, Typescript, Hanns Eisler Archives. Grabs notes (p. 113) that this was intended for publication in *New Music* and was published in a shortened version in the *Daily Worker*, New York, 5 December 1935 as 'The Composer in Society'.

# Chapter 23

Etchells

## Tim Etchells

## ON PERFORMANCE WRITING

**T**HIS PIECE ADDRESSES ITSELF to the task of making text for performance, especially within a collaborative process. It is a revised version of a presentation I made in Dartington (UK) at a 1996 conference entitled 'Performance Writing'. I was keen to open the door to a broad, adventurous description of what writing for performance might mean – beyond ideas of playwrighting which is still, sadly, the measure too often employed in the UK, despite a rich history of writers in theatre spaces who are doing something quite different. The piece talks about physical action and set construction as forms of writing, it talks about writing words to be seen and read on-stage rather than spoken, it talks about lists, about improvisation, about reading, about whispering and about collage as a form – in each case implying a critical dialogue with more traditional notions of theatre or performance writing.

Obsessed in any case with lists and indexes, he tried one night to write a list of the texts that he had made, or else texts that he might make. Or of texts that he could make. Through the night the list would slip and slide – breaking up into stories and speculations and then returning to listing again.

Which text should go first in the list? A real one or a possible one.

I chose a real one, remembering that I'd left my son at home ill, to come to a conference. And deciding to talk about him, sometimes, in the list.

177

1. A text to be whispered by the bedside of a sleeping child.
2. A text to be yelled aloud by a single performer in a car park at dawn.
3. A text to be left on the ansaphones of strangers.
4. A text to be spoken while fucking secretly the partner of a good friend.
5. A text for megaphone.
6. A text which could be used as a weapon.

Remember that prison I told you about? The troops found it deserted, jailers and torturers fled, their prisoners/victims executed in haste, dead in the cells.

And how in one room, stored amongst the bloody implements and signed confessionals, they discovered a strange and endless non-sensical near-gibberish text. How it transpired that the jailers would sit outside their prisoners' doors in the dead of the night and read this text aloud to them repeatedly – denying them sleep and, by destroying language or demolishing sense, attacking the very bounds which tied their charges to the earth and to sanity.

A true story. I keep wondering about those men knelt on the floor of a corridor and reading strange language to their prisoners. Did they think of themselves as performers? Did they chat, in the kitchen or the bar after work, discussing how well or badly their reading work had gone? Did they think about the pauses, the language, the emphasis? Did the reading drive them crazy too? Perhaps.

I think about the text they read from, and at night sometimes in a dream of a handwritten page, I think I can see it but I cannot read the words.

1. A text of lines from half-remembered songs.
2. A love letter written in binary.
3. A text composed of fragments.

In bed, early, Miles is jabbering and making jokes about breakfast and porridge in particular. He tells me that for breakfast we will have spider porridge, and I ask, 'What's that?' and he says *'spider porridge* – with *spiders* in it . . .' and I say I will feed him helicopter porridge, or something like that, and he threatens me with many other kinds of porridge until at last he gets to this one: radio porridge. He says we will have radio porridge with voices in it.

All summer we lived in the house with the stars up above it and the earth down below and we ate of radio porridge. Immensely filling, the porridge satisfied hunger but left one haunted with voices under the skin.

Who puts those voices in radio porridge?

No one.

Whose are the voices in radio porridge?

The voices in radio porridge come from the dead. They come from stray signals, lost letters. They come from the people who wrote graffiti on all the walls in town, or the people in books and stories we'd read, and many other places.

1. A text for people to find in their wallets, days later, when you are forgotten.
2. A text to come through people's doors – perhaps a letter.
3. A text for someone to find in the street, caught in one of those eddypools of blown leaves and ragged polythene bags.

One day in New York I am walking along, see a note on the floor, blowing past me in the wind, pick it up. The note says this:

'What in the World are You Doing, why are you taking some much time with the . . .'

A voice like that is the linkman in radio porridge.

It's radio porridge or something like it that speaks in all of the shows. I couldn't get excited about a deep voice or an authentic voice, but I could get excited by a gabbling voice composed of scraps and layers, fragments, quotations. No editorial, or at least no centre. Like I don't have a voice – I'm just a space this other stuff is flowing through and lodged inside.

1. A text written in condensation.
2. A text written, learned and performed to pass a polygraph test.
3. A series of texts written on a lover. In biro, in lipstick, in permanent marker, in blood, and semen.
4. An invisible text.
5. The same text written every day for a year, in different places, in different locations.
6. A text written on the floor of an old factory.

Ending the coach tour of Sheffield we made – a piece called *Nights in This City* (1995) – the bus arrived at a huge building – a building that served first as the tram depot for the city and then as the main bus depot and which is now disused. In this space, upon the floor we had written out the entire A-Z of the city – an alphabetical text in ten 75-metre-long columns – chalk on concrete floor. Climbing off the bus people would see the exit far down the end of the room, walk towards it, realise they were walking on something and then, in the end, realise what it was – often slowing down to walk and find their own street names, taking people to see where they had once lived, even having their photographs taken next to the name of their streets. In some way this index on the floor served the purpose of a reprise, where the city explored in the performance was laid out in textual miniature for people to survey as a whole.

Very often in the shows there were these lists or catalogues. Sometimes ordered, sometimes chaotic. Language like a camera on endless tracks, zooming everywhere, close-up, wide-shot, tracking shot, point of view. Language jumping you from one story, one world, one discourse to another.

1.  A text written at 3 am in the middle of a war.
2.  A text written in the fast food court of a large European shopping mall.
3.  A text which raises questions of ownership.

I come into the front room one afternoon and the TV is playing, and I am shocked beyond belief to find that the characters are speaking words stolen directly from our piece *Some Confusions in the Law about Love* (1989).

Moments pass, and then I realise, in a slow internal turning round, that this is some nameless film I must've flipped through five years ago or more and that I stole the lines from it, scrawling them on a newspaper, transferring them to notebook and then at some later point writing them into the work. Still, watching the film from this point on I am gripped by a feeling of strange violation as a handful of moments from our show *Some Confusions* are repeated, out-of-context, out of character and out of costume.

> 'Come here honey . . .' the drunk vamp woman says to her boss's hench-man turned betrayer/ lover 'If you'd like to see me again I'll give you a list of the times that Charlie's always out . . .'

The house full of shelves, full of notebooks, full of overheard and copied lines – film, life, dreams, literature. Anything. Shit – I'm like some teen-burglar – 'I nicked so much stuff I can't even remember what is mine anymore'. And of course Miles is already the same, since his stories when he tells them just recycle verbatim the best lines and characters from the stories he's heard. One night he was feeding the birds in one picture book with bread taken from the pages of another. A kind of gorgeous economy in his madness.

A thieving machine.

When provoked into discussing where their writing 'comes from', some of my students will invoke the notion of a voice. To be looked for intently and nurtured when found, this voice lives in them somewhere, deep down inside. When they find it they want to write in it. This voice is authentic in some way, by its very nature profound. It is knotty, connected to the body. It comes *from them*. Often at night.

And whilst I've done my share of night writing, I never know exactly what they mean.

Because for me writing was so often about collecting, sifting and using from bits of other people's stuff – copied language like precious stones. Authentic has not really been in it.

Working in performance they were always tempted to think about writing (or even speaking) as a kind of trying on of other peoples clothes – a borrowing of power. I speak for a moment like my father. I assume the language of a teacher. I speak for one moment like they do in some movie. I borrow a phrase from a friend, a sentence construction from a lover. A writing that's more like sampling. Mixing, matching, cutting, pasting. Conscious, strategic and sometimes unconscious, out of control. I'm quoting and I don't even know it. Perhaps it's best to think of one's relationship to language like this, as the novelist Michael Moorcock once described a character 'skipping through fragments of half-remembered songs like a malfunctioning juke-box'.

And when my students mention this *voice* (a frighteningly singular thing) which comes from *themselves* I always have a second problem, because not knowing the voice I also fail to recognise (at least not with the same confidence) the 'self' of which they are speaking. For us, in the work and out of it, this notion of self has often seemed after all to be simply a collection of texts, quotations, strategic and accidental speakings – not a coherent thing, much less the single-minded author of some text. What I am, in this text (now) at least, is no more (and no less) than the meeting-point of the language that flows into and flows out of me (these past years, months, days) – a switching station, a filtering and thieving machine, a space in which collisions take place.

Any regrets?

I once asked Ron Vawter (Wooster Group) if he ever wished they could deal with new texts instead of (as he described it to me) going back over the tapes of the twentieth century to see what had happened, to see what had gone wrong. He said yes, he could see a time when that might be fun, but for the moment at least there was so much work left to do. There's so much stuff left in the archives.

1. A broken text.
2. A discredited text.
3. A text to be utterly disowned by all those that perform it.
4. A series of texts in a language that doesn't work.

Perhaps our first subject was always this inadequacy of language. Its unsuitability for the job it has to do, its failure. And in this failure – by definition language is not and cannot express what it seeks to describe – an admission of the struggle in everyday life – to get blunt tools to do fine work, to carve out a life in, around, despite of and through what passes for culture in the late twentieth century.

And in this love of the blunt edges and limits of language he always cared most for illegitimate texts, finding hope and inspiration in the clichés of straight-to-video films, the tortuous prose of a book of instructions for chemistry experiments, a catalogue of the contents of a museum of curious, the simple language of cartoons, comic-strips, the disposable ease of plot summaries for a soap opera or the antiquated text of a fairy story or some mythical tale. The words 'good' and 'writing' never went together that well for us. Bad writing was always more our style. Language transfixed on its own inadequacy. Language at the point of breakdown, at the edges of sense, on the edge of not coping at all.

A writer of nonsense.

A writer of shapes that only look like letters.

A writer of filthy words.

Working on *Pleasure* (in summer 1997) we loved a text I downloaded from the Internet – a huge list entitled simply '*2,334 Filthy Words and Phrases*' – a pedant's catalogue of obscenities, slang words and descriptions containing some 500 alternative ways to say masturbate. First time I printed this list I left it running on the printer and on returning to the office some 20 minutes later found that people there had stopped work and were gathered around the printer from which the text was still spewing. They were poring over the words like so many scholars and obsessives. They were, in a mixture of fascination and repulsion, reading out the lists to each other, revelling in the awfulness, the unsayableness, the unwriteableness of:

YANK THE MEAT

PISS-FLAPS

GET SOME HOLE

PUSH SHIT UPHILL

EAT HAIR PIE

BURP THE WORM

Language at the edges of sense, on the edge of not coping at all.

Our favourite game, working from this text in *Pleasure* rehearsals, was to write these words and others like them on a blackboard on the stage – a piece of kids' language instruction gone wrong, or a foreign language course with a bitter little twist. The words written calmly in capitals, the performers stood beside the blackboard, owning the text written up there, meeting the gaze of the audience like 'this is your lesson for today'.

Months afterwards we made a film *Filthy Words & Phrases* (1998) of Cathy writing each of these words, on a blackboard, in an old abandoned schoolroom. We shot in one continuous seven-hour take and by the end of it Cathy (and crew) were blank with exhaustion and white from the chalk dust. We premiered the film in a Rotterdam porn cinema and could never quite decide if the film was an attack on the profligate redundancy of language or a hymn of sorts to its absurd inventiveness and its complete commitment to change – a marathon naming of the parts in which language proliferates around a crisis.

1.   A text for email.
2.   A text to be written in blood.
3.   A text in a made-up language.

Using gibberish in (*Let the Water Run its Course*) *to the Sea that Made the Promise* (1986) we used to talk a lot about the sound of voices coming through walls – like the blurred and awful sound of people arguing in the flat downstairs, the sounds of voices gabbling madly in a party – language reduced to its raw shapes, where listening, you do not know the words but you can guess what is being spoken of.

In *Hidden J* (1994) Cathy and Robin speak a version of this gibberish too – only here it has become most definitely foreign – not a fucked-up English, but a shattering of languages from broken Europe – Serb, Russian, Polish swinging to Italian in places. Cathy invisible in the house centre-stage and curtains drawn, speaking down the telephone – and incomprehensible – railing and whispering, yelling and urging, demanding, accusing. And outside the house all we see are the other performers waiting, some of them messing around, Richard peering, upstaging, but in the end all of them heads down, listening. It's not just the audience that listen to the text. Cathy railing and whispering, yelling and urging, demanding, accusing.

And for these moments the two cultures of the piece – drunk git English and war-zone Mainland – sit in their most appalling relationship – the one can neither see, help or understand the other at all. It's the opposite of those British Telecom ads where Bob Hoskins implores one that 'it's good to talk'; in this case it is no fucking good to talk.

A list of streets:

1.   Hope Street
2.   Furnace Lane
3.   Winter Hill
4.   Market Street. San Francisco's Oxford Street of lunacy and the wheel-chair homeless – drunk and drugged crazies on every street corner; those that aren't lying in comatose sleep in doorways, or propped against the sides of buildings are the ones too fast for sleep – the ones each dancing to some inaudible tune – jigging, walking, twisting,

turning (one woman beating the side of a trash can with glee in some unfinished, neverending symphony of noise) – and all of them muttering in some individual yet strangely collective voice – whispers, threats, assumptions, delusions – random samplings from the last days of the mechanical age . . .

. . . that was, pretty well, the kind of theatre or performance text I had in mind.

Or at least not the spectacle of 'new playwrights' at a 1997 conference in London's Royal Court Theatre whose biggest (almost only) topic of conversation seemed to be long long pontifications on the understanding of a comma. How directors and actors can't understand a comma these days. The terrible shame of it.

Hard for me to understand, having never much cared for punctuation.

I mean I'd rather say:

here are 26 letters:

a b c d e f g h i j k l m n o p q r s t u v w x y z

now write a text for performance.

Never cared much for playwrights. And in any case in some recent shows the text was generated in good part by performer improvisation – in reaction to written stimulus or without it. In this way a two-paragraph fragment becomes a ten-minute monologue – a growing, generative process of improvisation, negotiation, discussion, more writing and eventual fixing. A kind of speaking that becomes writing.

Working in this way – around the rhythms of text that's at least half made-up on the spot he was interested in precisely those textures – of thought, repetition, self-correction, hesitation, and so on – in which speech excels and which writing can only begin to approximate. Working with video-tape and transcripts of improvisations they were concerned to capture some of that sense, in speech, of how a voice finds itself, of how language stumbles, corrects and then flies – explorations of the struggle and process of language itself. A concern with language not as text then, but as event.

A series of spells:

1. To Bewitch a Service Station at Midnight.
2. To Exorcise a Bad Spirit from a Housing Estate.
3. To Escape from Prison or Some Terrible Place.
4. To Bring Some Ecstasy Kid from a Coma
5. To Combat Insincerity in a Soap Opera
6. To Summon the Power of Angels.

In *200% & Bloody Thirsty* (1987/8) the characters try on the voices of angels as if by speaking like them they might have power to raise the dead. Borrowing language for your own purposes, for its power and authority, for its style. Language is always a suit of someone else's clothes you try on – the fit is not good but there's power in it.

Football fans on a train some months ago boasting about their drunken exploits at a previous game: 'We *proceeded* to the White Hart pub and we were there *observed* to drink several pints of lager.' The whole conversation taking place in the style of an arresting officer's report. Stealing other people's language to bolster your own power.

In performance we use the struggle to feel right in the text, and the distance between the performer and her text is always visible. In recent shows this gap is all the more visible because the text features as paper or script – a physical object which can be picked up, handled, subjected to scrutiny, curiosity, indifference, contempt. In the work you can see the performers eyeing up the text, wondering about it, knowing that whatever it is it isn't them.

Or, if the fit is good between performer and text, it is a good fit that has to be struggled for and a fit that makes surprising use of the original material – the scenes of clichéd TV cop shit and emotion-drama in *Club of No Regrets* (1993/4) are smashed to pieces in Terry's final exertions as the 'character' Helen X – she jumbling the phrases, cuts from one scene to another, regardless of one sense whilst making another. It *is* like getting blood out of a stone but in the end she does get the material to mean for her, even if it is almost destroyed in the process.

The characters/performers always moving from outside language to a relationship in which they seem to own it.

Back on market.

One wrecked woman goes past me, her eyes wide, her arms folded tight across herself like she's a parcel wrapped too tight – she catches my eye and without breaking pace with her whisper, threatens out loud: 'Don't look at me you fucking psycho-killer.'

And I say: 'It takes one to know one.'

She follows me.

1. A text of obvious lies.
2. A text of promises.
3. A text of accusations.

How does Claire begin in *Hidden J* (1994)?

> Long ago and far away there was a country and all the people there were a bunch of fucking cunts . . .

and of course she is talking about England and all the people on the stage.

1.     Write like the text were by someone else.
2.     Adopt another's handwriting.
1.     Use a different pen.
1.     Write the text on cardboard, as if this were the only thing you had left, scrawl on the cardboard like urgency erased all style.
       and,
2.     Write about personas.

I should talk about Mark E. Smith here. Better yet, read the back of The Fall's 1978 or 1979 *Totale's Turns* live album recorded in Working Men's Clubs in Wakefield, Doncaster, etc.

> CALL YOURSELVES BLOODY PROFESSIONALS?
> Was one of the shower-cum-dressing room comments The Fall received after completing their 'turn' which makes up side one of this record, along with 'everybody knows the best groups cum from London' and 'You'll never work again'.
> Enough, Side 1 was recorded in front of an 80% disco-weekend-mating audience, but we never liked preaching to the converted anyway. Side 2 other places — 'New Puritan' at home, during which said home was attacked by a drunk, which accounts for the tension on that track.
> I don't particularly like the person singing on this LP. That said I marvel at his guts. This is probably the most accurate document of The Fall ever released, even though they'll have a hard time convincing their mams and dads about that, ha ha.
> R. Totale XVII
> Honorary Member
> Wakefield Young Drinkers Club.

Smith always casting himself in other personas, as other people, as fucked up narrators with a bad attitude. Like Ballard's central character in his science fiction books who are always called Traven or Travis or Trabert or Talbot, sometimes called by all of these names in the space of one chapter. Always some version of the same bloke, whose name, like his identity is forever in question. Like I don't particularly like the person writing this text.

1.     A text which sticks in the mouth, begging you not to say it.
2.     A text that spills and slips and runs.
3.     A text that no-one will ever hear.

In *Marina & Lee* (1990/91) Cathy delivered several of her texts at an ever-decreasing volume so that the final sections of each were completely inaudible.
I had to write these texts anyway but was puzzled for weeks about what to put in them. In some ways it didn't seem to matter at all but in other ways these

seemed like the most important texts in the piece. What might one wish to say, but have no one hear?

1.   A text where the voice is clear and sharp.
2.   A text where the voice is compromised.
3.   A text where the voice is under heavy pressure.

Watching the film *Performance* (Nicholas Roeg and Donald Cammell) and watching the 'character' of James Fox – East End gangster plunged into the underworld of drugs, rock 'n' roll, hippie sexuality. Like Jack the Lad cannot cope. Like his voice cannot deal with the things it has to describe.

That's the thing you have to do with a voice after all – make it speak of the things that it cannot deal with – make it speak of the illegal.

I'm a man, I'm a man, I'm all fuckin man . . .

James Fox as drugged out gangster transformed in wig, kimono and makeup, not able to cope.

That was something we always loved to do – play a gap between the voice and the bodies from which it arises. The teenage shop-girls were making physics lectures and then slipping into descriptions of long Russian winter romances. The bloke at a wedding was making an announcement about bombs in the car park. The clumsy pantomime skeletons were performing a very old poetic text. Like all the time these texts take the people who speak them by surprise.

Round midnight he made an end to his listing of texts and tried instead to think about silence. It was silent in the house. He made a list of silences, like the list from *Pleasure* (1998).

The kind of silence you sometimes get in phone calls to a person that you love.

The kind of silence people only dream of.

The kind of silence that is only for waiting in.

The kind of silence as a thief makes away with the gold.

The kind of silence that follows a car crash.

The kind of silence in a crowded house when everyone is asleep.

The kind of silence between waves at the ocean.

The kind of silence which follows a big argument.

The kind of silence that happens when you put your head under the water of the bath.

The kind of silence that only happens at night.

The kind of silence that happens when you close the curtains and climb into bed.

The kind of silence that has everything in it.

■   ■   ■

## Source

Etchells, T. (1999) *Certain Fragments*, London: Routledge.

## Tim Etchells (1956–)

Tim Etchells is the director of the UK performance company known as Forced Entertainment, which has been described as 'Britain's most brilliant experimental theatre company'. The company was founded in 1984, and is responsible for some of the most challenging theatrical responses to the urban experiences of its audiences, which also include the effects of the mediatization of culture and the issues and problems of contemporary identity. Forced Entertainment owes something to the work of the New York-based Wooster Group, as well as to the work of Pina Bausch. In the years of the company's existence they have produced a series of works which are only unclassifiable in that they reject nearly all the conventional theatre conventions, preferring to attempt, as Peggy Phelan has put it, 'to expose the illusions that prop up the fiction of "the real world"'. The group also makes durational work and work for digital media, galleries and unusual sites. Samples of the work, all of which have texts by Etchells, include *Emmanuelle Enchanted* (1992), *Club of No Regrets* (1993/4), *Hidden J* (1994). In 1995 they produced *Speak Bitterness*, a five-hour piece created for the National Review of Live Art, which used multiple traditions of confessions to produce a set of seamless statements by the line of performers from behind a long table in a brightly lit space. *Quizoola* (1996), another durational piece, involves a 4/5 hour series of quiz questions which the three performers struggle to answer or not, while the audience files in and out during the period of the performance. Forced Entertainment have had work commissioned by festivals and organisations in Europe, as well as making CD-ROM pieces such as *Nightwalks* and *Spin*, with the artist Hugo Glendinning.

Etchells has published books of essays as well as fiction (*Endland Stories*, 1998) and *The Dream Dictionary* (2001). The essay reproduced here is from his collection published in 1999 where he puts forward his theory of writing texts for performance in a collective context, where the text can often be a text *for* something, rather than, as in the traditional theatre world, as a text *about* something. As such it becomes a directory of possibilities for writing for performance in the twenty-first century, where the text may be one part of a total performance whole.

## Compare this article with writings by the following authors in this reader

**Bausch** – a choreographic approach to disrupting expectations
**Brecht and Foreman** – the writer as director
**Kaprow** – for diverse sources and spaces for performance
**LeCompte** – a US-based collective approach to theatre

## Further reading

Etchells, T. and Glendinning, H. (1996) 'A Decade of Forced Entertainment', *Performance Research*, Vol. 1 No. 1.

Harvie, J. (2009) *Theatre and the City*, London: Palgrave Macmillan.

Helmer, J. (2004) *'Not Even a Game Anymore': The Theatre of Forced Entertainment*, Berlin: Alexander Verlag.

Kaye, N. (ed.) (1996) 'Tim Etchells and Richard Lowden', *Art into Theatre*, Amsterdam: Harwood.

Tushingham, D. (ed.) (1996) 'How Long Do You Have to Have Lived Somewhere Before You're Allowed to Lie About It?', *Live Four*, London: Methuen.

http://www.forcedentertainment.com

# Chapter 24

# Karen Finley

## HELLO MOTHER/IT'S MY BODY
### (from *A Certain Level of Denial*)

**HELLO MOTHER**

Hello Mother,
Your son is dying. You knew—no, don't hang up. Your son is dying.

Hello gallery—SoHo—bullshit—
Hello art magazine cover crap,
Hello trendy East Villagers with rich parents—
Your friend, your artist is dying.
Where are you now?
Where are you now?

Hello ambulance,
Can you hear me? Today the I.V. of one of your clients came out and he was bleeding—yeah bleeding—all over, and you could give a shit. And as he was bleeding more and more, this ambulance didn't even know the way to the hospital.

Hello emergency room,
Don't bother helping someone sick. Don't bother helping someone dying. He's a leper. He's going to die anyway.

Hello admitting,
A patient is puking and bleeding in your mauve room.
Hey, there's no one to admit him. There's no one to admit him.

Hello hospital,
There's a patient who needs a wheelchair—but there ain't one.
There's a patient who needs a blanket—but there ain't one.
There's a patient caked in his own blood. Throw him a rag.

Hello society—
No answer.

Hello America—
No answer.

## IT'S MY BODY

LAST NIGHT I heard crying—it was a piercing cry—and I awoke, and in my room were hundreds and hundreds of women. And they were all crying, all weeping, all marching.

I saw the Virgin Mary and she carried a sign that read "PRO-CHOICE." I saw Cleopatra and she wore a T-shirt that read, "VAGINAL PRIDE." I saw Joan of Arc and she wore a button that said, "THE POPE IS SATAN." I saw Josephine Baker and she held a sign that read, "U.S. OUT OF MY UTERUS."

And then I saw my Aunt Mandy and she was screaming. She came up to me and I said, "I'm sorry that you died from cancer of the uterus," and she said, "Child, I died of an illegal abortion at fifty with this damn gag in my throat. When you die like I died, they don't even let you scream. Bled to death, I did. Rats ate my insides out. I was fifty."

Then I saw the ghost of my childhood friend, Pam, who died by her own hands. She just didn't have the money to go to New York City, where abortion was legal in 1973. She didn't have the money. So one day she opened a can of Drano and poured it into her. She thought she could just burn it out. But she was only twelve. She was only twelve.

Let me tell you about children dying. Let me tell you about the sanctity of life. The infant mortality rate in Harlem is higher than it is in some Third World countries.

The Far Right wants women to obey a Patriarchal Disorder. Well we women aren't going back to our only choice is to clean up after men.

Our choice is a woman becoming President. A woman becoming Pope. Whether these male control freaks like it or not, we're going to feminize this planet. Baby, we're going to show them HYSTERIA, we're going to show them OUT OF CONTROL, CRAZY, HELL-BENT, OVER-EMOTIONAL, PMSed, IRRATIONAL WOMEN united in rage to overturn this male control of our lives.

No one is controlling me.

Say it, sister.

NO ONE IS CONTROLLING MY BODY.

We've been raped.

We've been discriminated against.

We've been oppressed.

We've been persecuted.

We've been controlled.

MEN ARE NOT CONTROLLING US ANY LONGER.

And the spirits of women are remembering when men would gag women as they performed their hatchet jobs, and the men would say, "I'll kill you if you scream."

But this time we're screaming.

This time we're screaming.

■  ■  ■

## Source

Finley, K. (2000) *A Different Kind of Intimacy: The Collected Writings of Karen Finley*, New York: Thunder's Mouth Press.

## Karen Finley (1956–)

Karen Finley is a performance artist who creates spoken word performances, installations and public events. She works in film, television and print as well as in live performance spaces and galleries. Born in Chicago and educated at the San Francisco Art Institute where she gained an MFA and honorary PhD, she works as a professor at New York University in the Tisch School and frequently lectures at the Guggenheim Museum, New York.

She was notably one of the NEA Four, four performance artists whose grants from the National Endowment for the Arts were vetoed in 1990 after the process was condemned by Senator Jesse Helms under "decency" issues.

Although she has collaborated with various artists and groups, she works predominantly as a solo artist and is perhaps most well known for her spoken word performances, where she often goes into a trancelike voice and verbally juggles different characters and voices. Her vocal practice often sounds like spirit channelling and possession. Many of her monologues deal with issues of sexual abuse, violence towards women, emotional despair and a sense of loss and disenfranchisement. In dealing with emotional and often "unspeakable" subjects, Finley's work is closely aligned with other politicized female solo performance artists. She has seen her share of international controversy and has been described as America's most controversial artist.

In *A Different Kind of Intimacy*, Finley said that she smeared herself in chocolate to commemorate Tawana Brawley, a young woman who alleged that some police officers raped her and smeared her with faeces.

Her poem *The Black Sheep* is among her best-known works, and has been immortalized on a sculpture in New York City. Her performance texts of vocal recordings are published. In 1994, she released a double-disc set of *A Certain Level of Denial*, a studio version of the performance piece.

She has authored and/or edited six books including *Shock Treatment* (City Lights 1990), *Enough is Enough* (Poseidon, Simon and Schuster 1993), *Living It Up* (Doubleday 1996), *Pooh Unplugged* (Smart Art Press 1999), *A Different Kind Of Intimacy: The Collected Writings of Karen Finley* (Thunder's Mouth Press 2000).

In these two performance text extracts, we see an example of the immediacy and tone of her writing register. She articulates clearly the strength of feeling and despair that is present in the contemporary world. Hearing her voice performing these texts gives the reader a stronger sense of the power of the work beyond the written words.

## Compare this article with writings by the following authors in this reader

**Baker** – for domesticity
**Richter** – for exploratory and performative use of the voice
**Schneemann** – for reference to and use of the explicit body

## Further reading

Finley, K. (1991) *Shock Treatment,* San Francisco: City Lights.
Finley, K. (2006) *George and Martha,* London and New York: Verso.
Harris, G. (1999) *Staging Femininities: Performance and Performativity,* Manchester and New York: Manchester University Press.
http://karenfinley.com/

# Chapter 25

# Richard Foreman

## HOW TO WRITE A PLAY (IN WHICH I AM REALLY TELLING MYSELF HOW, BUT IF YOU ARE THE RIGHT ONE I AM TELLING YOU HOW, TOO)

make a kind of beauty that isn't an
ALTERNATIVE to a certain environment
(beauty, adventure, romance, dream, drama all
take you out of your real world and into their
own in the hope you'll return refreshed, wiser,
more compassionate, etc.)
                    but rather

makes GAPS in the non-beautiful, or look carefully at the structure of
the non-beautiful, whatever it is (and remember that structure is always a
combination of the
THING
and the
PERCEIVING of it)

and see where there are small points, gaps, unarticulated or un-mapped places
within it
(the non-beautiful)
which un-mapped places must be the very places where beauty CAN be
planted in the midst of the heretofore unbeautiful.

Because the mind's PROJECTED beauty (which is the only beauty) . . . can
either find itself in the already beautiful (so agreed upon) or it can MAKE
Conquer new territories.

                But: while in the midst of the heretofore
still un-redeemed 'non-beautiful' the projection of the will-to-beauty can

either be a pure act of will in which there is a pure, willed reversal of values

(which can have great strategic value but creates art that DOES tend to 'wear out' — not, you understand, a negative judgement)

or

our method.

find the heretofore un-mapped, un-notated crevices
in the not-yet-beautiful landscape (which is a
collaboration between perceiving mind and world)
and widen the gaps
and plant the seed in those gaps
and make those gaps flower . . . and the plant
over-runs the entire landscape.

What this amounts to is a DECISION

to view non-beautiful material in such a way that what was foreground is now background . . . and the desired beauty is then projected, as the creative act, into the midst of the heretofore rejected (non-beautiful, un-interesting, cliched, etc.).

---

Delight is delight.

It aims us to whatever it is that delights us.

Can we make a more CONTROLLED use of that energy of 'being-aimed' by willfully choosing to have a certain object be the one which arouses that delight-energy? ANY object?

Of course. That's the task — discover how to be in control, how to CHOOSE.

which object shall provoke the delight phenomenon

(and so increase that per-centage of the world we can say 'yes' to, and thereby gain an inexhaustible fund of 'delight-fuel')

Here's how.

Normally, let us assume we are delighted by a sunset
We are not delighted by a corpse.
But if we place the corpse within a certain composition, let us say — we are then delighted by the composition of which the corpse is a part.

So — while we are still not delighted by a corpse, we can be delighted by something (made or found) of which the corpse is a part.

The task of art is to find what heretofore does not delight us, and make that part of some kind of composition in such a way that delight results.

Now, the composition need not be a composition in the expected sense, that is, need not be something that is defined or defines the artwork itself –

The composition may be any 'context' in which the material is placed. In much art today, for instance, the context-composition is 'the inherited history of Western art.' So that the reason a minimalist gesture such as a Morris black box is 'delightful' is because we understand it as an intelligent next move chosen in the context of an evolving 'game' which has been the game (move and countermove) of Western art.

So in the theatre, which is always behind the times, one must ask 'ah – what can we include in the on-going context composition which heretofore has been de-valued and kept out, etc., etc., and few people in the theatre ask that question and do that thing and so the theatre is rarely art, and when it is it creates problems for itself since its audience is not an audience interested in art but in entertainment.

Which means, its audience is interested in being delighted by what they already know in themselves as delightful. And their response to the attempt to include NEW material in the composition – material which they heretofore have categorized as non-delightful – their response is generally negative because they have never been trained to be composition perceivers rather than object perceivers. When they look at theatre, they use daily-life perceptual modes and so see things, and not patterns and contexts and compositions.

The rallying cry must be – stop making objects that men can worship.

Art shouldn't add new objects to the world to enslave men. It should begin the process of freeing men by calling into doubt the solidity of objects – and laying bare the fact that it is a web of relations that exists, only; that web held taut in each instance by the focal point of consciousness that is each separate individual consciousness.

In my work, I show the traces of one such web. (The assumption herein is not idealism, because the consciousness is a constructed thing also, on a different level subject to the same laws of configuration as the world outside, a collection of trace elements, not a self-sufficient constituting agent: but the relation between consciousness and 'world' is the relation between two intersecting force fields, neither of which is a thing, both of which are a system of relations.)

I show the traces of such web intersections – and by seeing that, you are 'reminded' to tune to your own. Find objects in a sense interchangeable (and, in another sense, poignant for that reason). But most of all. find exhilaration and freedom and creative power, for when you see the web of relatedness of all things – which is in a certain ever-alive relation to a 'your own web' of consciousness – you then are no longer a blind, hypnotized worshiper of 'objects' – but a free man. Capable of self-creation and re-creation in all moments of your life.

Most audiences and critics want to be moved, knocked out. That is a sign of their illness, blindness, need to remain children. Most audiences want a perceivable, nameable content. That is, they want to be able to reduce the experience of the work to a gestalt of some sort that they can carry away from the theatre with them.

That means, they want to feel that they have extracted property, capital, from the investment of time in the experience.

NO! The art experience shouldn't ADD to our baggage, that store of images that weighs us down and limits our clear view to the horizons. The art experience should rather (simply) ELIMINATE what keeps us moored to hypnotizing aspects of reality.

Or better – by showing how reality is always a 'positive' which is but a response to (an extraction from) a 'negative' background, it allows us, in terms of this continual, now revealed polarity, to make contact with the reality that is really-there. Not by social fiat, but by operating at the constituting heart of things.

It is not a matter of getting BEYOND, DEEPER, HIGHER than everyday, normal, agreed on culturally-determined reality, it is a matter of – within the confines of the art experience – allowing ourselves to partake of the 'taste' of a perceptive mode that strategically subverts the very OBVIOUS aspects of the gross and childish conditioned perception used to 'brow beat us' through life. The gross mode of perception that supresses the contradiction at the heart of each consciously posited 'object.'

---

The artist must search for what has never been seen before.
   BUT
Not simply a new 'monster.' Not a new 'that knocks me out like . . . '
(a pyramid, Shakespeare, sex, etc.)
    But
a new
object which once found
is hard to see. Maybe it's not even 'there.'

---

We live in a world of traces. Things leave traces. We must never try to make man believe that what is by definition constituted as a 'trace,' has indeed a different kind of reality – that of 'object.'

The emotion must never come, as it usually does, through our being convinced of the reality of the image or event presented, but only the ecstatic emotion of one's own seeing of things. Delight in one's own energy.

197

NEVER awe or delight in the 'worshipful way' we feel emotion when we are awed or moved by the 'other' which seems like an alien other in which we 'wish' we could partake (all romantic art).

---

## Need for Confrontation

Art += to CONFRONT the object

Kitsch=  atmosphere replaces object
distance between you and object
de-creased by atmosphere
which makes you FEEL
at one with the object
because the atmosphere
is felt to be that exuded
by the object. But then
object and you (feeling)
are one and there is
no ENCOUNTER, and no
seeing. (To play the
subtext, rather than
the object, for instance.)

What is the object?
The encountered object,
encountered in making
the work: the 'real'
chair, body, word,
noise, etc.

The constructed object
end with (art) is the we
STRUCTURE of the
articulating process. The
MAKING A THING BE-
THERE AS ITSELF
(in its web of relations).
Process.

The artist doesn't explain, analyze the object . . . but he sets it up so that one CONFRONTS in the realist fashion it's BEING-THERE which is a confrontation to your own BEING-THERE.

PARADOX
The way to confront the object is to allow it its own life — let it grow its own shoots in directions that do not re-inforce it's being-in-life for use as a tool, but that suggests a compositional scheme not centered on useful human expectations. So, let the chair that is for sitting have a string run from it to an orange, because if chair was just 'chair for sitting' we would not 'confront' as we not-confront in kitsch because we are too close to the chair, its meaning is too much OUR meaning; but now chair-connected-to-orange is an 'alien' chair that we must CONFRONT.

(To reveal an object or act, gesture, emotion, idea, sound.
To make it seizable
To speak its name you must
make it part of a system not
its own. Involve it compositionally with
another realm, which is YOUR realm of pattern
making isomorphic with your
mind-process. THEN there is confrontation.)

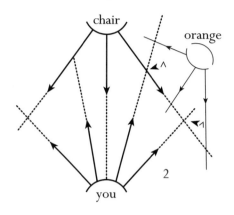

KITSCH
(and sleep) as
the moment of
contact between
you and object
is one dimensional
and you are
in a state of
identification
(hypnotized by)
with that face
of itself the
object presents
to you.

ART
(and awakedness)
        as
the moment of
contact between
you and object
is multifaceted and
often 'distant' (point A)
from the object.

        also
in 2 (as opposed to 1)
your mind-pattern-
process is being as-it-is:
and THAT structure
inter-acts with the
object structure as-it-is.

In 1 the mind forgets
its own working and there
is no real meeting, only
a 1-dimensional (1 'presented'

face to another) moment of
'official' (cliched)
  'something'
that is too mindless: i.e. one dimensional
(lacking points 'A' of 2)
to be a real encounter.

*Diagram 2 explains, once and for all, all of my plays!*

---

The message must be 'To choose either turbulence or serenity is an error. To choose either knowing or doing is an error.' So . . . in the play . . . inject disruption into knowing, and order into passion.

---

The play is a lecture in which you don't say 'This is so . . . ' but rather . . . 'This occurs to me and it occurs to me that the reason it occurs to me is this act, which occurs to me,' and so on and so on, deeper and deeper.

---

My message is 'filling the space with the idea.' Free play within the idea. Ability to treat the 'field' of the idea as an area for work and discovery. Idea as a field . . . in which something that is not idea (but more physical, sensual, ecstatic) can emerge.

---

I write to make life handle-able.

The deflection inherent in time. Space —
one makes art to be able to decide what goes into you
                     and what goes out of you.
    To be in control of what goes into you and out
    of you is why you decide to make your own art.
    Of course . . . as it goes in and out, space and time
    give it an uncontrollable 'twist.'

---

Lived experience is a certain kind of focus. You focus on an aimed-at while living, and because you are focused on that, you don't see your own gestures, Art: is trying to see your own gestures.

My gesture has always been to pull away, to change what came into me, to make something BETTER, that could then go into me instead of the thing that did go into me. Hence, to find a way to make better FOOD for myself than was provided by others. My art then (one's art) is a way of being-in-the-world so that the INPUT is the best possible input . . . into me.

Journalism is trying to imitate life. Art is an amplification of the effects encountered in trying to make art.

---

Art: a machine to effect input. To provide awakening, energy-giving discontinuities. To fight entropy. Art is NOT comment on life. It is fighting the entropy of life-that-seeks equilibrium, that seeks-not-stress, which would lead (as life does) to death. (Inject quantum shocks, discontinuities, to keep twisting us away from sleep, death, into what is 'artificially' sustained . . . AWAKENED LIFE, CONSCIOUSNESS!

---

Form in art – form isn't a container (of content) but rather
   a rule for generating a possible 'next move.'
         That's where the subject is (in that next move, dictated or made pos-
         sible by the form). The commonly-thought-of content or subject is the
         pretext to set a process in operation, and that process is the real subject.
The text is me
It grows like I grow
It extends itself, falls, stumbles over . . . something.
   Recovers. It projects itself as it will. Encounters resistance of various sorts,
   but those resistances turn out to be steps affording a new advance
stretch   extension   twist
stage it: Try to make the compositional aspects be
in relief. The **structure** as it were. Not the structure
in time, but the structure of the moment.
   (time doesn't exist. It's all **now**
   There's memory-now-future.
   Now doesn't exist
   It's a pivot point
   Make things structured in that pivot point.
   (I.E. frame now, frame not-there)
People who work in time are making things for memory
   Are not clear about here and now
      Proper analysis here & now
         What am I doing now
Man is future-oriented, but life is collision in now between project and what resists it
So: each movement show what interferes with, contradicts, projects – from other levels. Not just conflict of people. What contradicts the 'play' itself and its mode-of-being-present.

---

That privileged object which is the ONE object that must be studied . . . (so that man can study what it is most important he study) . . . that object is not yet 'available.' Not yet there.

In making a play I am trying to make that important object that is not yet there.

■　■　■

## Source

Foreman, R. (1985) 'How to Write a Play', in *Reverberation Machines*, New York: Station Hill.

## Richard Foreman (1937–)

The long-term artistic director of his own theatre, the Ontological-Hysteric Theater, founded in New York in 1968, Foreman is one of the most long-serving examples of the American avant-garde of the 1960s, with links to the worlds of John Cage and Merce Cunningham on the one hand, and to the Wooster Group on the other. From 1979 to 1985 a branch of his theatre was established in Paris and funded by the French government. The theatre is currently located in New York's East Village in St Mark's Church, where Foreman rehearses and produces a newly devised and written play each year, performing for 16 weeks each winter. In addition Foreman directs major productions of operas, classical plays, and contemporary work around the world. Foreman's method of writing his plays consists of 'writing snatches of dialogue, and then in rehearsal distributing individual lines to individual performers'. His writing defies narrative norms and character, instead his plays are the outcome of a process in which the circulation of verbal and psychological energies can be recombined in many different patterns. The words therefore become an aspect of the scenography of the final product, while Foreman is an example of a theatre artist who uses a collection of theatre elements to produce a total scenographic whole. In this respect he has links with artists such as Tadeusz Kantor, Gordon Craig, Robert Wilson, and of course John Cage, whose theatre work similarly used the word as but one scenographic element. Recent works have included *Paradise Hotel (Hotel Fuck)* (1998), which toured to Europe, *Bad Boy Nietzsche* (2000), and *Now that Communism is Dead* (2001), which played in New York and in Europe. Many of the scenic and prop elements in Foreman's productions come from second-hand shops: there is a deliberate attempt to subvert the idea of comfortable, well-heeled theatre. There are also the characteristic strings which criss-cross the stage and auditorium, disrupting the audience view so that there is no illusion but a theatrical illusion to face the audience. Like Brecht's audience we are never allowed to forget that we are in a theatre and that what is being presented is the workings of an artist's mind made three-dimensional. Spectators have to work at a Foreman production as they might have to work at an exhibition of contemporary art. In this essay he outlines some of his strategies.

## Compare this article with writings by the following authors in this reader

**Brecht** – an earlier attempt to subvert audiences
**Craig** – the precursor of visual theatre
**Kantor** – a Polish visual artist/theatre maker
**LeCompte** – another New York-based theatre artist
**Wilson** – a primarily visual director

## Further reading

Cole, S.L. (1992) *Directors in Rehearsal*, London: Routledge.
Davy, K. (1981) *Richard Foreman and the Ontological Hysteric Theatre*, Ann Arbor, Mich.: UMI Research Press.
Foreman, R. (2013) *Manifestos and Essays*, New York: Theatre Communications Group.
Kaye, N. (1994) *Postmodernism and Performance*, London: Macmillan.
Rabkin, G. (1999) *The Theatre of Richard Foreman*, New York: Johns Hopkins Press.
Rabkin, G. (ed.) (1999) *Richard Foreman*, Baltimore: Johns Hopkins University Press.
http://www.ontological.com

# Philip Glass

## NOTES ON *EINSTEIN ON THE BEACH*

## Part 1

The music for *Einstein on the Beach* was written in the spring, summer and fall of 1975. Bob Wilson and I worked directly from a series of his drawings which eventually formed the designs for the sets. Prior to that period, we had reached agreement on the general thematic content, the overall length, its divisions into 4 acts, 9 scenes and 5 connecting 'knee plays.' We also determined the makeup of the company – 4 principal actors, 12 singers, doubling when possible as dancers and actors, a solo violinist, and the amplified ensemble of keyboards, winds and voices with which my music is usually associated.

The three main recurring visual themes of the opera (Train/Trial/Field with Spaceship) are linked to three main musical themes. The overall thematic divisions of the opera are as follows:

KNEE PLAY 1 (Chorus and electric organ)
 Act I  Scene 1 TRAIN (ensemble with solo voice and chorus
          joining at the end)
      Scene 2 TRIAL (chorus, violin, electric organ and flutes)

KNEE PLAY 2 (Violin solo)
 Act II  Scene 1 DANCE 1 – Field with Spaceship (ensemble with
          solo voice/dancers)
      Scene 2 NIGHT TRAIN (2 voices, chorus and small ensemble)

KNEE PLAY 3 (Chorus *a capella*)
 Act III Scene 1 TRIAL/PRISON (chorus and electric organ,
          ensemble at the end)
      Scene 2 DANCE 2 – Field with Spaceship (6 voices, violin,
          electric organ)

KNEE PLAY 4 (Chorus and violin)
   Act IV   Scene 1   BUILDING/TRAIN (chorus and
                             ensemble)
           Scene 2   BED (solo electric organ and voice)
           Scene 3   SPACESHIP (chorus and ensemble)

KNEE PLAY 5 (Women's chorus, violin and electric organ)

The most important musical material appears in the knee plays and features the violin. Dramatically speaking, the violinist (dressed as Einstein, as are the performers on stage) appears as a soloist as well as a character in the opera. His playing position – midway between the orchestra and the stage performers – offers a clue to his role. He is seen then, perhaps as Einstein himself, or simply as a witness to the stage events; but, in any case, as a musical touchstone to the work as a whole.

It might be useful to delineate some of the visual/musical transformation of the material which makes up the opera:

The image of the train appears three times – first in Act I, Scene 1, then in Act II, Scene 2 (as the Night Train), and finally in Act IV, Scene 1, where it appears in the same perspective as the Night Train, but this time transformed into a building. The music for the first train is in three parts, or 'themes.' The first theme (based on the super-imposition of two shifting rhythmic patterns, one changing and one fixed) makes up most of the music of this scene.

The second appearance of the train image, the Night Train, is a reworking of the first theme, this time with a larger complement of voices. The music for the Building is a development of the second theme, recognizable by its highly accented rhythmic profile, in which the repeated figures form simple arithmetic progressions.

The third theme is a rhythmic expansion of a traditional cadential formula. This 'cadence' theme forms the principal material of the opera, being used for the 2nd, 3rd and 4th Knee Plays, as well as almost the entire music for Act IV, Scene 3, the Spaceship.

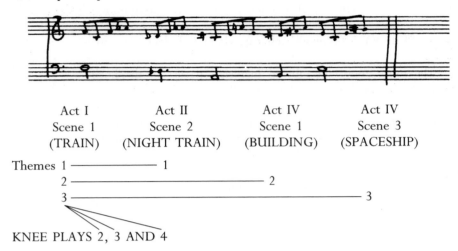

| Act I | Act II | Act IV | Act IV |
|---|---|---|---|
| Scene 1 | Scene 2 | Scene 1 | Scene 3 |
| (TRAIN) | (NIGHT TRAIN) | (BUILDING) | (SPACESHIP) |

Themes 1 ——————— 1
       2 ———————————————— 2
       3 ———————————————————— 3

KNEE PLAYS 2, 3 AND 4

The second major visual image, the Trial, also appears three times in the opera – first in Act I, Scene 2, then in Act III, Scene 1 where, after the first few minutes, the stage divides, becoming half-trial/half-prison, and finally in Act IV, Scene 2, where the bed which has been in the center of the trial, and in half of the trial/prison, now occupies the entire stage. Here again the trial music is in three parts, or 'themes.' After the opening of the first trial we hear the violin, accompanied by men's voices, playing a simple, harmonically stable rhythmic pattern which, through an additive process, slowly expands and contracts.

Later, the women's voices join in, producing a somewhat thicker texture. Toward the end of this scene, during the judge's speech, the second theme is heard, more chordal in nature, for solo electric organ.

The Trial/Prison begins musically in the same way as the first Trial. After the stage divides, the third theme is heard — numbers sung by the men and women in the jury box and lightly accompanied by harmonically shifting arpeggios on electric organ. Toward the end of the scene, the witness remaining alone on the stage speaks and, as the scenery is removed, the second (chordal) theme appears — this time in soprano saxophone and bass clarinet.

The Bed scene begins with a cadenza for electric organ. As the bed lifts to a vertical position and flies upwards, we hear the first theme again. Then, for the last time, the second (chordal) theme is heard, now accompanied by a solo singing voice.

| Act I, Scene 2 | Act III, Scene 1 | Act IV, Scene 2 |
|:---:|:---:|:---:|
| (TRIAL) | (TRIAL/PRISON) | (BED) |
| Theme 1 | 1 | 1 |
| | Theme 3 | |
| Theme 2 | 2 | 2 |

The first two appearances of the Field image are given over to dance and can be heard as similar reflections of the same musical material. For me they are two pillars equidistant from either end of the opera, sharing only superficial features with the musical content of the other scenes. During the first dance in Act II, Scene 1, a spaceship is seen in the distance. In the second dance, Act III, Scene 2, the spaceship appears closer. The third appearance of the Field, Act IV, Scene 3 takes place inside the spaceship and, as indicated earlier, the music comes from the third theme of the train music.

The Knee Plays are the short connecting pieces which appear throughout the work much as prelude, interludes and postlude. Taken together, they form a play in themselves. They can also be seen as the seeds which flower and take form in the larger scenes. In the first four Knee Plays, two characters are seen in a room, sitting at two tables, then sitting side-by-side in two chairs, next standing together in front of a large control board and then lying on top of two large glass tables. In the final knee play, the last moment of the opera, they are seen sitting on a bench waiting for a bus.

The musical structure of the Knee Plays can be seen in the following diagram:

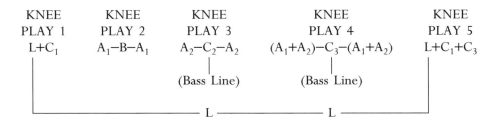

207

The 2nd, 3rd and 4th Knee Plays share the same form — first theme, second theme and return to first theme. The 'cadence' theme of the first train (Act I, Scene 1) makes up the first theme in all of these Knee Plays, either expressed as violin arpeggios ($A_1$), in a chorale setting for voices ($A_2$), or, in the 4th Knee Play, as a combination of the two ($A_1 + A_2$). The middle theme (B) of the 2nd Knee Play, based on simple scale passages, reappears during the second dance and in the middle section of the Spaceship music. The middle themes of the 3rd Knee Play ($C_2$) and the 4th Knee Play ($C_3$) are different arrangements of the same material, easily recognizable by its highly lyrical character.

The root movement (implied bass line) of this material is A-G-C. This becomes, in the pedal of an electric organ, the opening descending bass line (L) of the 1st Knee Play.

After a very extended beginning, during which the audience enters, the first vocal setting ($C_1$) of these harmonies appears. The descending bass line (L) reappears for the 5th Knee Play, joined shortly thereafter by women's voices singing the vocal music of the 1st Knee Play ($C_1$), and then by the violin, playing the middle theme of the 4th Knee Play ($C_3$).

The vocal texts used throughout the opera are based on numbers and solfege ('do, re, mi . . .') syllables. When numbers are used, they represent the rhythmic structure of the music. When solfege is used, the syllables represent the pitch structure of the music. In either case, the text is not secondary or supplementary, but is a description of the music itself.

To conclude this part of the notes, one might say that, in a general way, the opera begins with a 19th Century train and ends with a 20th Century spaceship. Events occur en route — trials, prison, dances — and throughout, the continuity of the Knee Plays. A number of principal characters appear and reappear in different combinations, often carrying with them an identifying gesture. The violinist, one of the Einsteins of the opera, remains (even during the final scene, the Spaceship, when the entire company is on stage) seated apart, a witness.

## Part 2

'Einstein on the Beach' is part of an ongoing musical project begun with 'Another Look at Harmony' in the spring of 1975. This, in turn, is based on 'Music in 12 Parts' (completed 1974) which developed a vocabulary of techniques (additive processes, cyclic structure and combinations of the two) to apply to problems of rhythmic structure. 'Another Look at Harmony' turns to problems of harmonic structure or, more accurately, structural harmony – new solutions to problems of harmonic usage, where the evolution of material can become the basis of an overall formal structure intrinsic to the music itself (and without the harmonic language giving up its moment-to-moment content and 'flavor').

My main approach throughout has been to link harmonic structure directly to rhythmic structure, using the latter as a base. In doing so, easily perceptible 'root movement' (chords or 'changes') was chosen in order that the clarity of this relationship could be easily heard. Melodic material is for the most part a function, or result, of the harmony, as is true in earlier periods of Western music. However, it is clear that some of the priorities of Western music (harmony/melody first, then rhythm) have been reversed. Here we have rhythmic structure first, then harmony/melody. The result has been a reintegration of rhythm, harmony and melody into an idiom which is, hopefully, accessible to a general public, although, admittedly, somewhat unusual at first hearing.

Parts 1 and 2 of 'Another Look at Harmony' became the basis of Act I, Scene 1 (Train) and Act II, Scene 1 (Field) of the opera and were the starting points from which additional material and devices were developed.

The musical material of the opera is made up of series of 5 chords, 4 chords, 3 chords, 2 chords and 1 chord. Following is a brief description of each series and the techniques relevant to its use.

The most prominent 'theme' of the opera is made from the following progression of 5 chords:

$$
\begin{array}{c}
\text{key of f} \\
\text{f} - \text{D}^{\flat} - \text{B}^{\flat\flat} \\
\text{(i)} \quad \text{(VI)} \quad \text{(IV}^{\flat}\text{)}
\end{array}
$$

$$
\begin{array}{c}
\text{A} - \text{B} - \text{E} \\
\text{(IV)} \quad \text{(V)} \quad \text{(I)} \\
\text{key of E}
\end{array}
$$

This combines both a familiar cadence and a modulation in one formula. What makes the formula distinctive and even useful is, of course, the way in which the IV$^{\flat}$ (B$^{\flat\flat}$) becomes IV (A) of the new key, thereby making the phrase resolve a half-step lower. This, in turn, provides the leading tone for the original i (f). As it is a formula which invites repetition, it is particularly suited to my kind of musical thinking. It can be heard in the opera as the third theme of the Train music (Act I, Scene 1,) with ensemble and chorus, then in arpeggio form as a violin solo in Knee Play 2, next in chorale form for chorus *a capella* in Knee Play 3, then in both arpeggio form and chorale form in Knee Play 4, and finally combining all the previous arrangements in the Spaceship (Act IV, Scene 3).

The progression of 4 chords appears at the end of the Trial (Act I; Scene 2), Trial/Prison (Act III, Scene 1) and Bed (Act IV, Scene 2). It is a rhythmic expansion of the 4 chords:

$$f - E^b - C - D$$

As indicated, the f and C harmonies are 'paired' rhythmically, as are the $E^b$ and D harmonies. Beginning with a simple pattern of eighth notes,

$$(f)(E^b)(C)(D)$$
$$4 - 3 - 4 - 3,$$

the phrase gradually expands, each new phrase being played twice, until quite a long and elaborate final figure is produced. An example of the rhythmic/harmonic expansion in its early stage is as follows:

|      | (f)       | ($E^b$)   | (C)       | (D)       |
|------|-----------|-----------|-----------|-----------|
| (1)  | 4         | 3         | 4         | 3         |
| (2)  | (4+3)     | 4         | (4+3)     | (4)       |
| (3)  | (4+3)     | (4+3)     | (4+3)     | (4+3)     |
| (4)  | (4+3+2)   | (4+3)     | (4+3+2)   | (4+3)     |

etc.

The material involving the series of 3 chords makes up the music of the two dance sections (Act II, Scene 1 and Act III, Scene 2). The procedure here is quite different, setting three key centers (A, $e^7$ and $B^b$) 'around' a central key of d. At the beginning, each of the key centers is associated with its own meter and all are played over a common rhythmic pattern of 6/8. (This, incidentally, creates a secondary polymetric 'flavor' throughout the music.) The key of A appears in dotted quarters, $e^7$ in eighth notes (a substitute key of $C^7$ appears later) and $B^b$ in half notes. After an excursion into one of these key centers the music returns, always, to the central key of d. As the music develops, the key centers begin to exchange metrical character. Later, these form complex accumulations of meters in the same key before returning to the central key, d. This accumulative process continues until the original key/meter associations are lost in an overall texture of harmonies and meters.

The sequence of two chords is found in the Trial/Prison music. The two harmonies, $a^7$ and $g^7$, are first heard as two alternating arpeggiated figures in 6/8 (played on electric organ with voices chanting numbers representing the rhythmic patterns). The music develops as each 'half' of the figure undergoes a process of rhythmic fragmentation (wherein small increments of the original figure are added to itself). At first the process occurs equally in both halves (represented by the two harmonies) of the figure, thereby maintaining an exact overall symmetry. Gradually, the two halves begin to differ rhythmically, reaching a point where they are completely different and the figure is asymmetrical. At this point two successive asymmetrical figures in the music begin to act as mirror images of each other, thereby seeming to form one doubly-long symmetrical pattern.

The music based on one chord is first heard in the Trial (Act I, Scene 2). The violin, playing a figure in 7/8, outlines an $a^7$ harmony. A simple additive process begins as each successive figure adds a single eighth note, thereby changing its overall rhythmic character and causing the figure to gradually expand. The figure later contracts when the process is reversed, returning finally to its original form. The same process is heard later at the beginning of the Trial/Prison (Act III, Scene 1) and finally in the Bed (Act IV, Scene 2).

■　■　■

## Source

Glass, P. (1976) 'Notes on *Einstein on the Beach*', booklet accompanying *Einstein on the Beach*, New York: CBS: 9–11.

## Philip Glass (1937–)

Composer; studied at the University of Chicago and at the Juilliard School, New York. He worked with Ravi Shankar (Paris 1965) and then travelled to India (1965–66), where he developed an interest in Indian music; at the same time, he began composing 'minimalist' works. He gave his first concert in 1967, which was followed by the formation of the Philip Glass Ensemble, in 1968. His work was first recorded in 1971, and his first opera performed in 1976.

Glass's work has been noted for its contribution to 'minimalism', especially his compositions of the period 1965–75, including *Music in 12 Parts* (1971–74). His subsequent work has included many collaborations with theatre devisers, choreographers and film makers. He worked with Robert Wilson and Lucinda Childs on *Einstein on the Beach* (1976) and with Wilson again on *Satyagraha* (1980), *Akhnaten* (1984) and *CIVIL warS* (1984). He collaborated again with Childs, *Dance nos. 1–5* (1979), and with Jerome Robbins, *Glass Pieces* (1983). His film music includes *North Star* (1977) for *North Star: Mark di Suvero* and the soundtrack for Godfrey Reggio's *Koyaanisqatsi* (1983).

The extract here includes Glass's notes for the New York production of *Einstein on the Beach*. The work was premièred at Avignon, France, on 25 July 1976. Its New York première (21 November 1976), at the Metropolitan Opera, helped make Glass famous. The opera also established many precedents for its staging, choreography and manner of collaboration. The notes are of particular interest in the way they detail how the composer has approached the music for a collaborative theatre piece. They are clearly written with the totality of the performance in mind.

## Compare this article with writings by the following authors in this reader

**Brown** – a dancer working with concerns for structure and processes
**Cage** – a different approach to twentieth-century composition
**Eisler** – another theatre composer
**Rainer** – comparison with her ideas of minimalism
**Wilson** – a theatre collaborator

## Further reading and listening

Glass, P. (1977) *North Star*, Virgin.
Glass, P. (1983) *Glassworks*, CBS.
Jones, R.T. (ed.) (1988) *Opera on the Beach: Philip Glass on His New World of Music Theatre*, London: Faber.
Maycock, R. (2002) *Glass: A portrait*, London: Sanctuary Publishing Ltd.
Potter, K. (2002) *Four Musical Minimalists*, Cambridge University Press.
http://www.philipglass.com

# Chapter 27

# RoseLee Goldberg

## PERFORMANCE ART FROM FUTURISM TO THE PRESENT

**P**ERFORMANCE became accepted as a medium of artistic expression in its own right in the 1970s. At that time, conceptual art – which insisted on an art of ideas over product, and on an art that could not be bought and sold – was in its heyday and performance was often a demonstration, or an execution, of those ideas. Performance thus became the most tangible art form of the period. Art spaces devoted to performance sprang up in the major international art centres, museums sponsored festivals, art colleges introduced performance courses, and specialist magazines appeared.

It was during that period that this first history of performance was published (1979), demonstrating that there was a long tradition of artists turning to live performance as one means among many of expressing their ideas, and that such events had played an important part in the history of art. It is interesting that performance, until that time, had been consistently left out in the process of evaluating artistic development, especially in the modern period, more on account of the difficulty of placing it in the history of art than of any deliberate omission.

The extent and richness of this history made the question of omission an even more insistent one. For artists did not merely use performance as a means to attract publicity to themselves. Performance has been considered as a way of bringing to life the many formal and conceptual ideas on which the making of art is based. Live gestures have constantly been used as a weapon against the conventions of established art.

Such a radical stance has made performance a catalyst in the history of twentieth-century art; whenever a certain school, be it Cubism, Minimalism or conceptual art, seemed to have reached an impasse, artists have turned to performance as a way of breaking down categories and indicating new directions. Moreover, within the history of the avant garde — meaning those artists who led the field in breaking with each successive tradition — performance in the twentieth century has been at the forefront of such an activity: an avant avant garde. Despite the fact that most of what is written today about the work of the Futurists, Constructivists, Dadaists and Surrealists continues to concentrate on the art objects produced by each period, it was more often than not the case that these movements found their roots and attempted to resolve problematic issues in performance. When the members of such groups were still in their twenties or early thirties, it was in performance that they tested their ideas, only later expressing them in objects. Most of the original Zurich Dadaists, for example, were poets, cabaret artistes and performers who, before actually creating Dada objects themselves, exhibited works from immediately preceding movements, such as the Expressionists. Similarly, most of the Parisian Dadaists and Surrealists were poets, writers and agitators before they made Surrealist objects and paintings. Breton's text *Surrealism and Painting* (1928) was a belated attempt to find a painterly outlet for the Surrealist idea, and as such it continued to raise the question: 'What is Surrealist painting?' for some years after its publication. For was it not Breton who, four years earlier, had stated that the ultimate Surrealist *acte gratuit* would be to fire a revolver at random into a crowd on the street?

Performance manifestos, from the Futurists to the present, have been the expression of dissidents who have attempted to find other means to evaluate art experience in everyday life. Performance has been a way of appealing directly to a large public, as well as shocking audiences into reassessing their own notions of art and its relation to culture. Conversely, public interest in the medium, especially in the 1980s, stems from an apparent desire of that public to gain access to the art world, to be a spectator of its ritual and its distinct community, and to be surprised by the unexpected, always unorthodox presentations that the artists devise. The work may be presented solo or with a group, with lighting, music or visuals made by the performance artist him or herself, or in collaboration, and performed in places ranging from an art gallery or museum to an 'alternative space', a theatre, café, bar or street corner. Unlike theatre, the performer *is* the artist, seldom a character like an actor, and the content rarely follows a traditional plot or narrative. The performance might be a series of intimate gestures or large-scale visual theatre, lasting from a few minutes to many hours; it might be performed only once or repeated several times, with or without a prepared script, spontaneously improvised, or rehearsed over many months.

Whether tribal ritual, medieval passion play, Renaissance spectacle or the 'soirées' arranged by artists in the 1920s in their Paris studios, performance has provided a presence for the artist in society. This presence, depending on the nature of the performance, can be esoteric, shamanistic, instructive, provocative or entertaining. Renaissance examples even show the artist in the role of creator and director of public spectacles, fantastic triumphal parades that often required the construction of elaborate temporary architecture, or allegorical events that utilized the multi-media abilities attributed to Renaissance Man. A mock naval battle, designed by Polidoro da Caravaggio in 1589, took place in the specially flooded courtyard of the Pitti Palace in Florence; Leonardo da Vinci dressed his performers as planets and had them recite verses about the Golden Age in a pageant entitled *Paradiso* (1490); and the Baroque artist Gian Lorenzo Bernini staged spectacles for which he wrote scripts, designed scenes and costumes, built architectural elements and even constructed realistic flood scenes, as in *L'Inondazione* ('The Inundation of the Tiber', 1638).

The history of performance art in the twentieth century is the history of a permissive, open-ended medium with endless variables, executed by artists impatient with the limitations of more established art forms, and determined to take their art directly to the public. For this reason its base has always been anarchic. By its very nature, performance defies precise or easy definition beyond the simple declaration that it is live art by artists. Any stricter definition would immediately negate the possibility of performance itself. For it draws freely on any number of disciplines and media – literature, poetry, theatre, music, dance, architecture and painting, as well as video, film, slides and narrative – for material, deploying them in any combination. Indeed, no other artistic form of expression has such a boundless manifesto, since each performer makes his or her own definition in the very process and manner of execution.

This book is a record of those artists who use performance in trying to live, and who create work which takes life as its subject. It is also a record of the effort to assimilate more and more the realm of play and pleasure in an art which observes less and less the traditional limitations of making art objects, so that in the end the artist can take delight in almost any activity. It is, finally, about the desire of many artists to make art that functions outside the confines of museums and galleries.

In tracing an untold story, this first history inevitably works itself free of its material, because that material continues to raise questions about the very nature of art. It does not pretend to be a record of every performer in the twentieth century; rather, it pursues the development of a sensibility. The goal of this book is to raise questions and to gain new insights. It can only hint at life off the pages.

■　■　■

## Source

Goldberg, R. (1979, 1988) 'Foreword', *Performance Art from Futurism to the Present*, London: Thames & Hudson: 7–9. First published in 1979 as *Performance: Live Art 1909 to the Present.*

## RoseLee Goldberg

Performance historian and writer on art. She graduated from the Courtauld Institute, London, and became Director of the Royal College of Art Gallery, London, and then Curator of the Kitchen Centre for Video, Music, and Performance, New York. She has published in both the UK and the US.

Goldberg's first edition of *Performance* in 1979 was a groundbreaking history of twentieth-century 'live art' that established a precedent for later histories. In it she says that 'performance has only recently become accepted as a medium of artistic expression in its own right' (1979: 6). By the time the second edition was published she could confidently say that it 'became accepted. ... in the 1970s'. Among the reasons for this acceptance was precisely her popularisation of the idea.

Both editions of her history cover the twentieth century. Both editions, despite different titles, identify the first futurist manifesto of 20 February 1909 as a starting point. The first concludes with Robert Wilson and *Einstein on the Beach*. The second completely rewrites the recent period as 'the art of ideas and the media generation' and includes not only Wilson but also Anderson, Bausch and Butoh.

Goldberg has since published (1998) *Performance: Live Art Since the 60s*. Here she gives a wide ranging and comprehensive illustrated account of performance forms whose scope and examples have consistencies with the account in this reader. She includes, for instance, Abramovic, Anderson, Bausch, Brown, Cage, Cunningham, Etchells, Foreman, Kaprow, Lepage, Rainer, Stelarc and Wilson.

Her most recent work is on *Laurie Anderson* (2001).

## Compare this article with writings by the following authors in this reader

**Anderson** – on performance
**Barba, Brown, Duncan, Rainer and Schlemmer** – the performer as artist
**Marinetti** – the historical futurist viewpoint on performance art
**Richter** – the founding of Dada
**Schechner** – a theatre/performance point of view

## Further reading

Goldberg, R. (1990) *High and Low: Modern Art and Popular Culture*, New York: Museum of Modern Art.

Goldberg, R. (1998) *Performance: Live Art Since the 60s*, London: Thames and Hudson.

Goldberg, R. and Anderson, L. (2001) *Laurie Anderson*, New York: Harry N. Abrams Publishers.

# Chapter 28

# Guillermo Gómez-Peña

## THE ART OF CAMOUFLAGE
## (Performing in extremely
## unusual contexts)

*The following text chronicles four collaborative performance projects which took place in unusual contexts: cable TV, a Natural History museum, malls and an opera house. Each of these contexts presented particular challenges to me and my collaborators, and demanded that we adopt different tactics and strategies. These otherwise highly diverse projects are unified primarily by a goal of destabilizing and subverting problematic notions of "racial" and cultural authenticity. I am well aware that my wonderful collaborators would probably construct very different accounts of these experiences, and I deeply respect their diverse experiences and interpretation of events, but the narratives I present here are as "true" as memory allows.*

## 1 Information Super-highway "bandits"
### Performing for Cable TV

On Thanksgiving Day, 1994, the evening news of over 3.5 million American households was suddenly interrupted by two "cyber-Aztec TV pirates," transmitting their bizarre views on American culture and identity direct from their underground vato-bunker, somewhere between New York, Miami and Los Angeles. In actuality, what the viewers were watching was an experiment in interactive television via satellite. Roberto Sifuentes and I had teamed with filmmakers Adrienne Jenik, Philip Djwa and Branda Miller from Eye-Ear Studio at Rennselear Polytechnic, New York

State, to broadcast a simulacrum of a pirate TV intervention to hundreds of cable television stations across the US. Our amazing publicist had managed to persuade over 400 program directors from all over the country to advertise the time slot under a fictional title. Initially, as far as the viewers were concerned, what they were witnessing was a "true" pirate TV intervention, though they slowly became aware of the artifice behind our performance strategies.

The style of the broadcast was influenced by MTV, with five hand-held cameras in constant motion. The content was a unique blend of radical politics, autobiographical material, "Spanish lessons for xenophobic Americans," and out-rageous parodies of traditional TV. Roberto and I spoke in English, Spanglish, Franglais, and an invented "Nahuatl." During the broadcast, we demonstrated a "Chicano virtual reality machine" by means of which the viewer could (in the context of the fiction) request "instant visualization of personal and historical memories;" these were in fact pre-produced segments utilizing home movie footage and videos from past performances. The broadcast also featured a "Chicano virtual reality bandana," that would allow (Anglo) users to vicariously experience racism. We also received "live" reports from writer Ruben Martinez via PictureTel (video telephone) from the Electronic Cafe in Santa Monica. Footage of other types of broadcasting intercut with our performance video were meant to suggest to the viewer that the "legitimate" broadcasters were attempting to regain the airwaves, but we ultimately managed to maintain control.

For an hour and a half, the "TV pirates" invited perplexed viewers to call in and respond to the broadcast. We encouraged them to be intelligent, poetical, and performative in their responses. The performance was also transmitted over computer networks via "M-Bone," and those watching in cyberspace could interact with us (and each other) by posting images and written comments. We received dozens of phone calls and computer messages, and probably broke many FCC rules.

Roberto and I were scared shitless of the possible legal repercussions of our TV experiment. For weeks after the event, we waited in dread for the arrival of a mythical FCC inspector in a trenchcoat. But instead of the scary repercussions we expected, it turned out that the experiment was so successful and "hip" that many cable stations who originally refused to go along with our fictitious premise decided to air the broadcast a few months later. When this happened, we were flattered, but uneasy. What did it mean to re-broadcast a supposed pirate TV intervention that was a simulacrum in the first place? We became obsessed with this dilemma. Our unexpected success could mean two entirely different things: either we had managed to find "a crack in the system" and accidentally kicked ass, or the system was completely immune to radical content, and only concerned with the high production value and aesthetic hipness of the project. If this was the case, we asked ourselves, wasn't this the ultimate paradox of contemporary "radical" performance? Our perplexity continued to increase. After the national re-broadcast of *Naftazteca: Cyber-TV for the year 2000 AD*, a one-hour, edited version of the project won first prize in the category of "best experimental video" at the Guadalupe Film Festival in San Antonio. At that point, I could only conclude that

American culture has always had a place for the anti-hero, the accepted iconoclast, and that nowadays perhaps some performance artists occupy that place.

## 2 "The Shame-man meets El Mexican't at the Smithsonian Motel and Golf Course." Performing in Museums of Natural History

Native American performance artist James Luna and I have known each other since the mid 1990s. Our work is stylistically very different; James practices an aesthetic of simplicity, whereas (according to critics) the style of my performance work is "excessive" and "neo-baroque." But we share similar political and theoretical concerns: we both theorize our own artistic practice; we are both critical of the way indigenous and ethnic identities are portrayed by mainstream cultural institutions and commodified by pop culture, tourism and self-realization movements; and we both utilize melancholic humor and tactics of "reverse anthropology" as strategies for subverting dominant cultural projections and representations of Mexicans and Native peoples.

My friendship and conceptual kinship with James has engendered many projects. From 1993 to 1996, he and I engaged in one collaborative project per year under the title "The Shame-man meets El Mexican't at [name of the host organization]." One project in particular stands out for me . . .

### From my performance diaries

"It's Friday morning. Luna and I share a diorama space at the Smithsonian's Natural History Museum. We are inside an ethnographic prison cell. I sit on a toilet costumed as a mariachi in a straitjacket with a sign around my neck that reads 'There used to be a Mexican inside this body' I attempt unsuccessfully to get rid of my straitjacket in order to 'perform' ('entertain' or 'educate' my audience). A Mexican waltz mixed with rap contributes to the pathos of my tableau. Meanwhile, James paces back and forth, changing personas. At times he is an 'Indian shoe-shiner', offering to shine the shoes of audience members. At other times, he becomes a 'diabetic Indian,' shooting insulin directly into his stomach. He then transforms into a 'janitor of color' (like most of the janitors in this, and other US museums) and sweeps the floor of the diorama. Hundreds of visitors gather in front of us. They look very sad . . . Next to us, the 'real' Indian dioramas speak of a mute world outside of history and social crises. Strangely, next to us, they appear much less 'authentic'. The visibly nervous museum staff makes sure the audience understands that 'this is just performance art . . . and they are famous artists.'"

"James and I have been rehearsing our next 'intervention' at the Natural History Museum. The piece consists of a selection of irreverent monologues, songs, dances, and staged conversations that problematize our bittersweet relationship with mainstream cultural institutions. This time the performance will take place in the main auditorium. It's 10 p.m., and James and I decide to take a break in our dressing room. Roberto and our producer, Kim Chan, are with us. James lights up some sage. I light up a Marlboro. Minutes later, several security guards break in and try to bust us for 'smoking dope.' When they finally realize it's just sage, they feel embarrassed and leave. I write in the margins of my script: *'The performance is never over for us. No matter how much we understand that ethnic identity is a cultural and ideological construction, and that as performance artists we have the power to alter it at will, nevertheless, we are always confronted in the most unexpected moments by the guardians of fetishized identity and the enforcers of stereotype.'*

When Aleta Ringlero, the curator of Native American art, finds out what happened, she gets furious, calls each and every Smithsonian undersecretary, and lets them have it. James, Roberto, Kim and I prefer to have a drink at a bar. It's just another day in our neverending pilgrimage towards the end of Western civilization."

## 3 Ethnic Talent for Export Performing in Malls

When the controversial North American Free Trade Agreement (NAFTA) was finally approved in January, 1994, the side effects of the rapid globalization of economy and culture became an important subject in the work of many Mexican, Chicano and Canadian artists. Cultural institutions on both sides of the two borders began to engage in a depoliticized exchange of what, at the time, I termed "Naftart." As a direct response to the pervasive trans-cultural hype, Cuban-American writer and artist Coco Fusco and I decided to invent a (fictional) post-NAFTA multinational corporation to market and distribute ethnic talent worldwide. We named it "Mexarcane International (Ethnic Talent for Export)." We decided that the logical location for this fictitious enterprise would be trendy shopping malls, the ultimate space for performance in globalized commodity culture. We placed our exhibition stand and temporary "office" in highly visible mall locations, usually next to the food court. This project was first presented at the National Review of Live Arts (Glasgow), and then taken to Dufferin Mall in Toronto and to Whiteley's Mall in London as part of LIFT '95.

Persuading mall administrators to let us stage an experimental performance art piece was not a problem, especially if we were backed by a prestigious art organization or festival. The management couldn't care less about the content of the project. All they wanted to know was if the *show* would bring in more people. We answered affirmatively. Our original idea was to mimic the "friendly tribalism" of corporations like Benetton, Banana Republic and The Body Shop. For this purpose, our presentational style and overall design needed to be sleek and yet ambiguous enough to generate a doubt in the viewer's mind: "Are they for real?" (whatever "real" meant in such a context) "Maybe it's an interactive advertisement for a new store or an upcoming product." We quickly discovered our presentation needed to be hyperstylized so as not to be to be engulfed and erased by the lush environment of consumer entertainment and fake tolerance.

For the performance, we set up a corporate-style backdrop (created by a professional corporate designer), complete with "explanatory" texts written in imitation corporate jargon, and images of "happy natives" from around the world. Coco was seated at a desk in front, dressed as the Aztec girlfriend of Mr Spock. Across from her, approximately 20 feet away, was my cage. For four to six hours a day, over three-day periods, I exhibited myself seated inside a tiny gilded or bamboo cage as an exotic "multicultural Frankenstein." Each detail and element of my costume came from a different culture in the Americas. I was "a living sample of Mexarcane's products for export," a composite "primitive" ready to fulfill the consumer's desire for exotica. Mall visitors were encouraged to "activate" me in order to experience my "incredible ethnic talents." My "live demonstrations" included: commercials for chile shampoo, "Ancient Grains" cereal, and other organic products, modeling tribal wear (in hopes that someone would hire me "for a rock video shoot or a kinky catering service"); posing in attitudes of martyrdom, despair, and poverty "for German documentary photographers"; doing shamanistic rituals and playing new age tribal music concerts (on toy instruments) "for confused suburbanites"; and (the most popular of all) demonstrating "pre-Columbian condoms," using a clay dildo as a proxy. During these demonstrations, Coco conducted interviews and surveys to determine the "ethnic desires" of the audience. After each interview, she would decide which "demonstration" was most appropriate for a particular consumer, who was then instructed to approach the "composite Indian" and ask me to "perform". Since I was not supposed to speak English (after all, I was an "authentic primitive"), the person who approached me had to mouth their request slowly and carefully, one syllable at a time, as if talking to an infant or a trained animal.

Contrary to our original expectations, our presence in the mall was not considered particularly outrageous. An eerie kind of "normality" and cool indifference seemed to surround the event. People participated very actively, critically and without self-consciousness, in much the same way they were used to participating in other interactive displays in the mall. Those who expressed strong feelings about the piece were primarily immigrants and people of color, but these emotional reactions never went beyond shedding a tear, or leaving us a supportive written note. Usually, by the third day of a performance, the management finally figured the real implications of a piece, and was extremely happy to see us leave for good.

## 4 The first, the last, the only "Lowrider Spanglish Opera."
"There Goes the Opera House . . ."

When Los Angeles producer Michael Milenski first contacted me in late 97 to ask if I wanted to direct an opera for the Long Beach Opera House, I truly thought he was kidding. The proposed piece was *The Indian Queen*, a seventeenth-century British baroque opera with text by Dryden and music by Purcell. Before accepting, I asked him two things: to fax me the libretto, and to become more familiar with my work by reading some of my books.

Dryden's text is filled with outrageous racist stereotypes and Eurocentric constructions of otherness. Set in an imaginary pre-contact Mexico, it describes a fictional conflict between Aztecs who behave like British royalty, and Incas who behave like mythical Scots. (In the seventeenth century British imagination, Scots were perceived as savages.) The Indian Queen herself is the personification of *America salvaje*, an oversexed, gluttonous female primitive, hungry for war and quick to betray her family and people.

The thought of "inverting" the script was so seductive that I couldn't resist. I got so nervous I developed acute insomnia. My initial proposal to Milenski was as follows. I wanted to rewrite the libretto in Spanglish, set it in a contemporary Californian mediascape, work with both symphonic and Mexican pop musicians, and create a cast using mainly Chicano performers and experimental artists, including many of my close collaborators. My demands were so outrageous that I felt sure they would be rejected (maybe deep inside that's precisely what I wanted) but Milenski reluctantly agreed. Just to make sure he really knew what he was getting into, I invited him to a performance of *Mexterminator* in San Francisco. After seeing the performance, he still insisted that he wanted to go forward with the project.

Since I didn't know much about opera, my very first task was to assemble a team of collaborators whose work I knew well and whose aesthetic vision was compatible with mine. City Lights editor Elaine Katzenberger agreed to be dramaturg for the project and work with me in writing the new Spanglish version of the libretto. Sara Shelton-Mann was hired to choreograph the ritual dances of the "primitives" (in our "inverted" version, the Aztec dancers were depicted as "blue savages" out of Celtic legend). Chicano filmmaker Gustavo Vázquez was commissioned to make a film including excerpts of B-movies, Mexican soap operas, and racist ethnographic documentaries, that was intended to comment on the live action and create a sort of ongoing "meta-reality." Milenski approached conductor Andreas Mitisek from the Salzburg Philarmonic, who got a kick out of the idea of directing an orchestra dressed á la "Chippendale's Aztec," and agreed to be part of our adventure for very little money. We knew that we also needed a staging director with experience in opera, someone with the skills to handle the difficult challenge of bringing together the work of actors, musicians, singers, and dancers, and who would agree to carry out our aesthetic and political vision rather than imposing his own. Los Angeles Maestro David Schweitzer was a logical choice.

Elaine, Sara and I had already shared a number of professional adventures and knew each other well. We clicked with David from day one. We shared an irreverent sense of humor and a fascination with perverse pop culture, high kitsch and sharp-edged politics. Perhaps the hardest task facing us was the need to create a new collaborative model with an unusual division of labor specific to the project. We had to learn to trust each other's sensibilities and decisions, Though Elaine and I did most of the rewriting and conceived the main concepts for the production, it was David who eventually had to work out most of the actual details of the staging and assemble the whole enchilada. For my friends and I, this was a radical exercise in ceding authority. The situation was made even more complicated by the fact that Sara and I were already committed to another project that overlapped with the rehearsal period for the opera: an extremely intensive, month-long residency in New York, which included performances of *Mexterminator* at Museo del Barrio and a number of performative events and interventions produced by Creative Time. Whenever Sara and I could manage a couple of days off from our multiple projects and commitments in New York, one or both of us flew back to California to work on the opera. It was an extremely chaotic and nerve-wracking experience, and our sense of ourselves as "trespassers" in the high-cultural, Eurocentric domain of opera made matters even worse. The unusual collaborative structure and fragmented working conditions made us fear that we could lose aesthetic control and end up with a project so eclectic that it would be an epic flop.

Auditions came. The team agreed that Moctezuma needed to be cast as a Chicano wrestler. Since Dryden's Indian Queen was a cultural transvestite, we decided to cast the role as a "clepto-Mexican" Anglo (not a Chicana) who purposely mispronounces her Spanish lines. The Queen's confused son, Acasius, became a soft-hearted, liberal Californian surfer. The Queen's arch enemy, an Inca tyrant, became a Miami narco-politico, and his daughter an archetypal assimilationist Indian collaborator — a folkloric "Mexican señorita" sponsored by the Department of Tourism whose job was to welcome the enemy into her culture.

The set was pure Aztec High-tech in Vegas. It involved a huge metallic pyramid, a lowrider car in the shape of a red stiletto shoe (the throne of *our* Indian Queen), and a "pre-Columbian nightclub" made out of Styrofoam that looked kind of like the Mexican pavilion at Disney's EPCOT, a place where yuppie cultural tourists could drink margaritas and enjoy a taste of "exotic Mexico."

While we were finishing revisions of the script and assembling the final company of actors, dancers and singers, the list of restrictions coming from above became increasingly longer. Magister Dixit: The spoken parts of Dryden's text could be rewritten in Spanglish, but all the sung parts needed to remain in archaic English. We couldn't have any musical intervention from outside sources, which meant no mariachi band, rap group, or Tex-mex accordionist — not even special sound effects. Full nudity for the "blue savages" was out of the question (g-strings were OK). Every day we had to (politely and indirectly but firmly) fight to defend and re-conquer every inch of the creative freedom we needed in order to stage an event that would genuinely merge performance art and opera with a strong Chicano sensibility.

Rehearsals began. In the highly specialized hierarchy of Opera, the roles of Sara, Elaine and I were extremely restricted. We weren't allowed to participate openly in the rehearsal process, and were instead restricted to writing notes and passing them on to David in private meetings so as not to undermine his authority in the eyes of the actors and singers. Actors, dancers and singers all rehearsed separately for most of the process, and it was only in the last two days of rehearsal that everything came together, which made it almost impossible to foresee the end result of such an unprecedented collaborative project. This process severely tested my tolerance and creative will, and of necessity increased my blind faith in my collaborators.

Opening night arrived. The Carpenter Center was packed. My colleagues and I were experiencing a combination of childish excitement and acute panic. If the piece didn't work, I knew I would be forced to go into hiding for at least a year. To our amazement, the performance was not only successful, but according to the press, "it shined". At the end of the piece, the audience applauded like crazy. None of us were prepared for what the LA Times reviewer said about the project the following day: "There is something in *The Indian Queen* to offend just about everyone. There is also something in it that should delight and astonish just about everyone as well. It's a mess. But it's a dazzling mess. It utterly, totally, unapologetically undoes just about everything its authors, composer Henry Purcell and poet John Dryden, set out to do in 1695. But it saves a work that probably could survive in no other reasonable way. It brings something new to opera at a time when you might think just about everything imaginable has already been done."

In the weeks after closing night, we were all high. There was talk about taking the opera to other places, and the critical buzz about the piece was extremely positive. However, I went into a pensive and anti-social mood for a while. With the opera, as with the other projects previously discussed in this chapter, I became hyper-aware of my privileged "experimental populist" status. Despite my utopian attempts "to cross over with dignity" into other realms and hopefully leave the door open behind me for other Mexicans, Chicanos, and artists of color to get in as well, it became clear that not many people were going to be given these opportunities. Most likely, the door would slam closed behind me, and the performances would become exotic anecdotes in the history of the institutions.

■　■　■

## Source

Gómez-Peña, G. (2000) *Dangerous Border Crossers . . . The Artist Talks Back*, London: Routledge.

## Guillermo Gómez-Peña (1955–)

Guillermo Gómez-Peña is a performance artist, writer, activist, radical pedagogue and director of the performance troupe La Pocha Nostra.

Born in Mexico City, he moved to the US in 1978 and currently resides in San Francisco. Educated at the Universidad Nacional Autonima de Mexico (UNAM) and at the California Institute for the Arts (Calarts), Valencia CA, Gómez-Peña works across and between the mediums to which he has access, and these include live performance, installation, film, radio, journalism, theory, the internet, direct political action and conversation. His work explores cross-cultural issues, immigration, the politics of language, the colonised body and new technology. Because of this diverse, prolific and ambitious portfolio, his work is sometimes difficult to characterise and he is continually pioneering, re-inventing and experimenting with and challenging new forms of artistic practice. His performances often involve collaboration with other artists and employ audience participation, elaborate costuming and environments, and interactive technologies.

His performance, installation and video work has been presented extensively at over 700 venues across the United States, Canada, Mexico, Europe, Australia, Russia, Colombia, Puerto Rico, Cuba, Brazil, Peru, Venezuela and Argentina. Some of his performance art pieces include *Border Brujo* (1988–89), *The Couple in the Cage* (1992–93), *The Cruci-Fiction Project* (1994), *The Temple of Confessions* (1995–96), *The Mexterminator Project* (1997–99), *The Living Museum of Fetishized Identities* (1999–2002) and the *Mapa/Corpo* series (2004–8).

He has lectured extensively at universities in America and Europe and has authored numerous books including *Dangerous Border Crossers* (2000), *Codex Espangliensis* (2000) and *The New World Border* (1996), for which he won the American Book Award in 1997.

He is a MacArthur fellow, a regular contributor to National Public Radio, a writer for newspapers and magazines in the United States and Mexico, and a contributing editor to *The Drama Review* (NYU-MIT). His performance works, residencies and books have contributed to the debates on cultural diversity, border culture and US–Mexico relations.

He is Artistic Director of La Pocha Nostra, a transdisciplinary arts organisation made up of international artists, curators and intellectuals, which provides a support network and forum for artists of various disciplines, ethnicities and generations. The work focuses on artistic collaboration across borders of geography, race, gender and generation as a means to create 'ephemeral communities' of 'rebel artists'. Their collective work includes experimental art projects, lectures, public discussions, writings and pedagogy, and is reactive to changing political and global contexts.

The pedagogic dimension of La Pocha Nostra's practice is a defining aspect of the collective and includes regular workshops and residencies for students and artists from diverse cultural, ethnic and generational backgrounds. Difference and experimentation is encouraged within the work as well as the creation of new hybrid and interdisciplinary aesthetics that enable and empower each individual participant.

In the article presented here, Gómez-Peña recounts his experience and process of creating highly politicised collaborative artworks in a variety of live and mediatised contexts for different audiences. He identifies the struggles of attempting to operate across the borders of experimental and mainstream practices and describes how his strategies for intervention aim to 'destabilize and subvert problematic notions of "racial" and cultural authenticity'.

## Compare this article with writings by the following authors in this reader

**Boal** – for invisible theatre
**Brecht** – for a political stance
**Finley** – for addressing the US stranglehold
**Kaprow** – for art in close proximity to life
**Schlemmer** – for elaborate use of costume
**Wilson** – for connections to opera

## Further reading

Gómez-Peña, G. (1996) *The New World Border: Prophecies, Poems and Loqueras for the End of the Century*, San Francisco: City Lights.

Gómez-Peña, G. (2005) *Ethno-Techno: Writings on Performance, Activism and Pedagogy*, London: Routledge.

Gómez-Peña, G. and Levin, L. (ed.) (2011) *Conversations Across Borders* (Enactments), Chicago: University of Chicago Press.

Gómez-Peña, G. and Sifuentes, R. (2011) *Exercises for Rebel Artists: Radical Performance Pedagogy*, London: Routledge.

http://www.pochanostra.com/

# Chapter 29

## Matthew Goulish

# THE CREATURE FROM
# THE BLACK LAGOON

Goulish

## 6.1 THE CREATURE FROM THE BLACK LAGOON

> How does it feel to be the only woman in a company with three male performers?

An audience member once asked Karen Christopher this question at a Goat Island work-in-progress discussion. I don't remember her response as much as my own reaction. I felt the urgent need to answer the question by rephrasing it. Soon I heard myself interjecting:

> I do not consider myself a male performer. I consider myself The Creature from the Black Lagoon.

My dissatisfaction with the question must be understood in the context of our performance at that time. *Can't Take Johnny to the Funeral.* At various points in this piece I saw myself as:

> one of the six simple machines
> an illustration in a figure skating manual
> The Creature from the Black Lagoon
> Hanuman the Hindu Monkey Spirit
> an autistic child
> myself at age 6
> a microphone stand
> myself in the present moment
> an emergency room doctor
> an angel in a painting by Nicolas Poussin

This represents only a partial list of my would-be identities in this particular performance, and I know the other three performers had conceived of at least as many for themselves. In fact, my identities only came into existence in relation to their identities, or in relation to my sense of their identities, and only lasted as long as the performance provided a time/space proximity for us to share. And never, I realized, did I consider among my list of identities, that of 'male performer.' In fact, I did not even understand the term. And yet, I could also ask myself, "What difference does it make how *I think* of myself? The question makes it clear that when people watch me, *they think* they are watching a 'male performer.'" Things became confusing quickly, requiring that I turn to philosophy for clarification.

Zen Buddhism teaches that what we call personality derives from five aggregates.

> Body
> Feelings
> Perceptions
> Mental Formations
> Consciousness

With each of these five aggregates come three mistakes.

> First mistake: This is mine.
> Second mistake: This is me.
> Third mistake: This is the Self.

A more correct view might be: my body is not mine; my body is not me; my body is not myself. And the same holds true for the other four aggregates. But what then is my body? My body is a first principle, a basic constituent of the universe. My body represents an intersection between my small self and the larger self of everything else, such as air, water, earth, animals, events, other people, et cetera. Several years ago I was fortunate enough to survive an illness, the treatment for which required the surgical removal of portions of the inside of my body. It became clear to me, as I regained consciousness some moments after my first operation, that:

> My body is not mine.
> My body is not me.
> My body is not my Self.

Under anaesthetic I had dreamed I was dancing for a small outdoor audience in a farmer's sunny field in Nicaragua. I found myself recreating this dance some years later in *Can't Take Johnny to the Funeral*. In this brief solo I saw myself as Hanuman the Hindu Monkey Spirit.

Performance, like dreaming, presents us with intersections. In a performance, a performer is not a single entity. Instead of a unit, a performer is an identity in motion in a particular direction. A performer is a BECOMING. I am not a "male performer," but neither am I The Creature from the Black Lagoon. I am:

Myself BECOMING one of the six simple machines
Myself BECOMING an illustration in a figure skating manual
Myself BECOMING The Creature from the Black Lagoon
Myself BECOMING Hanuman the Hindu Monkey Spirit
Myself BECOMING an autistic child
Myself BECOMING myself at age 6
Myself BECOMING a microphone stand
Myself BECOMING myself in the present moment
Myself BECOMING an emergency room doctor
Myself BECOMING an angel in a painting by Nicolas Poussin

Goat Island, a performance group now ten years old under Lin Hixson's direction, can attribute its creative survival to a series of small miracles. We may think of Goat Island as the small self, and the small miracles result from the profound influences brought about by intersections with the larger self of everything else, such as air, water, earth, animals, events, other people, et cetera. In this series of microlectures, I will try to examine in brief but precise detail, three of those profound influences from three exceptional people. Since all three of these people can be considered women, by the end I hope to have offered some insights into the topic of the day. I hope, but I can't promise. I will at least try to offer:

a thought BECOMING an insight.

## 6.2 EVERYTHING ABOUT LIFE

It is the summer of 1984. Seventeen of us sit in a classroom on a campus outside of Los Angeles. The room is silent and full of light. Lin Hixson is there, Karen Christopher is there, and I am there. Everyone is writing. We are students in a playwrighting class taught by Maria Irene Fornes. The birth of Goat Island remains three years in the future. The idea exists unarticulated. For now, we each write a dialogue of our own invention. Irene picks up a book from the small pile of books she has brought to the workshop, and she instructs us, "Now one of your characters says to the other . . ." She opens the book at random and reads:

"Do you really imagine you know everything about life?"

Later many of us read our dialogues aloud. In all the variations of time, place, character, conflict, tone, theme – in each of them at one point, unexpectedly, one character says to another:

"Do you really imagine you know everything about life?"

And in each dialogue, the line fits perfectly.

I cannot imagine teaching, either alone or collaboratively, without my experience as a student of Irene Fornes. In a book of interviews with women playwrights, I recently found this passage in which she describes her approach.

> My Lab is a place where we do many experiments on writing. Unlike most workshops and classes that exist in universities, where you go home and write, bring your writing to class, have it read and get criticism, the Lab is all about inducing inspiration. I have never felt that criticism was the way to teach writing. In painting classes you paint *together*, you don't paint, bring your work to class and have it criticized. There is a model and everyone is working together. The important thing is to teach how to *work*, not how to criticize a finished piece. There is something about the atmosphere in a room full of people working. Each person's concentration is giving you something. Once you've experienced this phenomenon in the practice of another art form, you have a knowledge that it exists. If you've been exclusively a writer, I don't think this way of working would ever occur to you. In fact, most writers say, "I have to be alone to work." That's nonsense! They usually need to be completely alone because the other people around them are not writing. But if you experience working in a room with people who are also writing, there is no distraction. There is an exchange of energy and you know the other writers are not there for you to chat with. Even if you wanted to talk, you would be interrupting, so there is no temptation. No one is waiting for you, distracting you, and yet others are there. It has all the advantages of being alone, without the isolation. People who come to visit The Lab are always amazed by its peacefulness and the beautiful quality of the light.

It is the spring of 1994. I am reading Albert Camus' novel *The Plague* in my living room in Chicago. Goat Island is seven years old. We are in the process of our fourth performance work, *It's Shifting, Hank*. I reach the bottom of page 129. "I've little left to learn," says Mr Tarrou, and the doctor replies:

"Do you really imagine you know everything about life?"

## 6.3 SLOW THINKING

Arriving at the World Wide Web site of Germany's Pina Bausch and the Wupperthal Dance Theatre, one finds a button marked "Videos." Clicking on this option reveals the text, "No videos are available." Which live art practitioner has not, at some time point, wished to scrap the whole notion of video documentation?

Why is it that some performance works, and some aspects of all performances, translate so inaccurately to the television screen?

In *The New Dance Review*, critic Anita Finkel wrote,

> Photographs distort Bausch's work. Her work as depicted in photographs is uncomely and false – 'weird,' in fact . . . Her images, ultimately twentieth century things, are fluid and cannot be captured in stills.

We expect a certain kind of stillness from a photograph. Other kinds of stillness seem strange. We expect a certain kind of motion from a television screen, namely the motion of speed. Even the idiom of slow-motion not only presents a rapidly changing image of its own, but it also by definition implies speed. Slow-motion does not capture slowness.

In his novel *A Quiet Life*, Japanese writer Kenzaburo Oe narrates through the voice of his twenty-year-old daughter Ma-Chan. In one chapter Ma-Chan discusses with her two brothers *The Stalker* by Soviet director Andrei Tarkovsky. The three of them have watched the film on late-night television while their parents were away. Ma-Chan feels intimidated by both her brothers. Her younger brother she finds brilliantly intelligent. Her older brother, who has grown up since birth with severe brain damage, possesses an unearthly understanding of sound and music, and speaks about the film's soundtrack with startling precision. She feels she cannot compete with them in the discussion, and states the following:

> I don't think I have what it takes to make an overall comment. But in the grassland scene, for example, you have these people huddled together? With a host of other props placed unobtrusively at some distance from them? And this scene goes on and on. With scenes like this, I feel like I'm looking at a stage performance where you can watch each actor or actress any way you like. These scenes are good for people like me who don't think very quickly.

The scene Ma-Chan refers to occurs early in the film. In this way, it relates to composer Witold Lutoslawski's statement that the function of the first movement in his compositions is to make the audience impatient. In light of Ma-Chan's insight into Tarkovsky's film, and into her own method of perception, those who grow impatient may simply be thinking too fast. Tarkovsky's work may prove that the television screen can in fact communicate slowness, but the accompanying slowness of thought requires in individuals either: 1) slow thought by nature, 2) slow thought by practice, meaning patience; or 3) slow thought by sheer force of will, meaning courage. Most of us live in fear of slowing down our thinking, because of the possibility that if we succeed we might find that in fact nothing is happening. I guarantee this is not the case. Something is always happening. In fact, some things happen which one can *only* perceive with slow thinking. Thus Ma-Chan's slowness of thought, although initially seen as a personal weakness, can in fact be taken as a necessity.

In Pina Bausch's work, the performance unfolds durationally on a stage. The image repeats; the image rotates. To witness it, one must occupy the same room at the same time. One may only experience it by experiencing it. To generate such non-reproducable performative material, Bausch asks her company questions.

> "How many people or things do you know named Maria?"
> "What did you eat for Christmas dinner?"
> "How do you cry?"

The dancer's experience becomes the answer. The answer becomes the dance. The dance becomes the experience. The experience takes as long as it takes. It repeats, and it rotates, and it repeats. The experience deserves "respect" in the sense of the word's original Latin meaning, "to look twice." For, as the great slow thinker Pina Bausch has said, "We must look and look again."

## 6.4 BEAUTY

The highest responsibility of the artist is to hide beauty.

John Cage once quoted this statement in reference to the music of Morton Feldman. The statement implies that beauty, in order to be hidden, must be present. The proper attitude of the artist toward beauty might then be something like: I know it's here somewhere.

In published comments on the theatre piece *Brace Up!*, Wooster Group director Elizabeth LeCompte referred to the transformation of the actors from self to more-self. To describe the medium for this transformation one might use the word *artificial*. LeCompte quotes film director Robert Bresson.

> On stage a horse or a dog that is not plaster or cardboard causes uneasiness. In the theatre, looking for truth in the real is fatal.

The "horse or dog" in question we may consider the stand-in for *the more-self*, or even for *the beautiful*. The "plaster or cardboard" represents the chosen medium of transformation, the journey from the less to the more. The corollary medium here, I might suggest, is the spoken word. In the example of *Frank Dell's The Temptation of Saint Antony*, those words included extracts from:

> Ingmar Bergman's film *The Magician*
> Gustave Flaubert's play *The Temptation of Saint Antony*
> Geraldine Cummins's book *The Road to Immortality*
> Recordings and films of performances of Lenny Bruce
> Original writing by playwright James Strahs.

Although LeCompte's approach appears fundamentally deconstructive, one sees how the process of gathering, altering, and recombining texts easily lends itself to the construction of *the more-self*. The texts become a layer on the surface of the actors, and that surface then becomes *the more-self*. This may be what Gilles Deleuze meant when he spoke of, in contrast to Jung's "collective unconscious," the existence of the "constructed unconscious" and its imminence to creativity.

> I think I'm a better ghost than I am a human being.

I can't repeat this line from Bergman's film *The Magician* without thinking of Ron Vawter, the actor who for so many years populated LeCompte's productions, until his AIDS-related death in 1994. Before his *death*, however, there was his *near-death* in 1986, during which he fell into a coma. At that time LeCompte, along with Wooster Group members Peyton Smith and Kate Valk, sat beside his hospital bed and read aloud for hours from the plays in which he had appeared, hoping to connect to him through the words to which he had devoted his life. After four days, Vawter suddenly awakened. Recalling again this famous story tells us exactly how much is at stake in LeCompte's work, wherein the texts, layered over *the self*, generate *the more-self*. We see the power of *the more-self* itself.

> I think I'm a better ghost than I am a human being, because I am still living, but have already begun to haunt.

The ghost is always present, but the human being only appears as a result of labor. In the process is *beauty*. I know it's there somewhere.

## 6.5 BODY THROUGH WHICH THE DREAM FLOWS

I have come to the end of my discussion of women and directing, but I don't know what I have said on the subject. I do however have an idea of what I did not say. I did not say that the details I singled out arose from some innate quality that my subjects share because they are women. I also did not indicate any commonality between these methods because their practitioners are women. Nor did I say that since Goat Island's director is also a woman, that we only look to other women directors as examples, or that Lin as a woman inevitably draws from the work of other women.

So what exactly *did* I say? Maybe I didn't say anything, and am in fact only out to confuse everybody. I am after all a man speaking at a woman's conference. It's bad enough they invited a man at all, let alone a man who begins his talk by confessing that gender definitions confuse him. Perhaps I feel that if I draw enough people into the vortex of my own personal confusion, a spontaneous illusion of order will arise, and then I will no longer appear confused.

I will illustrate this point with a story. A young music student at a midwestern college signed up to study with visiting composer George Crumb for the semester. The student faithfully attended Crumb's lectures and workshops, taking in his severe and challenging ideas on aesthetics and music. In the climactic event of the residency, an ensemble premiered a new work of Crumb's, and the excited student attended the crowded concert. As the music progressed, the audience grew more and more restless, until finally, pushed beyond their tolerance limit, a few individuals began shouting their displeasure. Very quickly the protests spread and grew to near-riot proportions. Audience members stood up, calling for the music to stop, tearing their programs, and hurling objects at the stage. In the midst of this spectacle, the student suddenly spotted the composer, unrecognized by those around him in the auditorium. To the student's horror, Crumb himself was also on his feet shouting, tearing his program, and hurling objects at the stage. The next day, the student approached Crumb in amazement. "How could you publicly revile your own work in this way?" he asked. Crumb replied, "When everyone else started doing it, it just looked like so much fun."

In the discourse of Zen Buddhism, this is what's known as *enlightenment by mistake*. Through his anonymous presence among the dissatisfied audience, Crumb accidentally learned his music was not his, was not him, and was not himself.

I'll finish by quoting another composer, John Adams, who recently wrote a violin concerto, the second movement of which he titled

> Body through which the dream flows.

Adams explained that he took the line from a poem by Robert Haas because it provided an image for the entire concerto: the orchestra as the organized, delicately articulated mass of blood, tissues, and bones; the violin as the dream that flows through it.

> This body is not mine.     This dream is not mine.
> This body is not me.       This dream is not me.
> This body is not my Self.  This dream is not my Self.

Since I began this talk with a story about my body and a dream, I may now be ready to conclude by rephrasing the question in a way that offers some order amid the confusion.

> How does the dream divide from the body;
> how does the body divide from the dream?

I can't answer. But as a performer, I know that I have my own body and my own dreams, and the bodies of others and the dreams of others. In order to continue, I need them all.

■   ■   ■

## Source

Goulish, M. (2000) *39 Microlectures: In Proximity of Performance*, London: Routledge.

## Matthew Goulish (1960–)

Matthew Goulish is a performer, a collaborator, a teacher and a writer of perform-
ance. He received his BA in theatre from Kalamazoo College. He co-founded both the
Chicago-based collaborative performance group Goat Island (1987–2009) and Every
House has a Door in 2008. He teaches on the MFA and BFA Writing Programs of the
School of the Art Institute of Chicago.

Collaboration is a key term in the body of work that Goulish has co-created to
date and his interest in inclusive discursiveness is regularly evidenced across and
through his identity and practice as a performance maker, a writer and a teacher.

Goat Island's performances involved all members of the ensemble in the conception, choreography, writing and editing of the material. The work often involved
lengthy research processes with members developing a dialogue through the passing
back and forth of creative responses which eventually resulted in the formation of a
performance ready to show to an audience.

Goat Island toured extensively in the United States, Canada and Europe with
nine full-length performances including *Can't Take Johnny to the Funeral* (1991);
*How Dear To Me the Hour When Daylight Dies* (1996); *When Will the September Roses
Bloom? Last Night Was Only a Comedy* (2004); *The Lastmaker* (2007). Goulish's
current collaboration with Lin Hixson, Every House has a Door, intends to create project-
specific collaborations with invited guests from different countries and cultures.

Goulish wrote *39 Microlectures: In Proximity of Performance* (2000), and co-
edited with Stephen Bottoms *Small Acts of Repair: Performance, Ecology, and Goat
Island* (2007). He was awarded a Lannan Foundation Writers' Residency in 2004,
and in 2007 he received an honorary PhD from Dartington College of Arts, University
of Plymouth. Goulish is Provocations editor for *The Drama Review*.

Goulish also collaborates with Tim Etchells, director of Forced Entertainment,
as co-directors of the Institute of Failure website, dedicated to the study, documentation and theorization of failure. The site contains documentation of performed lectures
and essays created by the co-founders alongside contributions from other honorary
scholars. His most recent book, *The Brightest Thing in the World: Three Essays from
the Institute of Failure*, is a collection of essays which weave together stories about
Dick Cheney, cuckoo clocks, the Fibonacci series, butterflies and old friends. Goulish
describes his writing as 'an act of extending other people's writing that I loved, into a
language and shape with the task of addressing a question'.

In this extract, Goulish approaches a number of conversations about gender,
identity, documentation, creative writing and musicality through a series of intercon-
nected stories. He recounts his own personal experiences, making connections along
the way with other artists and their work – including writer Irene Fornes, composer

John Cage, choreographer Pina Bausch and director Liz LeCompte. This microlecture is a typical example of how Goulish addresses key questions relating directly to performance by mixing philosophical thinking with lived experience and stories he has both read and heard along the way. He writes like a tour guide and interpreter whose job is to point up key landmarks, which serves to enhance the quality of our journey.

## Compare this article with writings by the following authors in this reader

**Baker** – for work which foregrounds the creative process
**Bausch, Cage and LeCompte** – whom he makes reference to in his extract
**Etchells** – for approaches to writing about performance
**Stein** – for compositional writing

## Further reading

Bailes, S.J. (2011) *Performance Theatre and the Poetics of Failure*, London: Routledge.
Bottoms, S. and Goulish, M. (2007) *Small Acts of Repair: Performance, Ecology, and Goat Island*, London: Routledge.
Goulish, M. (2012) *The Brightest Thing In the World: Three Essays from the Institute of Failure*, Chicago: Green Lantern Press.
http://www.goatislandperformance.org/
http://www.everyhousehasadoor.org/about.html

# Chapter 30

# Martha Graham

## GRAHAM 1937

THROUGHOUT TIME DANCE HAS NOT CHANGED in one essential function. The function of the dance is communication. The responsibility that dance fulfill its function belongs to us who are dancing today.

To understand dance for what it is, it is necessary we know from whence it comes and where it goes. It comes from the depths of man's inner nature, the unconscious, where memory dwells. As such it inhabits the dancer. It goes into the experience of man, the spectator, awakening similar memories.

Art is the evocation of man's inner nature. Through art, which finds its roots in man's unconscious—race memory—is the history and psyche of race brought into focus.

We are making a transition from 18th to 20th century thinking. A new vitality is possessing us. Certain depths of the intellect are being explored. Great art never ignores human values. Therein lies its roots. This is why forms change.

No art can live and pass untouched through such a vital period as we are now experiencing. Man is discovering himself as a world.

All action springs from necessity. This necessity is called by various names: inspiration, motivation, vision, genius. There is a difference of inspiration in the dance today.

Once we strove to imitate gods—we did god dances. Then we strove to become part of nature by representing natural forces in dance forms—winds—flowers—trees.

Dance was no longer performing its function of communication. By communication is not meant to tell a story or to project an idea,

but to communicate experience by means of action and perceived by action. We were not speaking to that insight in man which would elevate him to a new strength through a heightened sense of awareness. Change had already taken place in man, was already in his life manifestations. While the arts do not create change, they register change.

This is the reason for the appearance of the modern dance. The departure of the dance from classical and romantic delineations was not an end in itself, but the means to an end. It was not done perversely to dramatize ugliness, or to strike at sacred tradition—to destroy from sheer inability to become proficient in the technical demands of a classical art. The old forms could not give voice to the more fully awakened man. They had to undergo metamorphosis—in some cases destruction—to serve as a medium for a time differently organized.

The modern dance, as we know it today, came after the World War. This period following the war demanded forms vital enough for the reborn man to inhabit. Because of the revitalized consciousness came an alteration in movement—the medium of dance, as tone is medium. Out of this came a different use of the body as an instrument, as the violin is an instrument. Body is the basic instrument, intuitive, instinctive. As a result an entirely contemporary set of technics was evolved. While it had points of similarity with the old, that was because it was based on the innate co-ordination of the body which is timeless. With this enhanced language, and the more vitally organized instrument, the body, we are prepared for a deep, stirring creative communication.

All of this has nothing to do with propaganda as known and practiced. It only demands the dance be a moment of passionate, completely disciplined action, that it communicate participation to the nerves, the skin, the structure of the spectator.

For this to be accomplished, however, it means that the communication be valid to the twentieth century man. There has been swift transition in this present recurrence of the modern dance. There was a revolt against the ornamented forms of impressionistic dancing. There came a period of great austerity. Movement was used carefully and significantly. Subject matter began to diverge—the dancer emerged from the realm of introspection. The dance began to record evolution in man's thinking. An impassioned dynamic technic was needed and gradually appeared. Dance accompaniment and costume were stripped to essentials. Music came to be written on the dance structure. It ceased to be the source of the emotional stimulus and was used as background. Music was used almost in the same sense that decor had been used in the older dance to bring the emotional content of the movement into focus for the spectator. As dance evolved into larger forms, music began to evolve also. The composer gained a greater strength and a more significant line from composing to meet the passionate requirements of the dance.

Then arose a danger. With music no longer acting in that capacity, what means to employ for focus—a focus suited to the eyes of today? Dance can remain for a time an authentic, creative experience for the comparative few. There are those for whom focus is possible—because of their awareness and their response to the artist and his medium. But for the many the focus is not sharp enough to permit clear vision. At this point the responsibility rests with the dancer-choreographer. Now it seems necessary that the focus be made through sight.

While music for the dance is still transparent and exciting as an element, we still use the perennial black velvet curtain of another period as background. They were first used for the dance I believe by Isadora Duncan. She used them, from the same need we have today, to bring focus upon the dance, and she succeeded. But the dance today is another dance, brought into emergence by another orientation. Perhaps what Arch Lauterer calls "space man" will be as necessary to the dance of the future as the composer. All of life today is concerned with space problems, even political life. Space language is a language we understand. We receive so much of sensation through the eye.

It is understood without question that presentation can never take the place of the dance. It can only cover bad and unauthentic dancing as music was long able to do. But this evolved presentation will have nothing to do with dance decor in the older sense, which was basically a painting enlarged for the stage. At best it can only be an *accent* for the dance, evolved after the dance is finished. Dance decor can, I believe, serve as a means of enhancing movement and gesture to the point of revelation of content.

I refuse to admit that the dance has limitations that prevent its acceptance and understanding—or that the intrinsic purity of the art itself need be touched. The reality of the dance is its truth to our inner life. Therein lies its power to move and communicate experience. The reality of dance can be brought into focus—that is into the realm of human values—by simple, direct, objective means. We are a visually stimulated world today. The eye is not to be denied. Dance need not change—it has only to stand revealed.

■　■　■

## Source

Graham, M. (1980) 'Graham 1937', *The Vision of Modern Dance*, ed. J.M. Brown, London: Dance Books: 50–53.

## Martha Graham (1894–1991)

The founder of modern dance, Graham was born near Pittsburgh and began her career by working at the Denishawn school, founded by American dancers Ruth St Denis and Ted Shawn in 1915. Graham made her debut there in 1919 and remained there till 1923. Her first independent performance was given in New York in 1926, and consisted of eighteen dances, performed by herself and three other women. She founded the Martha Graham School of Contemporary Dance in New York in 1927. By this time the term 'modern' had become 'contemporary', which showed Graham's already expressed intentions that dance should be what she called 'an evocation of man's inner nature'. In this emphasis she shows how far she has moved from the ballet traditions of telling age-old stories and set to mostly nineteenth-century music.

In every Graham dance there is a feeling of wishing to reach out to new audiences with new perspectives on the connection between dance and contemporary concerns. The Graham technique is now taught in dance schools worldwide, concentrating on developing dances that are influenced by national characteristics. The technique concentrates on floor work, in contrast to ballet exercises, which concentrate on standing exercises on the barre. Some of her most famous dance pieces are connected with the sculptures of Isamu Noguchi (Japanese/American sculptor) and with the native traditions of the USA – *El Penitente* of 1940 is an example. This, an evocation of the visual images of the Navajo Indian rituals, was first performed in the middle of the Second World War, and is seen as an example of American art transcending history. But in 1990, a year before her death, she produced *Maple Leaf Rag*, a celebration of American popular culture.

At one point in her career she said 'No artist is ahead of his time. He is his time; it's just that others are behind the time', a statement that has been accepted as one of the major artistic analyses of our time, along with Claire MacDonald's categorization of contemporary performance as 'a constellation of practices', a phrase that sums up much of the content of this book.

Graham's concerns chime with other European artists of her time, who were also questioning accepted practices and performances, and wished to explore alternative possibilities. Thus Graham can be seen as a major exemplar, along with Kandinsky, the Futurists, Brecht, and many others of her earlier European contemporaries, of those twentieth-century artists who have seen a need to articulate a change in attitudes of audiences/spectators to performance practice.

## Compare this article with writings by the following authors in this reader

**Bausch** – as revolutionary in her subject matter as was Graham with hers
**Brecht** – a contemporary theatre experimentalist
**Cunningham** – a collaborator and later follower of Graham
**de Keersmaeker** – an extension of Graham's world
**Duncan** – an earlier pioneer of dance concerns
**Kandinsky** – who sought a new all-encompassing art form
**Marinetti** – who was also searching for a new twentieth-century art form
**Newson** – a contemporary choreographer owing much to Graham

## Further reading

Graham, M. (1973) *The Notebooks of Martha Graham*, New York: Harcourt Brace, Jovanovich.
De Mille, A. (1992) *Martha: The Life and Work of Martha Graham*, London: Hutchinson.
http://www.marthagraham.org

# Chapter 31

# Jerzy Grotowski

## STATEMENT OF PRINCIPLES

### I

THE RHYTHM OF LIFE in modern civilization is characterized by pace, tension, a feeling of doom, the wish to hide our personal motives and the assumption of a variety of roles and masks in life (different ones with our family, at work, amongst friends or in community life, etc.). We like to be 'scientific', by which we mean discursive and cerebral, since this attitude is dictated by the course of civilization. But we also want to pay tribute to our biological selves, to what we might call physiological pleasures. We do not want to be restricted in this sphere. Therefore we play a double game of intellect and instinct, thought and emotion; we try to divide ourselves artificially into body and soul. When we try to liberate ourselves from it all we start to shout and stamp, we convulse to the rhythm of music. In our search for liberation we reach biological chaos. We suffer most from a lack of totality, throwing ourselves away, squandering ourselves.

Theatre – through the actor's technique, his art in which the living organism strives for higher motives – provides an opportunity for what could be called integration, the discarding of masks, the revealing of the real substance: a totality of physical and mental reactions. This opportunity must be treated in a disciplined manner, with a full awareness of the responsibilities it involves. Here we can see the theatre's therapeutic function for people in our present day civilization. It is true that the actor accomplishes this act, but he can only do so through an encounter with the spectator

– intimately, visibly, not hiding behind a cameraman, wardrobe mistress, stage designer or make-up girl – in direct confrontation with him, and somehow 'instead of' him. The actor's act – discarding half measures, revealing, opening up, emerging from himself as opposed to closing up – is an invitation to the spectator. This act could be compared to an act of the most deeply rooted, genuine love between two human beings – this is just a comparison since we can only refer to this 'emergence from oneself' through analogy. This act, paradoxical and border-line, we call a total act. In our opinion it epitomizes the actor's deepest calling.

## II

Why do we sacrifice so much energy to our art? Not in order to teach others but to learn with them what our existence, our organism, our personal and unrepeat-able experience have to give us; to learn to break down the barriers which surround us and to free ourselves from the breaks which hold us back, from the lies about ourselves which we manufacture daily for ourselves and for others; to destroy the limitations caused by our ignorance and lack of courage; in short, to fill the emptiness in us: to fulfil ourselves. Art is neither a state of the soul (in the sense of some extraordinary, unpredictable moment of inspiration) nor a state of man (in the sense of a profession or social function). Art is a ripening, an evolution, an uplifting which enables us to emerge from darkness into a blaze of light.

We fight then to discover, to experience the truth about ourselves; to tear away the masks behind which we hide daily. We see theatre – especially in its palpable, carnal aspect – as a place of provocation, a challenge the actor sets himself and also, indirectly, other people. Theatre only has a meaning if it allows us to transcend our stereotyped vision, our conventional feelings and customs, our standards of judgement – not just for the sake of doing so, but so that we may experience what is real and, having already given up all daily escapes and pretences, in a state of complete defenselessness unveil, give, discover ourselves. In this way – through shock, through the shudder which causes us to drop our daily masks and mannerisms – we are able, without hiding anything, to entrust ourselves to something we cannot name but in which live Eros and Charitas.

## III

Art cannot be bound by the laws of common morality or any catechism. The actor, at least in part, is creator, model and creation rolled into one. He must not be shameless as that leads to exhibitionism. He must have courage, but not merely the courage to exhibit himself – a passive courage, we might say: the courage of the defenseless, the courage to reveal himself. Neither that which touches the interior sphere, nor the profound stripping bare of the self should be regarded as evil so long as in the process of preparation or in the completed work they produce an act of creation. If they do not come easily and if they are not signs of outburst but of mastership, then they are creative: they reveal and purify us **while we transcend ourselves**. Indeed, they improve us then.

For these reasons every aspect of an actor's work dealing with intimate matters should be protected from incidental remarks, indiscretions, nonchalance, idle comments and jokes. The personal realm – both spiritual and physical – must not be 'swamped' by triviality, the sordidness of life and lack of tact towards oneself and others; at least not in the place of work or anywhere connected with it. This postulate sounds like an abstract moral order. It is not. It involves the very essence of the actor's calling. This calling is realized through carnality. The actor must not **illustrate** but **accomplish** an 'act of the soul' by means of his own organism. Thus he is faced with two extreme alternatives: he can either sell, dishonour, his real 'incarnate' self, making himself an object of artistic prostitution; or he can give himself, sanctify his real 'incarnate' self.

## IV

An actor can only be guided and inspired by someone who is whole-hearted in his creative activity. The producer, while guiding and inspiring the actor, must at the same time allow himself to be guided and inspired by him. It is a question of freedom, partnership, and this does not imply a lack of discipline but a respect for the autonomy of others. Respect for the actor's autonomy does not mean lawlessness, lack of demands, never ending discussions and the replacement of action by continuous streams of words. On the contrary, respect for autonomy means enormous demands, the expectation of a maximum creative effort and the most personal revelation. Understood thus, solicitude for the actor's freedom can only be born from the plenitude of the guide and not from his lack of plenitude. Such a lack implies imposition, dictatorship, superficial dressage.

## V

An act of creation has nothing to do with either external comfort or conventional human civility; that is to say, working conditions in which everybody is happy. It demands a maximum of silence and a minimum of words. In this kind of creativity we discuss through proposals, actions and living organisms, not through explanations. When we finally find ourselves on the track of something difficult and often almost intangible, we have no right to lose it through frivolity and carelessness. Therefore, even during breaks after which we will be continuing with the creative process, we are obliged to observe certain natural reticences in our behaviour and even in our private affairs. This applies just as much to our own work as to the work of our partners. We must not interrupt and disorganize the work because we are hurrying to our own affairs; we must not peep, comment or make jokes about it privately. In any case, private ideas of fun have no place in the actor's calling. In our approach to creative tasks, even if the theme is a game, we must be in a state of readiness — one might even say 'solemnity'. Our working terminology which serves as a stimulus must not be dissociated from the work and used in a private context. Work terminology should be associated only with that which it serves.

A creative act of this quality is performed in a group, and therefore within certain limits we should restrain our creative egoism. An actor has no right to mould his partner so as to provide greater possibilities for his own performance. Nor has he the right to correct his partner unless authorized by the work leader. Intimate or drastic elements in the work of others are untouchable and should not be commented upon even in their absence. Private conflicts, quarrels, sentiments, animosities are unavoidable in any human group. It is our duty towards creation to keep them in check in so far as they might deform and wreck the work process. We are obliged to open ourselves up even towards an enemy.

# VI

It has been mentioned several times already, but we can never stress and explain too often the fact that we must never exploit privately anything connected with the creative act: i.e. location, costume, props, an element from the acting score, a melodic theme or lines from the text. This rule applies to the smallest detail and there can be no exceptions. We did not make this rule simply to pay tribute to a special artistic devotion. We are not interested in grandeur and noble words, but our awareness and experience tell us that lack of strict adherence to such rules causes the actor's score to become deprived of its psychic motives and 'radiance'.

# VII

Order and harmony in the work of each actor are essential conditions without which a creative act cannot take place. Here we demand consistency. We demand it from the actors who come to the theatre consciously to try themselves out in something extreme, a sort of challenge seeking a total response from every one of us. They come to test themselves in something very definite that reaches beyond the meaning of 'theatre' and is more like an act of living and way of existence. This outline probably sounds rather vague. If we try to explain it theoretically, we might say that the theatre and acting are for us a kind of vehicle allowing us to emerge from ourselves, to fulfil ourselves. We could go into this at great length. However, anyone who stays here longer than just the trial period is perfectly aware that what we are talking about can be grasped less through grandiose words than through details, demands and the rigours of work in all its elements. The individual who disturbs the basic elements, who does not for example respect his own and the others' acting score, destroying its structure by shamming or automatic reproduction, is the very one who shakes this undefinable higher motive of our common activity. Seemingly small details form the background against which fundamental questions are decided, as for example the duty to note down elements discovered in the course of the work. We must not rely on our memory unless we feel the spontaneity of our work is being threatened, and even then we must keep a partial record. This is just as basic a rule as is strict punctuality, the thorough memorizing of the text, etc. Any form of shamming in one's work is completely inadmissible. However it does sometimes happen that an actor has to go through a scene, just outline it, in order to check its organization and the elements of his partners' actions. But even then he must follow the actions carefully, measuring himself against them, in order to comprehend their motives. This is the difference between outlining and shamming.

An actor must always be ready to join the creative act at the exact moment determined by the group. In this respect his health, physical condition and all his private affairs cease to be just his own concern. A creative act of such quality flourishes only if nourished by the living organism. Therefore we are obliged to take daily care of our bodies so we are always ready for our tasks.

We must not go short of sleep for the sake of private enjoyment and then come to work tired or with a hangover. We must not come unable to concentrate. The rule here is not just one's compulsory presence in the place of work, but physical readiness to create.

## VIII

Creativity, especially where acting is concerned, is boundless sincerity, yet disciplined: i.e. articulated through signs. The creator should not therefore find his material a barrier in this respect. And as the actor's material is his own body, it should be trained to obey, to be pliable, to respond passively to psychic impulses as if it did not exist during the moment of creation – by which we mean it does not offer any resistance. Spontaneity and discipline are the basic aspects of an actor's work and they require a methodical key.

Before a man decides to do something he must first work out a point of orientation and then act accordingly and in a coherent manner. This point of orientation should be quite evident to him, the result of natural convictions, prior observations and experiences in life. The basic foundations of this method constitute for our troupe this point of orientation. Our institute is geared to examining the consequences of this point of orientation. Therefore nobody who comes and stays here can claim a lack of knowledge of the troupe's methodical programme. Anyone who comes and works here and then wants to keep his distance (as regards creative consciousness) shows the wrong kind of care for his own individuality. The etymological meaning of 'individuality' is 'indivisibility' which means complete existence in something: individuality is the very opposite of half-heartedness. We maintain, therefore, that those who come and stay here discover in our method something deeply related to them, prepared by their lives and experiences. Since they accept this consciously, we presume that each of the participants feels obliged to train creatively and try to form his own variation inseparable from himself, his own reorientation open to risks and search. For what we here call 'the method' is the very opposite of any sort of prescription.

## IX

The main point then is that an actor should not try to acquire any kind of recipe or build up a 'box of tricks'. This is no place for collecting all sorts of means of expression. The force of gravity in our work pushes the actor towards an interior ripening which expresses itself through a willingness to break through barriers, to search for a 'summit', for totality.

The actor's first duty is to grasp the fact that nobody here wants **to give** him anything; instead they plan **to take** a lot from him, to take away that to which he is usually very attached: his resistance, reticence, his inclination to hide behind masks, his half-heartedness, the obstacles his body places in the way of his creative act, his habits and even his usual 'good manners'.

## X

Before an actor is able to achieve a total act he has to fulfil a number of requirements, some of which are so subtle, so intangible, as to be practically undefinable through words. They only become plain through practical application. It is easier, however, to define conditions under which a total act cannot be achieved and which of the actor's actions make it impossible.

This act cannot exist if the actor is more concerned with charm, personal success, applause and salary than with creation as understood in its highest form. It cannot exist if the actor conditions it according to the size of his part, his place in the performance, the day or kind of audience. There can be no total act if the actor, even away from the theatre, dissipates his creative impulse and, as we said before, sullies it, blocks it, particularly through incidental engagements of a doubtful nature or by the premeditated use of the creative act as a means to further his own career.

■   ■   ■

## Source

Grotowski, J. (1968, 1969) 'Statement of Principles', *Towards a Poor Theatre*, trans. M. Buszewicz and J. Barba, ed. E. Barba, London: Methuen: 211–218.

# Jerzy Grotowski (1933–1999)

Polish director. Along with Stanislavski and Brecht, he is credited with establishing a new form of actor training for the twentieth century. His purpose was always more philosophical – 'the quest for what is most essential in life . . . something like a second birth'. Grotowski, with his Theatre of Thirteen Rows (Opole, 1959–62), then transformed into the Laboratory Theatre (1962–84), revolutionised the art of performance.

He insisted that the actor should be the prime energy and source of any theatre production and, moreover, that the space should be adapted to suit the dynamic of the individual theatre piece. From 1959 to 1970 he developed exercises and vocal techniques which produced some of Europe's most intense performances, such as *Kordian* (1962), *Akropolis* (1962), *Dr Faustus* (1963), and *The Constant Prince* (1965), most of which were played in a small upper space in the centre of Wroclaw, from where the Laboratory Theatre toured extensively both within and outside Europe. *Apocalypsus Cum Figuris* (1969), which ran for over twelve years – a quasi-mystic collage of theatrical ideas – has been described by those few who saw it as one of the great theatrical productions of the twentieth century. Through the shock of exposure to Grotowski's theatre, audiences were expected to be transformed, and many throughout Europe have testified to its power. In 1984 the Laboratory Theatre was dissolved and its members went their individual ways, one of which led to the establishment of the Gardzienice Association under the leadership of Wlodzimierz Staniewski. Grotowski himself, after a period in the USA, established a centre in Pontedera, Italy, where he concentrated in his final years on developing the para-theatrical work that formed the last stage of the Laboratory's work.

In this 'Statement' Grotowski outlines his belief that theatre can act as a catalyst for transcendence, and that the actor must, through his training, be a conduit for this change. The text was written for actors of the Laboratory Theatre undergoing a period of trial before being accepted as full members.

## Compare this article with writings by the following authors in this reader

**Artaud** – for a similar messianic role for theatre
**Barba** – a student of Grotowski's, published his first book
**Brook** – acknowledged him as 'unique'
**Brecht, Stanislavski and Meyerhold** – comparison with other European systems of training
**Copeau** – another concern for the actor
**Hijikata** – a contemporary, comparable Japanese account of the performer's role
**Kantor** – a Polish artist contemporary with Grotowski
**Rainer** – an approach to performance in many ways completely antithetical
**Soyinka** – a West African perspective on ritual

## Further reading

Allain, P. (ed.) (2009) *Grotowski's Empty Room,* London: Seagull Books.
Bradby, D. and Williams, D. (1988) *Directors' Theatre,* London: Macmillan.
Kumiega, J. (1985) *The Theatre of Grotowski,* London: Methuen.
Mitter, S. (1992) *Systems of Rehearsal,* London: Routledge.
Richards, T. (1995) *At Work with Grotowski on Physical Actions,* London: Routledge.
Schechner, R. and Wolford, L. (1997) *The Grotowski Sourcebook,* London: Routledge.

# Chapter 32

## Tatsumi Hijikata

## MAN, ONCE DEAD, CRAWL BACK!

**A**NXIETY has sown itself everywhere. It lies always ahead of the action, just like the school kid who pisses in his pants just as the whistle blows at the school races.

This form of anxiety is growing — anxiety over the present, anxiety over the future. However, there is not the slightest trace of fear in this condition. I wonder how it can be that this situation arose.

There is a lot of anxiety present at my dance lessons: one finds there many people festering due to their own turbid eroticism. All kinds gather at the studio, some forlorn, some just passing through. In teaching butoh my aim is to make them aware of a part of themselves that they have lost contact with, by making them study themselves body and soul. They are inhibited by their anxieties, but through the means of dance they can share their anxieties with each other.

Learning dance is not a matter of where to position an arm or a leg. Since I believe neither in a dance teaching method nor in controlling movement, I do not teach in this manner. I have never believed in these systems; I have been mistrustful of them since the day I was born.

Recently, it is possible to distinguish between the fighters and the pleasure seekers in this life. On the one hand, those who throw bombs, and on the other hand, those who are completely indifferent. Superficially they seem to be at extremes, but they share one thing in common: their homogeneity. They are mistaken in thinking that hurling bombs or turning away makes them diametrically opposed. One should do both!

As an example, the troops that fight continually in battle tire quickly. If they were immersed in the spirit of butoh, one man would be able to do the work of two and recovery would be quicker. This butoh spirit is what I try to impart during lessons in my studio. Younger people start with great enthusiasm in some endeavor, but their ardor quickly cools off. This is because they are acquainted only with the superficial and ostentatious aspects of life. Through immersing oneself wholly in dance one can encounter the butoh spirit. It is here, rather than in the stage performance, that one finds the real meaning of butoh.

When one considers the body in relation to dance, it is then that one truly realizes what suffering is: it is a part of our lives. No matter how much we search for it from the outside there is no way we can find it without delving into ourselves.

We are broken from birth. We are only corpses standing in the shadow of life. Therefore, what is the point of becoming a professional dancer? If a man becomes a laborer and a woman a servant, isn't that enough in itself!

That is the essence of butoh — and that is how I lead my communal life.

We should live in the present. We should do what we have to do now and not keep putting it on the long finger as the majority of adults do. This is why they exhaust themselves. For children, there is only the present. They are not afraid. Fear envelops us in a fine mesh. We must remove this mesh.

There is nothing to fear in the avant-garde; it's only a dry intellectual comprehension. We *should* be afraid! The reason that we suffer from anxiety is that we are unable to live with our fears. Anxiety is something created by adults. The dancer, through the butoh spirit, confronts the origins of his fears: a dance which crawls towards the bowel of the earth. I don't believe this is possible with European dance.

The body is fundamentally chaotic; the Japanese body particularly, which in comparison with the coherent body of the Occidental (both religiously and culturally), is unsure in its stance. Occidentals have their feet planted firmly on the ground, forming a pyramid, whereas the Japanese seem to be performing acrobatic feats on oil paper. Therefore, they have to find their balance on twisted legs.

For my next performance I plan to use *geta* (wooden sandals). There are now only seven artisans in Tokyo capable of inserting the 'teeth' for the foot strap. Eventually I will have to ask the craftsmen of the Osaka area. Gradually the environment in which we live is becoming a toothless one in every sense of the word.

Once fallen, man must rise again. It is not only a matter of straightening one's back and facing the sun. I am not interested in having an ordinary theater troupe, but rather a troupe which has experienced the vagaries of this world. Once, there was a very noticeable change in a member of the troupe who had returned after a period of absence. On being asked what had happened to him, he replied that he had been washing dishes! For these kind of people dance is a way of helping them from burning up; it acts as a lubricant. That is why I do not see any value in either literature or painting that does not contain the essence of butoh.

I abhor a world which is regulated from the cradle to the grave. I prefer the dark to the dazzling light. Darkness is the best symbol for light. There is no way that one can understand the nature of light if one never observes deeply the darkness. A proper understanding of both requires that both their inherent natures be truly understood.

One does not need to be dazzling like an alien from another star. I would like to construct a huge countryside in Tokyo.

The young should not become sensual addicts. They need a real desire and must act in accordance with it — dance with it, without imposing regulations on themselves.

Don't mince your steps, take a giant step!
One should believe in the energy born in oneself out of suffering.
One shouldn't become a *bonsai* (miniature tree).
Believe in your own energy and don't let yourself be affected by others.

■ ■ ■

## Source

Hijikata, T. (1988) 'Man, once dead, crawl back!', *Butoh: Shades of Darkness,* ed. N. Masson-Sekine, Tokyo: Shufonotomo: 186–189.

## Tatsumi Hijikata (1928–86)

Japanese dancer and choreographer. His early training in techniques derived from modern dance, notably with Kazuko Matsumura, whose work derived, via Takaya Eguchi, from Wigman. He began to present his own work in 1959, with *Kinjiki* (Forbidden Colours), based on a novel by Yukio Mishima (1915–70). In 1960 he termed his work Ankoku Buyo (Dance of Darkness), later Ankoku Butoh. He worked with Kazuo Ohno, who became his pupil and collaborator. From the late 1960s he also worked with Yoko Ashikawa, Saga Kobayashi and Monoko Hinura among others.

Hijikata developed a form, which was both uniquely Japanese and contemporary — Butoh. It could be seen as the antithesis of the liberation sought during the same period by contemporary Western dancers. In both its themes — cruelty, death, darkness, sexual perversion — and its concomitant attitude towards the body as 'fundamentally chaotic' it is a dance of denial. This is seen in *Saint Marquis – Dance of Darkness* (1960), *Secret Ceremony for an Hermaphrodite* (1961) and *Butoh Genet* (1967). His work with Kazuo Ohno included the celebrated *Admiring La Argentina* (1977) and with Ashikawa, *Nippon No Chibusa* (Breasts of Japan) (1983). Hijikata is ranked alongside

Ohno as the co-founder of Butoh. The many dance artists who followed him acknow-ledge his enormous influence. His work began to be seen more widely in the West in the early 1980s; as he said, 'we bring to the bright summer of Europe a little bit of violent darkness from Japan'.[1]

Hijikata comments here on his philosophy of dance. In this sense he outlines his attitude towards performance, rather than detailing process. Indeed, he speaks against a systematic approach to dance. His statements on the body will find resonance with those attracted by chaos as a defining feature of the postmodern condition, but not with those for whom reason is a virtue.

## Compare this article with writings by the following authors in this reader

**Artaud and Marinetti** – early European celebrations of the irrational
**Brown and Rainer** – completely antithetical, contemporary views of dance
**Grotowski and Barba** – contemporary European parallels
**Kantor** – a contemporary view of a theatre of death
**Richter** – an earlier, Western view of chaos
**Schechner** – a Western view of the role of the avant-garde
**Soyinka** – different views on the place of traditional forms

## Further reading

Baird, B. (2012) *Hijikata Tatsumi and Butoh: Dancing in a Pool of Gray Grits*, London: Palgrave Macmillan.
Barber, S. (2010) *Hijikata: Revolt of the body*, Washington, D.C.: Solar.
Blackwood, M. (1990) *Butoh: Body on the Edge of Crisis*, New York: Michael Blackwood.

## Note

1    Hijikata, T. (1983) *Ankoku Buto*, Programme, Festival of Japanese Arts, Not-tingham Playhouse, 24 June–1 July 1983.

# Chapter 33

# Alfred Jarry

## OF THE FUTILITY OF THE 'THEATRICAL' IN THEATER

I THINK THE QUESTION of whether the theater should adapt itself to the public, or the public to the theater, has been settled once and for all. The public only understood, or looked as if they under-stood, the tragedies and comedies of ancient Greece because they were based on universally known fables which, anyway, were explained over and over again in every play and, as often as not, hinted at by a character in the prologue. Just as nowadays they go to hear the plays of Molière and Racine at the Comédie Française because they are always being played, even though they certainly don't really understand them. The theater has not yet won the freedom to eject forcibly any member of the audience who doesn't understand, or to comb out the potential hecklers and hooligans from the auditorium during each interval. But we can content ourselves with the established truth that if people do fight in the theater it will be a work of popularization they are fighting over, one that is not in the least original and is therefore more readily accessible than the original. An original work will, at least on the first night, be greeted by a public that remains bemused and, consequently, dumb.

But first nights are attended by those capable of understanding!

If we want to lower ourselves to the level of the public there are two things we can do for them – and which *are* done for them. The first is to give them characters who think as they do (a Siamese or Chinese ambassador seeing *The Miser* would bet anything that the miser would be outwitted and his money box stolen), and whom they understand perfectly. When this is the case they receive two

impressions; firstly they think that they must themselves be very witty, as they laugh at what they take to be witty writing – and this never fails to happen to Monsieur Donnay's audiences. Secondly they get the impression that they are participating in the creation of the play, which relieves them of the effort of anticipating what is going to happen. The other thing we can do for them is give them a commonplace sort of plot – write about things that happen all the time to the common man, because the fact is that Shakespeare, Michelangelo, or Leonardo da Vinci are somewhat bulky; their diameter is a bit difficult to traverse because genius, intelligence, and even talent are larger than life and so inaccessible to most people.

If, in the whole universe, there are five hundred people who, compared with infinite mediocrity, have a touch of Shakespeare and Leonardo in them, is it not only fair to grant these five hundred healthy minds the same thing that is lavished on Monsieur Donnay's audiences – the relief of not seeing on the stage what they don't understand; the *active* pleasure of participating in the creation of the play and of anticipation?

What follows is a list of a few things which are particularly horrifying and incomprehensible to the five hundred, and which clutter up the stage to no purpose; first and foremost, the *decor* and the *actors*.

Decor is a hybrid, neither natural nor artificial. If it were exactly like nature it would be a superfluous duplication. . . . (We shall consider the use of nature as decor later.) It is not artificial, in the sense that it is not, for the five hundred, the embodiment of the outside world as the playwright has seen and re-created it.

And in any case it would be dangerous for the poet to impose on a public of artists the decor that he himself would conceive. In any written work there is a hidden meaning, and anyone who knows how to read sees that aspect of it that makes sense for him. He recognizes the eternal and invisible river and calls it *Anna Perenna*.[1] But there is hardly anyone for whom a painted backdrop has two meanings, as it is far more arduous to extract the quality from a quality than the quality from a quantity. Every spectator has a right to see a play in a decor which does not clash with his own view of it. For the general public, on the other hand, any 'artistic' decor will do, as the masses do not understand anything by themselves, but wait to be told how to see things.

There are two sorts of decor: indoor and outdoor. Both are supposed to represent either rooms or the countryside. We shall not revert to the question, which has been settled once and for all, of the stupidity of *trompe l'œil*. Let us state that the said *trompe l'œil* is aimed at people who only see things roughly, that is to say, who do not see at all: it scandalizes those who see nature in an intelligent and selective way, as it presents them with a caricature of it by someone who lacks all understanding. Zeuxis is supposed to have deceived some birds with his stone grapes, and Titian's virtuosity hoodwinked an innkeeper.

Decor by someone who cannot paint is nearer to abstract decor, as it gives only essentials. In the same way simplified decor picks out only relevant aspects.

We tried *heraldic* decors, where a single shade is used to represent a whole scene or act, with the characters poised harmonically *passant* against the heraldic field. This is a bit puerile, as the said color can only establish itself against a colorless background (but it is also more accurate, since we have to take into account the prevailing red-green color blindness, as well as other idiosyncrasies of perception). A colorless background can be achieved simply, and in a way which is symbolically accurate, by an unpainted backdrop or the reverse side of a set. Each spectator can then conjure up for himself the background he requires, or, better still, if the author knew what he was about, the spectator can imagine, by a process of exosmosis, that what he sees on the stage is the real decor. The placard brought in to mark each change in scene saves the onlooker from being regularly reminded of base 'reality' through a constant substitution of conventional sets which he really only sees properly at the moment the scene is being shifted.

In the conditions we are advocating, each piece of scenery needed for a special purpose – a window to be opened, for instance, or a door to be broken down – becomes a prop and can be brought in like a table or a torch.

The actor adapts his face to that of the character. He should adapt his whole body in the same way. The play of his features, his expressions, etc., are caused by various contractions and extensions of the muscles of his face. No one has realized that the muscles remain the same under the make-believe, made-up face, and that Mounet and Hamlet do not have the same zygomatics, even though in anatomical terms we think that they are the same man. Or else people say that the difference is negligible. The actor should use a mask to envelop his head, thus replacing it by the effigy of the CHARACTER. His mask should not follow the masks in the Greek theater to indicate simply tears or laughter, but should indicate the nature of the character: the Miser, the Waverer, the Covetous Man accumulating crimes. . . .

And if the eternal nature of the character is embodied in the mask, we can learn from the kaleidoscope, and particularly the gyroscope, a simple means of *illuminating*, one by one or several at a time, the critical moments.

With the old-style actor, masked only in a thinly applied make-up, each facial expression is raised to a power by color and particularly by relief, and then to cubes and higher powers by LIGHTING.

What we are about to describe was impossible in the Greek theater because the light was vertical, or at least never sufficiently horizontal, and therefore produced a shadow under every protuberance in the mask; it was a blurred shadow, though, because the light was diffused.

Contrary to the deductions of rudimentary and imperfect logic, there is no clear shadow in those sunny countries; and in Egypt, below the tropic of Cancer, there is hardly a trace of shadow left on the face. The light was reflected vertically as if by the face of the moon, and diffused by both the sand on the ground and the sand suspended in the air.

The *footlights* illumine the actor along the hypotenuse of a right-angled triangle, the actor's body forming one of the sides of the right angle. And as the footlights are a series of luminous points, that is to say a line which, in relation to the narrowness of the front view of the actor, extends indefinitely to right and left of its intersection with the actor's plane, these footlights should be considered as a single point of light situated at an indefinite distance, as if it were *behind* the audience.

It is true that the footlights are less than an infinite distance away, so that one cannot really regard all the rays reflected by the actor (or facial expressions) as traveling along parallel lines. But in practice each spectator sees the character's mask *equally*, with the differences which are certainly negligible compared to the idiosyncrasies and different perceptive attitudes of the individual spectator. These differences cannot be attenuated, though they cancel each other out in the audience *qua* herd, which is what an audience is.

By slow nodding and lateral movements of his head the actor can displace the shadows over the whole surface of his mask. And experience has shown that the six main positions (and the same number in profile, though these are less clear) suffice for every expression. We shall not cite any examples, as they vary according to the nature of the mask, and because everyone who knows how to watch a puppet show will have been able to observe this for himself.

They are simple expressions, and therefore universal. Present-day mime makes the great mistake of using conventional mime language, which is tiring and incomprehensible. An example of this convention is the hand describing a vertical ellipse around the face, and a kiss being implanted on this hand to suggest a beautiful woman – and love. An example of universal gesture is the marionette displaying its bewilderment by starting back violently and hitting its head against a flat.

Behind all these accidentals there remains the essential expression, and the finest thing in many scenes is the impassivity of the mask, which remains the same whether the words it emits are grave or gay. This can only be compared with the solid structure of the skeleton, deep down under its surrounding animal flesh; its tragicomic qualities have always been acknowledged.

It goes without saying that the actor must have a special *voice*, the voice that is appropriate to the part, as if the cavity forming the mouth of the mask were incapable of uttering anything other than what the mask would say, if the muscles of its lips could move. And it is better for them not to move, and that the whole play should be spoken in a monotone.

And we have also said that the actor must take on the body appropriate to the part.

Transvestism has been forbidden by the Church and by art. Witness Beaumarchais, who in one of his prefaces wrote: 'The young man does not exist who is sufficiently developed to . . .' And since women are beardless and their voices shrill all their lives, a boy of fourteen is traditionally played on the Paris stage by a twenty-year-old woman who, being six years older, has much more experience. This is small compensation for her ridiculous profile and unesthetic walk, or for the way the outline of all her muscles is vitiated by adipose tissue, which is odious because it has a function – it produces *milk*.

Given the difference in their brains, a boy of fifteen, if you pick an intelligent one, will play his part adequately (most women are vulgar and nearly all boys are stupid, with some outstanding exceptions). The young actor Baron, in Molière's company, is an example, and there is also the whole period in the English theater (and the whole history of the Greek theater) when no one would have dreamed of trusting a part to a woman.

A few words on natural decors, which exist without duplication if one tries to stage a play in the open air, on the slope of a hill, near a river, which is excellent for carrying the voice, especially when there is no awning, even though the sound may be weakened. Hills are all that is necessary, with a few trees for shade. At the moment *Le Diable Marchand de Goutte* is being played out of doors, as it was a year ago, and the production was discussed some time ago in the *Mercure* by Alfred Vallette. Three or four years ago Monsieur Lugné-Poe and some friends staged *La Gardienne* at Presles, on the edge of the Isle-Adam forest. In these days of universal cycling it would not be absurd to make use of summer Sundays in the countryside to stage a few very short performances (say from two to five o'clock in the afternoon) of literature which is not too abstract – *King Lear* would be a good example; we do not understand the idea of a people's theater. The performances should be in places not too far distant, and arrangements should be made for people who come by train, without previous planning. The places in the sun should be free (Monsieur Barrucand was writing quite recently about the free theater), and as for the props, the bare necessities could be transported in one or several automobiles.

## Note

1    Dido's sister, who came to Rome and drowned in a river, of which she became the nymph. *Amne perenne latens, Anna Perenna vocor.*
(Ovid, Fasti, Book III, 1. 654.) [Translator's note.]

■    ■    ■

## Source

Jarry, A. (1896, 1985) 'Of the Futility of the "Theatrical" in the Theater', *Selected Works of Alfred Jarry*, trans. B. Wright (eds) R. Shattuck and S. Watson Taylor, London: Methuen: 69–75.

## Alfred Jarry (1873–1907)

The first performance of Jarry's *Ubu Roi* on 10 December 1896 in many ways marks the beginning of the modernist play. A wild parody of Shakespeare, it was originally written for marionettes, and its performance by actors with masks and sets by Pierre Bonnard, Toulouse-Lautrec and others, directed by Lugné-Poe at the Théâtre de l'Œuvre, provoked scenes of violence and pandemonium in the audience. Jarry's work, in plays, essays and fiction, was perceived as a direct attack on the fundamental concepts of Western civilisation. He promoted a bitingly satiric denigration of bourgeois values via parodies of existing nineteenth-century theatrical styles. *Ubu*, and the writings surrounding it – *Ubu Cocu, Ubu's Almanac* (1901), *Days and Nights* (1897), and *César Antéchrist* – are the key works in which Jarry questions all forms of rational thought and structure. *Père Ubu* was seen as a monstrous symbol of modern bourgeois society, which thus stands condemned by its own actions. Jarry eventually completely identified with *Ubu*, taking on the persona of *Ubu* himself, and invented the science of 'pataphysics,[1] which he defined as 'the science of imaginary solutions' and 'the science of the laws governing exceptions'.

Jarry's essay proposes to do away with realistic decor, to create a physical acting style that can utilise masks, and vocal skills that can produce emblematic performances that eschew all naturalistic devices. In other words the curse of theatre is its bogus theatricality, and the public needs more immediacy and less artifice, as society needs, in similar manner, to shed its bourgeois pretensions.

## Compare this article with writings by the following authors in this reader

**Artaud** – who wished for a theatre, which would stir audiences from their apathy
**Beck** – a later revolutionary view of change through theatre
**Copeau** – a French parallel
**Richter** – for the origins of Dada, which owed much to Jarry's absurdist ideas
**Marinetti** – for another view of the necessity of change

## Further reading

Esslin, M. (1961) *The Theatre of the Absurd*, London: Anchor Books.
Fell, J. (2010) *Alfred Jarry*, London: Reaktion Books.
Shattuck, R. (1958) *The Banquet Years*, London: Harcourt Brace.

## Note

1    This introduction to Jarry has been approved by the Collège de 'Pataphysique.

# Chapter 34

# Wassily Kandinsky

## ON STAGE COMPOSITION

**E**ACH ART HAS ITS OWN LANGUAGE, that is, its own methods.

Each art is something complete in itself. Each art leads a life of its own. It is an empire in itself.

Therefore the methods of the various arts are completely different externally. Sound, color, word! . . .

*In their innermost core* these methods are wholly identical: their final goal obliterates external differences and reveals their inner identity.

The *final* goal (knowledge) is reached through delicate vibrations of the human soul. These delicate vibrations are ultimately identical, although their inner motions are different.

The undefinable and still distinct spiritual action (vibration) is the goal of the various methods of art.

A distinctive complex of vibrations is the goal of a work.

The refinement of the soul through the accumulation of distinctive complexes—this is the goal of art.

*Art is*, therefore, indispensable and *practical*.

When the artist finds the appropriate means, it is a material form of his soul's vibration, which he is forced to express.

If the method is appropriate, it causes an almost identical vibration in the soul of the audience.

This is inevitable. But this secondary vibration is complicated. It may be strong or weak; this depends on the audience's level of development and on the influence of the times (the absorbed soul). Second, these vibrations in the audience's soul will also cause other strings to vibrate in turn. This is a stimulation of the audience's "fantasy," which "continues to create" the work.[1] These strings of the soul, which vibrate frequently, will also vibrate when other strings are sounded. And sometimes so intensely that they drown out the original sound. Some people are moved to tears when listening to "happy" music and vice versa. Therefore particular effects of a work are more or less colored by their different receptions.

But in this case the original sound is not destroyed. It lives on and continues—even if unnoticed—to work on the soul.[2]

There is no man who does not respond to art. Each work and each method of work causes in every man without exception a vibration fundamentally identical to that felt by the artist.

The inner, eventually discoverable identity of the separate methods in the various arts has been the basis for an attempt to strengthen a specific sound in one art with an identical sound in another art, to reinforce it and thus to obtain an especially powerful effect. This is one way of producing effect.

But the repetition of one method of one art (e.g., music) by means of an identical method of another art (e.g., painting) is only *one* case, only *one* possibility. When this possibility is also used as an inner method (e.g., in Scriabin),[3] we first consider the sphere of contrast and complicated composition as the opposite of this repetition and later as a series of possibilities that lie between effect and counter-effect. The material is inexhaustible.

The nineteenth century is distinguished as a period that lay far from inner creation. Its concentration on material appearances and on the material aspects of appearances logically caused internal creative powers to decline to the point of their virtual disappearance.

This one-dimensionality naturally caused other manifestations of one-dimensionality to develop.

So it was also with the theater:

1. Here perforce (as in other fields) already existing parts (created earlier) were minutely elaborated and distinctly separated from one another, because it seemed convenient to do so. This reflects the specialization that always arises immediately when no new forms are being created, and

2. The positive character of the spirit of the time could lead only to a form of combination that was likewise positive. People thought: two is more than one, and they tried to strengthen each effect by repeating it. With inner effects this may be reversed, and often one is more than two. In mathematics $1 + 1 = 2$. In the soul it is possible that $1 - 1 = 2$.

Elaboration to 1. Specialization and the further external elaboration of parts is the *first consequence of materialism*. As a result three groups of stage works arose and became petrified, separated from one another by high walls: (a) drama, (b) opera, (c) ballet.

(a) Drama of the nineteenth century is, in general, a more or less subtle and profound account of events of a more or less personal character. Usually it is a description of external life; the spiritual life played a part only when it was connected with the external life.[4] *The cosmic element was entirely missing.*

*The external action and the external connection of the plot is the form of contemporary drama.*

(b) Opera is drama to which music has been added as the principal element, causing the subtlety and profundity of the dramatic aspect to suffer severely. The two parts are connected only externally. This means that either the music illustrates (or strengthens) the dramatic action, or the dramatic action helps to explain the music.

This sore spot was recognized by Wagner, and he tried to improve it by various means. His basic idea was to connect the parts organically and in this way to create a monumental work.[5]

Wagner tried to intensify the means and bring the work to a monumental height by repeating one and the same external movement in two concrete forms. His mistake was to believe that he had a universal method at his command. Actually his method is only one of a series of even more powerful possibilities of monumental art.

Parallel repetition is only *one* method, and an external repetition at that. Wagner nonetheless gave it a new form that had to lead to other forms. Before Wagner movement, for example, was entirely external and superficial in opera (perhaps only decadent). It was a naive appendage to opera: pressing the hands against the chest—love; lifting the arms—prayer; extending the arms—strong emotion, etc. Such childlike forms (which can still be seen every night) were externally connected with the libretto, which again was illustrated by the music. Wagner connected movement and musical beat directly (artistically): the movement was subordinated to the beat.

This connection is still external. The inner sound of the movement plays no part.

In the same artistic but still external fashion Wagner subordinated the music to the libretto, that is, to the movement in a broad sense. He represented musically the hissing of glowing iron in water, the beating of a hammer in the smithy, etc.

This *interchanged* subordination increased the methods, leading thereby to further combinations.

On the one hand Wagner increased the effect of one method, and on the other hand he decreased the inner sense, the purely artistic inner meaning, of the auxiliary method.

These forms are only mechanical reproductions (not internal parallel effects) of purposeful actions in the plot. The second connection of music and movement (in the broad sense of the word) is similar; it is the musical "characterization" of various roles. The stubborn recurrence of a motif whenever the protagonist appears on the stage is finally losing its power. It affects the ear in the same way as a well-known label on a bottle affects the eye. Feeling ultimately rebels against such a consistent programmatic use of one and the same form.[6]

Finally Wagner uses the word to tell the story or to express his thoughts. However, he does not create an appropriate milieu for his purposes, because the words are usually drowned out by the orchestra. It is not enough to let the word sound in numerous recitatives. But the attempt to interrupt the incessant singing has already dealt a powerful blow to the "unity." Nevertheless, the external action remains untouched by it.

Despite Wagner's efforts to create a libretto (movement), he still completely followed the old tradition of the external, and he did not consider the third element, which is sporadically used today in a still-primitive form[7]—color and, connected with it, pictorial form (decoration).

*The external action, the external connection of the various parts and of the two methods (drama and music) is the form of contemporary opera.*

(c) Ballet is a drama with all the characteristics mentioned above and with the same content. The seriousness of the drama is lost, even more so than in opera. Opera has themes other than love: religious, political, and social relationships are the grounds for enthusiasm, despair, honesty, hate, and similar feelings. Ballet contents itself with love in a childlike fairy-tale form. Besides music, single and group movements are made use of. Everything remains in a naive form of external connection. It is even customary for various dances to be inserted or omitted at will. The "whole" is so problematic that such practices go entirely unnoticed.

*The external action, the external connection of the various parts and of the three methods (drama, music, and dance) is the form of contemporary ballet.*

Elaboration to 2. Through the *second consequence of materialism*, i.e., positive addition (1 + 1 = 2, 2 + 1 = 3), only one form of combination (or intensification) was brought about, and this demanded the same kind of methods. Thus powerful emotion was instantly underlined by a fortissimo in music. *This mathematical principle constructs the forms of effect on an entirely external basis.*

All the *forms* mentioned, which I call forms of substance (drama—word, opera—sound, ballet—movement), and the combination of various methods, which I call methods for effect, were constructed to form an *external unity. All these forms originated from the principle of external necessity.*

The logical result of this is the limitation, the one-dimensionality (= impoverishment) of forms and methods. Gradually they become orthodox and each tiny change appears to be revolutionary.

Let us start on the basis of the internal. The whole state of affairs changes fundamentally.

1. Suddenly the external appearance of each element vanishes, and its inner value sounds fully.

2. Clearly, when the criterion of the inner sound is applied, the outer action obviously is not only unimportant but also creates harmful obscurity.

3. The external connection appears in its proper value, i.e., setting up unnecessary limits and weakening the inner effect.

4. Automatically the feeling of the necessity of *internal unity* is aroused. This is supported and even caused by external irregularities.

5. It opens up the possibility for each element to keep its own external life, even if it contradicts the external life of another element.

If we make practical discoveries out of these abstract ones, we see that it is possible:

Elaboration to 1. To use as a method the inner sound of only one element.

Elaboration to 2. To eliminate the external action (= plot) so that

Elaboration to 3. The external connection collapses of its own accord, just like

Elaboration to 4. The external unity, and

Elaboration to 5. That the inner unity gives rise to an endless series of methods that earlier could not exist.

*The inner necessity becomes the only source.*

The following little stage composition is an attempt to draw upon this source.

There are three elements that as external methods serve the *inner value*:

1. The musical sound and its movement,

2. The physical-psychical sound and its movement, expressed through people and objects,

3. The colored tone and its movement (a special possibility for the stage).

The drama finally consists of the complex of inner experiences (soul = vibrations) of the audience.

Elaboration to 1. Music, the main element and source of the inner sound, was taken from opera. It should never be externally subordinated to the action.

Elaboration to 2. Dance was taken from ballet. It is involved with inner sound as abstract effective movement.

Elaboration to 3. The colored tone has an independent importance and is treated as a method with equal rights.

All three elements play equally important roles; they remain externally independent and are treated equally, i.e., they are subordinated to the inner goal.

Music, for example, may be entirely pushed into the background or played offstage when the effect of the movement is expressive enough, and powerful musical collaboration would only weaken it. An increase of musical movement may correspond to a decrease of dance movement; in this way both movements (the positive and the negative) enhance their inner value. There are numerous combinations between these two poles: collaboration and contrast. Graphically speaking, the three movements could run in entirely separate, externally independent directions.

The word, independent or in sentences, was used to create a certain "atmosphere" that frees the soul and makes it receptive. The sound of the human voice was also used pure, i.e., without being obscured by words, or by the meaning of words.

The reader is asked to attribute the weaknesses of the following little composition, *The Yellow Sound*, not to the principle of stage compositions, but to its author's account.

### Notes

1    This "collaboration" is counted on especially in theatrical productions nowadays, although it has naturally always been planned for by the artist. This produces the desire for a certain free space between the work and its ultimate expression. This "do-not-utter-the-ultimate" was demanded by Lessing and Delacroix, among others. Space is left free for the work of fantasy.

2    Therefore each work is correctly "understood" in the course of time.

3    See L. Sabaneiev's article in this volume.

4    There are few exceptions. Even these few (e.g., Maeterlinck, Ibsen's *Ghosts*, Andreyev's *Life of Man*, etc.) are under the spell of external events.

5    It has taken Wagner's idea more than half a century to cross the Alps. Now it is authoritatively expressed there in the form of articles. Take the musical "manifesto" of the futurists: "We proclaim as an absolute necessity that the composer must be the author of a dramatic or tragic poem that he has to set to music" (May 1911, Milan).

6    This programmatic use penetrates Wagner's work. Probably it may be explained not only by the artist's character, but also by his intention to discover a precise form for his new kind of creativity. The spirit of the nineteenth century gave it the "positive" stamp.

7    See Sabaneiev's article.

■　■　■

### Source

Kandinsky, W. (1974) 'On Stage Composition', *The Blaue Reiter Almanac*, ed. W. Kandinsky and F. Marc, London: Thames and Hudson: 190–206.

### Wassily Kandinsky (1866–1944)

Russian artist who was born in Moscow, lived in Odessa and became a French citizen in 1939, dying there in 1944. He is credited with being the first painter to work with abstraction in the 'direction of open, molten, and dissolved form'. His painting became the first consciously non-objective work, derived in the main from his belief that certain colours evoke certain responses in the viewer. 'In time it will become possible for us to speak through purely artistic means . . .' He was part of the generation of artists in revolt against established forms just before the First World War, and was a member of the Blaue Reiter collective of artists who wished for a total synthesis of international culture. His interest in the synthesis of the arts led him to write a series of 'colour-tone' dramas of which the most famous is *The Yellow Sound* of 1909, the scenario of which was published in the Blaue Reiter Almanac of 1912, from which his essay on Stage Composition comes. In it he introduces his ideas for 'the cosmic element' in drama, which would liberate it from 'accounts of a more or less personal character'. He wanted art to produce a 'spiritual vibration' in the viewer, for which it would need to be free from all associations with naturalism, thus becoming autonomous. Here he is linked with the ideas of Tadeusz Kantor, who also wanted a theatre free from all accepted naturalistic connections. Kandinsky's ideas also owe a lot to the then experimental ideas of the composer Richard Wagner (1813–1883), who had postulated the project of the Gesamtkunstwerk, or Total World Work, as being a theatrical form which would unite all the arts. Much of Kandinsky's essay is concerned with art that can deal with both the external and internal in a form that is unclassifiable, and so chimes in with many of today's current performance ideas. There are also links with the Italian Futurists, who wanted a new music that embraced ideas of 'sound' as exemplified in Luigi Russolo's sound machines of the period before and during the First World War.

From 1922 to 1933 Kandinsky taught at the famous Bauhaus School of Art in Weimar and Dessau, at the same time as Oscar Schlemmer, who was pioneering a stage course with similar ideas. In fact Schlemmer's *Triadic Ballet* was created in the same year that Kandinsky joined the school, though there is no record of his thoughts on it nor on any meeting between these two great pioneers. However, Kandinsky did some analytical drawings of the dances of Gret Palucca, a dancer who had Bauhaus contacts. Kandinsky left the Bauhaus in 1933, when the Nazis closed it down, but had by that time become disaffected with its changes.

*The Yellow Sound*, however, together with three other dramas, was never produced in his lifetime, finally reaching the stage only in 1972 in a performance at the Guggenheim Museum in New York.

## Compare this article with writings by the following authors in this reader

**Graham** – for ideas of contemporary dance
**Kantor** – for ideas of non-naturalistic theatre
**Marinetti** – for the synthesis ideas of the Futurists
**Newson** – for a contemporary dance/theatre company
**Schlemmer** – another Bauhaus teacher

## Further reading

Duchting, H. (1999) *Wassily Kandinsky: 1866–1944 A Revolution in Painting*, Köln: Taschen.
Lindsay, K. and Vergo, P. (1994) *Kandinsky: Complete Writings*, Boston, Mass.: Da Capo Press.

# Chapter 35

# Tadeusz Kantor

## THE THEATRE OF DEATH: A MANIFESTO

*1 Craig's Postulate: to bring back the marionette. Eliminate the live actor. Man — a creature of nature — is a foreign intrusion into the abstract structure of a work of art.*

According to Gordon Craig, somewhere along the banks of the Ganges two women forced their way into the shrine of the Divine Marionette, which was jealously hiding the secrets of the true THEATRE. They envied the ROLE of this Perfect Being in illuminating human intellect with the sacred feeling of the existence of God, its GLORY; they spied on its Movements and Gestures, its sumptuous attire and, by cheap parody, began to satisfy the vulgar taste of the mob. At the moment when they finally ordered a similar monument built for themselves — the modern theatre, as we know it only too well and as it has lasted to this day, was born. A clamorous Public Service Institute. With it appeared the ACTOR. In defence of his theory Craig cites the opinion of Eleanor Duse: 'to save the theatre, it must be destroyed, it is necessary for all actors and actresses to die of plague . . . for it is they who render art impossible . . . .'

*2 Craig's Version: Man — the actor ousts the marionette, takes its place, thereby causing the demise of the theatre.*

There is something very impressive in the stand taken by the great Utopian, when he says: 'In all seriousness I demand the return to the theatre of the imagination of the super-marionette . . . and when it appears people will again, as before, be able to worship the happiness of Existence, and render divine and jubilant homage to DEATH . . .' Craig, inspired by the aesthetics of SYMBOLISM, considered man to be subject to unpredictable emotions, passions, and consequently to chance as an element completely foreign to the homogenous nature and structure of a work of art, which destroys its principal trait; cohesion.

Not only Craig's idea but also that whole elaborate programme of symbolism – impressive in its own time – had in the 19th century the support of isolated and unique phenomena announcing a new era and new art: Heinrich von Kleist, Ernst Theodor Amadeus Hoffman. Edgar Allan Poe. . . . One hundred years earlier, Kleist for the same reasons as Craig, demanded the substitution of the actor by the marionette: he regarded the human organism, which is subject to the laws of NATURE, as a foreign intrusion into Artistic Fiction, based on the principle of Construction and Intellect. This accounts for his reproaches stressing the limited capabilities of man and charges of an incessantly controlling consciousness, which excludes the concepts of grace and beauty.

### 3 From the romantic mysticism of mannequins and the artificial creations of man in the XIX century – to the rationalism of XX century abstract thought.

On what seemed to be the safe road traversed by the man of Enlightenment and Rationalism there appears out of the darkness, suddenly and in increasingly greater numbers, DOUBLES, MANNEQUINS, AUTOMATONS, HOMUNCULI. Artificial creations, a mockery of the creatures of NATURE, bearers of absolute degradation, ALL human dreams, DEATH, Horror and Terror. There is born a faith in the unknown powers of MECHANICAL MOVEMENT, a maniacal passion for the invention of a MECHANISM surpassing in perfection and severity the human organism and all its weaknesses.

And all this with an aura of demonism, on the brink of charlatanism, illegal practices, magic, transgression and nightmare. This was the SCIENCE FICTION of those days, in which the demonic human brain created ARTIFICIAL MAN.

At the same time all of this signified an abrupt loss of faith in NATURE and in that realm of man's activity which was closely tied with nature. Paradoxically, from these extremely romantic and diabolical efforts to take away nature's right of creation – there evolved a movement increasingly independent and more and more dangerously distant from NATURE – A RATIONALISTIC, even MATERIALISTIC MOVEMENT of a 'WORLD OF ABSTRACTION', CONSTRUCTIVISM, FUNCTIONALISM, MACHINISM, ABSTRACTION, finally PURIST VISUALISM, recognising only the 'physical presence' of a work of art. This risky hypothesis, whose origin is none too attractive for an age of technology and scientism. I take upon my conscience and for my personal satisfaction.

## 4 Dadaism, introducing 'ready-made' elements of life, destroys the concepts of homogeneity and cohesion in a work of art, as postulated by symbolism. Art Nouveau and Craig.

But let us return to Craig's marionette. Craig's idea of replacing the live actor with a mannequin — an artificial and mechanical creation — for the sake of preserving perfect cohesion in a work of art, is today invalid.

Later experience destroyed the unity of structure in a work of art by introducing FOREIGN elements in collages and assemblages; the acceptance of 'ready-made' reality, full recognition of the role of CHANCE, and the placing of a work of art on the sharp borderline between the REALITY OF LIFE AND ARTISTIC FICTION — made irrelevant those scruples from the beginning of this century, from the period of Symbolism and Art Nouveau. The two possible solutions — either autonomous art and intellectual structure, or naturalism — ceased to be the ONLY ones. When the theatre, in its moments of weakness, submitted to the live organism of man and his laws — it automatically and logically agreed to the form or imitation of life, its presentation and re-creation. In the opposite circumstances, when the theatre was strong and independent enough to free itself from the pressure of life and man, it created artificial equivalents to life which turned out to be more alive, because they submitted easily to the abstractions of space and time and were capable of achieving absolute unity.

Today these possibilities are neither appropriate nor valid alternatives. For a new situation and new conditions have arisen in art. The appearance of the concept of READY-MADE REALITY, extracted from life — and the possibilities of ANNEXING it, INTEGRATING it into a work of art through DECISION, GESTURE or RITUAL — has become a fascination much stronger than (artificially) CONSTRUED reality, than the creation of ABSTRACTION, or the surrealistic world, than Breton's MIRACU-LOUSNESS. Happenings, Events and Environments with their colossal momentum, have achieved the rehabilitation of whole regions of REALITY, disdained until this time, cleansing it of the ballast of life's intentions.

This 'DECALAGE' of life's reality, its derailment from life's practices, moved the human imagination more strongly than the surrealistic reality of dreams. As a result, fears of direct intervention by life and man in the scheme of art — became irrelevant.

## 5 From the 'Ready-Made Reality' of the happening — to the dematerialization of the elements of a work of art.

However, as with all fascination, so too this one, after a time, was transformed into a convention practised universally, senselessly and in a vulgar manner. These almost ritualistic manipulations of Reality, connected as they are with the contestation of ARTISTIC STATUS and the PLACE reserved for art, gradually started to acquire different sense and meaning. The material, physical PRESENCE of an object and PRESENT TIME, the only possible context for activity and action – turned out to be too burdensome, had reached their limits. The TRANSGRESSION signified: depriving these conditions of the material and functional IMPORTANCE, that is, of their COMMUNICA-TIVENESS. Because this is the latest period, still current and not yet closed, the observations which follow derive from and are tied with my own creativity.

The object (*The Chair*, Oslo, 1970) became *empty*, deprived of *expression*, *connections*, *references*, characteristics of programmed *communication*, its '*message*' directed 'nowhere', it changed into a *dummy*.

Situations and activities were locked into their own CIRCUMFERENCE: the ENIGMATIC (theatre of the impossible, 1973), in my manifesto entitled 'Cambriollage', followed the unlawful INTRUSION into that terrain where tangible reality was transformed into its INVISIBLE EXTENSIONS. The role of THOUGHT, memory and TIME becomes increasingly clear.

## 6 The rejection of the orthodoxy of conceptualism and the 'Official Avant-garde of the Masses'.

The certitude which impressed itself upon me more and more strongly that the concept of LIFE can be vindicated in art only through the ABSENCE OF LIFE in its conventional sense (again Craig and the Symbolists!), this process of DEMATERIALIZATION SETTLED on a path which circumvented in my creative work the whole orthodoxy of linguistics and conceptualism. This was probably caused in part by the colossal throng which arose on this already official course and which will unfortunately become the latest instalment of the DADAIST current with its slogans of TOTAL ART, EVERYTHING IS ART, ALL ARE ARTISTS, ART IS IN THE MIND, etc.

I hate crowds. In 1973 I wrote a draft of a new manifesto which takes into consideration this false situation. This is its beginning:

From the time of Verdun, Voltaire's Cabaret and Marcel Duchamp's Water-Closet, when the 'status of art' was drowned out by the roar of Fat Bertha – DECISION became the only remaining human possibility, the reliance on something that was or is unthinkable, functioning as the first stimulant of creativity, conditioning and defining art. Lately thousands of mediocre individuals have been making decisions, without scruples or any hesitation whatever. We are witnesses of the banalization and conventionalization of decision. This once dangerous path has become a comfortable freeway with improved safety measures and information. Guides, maps, orientation tables, directional signs, signals, centres, Art Co-operatives guarantee the excellence of the functioning of creativity. We are witnesses of the GENERAL MOVEMENT of artist-commandos, street fighters, artist-mediators, artist-mailmen, epistologs, pedlars, street magicians, proprietors of Office and Agencies. Movements on this already official freeway, which threatens with a flood of graphomania and deeds of minimal significance, increases with each passing day. It is necessary to leave it as quickly as possible. This is not easily done. Particularly at the apogee of the UNIVERSAL AVANT-GARDE – blind and favoured with the highest prestige of the INTELLECT, which protects both the wise and the stupid.

## 7 On the side streets of the official avant-garde, Mannequins appear.

My deliberate rejection of the solutions of conceptualism, despite the fact that they seemed to be the only way out from the path upon which I had embarked, resulted in my placing the above-mentioned facts of the latest stage of my creativity and attempts to describe them, on side streets which left me more open to the UNKNOWN!!!

I have more confidence in such a situation. Any new era always begins with actions of little apparent significance and little note, incidents having little in common with the recognised trend, actions that are private, intimate, I would even say – shameful. Vague. And difficult! These are the most fascinating and essential moments of creativity.

> All of a sudden I became interested in the nature of
> MANNEQUINS
> The mannequin in my production of THE WATER HEN 1967 and the mannequins in THE
> SHOEMAKERS 1970, had a very specific role: they were like a non-material extension,
> a kind of ADDITIONAL ORGAN for the actor, who was their 'master'. The mannequins
> already widely used in my production of Slowacki's Balladyna were DOUBLES of live
> characters, somehow endowed with a higher CONSCIOUSNESS, attained 'after the
> completion of their lives'.

These mannequins were already clearly stamped with the sign of DEATH.

## 8 The mannequin as manifestation of 'REALITY OF THE LOWEST ORDER'.

The mannequin as dealings of TRANSGRESSION.

The mannequin as EMPTY object. The DUMMY. A message of DEATH. A model for the actor.

The mannequin I used in 1967 at the Cricot 2 Theatre (*The Water Hen*) was a successor to the 'Eternal Wanderer' and 'Human Ambellages', one which appeared naturally in my 'Collections' as yet another phenomenon consistent with my long-held conviction that only the reality of the lowest order, the poorest and least prestigious objects are capable of revealing their full objectivity in a work of art.

Mannequins and Wax Figures have always existed on the peripheries of sanctioned Culture. They were not admitted further; they occupied places in FAIR BOOTHS, suspicious MAGICIANS' CHAMBERS, far from the splendid shrines of art, treated condescendingly as CURIOSITIES intended for the tastes of the masses. For precisely this reason it was they, and not academic, museum creations, which caused the curtain to move at the blink of an eye.

MANNEQUINS also have their own version of TRANSGRESSION. The existence of these creatures, shaped in man's image, almost 'godlessly', in an illegal fashion, is the result of heretical dealings, a manifestation of the Dark, Nocturnal, Rebellious side of human activity. Of Crimes and Traces of Death as sources of recognition. The vague and inexplicable feeling that through this entity so similar to a living human being but deprived of consciousness and purpose there is transmitted to us a terrifying message of Death and Nothingness – precisely this feeling becomes the cause – simultaneously – of that transgression, repudiation and attraction. Of accusation and fascination. All arguments have been exhausted in accusations. The very mechanism of action called their attention to itself, that mechanism which, if taken as the purpose, could easily be relegated to the lower forms of creativity! IMITATION AND DECEPTIVE SIMILARITY, which serve the conjurer in setting his TRAPS and fooling the viewer, the use of 'unsophisticated' means, evading the concepts of aesthetics, the abuse and fraudulent deception of APPEARANCES, practices from the realm of charlatans.

To make matters complete, the entire proceedings were accompanied by a philosophical world-view which, from the time of Plato to this day, often regards as the purpose of art the unmasking of Being and a Spiritual Sense of Existence and not involvement in the Material Shell of the world, in that faking of appearances which are the lowest stage of being.

I do not share the belief that the MANNEQUIN (or a WAX FIGURE) could replace the LIVE ACTOR, as Kleist and Craig wanted. This would be too simple and naive. I am trying to delineate the motives and intent of this unusual creature which has suddenly appeared in my thoughts and ideas. Its appearance complies with my ever-deepening conviction that it is possible to express *life* in art only through the *absence of life*, through an appeal to DEATH, through APPEARANCES, through EMPTINESS and the lack of a MESSAGE.

The MANNEQUIN in my theatre must become a MODEL, through which pass a strong sense of DEATH and the conditions of the DEAD. A model for the live ACTOR.

### 9 My elucidation of the situation described by Craig. The appearance of the LIVE ACTOR as a revolutionary moment. The discovery of the IMAGE OF MAN.

I derive my observations from the domain of the theatre, but they are relevant to all current art. We can suppose that Craig's suggestively-depicted and disastrously-incriminating picture of the circumstances surrounding the appearance of the Actor — was composed for his own use, as a point of departure for his idea of the 'SUPER-MARIONETTE'. Despite the fact that I remain an admirer of Craig's magnificent contempt and passionate accusations (especially since I see before me the absolute downfall of today's theatre) and then only after my full acceptance of the first part of his Credo, in which he denies the institutionalised theatre any reason for artistic existence — I dissociate myself from his renowned decisions on the fate of the ACTOR.

For the moment of the ACTOR's first appearance before the HOUSE (to use current terminology) seems to me, on the contrary: *revolutionary* and *avant-garde*. I will even try to compile and 'ascribe to History' a completely different picture, in which the course of events will have a meaning quite the opposite. . . .! From the common realm of customary and religious rituals, common ceremonies and common people's activities advanced SOMEONE, who made the risky decision to BREAK with the ritualistic Community. He was not driven by conceit (as in Craig) to become an object of universal attention. This would have been too simplistic. Rather it must have been a rebellious mind, sceptical, heretical, free and tragic, daring to remain alone with Fate and Destiny. If we also add 'with its ROLE', we will then have before us the ACTOR. This revolt took place in the realm of art. Said event, or rather manifestation, probably caused much confusion of thought and clashing of opinions. This ACT was undoubtedly seen as a disloyalty to the old ritualistic traditions and practices, as secular arrogance, as atheism, as dangerous subversive tendencies, as scandal, as amorality, as indecency; people must have seen in it elements of clownery, buffoonery, exhibitionism and deviation. The author himself, set apart from society, gained for himself not only implacable enemies, but also fanatical admirers. Condemnation and glory simultaneously. It would be guilty of a ludicrous and shallow formalism to interpret this act of SEVERANCE (RUPTURE) as egotism, as a lust for glory or latent inclinations toward acting. It must have implied something much greater, a MESSAGE of extraordinary import. We will try to illustrate this fascinating situation: OPPOSITE those who remained on this side there stood a MAN DECEPTIVELY SIMILAR to them, yet (by some secret and ingenious 'operation') infinitely DISTANT, shockingly FOREIGN, as if DEAD, cut off by an invisible BARRIER — no less horrible and inconceivable, whose real meaning and THREAT appears to us only in DREAMS. As though in a blinding flash of lightning, they suddenly perceived a glaring, tragically circus-like IMAGE OF MAN, as if they had seen him FOR THE FIRST TIME, as if they had seen THEIR VERY SELVES. This was certainly a shock — a meta-physical shock, we might even say. The live effigy of MAN emerging out of the shadows, as if constantly walking ahead of himself, was the dominant MESSAGE of its new HUMAN CONDITION, only HUMAN, with its RESPONSIBILITY, its tragic CONSCIOUSNESS, measuring its FATE on an inexorable and final scale, the *scale of DEATH*. This revelatory MESSAGE, which was transmitted from the realm of DEATH, evoked in the VIEWERS (let us now call them by our own term) a metaphysical shock. And the reference to DEATH, to its tragic and MENACING beauty, were the means and art of that ACTOR (also according to our own terminology).

It is necessary to re-establish the essential meaning of the relationship:
VIEWER and ACTOR.

IT IS NECESSARY TO RECOVER THE PRIMEVAL FORCE OF THE SHOCK TAKING PLACE AT
THE MOMENT WHEN OPPOSITE A MAN (THE VIEWER) THERE STOOD FOR THE FIRST TIME A
MAN (THE ACTOR) DECEPTIVELY SIMILAR TO US YET AT THE SAME TIME INFINITELY FOREIGN,
BEYOND AN IMPASSABLE BARRIER.

## 10 Recapitulation.

Despite the fact that we may be suspected and even accused
of a certain scrupulousness, inappropriate under the circumstances,
in destroying inborn prejudices and fears,
for the sake of a more precise picture
and possible conclusions
let us establish the limits of that boundary, which has the name:
THE CONDITION OF DEATH
for it represents the most extreme point of reference,
no longer threatened by any conformity,
FOR THE CONDITION OF THE ARTIST AND ART

. . . this specific relationship
terrifying
but at the same time compelling
the relationship of *the living to the dead*
who not long ago, while still alive, gave not the slightest
reason for the unforseen spectacle
for creating unnecessary separation and confusion:
they did not distinguish themselves
did not place themselves above others
and as a result of this seemingly banal
but, as would later become evident, rather essential
and valuable attribute
they were simply, normally
in no way transgressing universal laws
*unremarkable*
and now suddenly
*on the other side*
*opposite*
they astound us
as though we
*were seeing them for the first time*
set on display
in an ambiguous ceremony:

pointless
and at the same time repudiated,
irrevocably different
and infinitely foreign
and more: somehow deprived of all meaning
of no account
without the meanest hope of occupying some position
in our 'full' life relationships
which to us alone are accessible, familiar
comprehensible
but for them meaningless.
If we agree that a trait
*of living people*
is the ease and ability
with which they enter into mutual and manifold
*life relationships*
only then
with regard to the dead
is there born in us a sudden and startling
realisation of the fact that
this basic trait of the living
is brought out and made possible by
their complete
*lack of differentiation*
by their
*indistinguishability*
by their universal *similarity*
mercilessly abolishing all other opposing delusions
common
consistent
all-binding.
Only then do the *dead*
become (for the living)
*noteworthy*
for that highest price
achieving
their individuality
distinction
their CHARACTER
glaring
and almost
circus-like.

■　■　■

## Source

Kantor, T. (1984) 'The Theatre of Death: A Manifesto', *Twentieth Century Polish Theatre*, trans. V.T. and M. Stelmaszynski, ed. B. Drozdowski, English trans. and ed. C. Itzin, London: John Calder: 97–106.

## Tadeusz Kantor (1915–90)

Polish designer, artist and director. He became one of the century's most extraordinary practitioners through the creation of relatively few, but highly travelled productions. Starting as a painter and stage designer, he soon moved towards theatrical form with a series of 'happenings' in Warsaw and on the Baltic coast in the early 1960s. He sought to redefine the language of theatre through a constant questioning of the relationship between the performance space and the performers. Like Wagner, Kantor created total theatre pieces, devised and controlled by himself. In 1955 he formed his performance company, Cricot[2], in Krakow, in conjunction with other visual artists. In 1975 he produced his most famous piece, *The Dead Class*, a surrealist evocation of a 'dead' Polish past, by a cast of artists of all ages, which toured Europe and the USA, receiving awards and prizes. This was followed by, *Wielopole, Wielopole* (1982), *Let the Artists Die* (1985), and *I Shall Never Return* (1989). Kantor continued to produce work with Cricot[2] until his death in 1990, rehearsing his last piece, *Today is My Birthday*.

Kantor's 'Manifesto' shows how he departs from all the main traditions of European theatre in advocating non-linear form. He encapsulates his concern with the theatrical object, and with the actor as object, emphasising his roots in the visual arts. He expresses his concept of theatre as vision; as a process of parallel actions and events folding back on themselves; continuously commenting on Polish life under the domination of communism, and on its collective memory and nationality.

## Compare this article with writings by the following authors in this reader

**Craig** – to whom he refers at length
**Foreman and Wilson** – other approaches to non-linear theatre
**Grotowski** – a contemporary Polish artist
**Kaprow** – a parallel interest in 'happenings'
**Hijikata** – a contemporary concern with death
**Schlemmer** – theatre as sculptural object

## Further reading

Drozdowski, B. (ed.) (1979) *Twentieth Century Polish Theatre*, London: John Calder.
Klossiwicz, J. (1986) 'Tadeusz Kantor's Journey' *Drama Review* 30, T111: 4.

Kobialka, M. (trans. and ed.) (1993) *A Journey Through Other Spaces: Essays and Manifestos by Tadeusz Kantor,* Berkeley, Calif.: University of California Press.

Kobialka, M. (2010) *Further on, Nothing*, University of Minnesota Press.

Murawska-Muthesius, K. and Zarzecka, N. (eds) (2011) *Kantor Was Here*, London: Black Dog Publishing.

Plesniarowicz, K. (2000) *The Dead Memory Machine*, Aberystwyth: Black Mountain Press.

Witts, N. (2010) *Tadeusz Kantor*, London: Routledge.

http://www.cricoteka.pl

# Chapter 36

# Allan Kaprow

## ASSEMBLAGES, ENVIRONMENTS AND HAPPENINGS

(A) *The line between art and life should be kept as fluid, and perhaps indistinct, as possible.* The reciprocity between the man-made and the ready-made will be at its maximum potential this way. Something will always happen at this juncture, which, if it is not revelatory, will not be merely bad art – for no one can easily compare it with this or that accepted masterpiece. I would judge this a foundation upon which may be built the specific criteria of the Happenings, as well as the other styles treated in this book.

(B) *Therefore, the source of themes, materials, actions, and the relationships between them are to be derived from any place or period except from the arts, their derivatives, and their milieu.* When innovations are taking place it often becomes necessary for those involved to treat their tasks with considerable severity. In order to keep their eyes fixed solely upon the essential problem, they will decide that there are certain 'don'ts' which, as self-imposed rules, they will obey unswervingly. Arnold Schoenberg felt he had to abolish tonality in music composition and, for him at least, this was made possible by his evolving the twelve-tone series technique. Later on his more academic followers showed that it was very easy to write traditional harmonies with that technique. But still later, John Cage could permit a C major triad to exist next to the sound of a buzz saw, because by then the triad was thought of differently – not as a

musical necessity but as a sound as interesting as any other sound. This sort of freedom to accept all kinds of subject matter will probably be possible in the Happenings of the future, but I think not for now. Artistic attachments are still so many window dressings, unconsciously held onto to legitimize an art that otherwise might go unrecognized.

Thus it is not that the known arts are 'bad' that causes me to say 'Don't get near them'; it is that they contain highly sophisticated habits. By avoiding the artistic modes there is the good chance that a new language will develop that has its own standards. The Happening is conceived as an art, certainly, but this is for lack of a better word, or one that would not cause endless discussion. I, personally, would not care if it were called a sport. But if it is going to be thought of in the context of art and artists, then let it be a distinct art which finds its way into the art category by realizing its species outside of 'culture.' A United States Marine Corps manual on jungle-fighting tactics, a tour of a laboratory where polyethylene kidneys are made, the daily traffic jams on the Long Island Expressway, are more useful than Beethoven, Racine, or Michelangelo.

(C) *The performance of a Happening should take place over several widely spaced, sometimes moving and changing, locales.* A single performance space tends toward the static and, more significantly, resembles conventional theatre practice. It is also like painting, for safety's sake, only in the center of a canvas. Later on, when we are used to a fluid space as painting has been for almost a century, we can return to concentrated areas, because then they will not be considered exclusive. It is presently advantageous to experiment by gradually widening the distances between the events within a Happening. First along several points on a heavily trafficked avenue; then in several rooms and floors of an apartment house where some of the activities are out of touch with each other; then on more than one street; then in different but proximate cities; finally all around the globe. On the one hand, this will increase the tension between the parts, as a poet might by stretching the rhyme from two lines to ten. On the other, it permits the parts to exist more on their own, without the necessity of intensive coordination. Relationships cannot help being made and perceived in any human action, and here they may be of a new kind if tried-and-true methods are given up.

Even greater flexibility can be gotten by moving the locale itself. A Happening could be composed for a jetliner going from New York to Luxembourg with stopovers at Gander, Newfoundland, and Reykjavik, Iceland. Another Happening would take place up and down the elevators of five tall buildings in midtown Chicago.

The images in each situation can be quite disparate: a kitchen in Hoboken, a *pissoir* in Paris, a taxi garage in Leopoldville, and a bed in some small town in Turkey. Isolated points of contact may be maintained by telephone and letters, by a meeting on a highway, or by watching a certain television program at an appointed hour. Other parts of the work need only be related by theme, as when all locales perform an identical action which is disjoined in timing and space. But none of these planned ties are absolutely required, for preknowledge of the Happening's cluster of events by all participants will allow each one to make his own connections. This, however, is more the topic of form, and I shall speak further of this shortly.

(D) *Time, which follows closely on space considerations, should be variable and discontinuous.* It is only natural that if there are multiple spaces in which occurrences are scheduled, in sequence or even at random, time or 'pacing' will acquire an order that is determined more by the character of movements within environments than by a fixed concept of regular development and conclusion. There need be no rhythmic coordination between the several parts of a Happening unless it is suggested by the event itself: such as when two persons must meet at a train departing at 5:47 PM.

Above all, this is 'real' or 'experienced' time, as distinct from conceptual time. If it conforms to the clock used in the Happening, as above, that is legitimate, but if it does not because a clock is not needed, that is equally legitimate. All of us know how, when we are busy, time accelerates, and how, conversely, when we are bored it can drag almost to a standstill. Real time is always connected with doing something, with an event of some kind, and so is bound up, with things and spaces.

Imagine some evening when one has sat talking with friends, how as the conversation became reflective the pace slowed, pauses became longer, and the speakers 'felt' not only heavier but their distances from one another increased proportionately, as though each were surrounded by great areas commensurate with the voyaging of his mind. Time retarded as space extended. Suddenly, from out on the street, through the open window a police car, siren whining, was heard speeding by, *its* space moving as the source of sound moved from somewhere to the right of the window to somewhere farther to the left. Yet it also came spilling into the slowly spreading vastness of the talkers' space, invading the transformed room, partly shattering it, sliding shockingly in and about its envelope, nearly displacing it. And as in those cases where sirens are only sounded at crowded street corners to warn pedestrians, the police car and its noise at once ceased and the capsule of time and space it had become vanished as abruptly as it made itself felt. Once more the protracted picking of one's way through the extended reaches of mind resumed as the group of friends continued speaking.

Feeling this, why shouldn't an artist program a Happening over the course of several days, months, or years, slipping it in and out of the performers' daily lives. There is nothing esoteric in such a proposition, and it may have the distinct advantage of bringing into focus those things one ordinarily does every day without paying attention – like brushing one's teeth.

On the other hand, leaving taste and preference aside and relying solely on chance operations, a completely unforeseen schedule of events could result, not merely in the preparation but in the actual performance; or a simultaneously performed single moment; or none at all. (As for the last, the act of finding this out would become, by default, the 'Happening.')

But an endless activity could also be decided upon, which would apparently transcend palpable time – such as the slow decomposition of a mountain of sandstone . . . In this spirit some artists are earnestly proposing a lifetime Happening equivalent to Clarence Schmidt's lifetime Environment.

The common function of these alternatives is to release an artist from conventional notions of a detached, closed arrangement of time-space. A picture, a piece of music, a poem, a drama, each confined within its respective frame, fixed number of measures, stanzas, and stages, however great they may be in their own right, simply will not allow for breaking the barrier between art and life. And this is what the objective is.

(E) *Happenings should be performed once only*. At least for the time being, this restriction hardly needs emphasis, since it is in most cases the only course possible. Whether due to chance, or to the lifespan of the materials (especially the perishable ones), or to the changeableness of the events, it is highly unlikely that a Happening of the type I am outlining could ever be repeated. Yet many of the Happenings have, in fact, been given four or five times, ostensibly to accommodate larger attendances, but this, I believe, was only a rationalization of the wish to hold onto theatrical customs. In my experience, I found the practice inadequate because I was always forced to do that which *could be repeated*, and had to discard countless situations which I felt were marvelous but performable only once. Aside from the fact that repetition is boring to a generation brought up on ideas of spontaneity and originality, to repeat a Happening at this time is to accede to a far more serious matter: compromise of the whole concept of Change. When the practical requirements of a situation serve only to kill what an artist has set out to do, then this is not a practical problem at all; one would be very practical to leave it for something else more liberating.

Nevertheless, there is a special instance of where more than one performance is entirely justified. This is the score or scenario which is designed to make every performance significantly different from the previous one. Superficially this has been true for the Happenings all along. Parts have been so roughly scored that there was bound to be some margin of imprecision from performance to performance. And, occasionally, sections of a work were left open for accidentals or improvisations. But since people are creatures of habit, performers always tended to fall into set patterns and stick to these no matter what leeway was given them in the original plan.

In the near future, plans may be developed which take their cue from games and athletics, where the regulations provide for a variety of moves that make the outcome always uncertain. A score might be written, so general in its instructions that it could be adapted to basic types of terrain such as oceans, woods, cities, farms; and to basic kinds of performers such as teenagers, old people, children, matrons, and so on, including insects, animals, and the weather. This could be printed and mail-ordered for use by anyone who wanted it. George Brecht has been interested in such possibilities for some time now. His sparse scores read like this:

## DIRECTION

Arrange to observe a sign
indicating direction of travel.

- travel in the indicated direction
- travel in another direction

But so far they have been distributed to friends, who perform them at their discretion and without ceremony. Certainly they are aware of the philosophic allusions to Zen Buddhism, of the subtle wit and childlike simplicity of the activities indicated. Most of all, they are aware of the responsibility it places on the performer to make something of the situation or not. As we mentioned before in connection with another of Brecht's pieces, this implication is the most radical potential in all of the work discussed in this book. Beyond a small group of initiates, there are few who could appreciate the moral dignity of such scores and fewer still who could derive pleasure from going ahead and doing them without self-consciousness. In the case of those Happenings with more detailed instructions or more expanded action, the artist must be present at every moment, directing and participating, for the tradition is too young for the complete stranger to know what to do with such plans if he got them.

(F) *It follows that audiences should be eliminated entirely.* All the elements – people, space, the particular materials and character of the environment, time – can in this way be integrated. And the last shred of theatrical convention disappears. For anyone once involved in the painter's problem of unifying a field of divergent phenomena, a group of inactive people in the space of a Happening is just dead space. It is no different from a dead area of red paint on a canvas. Movements call up movements in response, whether on a canvas or in a Happening. A Happening with only an empathic response on the part of a seated audience is not a Happening but stage theatre.

Then, on a human plane, to assemble people unprepared for an event and say that they are 'participating' if apples are thrown at them or they are herded about is to ask very little of the whole notion of participation. Most of the time the response of such an audience is halfhearted or even reluctant, and sometimes the reaction is vicious and therefore destructive to the work (though I suspect that in numerous instances of violent reaction to such treatment it was caused by the latent sadism in the action, which they quite rightly resented). After a few years, in any case, 'audience response' proves to be so predictably pure cliché that anyone serious about the problem should not tolerate it, any more than the painter should continue the use of dripped paint as a stamp of modernity when it has been adopted by every lampshade and Formica manufacturer in the country.

I think that it is a mark of mutual respect that all persons involved in a Happening be willing and committed participants who have a clear idea what they are to do. This is simply accomplished by writing out the scenario or score for all and discussing it thoroughly with them beforehand. In this respect it is not different from the preparations for a parade, a football match, a wedding, or religious service. It is not even different from a play. The one big difference is that while knowledge of the scheme is necessary, professional talent is not; the situations in a Happening are lifelike or, if they are unusual, are so rudimentary that professionalism is actually uncalled for. Actors are stage-trained and bring over habits from their art that are hard to shake off; the same is true of any other kind of showman or trained athlete. The best participants have been persons not normally engaged in art or performance, but who are moved to take part in an activity that is at once meaningful to them in its ideas yet natural in its methods.

There is an exception, however, to restricting the Happening to participants only. When a work is performed on a busy avenue, passersby will ordinarily stop and watch, just as they might watch the demolition of a building. These are not theatre-goers and their attention is only temporarily caught in the course of their normal affairs. They might stay, perhaps become involved in some unexpected way, or they will more likely move on after a few minutes. Such persons are authentic parts of the environment.

A variant of this is the person who is engaged unwittingly with a performer in some planned action: a butcher will sell certain meats to a customer-performer without realizing that he is a part of a piece having to do with purchasing, cooking, and eating meat.

Finally, there is this additional exception to the rule. A Happening may be scored for *just watching*. Persons will do nothing else. They will watch things, each other, possibly actions not performed by themselves, such as a bus stopping to pick up commuters. This would not take place in a theatre or arena, but anywhere else. It could be an extremely meditative occupation when done devotedly; just 'cute' when done indifferently. In a more physical mood, the idea of called-for watching could be contrasted with periods of action. Both normal tendencies to observe and act would now be engaged in a responsible way. At those moments of relative quiet the observer would hardly be a passive member of an audience; he would be closer to the role of a Greek chorus, without its specific meaning necessarily, but with its required place in the overall scheme. At other moments the active and observing roles would be exchanged, so that by reciprocation the whole meaning of watching would be altered, away from something like spoon-feeding, toward something purposive, possibly intense.

(G) *The composition of a Happening proceeds exactly as in Assemblages and Environments, that is, it is evolved as a collage of events in certain spans of time and in certain spaces.*

When we think of 'composition,' it is important not to think of it as self-sufficient 'form,' as an arrangement as such, as an organizing activity in which the materials are taken for granted as a means toward an end that is greater than they are. This is much too Christian in the sense of the body being inferior to the soul. Rather, composition is understood as an operation dependent upon the materials (including people and nature) and phenomenally indistinct from them. Such materials and their associations and meanings, as I have pointed out, generate the relationships and the movements of the Happening, instead of the reverse. The adage that 'form follows function' is still useful advice.

Otherwise, a sort of artistic schizophrenia can result if *any* subject matter and material is subjected to *any* interesting formal technique. It may be that some subjects, because of our familiarity with and wide use of them, allow for more alternatives of transformation and grouping than other subjects. An apple can be painted in the Neo-Classic, Realist, Impressionist, Expressionist, and Cubist styles and still be recognized as an apple, but an electron microscope cannot. The Impressionist mode, for instance, would blur it beyond recognition – and at that point the real subjects become light, optical sensation, and paint, and *not* the microscope.

Because the Happenings are occupied with relatively new (at least new for art) subject matter and materials, the stylistic conventions used by the other arts, or by such philosophical disciplines as logic, are best left alone. To illustrate why, several years ago I used serial methods related to Schoenberg's twelve-tone technique. A root-molecule of events was written down: 'a jam sandwich being eaten in a dining room, a person laughing outside a window, and an alarm clock going off periodically in the bedroom.' This was the basic cluster of situations that was to grow into the Happening. [ . . . ] I had in mind the very thorough way that the composer Karlheinz Stockhausen developed serialism, whereby all the elements of sound could be made mathematically consistent. But while this was possible in music, particularly electronic music, whose rudiments are relatively nonassociative, this was not possible with the materials of a Happening, with their high degree of everyday usage. And I did not want to lose all the advantages these provided by deliberately choosing more neutral events (about which I shall say more shortly). The worst difficulty to arise out of these procedures, however, was that as they became more exacting, performance became nearly impossible.

The results on paper were interesting enough, but in action (as far as any action was capable of being derived from the complicated scores) the effect was static and mechanical. The events were simply not eventful. A regimen unrelated to their natural qualities seemed to have been superimposed upon them. The scheme was self-evidently 'formal' but the subject matter was not; or it had some as yet unrevealed form that was hidden because it was not respected. I concluded that to do this at all, limits had to be observed in choosing the initial stuff of the Happening. And these limits were contrary to the principal direction the art was taking.

We generally mean by 'formal' art (the fugues of Bach, the sonnets of Shakespeare, Cubist paintings) an art that is primarily manipulative. As in a chess game, the manipulation is intellectual, whereby elements of the work are moved according to strict, sometimes self-imposed, regulations. The weaving of these elements into groupings, regroupings; the losing and finding of themes, subthemes, and counterthemes, seemingly disparate yet always dominated by the relentless inevitability that they shall resolve at the end, is the peculiar fascination of such an art.

Formal art must be made of a substance that is at once stable and general in meanings. A formalist cannot easily use the horrifying records of Nazi torture chambers, but he can use a simple statement like 'the sky is blue,' abstract shapes such as circles and squares, the raising and lowering of an arm that does nothing else. The impact of the imagery, the 'what,' is not as important as the intricacy and subtlety of the moves the imagery is put through.

A formalist who wishes to make a Happening must choose with discretion situations that can be freely manipulated without jarring the overtones of the imagery within them. A group of men all in white doing calisthenics, a ticking metronome, a sheet of paper being moved variously across the floor are obviously easily formalized. But for this to become truly great, I think that some time must elapse. The media are still too undigested for us to feel at home with them. This is essential: to be profitably involved in an activity of arrangements, the materials arranged must not command attention. At present, the media are all rather unstable because their meanings in their new context tend to arise more quickly than anything else. Kleenex may be a commonplace, but collected in quantity in a Happening they would immediately push into relief all that we have only half-consciously thought about Kleenex and its intimate uses.

Therefore, in making a Happening, it is better to approach composition without borrowed form theories, and instead to let the form emerge from what the materials can do. If a horse is part of a work, whatever a horse does gives the 'form' to what he does in the Happening: trotting, standing, pulling a cart, eating, defecating, and so forth. If a factory of heavy machinery is chosen, then the clanging of motorized repetition might easily cause the form to be steadily repetitive. In this way a whole body of nonintellectualized, nonculturized experience is opened to the artist and he is free to use his mind anew in connecting things he did not consider before.

Think of the following items: tires, doughnuts, Cheerios cereal, Life Savers candy, life preservers, wedding rings, men's and women's belts, band saws, plastic pools, barrel hoops, curtain rings, Mason jar gaskets, hangman's nooses – one could go on almost indefinitely. They are all obviously united by a common circular shape (an observation that could be made by a botanist or a standard auto parts salesman as well as by any painter; for the recognition and use of physical resemblances is not the special talent of artists alone, even if the tradition of form analysis would seem to tell us so). By juxtaposing any half dozen of these items, an idea for a Happening could emerge. And from this combination, meanings not normally associated with such things could be derived by minds sensitive to symbols. [ . . . ]

Shifting things around can be an excellent mode of *performance* as much as of composition. Just as an Environment or an Assemblage can be maintained in prolonged transformation by allowing its parts to be rearranged in numbers of ways, the same can apply to a Happening. This would simply continue the compositional process into the performance process and the two usually distinct phases would begin to merge as the caesura between them is pulled out. Suppose, for example, that three environments and five actions are selected, partly by taste and partly by chance methods. [ . . . ] Each action may be performed once or twice, and at one or two prescribed environments and at their respective times, as desired.

At no time is it known if actions will be performed at all of the three environments, since the choice is left to the performers, nor what the number and kind of actions will be at the environments chosen. [ . . . ] The ninety-six possible combinations are numerous and dramatic enough to make this small list of events both unexpected and sufficiently different in every case.

There are related ways of setting off rearrangements of fixed numbers of actions such as by *cueing*, in which performers are given a set of actions that are signaled, knowingly or unknowingly, by one another or by natural occurrences such as the sound of a car horn or a cloud formation. These cues also may be responded to in any one of a number of alternative ways in each instance, so here again the combinations are quite varied.

Finally, chance may determine nearly everything, and personal preference and the rumblings of the imagination will be put aside. I say chance operations may 'nearly' determine everything, for any sensitive mind will tend to make connections between the actions which he finds occurring and those in which he is taking part, even if he had no way of knowing them beforehand. [ . . . ] The advantage of chance methods, in my view, is that they free one from *customary* relationships rather than from any relationships. New ones will be noticed by the observant artist, whether he professes to like this or not. Most of the time he seems to like it.

The preceding discussion of composition has been a summary of all the rules-of-thumb raised respecting Happenings, rather than being merely technical. Problems of materials and content enter into the question at every stage and so I should like to re-emphasize the importance of a pervasive process which is manifestly organic and not divided into categories. Analytic writing, because of the very nature and history of the words we use, tends towards the broken-apart and divided and is necessary for the sake of convenience. But the only art that is so fractured is academic art, and thus I made it clear throughout the listing of the conditions I believe to be crucial to the Happening as an art, that they are not iron-clad rules but fruitful limits within which to work. As soon as they are found to be useless they will be broken, and other limits will take their place.

■   ■   ■

## Source

Kaprow, A. (1965) *Assemblages, Environments, and Happenings*, New York: Harry N. Abrams.

## Allan Kaprow (1927–2006)

American artist, founder of the so-called 'Happening' movement in the early sixties. Kaprow studied at New York University, at Columbia University, and at the New School of Social Research, New York, where he took John Cage's class in experimental music. He was producing performance art as a practitioner and theorist from the late 1950s until his death in 2006. Around 1956 Kaprow began making what he called Assemblages, which used found material from the surrounding environment, also creating Environments and Happenings, the latter of which were described by Michael Kirby as 'non-matrixed performances', a similar concept to that employed by the Dadaists, though without their anti-art overtones. The element of chance, which was often present in these early works, clearly came from working with Cage. Kaprow saw art in the streets and in the everyday actions of life as Cage had defined music, and the happenings were devised to sensitise audiences and participants to this, prefiguring current explorations of the 'performative' in everyday life on the one hand, and the work of Richard Foreman and Marina Abramovic on the other. Kaprow's *18 Happenings in 6 Parts* (1959) involved three rooms with chairs arranged in circles and rectangles forcing the audience to face in different directions. Each visitor was presented with a programme and cards with instructions as to actions they were to follow. The series of fragmented events were to be understood by the audience in any way, thus prefiguring the multiple meanings of postmodern performance. 'It is important' wrote Kaprow, 'to declare as art the total event comprising noise/object/ movement/colour and psychology'. In *Sweet Wall* (1970) participants built and then destroyed a wall made with bricks and held together by a mortar of bread and jam, just a few steps from the Berlin Wall, calling attention to the uselessness of the task in what was a materialist environment. Many of Kaprow's contemporaries undertook similar experiments, notably Claes Oldenberg, Dick Higgins and Yoko Ono, though none of them agreed the term 'Happening' and none produced manifestos or magazines. The idea of the audience was eliminated completely, integrating all elements into one experiential whole, prefiguring the breakdown in audience/performer relationship attempted by Grotowski or Boal. Thus Kaprow can be seen to be at the root of many contemporary attitudes to art and performance, his influence spreading throughout the performing arts. In this extract from his book Kaprow explains the origin of the field of the Happening, as well as giving some examples for his readers to follow.

## Compare this article with writings by the following authors in this reader

**Abramovic** – the heightening of the everyday
**Boal** – for the theatricality of the everyday
**Brecht** – for making the everyday strange
**Cage** – Kaprow's teacher
**Grotowski** – for audience/performer interaction
**Kantor** – a European interest in the 'Happening'
**Richter** – for the Dada experiments

## Further reading

Kirby, M. (ed.) (1965) *Happenings: An Illustrated Anthology*, New York: Dutton.
Meyer-Herman, E., Perchuk, A. and Rosenthal, S. (2008) *Allan Kaprow: Art as Life*, London: Thames and Hudson.
Rodenbeck, J. (2011) *Radical Prototypes: Allan Kaprow and the Invention of Happenings*, Cambridge, Mass.: MIT Press.
Sandford, M.S. (ed.) (1995) *Happenings and Other Acts*, London: Routledge.

# Chapter 37

# Elizabeth LeCompte

## INTERVIEW

*In developing* Brace Up! *(1990) did you work with the Japanese material before addressing* Three Sisters?

Yes.

*Was this material linked to the notion of a Japanese theatre troupe?*

I always use a framing device outside the material, so it's like an onion skin or a frame within a frame. In all the pieces there's some outside storyteller and there's a text within that story.

*Do you see specific connections between the Japanese material and the Chekhov?*

Well, I do after the fact, but it isn't something that informs the way we go about making the pieces. After the fact certain things become obvious, but they're never obvious to begin with. I didn't see any reason for them to be put together other than that I happen to be interested in the formal aspects of Japanese theatre and some of the Japanese pop culture stuff and that I happen to like Chekhov's writing. When I started working on *Route 1 & 9* (1981) I didn't have any idea that these routines from Pigmeat Markham would have anything to do with *Our Town*. I had no idea whatsoever that these two would go together. I was working on Pigmeat Markham material because I was interested in it formally, the way I'm interested in the Japanese material formally. Again, in a similar way, I was attracted to the writing, to Wilder's writing – specifically Wilder's writing as a sort of poetic text next to this popular material – 'poetic' in quotes – filled with sentimental meaning, but absolutely vacant of any *real* meaning taken apart from the characters. I then take these things as givens when we work. Of course, eventually – because I and the company are the catalysts for the two things coming together – I will see things.

*You seem to be describing a process that allows very different kinds of material to inhabit the same space while, in some respects, remaining very much apart.*

Yeah. Yeah, definitely. I think probably in *Brace Up!* they ended up coming too much together. I would really want something more disparate.

*The emphasis you place on the formal qualities of the material seems to be in opposition to the kind of psychological basis of Wilder and Chekhov's texts.*

I don't have a rejection of psychological motivation. I just have a rejection of psychological motivation existing in one form. I like to use the psychological motivation as a whole theatrical space. I can't imagine, in this day and age, not feeling the psychology in one way or another.

*Were you interested in any way in the association between Chekhov's work and naturalism? Perhaps in opposition to the Japanese material?*

You see, I don't know the history of the Chekhov. I hadn't, before I'd done this, seen a Chekhov play except in Dutch. I couldn't really tell what the psychology was. And the naturalism was – well, I don't speak the language. I don't have the history of that, I don't know what that is. I think I'm doing a naturalistic version of Chekhov.

*One of the conventional things about naturalism is that it creates one unified world.*

Yeah. That's what I think I'm doing. Perhaps Stanislavski was not – he was fragmenting it all into different characters – to me it's all one thing.

*Did you see any Noh theatre live?*

No. I did see some tapes in Japanese. I never saw it translated. I couldn't follow the content, but I could watch them come on and go off. That's very important. So, you know, I didn't read too

much about what Noh was or what it's supposed to be. I just watched tapes in Japanese. So I think I was probably drawn to that structure, that physical architectonic structure. How they moved, how they dealt with entrances and exits.

*Is it something you pursued in the piece particularly?*

Entrances and exits are extremely important. That's the defining thing, isn't it? In theatre. That's essential. It's the deepest, deepest place for me. But, I've said this before.

*One of the things that interests me about the use of Noh is its emphasis upon continuity — and so its reflection upon its own history. This seems to be reflected in the Wooster Group's work. Performances seem to comment on previous productions, images are re-used, rehearsal procedures are remembered or re-presented. Were you interested in Noh's concern with its own history?*

I don't know. I mean, I'm not a Japanese theatre artist. I don't study Japanese theatre. I don't have any academic interest in Japanese theatre.

*I'm just interested in what these appropriations might have to offer. Or what the juxta-position of the Japanese material against the Chekhov might be doing.*

I think we were getting to that when I said 'entrances and exits'.

**MW** [Marianne Weems, a Wooster Group associate, who was also present]: The way that I look at it is that it's more like a contrapuntal reading. The two things go, and sometimes connect in the audience member's mind and sometimes don't. But there's no didactic, polemical —

Attempt.

**MW:**    connection being made. There's no attempt to connect them, really. I think there's a rhythmic attempt to make them relate, or perhaps to let them relate in the space.

Yes. To allow them to be in the space together, without this *demand* for meaning. 'Meaning' in quotes — that you're dealing with, very strongly.

*Do you mean that I'm demanding meaning of you?*

Yes, absolutely. That's not what I'm about. My meaning is in the piece itself. I'm not going to now make meaning separately from that piece for you. Again, it's not a thing where I'm withholding that — I don't have it. It only happens for me in the space. In the moment of the theatrical act. Here I can just tell you the way

I came up with those images, the way they are brought to the stage. Then, I could, if I wanted to, spin off and say, Oh, yes, isn't it funny how this image looks good, or it's good with that sound. I could even, after the fact, probably – if I were a writer – write a whole thing on the meaning of Japanese culture and Western language. About meaning and lack of meaning, about Western poetry and Eastern poetry. But I don't have much interest in it.

*It may be that we don't have a language to talk with.*

It's possible.

*Which is, on the one hand, a shame, on the other hand, it may be instructive.*

I think it is. I think it's probably very instructive looking at the work next to other people's work, too, to be honest, just by my inability to grapple with whatever it is you're telling me. It has something to do with why the work is like it is.

*It's important, from my point of view, because I don't intend to demand a meaning for the piece.*

No, no. I know. Believe me, I'm not trying to be obfuscating. Maybe the language that you're using I don't use. Maybe you've talked to people who aren't as theatre-oriented as I am. That's why Joan Jonas came to work with us, because she wanted to make entrances and exits. She doesn't make them in her own work. I didn't come from theatre but from painting and film – which is, the cut, you know, entrances and exits again – when do you come into a scene and when do you leave it. It may be that.

*And this is also connected with framing.*

Well, of course. Again, I think what I'm saying to you is that form is extraordinarily important to me – certain kinds of theatrical form. And I'm always trying to see it in different ways. And of course I work to different theatre traditions – not only Japanese. I worked for a long time with vaudeville, American vaudeville. So –

*And the focus upon form is a key to these very disparate elements coinciding in the same space.*

Yes, absolutely. And anything can co-exist together – without, you know, losing its own uniqueness – without being absorbed and regurgitated. They are separate, and they can stay separate and at the same time inform each other – within the same work. At best, when the form is strong enough, that's what happens. If the form isn't strong enough, it's just chaos. That's the danger.

*That kind of focus doesn't offer itself to any kind of question I might ask about meaning or theme, does it?*

No. Again, you can talk to me about what's going on on the stage.

*I'm interested in the emphasis you place on 'presence'. You've said that you use whatever methods you can to try and make — or allow — the actor to become as present as possible.*

Yes.

*Is this a formal quality in the work?*

It can be. Usually that presence is something that I think is — kind of — always in conversation with the formal pattern. The formal pattern will tend to allow the performer to get lulled into feeling safe. Within this structure that I've made, there are always holes that pop up — that's part of the form. So you have to be vigilant, all the time. Vigilant. Tremendously vigilant. And be aware of everything behind you and in front of you, of the entire structure. Or you might drown. Drowning, I mean — you know, stop you from breathing — to fill you up with water so you can't breathe. I think the constant battle for me as a director is to find ways that an actor can be always present, always alive, always thinking this is the first and last moment that she's there — doing this thing — within a structure that is so strong and so sure.

*Do you think about the audience in the making of work?*

Yeah. I mean — it's like the audience is *there*. They're the air that you breathe. The audience is the other part of the exploration process for theatre. There is no theatre without audience, so there is no life without breath. It's that essential. But it's an involuntary thing, breathing. And my awareness of the audience is almost involuntary. Sometimes I'm conscious of it. Usually when they come in for the first time — it's like a pain in your chest. I become aware of them when things aren't working on the stage. When something's wrong, I become aware in a very conscious way. So then I work to become unaware of them in a way that I'm unaware of my breathing. It doesn't mean that I'm cutting them out. It's just that they should be part of the flow of the whole.

*It strikes me that if you concentrate on these formal elements in a way that keeps the possibilities of the piece open, that keeps these things colliding or existing at the same moment, then — because there are many languages being held up at the same time — the work resists being read through a single language. I wonder if, as a consequence of this, the viewer might become more open to this 'presence'?*

I know what you're saying – but I don't know. Again, I'm not always sure. It's no science. I was talking to a writer a while ago, who's a little older than me. He was saying how, you know, he now had become technically better. He could write more quickly. He knew when things weren't working. He'd acquired technique. And I had to realise when I was talking to him that I still don't know how to get that presence on the stage, that every time I go down for a new piece it's the same battle as it was for *Sakonnet Point* in 1975. That I had not gotten any clearer about how to get that presence, how to keep it, how to make the form balance with the –

*Do you think it can succumb to technique?*

Well, I don't know. I don't know. I wish I had the technique, because it's harder to do it.

*Joe Chaikin tried to gear technique toward producing presence, didn't he?*

Yes, he did. That's a good point. I hadn't thought about Chaikin in a long time. But it's also – I'll tell you what else. And this is where I'm different from the other people you've talked to, with the exception of John Cage. I think what keeps me unable to get that technique down so that I can, you know, produce more quickly, more easily and more fluidly what I need – again, I use *need* in a spiritual way – on the stage is that I'm always working with other people and other texts, not my own texts. You know, Ping Chong writes his own texts. He's controlling them all the time. Joan Jonas makes up her own actions. She doesn't go to a script. She's writing her own material. I'm not. I'm having to come up against a new person and new people downstairs every single piece. So I have to rediscover, in every piece, what makes the balance. Because people are so different. Actors are so different. I think that that's part of it. And it's that unique place – that I'm making a new thing out of old material. I'm not just redecorating an old script. I'm not just going to do Chekhov. I'm trying to – I'm trying to make it present for me. Which means, literally reinventing. I mean – 'reinventing' it – it's an over-used word. I mean reinventing it from the ground up. From the way that the language resonates in the body on the stage – every way – to the way the psychology has to be – (Claps once) – has to be crashed up against and fragmented and then reformed. So it's got a double problem. I'm reinventing something and I'm having to come up against material that I don't necessarily understand – my actors, a text – and that I don't know how to manipulate. And because I think on stage – I don't think separately, I don't sit down with the text and say, 'Ah, this means this – if I get Joan Jonas to do this on stage, then I'll get what I want from this text.' What I want from the text is what Joan Jonas and Chekhov give to me on the stage! Only on the stage. Not inside my head. So it makes it particularly difficult. I've got the worst of both worlds.

*Does it not also mean that the work is difficult to talk about, in certain respects?*

Well. It depends on what you mean by 'talk about'. I don't think it does. I just can't talk about it in literary terms, in the same way that most people talk about it. I've discovered more recently that theatre people – especially directors – don't talk in the same way that I do. They talk as if I'm writing. Yet I'm not a writer. I'm using other people's writing. The process is akin to that – the process of reinventing – it's akin to writing. I just have my characters, my words, my colleagues, all materialised on the stage. Writers can do it in their head. I can't. I have to take my head – I'm very literal, as you can see – I have to take my head and put it on the stage and move the little elements of ideas around the stage to see what it means. Maybe it's a little unusual.

So I'm really a classical director in the sense that – I do plays. You know. (Laughs.) The most important thing in all of this is that – when I go downstairs I don't have any thematic ideas – I don't even have a theme. I don't have anything except the literal objects – some flowers, some images, some television sets, a chair, some costumes I like. In the last piece, something someone brought in by mistake. That's it. And then ideas come after the fact. It's a total reversal of most of the processes. And probably if I reversed it I'd do a lot more work and be a lot happier. (Laughs.) On that note –

*Thanks.*

*(The interviewer was Nick Kaye)*

■  ■  ■

## Source

LeCompte, E. and Kaye, N. (1993, 1995) 'Interview with Elizabeth LeCompte', *Art into Theatre*, London: Macmillan.

## Elizabeth LeCompte (1944–)

Founder and director of the Wooster Group (1976–), the New York-based perform-ance company, which broke away from Richard Schechner's Performance Group (1967–80). It grew out of a long tradition of rejection of American commercial theatre, redefining the position of the 'performer' and 'role', and the function of previously written playscripts, in particular plays by the established American and European writers, whose work often constitutes a base for the group's performance explorations. Creations such as *Sakonnet Point* (1975) and *Route 1 & 9 (The Last Act)* (1981) deliberately challenge the audience's expectations, through an essentially fragmentary and deconstructive approach. *Route 1 & 9* for example, juxtaposed extracts from Thornton Wilder's *Our Town* with the comedy routines of the black company of Pigmeat Markham, the Wooster Group performers being in blackface. *LSD . . . Just the High Points* (1984), attempted to confront Arthur Miller's *The Crucible* with a debate incorporating Timothy Leary, the drug guru of the 1960s. (Miller eventually forbade the use of his text.) In 1991 *Brace Up!* subverted the narrative and psychological slant of Chekhov's *Three Sisters* to produce a set of technologically brilliant comments on the play and its reception, at the same time taking its visual stimulus from Japanese theatre. Later work has included material using the work of Eugene O'Neill, Racine, and Gertrude Stein (*House/Lights*, 2000).

This interview with Nick Kaye, the postmodernist historian, attempts to elucidate LeCompte's 'meaning' in her work. It is illuminating for her refusal to adopt any explanations, which avoids the fact that she creates 'theatrical', not literary or philosophical, meaning, instead maintaining that the meanings of the Wooster Group's creations lie in the pieces themselves and nowhere else.

## Compare this interview with writings by the following authors in this reader

**Bausch** – a confrontational theatre approach
**Brecht** – the roots of an anti-psychological stance
**Etchells** – who acknowledges LeCompte as influence
**Foreman and Wilson** – other deconstructive approaches to narrative
**Lepage** – a similar eclectic approach to material
**Rainer** – a contemporary woman postmodernist with a similar concern for process
**Schechner** – North American antecedents

## Further reading

Callens, J. (2005) *The Wooster Group and its Traditions*, Brussels: Peter Lang.
Gray, S. and LeCompte, E. (1980) 'Rumstick Road', *Performing Arts Journal*, Vol. 111 No. 2.
Quick, A. (2007) *The Wooster Group Workbook*, London: Routledge.
Savran, D. (1988) *Breaking the Rules*, New York: Theatre Communications Group.
Shank, T. (1982) *American Alternative Theatre*, New York: Grove Press.
http://www.thewoostergroup.org

# Chapter 38

# Jacques Lecoq

## THE THEATRE OF GESTURE AND IMAGE

T HE THEATRE OF MOVEMENT AND GESTURE can be recognised throughout the world today through the emergence of original productions. Young performers get together in companies, exchange their cultures and mix art forms: their performances are brought alive through gesture, word, music, object, and the image. This theatre makes its appearance following the break-up of that 'ossified mime' which flourished in numerous countries after the 1950s. The image of mime then was characterised by routines such as walking on the spot, the imaginary wall, and the typical outfit of white face and black tights. Copying one another, mime artists got stuck in a formula – no words, no objects, no sets other than themselves – and they soon found their limit. The audience applauded the novelty and surprise value; this silent genre was exportable, which increased its audience and allowed mimes to repeat the same discoveries before crowds who had never seen them. Only a mime with the great talent of Marceau could raise the level through his personality and his own poetry. Every mime is, in him- or herself, inimitable. The art of mime is not discontinuous with theatre and dance. When they have become separated from one another, it is because theatre has lost its sense of movement and has failed to realise it. Now that theatre is beginning to understand this, the mime performer can restore this sense of movement. Mime will have served the role of preserving those qualities of movement and of silence that dramatic action had lost in its preoccupation with text. Mime will restore the power of the word to the art of theatre.

The tempting vision of a total theatre, combining oratory, song, mime and dance, each one retaining its own formal autonomy, has often been evoked and realised, notably by Jean-Louis Barrault. This form of performance, influenced by traditional eastern theatre, in particular the Noh theatre of Japan, has always fascinated theatre artists. The actor performs using speech, then miming and dancing, alternating with the chorus which supports him and takes over the spoken word. The chorus speaks and the actor mimes; then the chorus sings and the actor dances. The forms of expression shift between them according to the dramatic pitch and the theatrical action. These sublime types of theatre are consummate forms which are no longer capable of evolution and which are difficult to take as practical models in our period of change. Today Jerzy Grotowski, Maurice Béjart, Peter Brook, Ariane Mnouchkine and Bob Wilson are making the journey east. India, Bali, Japan, China inspire their approach. These theatres with their perfected forms, all so different from each other, have this in common: they stylise the acting, rely on the mask, and focus on the head and hands to the point of symbolic gesture. Their way of moving the hand and head mark the most accomplished form of physical expression, just as they are the most developed form of gestural theatre. To those who are tempted by such an approach, this quest for the mysterious secrets still possessed by the Orient holds out the possibility of emptying oneself and of opening oneself up in order to understand better what is enduring; it permits such people to rediscover a theatre where the whole human being can become one with the universe. But this isn't about asking a French actor to perform like a Kathakali actor: this would be like putting a Scotsman in the lotus position – an impossible task for his joints. It is the meaning rather than the form that can bring us what theatre needs.

The scream seeks out the sign when one has lost one's memory of the other – that two such different words should be side by side! In 1968 this urgent scream first uttered by Antonin Artaud was rediscovered. Artaud was also fascinated by eastern theatre, that of Bali – he had seen the Balinese dancers at the 1937 Colonial Exhibition in Paris. The juxtaposition of these two phenomena – the scream and the sign – so distant from one another was, in their sudden reunion, evidence of how they had been torn apart. The phenomenon of their reunion becomes elided with the initial separation, concealing the split. It requires much time and work before the living gesture can avoid, from the outset, being rushed into codified definitions, into closed systems. Between the two, scream and sign, there remains a territory to be discovered which will aid the passage between the pelvis and the head and thus restore the whole body.

In Japan in 1972 the Kanze brothers, great actors in the traditional theatre forms of Noh and Kabuki, decided to perform the work of a modern author for the first time. Samuel Beckett was chosen, with *Waiting for Godot*. Having attended one of their rehearsals I asked them: 'Why have you chosen this play as your first experience of modern theatre?' They replied: 'In Beckett's theatre it is just like Noh, you're always waiting for something, be it to live or to die.' Beckett holds a very important position in the theatre of movement and gesture. Already in 1962, at the first international festival of mime held in Berlin, his *Play without Words* was performed by the actor-dancer Derrick Mandel. Then, as a result of that, numerous mimes were chosen to perform Beckett so that his thoughts turned to Buster Keaton for his silent film called Film (1964).

The return to physical expression by actors who had been caught up in the great psychodrama of 1968 gave rise to a movement vocabulary which had, up to that point, remained concealed within. The body brought to the visible surface a gestural language which was 'imprecise' rather than 'expressive', and this marked what could be called a 'revolt of the hunchbacks', 'the why not me's?' Physical states that had been considered impossible to show in public were displayed naked on stage for the first time. Grotowski ritualised the body through his semi-private ceremonies in an elitist semi-voyeurism. He wrapped the body in a white sheet, the shroud of purity. Starting from a sort of physical ascesis the actor sought to overcome the limits of his own powers through an act of will, to the point of harming himself.

After 1968, so-called 'classical' mime collapses. Companies change and abandon the clichés of mime for a theatre of gesture and movement. I am thinking of Els Joglars, a Spanish company who presented *Adam and Eve* at the 1970 Frankfurt Mime Festival. It was the first festival that publicly espoused this change in mime and which buried the 'mime of picking flowers'. There were countless discussions which took place in an increasingly positive climate.

Mime shifted to such an extent that it lost its name. Pierre Byland was emblematic of this change a prophetic image of which appeared in 1964 in his show, *The Concert*.

Mimes moved into clowning and spread across the world. In the United States, the Two Penny Circus was one of the first groups to make this journey. During the same period Dimitri was already mixing mime and the clown in his acts, whilst at the same time retaining the white face and the black tear. He played under the big top of Circus Knie in Switzerland, followed by Pic, retracing the steps of the earliest mimes of nineteenth-century pantomime who went to the circus to enliven and entertain the audience in between the equestrian numbers.

In Czechoslovakia, at the 1971 Prague festival, Ctibor Turba presented a piece which marked the split with the official mime of the period represented by Fialka and his company.

Today the theatre of gesture and movement has varied its themes and styles with a greater concern for image and object, thereby rediscovering the plastic function of the stage and integrating this into a whole new style of performance. Dance has taken over into its territory the abstract and technical mime in which certain dancers had specialised.

This period of exchange and multiplicity makes it impossible to classify differences between productions in which movement has a role, for fear of overlooking what is being born at this time, and with which we are not yet familiar.

■   ■   ■

## Source

Lecoq, J. (2006) 'The Theatre of Gesture and Image', *Theatre of Movement and Gesture*, London: Routledge: 126–130.

## Jacques Lecoq (1921–1999)

Of the artists in this book who have also constructed systems of performance training – Stanislavski, Meyerhold, Grotowski, Cunningham, Graham – most have also been performers or directors of their own work, which lives on in the form of DVDs or videos. Jaques Lecoq is the exception in that he has, through his school in Paris, trained many contemporary performance practitioners, such as members of Theatre de Complicite, but has not left us a set of recorded performances which demonstrate the results of his teaching. As long ago as 1948, Lecoq was invited to teach movement at the University of Padua in Italy, which introduced him to the Italian mime tradition of commedia dell'arte. He then went on to become a friend and colleague of Dario Fo, probably the most important mime/physical theatre artist of twentieth-century Italy, whose work was to connect theatre with the communities in which it was created. Lecoq then went on to work with Georgio Strehler at the Piccolo Theatre in Milan, which was also concerned with reaching out to working-class audiences. In 1956, when he was then 35, Lecoq established his own school in Paris, which he directed until his death in 1999. Lecoq never saw himself as either director or guru. The brochure of the 1980s advertising the school talks about 'a school of dynamic creativity. It relies on knowledge of the organic and emotional dynamics of man and nature . . .', phrases which encapsulate Lecoq's approach. Much of Lecoq's training involved an understanding that we communicate only secondarily through the word, but that our physicality tells much more about us: 'Gesture precedes knowledge, Gesture precedes thought, Gesture precedes language'. This sums up Lecoq's philosophy, which was transmitted to students over a period of 40 years at the school in Paris. The legacy is a set of exercises concerned with the body as a repository of emotion on the one hand, and as a memory bank on the other. Through what Lecoq described as the neutral mask, the student is asked to engage with the world, and to create movement and character which reflects the world as observed.

In this extract from his very rare writings, he discusses the significance of mime and its relationship with dance and its implications for a view of 'total' theatre, where the word is not dominant. He links his obsession with movement to the theatre of the East – India, Bali, Japan. In so doing Lecoq establishes a link with non-Western traditions of theatre, much of which is stylised and precise. Like Artaud, Lecoq was fascinated by the East, and this explains the attraction of his school, which still exists in Paris, and which provides a performance training without geographical borders. Lecoq, without knowing it, created a twenty-first-century performance training framework.

## Compare this article with writings by the following authors in this reader

**Artaud** – another interest in Eastern art
**Cunningham** – for the importance of movement
**Kantor** – for the importance of non-verbal theatre
**Mnouchkine** – an exponent of the body as prime communicator

## Further reading

Murray, S. (2003) *Jaques Lecoq*, London: Routledge.
Lecoq, J. (2000) *The Moving Body*. London: Methuen.
Zarrilli, P. (1995) *Acting (Re)Considered*, London: Routledge.
http://www.ecole-jacqueslecoq.com

# Chapter 39

# Hans-Thies Lehmann

## PROLOGUE TO *POSTDRAMATIC THEATRE*

### *The stakes*

With the end of the 'Gutenberg galaxy' and the advent of new technologies the written text and the book are being called into question. The mode of perception is shifting: a simultaneous and multi-perspectival form of perceiving is replacing the linear-successive. A more superficial yet simultaneously more comprehensive perception is taking the place of the centred, deeper one whose primary model was the reading of literary texts. Slow reading as much as theatre, which is laborious and cumbersome, is in danger of losing its status compared to the more profitable circulation of moving images. Literature and theatre, which are aesthetically mutually dependent on each other in a productive relation of repulsion and attraction, are both being demoted to the status of minority practices. Theatre is no longer a mass medium. To deny this becomes increasingly ridiculous, to reflect on it increasingly urgent. In the face of the pressure created by the attraction of the united forces of speed and surface, theatrical discourse emancipates itself from literary discourse but at the same time draws nearer to it in terms of its general function within culture. For both theatre and literature are textures which are especially dependent on the release of active energies of imagination, energies that are becoming weaker in a civilization of the primarily passive consumption of images and data. Neither theatre nor literature is essentially characterized by reproduction but rather organized as a complex system of signifiers.

At the same time, the cultural 'sector' increasingly falls prey to the laws of marketability and profitability, and here an additional disadvantage becomes apparent: theatre does not produce a tangible object which may enter into circulation as a marketable commodity, such as a video, a film, a disc, or even a book. The new technologies and media are becoming increasingly 'immaterial' – 'Les Immatériaux' was the title of an exhibition organized in 1985 by Jean-François Lyotard. Theatre, by contrast, is especially distinguished by the 'materiality of communication'. Unlike other forms of artistic practice it is marked by the especially heavy weight of its resources and materials. Compared to the poet's pen and paper, or the painter's oils and canvas, it requires a lot: the continuous activity of living people; the maintenance of theatre spaces; organizations, administrations and crafts; in addition to the material demands of all the arts themselves that are united in the theatre. Nevertheless, this seemingly antiquated institution still finds a surprisingly stable cultural place in society next to technically advanced media (which are increasingly often incorporated into theatrical performance).

Theatre is the site not only of 'heavy' *bodies* but also of a *real gathering*, a place where a unique intersection of aesthetically organized and everyday real life takes place. In contrast to other arts, which produce an object and/or are communicated through media, here the aesthetic act itself (the performing) as well as the act of reception (the theatre going) take place as a real doing in the here and now. Theatre means the collectively spent and used up lifetime in the collectively breathed air of that space in which the performing *and* the spectating take place. The emission and reception of signs and signals take place simultaneously. The theatre performance turns the behaviour onstage and in the auditorium into a *joint text*, a 'text' even if there is no spoken dialogue on stage or between actors and audience. Therefore, the adequate description of theatre is bound to the reading of this total text. Just as much as the gazes of all participants can virtually meet, the *theatre situation* forms a whole made up of evident and hidden communicative processes. This study concerns itself with the question of how scenic practice since the 1970s has made use of this basic given of theatre, has specifically reflected on it and directly turned it into the content and theme of its presentation. For the theatre shares with the other arts of (post)modernity the tendency for self-reflexivity and self-thematization. Just as, according to Roland Barthes, in modernism every text poses the problem of its own possibility (can its language attain the real?), radical staging practice problematizes its status of illusory reality. At the mention of 'self-reflexivity' and 'auto-thematic structure' one may at first think of the dimension of the text, since it is language *par excellence* that opens up the free play of a self-reflexive use of signs. Yet in theatre the text is subject to the same laws and dislocations as the visual, audible, gestic and architectonic theatrical signs.

Its profoundly changed mode of theatrical sign usage suggests that it makes sense to describe a significant sector of the new theatre as 'postdramatic'. At the same time, the new theatre *text* (which for its part continually reflects its constitution as a linguistic construct) is to a large extent a 'no longer dramatic' theatre text. By alluding to the literary genre of the drama, the title 'Postdramatic Theatre' signals the continuing association and exchange between theatre and text. Nevertheless, the discourse of *theatre* is at the centre of this book and the text therefore is considered only as one element, one layer, or as a 'material' of the scenic creation, not as its master. In no way does this involve an a priori value judgment. Important texts are still being written, and in the course of this study the often dismissively used term 'text theatre' will turn out to mean a genuine and authentic variant of postdramatic theatre, rather than referring to something that has supposedly been overcome. However, in view of the wholly unsatisfactory theoretical analysis of the newly produced *scenic* discourses (in comparison with the analysis of *drama*), it seems appropriate to consider even the dimension of the text from the perspective of theatrical reality.

The 'principles of narration and figuration' and the order of a 'fable' (story) are disappearing in the contemporary 'no longer dramatic theatre text' (Poschmann).[1] An 'autonomization of language'[2] develops. Retaining the dramatic dimension to different degrees, Werner Schwab, Elfriede Jelinek, Rainald Goetz, Sarah Kane and René Pollesch, for example, have all produced texts in which language appears not as the speech of characters – if there still are definable characters at all – but as an autonomous theatricality. With her 'theatre as an oralic institution', Ginka Steinwachs tries to create the scenic reality as a heightened poetic-sensual reality of language. A concept that may illuminate what is happening here is Elfriede Jelinek's idea of juxtaposed 'language surfaces' (*Sprachflächen*) in place of dialogue. As Poschmann explains,[3] this form is directed against the 'depth' of speaking figures, which would suggest a mimetic illusion. In this respect, the metaphor of 'language surfaces' corresponds to the turning point of painting in modernity when, instead of the illusion of three-dimensional space, what is being 'staged' is the picture's plane-ness, its two-dimensional reality, and the reality of colour as an autonomous quality. The interpretation that this autonomization of language bears witness to a lack of interest in the human being,[4] however, is not a foregone conclusion. Is it not rather a matter of a changed perspective on human subjectivity? What finds articulation here is less intentionality – a characteristic of the subject – than its failure, less conscious will than desire, less the 'I' than the 'subject of the unconscious'. So rather than bemoan the lack of an already defined image of *the* human being in postdramatically organized texts, it is necessary to explore the new possibilities of thinking and representing the individual human subject sketched in these texts.

## *Intentions*

This study does not aim to be a comprehensive inventory. Rather it attempts to develop an aesthetic logic of the new theatre. That this has hardly been under-taken yet is – among other reasons – due to the fact that theoreticians whose thinking could correspond to the tendencies of radical theatre rarely encounter this theatre and engage with it. Philosophers, while contemplating the 'theatre' as a concept and idea with conspicuous frequency and even turning 'scene' and 'theatre' into key concepts of theoretical discourse, rarely write concretely about specific theatre forms or practitioners. Jacques Derrida's readings of Artaud, Gilles Deleuze's comments on Carmelo Bene or Louis Althusser's classic text on Bertolazzi and Brecht are the more notable exceptions confirming the rule.[5] The affirmation of a theatre-*aesthetic* perspective may, however, necessitate the remark that aesthetic investigations always involve *ethical*, moral, political and legal questions in the widest sense. Art, and even more so theatre which is embedded in society in multiple ways – from the social character of the production and the public financing to the communal form of reception – exists in the field of *real socio-symbolic practice*. While the common reduction of the aesthetic to social positions and statements remains empty, inversely all aesthetic interrogation is blind if it does not recognize the reflection of social norms of perception and behaviour in the artistic practice of theatre.

The description of all those forms of theatre that are here considered as postdramatic is intended to be useful. What is at issue is, on the one hand, the attempt to place the theatrical development of the twentieth century into a perspective inspired by the developments of the new and newest theatre – developments which are obviously still hard to categorize – and, on the other hand, to serve the *conceptual* analysis and *verbalization of the experience* of this often 'difficult' contemporary theatre and thus to promote its 'visibility' and discussion. For it cannot be denied: the new forms of theatre have certainly marked the work of some of the most significant directors and companies of our time. They have found a significant, mostly younger audience who have flocked and continue to flock to venues like the Mickery Theater (Amsterdam), Kaaitheater (Brussels), Kampnagel (Hamburg), Mousonturm und TAT in Frankfurt, Hebbel-Theater (Berlin), Szene Salzburg, the Edinburgh Festival, the Barbican's BITE series, Riverside Studios, BAC and the ICA in London, Arnolfini (Bristol), Chapter Arts Centre (Cardiff), Nuffield Theatre (Lancaster), Tramway (Glasgow), PS122 (New York), Walker Arts Centre (Minneapolis), Wexner Centre for the Arts (Ohio State University), MCA (Chicago), PICA (Portland), On the Boards (Seattle), Highways Performance Space (Los Angeles) and Performance Space (Sydney) to name but a few. They have received an enthusiastic reception among a number of critics and some of their aesthetic principles have managed to 'infiltrate' the established theatre (albeit mostly in a watered down form). Yet the majority of spectators, who – to put it crudely – expect from the theatre the illustration of classic texts, may well accept the 'modern' set but subscribe to a comprehensible fable (story), coherent meaning, cultural self-affirmation and touching theatre feelings. With this audience the postdramatic theatre forms of a Robert Wilson, Jan Fabre, Einar Schleef or Jan Lauwers – to name but a few of the more 'accepted' theatre practitioners of the 1980s and 1990s – have met with little understanding. But even spectators who are convinced of the artistic integrity and the quality of such theatre often lack the conceptual tools to articulate their perception. This is demonstrated by the predominance of purely negative criteria. The new theatre, one hears and reads, is not this and not that and not the other, but there is a lack of categories and words to define or even describe what it is in any positive terms. This study aims to go some way towards correcting this situation and at the same time encourage ways of working in the theatre that expand our preconceptions of what theatre is or is meant to be.

Furthermore, this essay aims to facilitate an orientation in the variegated field of the new theatre. Much of it is only briefly sketched and would already serve its purpose if it inspired more detailed analyses. A comprehensive 'overview' of the new theatre in all its variants is obviously impossible anyway, and not only because of its limitless diversity. This is indeed a study dedicated to 'contemporary theatre'[6] but only in so far as it attempts to define theoretically how we recognize what makes it truly contemporary. Only a fragment of the theatre of the last thirty years is being considered here. The goal was not to find a conceptual framework that accommodates everything. The task in each case was to decide whether an aesthetic attests to true 'contemporaneity' or whether it merely perpetuates old models with technical accomplishment. Classical idealistic aesthetics had the concept of the 'idea' at its disposal: the design of a conceptual whole which allows the details to concretize (to grow together) as they unfold simultaneously in 'reality' and in 'concept'. Every historical phase of a particular art could thus be regarded by Hegel as a concrete and specific unfolding of the idea of art, every work of art as a special concretization of the objective spirit of an epoch or 'artistic form'. The idea of an 'epoch' or a historical state of the world gave idealism its unifying key, which made it possible to place art historically and systematically. If the confidence in such constructions – for example in that of 'the' theatre, of which the theatre of a particular epoch is a specific unfolding – has disappeared, then the pluralism of phenomena forces us to recognize the unforeseeability and suddenness of the *invention*, its indeducible moment or event.

At the same time, the heterogeneous diversity of forms unhinges all those methodological certainties that have previously made it possible to assert large-scale causal developments in the arts. It is essential to accept the coexistence of divergent theatre forms and concepts in which no paradigm is dominant. A conceivable consequence would be to leave it at a purely additive description, which would at least seemingly do justice to all the variants of the new theatre. But we cannot be satisfied with restricting ourselves to an atomizing historico-empirical listing of everything that exists. This would only be the transferral of a historicist contentedness – according to which everything is worth attending to simply because it once existed – to the present. As theatre studies scholars, we must not approach our own present with the gaze of the archivist. Therefore we must find a way out of this dilemma, or at least an attitude to it. The academic industry only seemingly solves the difficulties arising from the disappearance of overarching historical and aesthetic ordering models: mostly through the splintering into pedantic specializations. These in themselves, however, can be nothing more than increasingly laboriously packaged pieces of data collection, no longer of interest or support even to theorists in neighbouring fields. Another answer consists in theatre studies placing its bets on the much called upon inter-disciplinarity. The impulses resulting from this orientation are certainly very important. Yet it has to be stated that especially under the banner of an interdisciplinary approach scholars often evade the very cause and *raison d'être* for the theorizing – namely the aesthetic experience itself in its unprotected and unsecured experimental character. The latter is often sidestepped as a disturbing element in favour of large (and, in the name of interdisciplinarity, increasingly larger-scale) strategies of categorization.

Not wanting to succumb to the metamorphosis of thought into the equally meaningless exercises of either archiving or categorizing, I propose a double path. On the one band, following Peter Szondi, I want to read the realized artistic constructions and forms of practice as answers to artistic questions, as manifest reactions to the representational problems faced by theatre. In this sense, the term 'post*dramatic*' – as opposed to the 'epochal' category of the 'postmodern' – means a concrete problem of theatre aesthetics: thus Heiner Müller could state that he found it increasingly difficult even to articulate himself in a dramatic form any longer. On the other hand, I will claim here a certain (controlled) trust in a personal – or, to quote Adorno, 'idiosyncratic' – reaction. Where theatre caused me 'shock' through enthusiasm, insight, fascination, inclination or curious (not paralysing) incomprehension, the field marked by my experiences was carefully surveyed. However, only the course of the explication itself will justify the leading selection criteria.

## Trade secrets of dramatic theatre

For centuries a paradigm has dominated European theatre that clearly distin-guishes it from non-European theatre traditions. For example, Indian Kathakali or Japanese Noh theatre are structured completely differently and consist essentially of dance, chorus and music, highly stylized ceremonial procedures, narrative and lyric texts, while theatre in Europe amounted to the representation, the 'making present' (*Vergegenwärtigung*) of speeches and deeds on stage through mimetic dramatic play. Bertolt Brecht chose the term 'dramatic theatre' to designate the tradition that his epic 'theatre of the scientific age' intended to put an end to. In a more comprehensive sense (and also including the majority of Brecht's own work), however, this term can be used to designate the core of European theatre tradition in modern times. Inherent in it is a certain conglomeration of motifs – partially conscious and partially taken for granted as self-evident – that is frequently still unquestioningly regarded as constitutive for 'the' theatre. Theatre is tacitly thought of as the *theatre of dramas*. Among its consciously theorized elements are the categories of 'imitation' and 'action'/'plot', as much as the virtually automatic intimate connection of the two. As an associated, rather unconscious motif of this classical theatre conception we can point out the attempt to form (or strengthen) a social bond through theatre, a community uniting the audience and the stage emotionally and mentally. 'Catharsis' is the displaced theoretical name for this – by no means primarily aesthetic – function of theatre: the bringing about of affective recognition and solidarity by means of the drama and the affects represented and transmitted to the audience within its frame. These traits cannot be separated from the paradigm of 'dramatic theatre', whose significance therefore reaches far beyond the validity of a simple genre classification.

Dramatic theatre is subordinated to the primacy of the text. In the theatre of modern times, the staging largely consisted of the declamation and illustration of written drama. Even where music and dance were added or where they predominated, the 'text', in the sense of at least the imagination of a comprehensible narrative and/or mental *totality*, was determining. Despite an ever increasing characterization of dramatis personae through the non-verbal repertoire of gesture, movement and psychologically expressive mime, the human figure even in the eighteenth and nineteenth centuries was still centrally defined through speech. The text, in turn, functioned primarily as role script. The use of choruses, narrators, interludes, plays-within-a-play, prologues and epilogues, asides, and a thousandfold more subtle openings of the dramatic cosmos – including in the end even the Brechtian repertoire of epic ways of playing – could all be incorporated and added to the drama without destroying the specific experience of dramatic theatre. Whether or not lyrical forms of language were effective within the dramatic texture, and to what degree epic dramaturgies were applied, made no difference in principle: the drama was able to incorporate all of these without losing its dramatic character.

Although it remains debatable to what degree and in what way the audiences of former centuries were taken in by the 'illusions' offered by stage tricks, artful lighting, musical background, costumes and set, it can be stated that dramatic theatre was the formation of illusion. It wanted to construct a *fictive cosmos* and let all the stage represent – be – a world (this inversion is the aesthetic implication of the Shakespearean 'All the world's a stage . . .') abstracted but intended for the imagination and empathy of the spectator to follow and complete the *illusion*. For such an illusion neither completeness nor even continuity of the representation is necessary. What is necessary, however, is the principle that what we perceive in the theatre can be referred to a 'world', i.e. to a totality. Wholeness, illusion and world representation are inherent in the model 'drama'; conversely, through its very form, dramatic theatre proclaims wholeness as the *model* of the real. Dramatic theatre ends when these elements are no longer the regulating principle but merely one possible variant of theatrical art.

## Caesura of the media society

One commonly held view is that the experimental forms of contemporary theatre since the 1960s all have models in the period of the historical avant-gardes. This study proceeds from the conviction, however, that the undoubtedly deep caesura caused by the historical avant-gardes around 1900, despite their revolutionary innovations, largely maintained the essence of the 'dramatic theatre'. The newly emerging theatre forms continued to serve the – now modernized – representation of textual worlds; they plainly sought to save the text and its truth from disfigurement through a theatre practice that had become conventional; only within limits did they question the traditional model of theatrical representation and communication. Certainly Meyerhold's means of staging 'alienated' the staged plays in an extreme manner but they were still presented in a cohesive totality. Certainly the theatre revolutionaries broke with almost all conventions but even in their turn towards abstract and alienating means of staging they mostly still adhered to the mimesis of action on stage. By comparison, the spread and then omnipresence of the *media* in everyday life since the 1970s has brought with it a new multiform kind of theatrical discourse that is here going to be described as *postdramatic theatre*, It will not be disputed that the important art and theatre revolution that occurred around the turn of the twentieth century historically paved the way – on the contrary, we will devote a whole section to the antecedents, first beginnings and anticipations of postdramatic theatre that were developed at this time. For all the similarities in expressive forms, however, one has to consider that the same means can radically change their meaning in different contexts. The formal languages developed since the historical avant-gardes have become an arsenal of expressive gestures, which in postdramatic theatre serve as theatre's response to changed social communication under the conditions of generalized information technologies.

One of the salutary effects of this study is that the demarcation of a new theatre continent with other criteria, values and processes has created the necessity to reveal a number of 'un-thought' implications of that which even nowadays shapes the common understanding of theatre. Apart from this critique of a series of – on closer inspection rather questionable – self-evident notions in the theory of theatre, it is necessary to postulate postdramatic theatre energetically as a concept contradictory to these seemingly self-evident concepts. Developed as a way of defining the contemporary, it can retroactively allow the 'non-dramatic' aspects of the theatre of the past to stand out more clearly. The newly developed aesthetic forms allow both the older forms of theatre *and* the theoretical concepts used to analyse them to appear in a changed light. To be sure: one always has to be cautious with the assertion of caesuras in the history of an art form, above all when they are of a very recent date. There may be a danger in overestimating the depth of the rupture postulated here: the destruction of the foundations of dramatic theatre – which after all have been valid for hundreds of years – and the radical transformation of scenic practice in the ambiguous light of media culture. But the obverse danger (especially in academia) of perceiving the new always as only a variant of the well known seems to threaten with yet more disastrous misjudgments and blindness.

## *Names*

The following list offers a kind of *panorama* of the field of study that opens up under the name of postdramatic theatre. It is concerned with phenomena of a most heterogeneous kind, with world famous theatre practitioners, as much as with companies hardly known beyond a small circle. Every reader will discover a more or less long list of names familiar to them. Not all of the practitioners have created a whole 'oeuvre' that can be considered postdramatic in its entirety – if we can use the term 'oeuvre' for directors, theatre companies, theatre productions and actions. Not all of them are extensively discussed in this book. Accordingly, the following belong among this, in every way incomplete, 'namedropping' for a postdramatic theatre: Robert Wilson, Jan Fabre, Jan Lauwers, Heiner Goebbels, Einar Schleef, Jürgen Manthey, Achim Freyer, Klaus Michael Grüber, Peter Brook, Anatoli Vassiliev, Robert Lepage, Elizabeth LeCompte, Pina Bausch, Reinhild Hoffmann, William Forsythe, Meredith Monk, Anne Teresa de Keersmaeker, Meg Stuart, En Knap, Jürgen Kruse, Christof Nel, Leander Hausmann, Frank Castorf, Uwe Mengel, Hans-Jürgen Syberberg, Tadeusz Kantor, Eimuntas Nekrosius, Richard Foreman, Richard Schechner, John Jesurun, Theodoros Terzopoulos, Giorgio Barberio Corsetti, Emil Hrvatin, Silviu Purcarete, Tomaz Pandur, Jerzy Grotowski, Eugenio Barba, Saburo Teshigawara, Tadashi Suzuki. Countless action theatres, performance artists, happenings and theatre styles inspired by happenings also belong here: Bobby Baker, Hermann Nitsch, Otto Mühl, The Wooster Group, Survival Research Laboratories, Squat Theatre, The Builders Association, Magazzini, Falso Movimento, Theatergroep Hollandia, Theatergroep Victoria, Matschappej Discordia, Theater Angelus Novus, Hotel Pro Forma, Serapionstheater, Sydney Front, Bak-Truppen, Remote Control Productions, Tg STAN, Suver Nuver, La Fura del Baus, Goat Island, DV8 Physical Theatre, Forced Entertainment, Station House Opera, Vincent Dance Theatre, Desperate Optimists, Reckless Sleepers, Théâtre de Complicité, Teatro Due, Societas Raffaello Sanzio, Théâtre du Radeau, Akko-Theater, Gob Squad. Numerous theatre companies, small, medium and large projects and productions, which are associated with one or more of the 'theatre languages' indicated by the named names. Younger theatre practitioners like Stefan Pucher, Helena Waldmann, René Pollesch, Michael Simon. Authors whose work is at least partially related to the postdramatic paradigm: in the German-speaking countries above all Heiner Müller, Rainald Goetz, the Vienna School, Bazon Brock, Peter Handke, Elfriede Jelinek . . .

## Paradigm

The plethora of phenomena in the theatre landscape of the last few decades that have challenged the traditional forms of drama and 'its' theatre with aesthetic consistency and inventiveness suggests that it is justified to speak of a new *paradigm of postdramatic theatre*. Paradigm is an auxiliary term used here to indicate the shared negative boundary demarcating the internally highly diverse variants of the postdramatic theatre from the dramatic. These works of theatre also become paradigmatic because they are widely recognized – albeit not always welcomed – as an authentic testimony of the times, and as such develop their own yardstick. The term paradigm is not intended to promote the illusion that art, like science, could conform to the developmental logic of paradigms and paradigm shifts. When discussing postdramatic stylistic moments one could easily point out those that the new theatre shares with the traditional dramatic theatre. In the emergence of a new paradigm, the 'future' structures and stylistic traits almost unavoidably appear mixed in with the conventional. An analysis that resigned itself to a mere inventory of the motley costumed styles and varieties would miss the actual underlying productive processes. Without the development of categories for stylistic traits, which in each case are only impurely realized, these traits would not even stand out. For instance, narrative fragmentation, heterogeneity of style, hypernaturalist, grotesque and neo-expressionist elements, which are all typical of postdramatic theatre, can also be found in productions which nevertheless belong to the model of dramatic theatre. In the end, it is only the constellation of elements that decides whether a stylistic moment is to be read in the context of a dramatic or a postdramatic aesthetics. One thing is certain: today a Gotthold Ephraim Lessing, who could develop 'the' dramaturgy of a postdramatic theatre, is unthinkable. The theatre of sense and synthesis has largely disappeared – and with it the possibility of synthesizing interpretation. Recommendations, let alone prescriptions, are no longer possible, merely partial perspectives and stuttering answers that remain 'works in progress'. The task of theory is to articulate, conceptualize and find terms for that which has come into being, not to postulate it as the norm.

## Postmodern and postdramatic

For the theatre of the time span we are concerned with here – roughly the 1970s to the 1990s – the term *postmodern theatre* has become established. This can be sorted in many ways: the theatre of deconstruction, multimedia theatre, restoratively traditionalist theatre, theatre of gestures and movement. The difficulty of comprehending such a wide field in terms of 'epoch' is evident in many studies that try to characterize the 'postmodern theatre' since 1970 through a long and impressive list of features. Some of the key words that have come up in the international postmodernism discussion are: ambiguity; celebrating art as fiction;

celebrating theatre as process; discontinuity; heterogeneity; non-textuality; plural-ism; multiple codes; subversion; all sites; perversion; performer as theme and protagonist; deformation; text as basic material only; deconstruction; considering text to be authoritarian and archaic; performance as a third term between drama and theatre; anti-mimetic; resisting interpretation. Postmodern theatre, we hear, is without discourse but instead dominated by mediation, gestuality, rhythm, tone. Moreover: nihilistic and grotesque forms, empty space, silence. Such keywords, as much as they often hit upon something real about the new theatre, can neither be cogent individually (much of it – ambiguity, resisting interpreta-tion, multiple codes – is obviously also true for previous forms of theatre), nor can they collectively offer more than catchphrases which necessarily have to remain very general (deformation) or name very heterogeneous traits (perver-sion, subversion). Much of it also provokes opposition: of course there is 'discourse' in postmodern theatre, for instance. Like any other artistic practice, it is not exempt from the modern development that analysis, 'theory', reflection and self-reflection invade art to a previously unknown degree. Postdramatic theatre knows not only the 'empty' space but also the overcrowded space. It can indeed be 'nihilistic' and 'grotesque' – but so is *King Lear*. Process, heterogeneity or pluralism in turn are true for all theatre – the classical, modern and 'postmodern'. When Peter Sellars staged *Ajax* in 1986 and *The Persians* in 1993, his productions, like his original stagings of Mozart operas, were called 'postmodern' merely because he rigorously and irreverently brought classical material into the contem-porary, everyday world.

## *Choice of term*

The term and subject of 'postdramatic theatre' that I introduced into the debate some years ago have been picked up by other theoreticians, so for this reason, too, it made sense to stay with this coinage. The present study takes up questions that could only be hinted at in my earlier opposition of the 'predramatic' discourse of Attic tragedy and 'postdramatic' contemporary theatre.[7] In passing, and related to but diverging from the emphasis attempted here, Richard Schechner has applied the word 'postdramatic' to happenings; he once spoke of the 'postdramatic theatre of happenings'.[8] Similarly *en passant* and with a view to Beckett, Genet and Ionesco, he also, somewhat paradoxically, talked about the 'postdramatic drama',[9] in which no longer the 'story' but what Schechner calls the 'game' becomes the 'generative matrix' – albeit within the frame of what, according to our use of terms, is a 'dramatic' structure of stage fiction and situation. With respect to newer theatre texts, scholars have talked about 'no longer dramatic theatre texts', as already mentioned, but what is still missing is an attempt to survey the new *theatre* and the diversity of its theatrical means in more detail in the light of postdramatic aesthetics.

One could cite other reasons in favour of the term 'postdramatic' – notwithstanding the understandable scepticism towards coinages with the prefix 'post'. (Heiner Müller once said he knew only one postmodern poet: August Stramm – a modern poet who worked at the post office.) This scepticism, however, seems to be more justified towards the concept of postmodernism, which claims to achieve the definition of a whole epoch. Many traits of theatre practice that are called postmodern – from the seeming to the real randomness of means and quoted forms, to the unabashed use and combination of heterogeneous styles, from a 'theatre of images' to mixed media, multimedia and performance – by no means demonstrate a renunciation of modernity on principle. Yet they do show a renunciation of the traditions of dramatic form. The same is true for numerous texts by authors ranging from Heiner Müller to Elfriede Jelinek that have been labelled as 'postmodern'. When the progression of a story with its internal logic no longer forms the centre, when composition is no longer experienced as an organizing quality but as an artificially imposed 'manufacture', as a mere sham of a logic of action that only serves clichés (something Adorno abhorred about the products of the 'culture industry'), then theatre is confronted with the question of possibilities beyond drama, not necessarily beyond modernity. Heiner Müller said in a conversation with Horst Laube in the mid-1970s:

> Brecht thought epic theatre was impossible; it would only become possible if the perversion of turning a luxury into a profession were to cease – the constitution of theatre out of the division of stage and auditorium. Only if this is abolished, at least in tendency, does it become possible to make theatre with a minimum of dramaturgy, almost without dramaturgy. And that's what it's about now: to produce a theatre without effort. I realize when I go to the theatre that it is increasingly boring to me to follow one plot for an evening. That is actually no longer interesting to me. If one plot starts in the first image, and then an entirely different one is continued in the second one, and then a third and a fourth starts, then it's entertaining and pleasurable, but it's no longer the perfect play.[10]

In the same context, Müller bemoans that the method of collage is not yet sufficiently utilized in theatre. While the large theatres, under the pressures of conventional norms of the entertainment industry, tend not to dare to deviate from the unproblematic consumption of fables, the newer theatre aesthetics practise a consistent renunciation of the one plot and the perfection of drama without this implying a renunciation of modernity *per se*.

## Tradition and the postdramatic talent

The adjective 'postdramatic' denotes a theatre that feels bound to operate beyond drama, at a time 'after' the authority of the dramatic paradigm in theatre. What it does not mean is an abstract negation and mere looking away from the tradition of drama. 'After' drama means that it lives on as a structure – however weakened and exhausted – of the 'normal' theatre: as an expectation of large parts of its audience, as a foundation for many of its means of representation, as a quasi automatically working norm of its drama-turgy. Müller calls his postdramatic text *Description of a Picture*,[11] a 'landscape beyond death' and 'explosion of a memory in a withered dramatic structure'. This describes postdramatic theatre: the limbs or branches of a dramatic organism, even if they are withered material, are still present and form the space of a memory that is 'bursting open' in a double sense. Even in the term 'postmodern', wherever it is used in more than a token sense, the prefix 'post' indicates that a culture or artistic practice has stepped out of the previously unquestioned horizon of modernity but still exists with some kind of reference to it. This may be a relation of negation, declaration of war, liberation, or perhaps only a deviation and playful exploration of what is possible beyond this horizon. Similarly, one can speak of a 'post-Brechtian theatre', which is precisely not a theatre that has nothing to do with Brecht but a theatre which knows that it is affected by the demands and questions for theatre that are sedimented in Brecht's work but can no longer accept Brecht's answers.

Postdramatic theatre thus includes the presence or resumption or continued working of older aesthetics, including those that took leave of the dramatic idea in earlier times, be it on the level of text or theatre. Art in general cannot develop without reference to earlier forms. It is only a question of the level, conscious-ness, explicitness and special manner of reference. Nevertheless, one has to distinguish between the recourse to earlier forms within new forms and the (false) appearance of the continued validity and necessity of the traditional 'norms'. The claim that postmodern theatre needed classical norms in order to establish its own identity by way of a polemical distancing from it[12] could be based on a confusion between the perspective from outside and the internal aesthetic logic. For, it is often rather the critical talk *about* the new theatre that seeks such recourse. What is actually hard to shake off is the classical *terminology* that turns the power of tradition into aesthetic norms. It is true that new theatre practice often establishes itself in the public consciousness through polemical differentiation from customary practice and thus creates the appearance that it owes its identity to the classical norms. Provocation alone, however, does not make a form; even provocative, negating art has to create something new under its own steam. Through this alone, and not through the negation of classical norms, can it obtain its own identity.

## Notes

1   G. Poschmann, *Der nicht mehr dramatische Theatertext: Aktuelle Bühnenstücke und ihre dramatische Analyse*, Tübingen: Niemeyer, 1997, p. 177. (Unless otherwise indicated, all quotations in this book have been translated by K. Jürs-Munby.)

2   Ibid., p. 178.

3   Ibid., p. 204ff.

4   Ibid.

5   See the useful anthology of politico-philosophical texts on the theatre by T. Murray (ed.), *Mimesis, Masochism and Mime: Politics of Theatricality in Contemporary French Thought*, Ann Arbor: University of Michigan Press, 1977.

6   W. Floeck (ed.), *Tendenzen des Gegenwartstheaters*, Tübingen: Francke, 1998.

7   H.-T. Lehmann, *Theater und Mythos: Die Konstitution des Subjekts im Diskurs der antiken Tragödie.* Stuttgart: Metzler, 1991.

8   R. Schechner, *Performance Theory*, New York: Taylor and Francis, 1988, p. 21.

9   Ibid., p. 22.

10  H. Müller, *Gesammelte Irrtümer*, Frankfurt am Main: Verlag der Autoren, 1986, p. 21.

11  H.-T. Lehmann, 'Theater der Blicke: Zu Heiner Müller's "Bildbeschreibung"', in U. Profitlich (ed.), *Dramatik der DDR*, Frankfurt am Main: Suhrkamp, 1987, pp. 186–202.

12  P. Pavis, 'The Classical Heritage of Modern Drama: The Case of Postmodern Theatre', in *Modern Drama*, vol. 29, 1986, p. 1. 'Avant-garde theatre', Pavis says here, 'needs classical norms to establish its own identity.'

■  ■  ■

## Source

Lehmann, H.-T. (2006) *Postdramatic Theatre*, London: Routledge.


## Hans-Thies Lehmann (1944–)

Hans-Thies Lehmann is Professor of Theatre Studies at the Johann Wolfgang University, Frankfurt am Main, Germany. Lehmann, in *Postdramatic Theatre*, characterises much contemporary 'theatre' practice as being 'postdramatic', by which he means that the twentieth century has seen a major shift from the notion of 'drama' as being a writer's text (to be interpreted by actors, directors, etc.) to the idea of theatre as a performance phenomenon in which a written text – if it exists at all – is simply one of the signifying factors that form the notion of twentieth-century performance. As such Lehmann is of interest to us inasmuch as he is the first critic to elaborate this idea, though such writers as Schechner and Carlson had already explored this, as had RoseLee Goldberg in her two books *Performance Art* and *Performance*. The importance of Lehmann's insight is that it seeks to locate what are seen as conventional approaches to drama as simply part of a wider phenomenon of a world of 'performance'. The extract from his book that we include here shows how much of this varied world of performance Lehmann himself has seen, and how, by inventing the term 'postdramatic' he allows traditional ideas of 'drama' to be incorporated into the world of performance that this reader encompasses.

The list of names, companies, and artists that Lehmann gives us forms a catalogue of the major performance artists of both the twentieth and twenty-first century. The traditional worlds of theatre, dance, music, writing, production have formed a now established framework within which we can look across boundaries to the new world of performance that has emerged in the late twentieth century.

## Compare this article with writings by the following authors in this reader

**Goldberg** – a visual catalogue of performance artists
**Goulish** – an interpretation of 'writing'

## Further reading

Carlson, M. (1996) *Performance: a Critical Introduction*, London: Routledge.
Fischer-Lichter, E. and Jain, S.I. (2008) *The Transformative Power of Performance: A New Aesthetics*, London: Routledge.

Chapter 40

# Robert Lepage

## ROBERT LEPAGE IN DISCUSSION

**RE**   This is the end of a long but quite ordinary day for Robert: he's been rehearsing *A Midsummer Night's Dream* since 10.30 this morning, re-rehearsing his show *Needles and Opium*, which he has just performed, and is now rounding off the day with a light ten-mile jog through this Platform. I've been seeing Robert's work for maybe six years, since he brought a show to the ICA. Last year I was in a position to exercise my patronage – put the taxpayers' money where my heart is – and invite *Tectonic Plates* to the National. In addition, I've been able to pursue the real passion of a fan and ask Robert to direct a show for the National. This all begs the question of why I think Robert's work is so singular and so attractive. I think it's because the more I work in the theatre and the more theatre I see, the more I treasure and admire the characteristics about the theatre that can't be translated into any other medium. Robert Frost said that poetry is the bit that can't be translated, and that's what I think about theatre. I don't like theatre when it's a surrogate for TV or for debate or anything else. I like it when it's the thing itself and it happens to a live audience and employs a vocabulary of speech, gesture, music, space and light as the servants of expression and content. They are all things that you see in spades in the work of Robert Lepage. His work has a characteristic of the best art: it converts the commonplace into the magical and makes the magical real and accessible. He is a purveyor of dreams, and what's encouraging and exciting for me is that it's not that he works in a language or syntax that belongs to the world of performance art. It's absolutely, irreducibly, theatre. It uses sometimes very simple, very primitive theatrical methods and translates into a language that is entirely original. His work also places a very strong emphasis on the work of actors and on the human being. It's very humane, funny, touching, and I think entirely wonderful.

A bit of biography: Robert has worked since the beginning of the eighties with a company called Théâtre Repère. He's an actor – you may have seen him in *Jesus of Montreal* – director, writer, musician. He's also the artistic director of the French Theatre of the Canadian National Arts Centre, which effectively means he's responsible for the National Theatre. And what he does in his spare time, I can't imagine.

Robert, how did you get interested in theatre?

**RL**   I've never really been interested in theatre as such. In my adolescence I was more interested in theatricality. The reason, in my opinion, there's such a big difference between theatre and theatricality is that where I come from theatrical history is extremely young – about 50 years old or so – so we don't have any classics, our classics are borrowed. Also the fact that Canada's a bi-cultural country – two cultures that are *starting* to talk to each other. We did have a pool of good authors 20 years ago when I started to be interested in theatre. When I say that I'm more interested in theatricality, it's because I think the taste for young creators, actors or directors in Quebec, at least in the seventies, came much more from seeing rock shows, dance shows, performance art, than from seeing theatre, because theatre is not as accessible as it is here in Britain. And the theatre that was there was a theatre that was already dead: not reflecting anybody's identity, not actually staging the preoccupations of the people. I always come back to political things because it's important to understand what Canada's about culturally. For a long time anybody in English Canada who was an artistic director of a big theatre company had a British accent, and in Quebec those people had a French accent from France. I don't want to sound racist or xenophobic but it took some time before young theatre people became artistic directors or even directors. There's not a theatrical tradition but there's a lot of theatricality. A lot of my taste for theatre came from seeing concerts of Genesis and Jethro Tull. It sounds pretty superficial now, but theatre for a long time, at least in North America, has been dispossessed from its theatricality. It started to imitate film more and more and got stuck with cinematic realism. The theatrical fun was when Pina Bausch started to do tours and festivals in Toronto. In the late seventies or early eighties there was this movement of all these new directors who were theatrical, and it became a more exciting place to be.

**RE**   I think a lot of your generation here felt that theatre was in some way an inadequate substitute for film. They thought film is where the action is, film is the language of the 20th century, theatre is the language of the 19th century. Certainly in the States that was a strong feeling, and you didn't feel that?

317

**RL**  I think that film is an extraordinarily exciting place to be, to work in or to see. I think it's as exciting as theatre. But I think that it's more interesting to work in theatre and to borrow from film artistic ways of showing things or telling stories. For a long time theatre had been only using the naturalism from film – saying we need real food on stage, we need to pretend that there's a fourth wall. That's wrong. Theatre's theatre. There's no fourth wall; it's live, it changes every night. What I'm trying to say is that theatre borrowed all the wrong things from film. We're facing an audience now that knows what a flash-back or a flash-forward is, that has a very strong culture and education in how to tell stories in many different ways because of film and TV. Theatre has to go along with that and use that in a theatrical way. I'm afraid I see a lot of theatre that only borrows the realism, and only the people in the front rows get to appreciate it.

**RE**  I don't know the origin of Théâtre Repère, but is that why you started to write your own work, because you felt existing texts were somehow too linear?

**RL**  Not necessarily. I thought a lot of texts were inadequate because they didn't correspond to the time and place I was evolving in. That was a phenomenon that was happening in Montreal and Quebec City, where language was such a political debate. Words were so coloured with politics, at least in the seventies, that people turned to non-verbal theatre to try and get other messages across. Politics was so present in Canadian life in the seventies that a lot of the creative work in Canada was based only on politics of the mind, not politics of the body, of emotion, of relationships. I think an artist sometimes has to put words aside, to explore these types of politics. Also I got interested because I was very good at mime. I never thought I'd be working as an actor and as a director.

**RE**  You went to the Jacques Lecoq School in Paris?

**RL**  No, not to that school, I went to Alain Knapp who had something called the Institut de la Personalité Créatrice – translated as a place for good manners. I wasn't there a full year, only a part. He had a way of approaching theatre in a very creative way. He never distinguished what a director and an actor do. He worked mainly on improvisations – things would happen spontaneously and had to be written as they were going. So you learned to be an actor and at the same time be a director because you had to see what you were composing, and you had to be a writer so that the structure was also working. His goal was to try to make total theatrical creators. Later on I started to move on to improv games and things like that. I went to school at Quebec City Conservatory, almost a monastery, for three years. Most of the teachers there had done Lecoq and worked in Lecoq's way and philosophy. The school was based a lot on physical work. When I came out of school, I was very good physically, but at that point the bourgeoisie had incorporated clowns and Commedia and all of that. There's a company in Canada called Direct Film, that processes Kodak stuff. They have these clowns – so the only job you could get as a clown was with them.

So anyway, all the things I'd learned in school had been incorporated by the *théâtre bourgeois*. I had to find a way of using what I knew. I think my main talent was the ability to gather people around an idea and devise pieces, and slowly we developed this group called Théâtre Repère. It's rather strange because now I have this burden on my shoulder of having all of the success, the merit of this thing, but also all the criticism; in fact it's a collective venture. I'm not trying to be falsely humble or coy or whatever (and that wouldn't be very convincing in the mouth of someone who just did a solo piece) but I truly believe that theatre is a meeting place. I don't think film is, necessarily. Film is a much more individual-istic type of event. I believe that we can go through another renaissance in theatre. I'm not saying I'm trying to create a renaissance in what I'm doing, but I believe in the spirit of Renaissance, I think it's still alive and still possible. A lot of structures in the way our society permits or organises culture do not allow that, but as artists we can allow that to ourselves.

**RE**  In each of Robert's shows, there is at least one, but generally about thirty images which really burn themselves on the memory. One of the things about your work, for a fellow director, is that one just feels very jealous. You sit there thinking 'I wish I'd thought of that'. But it's partly because these moments are all very simple. Anyone can think of a Lycra screen doing all those things (in *Needles and Opium*) – it's in a sense a traditional device – but anyone didn't think of it. Let me take a moment in *Dragons' Trilogy* which was recently at Riverside Studios. There's an extraordinarily moving moment (I can't tell you the whole story, it would take four and a half hours) but there's a Chinese man, married to a French Canadian woman who has been won in a bet. They have a retarded daughter, and a French-speaking Chinese nun comes to this rather unhappy couple to take away the daughter to a special home. This nun chatters away in a mixture of Chinese, English and French for a long time; it's a funny and touching scene. The child's suitcase is brought out, and gradually, as the nun speaks, the mother starts to put the child's clothes into the suitcase. She takes off the nun's habit, puts it in the suitcase, and the nun becomes this retarded child. It's the most extraordinary metamorphosis, terribly moving, and the most brilliant piece of bravura acting and direction. I was asking Robert how it came about and he said 'I think it was because we didn't have enough actors to go round'. I'm also fascinated by a moment in *Tectonic Plates* which, as an idea and as a realisation of that idea, made me cry because it was so perfect. There was a pit of water in the Cottesloe theatre. The story was a complicated interweaving, including Chopin, George Sand, Jim Morrison and the Doors and many other things, some of it set in Venice. There was an image in the second half when you were in Père Lachaise cemetery and a statue came to life. The shroud was taken off this statue and laid into the pool, and as it was laid there, a huge image of George Sand appeared on it. Of course it was just a simple carousel projector from above with a small slide.

It was exquisitely beautiful because it was there on the water but only realised because the sheet was there. Now, I want to know how do you arrive at that? I don't think you sit at home thinking 'That's a good idea, how can I work it into the show' . . .

**RL**  I think there's an important word that has lost its sense in the theatre, and that's the word 'playing'. It's become a profession, a very serious word, but the concept of playing has disappeared from the staging of shows. The only way you can attain these ideas is if you play. I think we're trying to be grown-ups and taken seriously and all of that, and everything that's childish or inventive about us we put aside. I always give this example, and you probably all went through similar things . . . My father was a cab driver so he didn't have any money, but at Christmas they would buy some sophisticated toy I'd wanted badly, and I'd start playing around with it and after three days I'd be completely bored and have more fun with the box it came in. If you play around you get these ideas. Text and story-writing is very sacred, but, the thing with the nun really came about because she was playing both parts and didn't have time to go out and come in again, so we used that to become a moment of poetry. For it to work it meant that every element of clothing that we took off her had a line that went with it – we wrote to justify the costume change, which is a sacrilege in the world of writing for the theatre. You never start from form. You always work by the sacred word and of course you have problems if you don't reinvent it. I'm not saying it works every time, but I think theatre is a place of form. You explore mediums until one day you express something very profound that has some echo in the audience. Sometimes it doesn't work but at least if you put that word 'play' back, the audience is much more moved and feels much more stimulated and excited by something that allows them to be inventive with the actor. There are two ways of being attentive to a show, either you can watch in a very passive way or in a very active way. We have learnt, probably for budget reasons, that we want to give the audience their money's worth. We say 'They come here to relax, they don't want to think.' But it's not true. I believe in the intelligence of the audience, I believe that the audience wants to create. You have to give the audience food, not things that are already masticated and organised and painted. Sometimes I think I can do beautiful, magical images that are very stunning but they're too high-tec, they don't give the audience the opportunity to invent them. I think I've achieved something when it's extremely simple but triggers in 300 people in the house 300 different versions, like a word does.

**RE**  The pool in *Tectonic Plates*, you said that Michael Levine, the designer said you must have this pool . . .

**RL**  Of course if, after a while the pool gets in the way, we put it aside, we don't suffer. I believe a lot in intuition and in spontaneous propositions, mainly from actors because actors are extremely intuitive people. They often stutter and can't clearly explain theatrical ideas as well as writers or directors, but they can actually express intuitions, and that's what we have to look for in theatre. Sometimes it's completely clumsy, you come in with this image and you work on it and consider it and at some point it always comes out, that there's this inner connection between us, all these layers underneath our feet, secret connections that we have to discover. Then we work on the coincidences. When you work alone it's more difficult because it's much more egocentric, almost therapeutic. But these ideas come from coincidence and intuition. For *Needles and Opium*, I was interested in Jean Cocteau and fascinated by the fact that he wrote a book on a plane. In those days it took 15 hours to fly from New York City to Paris, so he had time to write a book. I was amazed because I only deliver one tenth of the contents of the book, but it's very fascinating. I read it on a plane to Barcelona and had the physical sensation of flying while this guy was on this old 1949 plane. So you start to investigate the effects it has on you, the coincidences. You say, how come I feel moved and inspired by this piece of work, which I might just have read, found interesting and put aside? It's the fact that you're in midair, in a privileged place, these events indicate to you what you should be using. I've done it so much, and worked with so many people that I don't have as much fear or apprehension about going into it. Of course, a lot of actors or writers who participate in my works are often destabilised when we start.

Talking about *Tectonic Plates*, I can't explain it, it made an impression on me intellectually, this thing of continents that are moving. It's just an intuition. Then everyone in the company gives their impression and at one point we see all these story lines. I didn't know anything about Romanticism before we did this show, or about Jim Morrison or Chopin. I mean, I knew *something* – I'm not totally uncultivated – but then you get so obsessed and so creative when you delve into a world you don't know. The thing that's interesting is to discover a text, an author. That's something I do when I direct actors. The main indication I give when I work on a text is: Discover what you're saying. The audience wants to discover things and it's in a state of discovery that the actor is on the wing.

**RE**   You've had prolonged experience of directing conventional existing texts, some classics, in large theatres not dissimilar from the National, and at the moment you're working on an existing text (*A Midsummer Night's Dream*), which you have directed before, in Victor Hugo's French translation. If you've got a given text, is that an inhibition or is it simply like the pool?

**RL**   It depends on the text of course. Dealing with Shakespeare we're dealing with an avalanche of resources, a box of toys to be taken out. There are some authors that are so infinitely rich and give so much permission, because theatre is the platform of allowing things to be expressed, emotions to meet. What's so extraordinary about Shakespeare is that this man was so intuitive, he gives us the story of mankind. I think he offers a lot of permission to the actor, the translator, the director. You don't feel in a literal environment when working with Shakespeare,

Dante or authors like that. Probably that's also one of the responses to the theatrical crisis in the past decade. In France for example, Mnouchkine is restaging all the Greeks – people are going back to these fundamental texts.

**RE**   Is that because they're poetic texts and the verbal imagery in the text resonates sufficiently . . .

**RL**   Yes but also there's something about these texts that are doubtful. I did the Scottish play two months ago in Toronto, the first time I directed Shakespeare in English. There are all of these theories about how maybe Shakespeare did not exist and these fifteen women wrote the plays . . . there's something doubtful about the property and the invention. The essence of Romanticism and the Renaissance is that you're building a new world on the ruins of the old one, and that's creative, that's rich. All these people. Shakespeare and the Greeks, built a new world on an old one.

**RE**   That's a wonderful metaphor for the whole continuing process of theatre, isn't it, particularly in this country where you're very conscious of the mountainous tradition, and every time you do a Shakespeare play you've got this huge baggage piled up behind you and you are building on the old world.

**RL**   I think also it's something about the global theatrical community. Theatre's a world that is built on ripping other people off. It's a normal tradition. Mummenschanz, an extraordinary mask and mime company from Switzerland, have this recipe for this kind of plasticine they use for their masks. Everyone wants to know the recipe. You have to show the strings. If you don't see the strings, at some point you have to understand that there *are* strings, there are people taking make-up off. You have to share that.

**RE**   One of the things I like about working in the theatre is that it's completely pragmatic, it's empirical, and you always say 'Does it work?' That's why I like British actors a lot, because they come from a completely empirical tradition. Some people, certainly from the perspective of German theatre, they're pragmatic to a fault. Is that your experience of working with British actors (and you're indemnified against slander)?

**RL**   I think the first thing you identify when you start working with British actors is that they're so professional, the system is centuries old, and you're shocked by how available actors are to the director. You want them to be crazy, to say shut up, listen to me. That's what they do where I come from – there's all these crazy people running round the room and you say 'Hey, focus.' British actors are extremely focused. It's an interesting phenomenon, not just in the theatre but British society in general has the reputation of this cliche of phlegmatism. Is that an English word?

**RE**  Yeah.

**RL**  Most certainly is. There's this theory that England's history, not in its theatre, but its history is so bloody – Jack the Ripper, Richard III – the culture is so bloody that it kind of assassinated death. It took the sexy thing of violence out of it. I'm amazed when I see British productions of a Shakespearean tragedy, to see this extraordinary balance between seeming cold but actually boiling inside, as if the British theatre is also referring to this extremely boiling and violent past but is actually living in a very organised and cold society. I think that the British actors I love have that quality – it's very close to Japanese theatre where everything is happening inside and it takes half an hour for an actor to cross the stage. You can feel the intensity and it's something that is lacking in North America because we're used to doing theatre or film that is crazy. An actor has to be crazy, to be generous, and there's a modesty that has been lost in theatre in North America.

**RE**  I think it's something to do with our greatest export being class and our obsession with class. As an English person you grow up being taught that you have to take on class roles that are allocated. There's a sense in which every English person is educated as an actor.

**RL**  It's very present in the theatre, that hierarchy. In the rehearsal room there's a hierarchy which you don't necessarily feel in other countries. Here, using words betrays where you're from, what part of the country you're from, it's very distinct. People don't talk a lot here. They don't say things before they can formulate them into very organised and pristine sentences.

**RE**  That's not entirely my experience. You must have some very articulate actors in your company.

**RL**  It all depends with whom you hang out.

**RE**  I don't know if you've worked in Germany, but if you think the British theatre is hierarchical, the German one is virtually feudal. The autocracy of the director is extreme.

**RL**  Yes, in France and Germany right now the new auteur is the director. People don't talk about the piece, they say the new Chéreau or the new Stein. It's interesting, for example the Latin countries like metaphors. They like this show, *Needles and Opium*, because it's a metaphoric kind of storytelling, but they're not as excited by something like the *Dragons' Trilogy* which is more a traditional way of telling a story, where you follow characters in chronology. That seems to appeal more to the anglophone countries. I wonder if it's to do with the language or culture. In the past six years maybe half and half of the shows I've produced have been either like this or like the *Dragons' Trilogy*, and it's difficult because even if you are fascinated by multicultural casting as I am, it's difficult to have a show to tour all the countries. Even if you think of Europe getting together and merging, in fact there are very strong cultural ways of telling stories and approaching theatre and it will take centuries before they change.

## Audience question

What do you want to do in three years' time?

**RL**   I don't really know – I guess I'll always work in a very spontaneous way and I'm booked for the next three years on a lot of things, but I can never envision the future. I don't have any future projects. I have commitments but I don't have any things I want to explore. I always bump into other people's good ideas.

■   ■   ■

## Source

Lepage, R. (1992) 'Robert Lepage in Discussion with Richard Eyre', *Platform Papers 3*, London: Royal National Theatre: 23–32.

## Robert Lepage (1957–)

Artistic Director of the French Theatre of the Canadian National Arts Centre. Born in Quebec, he graduated from the Quebec Conservatoire in 1978, and in 1982 joined Théâtre Repère, where he has pioneered his major work, which has been seen in Europe: *Polygraph (1981), Tectonic Plates (1988),* and *Needles and Opium* (1991), his one-man show. In 1992 he directed Shakespeare's *A Midsummer Night's Dream* for London's Royal National Theatre, which caused a certain outrage among the conservative UK critics by setting the play in a mudbath. He has continued producing theatre, which has the logic of a dream, using the technology of the stage, film and video to achieve his ends, which are often concerned with intuition rather than literal ideas and themes. He often writes his own material and constructs visually powerful images against which to perform. He is interested in the colliding, clashing, meeting and overlapping of ideas, hence his major work *Tectonic Plates* utilises the ideas of continents, cultures and personalities colliding in the act of transformation. He works often from improvisation, and is a representative of a Canadian generation that is post-nationalist and open to the world. His work has an originality that uses traditional theatre means to produce performances of strong visual and conceptual complexity. Even when he works with established texts such as Shakespeare, Lepage creates a performance where he has become the author of the total artefact, often illuminating where others merely interpret.

In this interview with Richard Eyre, then director of the Royal National Theatre, Lepage talks about his disillusion with modern theatre writing, leading to the devising of his own work. He also stresses the element of 'play' in theatre, which creates the eclecticism of his performances.

## Compare this interview with writings by the following authors in this reader

**Appia** – an earlier visual approach to theatre
**Bausch** – a comparable approach to staging dance theatre
**Beck** – an oppositional view of the function of performance
**LeCompte** – a similarly eclectic approach to material
**Wilson and Anderson** – similar concerns with visual theatre

## Further reading

Charest, R. (1997) *Robert Lepage, Connecting Flights: In Conversation with Remy Charest*, London: Methuen.
Dundjerovic, A. (2009) *Robert Lepage*, London: Routledge.
Lavender, A. (2001) *Hamlet in Pieces – Shakespeare Reworked: Peter Brook, Robert Lepage, Robert Wilson*, London: Nick Hern Books.
http://www.lacaserne.net

# Chapter 41

# George Maciunas

## EXPANDED FLUXUS DIAGRAM

### Introduction to diagram

The diagram [below] categorizes and describes planometrically the development of various "Expanded performing arts" movements. It describes movements rather than individuals and therefore should not be taken as a catalogue of names. Except for the Fluxus group, none others are complete. By the next edition it is hoped this diagram can be expanded to include more artists. Any comments, suggested additions and/or changes from readers will be welcome. The grouping of various artists was determined in most cases from statements of the artists themselves. When such statements were unobtainable, their work was studied to provide clues. Some controversial subjects such as sensationalism or pseudotechnology were based on careful observations of many performances rather than hearsay. Disrobing in public or lowering own pants to expose own bare bottom, or urinating in public, any such acts are considered by any dictionary definition exhibitionistic. Throwing oneself into water or covering self with cream etc., etc., can be considered as masochistic acts. Examples of preoccupation with sex and perversion are too numerous as to mention. All these stratagems are intended to arouse strong emotional response from the audience (and attention from the press of course), which may be a main motivation for such stratagems. Pseudotechnology or "engineering" (in quotes) has been derived from the fact that artists at best can acquire technical knowledge or understanding comparable to that of a technician (TV repairman or the like) rather than that of an engineer or scientist who speeds many years studying his specialty (just like artists spending many years on producing art). Such knowledge among these artists at best represent understanding wiring diagrams, function of basic electronic components, mechanism of electric motors, simple engines, determinate structures and the like. Unfortunately the technology among most of the artists employing that term is of the radio shop variety. Collaboration with engineers can achieve only a level of sophistication comprehended by the artist since

(1)    artist's new ideas or concepts will be affected or rather limited by his own past and recent technical-scientific knowledge rather than the uncommunicated knowledge of the engineer.
(2)    the collaborating engineer meanwhile, can't very well communicate a sophisticated technical and scientific knowledge to the artist without giving him a four year university course on related subjects.

Categories are ordered on the vertical scale to some degree within a spectrum of artificiality. Thus most "artistic" or cultural or serious are at the bottom and least so at the top ending with anti-art at the very top. The horizontal scale is chronological. Influences upon various movements is indicated by the source of influence and the strength of this influence (varying thicknesses of connecting links). Another vertical column indicates outlets, or major organizations, events, publications or institutions associated with the particular movement or group. Lines leading in and out of each persons name indicate various changes in the persons associations or chronological continuity of his work within any particular movement or group. Thus within Fluxus group there are 4 such categories: 1) individuals active in similar activities prior to formation of Fluxus collective, then becoming active within fluxus and still active up to the present day, (only George Brecht and Ben Vautier fill this category). 2) individuals active since the formation of Fluxus and still active within Fluxus. 3) individuals active independently of Fluxus but presently associated with Fluxus. 4) individuals active within Fluxus since the formation of the collective but having since then detached themselves. (Higgins, Patterson, Paik, Schmit, Williams, Flynt etc.) Some of them have even published own statements confirming their exodus.

George Maciunas

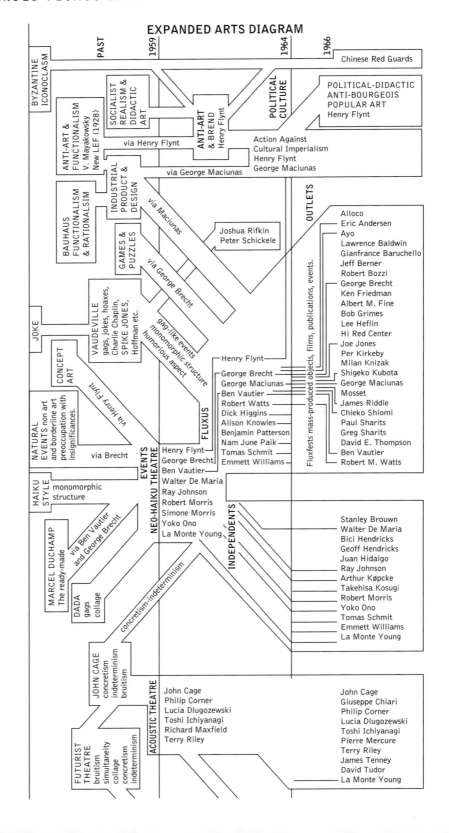

EXPANDED ARTS DIAGRAM

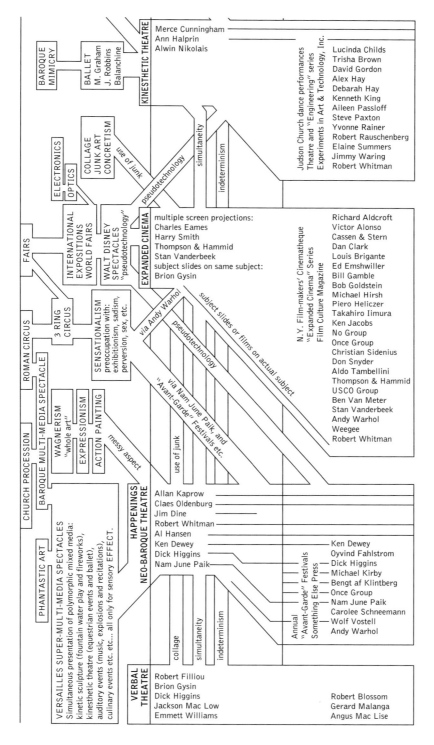

## Source

Maciunas, G. (2004) *Learning Machines*, ed. A. Schmidt-Burkhardt, Berlin: Vice Versa Verlag, and Detroit: Gilbert and Lila Silverman Fluxus Collection.

## Fluxus, Expanded Arts Diagram, 1966

This was a 1960s movement of composers, artists, designers, whose aim was to enable art to cross boundaries of both media and time. The founding member was George Maciunas (1931–1978), a Lithuanian-born American artist, who stated that Fluxus events 'strive for the monostructural and nontheatrical qualities of the simple natural event, a game or a gag. It is the fusion of Spike Jones, vaudeville, gag, children's games and Duchamp . . .'. Many of Fluxus's manifestations were performative and often consisted of scores to be followed and actions to be interpreted. There were clear links with both the Happenings activities of Alan Kaprow and the musical compositions of John Cage. Many of Fluxus's cross-disciplinary concerns formed a background to the innovative Black Mountain College, founded in 1933, with an overtly interdisciplinary approach to education. It was here that Merce Cunningham first gave his dance performances.

One of the key members of Fluxus – although it was never formalised as a movement – was George Brecht, who wrote '[i]n Fluxus there has never been any attempt to agree on aims or methods; individuals with something unnameable in common have simply naturally coalesced to publish and perform their work. Perhaps this common something is a feeling that the bounds of art are much wider than they have conventionally seemed, or that art and certain long-established bounds are no longer very useful'. Brecht's titles alone exemplify the Fluxus philosophy: *Comb Music, Three Gap Events, Spanish Card Piece for Objects, Drip Music*, etc. Another artist involved was the composer LaMonte Young, who was influenced by the music and ideas of John Cage, who had pioneered the idea of music as sound, unlimited and often unstructured. Cage's composition class in the 1950s formed a focus for what became a radical mixing of ideas from different sources – music, movement, objects, boxes, films. There was a clear relationship also with Dada and Futurism. Other artists associated with Fluxus include Yoko Ono, Nam June Paik, and for a short time Joseph Beuys, but also many artists all over the globe.

Maciunas published a series of manifestos in the form of diagrams that attempt to chart what he described as 'the art of networked thought'. It is clear that Fluxus presaged many of our current concerns about the mixing and de-categorisation of art forms. It is one of these diagrams that we present here.

## Compare this article with writings by the following authors in this reader

**Beuys** – as total educator
**Cage** – music as sound
**Cunningham** – dance pioneer
**Kaprow** – pioneer of the Happening
**Marinetti** – Futurism's founder
**Richter** – on the Dada connection

## Further reading

Bass, J. (ed.) (2011) *Fluxus and the essential questions of life,* University of Chicago Press.
Friedman, K. (ed.) (1998) *The Fluxus Reader,* Chichester: John Wiley and Sons.
Higgins, H. (2002) *Fluxus Experience,* University of California Press.
Kellein, T. (2007) *The Dream of Fluxus,* London: Thames and Hudson.
http://www.fluxus.org

# Chapter 42

# F.T. Marinetti

## THE FOUNDING AND MANIFESTO OF FUTURISM

W<small>E HAD STAYED UP ALL NIGHT</small>, my friends and I, under hanging mosque lamps with domes of filigreed brass, domes starred like our spirits, shining like them with the prisoned radiance of electric hearts. For hours we had trampled our atavistic ennui into rich oriental rugs, arguing up to the last confines of logic and blackening many reams of paper with our frenzied scribbling.

An immense pride was buoying us up, because we felt ourselves alone at that hour, alone, awake, and on our feet, like proud beacons or forward sentries against an army of hostile stars glaring down at us from their celestial encampments. Alone with stokers feeding the hellish fires of great ships, alone with the black spectres who grope in the red-hot bellies of locomotives launched down their crazy courses, alone with drunkards reeling like wounded birds along the city walls.

Suddenly we jumped, hearing the mighty noise of the huge double-decker trams that rumbled by outside, ablaze with coloured lights, like villages on holiday suddenly struck and uprooted by the flooding Po and dragged over falls and through gorges to the sea.

Then the silence deepened. But, as we listened to the old canal muttering its feeble prayers and the creaking bones of sickly palaces above their damp green beards, under the windows we suddenly heard the famished roar of automobiles.

'Let's go!' I said. 'Friends, away! Let's go! Mythology and the Mystic Ideal are defeated at last. We're about to see the Centaur's birth and, soon after, the first flight of Angels! . . . We must shake the gates of life, test the bolts and hinges. Let's go! Look there, on the earth, the very first dawn! There's nothing to match the splendour of the sun's red sword, slashing for the first time through our millennial gloom!'

We went up to the three snorting beasts, to lay amorous hands on their torrid breasts. I stretched out on my car like a corpse on its bier, but revived at once under the steering wheel, a guillotine blade that threatened my stomach.

The raging broom of madness swept us out of ourselves and drove us through streets as rough and deep as the beds of torrents. Here and there, sick lamplight through window glass taught us to distrust the deceitful mathematics of our perishing eyes.

I cried, 'The scent, the scent alone is enough for our beasts.'

And like young lions we ran after Death, its dark pelt blotched with pale crosses as it escaped down the vast violet living and throbbing sky.

But we had no ideal Mistress raising her divine form to the clouds, nor any cruel Queen to whom to offer our bodies, twisted like Byzantine rings! There was nothing to make us wish for death, unless the wish to be free at last from the weight of our courage!

And on we raced, hurling watchdogs against doorsteps, curling them under our burning tyres like collars under a flatiron. Death, domesticated, met me at every turn, gracefully holding out a paw, or once in a while hunkering down, making velvety caressing eyes at me from every puddle.

'Let's break out of the horrible shell of wisdom and throw ourselves like pride-ripened fruit into the wide, contorted mouth of the wind! Let's give ourselves utterly to the Unknown, not in desperation but only to replenish the deep wells of the Absurd!'

The words were scarcely out of my mouth when I spun my car around with the frenzy of a dog trying to bite its tail, and there, suddenly, were two cyclists coming towards me, shaking their fists, wobbling like two equally convincing but nevertheless contradictory arguments. Their stupid dilemma was blocking my way – Damn! Ouch! . . . I stopped short and to my disgust rolled over into a ditch with my wheels in the air. . . .

O maternal ditch, almost full of muddy water! Fair factory drain! I gulped down your nourishing sludge; and I remembered the blessed black breast of my Sudanese nurse. . . . When I came up – torn, filthy, and stinking – from under the capsized car, I felt the white-hot iron of joy deliciously pass through my heart!

A crowd of fishermen with handlines and gouty naturalists were already swarming around the prodigy. With patient, loving care those people rigged a tall derrick and iron grapnels to fish out my car, like a big beached shark. Up it came from the ditch, slowly, leaving in the bottom, like scales, its heavy framework of good sense and its soft upholstery of comfort.

They thought it was dead, my beautiful shark, but a caress from me was enough to revive it; and there it was, alive again, running on its powerful fins!

And so, faces smeared with good factory muck – plastered with metallic waste, with senseless sweat, with celestial soot – we, bruised, our arms in slings, but unafraid, declared our high intentions to all the *living* of the earth:

## Manifesto of Futurism

1   We intend to sing the love of danger, the habit of energy and fearlessness.

2   Courage, audacity, and revolt will be essential elements of our poetry.

3   Up to now literature has exalted a pensive immobility, ecstasy, and sleep. We intend to exalt aggressive action, a feverish insomnia, the racer's stride, the mortal leap, the punch and the slap.

4   We affirm that the world's magnificence has been enriched by a new beauty: the beauty of speed. A racing car whose hood is adorned with great pipes, like serpents of explosive breath – a roaring car that seems to ride on grapeshot is more beautiful than the *Victory of Samothrace*.

5   We want to hymn the man at the wheel, who hurls the lance of his spirit across the Earth, along the circle of its orbit.

6   The poet must spend himself with ardour, splendour, and generosity, to swell the enthusiastic fervour of the primordial elements.

7   Except in struggle, there is no more beauty. No work without an aggressive character can be a masterpiece. Poetry must be conceived as a violent attack on unknown forces, to reduce and prostrate them before man.

8   We stand on the last promontory of the centuries! . . . Why should we look back, when what we want is to break down the mysterious doors of the Impossible? Time and Space died yesterday. We already live in the absolute, because we have created eternal, omnipresent speed.

9   We will glorify war – the world's only hygiene – militarism, patriotism, the destructive gesture of freedom-bringers, beautiful ideas worth dying for, and scorn for woman.

10   We will destroy the museums, libraries, academies of every kind, will fight moralism, feminism, every opportunistic or utilitarian cowardice.

11   We will sing of great crowds excited by work, by pleasure, and by riot; we will sing of the multicoloured, polyphonic tides of revolution in the modern capitals; we will sing of the vibrant nightly fervour of arsenals and shipyards blazing with violent electric moons; greedy railway stations that devour smoke-plumed serpents; factories hung on clouds by the crooked lines of their smoke; bridges that stride the rivers like giant gymnasts, flashing in the sun with a glitter of knives; adventurous steamers that sniff the horizon; deep-chested locomotives whose wheels paw the tracks like the hooves of enormous steel horses bridled by tubing; and the sleek flight of planes whose propellers chatter in the wind like banners and seem to cheer like an enthusiastic crowd.

It is from Italy that we launch through the world this violently upsetting incendiary manifesto of ours. With it, today, we establish *Futurism*, because we want to free this land from its smelly gangrene of professors, archaeologists, *ciceroni* and anti-quarians. For too long has Italy been a dealer in second-hand clothes. We mean to free her from the numberless museums that cover her like so many graveyards.

Museums: cemeteries! . . . Identical, surely, in the sinister promiscuity of so many bodies unknown to one another. Museums: public dormitories where one lies forever beside hated or unknown beings. Museums: absurd abattoirs of painters and sculptors ferociously slaughtering each other with colour-blows and line-blows, the length of the fought-over walls!

That one should make an annual pilgrimage, just as one goes to the graveyard on All Souls' Day – that I grant. That once a year one should leave a floral tribute beneath the *Gioconda*, I grant you that. . . . But I don't admit that our sorrows, our fragile courage, our morbid restlessness should be given a daily conducted tour through the museums. Why poison ourselves? Why rot?

And what is there to see in an old picture except the laborious contortions of an artist throwing himself against the barriers that thwart his desire to express his dream completely? . . . Admiring an old picture is the same as pouring our sensibility into a funerary urn instead of hurling it far off, in violent spasms of action and creation.

Do you, then, wish to waste all your best powers in this eternal and futile worship of the past, from which you emerge fatally exhausted, shrunken, beaten down?

In truth I tell you that daily visits to museums, libraries, and academies (cemeteries of empty exertion, Calvaries of crucified dreams, registries of aborted beginnings!) are, for artists, as damaging as the prolonged supervision by parents of certain young people drunk with their talent and their ambitious wills. When the future is barred to them, the admirable past may be a solace for the ills of the moribund, the sickly, the prisoner. . . . But we want no part of it, the past, we the young and strong *Futurists*!

So let them come, the gay incendiaries with charred fingers! Here they are! Here they are! . . . Come on! set fire to the library shelves! Turn aside the canals to flood the museums! . . . Oh, the joy of seeing the glorious old canvases bobbing adrift on those waters, discoloured and shredded! . . . Take up your pickaxes, your axes and hammers and wreck, wreck the venerable cities, pitilessly!

The oldest of us is thirty: so we have at least a decade for finishing our work. When we are forty, other younger and stronger men will probably throw us in the wastebasket like useless manuscripts – we want it to happen!

They will come against us, our successors, will come from far away, from every quarter, dancing to the winged cadence of their first songs, flexing the hooked claws of predators, sniffing doglike at the academy doors the strong odour of our decaying minds, which will already have been promised to the literary catacombs.

But we won't be there. . . . At last they'll find us – one winter's night – in open country, beneath a sad roof drummed by a monotonous rain. They'll see us crouched beside our trembling aeroplanes in the act of warming our hands at the poor little blaze that our books of today will give out when they take fire from the flight of our images.

They'll storm around us, panting with scorn and anguish, and all of them, exasperated by our proud daring, will hurtle to kill us, driven by a hatred the more implacable the more their hearts will be drunk with love and admiration for us.

Injustice, strong and sane, will break out radiantly in their eyes.

Art, in fact, can be nothing but violence, cruelty, and injustice.

The oldest of us is thirty: even so we have already scattered treasures, a thousand treasures of force, love, courage, astuteness, and raw will-power; have thrown them impatiently away, with fury, carelessly, unhesitatingly, breathless, and unresting. . . . Look at us! We are still untired! Our hearts know no weariness because they are fed with fire, hatred, and speed! . . . Does that amaze you? It should, because you can never remember having lived! Erect on the summit of the world, once again we hurl our defiance at the stars!

You have objections? – Enough! Enough! We know them. . . . We've understood! . . . Our fine deceitful intelligence tells us that we are the revival and extension of our ancestors – Perhaps! . . . If only it were so! – But who cares? We don't want to understand! . . . Woe to anyone who says those infamous words to us again!

Lift up your heads!

Erect on the summit of the world, once again we hurl defiance to the stars!

■　■　■

## Source

Marinetti, F.T. (1909, 1973) 'The Founding and Manifesto of Futurism', *Marinetti: Selected Writings*, trans. R.W. Flint, New York: Farrar, Straus and Giroux: 19–24. First published in *Le Figaro* (Paris), 20 February 1909, translated into English 1973.

## F.T. Marinetti (1876–1944)

Performance as an act of engagement with its time found its most intense expression in the Italian futurist movement, a collection of artists, writers, composers, theatre makers, whose first manifesto, written by Marinetti, was printed in *Le Figaro* on 20 February 1909. This proclaimed a new and sensational world of speed, dynamism and aggression. Futurism was the first cultural movement of the twentieth century, and

Marinetti was a new kind of arts entrepreneur – artist, writer, publicist, promoter – without whose skills the movement would have foundered. Futurism, although it produced art, was more of an ideology, whose essential element was rebellion against the past, especially the stultifying past of Italian art, and against Italian cultural stagnation. The movement embraced industrialisation, technical invention, and ultimately Mussolini's fascism, hence its low profile in cultural historical terms until recent years. Futurism was organised like a political campaign; it embraced painting, music, plays, film, scenic design, dance and, for one of its members, Valentine de Saint Point, lust – 'the quest of the flesh for the unknown'. Theatre, as a major performance form, was of interest because of its immediacy, and the potential physical involvement of the spectators; it was able to maximise the sensory and minimalise the intellectual. Many of the performance scenarios – by Cangiullo, Boccioni, Balla, Settimelli and others – were far in advance of their time in their use of simultaneity and compression, synthesising actions and events into the fewest numbers of dynamic words and sound.

In this first manifesto of futurism, Marinetti describes the excitement and potential of a new artistic dynamism, in words which are clearly intended to provoke readers to action which will sweep away the cobwebs of the past, and points to the necessity for the twentieth century to embrace radical forms of art.

## Compare this article with writings by the following authors in this reader

**Artaud** – who also wished to sweep away logic and embrace physicality and sensuality
**Beck** – a similar messianic view of art's importance
**Duncan** – another voice heralding the new century
**Goldberg** – the historical importance of futurism
**Hijikata** – Butoh also rejects the rational
**Rainer** – another, later, 'manifesto'
**Richter** – the founding of Dada, a contemporary movement of disgust

## Further reading

Berghaus, G. (1998) *Italian Futurist Theatre*, Oxford: Clarendon Press.
Kirby, M. (1971) *Futurist Performance*, New York: Dutton.
Marinetti, F.T. and Berghaus, G. (2008) *Critical Writings*, New York: Farrar, Straus and Giroux.
Perloff, M. (2003) *The Futurist Moment*, University of Chicago Press.
Tisdall, C. and Bozzolla, A. (1977) *Futurism*, London: Thames & Hudson.

# Chapter 43

# Vsevolod Meyerhold

## FIRST ATTEMPTS AT
## A STYLIZED THEATRE

THE FIRST ATTEMPTS to realize a Stylized Theatre as conceived by Maeterlinck and Bryusov were made at the Theatre-Studio. In my opinion, this first experimental theatre came very near to achieving ideal stylized drama with its first production, *The Death of Tintagiles*; so I think it is appropriate to describe the work of the directors, actors and designers on this play, and to consider the lessons learnt during its production.

The theatre is constantly revealing a lack of harmony amongst those engaged in presenting their collective creative work to the public. One never sees an ideal blend of author, director, actor, designer, composer and property-master. For this reason, Wagner's notion of a synthesis of the arts seems to me impossible. Both the artist and the composer should remain in their own fields: the artist in a special *decorative* theatre where he could exhibit canvases which require a stage rather than an art gallery, artificial rather than natural light, several planes instead of just two dimensions, and so on; the composer should concentrate on symphonies like Beethoven's Ninth, for the dramatic theatre, where music has merely an auxiliary role, has nothing to offer him.

These thoughts came to me after our early experiments (*The Death of Tintagiles*) had been superseded by the second phase (*Pelléas and Mélisande*). But even when we started work on *The Death of Tintagiles* I was plagued already by the question of disharmony between the various creative elements; even if it was impossible to reach agreement with the composer and the artist, each of whom was trying instinctively to delineate his own function, at least I hoped to unify the efforts of the author, the director and the actor.

It became clear that these three, the basis of the theatre, could work as one, but only if given the approach which we adopted in the rehearsals of *The Death of Tintagiles* at the Theatre-Studio.

In the course of the usual discussions of the play (before which, of course, the director acquainted himself with it by reading everything written on the subject), the director and actors read through Maeterlinck's verses and extracts from those of his dramas containing scenes corresponding in mood to *The Death of Tintagiles* (the play, itself, was left until we understood how to treat it, lest it became transformed into a mere exercise). The verses and extracts were read by each actor in turn. For them, this work corresponded to the sketches of a painter or the exercises of a musician. The artist must perfect his technique before embarking on a picture. Whilst reading, the actor looked for new means of expression. The audience (everybody, not just the director) made comments and assisted the reader to develop these new means. The entire creative act was directed towards finding those inflections which contained the true ring of the author's own voice. When the author was 'revealed' through this collective work, when a single verse or extract 'rang true', the audience immediately analysed the means of expression which had conveyed the author's style and tone.

Before enumerating the various new aspects of technique developed through this intuitive method, and while I still retain a clear picture of these combined exercises of director and actors, I should like to mention two distinct methods of establishing contact between the director and his actors: one deprives not only the actor but also the spectator of creative freedom; the other leaves them both free, and forces the spectator to create instead of merely looking on (for a start, by stimulating his imagination).

The two methods may be explained by illustrating the four basic theatrical elements (author, director, actor and spectator) as follows:

1   A triangle, in which the apex is the director and the two remaining corners, the author and the actor. The spectator comprehends the creation of the latter two through the creation of the director. This is method one, which we shall call the 'Theatre-Triangle'.

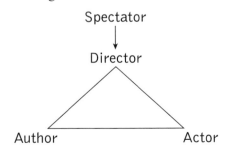

2  A straight, horizontal line with the four theatrical elements (author, director, actor, spectator) marked from left to right represents the other
method, which we shall call the 'Theatre of the Straight Line'. The actor
reveals his soul freely to the spectator, having assimilated the creation of the
director, who, in his turn, has assimilated the creation of the author.

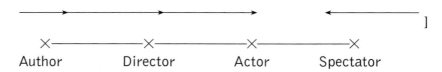

| Author | Director | Actor | Spectator |

1  In the 'Theatre-Triangle' the director explains his *mise en scène* in detail,
describes the characters as he sees them, prescribes every pause, and then
rehearses the play until his personal conception of it is exactly reproduced in
performance. This 'Theatre-Triangle' may be likened to a symphony orchestra
with the director acting as the conductor.

However, the very architecture of the theatre, lacking any provision for
conductor's rostrum, points to the difference between the two.

People will say that there are occasions when a symphony orchestra plays
without a conductor. Let us consider Nikisch[1] and the symphony orchestra which
has been playing under him for years with scarcely a change in its personnel; take
a composition which it has played several times a year over a period of ten
years. If Nikisch were absent from the conductor's rostrum on one occasion,
would the orchestra play the composition according to his interpretation? Yes,
it is possible that the listener would recognize it as Nikisch's interpretation. But
would the performance sound exactly as though Nikisch were conducting?
Obviously, it would be worse, although we should still be hearing Nikisch's
interpretation.

So I contend this: true, a symphony orchestra without a conductor is
possible, but nevertheless it is impossible to draw a parallel between it and the
theatre, where the actors invariably perform on the stage without a director. A
symphony orchestra without a conductor is possible, but no matter how well
rehearsed, it could never stir the public, only acquaint the listener with the
interpretation of this or that conductor, and could blend into an ensemble only to
the extent that an artist can re-create a conception which is not his own.

The actor's art consists in far more than merely acquainting the spectator with
the director's conception. The actor will grip the spectator only if he assimilates
both the director and the author and then gives of himself from the stage.

By contrast, an orchestral musician is distinguished by his ability to carry out
the conductor's directions precisely, by dint of his virtuoso technique and *by
depersonalizing himself*.

In common with the symphony orchestra, the 'Theatre-Triangle' must
employ actors with virtuoso technique, but at all costs lacking in indviduality, so
that they are able to convey the director's exact concept.

2   In the 'Theatre of the Straight Line', the director, having absorbed the author's conception, conveys his own creation (now a blend of the author and the director) to the actor. The actor, having assimilated the author's conception via the director, stands face to face with the spectator (with director and author behind him), and *freely* reveals his soul to him, thus intensifying the fundamental theatrical relationship of performer and spectator.

In order for the straight line not to bend[2], the director must remain the sole arbiter of the mood and style of the production, but nevertheless, the actor's art remains free in the 'Theatre of the Straight Line'.

The director describes his plan during the discussion of the play. The entire production is coloured by his view of it. He inspires the actors with his devotion to the work, and imbues them with the spirit of the author and with his own interpretation. But after the discussion all the performers remain completely independent. Then the director calls a further general meeting to create harmony from all the separate pieces. How does he set about this? Simply by balancing all the parts which have been freely created by the various individuals involved in the collective enterprise. In establishing the harmony vital to the production, he does not insist on the exact representation of his own conception, which was intended only to ensure unanimity and to prevent the work created collectively from disintegrating. Instead he retires behind the scenes at the earliest possible moment and leaves the stage to the actors. Then, either they are out of accord with the director or the author (if, say, they are not of the new school)[3] and 'set fire to the ship', or they reveal their souls through almost improvisatory additions, not to the text but to the mere suggestions of the director. In this way the spectator is made to comprehend the author and the director through the prism of the actor's art. *Above all, drama is the art of the actor.*

If you read any of the works of Maeterlinck, his poetry or his drama, his preface to the last collected edition,[4] his book *Le Trésor des Humbles*, where he speaks of the Static Theatre in a tone embodying all the colour and atmosphere of his works, you will see that he has no desire to evoke horror on the stage; nor does he seek to drive the spectator to such hysteria that he wants to flee in terror. On the contrary, he aims to provoke a fearful yet reasoning acceptance of the inevitability of life, to move the spectator to tears and suffering, and yet to soothe and console him. His first task is 'to alleviate our grief by implanting that hope which flags and then springs to life again'.[5] When the spectator leaves the theatre, life with all its pain resumes its course, but the pain no longer seems in vain; life flows on with its joys, its sorrows and its exigencies, but everything acquires meaning because we have seen that it is possible to emerge from the gloom, or at least to endure it without bitterness. Maeterlinck's art is healthy and life-giving. It summons people to a wise acceptance of the might of fate, and his theatre acquires all the significance of a temple. Pastore has good reason for extolling Maeterlinck's mysticism as the last refuge of apostates who refuse to recognize the temporal power of the Church yet cannot bring themselves to discard their free belief in another world. Such a theatre is fit for the presentation of religious subjects. No matter how sombre the colours of a work, so long as it is a *mystery*, it contains an indefatigable affirmation of life.

To us it seems that the whole mistake of our predecessors lay in their attempts at frightening the spectator instead of reconciling him with the inevitability of fate. 'At the foundation of my dramas' – writes Maeterlinck – 'lies the idea of a Christian God together with the ancient concept of Fate.' The author hears the words and lamentations of men as a muffled sound, as though they were falling into a deep abyss. He sees men from a vantagepoint beyond the clouds as faintly glittering sparks. All he desires is to overhear in their souls a few words of humility, of hope, of compassion, of terror, and to show us the might of the fate which guides our destiny.

Our aim was to ensure that our production of Maeterlinck produced the same effect of reconciliation in the spectator's mind as the author himself intended. A performance of Maeterlinck is a *mystery*; either there is a barely audible harmony of voices, a chorus of soft weeping, of muted sobs and a stirring of hope (as in *The Death of Tintagiles*), or there is an ecstasy which is transformed into a universal religious festival with dancing to the music of organ and trumpets, or a bacchanalia to celebrate a great miracle (as in Act Two of *Sister Beatrice*). The dramas of Maeterlinck are 'above all else a manifestation and purification of the spirit'. They are '. . . a chorus of souls singing *sotto voce* of suffering, love, beauty and death'. They have a *simplicity* which transports one to the realms of fantasy, a harmony which brings calm, a joy bordering on the ecstatic. It was with this understanding of the spirit of Maeterlinck's theatre that we began work on the rehearsal exercises.

What Muther[6] said of Il Perugino, one of the most fascinating painters of the Quattrocento, seems to me true of Maeterlinck: 'The contemplative lyrical character of his subjects, the quiet grandeur and archaic splendour of his pictures could only be achieved by a composition whose harmony is unmarred by the slightest abrupt movement or the merest harsh contrast.'

Proceeding from this general evaluation of Maeterlinck's art, our directors and actors intuitively established the following principles during the course of preliminary rehearsals:

## A  Diction

1   The words must be coldly 'coined', free from all tremolo and the familiar break in the voice. There must be a total absence of tension and lugubrious intonation.

2   The sound must always be 'reinforced'; the words must fall like drops into a deep well, the fall being clearly audible without any vibration in space. There must be no diffusion of sound, no drawing out of word-endings (as in the reading of the Decadents' verses).

3       The internal mystical vibration is more powerful than the histrionics of the old theatre, which were invariably uncontrolled and ugly to look at, with flailing of arms, beating of breasts and slapping of thighs. The internal mystical vibration is conveyed through the eyes, the lips, the sound and manner of delivery: the exterior calm which covers volcanic emotions, with everything light and unforced.

4       In the expression of the tragic sorrows of the soul the form is dictated by the content. Maeterlinck prescribes one form and no other in order to convey that which is so simple and so long-familiar.[7]

5       The dialogue should never be gabbled; this is permissible only in those *neurasthenic* dramas where much play is made with lines of dots. Epic calm does not exclude tragic emotions, which always possess a certain grandeur.

6       Tragedy with a smile on the lips. I did not grasp fully the need for this until I happened to read the following words of Savonarola:

> Do not assume that Mary cried out at the death of her Son and roamed the streets, tearing her hair and acting like a madwoman. She followed Him with great humility. Certainly she shed tears, but her appearance revealed not so much sheer grief as a combination of *grief and joy*. Even at the foot of the Cross she stood in grief and joy, engrossed in the mystery of God's great mercy.

If an actor of the old school wished to move the audience deeply, he would cry out, weep, groan and beat his breast with his fists. Let the new actor express the highest point of tragedy just as the grief and joy of Mary were expressed: with an outward repose, almost *coldly*, without shouting or lamentation. He can achieve profundity without recourse to exaggerated tremolo.

# B  Plasticity

1   Richard Wagner reveals inner dialogue through the orchestra; the sung musical phrase lacks the power to express the inner passions of his heroes. Wagner summons the orchestra to his assistance, believing that only the orchestra is capable of conveying what is ineffable, of revealing the mystery to the spectator. Like the singer's phrase in the 'Musikdrama', the actor's word in the drama is an insufficiently powerful means of conveying inner dialogue. Surely if the *word* were the sole means of conveying the essence of tragedy, everybody would be capable of acting in the theatre. But merely by declaiming words, even by declaiming them well, one does not necessarily *say* anything. We need some new means of expressing the ineffable, of revealing that which is concealed.

Just as Wagner employs the orchestra to convey spiritual emotions, I employ *plastic movement*. But the old theatre, too, regarded plasticity as an essential means of expression; one has only to consider Salvini[8] in *Othello* or

*Hamlet*. Plasticity itself is not new, but the form which I have in mind is new. Before, it corresponded closely to the spoken dialogue, but I am speaking of a *plasticity which does not correspond to the words*. What do I mean by this?

Two people are discussing the weather, art, apartments. A third – given, of course, that he is reasonably sensitive and observant – can tell exactly by listening to this conversation, which has no bearing on the relationship between the two, whether they are friends, enemies or lovers. He can tell this from the way they gesticulate, stand, move their eyes. This is because they move in a way unrelated to their words, a way which reveals their relationship.

The director erects a bridge between actor and spectator. He depicts friends, enemies or lovers, in accordance with the author's instructions, yet by means of movement and poses he must present a picture which enables the spectator not only to hear the spoken dialogue but to penetrate through to the *inner* dialogue. If he has steeped himself in the author's theme and grasped the music of this inner dialogue, he will suggest plastic movements to the actor which will help the spectator to perceive the inner dialogue as the actors and he, himself, understand it.

The essence of human relationships is determined by gestures, poses, glances and silences. Words alone cannot say everything. Hence there must be a *pattern of movement* on the stage to transform the spectator into a vigilant observer, to furnish him with that material which the two people in conversation yielded to the third, the material which helps him grasp the true feelings of the characters. Words catch the ear, plasticity – the eye. Thus the spectator's imagination is exposed to two stimuli: the oral and the visual. The difference between the old theatre and the new is that in the new theatre speech and plasticity are each subordinated to their own separate rhythms and the two do not necessarily coincide. However, it does not follow that plasticity has always to contradict speech; a phrase may be supported by a wholly appropriate movement, but this is no more natural than the coincidence of the logical and the poetic stress in verse.

2   Maeterlinck's images are archaized; the names are like the names on icons; Arkel[9] is like a picture by Ambrogio Borgognoni; Gothic arches; wooden statues, carved and polished like palissander. One senses the need for symmetrical groupings in the manner of Perugino, for thus do they resemble most closely the divine nature of the universe.

'Women, effeminate boys and harmless, weary old men best express the gentle, dreamlike thoughts' which Perugino was striving to convey. Is not the same true of Maeterlinck? It is this which prompted an iconic style of portrayal.

The unsightly clutter of the naturalistic stage was replaced in the New Theatre by constructions rigidly subordinated to rhythmical movement and to the musical harmony of colour masses.

An iconic style was employed, too, in the construction of scenery – before scenery was abolished altogether. And since plastic movement acquired primary importance as a means of revealing inner dialogue, it was essential that scenery should do nothing to distract attention from this movement. It was necessary to focus the spectator's entire attention on the actors' movements. Therefore, we employed only one backdrop in *The Death of Tintagiles*. When rehearsed against a plain canvas drop, the tragedy produced a powerful impression because the play of gestures was seen in such sharp relief. But when the actors were transferred to a stage with scenery and space in which to move about, the play suffered. Hence we developed the decorative panel. But when we tried it out in a number of plays (*Sister Beatrice, Hedda Gabler, The Eternal Story*[10]) it was a failure.[11] We found that it was no more effective than suspended scenery, against which the effect of plastic movement is dissipated because it is not seen in firm relief. In Giotto, nothing detracts from the fluidity of his lines, because all his work has a decorative rather than a naturalistic basis. But just as the theatre must not revert to naturalism, equally it must not become merely 'decorative' (unless the word be interpreted in the same sense as in the Japanese theatre).

Like symphonic music, the decorative panel serves its own specialized purpose, and if figures are necessary – as in a painting – they must be painted figures, or in the case of the theatre, cardboard marionettes – but not wax, wooden, or flesh-and-blood figures. A two-dimensional decorative panel demands two-dimensional figures.

The human body and the objects surrounding it – tables, chairs, beds, cupboards – are all three-dimensional; therefore the theatre, where the main element is the actor, must find inspiration in the plastic arts, not in painting. The actor must study *the plasticity of the statue*.

These were the conclusions reached at the close of the first cycle of experiments in the New Theatre. A historically vital circle was completed and yielded a fund of experience in stylized production, which gave rise to a new view of the role of decorative art in the theatre.

On learning that the theatre intends to reject the decorative principle, actors of the old school will be delighted, interpreting this as no less than a return to the old theatre. Surely, they will argue, the old theatre was the theatre of three dimensions. So this means – down with the stylized theatre!

My answer is that the placing of the decorative artist firmly in the decorative theatre and the musician in the concert hall signifies not the death of the stylized theatre but its adoption of an even bolder course.

In rejecting the decorative panel the New Theatre has not discarded the technique of stylized production; neither has it rejected the presentation of Maeterlinck in iconic terms. The means of expression must now be architectural, rather than pictorial as they were before. All our plans for stylized productions of *The Death of Tintagiles, Sister Beatrice, Hedda Gabler* and *The Eternal Story* have been preserved intact, but they have been translated into the terms of the liberated stylized theatre. Meanwhile, the painter has retired to a realm where actors and concrete objects are not admitted, because the aims of the actor and the non-theatrical painter are quite distinct.

**Notes**

1   Arthur Nikisch (1855–1922), celebrated conductor of the Leipzig Gewandhaus Orchestra.

2   Alexander Blok (*Pereval*, Moscow, 1906, no. 2) fears that the actors 'might set fire to the ship of the play', but to my mind, discord and disaster could occur only if the straight line were allowed to become crooked. This danger is eliminated if the director accurately interprets the author, accurately transmits him to the actors, and if they accurately understand him. [Meyerhold's note.]

3   The 'Theatre-Triangle' requires non-individualistic actors who none the less are outstanding virtuosi, regardless of their school. In the 'Theatre of the Straight Line' individual flair is most important, for without it free creativity is inconceivable. It needs a new school of acting, which must not be a school where new techniques are taught, but rather, one which will arise just once to give birth to a free theatre and then die.

　　'The Theatre of the Straight Line' will grow from a single school as one plant grows from one seed. As each succeeding plant needs a new seed to be sown, so a new theatre must grow every time from a new school.

　　'The Theatre-Triangle' tolerates schools attached to theatres which provide a regular stream of graduates, who imitate the great actors who founded the theatre, and fill vacancies in the company as they occur. I am convinced that it is these schools which are to blame for the absence of genuine, fresh talent in our theatres. [Meyerhold's note.]

4   Published in Russian in six volumes in Moscow, 1903–9.

5   Hannibale Pastore, 'Maurice Maeterlinck', in *Vestnik inostrannoy literatury*, September 1903.

6   Richard Muther, German art historian.

7   In practice, a question arose which I shall not attempt to answer, but content myself by merely stating: should the actor seek to discover the inner content of his part right from the start, give play to his emotions, and then shape it later into some form or other, or vice versa? At the time we adopted the procedure of restraining the emotions until the form was mastered, and that still seems to me the correct order. People will object that this only leads to the form fettering the emotions. This is not so. Our teachers, the actors of the old naturalistic school, used to say: if you do not want to ruin the part, start by reading it over to yourself, and do not read it aloud until it sounds right in your heart. One should approach a role in a realistic drama by first reading through the text to oneself; in a non-realistic drama one should master first the rhythm of the language and the movement – the same method is right for both. [Meyerhold's note.]

8   Tommaso Salvini: leading Italian Shakespearian actor. He toured in Russia on several occasions from 1880 to 1901.

9   In *Pelléas and Mélisande*.

10   By Przybyszewski.

11   All staged at Komissarzhevskaya's Theatre in 1906.

■　■　■

## Source

Meyerhold, V. (1908, 1969) 'First Attempts at a Stylized Theatre', *Meyerhold on Theatre,* trans. and ed. E. Braun, New York: Hill & Wang: 49–58. Written in 1907, first published in *Teatr, kniga o novom teatre,* Petersburg (1908), reprinted in Meyerhold's *O Teatre,* Petersburg (1913), English translation published (1969) by Hill & Wang.

## Vsevolod Meyerhold (1874–1940)

Russian theatre director. A colleague of Stanislavski, he stands in relation to modern theatre much as Schoenberg does to music. Through his work with the Moscow Art Studio, set up for him by Stanislavski, and in a variety of other ensembles, he explored and redefined the possibilities of theatre language in the twentieth century. Meyerhold reacted against naturalistic theatre from inside the fount of naturalism, holding that performers were capable of more than imitation by the extended and trained use of the body, for which he designed a system of exercises known as Bio-Mechanics.

The productions with which he was involved, via a variety of different performing groups, numbered over five hundred, and included a famous version of Gogol's play *The Government Inspector* (1926). His innovative work on the revolutionary plays of Mayakovsky – *Mystery Bouffe* (1921), *The Bedbug* (1929), and *The Bathhouse* (1930) – promotes a view of theatre where the performer and scenery became interchangeable; where the actor, combined with the dynamic form of constructivist settings, produced a totally new and physical theatre. Meyerhold's experiments, which took Russian theatre away from the great naturalist tradition, were such that, although revolutionary, they did not suit the aesthetic of the communist government. To the country's shame Meyerhold was tried in prison in 1940 and shot, after making a speech to the All-Union Conference of Theatre Directors, where he was bitterly attacked. It is only since the 1960s that his work has become known in translation in the West, thanks to the efforts of dedicated scholars, and to those who preserved the memory of his work in Russia. Now that his experiments are being rediscovered it is clear that Meyerhold foreshadowed much of the exciting visual and physical theatre of recent years.

In this essay he explains the possible new forms of relationship between the creative forces of the theatre, together with his physical principles for performers, from which many of his detailed exercises followed.

## Compare this article with writings by the following authors in this reader

**Appia, Craig and Schlemmer** – contemporary European visual perspectives
**Barba** – another, later, actor/director
**Brecht** – a similar anti-naturalist approach

**Copeau** – a later French view of actor/director training
**Cunningham** – the dancer as the total element of production
**Grotowski** – the physical training of the performer
**Stanislavski** – the naturalism that Meyerhold rejected
**Wilson** – a later example of total theatre

## Further reading

Braun, E. (1978) *The Theatre of Meyerhold,* London: Eyre Methuen.
—— (1978, 1995) *Meyerhold: A Revolution in Theatre,* 2nd edition, London: Methuen.
Leach, R. (1989) *Vsevolod Meyerhold,* Cambridge: Cambridge University Press.
Pitches, J. (2003) *Meyerhold,* London: Routledge.
http://www.meyerhold.ru

# Chapter 44

# Ariane Mnouchkine

## BUILDING UP THE MUSCLE OF THE IMAGINATION (An interview with Ariane Mnouchkine by Josette Féral)

*The following interview took place in March 1988 at the Cartoucherie, during a performance of* L'Indiade. *Mnouchkine reflects on some of the 'fundamental laws' governing performance, and on the interrelated roles of emotion, belief and imagination in the processes of acting.*

**JOSETTE FERAL:** I know right away that you're going to answer my first question by saying that there are no theories about acting.

**ARIANE MNOUCHKINE:** I don't know if I would say that. I know that I myself do not have any, maybe because I am not in the position to develop a theory on acting. I may not ever be capable of developing a theory on acting. Because in fact the idea of a theory of acting involves a written development of the theory of acting and a practice of acting. That is to say that we, directors and actors, put into practice the practice – we don't practise the theory.

I think that if there's no theory of acting, at least there are theoretical laws that we may find, curiously enough, in all traditions of acting. It is true that the term 'theory of acting' doesn't seem fundamentally wrong, but it always sounds somewhat imperialistic and pretentious. I prefer to use the term *fundamental laws*, laws which we sometimes recognise, but then sometimes lose and forget. It is only practice that can suddenly make law or tradition rise to the surface.

I will not say then that there is no theory of acting; on the contrary, there have been many of them. Of course, what interests me in these multiple theories are the essential laws that are common to all of them.

**F:** What are these laws?

**M:** Do you want me to make an inventory of them? How shall I tell you? They are so mysterious and so volatile. Sometimes we get the impression that a rehearsal goes by, and we've forgotten laws we thought we knew perfectly the day before. All of a sudden during a rehearsal, there's no more theatre, an actor cannot act, a director cannot help an actor any more. We ask ourselves why and we cannot understand. It seems to us that we're respecting the laws and actually all of a sudden we realize that we have lost the essentials: for example, *being in the present*.

I believe that theatre is the art of the present for the actor. There is no past, no future. There is only the present, the present act. When I see young students work on what they call the 'Stanislavski method', I am surprised to find out how much they go back to the past all the time. Of course, Stanislavski talks about the character's past: where does he come from? what is he doing? But the students are not able simply to find the present action. So they go back, and I always tell them, 'You enter leaning backwards, weighed down by all this past, while in the theatre only the moment exists.'

I think that the greatest law is probably the one that governs the mystery between inside and outside, between the state of being (or the 'feeling', as Jouvet would say) and the form. How do you give a form to a passion? How do you exteriorise without falling into exteriority? How can the autopsy of the body [*corps*] – I mean the heart [*coeur*] – be performed by the body. My slip of the tongue is revealing because the autopsy of the heart must be performed by the body. An actor worthy of the name is a kind of autoptist. His or her role is to show the inside [. . .]

## 'EMOTION COMES FROM RECOGNITION'

**F:** You talk about emotion from the actor's point of view, but doesn't emotion exist for the spectator as well?

**M:** The emotion is different in the two cases. For example, Indian theatre offers something very beautiful from this point of view. There are great theoretical books on the subject. There is Zeami, of course, but there is also an Indian book,[1] an enormous work that gives the theory of Indian theatre as a whole. It contains laws that I find extraordinary. For example, there are different words to define the emotion of the actor and the character [*bhava*], and the emotion of the spectator looking at the actor [*rasa*]. In Western theatre, in the acting style of certain actors, I find an ability to bring together what should be their emotion, which should be a part of the action, and what the emotion of the spectator should be. These are the good moments: when all of a sudden a spectator has tears in her eyes while what the actor performs is a moment of enthusiasm, happiness and laughter. Why do you suddenly start crying with joy or recognition?

**F:** Because you perceive at this very moment the exactitude of what is happening. It is the truth of the moment we experience, independently from what is expressed.

**M:** Exactly. The emotion comes from recognition. From the fact that it is true. [. . .]

**F:** How do you help an actor to be in the present? Do you use a technique, or method? Is your method a form of listening?

**M:** I believe that there are no techniques. There are methods, and every director has one, maybe an unconscious one. I believe I have one, but I do not know it.
The last word you said is very important: 'listening'. I believe that I know how to do that well. I love to listen, and I love to watch the actors with a passion. I think that's already a way of assisting them. They know that I never tire of listening to them, of watching them, but how do I help them? I don't know.

**F:** In one of your texts you wrote, 'One must build up the muscle of the actor's imagination.' The nourishment you feed the imagination is a form of assistance.

**M:** When I work with very young actors, one of the first questions I ask is. 'What do you think is the actor's most important muscle?' [. . .] It is the imagination, and it can be conditioned, worked on.

**F:** How do you proceed?

**M:** With sincerity, with emotion. By acting, by really acting. Not through memory, I don't believe in that. You have to be able to have visions little by little, to be a visionary – to see what they talk about, to see where they are going, where they are; to see the sky above them, the rain; to take in the emotion of another and to believe in it.
In reality, *the* essential theory is that you have to believe: believe in what you act, what you are, what you incarnate; and believe in what another incarnates; believe in the emotional turmoil, in one's strength, one's anger, one's joy, one's personality, one's love, one's hatred, whatever. But you have to believe in it. The common misinterpretation of Brecht is that we thought he said you shouldn't believe in it. Brecht never said that; he said you should not deceive.
I think there is something in the actor's work that obliges him or her, not to fall back into childhood, but to enter childhood. Actors must divest themselves of all made-up images which go against the work of the imagination; such images are clichés or crutches where there is no emotion [. . .]

## 'WE MUST HAVE THEATRE THE FIRST DAY'

**F:** Does work on character happen alone? In a group? In discussions?

**M:** Nothing ever happens alone. From the very beginning the work happens by acting. For us, there is never, never any work at a desk. We read the play once, and the next day we are already on the stage. The actors can decide to try all the characters they want for several weeks, even several months. They have old bits of costume at their disposal to disguise themselves, and they begin. And we act right away. We must have theatre the first day.

**F:** Do actors remember what they have done on-stage, so that the good things they have found during improvisation are retained? Or is it simply a period of exploration?

**M:** There is a period of exploration, but the good things remain when they are really good. This is what you were saying about the precision of gesture, what we call the *evidence* of gesture. The gesture is not what remains, because things are fixed much later; but we will know that such and such a character has that type of gesture, that he's a little like that. Then we will discover something else. Because one of our most important laws is to keep firmly in our mind the conviction that all of the characters – *all* of them – have a complete soul. We realise it's slightly dogmatic to say that each character in a play contains all the others. There is a little of Prince Hal in Falstaff, a little of the father in the son, a little of Juliet in the nurse, a little of the nurse in Juliet. Everyone is complete. Otherwise we do not progress. Which happens to us sometimes.

There were times when I realised that the concept of work on a character, the concept of character itself, could be very limiting, that we could often translate a character by limiting it instead of creating someone without limits who is always a surprise. There are character types, of course, but you always have to be able to go beyond the type.

**F:** Do you make a psychological study of the characters? I am asking you this because in *L'Indiade* we don't get the impression that the characters have a psychology. Instead the characters seem to be from the theatre, they are presented as theatrical constructions, with a complexity but without day-to-day psychology. They are emblems. They are motivated by signs rather than by psychology.

**M:** We flee daily life. We do not talk of psychology, but rather of the characters' souls. But they still have emotions, sensations; they are cold, hungry, proud, they want power, they don't want it, they're stubborn. Each one of them has their own way of being, their own world. Nicholas Boileau said, 'The truth is not always verisimilitude' – and verisimilitude is not necessarily true. This can be understood precisely in a historical play: that is, what happens, happens. These characters experienced it, oriented it, or made it happen. It was with their 'psychology', as you say, that the events took place.

But, and there's no question about it, the theatre is not supposed to represent psychology but *passions* – which is something totally different. Theatre's role is to represent the soul's different emotional states, and those of the mind, the world, history. In the Théâtre du Soleil, psychology has negative connotations; 'psychological' acting is a criticism. It means a performance does not reach truth; it is slow, complicated, narcissistic. Contrary to what we believe, psychology does not pull toward the interior, but toward the interior mask.

## 'ALL THEATRE IS ORIENTAL'

**F:** There is no tradition of gesture in the West. Many directors must look for this tradition in the East. You yourself in the Théâtre du Soleil have to find inspiration from Asian theatres. What are you looking for?

**M:** Theories that have marked all theatre people. Artaud, Brecht and all theatre people – because it is the source of theatre. I think that we go East to look for theatre. Artaud said, 'All theatre is oriental.' This thought goes very far. He doesn't say, 'There are oriental theories that are interesting for theatre'; he says, 'All theatre is oriental.' I believe Artaud is right. So I tell actors to look for everything in the East. Myth and reality, interiority and exteriorisation, and the autopsy of the heart by the body that we talked about.

We also go to look for non-realism or theatricality. The West has only given birth to the *commedia dell'arte* – and even this comes from Asia – and to a certain type of realism, from which great actors escape. It's true that great actors, even in a realistic theatre, succeed – and I don't quite know how – in not being realistic themselves. But it is difficult.

**F:** Is theatre in need of traditions?

**M:** It needs sources and memory. It needs to be worked on in order to allow the depths and origins to come to the surface. We have traditions. Lineages exist and they belong to us completely, even beyond national borders.

**F:** Why don't you put your theories about acting in writing?

**M:** First of all, my area is not writing. Also I sincerely think that everything has been said already and in an extraordinary fashion. Someone asked Jean-Jacques Lemêtre, our musician, if he invented instruments, and he replied: You do not invent instruments any more – you transform them, you rediscover more, but you don't invent them any more; they have all been invented.' I too reply that you do not invent theories of acting any more. The problem is that theories exist, but that they have been buried at the same rate as they have been pronounced. Let young students read Zeami, Artaud, Copean, Dullin, Jouvet, Brecht as well. Everything is there. And let them make theatre. We do not need to say more.

## Note

1   Mnouchkine is referring to Zeami's fifteenth-century treatises on the art of Noh, and the *Natyasastra*, a 2000-year-old Sanskrit text on theories and codifications of performance.

■   ■   ■

## Source

Mnouchkine, A. and Féral, J. (1999) 'Building up the Muscle of the Imagination', *Collaborative Theatre: The Théâtre Du Soleil Sourcebook*, ed. D. Williams, London: Routledge: 169–173.

## Ariane Mnouchkine (1939–)

Mnouchkine is one of Europe's major theatre creators. She created her company, the Théâtre du Soleil in 1964, since when its headquarters has been at the Cartoucherie, a former deserted site outside Paris, where most of the company's productions are rehearsed and performed. But Mnouchkine also works in non-conventional spaces, such as industrial buildings and gymnasia, and the work is toured internationally. Mnouchkine also has a view of theatre that it should be a collaborative effort between artists who might regard themselves as specialists, but who, when they work with her, become a major part of the creative process. Mnouchkine is on record as saying that 'the director has already achieved the greatest degree of power he has ever had in history. And our aim is to move beyond that situation by creating a form of theatre where it will be possible for everyone to collaborate without there being directors, technicians, and so on, in the old sense.' Her theatre usually has a political dimension, which allies it to the work of Bertolt Brecht, in that it wants its audience to engage with political ideas and events.

She is famous also for taking inspiration for much of her work from non-Western sources which often gives it an exotic visual dimension. Some of her major projects have been *1789* (1970–71), a piece about the French Revolution; *L'histoire terrible mais inachevée de Norodom Sihanouk, roi du Cambodge* (1985–86), a history of the destruction of a country; and *L'Indiade, ou L'Inde de leurs rêves* (1987–88), written by Helene Cixous, a piece which questioned the history of colonialist India. The recent work of the company, still based at their original headquarters, consists of collaborations with a theatre from Kabul, as well as profiling the work of emerging French companies. The Sihanouk piece embarked on a European tour in 2012.

Mnouchkine's work, in some ways, lies outside the accepted European traditions but has always – like that of her predecessors and contemporaries, such as Brecht, Grotowski, Schechner – been created over a major period of time, and she has become a director whose work is searched out by key theatre makers. This exemplifies the strength of the Théâtre du Soleil's traditions, which seek to show other countries' and international issues to European audiences.

In the interview above we see Mnouchkine talking about the influence of non-Western theatre on her ways of working with actors. She has no theories of acting, only possible ways of working with actors. She has no need of any more than to work practically with a creative ensemble of known artists.

## Compare this interview with writings by the following authors in this reader

**Barba** – for a contemporary long-standing company
**Bharucha** – for a non-Western view of theatre
**Brecht** – for theatre and political commitment
**Grotowski** – for a tight ensemble
**Kandinsky** – for a total view of theatre

## Further reading

Miller, J. (2007) *Ariane Mnouchkine*, London: Routledge.
Kernander, A. (1993) *Ariane Mnouchkine and the Théâtre du Soleil*, Cambridge University Press.

# Chapter 45

# Meredith Monk

## PROCESS NOTES ON *ATLAS*, 1989

THE BASIC THEME of "Ghost Stories" is the loss of wonder, mystery, and freshness in our contemporary life and the possibility of rediscovering it. As Joseph Campbell so eloquently says in "An Open Life": "The sense of the mystery, the gratitude for being alive, the sense of transcendent energy that unites all of us, coordinates our cities, coordinates our lives—that's all been lost. The work of the artist is to interpret the contemporary world as experienced in terms of relevance to our *inner life*." Since I work as a mosaicist, building my pieces out of modules of music, movement, character, light, image, text, and object, it is difficult to describe "Ghost Stories" in an absolute manner at this point in my process. I am at the stage of gathering my materials, discovering the strands that I will later weave together. What I am working with is three different manifestations of this basic theme. I am allowing the ideas to come for all three, knowing that possibly and probably they will combine in some way—these three islands will connect underwater to form one whole. There are similar motifs in all three:

1. There will be three acts with elements that recur or transform from act to act. For example, there will be the image of the Big Dipper, which will be seen in different perspectives in each act.

2. In each version, there is a cappella, pure, ethereal music for eight voices, which I began working on in 1987 under the name of "The Ringing Place." This music has the radiance and resonance that implies the existence of an invisible world that underlies what we think reality is but that we rarely notice or connect with.

3. Each version also has contrasting music sung by the characters which is robust, earthy, full in quality. This will be accompanied by the instrumentalists.

4.   Each deals with time—either jumping from period to period or showing the stages in one person's life that take place in three different times.
5.   Each is mythic and epic in its concept, but each will be realized in simple and essential means.

In order of my thinking process, the three approaches are as follows:

a. My first idea was to do a piece in three acts dealing with three "ghost stories." Each act would take place in a different location during a different period of time. The locales and eras that I had in mind included a contemporary urban section, a section of pioneers on the prairie during the mid-nineteenth century, and a traditional Japanese section (based on a story from Lafcadio Hearn's "Kwaidan"). Each section would have some similarities serving as constants throughout the piece—for example, each would take place at night; a ghost or phantom would enter and change each situation. There would also be images of other nights which would seep into the atmosphere—flappers from the 1920s would enter the urban section; the traditional Japanese section would be intruded upon by futuristic elements; prehistoric and Mexican elements would appear in the prairie section. The entire piece would work with perceptual contrasts both musically and visually, all within the framework of night.

b. These ideas transformed into a piece about reincarnation, focusing on the mystery and impermanence of life. The overture would take place in another world on which a harmonious society existed. Singing the ethereal music that conjures up images of the universe resonating, of planets spinning, the group would perform a ritual that ends in sending down one of their members to Earth to become part of the human race. A narrator or guide character conveys to him/her and to the audience before each of the acts, the current events of the period in which he/she is entering. The three locations and eras are: (1) Pompeii right before the disaster; (2) the Spanish Inquisition; (3) contemporary urban office. He/she forgets where he/she came from and becomes embroiled in human exist-ence. In each act, a ghost of phantom (from his world) delivers a message about how to avert a disaster that is occurring on Earth. He is the only one who can perceive this figure, but not until the last act is he aware of himself and where he comes from and then changes the course of events on Earth. In each act, he dies and becomes reborn in another incarnation (sometimes as a man, sometimes as a woman) in the next act. The hero-heroine can be identified by a constant costume element (such as red sleeves, for

example); similar movements and vocal themes recur in each act. At the end, he goes back to his world.

c. The third set of ideas is based on my interest in Tibet (and, by extension, other non-Western cultures) and in the life of Alexandra David-Néel—a female explorer who was one of the first Westerners to reach Tibet (in 1912); lived to be 101 years old; spoke fluent Tibetan in order to reach Lhasa undetected; spent years in hermitages meditating and becoming a Buddhist scholar. This piece is about the idea of search—the eternal quest for the *meaning* and transcendence *in life*. It is also about the cycle of one person's life, paralleling events in our century in which the notion of an uncorrupted or untouched society has been steadily eroded. The main character (which right now I'm thinking of as a man, but may be a female hero closer to the model of Madame David-Néel) is first seen in the first act as a child. There has been an overture of the ethereal, ringing music. The child is lonely and sensitive except for his or her fleeting glimpses of another existence (characterized by short phrases of the pure music of the overture). There is also a sense of his knowing that his destiny is to travel. In the piece, his physical wandering parallels his spiritual search. At the end of the first act, the child stands in the center of the space and is replaced by his adult self. The second act is the main act of the piece, which is his journey with and without companions to distant lands. He spends time alone as a hermit where he is visited by apparitions, temptations, and dreams. He finds places (untarnished by the fragmentation of industrial life) where other realities are allowed to exist as part of the culture. His journey is also marked by romances, follies, and misunderstandings. As the act goes on, we sense coming in around the edges, the threat of soldiers, tourists, intruders that begin to cause the destruction of the society. The act ends with the man in the center of the space being replaced by his older self. In the third act, the old man goes back to the place of his youth to revisit the world of his memories. Ruins and rubbish are all that remain. An old woman, who we realize is his wife, enters. He shows her the place and sings a song about his youth. They quietly walk to a table, where they perform a simple, tender scene, drinking coffee as the scenes of destruction around them go to black. After his search, tests, adventures, and romances, he finds utopia in the simple acts and tendernesses of the moment. The pure, ringing music that has been underlying the whole piece swells.

So, these are the ideas that I am playing with. I think of them as seeds that have been planted, ready to bloom when the time is right. My job is to cultivate them, water them, nurture them until the strongest ones come up. The process of making a piece is very much like a quest: you start out in the dark; you have a sense of the potential that opens out before you; there is a sense of danger because no one has gone this way before; you follow clues, listen to instincts, look for what is needed; soon, the way becomes apparent as more and more layers are added in and the piece takes on its own life.

■　■　■

## Source

Jowitt, D. (ed.) (1997) *Meredith Monk,* Baltimore: Johns Hopkins University Press.

## Meredith Monk (1942–)

Monk was born in Peru and is an American composer, director, vocalist, film maker, and choreographer – the cross-disciplinary artist par excellence. Since the 1960s she has created a series of works that unite what is now known as 'extended vocal techniques'. She possesses a three-octave range, which is used in some of her pieces. She studied at the Sarah Lawrence College in New York, has studied and taught eurythmics – the system of movement pioneered by Jaques-Dalcroze – and has performed with a variety of groups including the Kronos Quartet. In 1978 she founded the Meredith Monk Vocal Ensemble, modelled on the Philip Glass ensemble. Its music uses a variety of vocal techniques owing much to folk music, but also has explored new vocal mixtures. Her 1991 opera *Atlas* tells the story of Alexandra, who dreams of exploration, using few words but mostly assonant syllables. *Dolmen Music* (1980–81) produced a vocal style that enabled Monk 'to sing in complete abstraction'. It is claimed that her multidisciplinary style encapsulates much of the American avant-garde and has links with John Cage's ideas and with Allan Kaprow's Happenings, as well as with the Judson Dance Theatre, Merce Cunningham and Fluxus events.

Monk's process notes on *Atlas* delineate her multifaceted world and wide interests – in Tibet, ghost stories and reincarnation. The writing displays her constant quest for meaning, which links her also with Martha Graham and the ideals of theatre artists like Julian Beck and the Living Theatre. Like them, Monk symbolises a certain kind of American optimism.

## Compare this article with writings by the following authors in this reader

**Cunningham** – a dance contemporary
**Graham** – for American optimism
**Maciunas** – for unclassifiable events
**Glass** – for notes of music
**Eisler** – for an earlier musical revolutionary

## Further Reading

Cunningham, M., Monk, M. and Jones, B.T. (1978) *Art Performs Life,* Minneapolis: Walker Art Centre.
Jowitt, D. (ed.) (2011) *Meredith Monk,* Baltimore: Johns Hopkins University Press.
http://www.meredithmonk.org

# Chapter 46

# Heiner Müller

## 19 ANSWERS BY HEINER MÜLLER

*A couple of years ago you were invited to a conference on Postmodernism in New York. You couldn't attend the conference but submitted a paper defining your position versus some aspects of contemporary art. Could you explain what in your opinion would constitute a Postmodern drama, a Postmodern theatre?*

The only Postmodernist I know of was August Stramm, a modernist who worked in a post office.

*Language takes a central position in your work, much more than it usually does in contemporary American drama. Could you explain what you feel language's function is in the contemporary theatre?*

I would take issue with the premise in the first part of your question. Language is also important in American drama and other media but it is a different language, I think, with perhaps a different function. A film critic once asked me why stage and film productions in the GDR tend to use a poeticizing rather than what he called a naturalistic language, why the tendency toward stylization rather than realism. The extent to which that is valid comes from the fact that the GDR is not photographable, the fact that here actors cannot even say 'Guten Tag' without it sounding like a lie. Realism doesn't work at all, only stylization works — a variation of Brecht's remark that a photograph of the Krupp Works says nothing really about the Krupp Works. The actors in the West are much better at Naturalism, at working with photographic texts or plays or films. Here they are better in productions of the classics, i.e., in anything that entails a stylized removal from immediate reality.

*What is the role of language versus the rich visual imagery you employ to an ever increasing degree in your plays?*

The worst experience I had during my stay in the United States was a film I saw called *Fantasia*, by Disney. I had never heard of it and actually ended up watching it by mistake. There were three films playing in the same movie house and I went into the wrong one. The most barbaric thing about this film, something I learned later, was that almost every American child between the ages of six and eight gets to view it. Which means that these people will never again be able to hear specific works by Beethoven, Bach, Handel, Tchaikovsky, etc., without seeing the Disney figures and images. The horrifying thing for me in this is the occupation of the imagination by clichés and images which will never go away; the use of images to prevent experiences, to prevent the having of experiences.

*What has this got to do with your theatre?*

Wolfgang Heise, a philosopher here in the GDR, once said that theatre is a laboratory for the social imagination. I find that relevant for what we are talking about. If one starts with the assumption that capitalist societies, indeed every industrial society, the GDR included, tends to repress and instrumentalize imagination – to throttle it – then for me the political task of art today is precisely the mobilization of imagination. To return to our example of *Fantasia*, the metaphorical function of the Disney film is to reduce the symbolic force of images to one meaning, to make them immediately allegorical. The imagery one finds in the early Russian cinema, on the other hand, is like the torrent of metaphors at the heart of Elizabethan literature. Here metaphors are constructed as a kind of visual protection against a much too rapidly changing reality, a reality that can only be dealt with and assimilated in this very special way. A world of images is created that does *not* lend itself to conceptual formulation and that cannot be reduced to a one-dimensional metaphor. This is what I try to do in my theatre.

*You have written in other literary forms, poetry, short story, etc., but you always returned to the theatre, recently even as the director of your plays. Do you believe then that the theatre is a superior medium to investigate the complex problems of our time?*

I have a real difficulty writing prose. I don't believe in literature as a work of art to be read. I don't believe in reading. I couldn't imagine writing a novel.

*Where does your distrust of prose come from?*

Writing prose you are all alone. You can't hide yourself. I also don't think I can write prose in the third person. I can't write: 'Washington got up and went to 42nd Street.' I can only imagine writing prose in the first person. Writing drama you always have masks and roles and you can talk through them. That's why I prefer drama — because of the masks. I can say one thing and say the contrary. I have a need to get rid of contradictions and that is easier to do with drama.

*The theatre seems to have increasing difficulties in reaching wider audiences, larger sections of society, especially when it tries to interact with, or activate, its audiences. Where do you see reasons for this development and how should one cope with this danger of elitism?*

This 'elitism,' as you call it, this not being immediately accessible, can also have its advantages. For accessibility is often connected with commercialization. Art becomes commercial at precisely the moment when its time is past. The tension between success and impact, which Brecht spoke of, is important in this respect: that one is always overtaken by success before a real impact can occur. As long as a thing works it is not successful, and when success is there then the impact is over. This is because there can only be an impact if, as for example in the theatre, the audience is split, brought home to its real situation. But that means there will be no agreement, no success. Success happens when everybody is cheering, in other words, when there is nothing more to say. For me the theatre is a medium which still permits one to avoid that kind of success. In film that is difficult because of the money involved.

*But what about the GDR?*

In our country, theatre allows you to have 500 or 800 people together in one room reacting at the same time, in the same space, to what is happening on stage. The impact of the theatre here is based on the absence of other ways of getting messages across to people. Films are not as important either because there is so much control. As a result, the theatre here has taken over the function of the other media in the West. I don't believe theatre has a great impact in West Germany, for instance. (We can forget about the United States.) You can do anything on the stage there but it doesn't mean anything to the society. Here the slogan of the Napoleonic era still applies: Theatre is the Revolution on the march.

*In many of your texts you deal with topics which in this country would be defined as 'feminist'; and female characters often have a central place in your work. Could you explain how you think women should be presented on the contemporary stage?*

As a playwright I don't deal with 'isms' but with reality. Can you tell me what a real female character is?

*Your work is firmly rooted in history and/or mythology. American drama deals rarely with the past. What do you conceive as the function of mythology and history in the contemporary theatre?*

The dead are in the overwhelming majority when compared to the living. And Europe has a wealth of dead stored up on that side of the ledger. The United States, not satisfied just with dead Indians, is fighting to close the gap. Literature, as an instrument of democracy, while not submitting to, should nevertheless be respectful of, majorities as well as of minorities.

*Some of your critics maintain that at the center of your recent work is the conflict between the individual's desire 'to pursue happiness' and the individual's responsibility to history and mankind's progress. Do you agree with this view? If yes, could you speak to this contradiction and its present manifestations?*

'We Germans were not put here on earth to enjoy ourselves but to do our duty.' (Bismarck)

*If you disagree, what would you regard as a central issue in your recent texts?*

How should I know, and if I knew why should I tell you?

*If you reject this idea of a central issue, could you mention some of the interests you pursue in your writing?*

See above.

*Your plays have been performed in East and West Germany, in the United States, and in many other countries. You participated in many of these productions and recently have directed your plays in both Germanies. What difference could you observe in the theatrework of these different social and cultural systems, and what did they have in common?*

To answer this question I am going to have to wait for more performances in East and West.

*a) Where is the theatre, in your opinion, a more efficient instrument of social impact?*
*b) Where would you prefer to direct, and to watch, your plays on stage?*

a) In the East. b) I would like to stage MACBETH on top of the World Trade Center for an audience in helicopters.

*There has been a lot of attention given to the so-called 'New Subjectivity' in German letters, as exemplified by writers like Handke, Strauss, Laederach, etc. Do you see yourself in any relation to them and their work?*

No. Nor do I see any relation of them to each other.

*Terms like 'Despair,' 'Pessimism,' 'Guilt' are often used by critics writing about your work. Do you think these are adequate definitions of your intentions and/or values?*

Three times No.

*People familiar with your recent texts often complain about a total lack of hope in your writing. What is your opinion?*

I am neither a dope- nor a hope-dealer.

*Would you care to comment on your views about the future of our world which you paint so darkly in your work?*

The future of the world is not my future.
'Show me a mousehole and I'll fuck the world.' (Railworker at the soft-coal strip mine Klettwitz, GDR.)

■  ■  ■

## Source

Müller, H. (1984) 'Interview: 19 Answers by Heiner Müller. "I am Neither A Dope-Nor a Hope-Dealer"', *Hamlet Machine and Other Texts for the Stage*, ed. C. Weber, New York: Performing Arts Journal: 137–140.

## Heiner Müller (1929–1995)

German playwright; one of Europe's most radical, in his most innovative work equal in stature to Samuel Beckett. For most of its existence Müller was a citizen of the German Democratic Republic (GDR), and worked with Brecht at the Berliner Ensemble, of which he was a director since the collapse of the Berlin Wall. As an admirer of Brecht his theatre texts – he deliberately did not call them plays – do not attempt to dictate fixed meanings, instead allowing the individual performer and director free play with the collage of materials that he presents. His major pieces often have elliptical titles – *Hamletmachine* (1977), *Despoiled Shore Medeamaterial Landscape with Argonauts* (1982), *Gunding's Life Frederick of Prussia Lessings Sleep Dream Scream* (1976), *Germania Death in Berlin* (1973). He was interested in a totally different theatre from the predominantly interpretative theatre that grew up in Germany post-war. 'I have no message,' he says, 'I just want conflicts, even between the audience and the text.' Müller's work presents formidable challenges for performers and directors, who must, by choices, 'make' the performance out of the texts which he presents. The pieces are often collages of different ideas, assemblages of literary fragments 'to escape the prison of meaning' – essential for a citizen of a country where all meanings were decided by decree, a tendency that caught up with Brecht in his later years. This social tension nevertheless produced some of the most challenging texts of the century, hence Müller's inclusion in this book. His collaborations with Robert Wilson – most notably on *CIVIL warS* (1984) have brought to the fore attitudes that both artists have in common with Beckett – that a work of art is not about something – it is something. He was also an admirer of Pina Bausch, of whose work he said, 'the image is a thorn in our eye'. Similarly, this set of replies displays a typically Müllerian cast of thought.


## Compare this interview with writings by the following authors in this reader

**Bausch** – a dance theatre that Müller admired
**Brecht** – Müller's mentor and antecedent
**Richter** – the conflicts of Dada
**Wilson** – one of his major collaborators


## Further reading

Calandra, D. (1983) *New German Dramatists*, London: Macmillan.
Henning, M. von (ed.) (1995) *Theatremachine*, London: Faber.
Kalb, J. (2004) *The Theater of Heiner Müller*, New York: Limelight Editions.
Linders, J. (1996) 'Moliere + Muller', *Performance Research* Vol. 1. No. 2.
http://www.heinermueller.de

# Chapter 47

# Lloyd Newson

## CONVERSATION WITH
## JO BUTTERWORTH

*Can you give some insights into the points of departure for your choreography, about the artistic motivation for your work?*

Newson . . . I only create when I have something to say, and the work is generally about issues that concern or affect my life at a given time. I'm interested in provoking myself, questioning my own and the performers' thoughts, motivations and assumptions. Many of the themes I dealt with in the early works — as in *My Sex, Our Dance* (1986), *My Body, Your Body* (1987) and *Dead Dreams of Monochrome Men* (1988) — have been controversial. At the time I chose to examine these themes through physically challenging movement. However when we made *Strange Fish* (1992), the risk was not so much about physical danger, but whether dance can deal with complex emotional narrative, and whether tragi-comic theatre can in fact be created through dance alone. You can take risks without always being physical.

I have regularly challenged what is traditionally defined as dance, i.e., who can dance in terms of shape, size, age, and what dance can talk about. In order to keep my interest in dance it has to personally resonate with issues I experience directly in my life. I am not interested in making work that does not focus clearly on content. Content, rather than style drives DV8's work, which distinguishes it from a lot of other contemporary dance. Issues, rather than 'prettiness' or aesthetics, are important. Our work delves into how individuals relate to one another, emotionally and intellectually, rather than being about movement or design patterns per se; exploring the individual's actions, and looking at how these in turn reflect political and social issues.

*And what methods do you utilise to engage dancers in your choreographic process?*

My process involves making performers question how they engage in making work. I seek movement with intention and purpose. What are they/we trying to communicate? It is not that I am necessarily against using an arabesque, but you must know why you do it. Why is at the heart of DV8's work. It is closer in terms of intention, focus and subtext to the ways in which a theatre director works with a text.

DV8 is known as a company that fights hard for funding to engage in research and development processes in order to gain periods of experimentation. Can you give some insights into your approach?

Time for research and experimentation is our chance for rejuvenation. The climate has changed radically since the mid-eighties when we were first making work, when there was much more openness about experimentation. Therefore I have come to a point where I feel I can only really take risks and face possible failure in my research periods. Without this I would be fearful to try new ideas and work with new people. I invite new dancers/performers to participate in research periods to try and alter my approach to making work. For example, when I researched *Bound To Please* (1997) we explored the performers' psychological experiences as professional 'dancers'. This brought up an unexpected issue. What is their perceived value as people in relation to their value as dancers; were they only as good as the height of their leg?

Another research project centred on taking the performers into, and working in, a 'greasy spoon' café. The performers were asked to observe normal café users to see what information was conveyed through their body language. When they returned to the studio, I asked them to extrapolate what they had seen so that they could abstract it and use the principles of the movement patterns they had observed to make movement phrases. Most choreography is made in the rehearsal studio, yet this can be a sterile environment. My concern is for dance to connect with and talk about the real world, so it seemed logical to send the performers out of the dance environment, in order to observe and interact with it.

The research and development period for *Enter Achilles* (1995) occurred almost two years prior to the piece being completed. This gap suggests that sometimes there can be quite a significant delay between ideas being initiated and the work that emerges a few years later.

During a five-week R&D period in Glasgow in 1994, I found myself struggling creatively while investigating the distinction between subtleties of the spoken word and the equivalent subtleties in movement. The improvisations were quite frustrating and quite tough. Yet suddenly, I found a new direction for the experimentation. One day I went down for a drink with the performers after we had finished rehearsals; we were all sitting around rather tired, and I noticed that everybody was drinking pints of beer. Seeing the potential for both initiating and limiting movement exploration, I suggested bringing pint glasses to the studio the following day. As work progressed the glass became a metaphor for all sorts of things in the piece to do with masculinity and British culture.

It is obvious from the examples you have cited that the very different circumstances of the research periods lead to very different types of dance pieces. Is it challenging to make or find an appropriate vocabulary for each work?

Yes. Another example from the Glasgow R&D period exemplifies this. A situation was reported in the paper about a policeman who refused to hold the hand of a car accident victim because he feared being perceived as a homosexual. In exploring how I might represent something like that physically, I talked to some of the heterosexual guys from my company, asking them to walk hand in hand down Sauchiehall Street in Glasgow. They said no problem, but only managed to walk three blocks — they couldn't bear the tension and reaction from the locals. So I questioned how this tension might be shown in the piece. When is it acceptable for men to hold hands? In searching for a metaphor to explore these notions of acceptability, I started investigating trapeze work and we engaged a specialist to train our dancers. In the piece two men hold on to a suspended rope and dance a duet where they must hold hands in order not to fall. When they get down on the ground, and are still holding hands, it's extremely uncomfortable for them. One performer becomes very nervous and anxious because of the social stigma attached to men holding hands.

Also, with regard to DV8's physical vocabulary, in the company training DV8 bring in different people to develop new skills, if appropriate, for a new piece: in *My Body, Your Body* we did aerobics and long distance running to build up stamina, and in *Strange Fish* we brought in yoga teachers. Voice teachers have been employed at times to work on different pieces that use text; specialist trainers are brought in according to the subject matter. When we were looking at football, we questioned why it is considered acceptable for men to do footwork around a football, but not to do footwork around Irish dancing or ballet. So we brought in an Irish dancing teacher because I wanted to explore the difference between those two forms in relation to what is 'acceptable' and 'unacceptable' masculine movement.

If I cannot find appropriate movement, I will also use words. I am not a purist, and don't wish to limit my breadth of expression or to trade complex scenarios for purism. The fundamental principle in the work is to make it clear, to be specific and detailed. Throughout, my interest is in conveying stories or ideas through movement. The research and development periods are all videoed, and documented, so that I can go back and refer to them in preparation for the actual piece. Much will be rejected and not used at all.

What form does the actual rehearsal process take?

The form of the preparation for the rehearsal period rarely follows one set approach. For example, for *Enter Achilles* (1995), I made five or six particular choices from the five-week workshop and took these ideas into the rehearsal period. Another exploratory idea was that we should start experimenting with the idea of the men using one another as furniture; another, that we should look at fluids, play with the idea of men sharing fluids together and of intoxication, and the connotations of that. Or how a pint glass can represent beauty or danger, community or isolation. We looked at videos of documentary programmes about binge drinking in Wales on Friday and Saturday nights and the ensuing violence that occurs after drinking 8 or 9 pints in one evening. Essentially, we attempted to look out at the world and our experiences of men amongst men, and to reflect this back on our work. It must be added that by the time we came to rehearsals after the workshop, I had written a storyline, and we'd already designed and built a complicated set.

Since DV8 is not a permanent company you have the opportunity to choose new cast for each work. What do you look for in a performer?

I choose people who are appropriate to the needs of the subject matter being explored, and with whom I can collaborate; people who can bring an openness of attitude and thoughtfulness to the process. They have to be interested in the subject matter. I cast like a film director, according to what the script requires, so for example, in looking at the relationship between an older woman and a younger man the cast choices have to give some authenticity. So we chose Diana Payne-Myers — a woman and dancer who has worked on many different projects with us over the years — who is in her mid-seventies.

When making *Enter Achilles*, I was concerned to find guys who looked like regular guys in the street. When we made *MSM* (1993) about cottaging, I asked two things of those auditioning; they had to be prepared to be naked on the stage, and to go to places known for cottaging to observe the situation, to know how tense, or frightening, or funny it can be. It is the principle here that is relevant; without that openness of mind and vulnerability, I knew we would experience blocks in other areas during rehearsal.

Some of the most interesting people chosen to work with DV8 have generally done something else in their lives before they came to dance. Through working in computers, tiling ceramics, acting, or something as mundane as working in a supermarket, they brought other significant experience of the real world into dance. I find it frustrating that many dancers train from such an early age and lack exposure to other life experiences. Having Diana Payne-Myers naked on stage in *Bound To Please* for me was infinitely more beautiful than seeing a gorgeous woman doing a perfect arabesque, because it is the context and meaning that makes something beautiful and touching.

Do you have particular methods of structuring your work?

Since 1990, after DV8 finished *Dead Dreams* and made the film, I made a deliberate choice to leave behind that very intense, dark and exhausting physicality

369

of the earlier pieces. I decided to try and create more image driven, humorous theatre, the traces of which can be first seen in "if only . . ." (1990). I soon discovered that it was too frightening to go into a studio without having a pre-written story and structure. I needed some structure — though you also need to be free to throw that structure out. So from then on, for all the pieces, *Strange Fish*, *Enter Achilles*, *Bound To Please*, I wrote a scenario prior to starting rehearsals, not that I always ended up sticking to it.

Having research and development periods, becoming my own dramaturg and writing a loose structure before the rehearsals provides the company with the opportunity to build sets in advance. The performers can then work with the set and ensure it becomes embedded into the performance. The environment needs to be lived in, and the set explored before the production week(s). A script provides a guide in helping me structure the rehearsal period, both day to day and overall. For example, in *Enter Achilles* we did a whole range of improvisations based on what is acceptable male physical contact, about what is considered an acceptable way for a man to walk and talk. We played with the simple ideas of straight and bent movements, how these affect how we feel and how they were perceived externally. We looked at the pressures on men to play certain roles, particular sports; we talked about relationships with our fathers, our mothers, our best male friends, what we expect from them, and how that differs from our relationships with our female friends. Then we would get to specifics, because we can generalise and make all these theories, but it's the specific individual stories that are interesting.

In the end, the interest lies not so much in how we do it, but in how he or she does it. Specifics can often contradict convenient social theories, and are often very conflicting, which is more human, complex and revealing.

In order for really interesting, deep material to come up, like in analysis, the performer has to let go of his subconscious. That sometimes poses a problem for dancers. If somebody truly lets go in improvisation it is impossible for him to remember exactly what he did, as that is a conscious process. That is why we use a video camera. Obviously there are endless means of constructing work — task setting, observation and translations, working directly from text, occasionally I even come in with set steps. These methods combined with structured improvisation are my way of discovering new and appropriate dance content and of finding individual voices within the company, thus distinguishing how each performer moves differently, and how interesting and unique their differences are. Generally DV8's works are about seeing particular individuals on stage, therefore it is important to nurture the individual vocabulary, while providing a focus and boundaries for the improvisations and tasks.

Do you join in with these tasks and improvisations?

In the past when I was performing, yes, but generally I stand out to be the 'eye'. Once we had more than four people in our company I felt it was impossible to be on stage personally, and keep an eye on other people's performances, so I removed myself, and now I sit through almost every performance our company does, give notes and make changes. It continues throughout the tour. Without constant change and development, I feel that a work becomes dead for both performers and audience.

This became particularly evident when reworking and touring *Enter Achilles*. It was the first time that DV8 had remounted a past work, and some dancers had to learn previous roles. This became a particular challenge. Because the work is devised with a particular group of people in the first instance, introducing new cast members can result in quite radical changes to the piece. New performers have not experienced all the intense research, whereas someone who has, and who made movement unique to himself, generated the material. Thus getting somebody else to do exactly the same part does not work — I find myself working with the qualities of the new individuals and having to adapt material to suit them in order to sustain some truth. This process made me more aware of just how exactly every movement is built on an individual, consistent with their thoughts, intention, way of moving, etc. There are thirty different ways to pick up a glass, and each one says something different. Basically, I try to impart that realisation to the people that I work with . . . and once they start understanding that, we're half way there.

The other thing about dance making is that a lot of people I work with are really committed to new work, therefore they are not interested in being part of a repertory company, and the only reason we remounted *Enter Achilles* was to pay for the next research period. We want to keep making new work that is intricately linked to personal development. It is important now, for me at least, not to get stuck in remounting and touring old works, and the commercialisation that can go with this.

It seems that your role in the company is different to that of a traditional choreographer, in that the work is devised and collectively made.

Let me be clear, whatever ends up on stage, the subject matter, each individual step, I decide on. I see my role as stimulator, facilitator, editor and constructor, but equally I want to learn from my performers. I find it dull, boring and reductive bringing in steps for my dancers to learn — which is what I did in my early choreographic days. I have a responsibility to keep finding ways to open up and creatively stimulate performers in the company. Most people are capable of producing incredible performances, however some are reluctant to enter new territory. I can open gates, but at a certain point, unless they are prepared to let go of their psychological blocks, I can't do anything. DV8 have produced some exceptional performers who, prior to joining the company, hadn't fulfilled their potential. Of course, this also means that DV8 might then lose their most capable collaborators, but its great when the people I've worked with go off and create something of their own, empowered through their association with DV8.

■   ■   ■

## Source

Lloyd Newson in Conversation with Jo Butterworth — unpublished interview adapted from a 1998 interview on 7 July 2004.

## Lloyd Newson (1954–)

Australian choreographer and dancer, co-founder and director of DV8 Physical Theatre. He originally studied psychology and social work at Melbourne University, and his developing fascination and interest in dance led, in 1980, to a full scholarship at London Contemporary Dance School. He danced and/or choreographed with many companies — including Modern Dance Ensemble, Impulse Dance Theatre/New Zealand Ballet Company, One Extra Dance Theatre and Extemporary Dance Theatre. He danced with the Extemporary Dance Theatre 1981–85 and also choreographed pieces for the company. In 1986 he formed his own company and his work to date as Director of DV8 Physical Theatre has had a dynamic impact on contemporary dance and theatre. His work for DV8 includes *Dead Dreams of Monochrome Men* (1989), *If Only . . .* (1990), *Strange Fish* (1992), *MSM* (1993), *Enter Achilles* (1995), *Bound To Please* (1997), *Just for Show* (2005), *To Be Straight With You* (2007) and *Can We Talk About This?* (2011). He has also collaborated with film makers David Hinton and Clara von Gool to make award-winning films of several of his pieces for the company. Having a strong sense that DV8's work would translate well to film, he directed *The Cost of Living,* based on the stage production of the same name, which has subsequently won a large number of international awards including a Prix Italia and a Rose D'or.

Much of his stage and film work with DV8 has consistently received major awards and he and his company have developed a strong international reputation for the production of high-quality outputs across both forms. Newson has also created *Living Costs* (2003) a site-specific performance at the Tate Modern, London, and his most recent work *Can We Talk About This?* (2011) is as a verbatim theatre piece that uses real-life interviews and archive footage. Newson and DV8 have developed a strong reputation for experimentation and the production of high-quality performances that are often controversial and challenge assumptions around what dance can and should deal with. His interest is in conceiving new and original work that addresses important themes and issues rather than performing existing plays or reinterpreting classical ballets. He describes the importance of re-inventing dance that addresses social issues, and the company aims to make work that is radical yet accessible to a wide audience — dance that is 'about something'. His thematic explorations have included social taboos; sexual and gender politics; notions of perfection and the (im)perfect body; homophobia and freedom of speech.

The work is often process-driven, often resulting in lengthy research and development periods, and performers are selected according to their personal experience and connections to the material being explored as well as their interest in the subject matter. Despite Newson's emphasis on issue-based, content-driven dance, DV8's performance works can be situated within the European tradition of dance theatre where dance, text, theatricality, site and film are all drawn upon to create work that speaks using a multiplicity of languages rather than taking a purist stance regarding what dance should be.

In this clearly articulated and accessible interview, Newson discusses his research processes, his approach to the selection of performers, his position on form and content and how the role of choreographer functions within a collaborative context.

## Compare this interview with writings by the following authors in this reader

**Bausch** – an influential European contemporary of dance theatre
**Cunningham** – a collaborator and later follower of Graham
**de Keersmaeker** – a contemporary of Newson
**Graham** – for investigating the question of defining dance
**Grotowski** – for a different lineage of physical theatre
**Rainer** – for taking dance in new directions

## Further reading

Allegranti, B. (2011) *Embodied Performances: Sexuality, Gender, Bodies,* Hampshire: Palgrave Macmillan.
Bremser, M. and Sanders, L. (1999) *Fifty Contemporary Choreographers: A Reference Guide,* London: Routledge.
Murray, S. and Keefe, J. (2007) *Physical Theatres: A Critical Introduction,* London: Routledge.
http://www.dv8.co.uk/about_dv8/lloyd_newson

# Chapter 48

# Erwin Piscator

## EPIC SATIRE

### The theatrical form

This was the first time we had been faced with a novel and not with a play which, whether it was good or bad, was at least conceived in terms of dialogue and scenery, and with some regard for theatrical form. A novel, furthermore, where despite the passivity of the hero there is constant movement; Schwejk is sent to prison, then discharged from prison, Schwejk follows the curate as he celebrates Mass, Schwejk is wheeled on to parade in a wheelchair, Schwejk is dispatched to the front in a train, marches for days in search of his regiment — in short, things around him are always moving, always in flux. It is fantastic how the constant shifting of the plot seems to express the restless instability of war.

### *Sample of stage movements as used in 'Schwejk'*

II. 2 (Anabasis):
*Belt 1 from right to left:*
    Schwejk is marching. From left to right. Singing.
*On Belt 1 ( from right to left):*
    Old lady is carried on standing.
    Meeting.
*Belt 1 stops:*
    Dialogue to '. . . regiment hurries.'
*Belt 1 from right to left:*
    Schwejk marches on.
    Old lady travels out standing.

*Belt 1 carries on milestones, trees, signposts: village of Malchin.*
*Belt 2 from right to left:*
 A bar travels on.
*Belts 1 and 2 stop:*
 Scene to '. . . to the regiment as quickly as possible.'
*Belts 1 and 2 from right to left:*
 Bar travels off.
 Schwejk marches.
*On Belt 2 traveling on stage:*
 Haystack (snoring 8 sec.).
 Scene to '. . . if they hadn't deserted.'
*Belt 1 runs ($^1/_2$ min.).*
*Belt 2 moves left to right.*

Even when I first read the novel, long before we thought of dramatizing it, I had a mental picture of events following one another in a ceaseless, uninterrupted stream. Faced with the problem of putting this novel on the stage, this impression in my mind assumed the concrete form of a conveyor belt.

So here again the stage technique emerged ready-made from the subject of the play, or at least from what I like to call the artistic aggregate of the subject matter. The fact that this technique 'symbolized' a stage of society (the dissolution and decline of a social order) was secondary and fortuitous. And the stage technique in its turn predetermined the textual shape of the play.

> P. has a technical imagination the like of which we have never seen before; he releases all the power of the stage, he wheedles out all its secrets, his conveyor belt is more than a gimmick, P. has dissolved the classical unities of time, place and space and given the dimension of the marvelous, the magical back to the theater, thanks to his inspired mastery of the most modern technical devices.
>
> *Die Welt am Abend*, January 24, 1928 (Kurt Kersten)

## The dramatic principles of the conveyor belt

All previous attempts to put novels on the stage have essentially failed. In most cases they retained nothing but the figure of the hero whom they robbed of his characteristic atmosphere by placing him in a new plot and thus making him unconvincing as a character.

It was a doubly difficult task to dramatize Jaroslav Hašek's novel. For this was not a neatly constructed whole, but a huge agglomeration of anecdotes and adventures with no adequate conclusion. Schwejk's character was established at the beginning and did not develop at all in the course of the novel. He only ever appeared in a passive, never in an active role, and he could be imagined in any possible situation except the one in which he met his end. The action of the novel was determined solely by events from 1914 till the middle of the Great War. So even when one left aside the epic breadth of the book, all its other elements conspired to defy dramatization.

The first method we tried was dramatization in the traditional manner mentioned above. We extracted the figure of Schwejk from the novel and placed him in an action of our own invention. Predictably enough, this attempt produced nothing that could be used. We used all the best episodes in the original and still we deprived Schwejk of the atmosphere he needed. His stories and his gags were too abrupt. It was clear that they needed the build-up afforded by Hašek's involved style, and that dramatization could only shrink and diminish the events. The plot which we had superimposed on Schwejk (a love story, incidentally) also robbed Hašek's work of its political-theoretical dimension. His milieu and the people who make it work ceased to be decisive and were supplanted by the mechanical requirements of the comedy which produced its own inconsequential figures. Hašek's thrusts at the [Hapsburg] Monarchy, the Bureaucracy, the Military and the Church were thus robbed of their venom. We turned Schwejk, who takes everything so seriously that he makes it ludicrous, who obeys orders so literally that they turn into sabotage, who demolishes everything he supports, into an idiotic orderly whose witless efforts on behalf of his lieutenant eventually turn out for the best.

The failure of this attempt – and the adapters went as far as to produce an actable play – was further proof that this method of doctoring novels for the stage was wrong. So we abandoned the 'dramatization' of the hero and decided to stage sequences of the novel, instead of producing a play around the figure of Schwejk.

There was just one single objection to this plan: the form of the present-day stage. It seemed impossible to capture the epic movement of the novel with traditional theatrical techniques. With a fixed stage, the flow of Hašek's plot was bound to be chopped up into single scenes, and this would falsify the fluid character of the novel. Piscator overcame this problem by replacing the fixed stage floor with a moving floor, and with this one skillful touch he found the appropriate staging for the epic development of the novel: the conveyor belt.

And this solved our textual problems as well as our technical problems. The adapters no longer needed a framework other than the original story; they could limit themselves to choosing the most effective scenes in the novel and turning them into actable texts. The grouping of the action could follow Hašek's original closely, and the only problem left was how we could adequately stage Schwejk's environment, which had a decisive effect on him. And as usual, Piscator solved this question with film, but here with the difference that he had an animated cartoon made. At the beginning of each chapter where Hašek made direct general comments on his theme, Piscator projected cartoons, drawn by George Grosz. In this way he could effectively condense the forces which were opposed to Schwejk.

(It should be mentioned here that Piscator toyed for a while with the idea of making Schwejk the only figure to appear on the stage and representing all the other figures with cartoons.)

The figures alongside Schwejk, where they had no active part in the action, were represented by dolls or puppets. Originally these were to have been much more rigidly classified according to the various class ideologies of the figures.

Once the set and staging had been decided upon, the writers had only to compress the essentials of the novel – which at a conservative estimate takes twenty-four hours to read – into two and one-half hours without losing its particular style. (It is unfortunately impossible to spread Schwejk out over five evenings, as Piscator once suggested). The original novel had to be radically shortened and condensed and completely rearranged in places to make it playable at all. On the other hand, we strictly avoided using any material other than Hašek's original text.

The ending presented a special difficulty which was, in fact, never completely resolved. Hašek had died while writing the novel, without leaving any indication of a possible ending. Any ending we might contrive would seem to do violence to the original manuscript, and a natural ending was not effective theater. The controversial scene in Heaven, which in fact derived from one of Hašek's own passages, 'Cadet Biegler's Dream,' would have necessitated a disruptive reworking of the whole figure, since the novel did not afford all the material we would have needed. So for better or for worse, we had to adopt a compromise which was both effective theater and Schwejk-like.

The path followed here opens extraordinary prospects for the future. The intellectual revolution going on around us is not only radically transforming purely technical materials, but is also opening up new subjects and new forms. The theater can no longer restrict itself to a dramatic form which was once produced by a particular set of social and technical conditions, at a time when these very conditions are subject to far-reaching changes. A new form of play is evolving, one which is imperfect and transitional, but rich in new possibilities. Bourgeois art-historians may set out aesthetic principles which fortify the 'purity' of their art forms against the 'vandalism' of the rising classes. Piscator has captured the revolutionary novel for the stage, an achievement worth much more than all their wordy aestheticizing.

Gasbarra (*Welt am Abend*, January, 1928)

377

## The conveyor belt

We were also faced with new problems in acting technique. It was the first time an actor had been required to perform his entire role while he was being carried along or was walking or running. This made it imperative that the belts should function silently. During the first discussions the manufacturer accepted this basic condition. But when we heard the belts in action for the first time – on January 28, 1928 – they sounded like a traction engine under full steam. The belts rattled and snorted and pounded so that the whole house quaked. Even at the top of your voice you could hardly make yourself heard. The idea of dialogue on these raging monsters was quite unthinkable. I seem to remember we just sank into the orchestra seats and laughed hysterically. There were twelve days to opening night. The technicians assured us that they could cut down the noise, but there was no longer any mention of the silent operation that we had been promised. The process threatened to be long and put the production in jeopardy. As usual, I was made to see that only a fraction of my idea could be put into practice. And in this case the problem was more difficult because in Pallenberg we had an actor of unheard-of good will who would make any sacrifice to cooperate, but he was at the same time a very temperamental artist, and naturally apprehensive about the unusual apparatus, especially if it was not even going to work. The long, hard task of modifying the belts began; it occupied every minute that I did not need the stage for rehearsals. With huge quantities of graphite, soap and lubricating oil, by strengthening the stage floor with heavy wooden props, fitting new bearings, lining the chains with felt, and putting a felt underlay beneath the whole machine, the noise was reduced to a level where it no longer drowned the text completely. Nonetheless, the actors still had to keep their voices up to make themselves heard.

The rest of the set was utterly simple. The only things on the whole stage apart from the conveyor belts were two flats joined by borders, one behind the other and a cloth screen at the back. Some of the props were carried onto the open stage by the conveyor belt, others hung in the flies, so that everything could be put in and taken out quickly. It was the cleanest, simplest and most versatile set I had ever devised. Everything went off quickly as if by clockwork.

It seemed to me that this apparatus had a quality of its own; it was inherently comic. Every application of the machinery somehow made you want to laugh. There seemed to be absolute harmony between subject and machinery. And for the whole thing I had in mind a sort of knockabout style, reminiscent of Chaplin or vaudeville.

■　■　■

## Source

Piscator, E. (1929, 1980) 'Epic Satire: The Adventures of the Good Soldier Schwejk January 23, 1928 to April 12, 1928', *The Political Theatre*, trans. H. Rorrison, London: Eyre Methuen: 254–269. First published in 1929 in *Das Politische Theater*, first published in Great Britain 1980.

## Erwin Piscator (1893–1966)

The work of Piscator contains the most consistent set of experiments in staging, using all the possibilities that early twentieth-century stage technology allowed. Through his productions in Berlin throughout the 1920s and 1930s – *Sturmflut* (1926), *Hoppla, wir Leben!* (1927), *Der Kaisers Kulis* (1930) – in exile in America during the Second World War, and on his final return to Germany in the 1960s, Piscator showed a new awareness of the stage as a physical resource. He fought in the First World War, and became involved in many of the post-war Dada happenings in Berlin. The influence of Dada's harsh juxtapositions, grotesque masks, and attempts at immediacy gave Piscator's theatre a unique and exciting contemporaneity, in particular his production of Alfons Paquet's *Sturmflut (Tidal Wave)*, where the permanent setting was backed by a transparent screen with a black frame and variable aperture, onto which was projected film from four backstage projectors. In 1928 the Piscator-Bühne's greatest success was a free dramatisation of Jaroslav Hašek's novel *The Good Soldier Schwejk*, where Piscator cast a famous Viennese comedian, Max Pallenberg, as Schwejk. For the production he designed two electrically powered conveyor-belts, parallel to the line of the sets and backed by white flats. The background to Schwejk's progress across Europe was conveyed by naturalistic film and by means of a series of savage animated cartoons drawn by the satirist Georg Grosz.

After the war Brecht, who had collaborated with Piscator earlier, invited him back to Berlin to join in reviving the Berlin theatre. By this time Piscator had moved away from a directly political theatre, having also worked at the Dramatic Workshop of the New School of Social Research in New York (which trained such actors as Marlon Brando). However, in the last years of his life in West Germany he re-established himself as a master of theatrical staging in his work on a series of documentary plays such as Rolf Hochuth's *The Representative* (1964), Weiss's *The Investigation* (1965), and Kipphardt's *In the Case of Robert Oppenheimer* (1967).

In 1929 Piscator published his only book, *The Political Theatre*, from which this extract is taken. In it we see the directorial mind at work on one staging problem of the Schwejk play, the detail of which demonstrates how he maintained that theatre was a constant search 'for the basic artistic, philosophical, social, and political principles of human thought and action in our age'. The extract contains Piscator's own notes as well as extensive quotes from a contemporary account.

## Compare this article with writings by the following authors in this reader

**Appia and Craig** – similar concentration on the aesthetics of staging
**Brecht** – with whom Piscator sought for a new theatre
**Duncan** – a contemporary working in Europe in dance
**Foreman and Wilson** – visual theatre writer/directors
**Marinetti** – another radical view of theatre
**Richter** – Dada, early influences on his conception of staging
**Schlemmer** – a contemporary consideration of the staging of dance

## Further reading

Innes, C. (1972) *Erwin Piscator's Political Theatre*, Cambridge: Cambridge University Press.
Malina, J. (2012) *The Piscator Notebook*, London: Routledge.
Piscator, M.L. (1967) *The Piscator Experiment*, New York: James Heinemann.

# Chapter 49

# Yvonne Rainer

## A QUASI SURVEY OF SOME 'MINIMALIST' TENDENCIES IN THE QUANTITATIVELY MINIMAL DANCE ACTIVITY MIDST THE PLETHORA, OR AN ANALYSIS OF *TRIO A*

**A**LTHOUGH THE BENEFIT to be derived from making a one-to-one relationship between aspects of so-called minimal sculpture and recent dancing is questionable, I have drawn up a chart that does exactly that. Those who need alternatives to subtle distinction-making will be elated, but nevertheless such a device may serve as a shortcut to ploughing through some of the things that have been happening in a specialized area of dancing and once stated can be ignored or culled from at will.

It should not be thought that the two groups of elements are mutually exclusive ('eliminate' and 'substitute'). Much work being done today – both in theater and art – has concerns in both categories. Neither should it be thought that the type of dance I shall discuss has been influenced exclusively by art. The changes in theater and dance reflect changes in ideas about man and his environment that have affected all the arts. That dance should reflect these changes at all is of interest, since for obvious reasons it has always been the most isolated and inbred of the arts. What is perhaps unprecedented in the short history of the modern dance is the close correspondence between concurrent developments in dance and the plastic arts.

Isadora Duncan went back to the Greeks; Humphrey and Graham[1] used primitive ritual and/or music for structuring, and although the people who came out of the Humphrey-Graham companies and were active during the thirties and forties shared socio-political concerns and activity in common with artists of the period, their work did not reflect any direct influence from or dialogue with the art so much as a reaction to the time. (Those who took off in their own directions in the forties and fifties – Cunningham, Shearer, Litz, Marsicano, et al. – must be appraised individually. Such a task is beyond the scope of this article.) The one previous area of correspondence might be German Expressionism and Mary Wigman and her followers, but photographs and descriptions of the work show little connection.

Within the realm of movement invention – and I am talking for the time being about movement generated by means other than accomplishment of a task or dealing with an object – the most impressive change has been in the attitude to phrasing, which can be defined as the way in which energy is distributed in the execution of a movement or series of movements. What makes one kind of movement different from another is not so much variations in arrangements of parts of the body as differences in energy investment.

It is important to distinguish between real energy and what I shall call 'apparent' energy. The former refers to actual output in terms of physical expenditure on the part of the performer. It is common to hear a dance teacher tell a student that he is using 'too much energy' or that a particular movement does not require 'so much energy.' This view of energy is related to a notion of economy and ideal movement technique. Unless otherwise indicated, what I shall be talking about here is 'apparent' energy, or what is seen in terms of motion and stillness rather than of actual work, regardless of the physiological or kinesthetic experience of the dancer. The two observations – that of the performer and that of the spectator – do not always correspond. A vivid illustration of this is my *Trio A*: Upon completion two of us are always dripping with sweat while the third is dry. The correct conclusion to draw is not that the dry one is expending less energy, but that the dry one is a 'non-sweater.'

| **Objects** | **Dances** |
|:---:|:---:|
| *eliminate* | |
| *or* | |
| *minimize* | |
| | |
| 1 role of artist's hand | 1 phrasing |
| 2 hierarchical relationships of parts | 2 development and climax |
| 3 texture | 3 variation: rhythm, shape, dynamics |
| 4 figure reference | 4 character |
| 5 illusionism | 5 performance |

| 6 complexity and detail | 6 variety: phases and the spatial field |
|---|---|
| 7 monumentality | 7 the virtuosic feat and the fully extended body |

*substitute*

| 1 factory fabrication | 1 energy equality and 'found' movement |
|---|---|
| 2 unitary forms, modules | 2 equality of parts, repetition |
| 3 uninterrupted surface | 3 repetition or discrete events |
| 4 nonreferential forms | 4 neutral performance |
| 5 literalness | 5 task or tasklike activity |
| 6 simplicity | 6 singular action, event, or tone |
| 7 human scale | 7 human scale |

Much of the western dancing we are familiar with can be characterized by a particular distribution of energy: maximal output or 'attack' at the beginning of a phrase,[2] recovery at the end, with energy often arrested somewhere in the middle. This means that one part of the phrase – usually the part that is the most still – becomes the focus of attention, registering like a photograph or suspended moment of climax. In the Graham-oriented modern dance these climaxes can come one on the heels of the other. In types of dancing that depend on less impulsive controls, the climaxes are farther apart and are not so dramatically 'framed.' Where extremes in tempi are imposed, this ebb-and-flow of effort is also pronounced: in the instance of speed the contrast between movement and rest is sharp, and in the adagio, or supposedly continuous kind of phrasing, the execution of transitions demonstrates more subtly the mechanics of getting from one point of still 'registration' to another.

The term 'phrase' can also serve as a metaphor for a longer or total duration containing beginning, middle, and end. Whatever the implications of a continuity that contains high points or focal climaxes, such an approach now seems to be excessively dramatic and more simply, unnecessary.

Energy has also been used to implement heroic more-than-human technical feats and to maintain a more-than-human look of physical extension, which is familiar as the dancer's muscular 'set.' In the early days of the Judson Dance Theatre someone wrote an article and asked 'Why are they so intent on just being themselves?' It is not accurate to say that everyone at that time had this in mind. (I certainly didn't; I was more involved in experiencing a lion's share of ecstasy and madness than in 'being myself' or doing a job.) But where the question applies, it might be answered on two levels: 1) The artifice of performance has been reevaluated in that action, or what one does, is more interesting and important than the exhibition of character and attitude, and that action can best be focused on through the submerging of the personality; so ideally one is not even oneself, one is a neutral 'doer.' 2) The display of technical virtuosity and the display of the dancer's specialized body no longer make any sense. Dancers have been driven to search for an alternative context that allows for a more matter-of-fact, more concrete, more banal quality of physical being in performance, a context wherein people are engaged in actions and movements making a less spectacular demand on the body and in which skill is hard to locate.

It is easy to see why the *grand jeté* (along with its ilk) had to be abandoned. One cannot 'do' a *grand jeté*; one must 'dance' it to get it done at all, i.e., invest it with all the necessary nuances of energy distribution that will produce the look of climax together with a still, suspended extension in the middle of the movement. Like a romantic, overblown plot this particular kind of display – with its emphasis on nuance and skilled accomplishment, its accessibility to comparison and interpretation, its involvement with connoisseurship, its introversion, narcissism, and self-congratulatoriness – has finally in this decade exhausted itself, closed back on itself, and perpetuates itself solely by consuming its own tail.

The alternatives that were explored now are obvious: stand, walk, run, eat, carry bricks, show movies, or move or be moved by some *thing* rather than oneself. Some of the early activity in the area of self-movement utilized games, 'found' movement (walking, running, etc.), and people with no previous training. (One of the most notable of these early efforts was Steve Paxton's solo, *Transit*, in which he performed movement by 'marking' it. 'Marking' is what dancers do in rehearsal when they do not want to expend the full amount of energy required for the execution of a given movement. It has a very special look, tending to blur boundaries between consecutive movements.) These descriptions are not complete. Different people have sought different solutions.

Since I am primarily a dancer, I am interested in finding solutions primarily in the area of moving oneself, however many excursions I have made into pure and not-so-pure thing-moving. In 1964 I began to play around with simple one- and two-motion phrases that required no skill and little energy and contained few accents. The way in which they were put together was indeterminate, or decided upon in the act of performing, because at that time the idea of a different kind of continuity as embodied in transitions or connections between phrases did not seem to be as important as the material itself. The result was that the movements or phrases appeared as isolated bits framed by stoppages. Underscored by their smallness and separateness, they projected as perverse *tours-de-force*. Everytime 'elbow-wiggle' came up one felt like applauding. It was obvious that the idea of an unmodulated energy output as demonstrated in the movement was not being applied to the continuity. A continuum of energy was required. Duration and transition had to be considered.

Which brings me to *The Mind is a Muscle, Trio A*. Without giving an account of the drawn-out process through which this four-and-a-half-minute movement series (performed simultaneously by three people) was made, let me talk about its implications in the direction of movement-as-task or movement-as-object.

One of the most singular elements in it is that there are no pauses between phrases. The phrases themselves often consist of separate parts, such as consecutive limb articulations – 'right leg, left leg, arms, jump,' etc. – but the end of each phrase merges immediately into the beginning of the next with no observable accent. The limbs are never in a fixed, still relationship and they are stretched to their fullest extension only in transit, creating the impression that the body is constantly engaged in transitions.

Another factor contributing to the smoothness of the continuity is that no one part of the series is made any more important than any other. For four and a half minutes a great variety of movement shapes occur, but they are of equal weight and are equally emphasized. This is probably attributable both to the sameness of physical 'tone' that colors all the movements and to the attention to the pacing. I can't talk about one without talking about the other.

The execution of each movement conveys a sense of unhurried control. The body is weighty without being completely relaxed. What is seen is a control that seems geared to the *actual* time it takes the *actual* weight of the body to go through the prescribed motions, rather than an adherence to an imposed ordering of time. In other words, the demands made on the body's (actual) energy resources appear to be commensurate with the task – be it getting up from the floor, raising an arm, tilting the pelvis, etc. – much as one would get out of a chair, reach for a high shelf, or walk down stairs when one is not in a hurry.[3] The movements are not mimetic, so they do not remind one of such actions, but I like to think that in their manner of execution they have the factual quality of such actions.

Of course, I have been talking about the 'look' of the movements. In order to achieve this look in a continuity of separate phrases that does not allow for pauses, accents, or stillness, one must bring to bear many different degrees of effort just in getting from one thing to another. Endurance comes into play very much with its necessity for conserving (actual) energy (like the long-distance runner). The irony here is in the reversal of a kind of illusionism: I have exposed a type of effort where it has been traditionally concealed and have concealed phrasing where it has been traditionally displayed.

So much for phrasing. My *Trio A* contained other elements mentioned in the chart that have been touched on in passing, not being central to my concerns of the moment. For example, the 'problem' of performance was dealt with by never permitting the performers to confront the audience. Either the gaze was averted or the head was engaged in movement. The desired effect was a worklike rather than exhibitionlike presentation.

I shall deal briefly with the remaining categories on the chart as they relate to *Trio A*. Variation was not a method of development. No one of the individual movements in the series was made by varying a quality of any other one. Each is intact and separate with respect to its nature. In a strict sense neither is there any repetition (with the exception of occasional consecutive traveling steps). The series progresses by the fact of one discrete thing following another. This procedure was consciously pursued as a change from my previous work, which often had one identical thing following another – either consecutively or recurrently.

Naturally the question arises as to what constitutes repetition. In *Trio A*, where there is no consistent consecutive repetition, can the simultaneity of three identical sequences be called repetition? Or can the consistency of energy tone be called repetition? Or does repetition apply only to successive specific actions?

All of these considerations have supplanted the desire for dance structures wherein elements are connected thematically (through variation) and for a diversity in the use of phrases and space. I think two assumptions are implicit here: 1) A movement is a complete and self-contained event; elaboration in the sense of varying some aspect of it can only blur its distinctness; and 2) Dance is hard to see. It must either be made less fancy, or the fact of that intrinsic difficulty must be emphasized to the point that it becomes almost impossible to see.

Repetition can serve to enforce the discreteness of a movement, objectify it, make it more objectlike. It also offers an alternative way of ordering material, literally making the material easier to see. That most theatre audiences are irritated by it is not yet a disqualification.

My *Trio A* dealt with the 'seeing' difficulty by dint of its continual and unremitting revelation of gestural detail that did *not* repeat itself, thereby focusing on the fact that the material could not easily be encompassed.

There is at least one circumstance that the chart does not include (because it does not relate to 'minimization'), viz., the static singular object versus the object with interchangeable parts. The dance equivalent is the indeterminate performance that produces variations ranging from small details to a total image. Usually indeterminacy has been used to change the sequentialness – either phrases or larger sections – of a work, or to permute the details of a work. It has also been used with respect to timing. Where the duration of separate, simultaneous events is not prescribed exactly, variations in the relationship of these events occur. Such is the case with the trio I have been speaking about, in which small discrepancies in the tempo of individually executed phrases result in the three simultaneous performances constantly moving in and out of phase and in and out of synchronization. The overall look of it is constant from one performance to another, but the distribution of bodies in space at any given instant changes.

I am almost done. *Trio A* is the first section of *The Mind is a Muscle*. There are six people involved and four more sections. *Trio B* might be described as a VARIATION of *Trio A* in its use of unison with three people; they move in exact unison thruout. *Trio A* is about the EFFORTS of two men and a woman in getting each other aloft in VARIOUS ways while REPEATING the same diagonal SPACE pattern throughout. In *Horses* the group travels about as a unit, recurrently REPEATING six different ACTIONS. *Lecture* is a solo that REPEATS the MOVEMENT series of *Trio A*. There will be at least three more sections.

There are many concerns in this dance. The concerns may appear to fall on my tidy chart as randomly dropped toothpicks might. However, I think there is sufficient separating-out in my work as well as that of certain of my contemporaries to justify an attempt at organizing those points of departure from previous work. Comparing the dance to Minimal Art provided a convenient method of organization. Omissions and overstatements are a hazard of any systematizing in art. I hope that some degree of redress will be offered by whatever clarification results from this essay.

This article was written before the final version of *The Mind is a Muscle* had been made. (*Mat*, *Stairs*, and *Film* are not discussed.)

## Notes

1  In the case of Graham, it is hardly possible to relate her work to anything outside of theatre, since it was usually dramatic and psychological necessity that determined it.

2  The term 'phrase' must be distinguished from 'phrasing.' A phrase is simply two or more consecutive movements, while phrasing, as noted previously, refers to the manner of execution.

3  I do not mean to imply that the demand of musical or metric phrasing makes dancing look effortless. What it produces is a different kind of effort, where the body looks more extended, 'pulled up,' highly energized, ready to go, etc. The dancer's 'set' again.

■  ■  ■

## Source

Rainer, Y. (1968, 1974) 'A Quasi Survey of Some "Minimalist" Tendencies in the Quantitatively Minimal Dance Activity Midst the Plethora, or an Analysis of *Trio A'*, *Work 1961–73*, Halifax, Nova Scotia: The Press of the Nova Scotia College of Art and Design: 63–69. Written in 1966, first published (1968) in G. Battcock (ed.) *Minimal Art*.

## Yvonne Rainer (1934–)

American dancer and film maker, who began her dance training with Martha Graham in New York in 1957. In 1960 she did a summer workshop in San Francisco with Ann Halprin, where she met, amongst others, Trisha Brown and La Monte Young. She returned to New York, performed in work by Simone Forti and with James Waring and took Robert Dunn's workshop at the Cunningham Studio. In 1962 she formed Judson Dance Theatre with Steve Paxton and Ruth Emerson. Rainer made a number of dances between 1960 and 1966 that used a variety of vocabularies, props, forms and tasks. She presented *Dance for 3 People and 6 Arms* and *Ordinary Dance* as part of *A Concert of Dance* (1962), the first Judson performance.

In 1966 Rainer presented a short trio for Steve Paxton, David Gordon and herself at Judson Church, *The Mind is a Muscle, Part 1*. This four-and-a-half-minute phrase became known as *Trio A* and is celebrated as a 'paradigmatic statement of the aesthetic goals of post-modern dance' (Banes 1987: 44). Both the phrase itself and the context in which it was shown radically questioned ideas of theatricality that were current in modern dance. Its vocabulary, structure and function were democratic. It was recyclable and became part of seven of Rainer's other works in the late 1960s and in her last dance performance, *This is the Story of a Woman Who...* (1973). Between 1970 and 1973 Rainer was part of the improvisational collective, Grand Union, whose performances included her *Continuous Project Altered Daily*.

In the early 1970s she began to concentrate on film making, beginning with *Lives of Performers* (1972), *Film About a Woman Who...* (1974) and *Kristina Talking Pictures* (1976). She developed many of the concerns that had been first stated in her dance work, especially those concerned with formalism, narrative and gender. She returned to dancing in 1999 with a reconstruction of *Trio A* at Judson Memorial Church, three decades after the original.

Her 'analysis' was written shortly after the first performance of *Trio A*. She gives a detailed consideration of why she made the choices she did, comparing it to notions of minimalism then current in sculpture. She has frequently been misinterpreted and therefore regarded as a modernist. In fact, *Trio A* can be seen as an early postmodernist statement and it is the original context for this article that might have led to the confusion.

## Compare this article with writings by the following authors in this reader

**Bausch** – a different, European, perspective on dance
**Beck** – a contemporary, but contrasting, response to the times
**Boal** – whose work in a South American context stressed democracy as a political goal
**Brown** – a postmodern concern for process
**Cage** – an earlier North American statement on dance
**Grotowski and Hijikata** – antithetical approaches to the body
**LeCompte** – a contemporary woman postmodernist with a concern for process
**Marinetti** – an earlier manifesto that sought to sweep away the past

## Further reading

Banes, S. (1987) 'The Aesthetics of Denial', *Terpsichore in Sneakers: Post-Modern Dance*, Middletown: Conn.: 41–54.
Rainer, Y. (1974) *Work 1961–73*, Halifax: Nova Scotia: The Press of the Nova Scotia College of Art and Design.
Rainer, Y. (1999) *A Woman Who... Essays, Interviews, Scripts*, Baltimore: Johns Hopkins University Press.
Rainer, Y. (2006) *Feelings are Facts: A Life*, MIT Press.
Wood, C. (2007) *Yvonne Rainer: The Mind is a Muscle*, London: Afterall Books.

# Chapter 50

# Hans Richter

## HOW DID DADA BEGIN?

I N 1915, SOON AFTER the outbreak of the First World War, a rather undernourished, slightly pock-marked, very tall and thin writer and producer came to Switzerland. It was Hugo Ball, with his mistress Emmy Hennings who was a singer and poetry reader. He belonged to the 'nation of thinkers and poets', which was engaged, at that time, in quite different activities. Ball, however, had remained both a thinker and a poet: he was philosopher, novelist, cabaret performer, journalist and mystic.

> *I had no love for the death's-head hussars,*
> *Nor for the mortars with the girls' names on them,*
> *And when at last the glorious days arrived,*
> *I unobtrusively went on my way.*

(Hugo Ball)

It is impossible to understand Dada without understanding the state of mental tension in which it grew up, and without following in the mental and physical footsteps of this remarkable sceptic. (The diaries of this extraordinary man were published after his death in 1927, under the title *Flucht aus der Zeit* ['Flight from Time'].) Guided and perhaps plagued by his conscience, Ball became the human catalyst who united around himself all the elements which finally produced Dada.

It was not until many years later, when he already lay in his grave at San Abbondio, in Ticino, the little village where he had lived with his wife Emmy, that I learned about the latter part of his

life. He had renounced all the excesses of his youth, had become very devout, and had lived among poor peasants, poorer than they, giving them help whenever he could. Fourteen years after his death, people in Ticino still spoke with love and admiration of his nobility and goodness.

There can be no doubt of Ball's unswerving search for a *meaning* which he could set up against the absurd meaninglessness of the age in which he lived. He was an idealist and a sceptic, whose belief in life had not been destroyed by the deep scepticism with which he regarded the world around him.

On 1st February 1916, Ball founded the Cabaret Voltaire. He had come to an arrangement with Herr Ephraim, the owner of the Meierei, a bar in Niederdorf, a slightly disreputable quarter of the highly reputable town of Zurich. He promised Herr Ephraim that he would increase his sales of beer, sausage and rolls by means of a literary cabaret. Emmy Hennings sang *chansons*, accompanied by Ball at the piano. Ball's personality soon attracted a group of artists and kindred spirits who fulfilled all the expectations of the owner of the Meierei.

In the first Dada publication Ball writes:

When I founded the Cabaret Voltaire, I was sure that there must be a few young people in Switzerland who like me were interested not only in enjoying their independence but also in giving proof of it. I went to Herr Ephraim, the owner of the Meierei, and said, 'Herr Ephraim, please let me have your room. I want to start a night-club.' Herr Ephraim agreed and gave me the room. And I went to some people I knew and said, 'Please give me a picture, or a drawing, or an engraving. I should like to put on an exhibition in my night-club.' I went to the friendly Zurich press and said, 'Put in some announcements. There is going to be an international cabaret. We shall do great things.' And they gave me pictures and they put in my announcements. So on 5th February we had a cabaret. Mademoiselle Hennings and Mademoiselle Leconte sang French and Danish *chansons*. Herr Tristan Tzara recited Rumanian poetry. A balalaika orchestra played delightful folk-songs and dances.

I received much support and encouragement from Herr M. Slodki, who designed the poster, and from Herr Hans Arp, who supplied some Picassos, as well as works of his own, and obtained for me pictures by his friends O. van Rees and Artur Segall. Much support also from Messrs. Tristan Tzara, Marcel Janco and Max Oppenheimer, who readily agreed to take part in the cabaret. We organized a *Russian* evening and, a little later, a *French* one (works by Apollinaire, Max Jacob, André Salmon, A. Jarry, Laforgue and Rimbaud). On 26th February Richard Huelsenbeck arrived from Berlin, and on 30th March we performed some stupendous Negro music (toujours avec la grosse caisse: boum boum boum boum – drabatja mo gere drabatja mo bonoooooooooo –). Monsieur Laban was present at the performance and was very enthusiastic. Herr Tristan Tzara was the initiator of a performance by Messrs. Tzara, Huelsenbeck and Janco (the first in

Zurich and in the world) of simultaneist verse by Messrs. Henri Barzun and Fernand Divoire, as well as a *poème simultané* of his own composition, which is reproduced on pages six and seven. The present booklet is published by us with the support of our friends in France, *Italy* and Russia. It is intended to present to the Public the activities and interests of the Cabaret Voltaire, which has as its sole purpose to draw attention, across the barriers of war and nationalism, to the few independent spirits who live for other ideals. The next objective of the artists who are assembled here is the publication of a *revue internationale*. La revue paraîtra à Zurich et portera le nom 'Dada' ('Dada'). Dada Dada Dada Dada.

Zurich, 15th May 1916

I shall often quote from Ball's diaries, because I know of no better source of evidence on the moral and philosophical origins of the Dada revolt which started in the Cabaret Voltaire. It is entirely possible that any or all of the other Dadaists – Arp, Duchamp, Huelsenbeck, Janco, Schwitters, Ernst, Serner, or another – went through the same inner development, fought similar battles and were plagued by the same doubts, but no one but Ball left a record of these inner conflicts. And no one achieved, even in fragmentary form, such precise formulations as Ball, the poet and thinker.

To understand the climate in which Dada began, it is necessary to recall how much freedom there was in Zurich, even during a world war. The Cabaret Voltaire played and raised hell at No. 1, Spiegelgasse. Diagonally opposite, at No. 12, Spiegelgasse, the same narrow thoroughfare in which the Cabaret Voltaire mounted its nightly orgies of singing, poetry and dancing, lived Lenin. Radek, Lenin and Zinoviev were allowed complete liberty. I saw Lenin in the library several times and once heard him speak at a meeting in Berne. He spoke good German. It seemed to me that the Swiss authorities were much more suspicious of the Dadaists, who were after all capable of perpetrating some new enormity at any moment, than of these quiet, studious Russians . . . even though the latter were planning a world revolution and later astonished the authorities by carrying it out.

Press announcement, 2nd February 1916:

Cabaret Voltaire. Under this name a group of young artists and writers has formed with the object of becoming a centre for artistic entertainment. The Cabaret Voltaire will be run on the principle of daily meetings where visiting artists will perform their music and poetry. The young artists of Zurich are invited to bring along their ideas and contributions.

They brought them along.

On 5th February 1916, Ball writes: 'The place was full to bursting; many could not get in. About six in the evening, when we were still busy hammering and putting up Futurist posters, there appeared an oriental-looking deputation of four little men with portfolios and pictures under their arms, bowing politely many times.

'They introduced themselves: Marcel Janco the painter, Tristan Tzara, Georges Janco and a fourth, whose name I did not catch. Arp was also there, and we came to an understanding without many words. Soon Janco's opulent *Archangels* hung alongside the other objects of beauty, and, that same evening Tzara gave a reading of poems, conservative in style, which he rather endearingly fished out of the various pockets of his coat.'

Ball's night-club was an overnight sensation in Zurich.

### Cabaret

The exhibitionist assumes his stance before the curtain
and Pimpronella tempts him with her petticoats of scarlet.
Koko the green god claps loudly in the audience –
and the hoariest of old goats are roused again to lust.
Tsingtara! There is a long brass instrument.
From it dangles a pennant of spittle. On it is written: Snake.
All their ladies stow this in their fiddle-cases now
and withdraw, overcome with fear.

At the door sits the oily Camoedine.
She hammers gold coins into her thighs for sequins.
An arc-lamp puts out both her eyes;
And her grandson is crushed by the burning roof as it falls.

From the pointed ear of the donkey a clown catches
flies. His home is in another land.
Through little verdant tubes which bend
he has his links with barons in the city.

In lofty aerial tracks, where inharmonious
ropes intersect on which we whir away,
a small-bore camel makes platonic
attempts to climb; the fun becomes confused.

The exhibitionist, who in the past has tended
the curtain with a patient eye for tips,
quite suddenly forgets the sequence of events
and drives new-sprouted hordes of girls before him.

(Hugo Ball)

Readings of modern French poetry alternated with recitals by German, Russian and Swiss poets. Old music was played as well as new. This produced some unlikely combinations: Cendrars and van Hoddis, Hardekopf and Aristide Bruant, a balalaika orchestra and Werfel. Delaunay's pictures were exhibited and Erich

Mühsam's poems performed. Rubinstein played Saint-Saëns. There were readings of Kandinsky and Lasker-Schüler, as well as Max Jacob and André Salmon.

> He is a humble patron of a tenth-rate music-hall,
> where, florally tattooed, the devil-women stamp.
> Their pitchforks lure him on to sweet perditions,
> blinded and fooled, but always in their thrall.
>
> (Hugo Ball)

The poster for the Cabaret Voltaire was by the Ukrainian painter Marcel Slodki. He was later to participate from time to time, both through personal appearances and by submitting his works, but he never really belonged to Dada. He was a quiet, withdrawn individual whose voice could hardly be heard above the general uproar of the Cabaret Voltaire – or, later, that of the Dada movement.

Thus the Cabaret Voltaire was first of all a literary phenomenon. The creative energies of the group were devoted to the composition, performance and publication of poems, stories and songs. For each of these poems, songs and stories there was an appropriate style of delivery.

## Cabaret Voltaire: its members

Ball's qualities of thoughtfulness, profundity and restraint were complemented by the fiery vivacity, the pugnacity and the incredible intellectual mobility of the Rumanian poet Tristan Tzara. He was a small man, but this made him all the more uninhibited. He was a David who knew how to hit every Goliath in exactly the right spot with a bit of stone, earth or manure, with or without the accompaniment of witty *bons-mots*, back-answers and sharp splinters of linguistic granite. Life and language were his chosen arts, and the wilder the surrounding fracas, the livelier he became. The total antithesis between him and Ball brought out more clearly the qualities of each. In the movement's early, 'idealistic' period, these anti-*Dioscuri* formed a dynamic, even if serio-comic, unity.

What Tzara did not know, could not do, would not dare to do, had not yet been thought of. His crafty grin was full of humour but also full of tricks; there was never a dull moment with him. Always on the move, chattering away in German, French or Rumanian, he was the natural antithesis of the quiet, thoughtful Ball – and, like Ball, indispensable. In fact, each of these fighters for the spirit and anti-spirit of Dada was indispensable in his own way. What would Dada have been without Tzara's poems, his insatiable ambition, his manifestos, not to speak of the riots he produced in such a masterly fashion? He declaimed, sang and spoke in French, although he could do so just as well in German, and punctuated his performances with screams, sobs and whistles.

Bells, drums, cow-bells, blows on the table or on empty boxes, all enlivened the already wild accents of the new poetic language, and excited, by purely physical means, an audience which had begun by sitting impassively behind its beer-mugs. From this state of immobility it was roused into frenzied involvement with what was going on. This was Art, this was Life, and this was what they wanted! The Futurists had already introduced the idea of provocation into art and practised it in their own performances. As an art it was called Bruitism, and was later given musical status by Edgar Varèse, who followed up Russolo's discoveries in the field of noise-music, which was one of the basic contributions made by Futurism to modern music. In 1911 Russolo had built a noise-organ on which he could conjure up all the distracting sounds of everyday existence – the same sounds that Varèse later used as musical elements. This unique instrument was destroyed at the première of the Buñuel-Dali film *L'Age d'Or* at the *Cinéma 28* in Paris in 1930, when the *camelots du roi* and other reactionary groups threw stink-bombs at the screen on which this 'anti-' [Catholic] film was being shown, and then broke up the whole place: chairs, tables, pictures by Picasso, Picabia and Man Ray, and Russolo's 'bruitistic' organ, which was on show in the foyer along with the pictures. Bruitism was taken up again by the Cabaret Voltaire and gained a good deal from the furious momentum of the new movement: upwards and downwards, left and right, inwards (the groan) and outwards (the roar).

■　■　■

## Source

Richter, H. (1964, 1965) 'How Did Dada Begin?', *Dada: Art and Anti-Art*, trans. D. Britt, London: Thames & Hudson: 12–19. First published in 1964 by DuMont Schauberg, Köln, English edition 1965.

## Hans Richter (1888–1976)

Artist, film maker and writer. Together with fellow artists Hugo Ball, Hans Arp, Tristan Tzara, Marcel Janco and Richard Huelsenbeck, he launched the Dada movement in Switzerland in 1916, with the founding of the Cabaret Voltaire, in a run-down bar in Zurich. He became a film maker, and is noted especially for *Rhythmus 21* (1921), an early abstract film, and for *8X8* (1957). He was Director of New York City College Institute of Film Techniques (1942–52), and historian of the Dada movement.

Dada was essentially a reaction against what its participants saw as the meaninglessness of the war in Europe. Similarly its artistic manifestations – sound poems, collages, chance procedures, masks, dances – were anarchic reactions against established forms. The formation of the Cabaret gave a means of creating performance forms which could unite the arts, and from its beginnings in poetry and the visual arts, Dada was carried into film, music, typography, and articles of everyday use. The principle was for poetry to discard language as painting had already discarded the object, and in so doing to create provocative responses from the public: a logical destruction of logic in a futile world. Often chance became a major determinant in producing literature and performance poetry, the techniques of free association producing unexpected juxtapositions of words and sounds, seen as a creative basis on which to build a 'new and universal consciousness of art' (Huelsenbeck 1969). Dada ideas soon spread to Berlin, Cologne, Hanover, Paris and New York, where the influential presence of Marcel Duchamp became crucial in the development of American performance in dance and music.

There has always been confusion over the origins of Dada – its name, the individuals involved, its purpose and implications – and in 1964 Richter published his book to try and record what up to then had been subject to distorted accounts. In this essay he gives an apparently authoritative account of the founding of Dada, drawing largely on the diaries of Hugo Ball, the éminence grise behind the Dada idea.

## Compare this article with writings by the following authors in this reader

**Artaud** – whose theatre attempted to stir audiences from their apathy
**Cunningham** – an American approach which acknowledges Dada as an antecedent
**Goldberg** – locates the historical importance of Dada
**Hijikata** – a later exponent of chaos
**Jarry** – antecedent of Dada
**Marinetti** – the contemporary, futurist, viewpoint
**Müller** – later theatrical development of collage and conflict
**Piscator** – early staging was influenced by Dada
**Schlemmer** – another, contemporary, art perspective from the Bauhaus

## Further reading

Ball, H. (1974) *Flight Out of Time*, New York: Viking Press.
Foster, S. (2000) *Hans Richter: Activism, Modernism, and the Avant-Garde*, MIT Press.
Huelsenbeck, R. (1969) *Memories of a Dada Drummer*, New York: Viking Press.
Motherwell, R. (ed.) (1951) *The Dada Painters and Poets*, New York: Wittenborn, Schultz.
Richter, H. (1971) *Hans Richter*, ed. C. Gray, New York: Holt, Rinehart & Winston.

# Chapter 51

# Richard Schechner

## THE FIVE AVANT-GARDES OR...
## OR NONE?

### The five avant-gardes or ...

What the avant-garde has become during the past 100 years or so is much too complicated to be organized under one heading. There is an historical avant-garde, a current avant-garde (always changing), a forward-looking avant-garde, a tradition-seeking avant-garde, and an intercultural avant-garde. A single work can belong to more than one of these categories. The five avant-gardes have emerged as separable tendencies because 'avant-garde' meaning 'what's in advance of' — a harbinger, an experimental prototype, the cutting edge — no longer describes the multifid activities undertaken by performance artists, auteurs, directors, designers, actors, and scholars operating in one or more of the various 'worlds' the planet has been partitioned into. At this point, even as I use them, I voice my objection to these outdated categories. The end of the cold war dissolved the opposition between the first world and the second. The collapse of Soviet hegemony over Eastern Europe and even the territories of the USSR itself was not a spasm temporally limited to 1989–91 or spatially localized in Europe. A steady and long-term infiltration of possibilities and alternatives accompanied, forced, and highlighted the failure of Soviet communism to deliver the goods or permit an open play of ideas. Similar historical processes are at work eliding and topsy-turvying other apparently stable systems, including Europe, China, and that most stable of them all, the USA. If by 'new world order' George Bush means American hegemony (as he surely does), he is mistaken. The third and fourth worlds are everywhere. The pressures on America from the south are steadily increasing. There is a large and growing south in the USA, the UK, France, and other northern European countries. Change is coming both to China and the USA, forced on them by circumstances working themselves through in historical rather than journalistic time, As for the third world, it is character-ized by tumult and often uncontrollable transformations. The task for cultural workers is to express as clearly as we can both the emotional and the logical sense of the changes taking place. We need to find ways to celebrate individual and cultural differences, even as people work towards economic and political parity. Is such a differential egalitarianism possible?

The historical avant-garde took shape in Europe during the last decades of the nineteenth century. It soon spread to many places around the world. The plays of Ibsen, and the naturalistic style of presenting them, for example, affected the modernization of Japan and the liberation of China from the Qing Dynasty. But the first great modern avant-garde, naturalism, soon evoked its opposites in an explosion of heterodoxies: symbolism, futurism, cubism, ex-pressionism, dada, surrealism, constructivism . . . and many more with names, manifestos, and actions that came and went with such speed as to suggest their true aim: the propagation of artistic difference. Along with this was a political agenda, one of sharp opposition. Poggioli is near right when he detects in the historical avant-garde a 'prevalence of the anarchistic mentality . . . an eschatological state of mind, simultaneously messianic and apoca-lyptic' (1968: 99–100). Avant-gardists were on the left because the right was in power. When the left came to power, in the USSR for example, experimentalists were treated like kulaks, ripe for repres-sion and extermination. Look what happened to Mayakovsky and Meyerhold, who, among a host of others, were reclassified from 'revolutionary comrades' to 'enemies of the people.' Stalin pro-tected remnants of bourgeois culture, Stanislavski among them, and fostered the dullest kind of 'socialist realism.' Decades later, marching under the authority of Mao Zedong's 'little red book,' China's cultural revolution, orchestrated by Jiang Qing, actress and Mao's second wife, razed Chinese culture, both traditional and avant-garde. What Jiang produced were 'model operas,' brilliant but wooden performances expressing her own political and aes-thetic values. At present, categories like 'left' and 'right' have lost much of their meaning; they are useful only in very particular historical circumstances, not as general principles.

Regarding the historical avant-garde, Michael Kirby is on the mark when he says that

> 'avant-garde' refers specifically to a concern with the histori-cal *directionality* of art. An advanced guard implies a rear guard or at least the main body of troops following behind. . . . Some artists may accept the limits of art as

397

defined, as known, as given; others may attempt to alter, expand, or escape
from the stylistic aesthetic rules passed on to them by the culture.

(1969: 18–19)

What Kirby identifies as the avant-garde's 'impulse to redefine, to contradict, to continue the sensed directionality of art' (1969: 18–19) is the energy
source and connecting link holding together the disparate movements of the
historical avant-garde.

The historical avant-garde was characterized by the twin tendency to make
something new that was also in opposition to prevailing values. Since Romanticism, these values have been seen as social and political as well as aesthetic. The
Romantics introduced the idea that artists lived their lives in terms of their art —
that experience, display, and expression were inextricably linked, each one
functioning in terms of the others. 'Action,' whether poetic, personal, or political
(trying to affect the way society was organized) became key. Wordsworth's
description of poetry (in the 1800 'Preface' to his *Lyrical Ballads*) as the spontaneous overflow of powerful feelings . . . 'emotion recollected in tranquillity' was
soon replaced by Shelley's call for direct radical action. This affection for radical
thought, rhetoric, and action in opposition to accepted values was at the heart not
only of the historical avant-garde's politics, but also of its bohemian lifestyle.

Even the *ancien régime* was not hated as much as the new dominant class,
the bourgeoisie. Not only was the middle class in power, and to avant-gardists
therefore the cause of what was wrong with society, it was also uncultured,
grossly materialistic and greedy. Ironically, some of Shelley's heirs, in their hatred
of bourgeois values and manners, adopted aristocratic airs. Paris's Left Bank and
New York's Greenwich Village were famous as places where artists, dandies, and
radicals (not mutually exclusive categories) lived their eccentric and libidinous
lives, making art, mocking the bourgeoisie, and plotting revolution. Middle-class
people considered the artists to be neurotic, childlike, and savage — a trinity
formulated by Freud (in many ways an apologist for the Victorianism to whose
practices his 'talking cure' adjusted errants). From the bourgeois perspective,
artists were thought 'naturally' to be impetuous and irresponsible when it came
to money, sex, and politics.

After the Russian Revolution of 1917, the conjunction of revolutionary
thought and art grew stronger. Meyerhold was the most visible of a large cohort
who wanted to find a place for experimental performance in what he believed was
a new and progressive social order. For a time, until the paranoid 'man of steel'
Josef Stalin turned it off, light came from the East in the form of biomechanics,
constructivism, Russian futurism, montage, multimedia, and vibrant performance
styles combining the most recent technological innovations with traditional popular
entertainments, such as *commedia dell'arte*, circus, and the cabaret. And just as Germans fleeing Hitler in the 1930s and 1940s fertilized the artistic and intellectual
life of Great Britain and the Americas, so Russians (Czarists as well as progressives)
vitalized Western European and American theatre, film, and visual arts.

The 'current avant-garde' (second of the five types of avant-garde) is by definition what's happening *now*. Of course, 'now' is always changing – it will be different when this writing is published from what it is as I write in New York in November 1991. Today's current theatre avant-garde includes reruns of the historical avant-garde as well as the practices of formerly experimental artists whose work is by now 'classical' in terms of its predictability, solidity, and acceptance. You know what to expect from Robert Wilson, Laurie Anderson, Elizabeth LeCompte, Meredith Monk, Lee Breuer, Richard Foreman, Merce Cunningham, Pina Bausch, Rachel Rosenthal – and a bunch of younger people working in roughly the same ways as their predecessors and mentors; people like Anne Bogart, Julie Taymor, Bill T. Jones, and Martha Clarke.

The work of the current avant-garde is often excellent, virtuosic in its mastery of formerly experimental and risky materials and techniques. This mastery, coupled with a second and third generation of artists working in the same way, is what makes the current avant-garde classical. Over time, the historical avant-garde modulated into the current avant-garde: what were once radical activities in terms of artistic experimentation, politics, and lifestyles have become a cluster of alternatives open to people who wish to practice or see various kinds of theatrical art. The current avant-garde offers no surprises in terms of theatrical techniques, themes, audience interactions, or anything else. Like naturalism before it, 'avant-garde' has become a style, a way of working, rather than a bellwether. But unlike naturalism, the current avant-garde is not 'mainstream,' not what most theatres do. It is simply a menu of options drained of the fervor of their original impulses.

The current avant-garde certainly may be considered a 'new establishment.' As Graham Ley wrote, 'The continuing admiration for a select group of experimental practitioners prompts the question of whether we can have a theatrical avant-garde that would seem to be so well-established' (1991: 348). Ley identifies certain qualities of the current avant-garde that are antithetical to what drove the historical avant-garde. Chief among these are the heavy doses of money – most of it from government, big business, and foundations (where the robber barons and their descendants buried their pots of gold) – underwriting almost all of the established current avant-garde biggies from Robert Wilson and Peter Brook through to Grotowski and the Wooster Group. (Ley does not exclude me from the list of the subsidized, due to my long employment by first Tulane and then New York University.) Not only do well-known avant-gardists feed from various patrons (as did artists in the days before the marketplace), subsidy is what further generations of theatre, dance, and other artists expect as their birthright. One has to go to popular entertainments – pop music, sports, movies, and TV – to find arts conditioned by the rough-and-ready economics of the market. However 'vulgar' these entertainments, they are also often both lively and innovative, especially in the development of physical techniques (lighting, sound, ways of including the audience, 'special effects'). The current avant-garde is not only dominated by a group of oldsters (of which I am, for better or worse, one), but it is also quite clearly an established style of performance, one that in many ways is not distinguishable from orthodox theatre and dance. What innovation comes from the current avant-garde, is mostly emanating from performance art, where people are exploring such things as explicit sexual art and the combining of the extremely personal with the political.

Another wing of the current avant-garde is the activist political theatre – heir to the guerrilla and street theatre movements of the 1960s. This work is avant-garde because there has been free trade of techniques, persons, and ideas between the avant-garde and political theatre from the days of Meyerhold, Brecht, and dada. People and groups like the gay activists of ACT UP (AIDS Coalition to Unleash Power) who use guerrilla theatre to demand more AIDS research and treatment, the radical environmentalists of Greenpeace, and the 'theatre of the oppressed' of Augusto Boal are in the forefront of this kind of theatre. There are very active political theatres in Latin America, Africa, and Asia. ACT UP and Greenpeace work along two lines simultaneously: to get their message across graphically to the general public by using sudden, often disruptive, and dramatic means: and to instill solidarity among their members – nothing brings a group together faster or with more enthusiasm than collectively taking action in an atmosphere of risk. When ACT UP members lie down in the streets simulating the dead and dying of AIDS, or when a Greenpeace ship intercepts a polluting or nuclear arms-bearing vessel, not only does the media catch the event and broadcast it, but group members are also invigorated, reaffirming in public their belief in their cause and each other. In this way, the activist political theatre is a religious and ritual theatre, a theatre of 'witnesses' in the Buddhist, Christian, and Hindu sense. Indeed, the strategies of Gandhi live in the work of political theatres everywhere.

Boal's techniques, originating as opposition to Latin American fascists – Boal himself fled Brazil in the late 1960s and was later forced from Argentina; he is now based in Paris and back in Rio – are somewhat different from those of ACT UP, Greenpeace, and other guerrilla theatre operations. More than wanting to unmask, attack, and ridicule systems and people he feels are oppressive, Boal wants to empower the oppressed. To do this, he has developed, over nearly twenty-five years of work, a non-Aristotelian form of improvisational participatory performance. Boal has written extensively about his work. And his Center for the Theatre of the Oppressed in Paris regularly issues publications.

Political performance, formalist theatre, personal expression, meditative performances . . . and on through a long list of styles, objectives, social and political contexts, and venues: for a long time, since the late 1970s at least, the trend has been away from hegemony toward a situation where there are a number of styles, each of which is an alternative to all the others. Instead of fiercely contentious 'isms' struggling against the mainstream and each other (a characteristic of the historical avant-garde), the current avant-garde is one where producing organizations and particular venues celebrate their receptivity to various styles. So, for example, in New York, the Brooklyn Academy of Music's (BAM) 'Next Wave' festival is actually a compilation of many different kinds of nonnaturalistic theatre and dance, none of it really new, none of it about to replace everything that came before. BAM has no ideological or artistic program beyond presenting what Harvey Lichtenstein and his cohorts think is 'hot.' BAM titles its annual avant-garde festival the 'Next Wave,' an absurd appellation for artists most of whom have been on the scene for decades. Or take the 1991–2 season at the Public Theatre arranged by the organization's new artistic director, JoAnne Akalaitis, a Mabou Mines founder. Works range from solo pieces by people of color ('curated by George C. Wolf'), to performance art, to productions of Shakespeare, Ford, and Lorca, to Anne Bogart directing the Mabou Mines company in Brecht's *In the Jungle of Cities*. The former dominant mainstream – Broadway, the West End, regional theatres – for their part freely borrow techniques and people from the current avant-garde. Such willy-nilly eclecticism, a monoculturalist's nightmare, is the way things are going to be for a long time.

But it's not enough to divide the avant-garde in two, the historical and the current. Since at least the last great burst of new activity in performance, the late 1950s through the mid-1970s – the time of happenings (later to become performance art), environmental theatre, guerrilla theatre, ritual arts – there have been two strong themes within the avant-garde: the forward-looking and the tradition-seeking. Those who are forward-looking advocate and celebrate artistic innovation and originality. This branch of the avant-garde is heir to the historical avant-garde, on the lookout for new ideas and techniques – multimedia, video hookups and interactive telecommunications, megasound, laser light shows, cybernetics, and hyper or virtual time/space. The works of Robert LePage, Laurie Anderson, John Jesurun, and the Wooster Group come to mind. Naim June Paik and many performance artists are forward-looking in the way I am specifying; or those who showed their works at one of the PULSE shows (People Using Light, Sound, and Energy) in Santa Barbara, California. Often this kind of work fuses the avant-garde with popular entertainments because so much of pop culture is not only technologically driven but also where the money is.

The forward-looking avant-garde enacts a future that is both amazing and apocalyptic. The very technology that is celebrated is also feared; it obliterates even as it liberates. The film *Total Recall* very clearly shows this. In the movie the boundary between inner fantasy life and outer 'real' life is blurred. As in Indian tales where the dreamer wakes up into his own dream, the Schwarzenegger character in *Total Recall* doesn't know if his vacation to Mars – a violent, grotesque, and erotic place – is happening inside his mind or in ordinary time/ space. The movie ends with the hero and heroine barely escaping death as they witness the violently explosive terraforming of Mars. The old, desiccated planet is transformed into a new, fertile Edenic world. Unfortunately, this exciting denouement becomes pure Hollywood when it's stripped of its ambiguity and it's made clear that it's no dream; it's really happening.

The tradition-seeking avant-garde, so strongly present in Grotowski and Barba but visible as well in 'roots' movements and 'shamanic' performances, rejects fancy technology and cybernetics, preferring the 'wisdom of the ages,' most often found in nonWestern cultures. Jerzy Grotowski's journeys, both actual and conceptual, are paradigmatic of this tendency in the avant-garde. Grotowski's theatre education in Poland and the USSR was nothing unusual. He got his certificate in acting from the Krakow theatre school in 1955; from August 1955 until 1956 he studied directing in Moscow at the State Institute of Theatre Arts, where he became a 'fanatic disciple of Stanislavsky' and 'discovered Meyerhold' (Osinski 1986: 17–18). Then in the summer of 1956, he traveled through central Asia where, it seems, be experienced an epiphany. In Grotowski's own (translated) words:

> During my expeditions in Central Asia in 1956, between an old Turkmenian town, Ashkhabad, and the western range of the Hindu Kush Mountains, I met an old Afghan named Abdullah who performed for me a pantomime 'of the whole world,' which had been a tradition in his family. Encouraged by my enthusiasm, he told me a myth about the pantomime as a metaphor for 'the whole world.' It occurred to me then that I'm listening to my own thoughts. Nature – changeable, moveable, but permanently unique at the same time – has always been embodied in my imagination as the dancing mime, unique and universal, hiding under the glittering of multiple gestures, colors, and the grimace of life.
>
> (In Osinski 1986: 18)

Grotowski returned to Poland where he studied directing and became involved in the anti-Stalinist movements then gaining strength.

But his interest in things Asian and traditional continued. In 1957 he gave public lectures on 'The philosophical thought of the Orient,' including discussions of yoga, the Upanishads, Buddhism, Zen-Buddhism, Advaita-Vedanta, Taoism, and Confucius. In 1957 and again in 1959, Grotowski traveled to France where he saw works of Jean Vilar and Marcel Marceau, whom he greatly admired. All the while, Grotowski was directing Western works ranging from Ionesco's *The Chairs* and Chekhov's *Uncle Vanya* to an adaptation for radio of Mark Twain's *The White Elephant*. In 1959, Grotowski and critic-dramaturg Ludwik Flaszen took over Opole's Theatre of 13 Rows where they and their colleagues developed what was to be known as 'poor theatre' (see Grotowski 1968, Kumiega 1985, Osinski 1986). This style of performing – emphasizing the actors' psycho-physical abilities, refusing theatrical sets, redefining audience-performer interactions according to the needs of each production, constructing a textual montage from many sources (rather than interpreting a drama written by a single author) – was based on rigorous training founded at least initially on yoga and other principles Grotowski derived from his studies of Asian theatre and philosophies, combined with a deeply Polish Catholic and Hassidic mystic practice. In fact, Grotowski felt the similarity between these traditions, a similarity that Eugenio Barba some years later dubbed 'Eurasian theatre' (Barba: 1988). The stripped-down stage, the ritualized nature of the encounter between performers and spectators, the startling confrontation of extremely personal expression and totally composed face and body 'masks,' all were modeled to a degree after what Grotowski knew of Asian theatre, ritual, and thought. Grotowski's most audacious and experimental inventions are founded on tradition. What Artaud intuited and theorized, Grotowski researched and practiced.

In the late 1960s, Grotowski 'left the theatre.' He stopped directing plays. He began a series of research projects taking him to and putting him in touch with many artists and ritual specialists from different cultures in an attempt to find and express in specific theatrical ways – dances, songs, gestures, utterances, words – universals of performance. These research projects have had several names: theatre of sources, objective drama, ritual arts. The work is not yet complete and is probably uncompletable. It has taken Grotowski to Asia, the Americas, the Caribbean (and possibly other places too: Grotowski often travels incognito). Grotowski has not been silent regarding his work after poor theatre; and often enough he sounds classically avant-gardist:

> Art is profoundly rebellious. Bad artists *speak* of rebelling; real artists *actually* rebel. They respond to the powers that be with a concrete act: this is both the most important and the most dangerous point. Real rebellion in art is something which persists and is competent and never dilettante. When I began working with the Theatre of Sources (it was still the period of participatory theatre) it was quite clear that in certain traditional human activities – which may be called religious – from different cultures where tradition still existed, it was possible to see, in some cases, participatory theatre without banality. It soon became clear that not all the differences can be reduced, that we can't alter our own conditioning, that I shall never be a Hindu even if I am consecrated by the Hindus. One can, however, move toward what precedes the differences. Why do the African hunter from the Kalahari, the French hunter from the outskirts of Saintes, the Bengali hunter, and the Huichol hunter from Mexico all adopt the same body position when they go hunting, with the spinal backbone leaning slightly forward, and the knees slightly bent in a position that is sustained at the base by the sacrum-pelvis complex? And why can only one kind of rhythmic movement derive from this position? And what use can be made of this way of walking? There is a very simple, very easy level of analysis: if the weight of the body is on one foot and you move the other foot, you don't make any noise and you can also move very slowly without stopping. In this way certain animals remain unaware of your presence. But this isn't the important thing. What is important is that there exists a certain primary position of the human body. It's a position which goes back so far that it was probably the position not only of homo sapiens, but also of homo erectus, and connected in some way with the appearance of man. An extremely ancient position connected with what some Tibetans call the 'reptile' aspect. In the Afro-Caribbean culture this position is linked more precisely with the grass snake, and in the Hindu culture linked with the Tantra, you

have this snake asleep at the base of the backbone. We are now touching on something which concerns my present work [1985]. I began asking myself, at the end of the period of the Theatre of Sources, how people used this primary energy, how, through differing techniques elaborated in the traditions, people found access to this ancient body of man. I have traveled a lot, I've read numerous books, I have found numerous traces.

(Grotowski 1987: 30–5)

It is not necessary to summarize Grotowski's work over the past twenty-five years to note two things. It remains in the vanguard of experimental work concerning performance (if not strictly theatre in the Western sense); and it is deeply traditional in a way that Grotowski himself, among others, is defining.

Eugenio Barba, Grotowski's longtime colleague and the founder-director of Odin Teatret, one of Europe's leading experimental theatres, challenges Western orthodoxy with Asian practice.

Why in the Western tradition, as opposed to what happens in the Orient, has the actor become specialised [. . . instead of being able to act, dance, mime, and sing?]. Why in the West does the actor tend to confine herself within the skin of only one character in each production? Why does she not explore the possibility of creating the context of an entire story, with many characters, with leaps from the general to the particular, from the first to the third person, from the past to the present, from the whole to the part, from persons to things?

(1988: 126)

Barba proposes an experimental theatre of roots.

Here the term 'roots' becomes paradoxical: it does not imply a bond with ties to a place, but an ethos which permits us to change places. Or better: it represents the force which causes us to change our horizons precisely because it roots us to a center.

(1988: 128)

The roots movement is not only of the West. Re-examining and redefining tradition is a characteristic of the avant-garde in India, Japan, and elsewhere. Suresh Awasthi writes:

I am taking the risk of giving a label – 'theatre of roots' – to the unconventional theatre which has been evolving for some two decades in India as a result of modern theatre's encounter with tradition. . . . Directors like B.V. Karanth, K.N. Panikkar, and Ratan Thiyam have had meaningful encounters with tradition, and, with their work, reversed the colonial course of contemporary theatre. . . . It sounds paradoxical, but their theatre is both avant-garde in the context of conventional realistic theatre, and part of the 2,000-year-old *Natyasastra* tradition.

(1989: 48)

Awasthi points out that the 'theatre of roots' must be seen against the backdrop of more than a century of Western naturalistic theatre which is the mainstream in India. Some qualities of the 'theatre of roots' – rejection of the proscenium stage, closer contact between spectators and performers, integration of music, mime, gesture, and literary text – are identical to the experimental theatre program practiced by environmental theatre workers in the West. Of course, this would be so: many of the Western experiments were modeled on the kinds of performances directors like me studied and/or saw in India or elsewhere. That this same avant-garde impulse should now be affecting modern (that is, orthodox or mainstream) Indian theatre is only to be expected.

In Japan, butoh, a word which used to mean 'ancient dance,' now refers to an intense, physically extreme, and rebellious avant-garde performance art developed by Kazuo Ohno and the late Tatsumi Hijikata. Butoh is practiced by Kazuko Shiraishi, Min Tanaka, Natsuo Nakajima, and several groups (Dai Rakuda-kan, Muteki-sha, and Sankai Juku are the best known). Described by Bonnie Sue Stein as 'shocking, provocative, physical, spiritual, erotic, grotesque, violent, cosmic, nihilistic, cathartic, [and] mysterious' (1986: 111), butoh is closely linked to noh and kabuki as well as other traditional Japanese arts.

> Butoh is an anti-traditional tradition seeking to erase the heavy imprint of Japan's strict society and offering unprecedented freedom of artistic expression. . . . Nakajima said, 'We found that we were making the same discoveries as noh actors made, using some of the same terminology, but we had never learned these forms.'
>
> (Stein 1986: 111)

The images and actions butoh performers create are striking. Ohno in his eighties still performs the movements of a young coquette, her face painted white, her lips scarlet. 'He drapes himself across the edge of the stage in the serpentine curves of traditional femininity, then kicks his foot high like a carefree young lover. To the slow koto music, he skips, flutters, and poses' (Stein 1986: 107). Or Sankai Juku's nearly naked performers, their bodies powdered white, who dangle upside down far above the street, held aloft by ropes tied around their ankles. In Seattle in 1985, a rope broke and a Sankai Juku dancer plunged to his death. But risk is what butoh is about. Often performing outdoors in extremely harsh weather, forcing their bodies against rocks or into icy seawater, their teeth blacked out or painted, butoh performers awaken Japan's shamanic heritage, demonic mythology, and folk theatre. Butoh performers are also disruptive bohemians, canny city-based artists consciously playing out their subversive countertext mocking Japan's hyperorganized social life.

Examples like 'roots' from India and butoh from Japan could be multiplied from all around the world. There is no area, be it Micronesia, the Pacific Rim, West Africa, the Circumpolar Region, or wherever, which does not have artists actively trying to use, appropriate, reconcile, come to terms with, exploit, understand – the words and political tone vary, but the substance doesn't – the relationships between local cultures in their extreme particular historical development and the increasingly complex and multiple contacts and interactions not only among various cultures locally and regionally but on a global and interspecific scale. Fitfully, unevenly, and with plenty of cruelty, a planetary human culture is emerging which is aware of, if not yet acting responsibly toward, the whole geobiocultural system. Founded on certain accepted values which express themselves abstractly as mathematics and materially as technology, this planetary culture is engaging more and more scientists, social activists, and artists concerned with mapping, understanding, representing, and preserving the earth as an integrated geobiocultural system.

When I say 'accepted values' I don't mean these are God-given or inherent in nature or experience. They are constructed and imposed. These imposed values – mathematics and its expression in technology – can be used for good or bad. What constitutes good and bad is, of course, what philosophers, religious and spiritual people, and artists want to find out – and impose. No matter what is written or spoken at any given time – the Bible, the Koran, the Upanishads – history teaches that the question of good and bad is always open. Inquisitors used the Bible, bloody Muslim zealots the Koran, and the architects of the Indian caste system the Upanishads. Which leads me to the fifth kind of avant-garde, the intercultural. For whatever reasons – leftover colonialism, American imperialism, the hunger of people everywhere for material goods, the planetary spread of modernism, the ubiquity of a 'cosmopolitan style' in everything from airports to clothes – artists of the avant-garde are producing works on or across various borders: political, geographical, personal, generic, and conceptual. In a world where so-called universal values each day run up against deeply held local values and experiences, the result is clash, disturbance, turbulence, unease about the future, and hot argument about what the past was.

As intercultural performance artist Guillermo Gomez-Pena says:

> I physically live between two cultures and two epochs. . . . When I am on the US side, I have access to high-technology and specialized information. When I cross back to Mexico, I get immersed in a rich political culture. . . . When I return to California, I am part of the multicultural thinking emerging from the interstices of the US's ethnic milieus. . . . I walk the fibres of this transition in my everyday life, and I make art about it.
>
> (1991: 22–3)

This kind of uneasiness marks many in the intercultural avant-garde. It is not mostly a question of the artist not knowing where she lives. It is about belonging to more than one culture, subscribing to contradictory values, conflicting aesthetic canons. Salman Rushdie well knows the contradictions between Western liberal and Muslim fundamentalist values as they apply to literature and life. Rushdie has said he'd like to belong both to the Western and Islamic worlds. And within every nation many people are living difficult, sometimes exciting, multiple lives. The 'nation' no longer describes how or even where hundreds of millions of people live. As Sun Huizhu, aka William Sun, a leading young Chinese playwright who since the crushing of the democracy movement in Tiananmen Square in June 1989 has been unable to return to his native Shanghai, says:

> I would like to call on artists to pay more attention to an increasingly important reality. More and more people of different cultures are interacting and having problems in their interactions. As intercultural artists – often as ambassadors to other cultures – can we artists do something to address this issue and help solve some of those problems?[1]

Engaging intercultural fractures, philosophical difficulties, ideological contradictions, and crumbling national myths does not necessarily lead to avant-garde performances. Intercultural performances occur across an enormous range of venues, styles, and purposes. What is avant-garde is when the performance does not try to heal over rifts or fractures but further opens these for exploration. For example, I would say that Peter Brook's *The Mahabharata* was intercultural but not avant-garde, while Gomez-Pena's solo performances as *Border Brujo* or the *Warrior for Gringostroika* definitely are. The difference is that Brook wants to elide difference; he is looking for what unites, universalizes, makes the same. The conflicts in his Euro-Indic epic are philosophical, personal, familial, and religious – not intercultural. Brook assumes – as the English who own Shakespeare do – that certain works operate at the 'human' rather than cultural level. His *Mahabharata* does not interrogate the epic or subvert it; nor are spectators to regard with anything but liberal approval the 'international cast' Brook assembled to enact not only the epic story but also the universalist doctrine that under the skin all humans are the same. Don't get me wrong. I support nontraditional, color-blind, culture-blind casting (see Schechner 1989a). But in the case of Brook's *Mahabharata* such casting could have been the occasion for an exploration of the tensions between nonracialist universalism and the ethnic, nationalist, religious, and racial jungle of current world politics and personal relations.

## . . . Or none?

Of what use is dividing the avant-garde into five? These categories clearly overlap. The current avant-garde includes work that is forward-looking, tradition-seeking, and intercultural. But despite the rudeness of the division, the operation reminds us of how complex, how multiple, the avant-garde has become. We can also see how very far the current avant-garde is from the historical avant-garde. The current avant-garde is neither innovative nor in advance of. Like a mountain, it just is. Although the term 'avant-garde' persists in scholarship as well as journalism, it no longer serves a useful purpose. It really doesn't mean anything today. It should be used only to describe the historical avant-garde, a period of innovation extending roughly from the end of the nineteenth century to the mid-1970s (at most). Saying something is avant-garde may carry a cache of shock, of newness, but in the West, at least, there is little artists can do, or even ought to do, to shock audiences (though quite a bit can offend them). And why try to shock? There are no surprises in terms of technique, theme, or approach. Everything from explicit sex shows, site-specific work, participatory performance, political theatre and guerrilla theatre (of the kind Greenpeace or ACT UP now do), to postmodern dance, the mixing of personal narratives with received texts, the deconstruction of texts, the blurring of boundaries between genres and so on, has been done and done again many times, over the past forty years. And if the scope is opened to 100 years, what in today's performance world can be said to be new? But the question is not, 'Can anything new happen?', but 'Who cares? Does it matter?' Who today could write manifestos comparable to the febrile outpourings of Artaud, palpitating with hatred, rage, and hope? Who would want to? Is anyone waiting for an Artaud to come around again?

I doubt it. A Rubicon has been crossed. Events today are recorded, replayed, ritualized, and recycled. And if Artaud were to show up, he would be accepted, put in his proper place. The limitless horizons of expectations that marked the modern epoch and called into existence endless newness have been transformed into a global hothouse, a closed environment. I do not agree with Baudrillard that everything is a simulation. But neither do we live in a world of infinite possibilities or originalities. A long neomedieval period has begun. Or, if one is looking for historical analogies, perhaps neo-Hellenistic is more precise. A certain kind of Euro-American cultural style is being extended, imposed, willingly received (the reactions differ) by many peoples in all parts of the world. Exactly what shape this style will take, what its dominant modes of thought will be, are not yet clear. But it will be a conservative age intellectually and artistically. That does not mean reactionary or without compassion. Nor is the kind of conservatism I am talking about incompatible with democratic socialism. It is a conservatism based on the need to save, recycle, use resources parsimoniously. It is founded on the availability of various in-depth 'archives' of many different prior experiences, artworks, ideas, feelings, and texts. This stored and recallable prior knowledge is being used to avoid repeating certain kinds of events as well as to promote certain new kinds of events. Local violence increases, no one seems to care how many die if the bloodshed, starvation, or plague is 'limited' (not in danger of becoming pandemic). What those in control fear is global violence, a threat to the established order not simply emergent but already firmly in place. The world's peoples are reminded daily of what will happen if global violence – to the environment, to populations, to species – is not brought under control. At the same time, entertainment expands its scope to include almost anything that happens that is technically witnessed and can be edited and played back. Art comes in several mutually reinforcing varieties: that which passes the time of those with enough money to buy tickets; that which excites without satisfying the appetites of its consumers; that which shows off the wealth, power, and taste of its patrons; that which is acquired as an investment. Popular entertainment follows roughly the same path.

To recycle, reuse, archive and recall, to perform in order to be included in an archive (as a lot of performance artists do), to seek roots, explore and maybe even plunder religious experiences, expressions, practices, and liturgies to make art (as Grotowski and others are doing) is to ritualize; not just in terms of subject matter and theme, but also structurally, as form. Ethologists and psychologists have shown that the 'oceanic feeling' of belonging, ecstasy, and total participation that many experience when ritualizing works by means of repetitive rhythms, sounds, and tones which effectively 'tune' to each other the left and right hemispheres of the cerebral cortex (see d'Aquili et al. 1979; Eibl-Eibesfeldt 1979; Fischer 1971; and Turner 1983). This understanding of ritual, as a process applying to a great range of human activities rather than as something tethered to religion, is a very important development. The relatively tight boundaries that locked the various spheres of performance off from each other have been punctured. It is doubtful if these boundaries ever really functioned, in fact. Certainly they didn't in popular entertainments and religious rituals. The boundaries, in fact, are the ghosts of neoclassical and Renaissance readings of the Aristotelian 'unities.' Keeping each genre in its place is a last ditch regressive action mounted by some critics and academics.

The four great spheres of performance – entertainment, healing, education, and ritualizing – are in play with each other. This playing (and it can be a very serious matter) is the subject of this book. What used to be a tightly boundaried, limited field has expanded exponentially. Each of the performance spheres can be called by other names. Entertainment includes aesthetics, the arrangement and display of actions in ways that are 'satisfying' or 'beautiful' (according to particular and local cultural canons). Education includes all kinds of political performances designed to exhort, convince, and move to action. Healing performances include shamanism, the ostensive display of hi-tech medical equipment, the bedside manner, and all kinds of interactive psychotherapies.

As the writings in this book show, I am of at least two minds regarding all this. I am enthusiastic about the expanding field of performance and its scholarly adjunct, performance studies. Performative analysis is not the only interpretation possible, but it is a very effective method for a time of charged rhetorics, simulations and scenarios, and games played on a global scale. It has always been a good method for looking at small-scale, face-to-face interactions. The public display of these 'for fun' may be taken as an operative definition of drama. But only a small number of artworks relate creatively and critically to the worlds around them. These are what used to be the avant-garde, but which today, as I've been saying, barely owns its name. A century from now the world may be running on new fuels, the automobile may have passed away, human settlements may exist on the moon and elsewhere – and on through a list of as yet barely imaginable changes and technological improvements. The basic tendency of all these changes has already been set. That tendency is to use without using up; to reserve the ability to repeat; to test through modeling, virtual experience, and other kinds of mathematical and analogical rehearsing.

Where does that leave Jayaganesh?

The writings in this book all relate to aspects of what I have called the 'broad spectrum' of performance (see Schechner 1988, 1989b, 1990). The broad spectrum includes performative behavior, not just the performing arts, as a subject for serious scholarly study. This book is one contribution to this big project. How is performance used in politics, medicine, religion, popular entertainments, and ordinary face-to-face interactions? What are the similarities and differences between live and mediated performances? The various and complex relationships among players – spectators, performers, authors, and directors – can be pictured as a rectangle, a performance 'quadrilogue.' Studying the interactions, sometimes easy, sometimes tense, among the speakers in the quadrilogue is what performance studies people do. These studies are intensely interdisciplinary, intercultural, and intergenric. Performance studies builds on the emergence of a postcolonial world where cultures are colliding, interfering with, and fertilizing each other. Arts and academic disciplines alike are most alive at their ever-changing borders. The once distinct (in the West at least) genres of music, theatre, and dance are interacting with each other in ways undreamt-of just thirty-five years ago. These interactions are both expressive of and part of a larger movement culturally.

## Note

1   Sun made this statement during a five-day conference on intercultural performance held in Bellagio, Italy in February 1991. . . . Papers and proceedings from the conference will be published in 1994.

## References

Awasthi, S. (1989), '"Theatre of roots": encounter with tradition,' *TDR, The Drama Review* 33 (4): 48–69.

Barba, E. (1988), 'Eurasian theatre', *TDR, The Drama Review* 32 (3): 126–30.

d'Aquili, E.G., Laughlin, C.D. Jr., and McManus, J. (1979), *The Spectrum of the Ritual*, New York: Columbia University Press.

Eibl-Eibesfeldt, I. (1979), 'Ritual and ritualization from a biological perspective,' in M. von Cranach, K. Foppa, W. Lepenies and D. Ploog (eds) *Human Ethology*, Cambridge: Cambridge University Press.

Fischer, R. (1971), 'A cartography of the ecstatic and meditative states,' *Science* 174 (26 November): 897–904.

Gomez-Pena, G. (1991), 'A binational performance pilgrimage,' *TDR, The Drama Review* 35 (3): 22–45.

Grotowski, J. (1968), *Towards a Poor Theatre*, Holstebro: Odin Teatret Verlag.

—— (1987), 'Tu es le fils de quelqu'un [You are someone's son],' *TDR, The Drama Review* 31 (3): 30–41.

Kirby, M. (1969), *The Art of Time*, New York: E. P. Dutton.

Kumiega, J. (1985), *The Theatre of Grotowski*, London and New York: Methuen.

Ley, G. (1991), 'Sacred idiocy: the avant-garde as alternative establishment,' *New Theatre Quarterly* VII (28) (November): 348–52.

Osinski, Z. (1986), *Grotowski and His Laboratory*, New York: PAJ Publications.

Poggioloi, R. (1968), *The Theory of the Avantgarde*, Cambridge, Mass.: Harvard University Press.

Schechner, R. (1988), 'Performance Studies: the broad spectrum approach,' *TDR, The Drama Review* 32 (3): 4–6.

—— (1989a), 'Race free, gender free, body-type free, age free casting,' *TDR, The Drama Review* 33 (1): 4–12.

—— (1989b), '*PAJ* distorts the broad spectrum,' *TDR, The Drama Review* 33 (2): 4–9.

—— (1990), 'Performance Studies: the broad spectrum approach,' *National forum* 70 (3): 15–16.

Stein, B.S. (1986), 'Butoh: "Twenty Years Ago We Were Crazy, Dirty, and Mad,"' *TDR, The Drama Review* 30 (2): 107–26.

Turner, V. (1983), 'Body, brain and culture,' *Zygon* 18 (3): 221–45.

■  ■  ■

## Source

Schechner, R. (1993) 'Introduction: The five avant-gardes or . . . [and] . . . Or none?', *The Future of Ritual: Writings on Culture and Performance*, London: Routledge: 5–21.

## Richard Schechner (1934–)

Director, writer, theorist; founder of the Performance Group, New York (1967–80). His 1968 theatre piece, *Dionysus in '69*, introduced major elements of ritual into performance, one of his recurrent interests as both director and writer. He founded the influential *Tulane Drama Review* at Tulane University,[1] specifically to explore modes of non-verbal performance communication, and continues to edit *The Drama Review*. In *Commune* (1971) he selected at random fifteen members of the audience to act as villagers in a reconstruction of the Vietnam My Lai massacre, emphasising the Performance Group's interest in creating direct participation on the part of the spectators. Schechner coined the term 'Environmental Theatre' to describe performances which took inspiration from the specific reception conditions, and the work often blurred reality and performance as in his version of *The Balcony* (1979), the last of

411

the Performance Group's creations, after which it was dissolved. He is University Professor at New York University, Tisch School of the Arts.

Schechner's theoretical and critical writings are also of profound importance in the approach he adopts as a result of his practice as director. His distinctions between drama, theatre, script and performance relate the field to that of historians, archaeologists and anthropologists, and have influenced generations of Western practitioners and thinkers. For Schechner, therefore, the drama is 'what the writer writes'; the script is the code of a particular production; the theatre is 'the specific set of gestures performed by the performer in any given performance'; the performance is the totality of the event for both performers and audience. As both director and writer Schechner is concerned to make performers and audience aware of the interlinking of all these ideas and definitions, often taking examples from non-Western cultures, and drawing on his travels in Asia and the Far East. Schechner's essay attempts a historical and philosophical definition of the notion of the avant-garde. In doing so he refers to most of the figures included in this book. It is an excellent example of both the clarity and the importance of his theoretical writing, marking him out as one of the few director-theorists whose work is constantly breaking new boundaries in the analysis of performance.

## Compare this article with writings by the following authors in this reader

**Beck** – an American theatre contemporary
**Brook** – a European view of intercultural experiment
**Cage** – who also used non-Western thought and forms
**Goldberg** – an art historical view
**Hijikata** – a Japanese view of the avant-garde
**LeCompte** – who worked with Schechner before founding the Wooster Group

## Further reading

Schechner, R. (1978) *Environmental Theatre*, New York: Hawthorn.
Schechner, R. (1988) *Performance Theory*, London: Routledge.
Schechner, R. (2002) *Performance Studies: An Introduction*, London: Routledge.
Turner, V. (1969) *The Ritual Process*, Chicago: Aldine.

## Note

1    Then known as *The Tulane Drama Review*, later as *The Drama Review*, published from New York University, and now, usually, simply *TDR*.

# Oskar Schlemmer

## MAN AND ART FIGURE

T HE HISTORY of the theater is the history of the transfiguration of the human form. It is the history of *man* as the actor of physical and spiritual events, ranging from naïveté to reflection, from naturalness to artifice.

The materials involved in this transfiguration are form and color, the materials of the painter and sculptor. The arena for this transfiguration is found in the constructive fusion of *space and building*, the realm of the architect. Through the manipulation of these materials the role of the artist, the synthesizer of these elements, is determined.

One of the emblems of our time is *abstraction*. It functions, on the one hand, to disconnect components from an existing and persisting whole, either to lead them individually *ad absurdum* or to elevate them to their greatest potential. On the other hand, abstraction can result in generalization and summation, in the construction in bold outline of a new totality.

A further emblem of our time is *mechanization*, the inexorable process which now lays claim to every sphere of life and art. Everything which can be mechanized *is* mechanized. The result: our recognition of that which can *not* be mechanized.

And last, but not the least, among the emblems of our time are the new potentials of technology and invention which we can use to create altogether new hypotheses and which can thus engender, or at least give promise of, the boldest fantasies.

The theater, which should be the image of our time and perhaps the one art form most peculiarly conditioned by it, must not ignore these signs.

*Stage (Bühne)*, taken in its general sense, is what we may call the entire realm lying between religious cult and naïve popular entertainment. Neither of these things, however, is really the same thing as stage. Stage is *representation* abstracted from the natural and directing its effect at the human being.

This confrontation of passive spectator and animate actor preconditions also the form of the stage, at its most monumental as the antique arena and at its most primitive as the scaffold in the market place. The need for concentration resulted in the peep show or 'picture frame,' today the 'universal' form of the stage. The term *theater* designates the most basic nature of the stage: make-believe, mummery, metamorphosis. Between cult and theater lies 'the stage seen as a moral institution'; between theater and popular entertainment lie variety (vaudeville) and circus: the stage as an institution for the artiste. [See diagram opposite.]

The question as to the origin of life and the cosmos, that is, whether in the beginning there was Word, Deed, or Form – Spirit, Act, or Shape – Mind, Happening, or Manifestation – pertains also to the world of the stage, and leads us to a differentiation of:

the *oral or sound stage (Sprech-oder Tonbühne)* of a literary or musical event;
the *play stage (Spielbühne)* of a physical-mimetic event;
the *visual stage (Schaubühne)* of an optical event.

Each of these stage forms has its corresponding representative, thus:

the *author* (as writer or composer) who is the creator of the word or musical sound;
the *actor* whose body and its movements make him the player;
the *designer* who is the builder of form and color.

Each of these stage forms can exist for itself and be complete within itself.

The combination of two or all three stage forms – with one of them always predominating – is a question of weight distribution, and is something that can be perfected with mathematical precision. The executor of this process is the universal *regisseur* or *director*. E.g.:

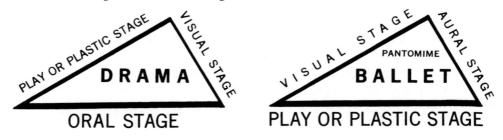

# SCHEME FOR STAGE, CULT, AND POPULAR ENTERTAINMENT ACCORDING TO:

| PLACE | PERSON | GENRE | SPEECH | MUSIC | DANCE |
|---|---|---|---|---|---|
| TEMPLE | PRIEST | RELIGIOUS CULT ACTIVITY | SERMON | ORATORIO | DERVISH |
| | | | | | |
| ARCHITECTURAL STAGE | PROPHET | | ANCIENT TRAGEDY | EARLY OPERA (e.g. Handel) | MASS GYMNASTICS |
| STYLIZED OR SPACE STAGE | SPEAKER | | SCHILLER ("BRIDE OF MESSINA") | WAGNER | CHORIC DANCE |
| THEATER OF ILLUSION | ACTOR | | SHAKESPEARE | MOZART | BALLET |
| WINGS AND BORDERS | PERFORMER (COMMEDIAN) | | IMPROVISATION—COMMEDIA DELL'ARTE | OPERA BUFFA OPERETTA | MIME & MUMMERY |
| SIMPLEST STAGE OR APPARATUS & MACHINERY | ARTISTE | | CONFERENCIER (M.C.) | MUSIC HALL SONG JAZZ BAND | CARICATURE & PARODY |
| PODIUM SCAFFOLD | ARTISTE | | CLOWNERY | CIRCUS BAND | ACROBATICS |
| FAIRGROUND SIDESHOW | FOOL JESTER | FOLK ENTERTAINMENT | DOGGEREL BALLAD | FOLK SONG | FOLK DANCE |

Center diagram (GENRE column):

PEEP SHOW ("picture frame")

ARENA — CONSECRATED STAGE / FESTIVAL STAGE — BORDERLINE — THEATER — BORDERLINE — CABARET / VARIETÉ / (Vaudeville) CIRCUS — ARENA

STAGE

From the standpoint of *material* the actor has the advantages of immediacy and independence. He constitutes his own material with his body, his voice, his gestures, and his movements. Today, however, the once noble type who was both the poet and the projector of his own word has become an ideal. At one time Shakespeare, who was an actor before he was a poet, filled this role — so, too, did the improvising actors of the *commedia dell' arte*. Today's actor bases his existence as player on the writer's word. Yet when the word is silent, when the body alone is articulate and its play is on exhibition — as a dancer's is — then it is free and is its own lawgiver.

The material of the author is *word or sound*.

Except for the unusual circumstance in which he is his own actor, singer, or musician, he creates the representational material for transmission and reproduction on the stage, whether it is meant for the organic human voice or for artificial, abstract instruments. The higher the state of perfection of the latter, the broader their formative potential, while the human voice is and remains a limited, if unique, phenomenon. Mechanical reproduction by means of various kinds of technological equipment is now capable of replacing the sound of the musical instrument and the human voice or of detaching it from its source, and can enlarge it beyond its dimensional and temporal limitations.

The material of the formative artist — painter, sculptor, architect — is *form and color*.

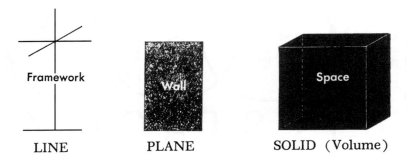

LINE      PLANE      SOLID (Volume)

These formative means, invented by the human mind, can be called *abstract* by virtue of their artificiality and insofar as they represent an undertaking whose purpose, contrary to nature, is order. Form is manifest in extensions of height, breadth, and depth; as line, as plane, and as solid or volume. Depending on these extensions, form becomes then linear framework, wall, or space, and, as such, rigid — i.e., tangible — form.

Non-rigid, intangible form occurs as light, whose linear effect appears in the geometry of the light beam and of pyrotechnical display, and whose solid- and space-creating effect comes through illumination. To each of these manifestations of light (which in themselves are already colored — only nothingness is without color) can be added coloring (*intensifying*) color.

416

Color and form reveal their elementary values within the constructive manipulation of architectonic space. Here they constitute both object and receptacle, that which is to be filled and fulfilled by Man, the living organism.

In painting and sculpture, form and color are the means of establishing these connections with organic nature through the representation of its phenomena. Man, its chief phenomenon, is both an organism of flesh and blood and at the same time the exponent of number and 'Measure of All Things' (the Golden Section).

These arts – architecture, sculpture, painting – are fixed. They are momentary, frozen motion. Their nature is the immutability of not an accidental but a typified condition, the stability of forces in equilibrium. And thus what may appear at first as a deficiency, particularly in our age of motion, is actually their greatest merit.

The stage as the arena for successive and transient action, however, offers *form and color in motion*, in the first instance in their primary aspect as separate and individual mobile, colored or uncolored, linear, flat, or plastic forms, but furthermore as fluctuating, mobile space and as transformable architectonic structures. Such kaleidoscopic play, at once infinitely variable and strictly organized, would constitute – theoretically – the *absolute* visual stage (*Schaubühne*). Man, the animated being, would be banned from view in this mechanistic organism. He would stand as 'the perfect engineer' at the central switchboard, from where he would direct this feast for the eyes.

Yet all the while Man seeks *meaning*. Whether it is the Faustian problem whose goal is the creation of Homunculus or the anthropomorphic impulse in Man which

created his gods and idols, he is incessantly seeking his likeness, his image, or the sublime. He seeks his equal, the superman, or the figures of his fancy.

Man, the human organism, stands in the cubical, abstract space of the stage. Man and Space. Each has different laws of order. Whose shall prevail?

Either abstract space is adapted in deference to natural man and transformed back into nature or the imitation of nature. This happens in the theater of illusionistic realism.

Or natural man, in deference to abstract space, is recast to fit its mold. This happens on the abstract stage.

The laws of cubical space are the invisible linear network of planimetric and stereometric relationships. (See above sketch.) This mathematic corresponds to the inherent mathematic of the human body and creates its balance by means of movements, which by their very nature are determined *mechanically and rationally*. It is the geometry of calisthenics, eurhythmics, and gymnastics. These involve the *physical attributes* (together with facial stereotypy) which find expression in acrobatic precision and in the mass calisthenics of the stadium, although there is no conscious awareness of spatial relationships here. (See sketch, p. 419, top.)

The laws of organic man, on the other hand, reside in the invisible functions of his inner self: heartbeat, circulation, respiration, the activities of the brain and nervous system. If these are to be the determining factors, then their center is the human being, whose movements and emanations create an imaginary space. (See sketch, p. 419, bottom.) Cubical-abstract space is then only the horizontal and vertical framework for this flow. These movements are *determined organically and emotionally*. They constitute the *psychical impulses* (together with the mimetics of the face), which find expression in the great actor and in the mass scenes of great tragedy.

*Invisibly involved with all these laws is Man as Dancer* (Tänzermensch). *He obeys the law of the body as well as the law of space; he follows his sense of himself as well as his sense of embracing space.* As the one who gives birth to an almost endless range of expression, whether in free abstract movement or in symbolic pantomime, whether he is on the bare stage or in a scenic environment constructed for him, whether he speaks or sings, whether he is naked or costumed, the *Tänzermensch* is the medium of transition into the great world of the theater (*das grosse theatralische Geschehen*). Only one branch of this world, the metamorphosis of the human figure and its abstraction, is to be outlined here.

The transformation of the human body, its metamorphosis, is made possible by the *costume*, the disguise. Costume and mask emphasize the body's identity or they change it; they express its nature or they are purposely misleading about it; they stress its conformity to organic or mechanical laws or they invalidate this conformity.

The native costume, as produced by the conventions of religion, state, and society, is different from the theatrical stage costume. Yet the two are generally

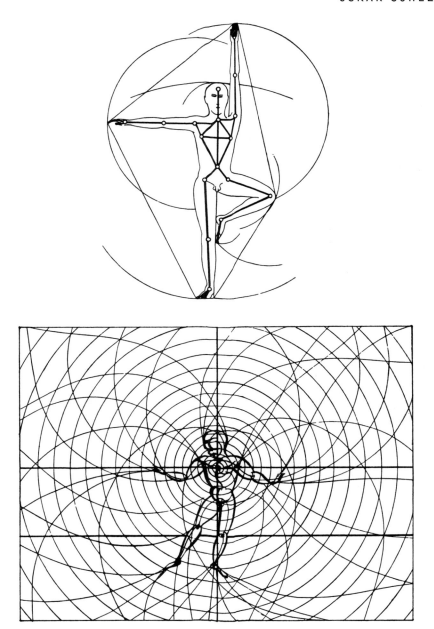

confused. Great as has been the variety of native costumes developed during the course of human history, the number of genuine stage costumes has stayed very small. They are the few standardized costumes of the *commedia dell' arte*: Harlequin, Pierrot, Columbine, etc.; and they have remained basic and authentic to this day.

419

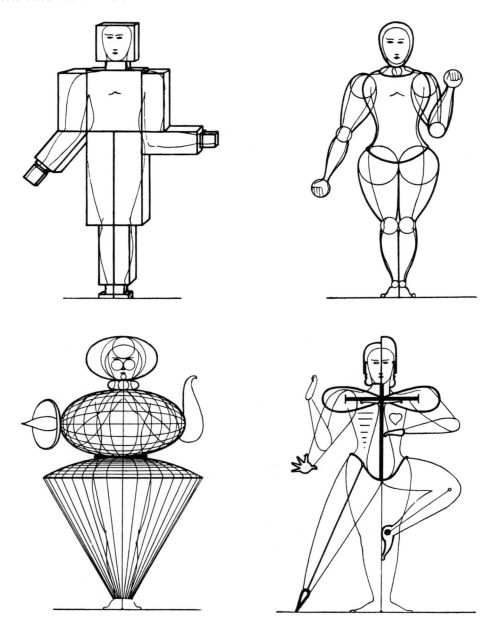

The following can be considered fundamentally decisive in the transformation of the human body in terms of this stage costume (see illustrations above).

These are the possibilities of Man as Dancer, transformed through costume and moving in space. Yet there is no costume which can suspend the primary limitation of the human form: the law of gravity, to which it is subject. A step is not much longer than a yard, a leap not much higher than two. The center of gravity can be abandoned only momentarily. And only for a second can it endure in a position essentially alien to its natural one, such as a horizontal hovering or soaring.

*Acrobatics* make it possible to partially overcome physical limitations, though only in the realm of the organic: the contortionist with his double joints, the living geometry of the aerialist, the pyramid of human bodies.

The endeavor to free man from his physical bondage and to heighten his freedom of movement beyond his native potential resulted in substituting for the organism the mechanical human figure (*Kunstfigur*): *the automaton and the marionette*. E.T.A. Hoffmann extolled the first of these, Heinrich von Kleist the second.

The English stage reformer Gordon Craig demands: 'The actor must go, and in his place comes the inanimate figure – the Übermarionette we may call him.' And the Russian Brjusov demands that we 'replace actors with mechanized dolls, into each of which a phonograph shall be built.'

Such, indeed, are two actual conclusions arrived at by the stage designer whose mind is constantly concerned with form and transformation, with figure and configuration. As far as the stage is concerned, such paradoxical exclusiveness is less significant than the enrichment of modes of expression which is brought about by it.

Possibilities are extraordinary in light of today's technological advancements: precision machinery, scientific apparatus of glass and metal, the artificial limbs developed by surgery, the fantastic costumes of the deep-sea diver and the modern soldier, and so forth. . . .

*Consequently, potentialities of constructive configuration are extraordinary on the metaphysical side as well.*

The artificial human figure (*Kunstfigur*) permits any kind of movement and any kind of position for as long a time as desired. It also permits – an artistic device from the periods of greatest art – a variable relative scale for figures: important ones can be large, unimportant ones small.

An equally significant aspect of this is the possibility of relating the figure of natural 'naked' Man to the abstract figure, both of which experience, through this confrontation, an intensification of their peculiar natures.

Endless perspectives are opened up: from the supernatural to the nonsensical, from the sublime to the comic. Precursors in the use of pathos, of the sublime, are the actors of ancient tragedy, monumentalized by means of masks, cothurni, and stilts. Precursors in the comic style are the gigantic and the grotesque figures of carnival and fair.

Wondrous figures of this new sort, personifications of the loftiest concepts and ideas, made of the most exquisite material, will be capable also of embodying symbolically a new faith.

Seen from this perspective, it might even be predicted that the situation will completely reverse itself: the stage designer will develop optical phenomena and will then seek out a poet who will give them their appropriate language through words and musical sounds.

And so, in accordance with idea, style, and technology, the following still await their creation:

| | |
|---|---|
| the *Abstract-Formal and Color*<br>the *Static, Dynamic, and Tectonic*<br>the *Mechanical, Automatic, and Electric*<br>the *Gymnastic, Acrobatic, and Equilibristic*<br>the *Comic, Grotesque, and Burlesque*<br>the *Serious, Sublime, and Monumental*<br>the *Political, Philosophical, and Metaphysical* | Theater |

*Utopia?* It is indeed astonishing how little has been accomplished so far in this direction, This materialistic and practical age has in fact lost the genuine feeling for play and for the miraculous. Utilitarianism has gone a long way in killing it. Amazed at the flood of technological advance, we accept these wonders of utility as being already perfected art form, while actually they are only prerequisites for its creation. 'Art is without purpose' insofar as the imaginary needs of the soul can be said to be without purpose. In this time of crumbling religion, which kills the sublime, and of a decaying society, which is able to enjoy only play that is drastically erotic or artistically *outré*, all profound artistic tendencies take on the character of exclusiveness or of sectarianism.

And so there remain only three possibilities for the artist in the theater today!

*He may seek realization within the confines of the given situation.* This means cooperation with the stage in its present form – productions in which he places himself at the service of writers and actors in order to give to their work the appropriate optical form. It is a rare case when his intentions coincide with those of the author.

*Or he may seek realization under conditions of the greatest possible freedom.* This exists for him in those areas of staging which are primarily visual display, where author and actor step back in favor of the optical or else achieve their effect only by virtue of it: ballet, pantomime, musical theater, and the like. It also exists in those areas – independent of writer and actor – of the anonymous or mechanically controlled play of forms, colors, and figures.

*Or he may isolate himself altogether from the existing theater* and cast his anchor far out into the sea of fantasy and distant possibilities. In this case his projects remain paper and model, materials for demonstration lectures and exhibitions of theater art. His plans founder on the impossibility of materialization. In the final analysis this is unimportant to him. His idea has been demonstrated, and its realization is a question of time, material, and technology.

This realization will come with the construction of the new theater of glass, metal, and the inventions of tomorrow.

*It depends as well upon the inner transformation of the spectator — Man as alpha and omega of every artistic creation which, even in its realization, is doomed to remain Utopia so long as it does not find intellectual and spiritual receptivity and response.*

■　■　■

## Source

Schlemmer, O. (1924, 1961) 'Man and Art Figure', in W. Gropius and A. Wensinger (eds) *The Theater of the Bauhaus*, Middletown, Conn.: Wesleyan: 17–32.

## Oskar Schlemmer (1888–1943)

German painter, choreographer, dancer, theorist, teacher. Schlemmer trained as a painter in Stuttgart, and became increasingly interested in the other arts and attracted to dance. He described ideas for a new type of dance as early as 1912.[1] In 1920 he became Master of the Stone Masonry Workshop at the newly created Bauhaus (1919) in Weimar, under Walter Gropius. He designed productions at Stuttgart Landestheater, including Kokoschka's *Murderer, Hope of Women*. His most famous choreography, *The Triadic Ballet*, was completed and premièred in Stuttgart on 30 September 1922. He was Head of the Bauhaus Stage Workshop 1923–29 in Dessau, working with Kurt Schmidt, Xanti Schawinsky and Wassily Kandinsky. He made a number of works, *Dances for the Experimental Stage*, including *Gesture Dance* (1926) and *Stick Dance* (1927). When Meyer took over the Bauhaus (1929), Schlemmer left, rather than sacrifice his ideals. *The Triadic Ballet* was restaged for Rolf de Maré's International Choreographic Competition, Paris (1932). Schlemmer became a professor at art schools in Breslau, then in Berlin. In 1933, following the ascendancy of Nazism (and attendant disapproval of modernism), he was dismissed as 'degenerate' by the authorities. The Bauhaus was dissolved in the same year. During the Second World War he was a worker in an enamel factory, before taking his life in 1943.

The Bauhaus was perhaps the most important art school of the twentieth century, certainly one of the most influential. Its example of democratising the distinctions between artists and craftsmen, theory and practice, and between the arts is unparalleled. Significantly, it had an experimental stage workshop; dance was central to this experiment, and there was a lively interface between choreography and art.[2]

In this article Schlemmer describes the theoretical foundations of theatre in terms of relationships between the stage, the performer, and its visual constituents. It ranges widely and is one of the most comprehensive such statements. It was written a year after *The Triadic Ballet* and reflects this as a definitive theatre experiment of its time.

## Compare this article with writings by the following authors in this reader

**Anderson, Foreman and Wilson** – later views of visual theatre
**Appia** – a contemporary on visual theatre
**Craig** – a contemporary, and to whom Schlemmer refers
**Cunningham and Cage** – the Black Mountain Connection
**Kantor** – a later concern with sculptural qualities of performance
**Meyerhold and Piscator** – concern with staging
**Richter** – a contemporary, but different, art perspective – Dada

## Further reading

Bitterberg, K.-G. (1968, 1975) *Bauhaus*, Stuttgart: Institut für Auslandsbeziehungen.
Scheyer, E. (1970) 'The Shapes of Space: The Art of Mary Wigman and Oskar Schlemmer', *Dance Perspectives*, Vol. 41, Spring.
Schlemmer, O. (1969, 1971) *Man: Teaching Notes from the Bauhaus*, trans. J. Seligman, London: Lund Humphries.
Whitford, F. (1984) *Bauhaus*, London: Thames and Hudson.

## Notes

1     Described in his diaries but not realised until 1916. Contemporaneous with Kandinsky's similar *Der Gelbe Klange* (1912) and with the first seasons of the Ballets Russe from 1909.
2     This valuable connection continued at Black Mountain College, USA in the 1950s (see Cage and Cunningham) and, more informally, at Judson in the 1960s.

# Chapter 53

# Carolee Schneemann

## MEAT JOY

### 1964

*Meat Joy* developed from dream sensation images gathered in journals stretching back to 1960. By February 1964, more elaborate drawings and notes accumulated as scraps of paper, on the wall over my bed, in tablets. I'd been concentrating on the possibility of capturing interactions between physical/metabolic changes, dream content, and my sensory orientation upon and after waking: an attempt to view paths between conscious and unconscious organization of image, pun, double entendre, masking, and the release of random memory fragments (often well-defined sounds, instructions, light, textures, weather, places from the past, solutions to problems). Because the transition between dream and waking, envisioning and practical function, became so attenuated, it was often difficult to leave the loft for my job or errands. My body streamed with currents of imagery: the interior directives varied from furtive to persistent, either veiling or so intensely illuminating ordinary situations that I continually felt dissolved, exploded, permeated by objects, events, persons outside of the studio, the one place where my concentration could be complete.

The drawings of movement, and notations on relations of color, light, sound, and language fragments, demanded organization, enaction, and that I be able to sustain the connection to this imagery for an extended time—through the search for space, performers, funds, painstaking rehearsals, and the complexities of production down to the smallest details—all to achieve a fluid, unpredictable performance.

*Meat Joy* has the character of an erotic rite: excessive, indulgent; a celebration of flesh as material: raw fish, chickens, sausages, wet paint, transparent plastic, rope, brushes, paper scrap. Its propulsion is toward the ecstatic, shifting and turning between tenderness, wildness, precision, abandon—qualities that could at any moment be sensual, comic, joyous, repellent. Physical equivalences are enacted as a psychic and imagistic stream in which the layered elements mesh and gain intensity by the energy complement of the audience. (They were seated on the floor as close to the performance area as possible, encircling, resonating.) Our proximity heightened the sense of communality, transgressing the polarity between performer and audience.

In precisely determined patterns, vertical, diagonal, and horizontal shafts of movement and lighting cut through the overall circular structures of *Meat Joy*. The popular songs occuring throughout most sequences are "circular" in their thematic and rhythmic three-minute disc-spun durations, and they introduce a literal, istoric time—popular "ritual" sound centering the sensory flow. Tapes of Paris street sounds were superimposed: the cries and clamorings of rue de Seine vendors selling fish, chickens, vegetables, and flowers beneath the hotel window where I first composed the actual performance score. These shouts dominate a layering of traffic noise and displace the songs' recognizable continuity, interfering with their associative range.

Certain parameters of the piece function consistently. Sequence, lights, sound, materials—these were planned and coordinated in rehearsal. Other components vary with each performance. Attitude, gesture, phrasing, duration, relationship between performers (and between performers and objects) became loosely structured in rehearsal and were expected to evolve. For instance, "The Paint Attack" was rehearsed as a *projective* exercise with brushes and dry sponges: the actual paint, fish, chickens, hot dogs introduced during performance came as a visceral shock.

Lighting is keyed to the larger rhythms of the work—sound and action—by washes and sudden concentrations of strong illumination on energy clusters. Here again, within certain determined bounds (I knew when I needed, for example, "a muddy light in a pool over there which turns to diffuse gold" or in another place, "something blue and wet-looking with a blast of green") the lighting and sound technicians were free to improvise. They followed formal cues but had to be able to make choices relating to energy shifts of both performers and audience. Four blackouts were used to compact or shatter sequences, to insert a *blank* in which perception is halted and the imagery settles into the mind.

As the audience enters, the tape of "Notes as Prologue" begins: a collage of my voice reading the written notes formative to *Meat Joy* (so that the work is verbally revealed before it begins, including discarded unrealizable imagery), beginning French exercises (from a book titled *Look and Learn* and a dictionary), a ticking clock, and the noises of the rue de Seine.

426

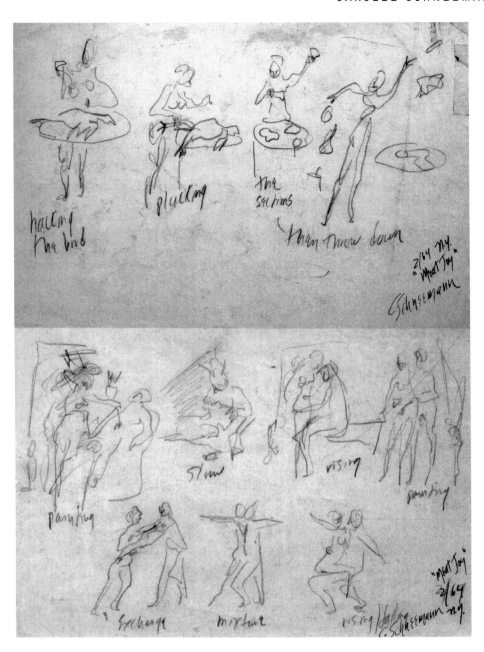

**Drawings for** *Meat Joy*, 1963.
Pencil on paper. 9 × 12 in.
Collection of Gilbert and Lila Silverman.
© ARS, NY and DACS, London 2013

*Meat Joy*, 1964. Performance: raw fish, chickens, sausages, wet paint, plastic, rope, paper scrap, 60–80 minutes.

**Performances**
Festival de la Libre Expression, Paris (May 29, 1964).
Dennison Hall, London (June 8, 1964).
Judson Church, New York (November 16–18, 1964).

■ ■ ■

## Source

Schneemann, C. (2002) *Imaging Her Erotics: Essays, Interviews, Projects*, London: MIT Press.

## Carolee Schneemann (1939–)

Carolee Schneemann from Pennsylvania is best described as a multidisciplinary artist and one of the original creators of performance art in America who began making events and 'happenings' in the 1960s.

She trained originally at Bard College and gained an MFA from the University of Illinois. She has taught at many universities, has a string of lifetime achievement awards, honorary doctorates and prestigious fellowships, and has published widely. She is noted for being a feminist figure, whose works explore subversive issues in art and acknowledge her expertise in art history. Books include *Cezanne, She Was a Great Painter* (1976), *Early and Recent Work* (1983), *More Than Meat Joy: Performance Works and Selected Writings* (1997) and *Imaging Her Erotics: Essays, Interviews, Projects* (2001).

Her extensive body of work, which has been presented throughout Europe and the United States, is broad in scope and ranges from painting, photography and film making through solo and group ensemble performances and multi-sensory visual events. Often situated in the field of Fluxus, neo-Dada and Happenings, her work is reported to be influenced by Simone de Beauvoir, Antonin Artaud, Wilhelm Reich and Allan Kaprow. She was involved in the Judson Memorial Church's art programme, where she participated in Oldenburg's *Store Days* (1962) and Robert Morris's *Site* (1964). The 1964 piece *Meat Joy* revolved around eight partially nude figures dancing and playing with various objects and substances including wet paint, sausage, raw fish, scraps of paper, and raw chickens. It was first performed in Paris and was later filmed and photographed as performed by her Kinetic Theater group at Judson Memorial Church. She described the piece as an 'erotic rite' and an indulgent Dionysian 'celebration of flesh as material'. In 1975, Schneemann performed the now seminal piece *Interior Scroll*, in which she used nudity, paint, action poses and read text from her book and a scroll extracted from her vagina. Her 1994 piece *Mortal Coils* commemorated 15 friends and colleagues who had died over the period of two years including Hannah Wilke, John Cage and Charlotte Moorman. The piece consisted of rotating mechanisms from which hung coiled ropes while slides of the commemorated artists were shown on the walls. *Terminal Velocity* (2001) consisted of a group of photographs of people falling to their deaths from the World Trade Center following the September 11, 2001 attacks.

Although Schneemann moved towards performance from painting she considers her photographic and body pieces to still be based in painting despite appearing otherwise on the surface. She has described herself as 'A painter who has left the canvas to activate actual space and lived time'. She contributed substantially to a redefinition of performance art practice, especially discourse on the body, sexuality and gender.

She uses her nude body in works, feeling that it needed to be seized back from the status of a cultural possession. Schneemann acknowledges that she is often labelled as a feminist icon and that she is an influential figure to female artists. 'I take the position that I do not ask anyone else to do what I myself would not do and using myself as subject . . . as material (I) want to displace the power and separation of the artist from what's made. In the masculine tradition the director, the producer is always outside of the work because he's above it.'

The photographic book *More Than Meat Joy* offers readers a significant context for performance art, as well as profiling Schneemann's important work.

## Compare this article with writings by the following authors in this reader

**Kaprow** – for Happenings
**Cage** and **Maciunas** – for Fluxus and Dada influences
**Finley** – for issues around gender and explicit use of the female body

## Further reading

Schneemann, C. (1997) *More Than Meat Joy: Performance Works and Selected Writings*, New York: McPherson & Co.
Schneider, R. (1997) *The Explicit Body in Performance*, London: Routledge.
Stiles, K. (ed.) (2011) *Correspondence Course: An Epistolary History of Carolee Schneemann and Her Circle*, Durham, NC: Duke University Press.
http://www.caroleeschneemann.com/

# Chapter 54

# Wole Soyinka

## THEATRE IN AFRICAN TRADITIONAL CULTURES: SURVIVAL PATTERNS

E VEN WHERE other resources of pre-colonial society are unevenly shared, culture tends to suggest a comparatively even-handed distribution or – perhaps more simply – mass appropriation. This may help to explain why it is always a primary target of assault by an invading force. As an instrument of self-definition, its destruction or successful attrition reaches into the reserves of racial/national will on a comprehensive scale. Conversely, the commencement of resistance and self-liberation by the suppressed people is not infrequently linked with the survival strategies of key cultural patterns, manifested through various art forms. The experience of West Africa has been no different. The history of West African theatre in the colonial period reveals itself therefore as largely a history of cultural resistance and survival. Confronted by the hostility of both Islamic and Christian values, in addition to the destructive imperatives of colonialism, it has continued until today to vitalize contemporary theatrical forms both in the tradition of 'folk opera' and in the works of those playwrights and directors commonly regarded as 'Westernized'.

We must not lose sight of the fact that drama, like any other art form, is created and executed within a specific physical environment. It naturally interacts with that environment, is influenced by it, influences that environment in turn and acts together with the environment in the larger and far more complex history of society. The history of a dramatic pattern or its evolution is therefore very much the history of other art forms of society. And when we consider art forms from the point of view of survival strategies, the dynamics of cultural interaction with society become even more aesthetically challenging and fulfilling. We discover, for instance, that under certain conditions some art forms are transformed into others – simply to ensure the survival of the threatened forms. Drama may give way to poetry and song in order to disseminate dangerous sentiments under the watchful eye of the oppressor, the latter forms being more easily communicable. On the other hand, drama may become more manifestly invigorated in order to counteract the effect of an alienating environment.

Nigeria offers a valuable example of the dual process of cultural attenuation and resurgence. For example, theatrical professionalism was synonymous, by the middle nineteenth century, with the artistic proficiency and organisation of a particular theatrical form which had emerged from the burial rituals associated with the Oyo monarchy, the *egungun*. The question of when a performed event became theatre as opposed to ritualism is of course a vexed one that we need not bother about in this context. It is, however, commonly agreed that what started out – probably – as a ritualistic ruse to effect the funeral obsequies of an Oyo king had, by the mid-century, evolved into a theatrical form in substance and practice. From an annual celebration rite of the smuggling-in of the corpse of that king and its burial, the *egungun* ancestral play became, firstly, a court re-enactment, then a secular form of performance which was next appropriated by the artists themselves. Its techniques were perfected by family guilds and township cults. About this time, however, Islam had begun its push southwards. The Oyo empire, already in disintegration from internal rivalries and other stresses, found itself under increasing military pressure from the Hausa-Fulani in the north, a situation which came on the heels of a rebellion of tributary states to the south. The fall of Oyo took down with it the security which the theatrical art had enjoyed under its patronage. The Muslims, victorious in northern Yorubaland, banned most forms of theatrical performance as contrary to the spirit of Islam. The *Agbegijo, Alarinjo* and allied genres, with their dramatic use of the paraphernalia of carved masks and other representations of ancestral spirits, came most readily under religious disapproval. It did not matter that, by now, they had lost most of their pretence to the mysterious or numinous.

Southern Nigeria and its neighbouring territories were, however, only temporary beneficiaries from this disruption of political life in the old Oyo empire. The Christian missionaries had also begun their northward drive, usually only a few steps ahead of the colonial forces. The philistinic task begun by the Moslems was rounded out by the Christians' ban on the activities of suspect cults. The Christians went further. They did not content themselves with banning just the dramatic performance; they placed their veto also on indigenous musical instruments – *bata, gangan, dundun* and so on – the very backbone of traditional theatre. It was into this vacuum that the returned slaves stepped with their Western (and therefore

Christian) instruments, their definitely Christian dramatic themes and their Western forms.

Another historical factor aided the temporary eclipse of indigenous theatre forms: the slave trade and its supply which involved inter-state wars, raids and casual kidnappings. The missionary compounds often offered the securest havens from these perennial hazards, just as did (in West Africa) submission to the protective spheres of the Muslim overlords. It is difficult to imagine a group of refugees from the old Oyo empire encouraged by their Muslim or Christian protectors to revert to the ways of their 'pagan art'. The records do not reveal any such acts of disinterested artistic patronage. Artistic forms might be appropriated, but only in the cause of religious promotion; thus, for example, the appropriation of musical forms by the nineteenth-century Christian missionaries in Buganda for hymns. This, however, was only a later refinement, a sensible strategy for rendering the patently alien words and sentiments less abrasive to the indigenes by coating them in traditional harmonies.

It is difficult to trace, at present, the effect of the Oyo *egungun* dispersal on the development of theatrical forms in neighbouring areas. This is always the case with any situation of artistic hiatus – a period, that is, when a particular form of art goes underground or disappears temporarily, especially under the pressures of a dominant political and artistic ethos. The records simply ignore them, or treat them merely as isolated nuisances. The substitution of new forms belonging to the dominant culture takes pride of place in records, and this is the situation we encounter in the development of Western 'concerts' and variety shows in the colonized territories of West Africa. At this point, therefore, let us clarify in our minds what theatre is. That this is more than a merely academic exercise is easily grasped if we refer to a sister art, sculpture, an achievement which the missionary-colonizer pioneers found convenient to deny to the African. The redressing assessment was made by other Europeans – the artists themselves, notably the Expressionists; they had no overriding reasons to deny the obvious, to ignore what was even a potential source of inspiration to their own creative endeavours. The vexed question of what constitutes drama and what is merely ritual, ceremony, festival and so on, while it continues to be legitimately argued, must always be posed against an awareness of early prejudiced reading of the manifestations encountered by culture denigrators, definitions which today still form the language of orthodox theatre criticism. To assist our own definition we need look only at any one cultural event within which diversified forms are found, forms which – through their visual impact – tend towards the creation of differing categories for a comparative description. In other words if, within one performance or cluster of performances (say, a festival or a celebration) in any given community, we discover consciously differing qualitative enactments, we are obliged to rummage around in our artistic vocabulary for categories that reflect such differences. Thus we find that, sooner or later, we arrive at the moment when only the expression 'drama' or 'theatre' seems apposite, and then the search is over. We will take an example from the Afikpo masquerades of south-east Nigeria.

A contrast between the *okumkpa* event and the *oje ogwu*, both being components of this Afikpo festival, actually furnishes us with the basic definition we need. This masquerade, which is the professional handiwork of a male initiation society, varies, we discover, from basically balletic sequences as contained in the *oje ogwu* to the *mimetic* as contained in the *okumkpa*. The latter is indeed performed as a climax to what appears to be the prominent *oje ogwu* turn by the masqueraders. Both are basically audience-oriented – in other words, we are not really concerned here with the complication of a *ritual* definition but one of performance and reception. The audience plays a prominent appreciative role in this outdoor performance, judging, booing or approving on purely aesthetic grounds. Whatever symbolism may be contained in the actual movements of the *oje ogwu* is of no significance in the actual judgement. What the audience looks for and judges are the finer points of leaps, turns, control and general spatial domination. The poorer performers are soon banished to the group sessions – which demonstrates the importance given to individual technical mastery.

The *okumkpa* event, by contrast, consists of satirical mimesis. Masks are also used but the *action* forms the basis of performance. This action consists of a satirical rendition of actual events both in neighbouring settlements and in the village itself. Personalities are ridiculed, the events in which they were involved are re-enacted. In short, events are transformed artistically both for audience delectation and for the imparting of moral principles. Additionally, however, one standard repertoire consists of the taking of female roles by the young male initiates, this role being of a rather derogatory character. The satirized female is invariably what we might call 'the reluctant bride'. As the young actor minces and prances around, sung dialogues accompany him, built around the same theme: 'How much longer are you going to reject all suitors on the grounds that they are not sufficiently handsome/strong/industrious etc., etc.?' Competition is keen among the initiates for the honour of playing this central female impersonator. The various sketches in this vein are rounded off in the end by a massed parade of the various actors in the *njenji* where the less accomplished actors have their own hour of glory and the entire female world is satirically lectured on the unkindness of keeping the male rooster waiting too long.

We will not examine the sociological motivation of this kind of drama except to point out that this example is actually more rewarding, in our search for an explanation of man's motives in *dramatizing*, than, for instance, the theory of the origin in the Oyo masquerade. Clearly, in the Afikpo masquerade we encounter a male-prejudiced device. It ensures man's claim to social superiority and creates guilt in the woman for not fulfilling on demand man's need for female companionship. It is of no more mystifying an order of things than, for instance, the disparagement by male undergraduates in their press of female undergraduates who have not submitted to their own desires – except, of course, that traditional society imposed heavy penalties on libellous fabrication (which is, by the way, a reliable indication of artistic barrenness). What we obtain from one, therefore, is genuine art; from their modern progeny, alas, only dirty pictures and fevered fantasies. The *okumkpa* provides us with drama — variety, satire. We are left with no other definition when we contrast it with its consciously differentiated companion piece — the *oje ogwu*.

Similarly, festivals such as the Ogun or Osun (River) festivals in Yorubaland provide us with multi-media and multi-formal experiences within which it is not at all difficult to find unambiguous examples of dramatic enactments. The high point of the festival of the Yoruba hero-deity Obatala is, for instance, undoubted drama, consisting of all the elements that act on the emotions, the excitations of conflict and resolution and the human appreciation of spectacle. We begin to understand now why dating the origin of African drama, locating it in a specific event, time and place is an impossible task — indeed, a meaningless one. In the study of art forms, it is clearly more appealing to look into extant material for what may be deduced as primitive or early forms of the particular art, noting along the way what factors have contributed to their survival in the specific forms. Festivals, comprising as they do such a variety of forms, from the most spectacular to the most secretive and emotionally charged, offer the most familiar hunting-ground. What is more, they constitute in themselves *pure theatre* at its most prodigal and resourceful. In short, the persistent habit of dismissing festivals as belonging to a 'spontaneous' inartistic expression of communities demands re-examination. The level of organization involved, the integration of the sublime with the mundane, the endowment of the familiar with properties of the unique (and this, spread over days) all indicate that it is into the heart of many African festivals that we should look for the most stirring expressions of man's instinct and need for drama at its most comprehensive and community-involving. Herbert M. Cole renders this point of view in penetrating terms:

> A festival is a relatively rare climatic event in the life of any community. It is bounded by a definite beginning and end, and is unified thereby, as well as being set apart from the above daily life. Its structure is built on a core or armature of ritual. The festival brings about a suspension of ordinary time, a transformation of ordinary space, a formaliser of ordinary behaviour. It is as if a community becomes a stage set and its people actors with a battery of seldom-seen props and costumes. Meals become feasts, and greetings, normally simple, become ceremonies. Although dependent upon life-sustaining rituals, the festival is an elaborated and stylised phenomenon which far surpasses ritual necessity. It often becomes the social, ritual and political apotheosis of community life in a year. At festival time one level of reality — the common and everyday — gives way to another, a more intense, symbolic and expressive level of reality.[1]

What this implies is that instead of considering festivals from one point of view only — that of providing, in a primitive form, the ingredients of drama — we may even begin examining the opposite point of view: that contemporary drama, as we experience it today, is a contraction of drama, necessitated by the productive order of society in other directions. That is, drama undergoes parallel changes with other structuring mechanisms of society. As communities outgrow certain patterns of producing what they require to sustain themselves or of transforming what exists around them, the structures which sustain the arts are affected in parallel ways, affecting in turn the very forms of the arts. That the earlier forms are not necessarily more 'primitive' or 'crude' is borne out by the fact that more and more of the highly developed societies are turning to the so-called 'primitive' forms of drama as representing the significant dramatic forms for contemporary society. These societies, which vary from such ideologically disparate countries as the United States and East European countries, are re-introducing on stage, in both formal theatre structures and improvised spaces, dramatic forms such as we have described, from the macro-conceptual (as represented in festivals) to the micro-conceptual, as ritual may be held to epitomize.

In this vein, what are we to make of the famous Return-to-the-Village Festival of the Koumina canton in Bobo-Dioulasso, Upper Volta?[2] Here we encounter a people who, like many others in West Africa, have experienced the culturally disrupting influences of Muslim and Christian cultures. The traders came first, the Mande traders, in the early sixteenth century. In their next significant migration, the mid-eighteenth century, they were accompanied by Muslim clerics, with the cultural results with which we are by now familiar. By 1775 proselytization had become so successful that an Imamate had been established by the famous Saghnughu family of scholars. The late nineteenth century saw the take-over by colonial administrators and Christian missionaries. Yet under this double assault, Bobo traditional arts have survived until today, and nowhere are they given more vital expression than in the 'Tagaho' season festival which marks the return of the Bobo to their village after their seasonal migrations to their farmsteads. The festival, which has for its core the funeral ceremonies for those who died during the period of farmland migration, has a far more important function for the living: the re-installation of the cohering, communal spirit and existential reality. Costumes are elaborately prepared, formal patterns both of 'ritual' and 'pageant' worked out and rehearsed, individual events enacted by masked figures for a delayed participation by the community as one entity. It is all of course a conscious performance, informed and controlled by aesthetic ideas, by the competitive desire also of 'showing off' dramatic skills. Simultaneously it is an affirmation of social solidarity. Can this form of theatre, considered in its most fundamental purpose and orientation, be viewed much differently from the theatre of 'happenings' which began in America and Europe in the sixties and is still encountered in parts of those societies today? To be sure, the former is more disciplined, formal and community-inspired, which are all attributes that we experience from unalienating forms of theatre.

At this point, it may be useful to consider instances where an art form evolves into another art form in one geographical/cultural area but fails to do so in another. The heroic tradition is one that is common to most parts of Africa (and, indeed, to most societies). Within this tradition may be grouped, at any level of its development, the epic, saga, praise-chants, ballads and so on, but here we are concerned with the performance aspect from which dramatization most naturally evolves. East, Central and South Africa are particularly rich in the tradition of the heroic recitative. Among the Luo of Kenya and Uganda, for instance, we may note the form known as the *pakrouk*, a kind of virtue-boasting which takes place at ceremonial gatherings, usually to the accompaniment of a harp. The individual performer emerges from the group, utters praises of his own person and his achievements, and is replaced or contended with by another. Similar manifestations are found among the Ankole tribes, while further south, among the Sotho and the Zulu, sustained lyrical recitations on important historical events have become highly developed.

Among the Ijaw people of south-eastern Nigeria, however, the same tradition has actually developed dramatic variants, has moved beyond the merely recited to the enacted, a *tour de force* sustained by a principal actor for over three days. The saga of *Ozidi*, the principal source for J.P. Clark's play of the same name, is an example. By contrast, the history of the performance arts in Central and Southern Africa reveals a tendency towards virtual stasis of the putative dramatic elements. Even the dramatic potential of such rituals as the *Nyasi-iye*, the boat-building and launching ceremonies of the Luo, with its symbolic cutting of the 'umbilical cord' as the boat is freed from its moorings, even the abundant parallelisms with nuptial rites, have somehow failed to move towards a truly dramatic rendering of the significance and life-intertwining role of the boats in the daily pre-occupations of the Luo. One need only contrast this with the various rites and festivals of the coastal and riverine peoples of West Africa, where both religious observances and economic practicalities of the same activity have taken on, over the centuries, a distinctly dramatic ordering. One may speculate at length on the reasons for this contrast; the reality remains, however, that drama as an integral phenomenon in the lives of the peoples of Central and Southern Africa has followed a comparatively meagre development.

Well then, let us, using one of our early examples, follow how traditional theatre forms adjusted or re-surfaced from the preliminary repressions of alien cultures. We find that the 'pagan' theatre ultimately withstood the onslaught, not only preserving its forms but turning itself consciously into a base of resistance against both dominating systems. We are able to witness the closing of a cycle of cultural substitution in a curious irony of this slavery-colonial experience. Having first broken up the cultural life of the people, the slave era, now in its dying phase in the first half of the nineteenth century, brought back the sons of the land with a new culture in place of the old. The returnees constituted a new elite: they possessed after all the cultural tools of the colonial masters. But – and now we emphasize the place of theatre among these cultural tools – even where they were fully assimilated into the cultural values of their erstwhile masters (or saviours), they found on their return company servants, civil servants, missionary converts who belonged in the same social class as themselves, but were culturally unalienated. These stay-at-homes had had what was more or less an equivalent colonial education, yet had also acquired a nationalist awareness which manifested itself in cultural attitudes. As the nineteenth century entered its last quarter, the stay-at-homes were able to provide a balancing development pattern to cultural life on the West coast which came predominantly under the creative influence of the returnee Christians, despite the latter's confidence in the superiority of their acquired arts and their eagerness to prove to the white population that the black man was capable not only of receiving but also of practising the refined arts of the European.

The cultural difference between the settlers of Liberia and Sierra Leone on the one hand, and the coastal societies of Ghana and Nigeria on the other can be translated in terms of the degree of cultural identification with, and adaptation of the authentic resources of the hinterland. To the former – mostly returnee slaves – the indigenous people remained savage, crude and barbaric, to be regarded only as material for missionary conversion and possible education. The converts who had remained at home, however, set off a process of schisms within social and religious institutions whose value-system was Eurocentric, delving again and again into the living resources of indigenous society. Naturally there were exceptions on both sides, but this dichotomy did hold in general. The direction of *new* forms of theatrical entertainment therefore followed an eastward pattern from the new returnee settlements; inevitably it received increasing native blood-transfusion as it moved further east away from the bastardized vaudeville of the 'Nova Scotians', so that by the time it arrived in Ghana, Dahomey (now Benin) and Nigeria, both in form and content, a distinct West African theatrical idiom had evolved.

'Academies', to begin with, were formed for the performance of concerts which were modelled on the Victorian music hall or the American vaudeville. The Christian churches organized their own concerts, schools were drawn into the concert rage – prize-giving days, visits of the District Officer, Queen Victoria's birthday and so on. The black missionaries refused to be outdone; Rev. Ajayi Crowther was a famous example, a black prelate who patronized and encouraged this form of the arts, while the Rev. James Johnson turned the famous Breadfruit church in Lagos into a springboard for theatrical performances. The Brazilian returnees added an exotic yet familiar flavour, their music finding a ready echo in the traditional melodies of the West Coast and the Congo whose urban suppression had not occurred long enough for such melodies to be totally forgotten. At the turn of the century and in the first decades of the twentieth century, Christmas and New Year saw the streets of the capital cities of Freetown and Lagos transformed by mini-pageants reminiscent of Latin fiestas, of which the 'caretta', a kind of satyr masquerade, appears to have been the most durable.

Cultural nationalism was, however, constantly at work against a total usurpation by imported forms. Once again religion and its institutions provided the base. Unable to accept the excesses of the Christian cultural imperialism, such as the embargo on African instruments and tunes in a 'universal' church, and the prohibition of drumming on tranquil Anglican Sundays, the breakaway movements began. The period 1888 to the early 1930s witnessed a proliferation of secessionist movements, mostly inspired by a need to worship God in the cultural mode of the forefathers. And now began also a unique 'operatic' tradition in West Africa, but especially Lagos, beginning with church cantatas which developed into dramatizations of biblical stories until it asserted its independence in secular stories and the development of professional touring troupes. The process, reminiscent of the evolution of the 'miracle' or 'mystery' plays of medieval Europe, is identical with the evolution of the Agbegijo theatre (then temporarily effaced) from the sacred funeral rites of the Alafin of Oyo to court entertainment and, thereafter, independent existence and geographical dispersion. From the genteel concerts of classical music and English folk songs by the 'Academy' of the 1880s to the historical play *King Elejigbo* of the Egbe Ife Church Dramatic Society in 1902, a transformation of thought and sensibility had recognizably taken place even among the Westernized elite of southern Nigeria. The Churches did not take kindly to it. They closed their churchyards and schools to the evolving art. Alas, they only succeeded in accelerating the defiant erection of theatre halls, specifically designed for the performing arts. It was in reality a tussle between groups of colonial elites, fairly balanced in the matter of resources. By 1912 the secularization of theatrical entertainment in southern Nigeria was sufficiently advanced for the colonial government to gazette a 'Theatre and Public Performance Regulations Ordinance', which required that performing groups obtain a licence before going before the public. In the climate of cultural nationalism which obtained in Lagos at that time, it is doubtful whether this disguised attempt at political censorship would have worked; it is significant that the ordinance was never made into law.

Ironically, yet another breakaway church, the Cherubim and Seraphim movement, swung the pendulum back towards a rejection of traditional forms and was followed shortly by other emulators in the Christian re-consecration of theatrical forms. The furthest these churches would go in the use of musical instruments was the tambourine; local instruments which had created a new tonality in the operettas now touring the West Coast – sekere, dundun, gangan, and so on – were damned as instruments of the Devil. Secular stories, even of historic personages and events, were banned and the new theatre halls, church halls and schoolrooms echoed once more to the Passion of Christ, the anguish of Nebuchadnezzar, the trials of Job, and other dramatic passages from the Bible. The Aladura, Cherubim and Seraphim, and their adherents did not however stop there. These 'prophetist' cults spread rapidly along the West Coast waging a crusade against all 'pagan' worship and their sacred objects. Descending on the provinces of the established churches, they ignited bonfires with their hot-gospelling in which perished thousands of works of art, especially in Nigeria, Cameroons, Ghana and the Ivory Coast. The vision of a fifteen-year-old girl, Abiodun Akinsowon, about 1921, was to prove a costly dream for the cultural heritage of West Africa, the heaviest brunt of which was borne by Yoruba sculpture. This period may also be justly said to constitute the lowest ebb in the fortunes of traditional theatre, participation in the cultural life even of the villages being subjected to lightning descents from the fanatical hordes of the prophetic sects. In the physical confrontations that often took place, the position of authority was predictable. Embarrassed as they sometimes were by the excesses of the sectarians, the European missionaries and their black priests had no hesitation about their alliances — and their voice was weighty in the processes of imposing the colonial peace.

But the 'vaudeville' troupes prospered. Names of groups such as we encounter in 'Two Bobs and their Carolina Girl' tell us something of the inspiration of much of these. Master Yalley, a schoolteacher, is credited with having begun the tradition of the vaudeville variety act in Ghana. His pupil Bob Johnson and his 'Axim Trio' soon surpassed the master and became a familiar figure on Ghana's cultural landscape, also later in Nigeria. More important still, Bob Johnson's innovations must be credited with having given birth to the tradition of the 'concert party' of Ghana, groups which specialize in variety routine: songs, jokes, dances, impersonations, comic scenes. However, the most notable achievement in the sense of cultural continuity was their thrusting on to the fore-state of contemporary repertoire a stock character from traditional lore, the wily trickster Anansi. This quickly developed into a vehicle for social and political commentary, apart from its popularity in comic situations.

The Jaguar Jokers, for example, transformed Anansi into the more urban character of Opia, while Efua Sutherland's more recent *The Marriage of Anansewa* takes this tradition into an even more tightly-knit and disciplined play format — the term 'disciplined' being employed here merely in the sense of reducing the areas of spontaneous improvization, without however eliminating them. Those who saw this piece during Festac 77 will have observed how attractively the element of formal discipline and free improvization blended together to encourage a controlled audience interaction. By the middle 1930s, Bob Johnson had become sufficiently established to take his brand of vaudeville to other West African cities. West Africa in this decade could boast of a repertoire of shows displaying the most bizarre products of eclectic art in the history of theatre. Even cinema, an infant art, had by then left its mark on West African theatre: some of Bob Johnson's acts were adaptations of Charlie Chaplin's escapades, not omitting his costume and celebrated shuffle. And the thought of Empire Day celebration concerts at which songs like 'Mini the Moocher' formed part of the evening musical recitals, side by side with 'God's Gospel is our Heritage' and vignettes from the life of a Liberian stevedore, stretches the contemporary imagination, distanced from the historical realities of colonial West Africa.

Again, another irony of colonial intentions: while Bob Johnson was preparing his first West African tour and Hubert Ogunde, later to become Nigeria's foremost 'concert party' leader, was undergoing his aesthetic formation from the vying forces of a clergyman father and a grandmother who was a priestess of the *Osugbo* cult, a European educationist, Charles Beart in Senegal, was beginning to reverse the policy of European acculturation in a leading secondary school in Senegal. The extent of this development — including also an appreciation of the slow pace of such an evolution — will be better grasped by recalling the educational charter of assimilationism, spelt in diverse ways by the publications of such dedicated African Francophiles as the Abbe Boillat, Paul Holle and so on. Boillat, in spite of extensive sociological research (*Esquisses senegalaises*),[3] the result of his examination of the culture and philosophy of the Bambara, Sarakole, Wolof, Serer, the Tukulor and Moorish groups in Senegal, found no lessons to be drawn from African society for modern cultural development, no future but to witness the fall of all those 'gross, if not dishonourable, ways known as the *custom of the country*'. If his addresses to the metropolitan centre of the French world did not become the cornerstone of French assimilationist policies, they undoubtedly played a key role in their formulation. Against this background, and ensuring decades of such conservatism, the Ecole William Ponty was founded. A famous teachers' college, it served Francophone Africa in the same way as did Achimota College in the Anglophone West and Makerere College in East Africa. They were all designed to provide a basic European education for would-be teachers and low-echelon civil servants. Such humanistic education as came into the curriculum of the Ecole William Ponty was of necessity French – French plays, poetry, music, art, history. Charles Beart, during his principalship, embarked however on a new orientation of the students' cultural instructions. From 1930 onwards the students were encouraged to return to their own societies for cultural directions. Assignments were given which resulted in the students' exploration of both the form and the substance of indigenous art. Groups from every colonial territory represented at William Ponty were then expected to return from vacation armed with a theatrical presentation based on their researches, the entire direction being left in the hands of the students themselves. Since the new theatrical sociology did not confine itself to the usual audiences of European officials and 'educated' Africans, nor to Senegal alone, its influence spread widely through different social strata of French-speaking Africa. Was it, however, a satisfying development of the culture from which it derived?

The answer must be in the negative, though the experiment was not without its instructive values. It would be too much to expect that, at that period, the classic model of French theatre could yield completely to the expression of traditional forms. The community represented by William Ponty was an artificial one. It was distanced from the society whose cultural hoard it rifled both in qualitative thought and material product. The situation was of course not peculiar to William Ponty since it also obtained in the other schools and institutions set up by the colonizer for the fulfilment of his own mission in Africa. Thus the theatre of William Ponty served the needs of exotic satisfaction for the community of French colonials. Even when it 'went to the people', and with their own material, it remained a curiosity that left the social life and authentic cultural awareness of the people untouched.

We will conclude with the 'new' theatre form which has proved the most durable; hybrid in its beginnings, the 'folk opera' has become the most expressive language of theatre in West Africa. What were the themes that mostly engaged the various groups spread along the Coast? The Nigerian Hubert Ogunde provides a convenient compendium, since he does appear to be more consistently varied in his dramatic fare than any comparable group to date in West Africa. His repertoire ranges from outright fantasy through biblical dramatizations to social commentary and political protest, both in the colonial and post-colonial era. A comparative study of the repertoire of the Jaguar Jokers, the Axim Trio, or the current Anansekrom groups of Ghana for example would reveal that these concentrate almost exclusively on social commentary, mostly with a moralistic touch – the evils of witchcraft, maladjustment in the social status of the cash-crop *nouveaux riches*, generational problems, changing status of women in society, sexual mores and so on, all of which also preoccupy the pamphlet drama of the Onitsha market literateurs. Hubert Ogunde explored these themes in his plays and more. His biblical adaptations became in effect a vehicle for direct commentaries on contemporary society. Reference is hardly necessary to those plays which have earned him the ire of colonial and post-colonial governments: *Bread and Bullets*, a play not merely on the famous Iva Valley strike by miners in eastern Nigeria but on the general inequity of labour exploitation; and *Yoruba Ronu*, an indictment of the corruption and repression of the government of the then Western Region. Both plays were proscribed by the affected governments. They have entered the lore of theatrical commitment in Nigeria.

And additionally, Hubert Ogunde exemplifies what we have referred to up until now as the survival patterns of traditional theatrical art. From the outset of his theatrical career, Ogunde's theatre belonged only partially to what we have described as the 'Nova Scotian' tradition. His musical instrumentation was all borrowed from the West, movement on stage was pure Western chorus-line night-club variety. Nevertheless, the attachment to traditional musical forms (albeit with Western impurities) gradually became more assertive. Encouraged no doubt by the appearance of more tradition-grounded groups such as Kola Ogunmola and Duro Ladipo, Hubert Ogunde in the early sixties began to employ traditional instruments in his performance, his music delved deeper into home melodies, and even his costumes began to eschew the purely fabricated, theatrically glossy, for recognizable local gear. Rituals appeared with greater frequency and masquerades became a frequent feature – often, it must be added, as gratuitous insertions. Ogunde's greatest contribution to West African drama – quite apart from his innovative energy and his commitment to a particular political line – lies in his as yet little appreciated musical 'recitative' style, one which he has made unique to himself. It has few imitators, but the success of his records in this genre of 'dramatic monologue' testifies to the responsive chord it elicits from his audience. Based in principle on the Yoruba *rara* style of chanting, but in stricter rhythm, it is melodically a modernistic departure, flexibly manipulated to suit a variety of themes. Once again, we find that drama draws on other art forms for its own survival and extension. It is no exaggeration to claim that Hubert Ogunde's highest development of the chanted dramatic monologue can be fixed at the period of the political ban on his *Yoruba Ronu*. Evidently all art forms flow into one another, confirming, as earlier claimed, that the temporary historic obstacles to the flowering of a particular form sometimes lead to its transformation into other media of expression, or even the birth of totally different groups.

This survey stops at the emergence of the latest forms of traditional drama. The finest representatives of this to date have been the late Kola Ogunmola (comedy and satire) and Duro Ladipo (history and tragedy). Their contribution to contemporary drama and their innovations from indigenous forms require a far more detailed study, just as Moses Olaiya (Baba Sala) demands a chapter of his own iconoclastic brand of theatrical wit. The foregoing attempts to highlight ways in which artistic forms return to life again and again after their seeming demise, ways by which this process emphasizes the fundamental unity of various art forms and the social environment that gives expression to them; how certain creative ideas are the very offspring of historic convulsions. Finally, while for purposes of demarcation we may speak of Nigerian, Ghanaian or perhaps Togolese drama, it must constantly be borne in mind that, like the economic intercourse of the people themselves, the various developments we have touched upon here in drama and the arts do not obey the laws of political boundaries though they might respond to the events within them. The various artistes we have mentioned had, and still enjoy, instant *rapport* with audiences far from their national and linguistic boundaries. Their art finds a ready response in most audiences since their themes are rooted in everyday experience, fleshed out in shared idioms of cultural adjustment.

## Notes

1    Herbert M. Cole in *African arts*, VIII (3).
2    Now renamed Burkina Faso.
3    Abbe Boillat, *Esquisses Sénégalaises*, 1858; new edition, Paris, 1984, Editions Karthala.

■    ■    ■

## Source

Soyinka, W. (1982, 1988, 1993) 'Theatre in African Traditional Cultures: Survival Patterns', *Art, Dialogue and Outrage*, ed. B. Jeyifo, London: Methuen: 134–146. Originally published in 1982 in *African History and Culture* and first republished in 1988 by New Horn Press.

## Wole Soyinka (1934–)

Nigerian playwright, novelist, critic, poet, essayist. He was born and educated in Nigeria, then in England where he lived (1954–70). He worked for the Royal Court, London (1957–59) where excerpts from his early plays were produced. *The Swamp*

*Dwellers* was produced in London in 1957, then in Ibadan, Nigeria with *The Lion and the Jewel* (1959). Soyinka produced plays in both Nigeria and England, notably *A Dance of the Forests* (1963). He worked at the University of Ife, then the University of Lagos, and in 1969 was appointed Head of Theatre at the University of Ibadan. He continued to write extensively there, then later at the University of Ife.

Soyinka's writing became recognised worldwide and in 1986 he was awarded the Nobel prize for literature, the first African to be so recognised. At the same time, in his own country, he was arrested and detained for his intellectual and political views on a number of occasions, especially for the two years 1967–69 (described in *The Man Died*, 1979). He has continued to speak out against injustice, however unpopular this has made him. He left Nigeria in 1994.[1] In 1996 he wrote a two-volume critique, *Open Sore of a Continent*, of the Nigerian regime that had executed his fellow playwright Ken Saro-Wiwa. The same regime pronounced the death sentence on him in 1997.

Soyinka's work is remarkable for the way it combines a profound understanding of the history and myths of the Yoruba and other African peoples and his ability to draw on a wide range of sources from both the European and Asian traditions. He is truly a pan-cultural writer and has been at the forefront of such a worldview for some thirty years.

This essay is about the resilience of West African theatre forms within the wider contexts of both Christian and Muslim colonisers. It shows a deep understanding of all three cultures and the interplay between them at the level of performance.

## Compare this article with writings by the following authors in this reader

**Artaud, Grotowski and Barba** – European notions of ritual
**Benjamin** – comparative, European intellectual stance
**Brecht and Piscator** – the theatre as a political force
**Hijikata** – different notions of the traditional

## Further reading

Gibbs, J. (1968) *Wole Soyinka*, London: MacMillan Education.
Jones, E.D. (1973) *The Writings of Wole Soyinka*, London: Heinemann.
Soyinka, W. (1974) *Collected Plays 1 and 2*, Oxford: Oxford University Press.
Soyinka, W. (2006) *You Must Set Out at Dawn*, London: Methuen.

## Note

1   The way in which he was treated as an intellectual in Nigeria was reported, after his departure, in S. Hughes (1994) 'Long road to freedom', *Times Higher Education Supplement*, No. 1151, 25 November: 1.

# Chapter 55

# Konstantin Stanislavski

## INTONATIONS AND PAUSES

### 1

IN THE AUDITORIUM of the school theatre we found, when we came in to-day, a large placard with the words 'Speech on the Stage'. As is his custom Tortsov congratulated us on reaching a new phase in our work:

'At our last lesson I explained to you that actors must acquire the feel of vowels and consonants of syllables, get inside them.

'To-day we go on, in the same way, to consider whole words and phrases. Do not expect me to read you a lecture on the subject, that is the job of a specialist. All I shall tell you concerns several aspects of the art of speaking on the stage that I have learned about in my own practical experience. It will help you in your approach to your new studies in the "laws of speech!"

'Many fine books have been written about these laws and about words. Study them carefully. The most appropriate to the needs of Russian actors is the well worked out book of S.M. Volkonski on *The Expressive Word*. I shall be constantly having recourse to it, I shall quote it and draw examples from it in these introductory lessons on stage speech. An actor should know his own tongue in every particular. Of what use will all the subtleties of emotion be if they are expressed in poor speech? A first-class musician should never play on an instrument out of tune. In this field of speech we need science but we must be intelligent and forehanded about acquiring it. There is no point in filling our heads with a lot of new ideas and rushing on the stage to exploit them before we have learned the elementary rules. That kind of a student will lose his head, he will either forget his science or think about it to the exclusion of everything else. Science can help art only when they support and complement each other.'

Tortsov reflected for a moment and then went on:

'You have often heard me say that each person who goes on to the stage has to re-train himself from the beginning: to see, walk, move about, hold intercourse with people and, finally, to speak. The vast majority of people make use of poor, vulgar ways of speaking in ordinary life, but they are not aware of this because they are accustomed to these defects in themselves and in others. I do not say that you are an exception to this rule. Therefore, before you begin your regular speech work it is absolutely necessary to be made aware of the deficiencies in your speech so that you can break yourselves permanently of the habit, widespread among actors, of giving their own incorrect everyday speech as an excuse for the slovenly ways of speaking on the stage.

'Words and the way they are spoken show up much more on the stage than in ordinary life. In most theatres actors are required to repeat the text half-way decently. Even this is done in a slipshod, routine way.

'There are many reasons for this and the first of them is that in ordinary life one says what one is obliged to, or what one desires to, for a purpose, to accomplish an end, because of necessity or, actually, for the sake of some real, fruitful, pointed verbal action. It even happens rather frequently that even when one chatters along without paying much attention to the words, one is still using them for a reason: to pass the time quickly, to distract the attention and so on.

'On the stage it is different. There we speak the text of another, the author's, and often it is at variance with our needs and desires.

'Moreover in ordinary life we talk about things we actually see or have in our minds, things that actually exist. On the stage we have to talk about things we do not see, feel, think about for ourselves but in the imaginary persons of our parts.

'In ordinary life we know how to listen, because we are interested in or need to hear something. On the stage, in most cases, all we do is make a pretence of attentive listening. We do not feel any practical necessity to penetrate the thoughts and words of our stage partner. We have to oblige ourselves to do it. And that forcing ends in over-acting, routine, clichés.

'There are other distressing circumstances too, which tend to kill lively human reactions. The lines, repeated so often in rehearsals and numerous performances, are parroted. The inner content of the text evaporates, all that is left is mechanical sound. In order to earn the right to be on the stage the actors have to be doing something. One of the things they do to fill up the blank spaces inside their parts is to engage in automatic repetition of their lines.

'The consequence of this is that actors acquire a habit of mechanical speech on the stage, the thoughtless parrot-like pronunciation of lines learned by heart without any regard for their inner essence. The more rein they give to this habit, the keener their mechanical memory, the more stubborn the habit of such prattle becomes. And gradually we see the development of a specifically stereotyped kind of stage speech.

'In ordinary life we also meet with mechanical expressions such as: "How do you do?" "Pretty well, thank you." Or "Good-bye. Best of luck!"

'What is a person thinking of while he is saying those automatic words? He is subject neither to the thought nor the feeling essentially contained in them. They just pop out of us while we are absorbed by entirely different interests. We see the same thing in school. While a pupil is reciting something he has learned by rote he is often thinking about his own affairs and the mark the teacher will give him. Actors are prone to the same habits.

'To such actors the feelings and ideas of a part are stepchildren. In the beginning, when they first read the play the words, both their own lines and those of the others who play opposite them, seem interesting, new; they have some point. But after they have heard them kicked around at rehearsal, the words lose all essential meaning. They do not exist in the hearts or even in the consciousness of the actors, but only in the muscles of their tongues. By then it makes little difference to him what his or anyone else's lines are. The only important thing is to keep going, never to stop in his tracks.

'How senseless it is when an actor on the stage, without even hearing out what is being said to or asked of him, without allowing a thought, even an important one, to be fully expressed to him, hurries to break in on his partner's lines. It also happens that the key word in a cue is so skimped that it does not reach the public, so that the sense of the reply to it is entirely lost, the partner has nothing to reply to. There is no use in his asking to have the question repeated because the first actor has no real comprehension of what he was asking in the first place. All these falsifications add up to conventional, cliché acting which kills all belief in the lines spoken and in their living content.

'The situation is worsened of course when actors consciously give an incorrect turn to their lines. We all know that many of them use their lines as a vehicle to exhibit some vocal attributes, diction, manner of recitation, the technique of their voice production. Such actors have no more relation to art than the salesman of musical instruments who brashly demonstrates his wares by pyrotechnical execution, not for the purpose of conveying the intent of the composer, but merely to sell the instrument.

'Actors do the same when they indulge in calculated cadences and technical effects by emphasizing individual letters of syllables, crooning over or bellowing them without any purpose other than to show off their voices, and to make the eardrums of their hearers tingle with pleasant admiration.'

## 2

Tortsov began with a question to-day: What do we mean by subtext? What is it that lies behind and beneath the actual words of a part?

He expressed his answer this way:

'It is the manifest, the inwardly felt expression of a human being in a part, which flows uninterruptedly beneath the words of the text, giving them life and a basis for existing. The subtext is a web of innumerable, varied inner patterns inside a play and a part, woven from "magic ifs", given circumstances, all sorts of figments of the imagination, inner movements, objects of attention, smaller and greater truths and a belief in them, adaptations, adjustments and other similar elements. It is the subtext that makes us say the words we do in a play.

'All these intentionally intertwined elements are like the individual threads in a cable, they run all through the play and lead to the ultimate super-objective.

'It is only when our feelings reach down into the subtextual stream that the "through line of action" of a play or a part comes into being. It is made manifest not only by physical movements but also by speech: it is possible to act not only with the body but also with sound, with words.

'What we call the through line as related to action has its equivalent in the subtext, as related to speech.

'It is superfluous to state that a word taken separately and devoid of inner content is nothing but an external name. The text of a part if it is made up of no more than that will be a series of empty sounds.

'Take as an example the word "love". For a foreigner it is only a strange combination of letters. It is an empty sound because it is devoid of all the inner connotations which quicken the heart. But let feelings, thoughts, imagination give life to the empty sound and an entirely different attitude is produced, the word becomes significant. Then the sounds "I love" acquire the power to fire a man with passion and change the course of his whole life.

'The word "onward" when inwardly coloured by patriotic emotion is capable of leading regiments to sure death. The simplest words, that convey complex thoughts affect our whole outlook on the world. It is not for nothing that the word has become the most concrete expression of man's thought.

'A word can arouse in him all five senses. One needs to do no more than recall the title of a piece of music, the name of a painter, of a dish, of favourite perfumes and so on and one immediately resurrects the auditory and visual images, tastes, smells or tactile sensations suggested by the word.

'It can bring back painful sensations. In *My Life in Art* a story about a toothache caused a toothache in the person who heard it.

'There should never be any soulless or feelingless words used on the stage. Words should no more be divorced from ideas there than from action. On the stage it is the part of the word to arouse all sorts of feelings, desires, thoughts, inner images, visual, auditory and other sensations in the actor, in those playing opposite him and through them together in the audience.

'This suggests that the spoken word, the text of a play is not valuable in and of itself, but is made so by the inner content of the subtext and what is contained in it. This is something we are prone to forget when we step on to the stage.

'We are also inclined to forget that the printed play is not a finished piece of work until it is played on the stage by actors and brought to life by genuine human emotions; the same can be said of a musical score, it is not really a symphony until it is executed by an orchestra of musicians in a concert. As soon as people, either actors or musicians, breathe the life of their own sentiment into the subtext of a piece of writing to be conveyed to an audience, the spiritual well springs, the inner essence is released – the real things which inspired the writing of the play, the poem, the score of music. The whole point of any such creation is in the underlying subtext. Without it the words have no excuse for being presented on the stage. When they are spoken the words come from the author, the subtext from the actor. If this were not so the public would not make the effort of coming to the theatre, they would sit at home and read the printed play.

'Yet it is only on the stage that a drama can be revealed in all its fullness and significance, Only in a performance can we feel the true spirit which animates a play and its subtext – this is recreated, and conveyed by the actors every time the play is given.

'It is up to the actor to compose the music of his feelings to the text of his part and learn how to sing those feelings in words. When we hear the melody of a living soul we then, and only then, can come to a full appreciation of the worth and beauty of the lines and of all that they hold concealed.

'From your earlier work in this school you are familiar with the inner line of a part with its progressive action leading to the super-objective. You know too how these lines are formed to create an inner state in which you live your part, and how you have recourse to the aids of psycho-technique when this does not occur spontaneously.

'This whole process is equally valid and necessary in the relation to the spoken word.'

■　■　■

## Source

Stanislavski, K. (1950), 'Intonations and Pauses', (parts 1 and 2), *Building a Character*, trans. E.R. Hapgood, London: Max Reinhardt: 109–115. Completed in 1930 and first published in English in 1950.

## Konstantin Stanislavski (1863–1938)

Russian actor and director. The work and teaching of Stanislavski have been the major influence on actor training in Europe in the twentieth century. It is still the only substantial and completely worked-out method of acting available. Brecht's and Meyerhold's attempts at recording their training methods are, by comparison, crude and partial. Stanislavski's System, as it has come to be known, is available in two major books, *An Actor Prepares*, and *Building a Character*, first published in English in 1936 and 1950 respectively. They are the result of a life of directing and training actors, mostly those of the Moscow Art Theatre, which Stanislavski founded with Vladimir Nemirovitch-Danchenko in 1898. The company became associated in particular with the plays of Anton Chekhov, and it is mainly to the problems of producing Chekhov's plays that much of the advice of the System refers. As such it is taught all over Europe and the USA, China, and parts of the rest of the world. In a modified form, known as the Method, it has trained many of the best North American performers, and has been a profound influence on Hollywood. In the UK most professional drama schools are still dedicated to exploring the implications of the System. It is thus the most pervasive performer training conducted in the Western world, and has held its own against the tide of anti-naturalist approaches unleashed in modern and postmodern contexts.

In this extract from *Building a Character* Stanislavski deliberately uses a fictional situation – the actors and teachers in a studio – in order to give the sense of a practical acting method. The book is essentially a guide to the attainment of a certain style, but it is interesting to note the emphasis that Stanislavski puts on observation and analysis of everyday human behaviour as a basis for discovering a way of internalising knowledge of which the results will be shown on stage. In this emphasis he agrees with Brecht, for whom observation was the paramount performer's skill.

## Compare this article with writings by the following authors in this reader

**Artaud** – a contemporary, but different, approach
**Beck** – similar intensity of purpose in training
**Boal, Barba and Copeau** – alternative training methods
**Brecht** – similar insights to opposing ends
**Craig** – the Hamlet collaboration
**Duncan** – a contemporary whom Stanislavski admired for her performance
**Meyerhold** – an opposing Russian method

## Further reading

Benedetti, J. (1988) *Stanislavski: A Biography*, London: Methuen.
Benedetti, J. (2008) *Stanislavski: An Introduction*, London: Methuen.
Merlin, B. (2007) *The Complete Stanislavsky Toolkit*, London: Nick Hern Books.
Nemirovitch-Danchenko, V. (1936) *My Life in the Russian Theatre*, trans. J. Conrad, New York: Theatre Arts Books.
Stanislavski, K. (1924) *My Life in Art*, trans. J.J. Robbins, London: Geoffrey Bles.

# Chapter 56

# Gertrude Stein

## COMPOSITION AS EXPLANATION

THERE is singularly nothing that makes a difference a difference in beginning and in the middle and in ending except that each generation has something different at which they are all looking. By this I mean so simply that anybody knows it that composition is the difference which makes each and all of them then different from other generations and this is what makes everything different otherwise they are all alike and everybody knows it because everybody says it.

It is very likely that nearly every one has been very nearly certain that something that is interesting is interesting them. Can they and do they. It is very interesting that nothing inside in them, that is when you consider the very long history of how every one ever acted or has felt, it is very interesting that nothing inside in them in all of them makes it connectedly different. By this I mean this. The only thing that is different from one time to another is what is seen and what is seen depends upon how everybody is doing everything. This makes the thing we are looking at very different and this makes what those describe it make of it, it makes a composition, it confuses, it shows, it is, it looks, it likes it as it is, and this makes what is seen as it is seen. Nothing changes from generation to generation except the thing seen and that makes a composition. Lord Grey remarked that when the generals before the war talked about the war they talked about it as a nineteenth-century war although to be fought with twentieth-century weapons. That is because war is a thing that decides how it is to be done when it is to be done. It is prepared and to that degree it is like all academies it is not a thing made by being made it is a thing prepared. Writing and painting and all that, is like that, for those who occupy themselves with it and don't make it as it is made. Now the few who make it as it is made, and it is to be remarked that the most decided of them usually are prepared just as the world around them is preparing, do it in this way and so I if you do not mind I will tell you how it happens. Naturally one does not know how it happened until it is well over beginning happening.

To come back to the part that the only thing that is different is what is seen when it seems to be being seen, in other words, composition and time sense.

No one is ahead of his time, it is only that the particular variety of creating his time is the one that his contemporaries who also are creating their own time refuse to accept. And they refuse to accept it for a very simple reason and that is that they do not have to accept it for any reason. They themselves that is everybody in their entering the modern composition and they do enter it, if they do not enter it they are not so to speak in it they are out of it and so they do enter it; but in as you may say the non-competitive efforts where if you are not in it nothing is lost except nothing at all except what is not had, there are naturally all the refusals, and the things refused are only important if unexpectedly somebody happens to need them. In the case of the arts it is very definite. Those who are creating the modern composition authentically are naturally only of importance when they are dead because by that time the modern composition having become past is classified and the description of it is classical. That is the reason why the creator of the new composition in the arts is an outlaw until he is a classic, there is hardly a moment in between and it is really too bad very much too bad naturally for the creator but also very much too bad for the enjoyer, they all really would enjoy the created so much better just after it has been made than when it is already a classic, but it is perfectly simple that there is no reason why the contemporary should see, because it would not make any difference as they lead their lives in the new composition anyway, and as every one is naturally indolent why naturally they don't see. For this reason as in quoting Lord Grey it is quite certain that nations not actively threatened are at least several generations behind themselves militarily so aesthetically they are more than several generations behind themselves and it is very much too bad, it is so very much more exciting and satisfactory for everybody if one can have contemporaries, if all one's contemporaries could be one's contemporaries.

There is almost not an interval.

For a very long time everybody refuses and then almost without a pause almost everybody accepts. In the history of the refused in the arts and literature the rapidity of the change is always startling. Now the only difficulty with the *volte-face* concerning the arts is this. When the acceptance comes, by that acceptance the thing, created becomes a classic. It is a natural phenomena a rather extraordinary natural phenomena that a thing accepted becomes a classic. And what is the characteristic quality of a classic. The characteristic quality of a classic is that it is beautiful. Now of course it is perfectly true that a more or less first rate work of art is beautiful but the trouble is that when that first rate work of art becomes a classic because it is accepted the only thing that is important from then on to the majority of the acceptors the enormous majority, the most intelligent majority of the acceptors is that it is so wonderfully beautiful. Of course it is wonderfully beautiful, only when it is still a thing irritating annoying stimulating then all quality of beauty is denied to it.

Of course it is beautiful but first all beauty in it is denied and then all the beauty of it is accepted. If every one were not so indolent they would realize that beauty is beauty even when it is irritating and stimulating not only when it is accepted and classic. Of course it is extremely difficult nothing more so than to remember back to its not being beautiful once it has become beautiful. This makes it so much more difficult to realize its beauty when the work is being refused and prevents every one from realizing that they were convinced that beauty was denied, once the work is accepted. Automatically with the acceptance of the time sense comes the recognition of the beauty and once the beauty is accepted the beauty never fails any one.

Beginning again and again is a natural thing even when there is a series.

Beginning again and again and again explaining composition and time is a natural thing.

It is understood by this time that everything is the same except composition and time, composition and the time of the composition and the time in the composition.

Everything is the same except composition and as the composition is different and always going to be different everything is not the same. Everything is not the same as the time when of the composition and the time in the composition is different. The composition is different, that is certain.

The composition is the thing seen by every one living in the living that they are doing, they are the composing of the composition that at the time they are living is the composition of the time in which they are living. It is that that makes living a thing they are doing. Nothing else is different, of that almost any one can be certain. The time when and the time of and the time in that composition is the natural phenomena of that composition and of that perhaps every one can be certain.

No one thinks these things when they are making when they are creating what is the composition, naturally no one thinks, that is no one formulates until what is to be formulated has been made.

Composition is not there, it is going to be there and we are here. This is some time ago for us naturally.

The only thing that is different from one time to another is what is seen and what is seen depends upon how everybody is doing everything. This makes the thing we are looking at very different and this makes what those who describe it make of it, it makes a composition, it confuses, it shows, it is, it looks, it likes it as it is, and this makes what is seen as it is seen. Nothing changes from generation to generation except the thing seen and that makes a composition.

Now the few who make writing as it is made and it is to be remarked that the most decided of them are those that are prepared by preparing, are prepared just as the world around them is prepared and is preparing to do it in this way and so if you do not mind I will again tell you how it happens. Naturally one does not know how it happened until it is well over beginning happening.

Each period of living differs from any other period of living not in the way life is but in the way life is conducted and that authentically speaking is composition. After life has been conducted in a certain way everybody knows it but nobody knows it, little by little, nobody knows it as long as nobody knows it. Any one creating the composition in the arts does not know it either, they are conducting life and that makes their composition what it is, it makes their work compose as it does.

Their influence and their influences are the same as that of all of their contemporaries only it must always be remembered that the analogy is not obvious until as I say the composition of a time has become so pronounced that it is past and the artistic composition of it is a classic.

And now to begin as if to begin. Composition is not there, it is going to be there and we are here. This is some time ago for us naturally. There is something to be added afterwards.

Just how much my work is known to you I do not know. I feel that perhaps it would be just as well to tell the whole of it.

In beginning writing I wrote a book called *Three Lives* this was written in 1905. I wrote a negro story called *Melanctha*. In that there was a constant recurring and beginning there was a marked direction in the direction of being in the present although naturally I had been accustomed to past present and future, and why, because the composition forming around me was a prolonged present. A composition of a prolonged present is a natural composition in the world as it has been these thirty years it was more and more a prolonged present. I created then a prolonged present naturally I knew nothing of a continuous present but it came naturally to me to make one, it was simple it was clear to me and nobody knew why it was done like that, I did not myself although naturally to me it was natural.

After that I did a book called *The Making of Americans* it is a long book about a thousand pages.

Here again it was all so natural to me and more and more complicatedly a continuous present. A continuous present is a continuous present. I made almost a thousand pages of a continuous present.

Continuous present is one thing and beginning again and again is another thing. These are both things. And then there is using everything.

This brings us again to composition this the using everything. The using everything brings us to composition and to this composition. A continuous present and using everything and beginning again. In these two books there was elaboration of the complexities of using everything and of a continuous present and of beginning again and again and again.

In the first book there was a groping for a continuous present and for using everything by beginning again and again.

There was a groping for using everything and there was a groping for a continuous present and there was an inevitable beginning of beginning again and again and again.

Having naturally done this I naturally was a little troubled with it when I read it. I became then like the others who read it. One does, you know, excepting that when I reread it myself I lost myself in it again. Then I said to myself this time it will be different and I began. I did not begin again I just began.

In this beginning naturally since I at once went on and on very soon there were pages and pages and pages more and more elaborated creating a more and more continuous present including more and more using of everything and continuing more and more beginning and beginning and beginning.

I went on and on to a thousand pages of it.

In the meantime to naturally begin I commenced making portraits of anybody and anything. In making these portraits I naturally made a continuous present an including everything and a beginning again and again within a very small thing. That started me into composing anything into one thing. So then naturally it was natural that one thing an enormously long thing was not everything an enormously short thing was also not everything nor was it all of it a continuous present thing nor was it always and always beginning again. Naturally I would then begin again. I would begin again I would naturally begin. I did naturally begin. This brings me to a great deal that has been begun.

And after that what changes what changes after that, after that what changes and what changes after that and after that and what changes and after that and what changes after that.

The problem from this time on became more definite.

It was all so nearly alike it must be different and it is different, it is natural that if everything is used and there is a continuous present and a beginning again and again if it is all so alike it must be simply different and everything simply different was the natural way of creating it then.

In this natural way of creating it then that it was simply different everything being alike it was simply different, this kept on leading one to lists. Lists naturally for a while and by lists I mean a series. More and more in going back over what was done at this time I find that I naturally kept simply different as an intention. Whether there was or whether there was not a continuous present did not then any longer trouble me there was or there was not, using everything no longer troubled me if everything is alike using everything could no longer trouble me and beginning again and again could no longer trouble me because if lists were inevitable if series were inevitable and the whole of it was inevitable beginning again and again could not trouble me so then with nothing to trouble me I very completely began naturally since everything is alike making it as simply different naturally as simply different as possible. I began doing natural phenomena what I call natural phenomena and natural phenomena naturally everything being alike natural phenomena are making things be naturally simply different. This found its culmination later, in the beginning it began in a center confused with lists with series with geography with returning portraits and with particularly often four and three and often with five and four. It is easy to see that in the beginning such a conception as everything being naturally different would be very inarticulate and very slowly it began to emerge and take the form of anything, and then naturally if anything that is simply different is simply different what follows will follow.

So far then the progress of my conceptions was the natural progress entirely in accordance with my epoch as I am sure is to be quite easily realized if you think over the scene that was before us all from year to year.

As I said in the beginning, there is the long history of how every one ever acted or has felt and that nothing inside in them in all of them makes it connectedly different. By this I mean all this.

The only thing that is different from one time to another is what is seen and what is seen depends upon how everybody is doing every thing.

It is understood by this time that everything is the same except composition and time, composition and the time of the composition and the time in the composition.

Everything is the same except composition and as the composition is different and always going to be different everything is not the same. So then I as a contemporary creating the composition in the beginning was groping toward a continuous present, a using everything a beginning again and again and then everything being alike then everything very simply everything was naturally simply different and so I as a contemporary was creating everything being alike was creating everything naturally being naturally simply different, everything being alike. This then was the period that brings me to the period of the beginning of 1914. Everything being alike everything naturally would be simply different and war came and everything being alike and everything being simply different brings everything being simply different brings it to romanticism.

Romanticism is then when everything being alike everything is naturally simply different, and romanticism.

Then for four years this was more and more different even though this was, was everything alike. Everything alike naturally everything was simply different and this is and was romanticism and this is and was war. Everything being alike everything naturally everything is different simply different naturally simply different.

And so there was the natural phenomena that was war, which had been, before war came, several generations behind the contemporary composition, because it became war and so completely needed to be contemporary became completely contemporary and so created the completed recognition of the contemporary composition. Every one but one may say every one became consciously became aware of the existence of the authenticity of the modern composition. This then the contemporary recognition, because of the academic thing known as war having been forced to become contemporary made every one not only contemporary in act not only contemporary in thought but contemporary in self-consciousness made every one contemporary with the modern composition. And so the art creation of the contemporary composition which would have been outlawed normally outlawed several generations more behind even than war, war having been brought so to speak up to date art so to speak was allowed not completely to be up to date, but nearly up to date, in other words we who created the expression of the modern composition were to be recognized before we were dead some of us even quite a long time before we were dead. And so war may be said to have advanced a general recognition of the expression of the contemporary composition by almost thirty years.

And now after that there is no more of that in other words there is peace and something comes then and it follows coming then.

And so now one finds oneself interesting oneself in an equilibration, that of course means words as well as things and distribution as well as between themselves between the words and themselves and the things and themselves, a distribution as distribution. This makes what follows what follows and now there is every reason why there should be an arrangement made. Distribution is interesting and equilibration is interesting when a continuous present and a beginning again and again using everything and everything alike and everything naturally simply different has been done.

After all this, there is that, there has been that that there is a composition and that nothing changes except composition the composition and the time of and the time in the composition.

The time of the composition is a natural thing and the time in the composition is a natural thing it is a natural thing and it is a contemporary thing.

The time of the composition is the time of the composition. It has been at times a present thing it has been at times a past thing it has been at times a future thing it has been at times an endeavour at parts or all of these things. In my beginning it was a continuous present a beginning again and again and again and again, it was a series it was a list it was a similarity and everything different it was a distribution and an equilibration. That is all of the time some of the time of the composition.

Now there is still something else the time-sense in the composition. This is what is always a feat a doubt and a judgement and a conviction. The quality in the creation of expression the quality in a composition that makes it go dead just after it has been made is very troublesome.

The time in the composition is a thing that is very troublesome. If the time in the composition is very troublesome it is because there must even if there is no time at all in the composition there must be time in the composition which is in its quality of distribution and equilibration. In the beginning there was the time in the composition that naturally was in the composition but time in the composition comes now and this is what is now troubling every one the time in the composition is now a part of distribution and equilibration. In the beginning there was confusion there was a continuous present and later there was romanticism which was not a confusion but an extrication and now there is either succeeding or failing there must be distribution and equilibration there must be time that is distributed and equilibrated. This is the thing that is at present the most troubling and if there is the time that is at present the most troublesome the time-sense that is at present the most troubling is the thing that makes the present the most troubling. There is at present there is distribution, by this I mean expression and time, and in this way at present composition is time that is the reason that at present the time-sense is troubling that is the reason why at present the time-sense in the composition is the composition that is making what there is in composition.

And afterwards.

Now that is all.

■   ■   ■

## Source

Stein, G. (1971) 'Composition as Explanation', *Look at Me Now and Here I am*, Harmondsworth: Penguin: 21–30.

## Gertrude Stein (1874–1946)

A key writer for many twentieth-century performance practitioners, among them the Wooster Group (*House Lights*) and Robert Wilson (*Dr Faustus Lights the Lights*), Stein was born in America and moved to Paris in 1903 with Alice B. Toklas, a friend who became her partner and lifelong secretary. Their home on the Left Bank in Paris became a meeting place for many contemporary artists such as Matisse, Picasso and Braque. Her interests were wide and eclectic and among her most famous writings are *The Making of Americans* (1925), *How to Write* (1931) and the *Autobiography of Alice B. Toklas*. Her writing is unique in its style and her interests led her to write poems, essays and plays. She, more than any other writer, crossed the boundaries of the fine arts and performance practice. She broke totally with literary convention, questioning what it is to write and how to write. Her essays and writings are performative in that they demand reading out loud to be understood. This is her attraction for many of today's performing artists. Far from being seen as a literary joke or merely an idiosyncratic literary side-show, in the late twentieth century she has moved to a position where she is seen, together with Samuel Beckett, Heiner Müller and James Joyce, as one of the great originals. She wrote a series of 'plays' that break with orthodox conventions of character and situation, some of which have been used as the basis of contemporary theatre practice.

In this wide-ranging essay, ostensibly about 'composition', she discusses how the world can be seen by different generations as a framework that can define and re-define perceptions and which can apply fine arts practice to life.

## Compare this article with writings by the following authors in this reader

**Foreman** – another idiosyncratic American writer
**Kandinsky** – a contemporary artist
**LeCompte** – director of the Wooster Group
**Wilson** – American director

## Further reading

Daniel, S. (2009) *Gertrude Stein*, London: Reaktion Books.
Knapp, B. (1990) *Gertrude Stein*, New York: Continuum Books.
Shaughnessy, N. (2007) *Gertrude Stein*, Tavistock: Northcote House.

# Chapter 57

# Stelarc

## INTERVIEW WITH NICHOLAS ZURBRUGG

INTERVIEW

Nicholas Zurbrugg

(Sydney, April 1996, Glasgow, April 1997, Leicester, June 1998)

N.Z. Perhaps I could begin by asking you what kind of experiences your most recent performances have been exploring? One of your most central concerns seems to be the attempt to enter an interface between technology and the body in order to look beyond dominant concepts of identity and the 'I'.

S. Yes, I think the query is 'How is that experience of the "I" generated' and 'How might new explanations of awareness be appropriate?'. I guess that I don't take the body as a given, and I don't take the 'I' or the 'self' as a necessary construct. Certainly, it's a convenient one, a seductive one, one that allows us to exist in the world, one that allows us to function with other bodies – in relationship to other bodies. But it seems clear that the conventional notion of 'awareness', as a possession of each and every individual body, can also be reconfigured as a sensation constantly reconstructed between individuals, rather than within each individual.

So what's important is what's occurring between you and I, in the medium of language and in the social institution, at this point in history, in this particular culture that we're functioning in. So I think of technology augmenting this mindless body of mine. And

I don't say that in a derogatory sense or in a belittling sense. But I think, 'Can we consider a body that can function with neither memory nor desire?' – 'Is it possible to navigate the world, to operate effectively, sense and communicate, in these kind of cool spaces displaced from the cultural spaces – the carbon-chemistry hot spaces – of emotion and of personal experience?'.

I'm intrigued by the way in which our psycho-social and historical and cultural development has always tended to perceive the notion of the split personality as pathological. We query whether it's possible to function with multiple personalities. But in our cyber realm of existence, it'll be an advantage to have a split personality – where one body might function in multiple and unconnected ways. Parts of your body will become alien to yourself. You see limbs move as alien arms remotely actuated by agents elsewhere. You have a split body – your right side collaborating with local awareness with the alien left side of your body. A two-way tele-Stimbod system would create both a possessed and a possessing body in the one physiology. A Stimbod would be a hollow body, a host body for the projection and performance of remote agents. Glove Anaesthesia and Alien Hand are pathological conditions in which the patient experiences parts of their body as not there, as not their own, as not under their own control – an absence of physicality on the one hand and an absence of agency on the other. In a Stimbod, not only would it possess a split physiology but it would experience parts of itself as automated, absent and alien. In our Platonic, Christian, Cartesian and Freudian pasts this might have been considered pathological. But in this terrain of cyber complexity that we now inhabit the inadequacy and the obsolescence of the ego-agent driven biological body cannot be more apparent. A transition from psycho-body to cybersystem becomes necessary to function effectively and intuitively in remote spaces, speeded-up situations and alien information beyond sensory experience.

Now, the issue here isn't one of 'remote control', because the body is not a robot – the body initiates a loop of awareness in this relationship. So what is important is not so much that you're remote-controlling my body, but rather that a movement that you make in London happens in my body in Melbourne. There's a physical displacement of a movement from one body to another body in another place. From my perspective, or from this body's perspective in this place, this body becomes a host for a remote agent. From your point of view, you become an agent that can extrude awareness and action into another body elsewhere – you can project your human presence in a physical action, through another body.

So this notion of 'fractal flesh' is the idea that you can project or extrude awareness and action into other bodies or bits of bodies, on the net – that your realm of operation goes beyond your biological boundaries and the local space that you function within, to an electronic space that connects other limbs, other people, in other places. These are the sorts of concerns and explorations in my work – there's no kind of ideological agenda that has to be constantly affirmed. I think that most artists – to make interesting art – make it in the realm of the open, of the divergent rather than the convergent, where what you're creating are contestable futures, not utopian ideals.

N.Z. Your own works don't reflect utopian ideals?

S. No, the performances are not about illustrating scifi yearnings, they are not about affirming a desired future. They are not about closure. There is an attempt to explore and elaborate, to experience and speculate through interfaces, simulations and stimulations. They do not affirm 'What it means to be human' but rather they undermine simplistic assumptions of 'what it means to be a body'. Is it meaningful to 'have a mind of your own' anymore? Must these genetic, personal and cultural memories continue to contain and condition us? What other strategies and trajectories can be plotted? We continue to map our outmoded metaphysical assumptions onto our new technologies. This is a seductive strategy as it is part of a process of affirmation (retro-human). New technologies are justified by obsolete desires. Perhaps what it means to be human is about not retaining our humanity.

N.Z. Do you ever feel that in the process of this kind of performance you're unexpectedly tuning in to some sort of field of collective memory?

S. Well, it depends what we mean by 'collective memory'. It's not so much a matter of 'tuning-in' but rather creating alternate interfaces and constructing an extended field of operation. And in functioning in this complex information structure unexpected possibilities are generated – and experienced. Certainly, the experience is fragmented, particular and peculiar to the instruments and interfaces you are connected to. There is no coherent, collective unconscious – what you manifest is what you mentally and physically experience and that's what becomes meaningful from moment to moment. The Internet can become not only a medium of information transfer and transmission, but rather it can become a transducer affecting physical action. Electronic space as a medium of action rather than information. The Internet as external nervous system for a multiplicity of bodies in different places – awareness and agency could be shifted and shared in a space of distributed intelligence, scaling up the subtlety, speed and complexity of human activity. The cyborg system would have a 'Fractal Flesh' – awareness and action would be extruded to bodies and bits of bodies in a vast network of interactive entities, augmented by agents and avatars on the Internet.

N.Z. Have any particular patterns of discovery emerged from these kinds of global link-up?

S. Bodies must now perform in techno-terrains and data-structures beyond the human-scale where intention and action collapse into accelerated responses. Bodies acting without expectation, being prompted to move with neither memory nor desire. Can a body act without emotion? Must a body continuously affirm its biological, emotional and social status quo? Perhaps what is necessary is electronic erasure with alternate, intimate and internalized interfaces to allow for the design of a body with more inputs and outputs for performance and awareness that it is augmented by search engines. Consider a body that is informed by spiders, robots and phantoms – whose awareness is exponentially, telematically scaled-up. Consider a body that is projected by surrogate robots in situations and spaces where no body could go.

For example, in 'Ping Body', the performance I did at Artspace the other night, instead of the body moving to the promptings of other bodies in other places, I was intrigued by the possibility of the body functioning to the statistical ebb and flow of Internet activity. We couldn't literally do that, but we came up with a procedure that enabled the structural, spatial and temporal parameters of the Internet – and also to an extent, the Internet activity – to impose and choreograph the body's movements. So using the UNIX Ping protocol we automatically, randomly and continuously live during the performance 'pinged' 30–40 remote computer domains. The reverberating signals returning to the host computer in Sydney took anywhere from several hundred to several thousand milliseconds depending on whether you were pinging China, Brazil, Europe or the USA.

The ping values were indicative not of spatial distance but of the complexity of the network, because the further your ping, the more complex the network that the signal travels through. So even if you were pinging one particular remote domain, from moment to moment the values would vary, indicating that the Internet activity had decreased or intensified, so that the more the activity, the longer the signal took to transmit back.

It was these values that were mapped onto the choreography of the body. We were telematically scaling the body to the point where its musculature is driven not merely by its internal nervous system but rather by this external data field – this data flow – of the Internet.

N.Z. Perhaps this could be described as a kind of telematic ballet. The Melbourne composer Warren Burt discusses rather more restrained interactive dance environments in which movement into certain areas activates sensors which alter sound or light, whereas here the whole Internet world seems to become the stage or environment for your performance.

S. Yes – and it's not only a special kind of space to perform in, but the structure of interaction and operation – and initiation – is very different. It's an electronic realm of millisecond values that can be reverberated in a global network. That doesn't necessarily guarantee its meaningfulness or even its significance – this can only be evaluated or authenticated by what happens in itself. I mean, if you walked into this performance and you were mesmerized by what was going on, as some people were, but didn't know the operational parameters, I would hope that the performance stands on its own. On the other hand, if you then went away, picked up this leaflet, and discovered a diagram that indicates a much more complex interaction, a much more global initiation of choreography, then perhaps – yes – you'd see this action in a very different way.

I remember once, at one of the Kassel Documentas, walking over a square bit of concrete sort of in the ground, with a circle of brass in the middle, which seemed to be a very minimal, simple, beautiful little piece. But then, going into the museum, I discovered that this was Walter De Maria's installation, and that brass circle was in fact a kilometer deep brass rod into the ground. And all of a sudden, you know, the kind of spatial dimensions and structural aesthetics of that piece exploded cerebrally!

N.Z. What you're doing sounds extremely exciting, doesn't it? From one point of view it's a choreographed performance or a dance performance, and from another point of view it's almost an enormous electronic/human sculpture of global proportions, setting up all these links and demonstrating their possibility.

S. Yes, yes. But I don't want to vindicate this performance by its global dimensions, but certainly, the spatial, structural and electronic nature of it does generate some new possibilities. The other issue – as in the Telepolis performance last year in Luxembourg, where we electronically linked the Pompidou Center in Paris, the Media Lab in Helsinki and the Doors of Perception Conference in Amsterdam – was the issue of a kind of physical intimacy between bodies without proximity. I was going to give an example of this using Werner Hammerstingl – the organiser of the Digital Aesthetics Symposium here in Sydney – as the other body, but I quickly spied Rachel Armstrong next to him, and decided to shift my attention to Rachel! It was a situation where the meaning of me touching my chest in Melbourne would effectively mean Rachel caressing her breast in London. In other words, there would be this kind of strange physical intimacy where if you were watching Rachel, it would appear as a kind of masturbatory act, as a kind of an act of self-gratification, but she would know that her hand was being remotely – and divinely! – guided!

If I then had feedback from Rachel, you would have an intimacy without proximity, but furthermore, you would have a intimacy with the added looped feedback of the other person's sensations mapped back onto your body. Ordinarily if I feel pleasure, it's a pleasure-loop in a sense that is wired within my body, although I can imagine that pleasure is extruded into the other body, and that by their sounds and movements somehow that there is pleasure given back to me in some kind of feedback. But what's happening in this sort of system is that in a sense you have electronically wired an added loop, where you initiate the intimacy, but that intimacy is felt not simply by you but through the feedback of the other body.

N.Z. Presumably this is not simply an erotic experiment elaborating phone sex?

S. No – this allusion to a kind of sexual intimacy is not a central issue. What I'm interested in are the possibilities of new physical interactions – new kinds of physical intimacies that don't rely on proximity, that are augmented by other sorts of feedback loops. I don't see these physical interactions as less than real experiences, but rather as alternate and possibly augmented experiences. The allusion to sex was simply a means of conveying the idea to you.

But imagine if we were electronically linked, and we could both receive and transmit stimulation – the movements you made in the right side of your body occur in my left side, the movements I make on my right side occur on your left side – or perhaps the movements I make with my arms occur in your legs, or vice versa. Here we have a situation where we can actuate a half of each other's body and create not only a symbolic and kind of mental relationship between our bodies, but we can establish direct internal stimulation and activation of our muscles. And of course, here we're only talking about driving the musculature of the body.

But imagine telematically scaling the body and augmenting Internet information in an optical sense, to augment your retinal images with this Internet data. But of course, at the moment, we can't make direct retinal feed into our nervous systems. We can do that with our muscles – we can transmit electronic pulses to stimulate the nerve-endings of the muscles – and the muscles contract and we move. But this notion of telematically scaling up the body will not be limited merely to the musculature of the body, but in the future will also include its sensory, cerebral and retinal inputs, giving the body extended inputs beyond its retinal scan.

The other experience that I've had with this remote activation of the body is that effectively, the left side of your body might be remotely guided, the right side locally initiated, so in one body you can collapse the operations of two agents, one remote, one local – and that experience is a very strange one. You watch your arm move, but you realise that it's remotely guided from elsewhere.

N.Z. Do you see this as a mind/body split, or perhaps as a kind of triangular mind/body/technology split?

S. No, I don't talk about the mind/body split, but about splitting the body. When we talk about the body here, we talk about the total physiological, phenomenological, cerebral package – we're not talking about a body opposed to a mind, because I don't want to make those kinds of distinctions. A body for me is a person, and a person is a thinking, moving, aware entity. I don't want to be immersed in those old metaphysical distinctions between the soul and the body, or the mind and the brain.

N.Z. How would you respond to Virilio's suggestion that in some respects you exemplify a body overtaken by technology and in consequence, a body suffering the loss of various kinds of direction and orientation?

S. Well, Virilio's one of my favourite writers, but I think that his critique in this instance is one that is in a sense obsessed with an ethical and a very human-based concern – he sees technology as a kind of threat to the body. But ever since we became hominids with bipedal locomotion, two limbs become manipulators and we began making artifacts, instruments and machines. Technology has always been part of the human trajectory. Technology is not an alien other. To be human is to be augmented, extended and enhanced by technology.

N.Z. Virilio himself emphasises that he's firmly in favour of technology, generally speaking.

S. But he then begins to draw distinctions. Technology outside the body might be OK, but he seems to see technology as more of a threat when it invades the body's tissues – as if it betrays a body operating with a capital 'I' – a body with a possessed mind, a body that is a possessed individual. This is just a query, but is it possible to consider a body without an 'I', without a self, in the traditional metaphysical way? Can a body operate without memory and desire? These are the central questions, I think.

N.Z. But I imagine you'd want to be more than a cosmic puppet responding to telematic strings?

S. Yes – this kind of notion of a puppet and strings installation or of a master/slave installation might be possible with a robot, but it's a very, very different situation with another body, or between bodies. Firstly, unless you were implanted at birth, you have the choice to sit down, turn on the computer, plug in the stimulation system, turn the voltage up and down in intensity, then log in. You have a choice, to begin with. Secondly, because you are aware of what's going on, this loop of consciousness creates the possibility of response and interaction. I would find no immediate value in a body that wasn't split. Just as I am a little concerned about a body with seemingly unbounded free agency, which we like to romantically imagine we have, I'm also concerned about the body as a total automaton.

N.Z. How does the issue of more or less free agency affect your performances? What for you are the most significant areas of choice allowing modification of the process?

S. Well, precisely in setting up a system of things, a system of operation, an interactive connection of the body with other bits of technologies and images and sounds, which might simulate or unexpectedly generate other kinds of alternate sorts of experiences.

N.Z. What would you say are the most interesting of these experiences?

S. Well, the ones that have already been experienced are the notions of your body becoming a host for a remote agent. Your body is moving, and you've neither initiated that movement nor are you yourself contracting your muscles to produce it. You realise because of your software program and your connection on the net, that you're manifesting the behaviour of another body elsewhere, and that's a strange situation. There may be twenty to thirty channels of interactive possibilities in the performance – the sounds that are generated, which are from a combination of electrodes, sensors, angle-transducers, ultrasound transmitters, which map the position/orientation and bending motion of the head, torso, limbs and fingers. The body also becomes the video switcher and mixer, inadvertently becoming the composing system for the images that are projected on the screen. In the performance the other night, movements initiated by the Internet activity were then in turn uploaded to a website on the net, so in a sense you're using the structural parameters of the net to activate the body, but then, in turn, to upload it. That kind of realisation, that kind of looping, uploading/downloading kind of operation, was a very intriguing one.

Sometimes, within these complexities of things, you're experiencing a kind of cerebral and bodily anaesthesia – a little like when you're driving a car, and all of a sudden you see that you've been out of it for a second, two seconds, ten seconds, thirty seconds, a minute – when the body seems to enter into a state of synchronicity with the technology's complexity. The body performs best when it performs automatically. Symbiosis with technology occurs when the degree of intimacy of interface seduces the body to experience the machine not merely as an addition, but rather as an appendage. Not distinguishing between the two the body forgets not only itself but the machine it is operating.

N.Z. Virilio also seems to discuss this kind of fusion with technology in terms of the way in which the pilot of a jumbo jet more or less becomes the plane, and enters into a state of identification with the plane that he equates with certain kinds of all-knowing, religious experience. I imagine that you'd be reluctant to share these kind of metaphysical categories?

S. The experience of symbiosis is similar to Virilio's description, but equating it to kinds of religious, all-knowing experiences is unnecessary. How is one to know what that means? All that analysis does is to obscure. A strategy for comprehension is categorisation. We understand by associating. And this is a common literary and textual strategy that tries to create convenient continuities in cultural experience by connecting. Sometimes this results in rather simplistic academic critique. In pointing back to past practices or experiences it does not only obscure, but it also affirms obsolete human yearnings. We need to reconsider outmoded metaphysical memes.

N.Z. One day I'd like to hear you enthuse about the compatibility of the new and the old! One day perhaps! But tell me – for now – about your most recent performance – 'Parasite'.

S. In 'Parasite', performed first for Virtual World Orchestra in Glasgow, a customised search engine has been constructed that scans, selects and optically displays images (medical, anatomical, robotic) off the WWW to the body via its head-mounted VR display. Analysis of the JPEG files provides data that is mapped to the body with a muscle stimulation system. The images you see are the images that move you. Representations of the body activate the physical body. The resulting motion is mirrored in a VRML space at the performance site and is also uploaded to a web site as potential and recursive source images for body react-ivation. RealAudio sequences were inserted into sounds generated by limb and finger movements with flexion, proximity, pressure, position and accelerometer sensors. Within this interactive field of Internet and video images the body's physicality provides feedback loops of muscles, transducers and the Third Hand mechanism. The prosthesis of the Third Hand is counterpointed by the prosthesis of the search engine software code. The body becomes split – its left side Internet actuated (voltage-in) whilst its right side operates with local agency and controls an extra hand (voltage-out). Augmented but involuntarily, extended and symbi-otic. Plugged-in, the body becomes a parasite sustained optically and stimulated electrically by an external and virtual nervous system.

■   ■   ■

## Source

Unpublished interview.

## STELARC (1946–)

Stelarc (formerly Stelios Arcadiou) was born in Australia and studied art at Monash and Melbourne universities. His work attempts to extend the boundaries of the perform-ative to include the use of medical instruments, prosthetics, robotics, virtual reality systems, and the internet, and to explore alternative, intimate and involuntary inter-faces with the body. The artist, he believes, can combine biology and technology to become 'an evolutionary guide' for the human body of the twenty-first century. He has performed with a third hand, a virtual arm, a virtual body, and a stomach sculpture, and has acoustically and visually probed the body – having amplified brain waves, blood-flow and muscle signals and filmed the inside of his lungs, stomach and colon. He has done twenty-five body suspensions with insertions into the skin, in different positions, and in varying situations in remote locations.

For *Fractal Flesh* (1995–8), as part of Telepolis, he developed a touch-screen interfaced Muscle Stimulation System, enabling remote access, actuation and choreography of the body. Performances such as *Ping Body* (1995–8) and *Parasite*

(1995–8) probe notions of telematic scaling and the engineering of external, extended and virtual nervous systems of the body using the internet. In 1998 he completed *Exoskeleton*, a pneumatically powered 6-legged walking machine actuated by arm gestures. Stelarc joins other artists, such as Marina Abramovic, Ulay, Orlan, and Herman Nitsch, in exploring solo material often concentrating on gestures, events and images, which were often unnerving and painful to watch. As RoseLee Goldberg points out, much of this material evokes a masochistic ethos, whereby artists have sought to measure their actions against the key texts of writers as diverse as Artaud or Baudrillard.

Stelarc's current projects include the *Extra Ear*, a surgically constructed ear as an additional facial gesture that coupled with a modem and a wearable computer acts as an internet antenna, able to hear RealAudio sounds. *Movitar* (2000) is an intelligent avatar that will be able to perform in the real world by possessing a physical body.

Stelarc has held several appointments and Fellowships at Carnegie Mellon University, Hamburg City and Nottingham Trent University, UK, where he is Principal Research Fellow in the Performance Arts Digital Research Unit.

## Compare this interview with writings by the following authors in this reader

**Artaud** – for a philosophy of extreme theatre
**Abramovic** – for a similar exploration of pain
**Bausch** – for a choreography often of extremes
**Hijikata** – dance as suffering

## Further reading

Bell, D. and Kennedy, B. (2000) *The Cybercultures Reader*, London: Routledge.
Dixon, J.B. and Cassidy, E. (1998) *Virtual Features*, London: Routledge.
Gardiner, H. (ed.) (2010) *Art Practice in a Digital Culture*, Farnham: Ashgate.
Heathfield, A. (1997) *Shattered Anatomies*, Bristol: Arnolfini Live.
Smith, M. (ed.) (2007) *Stelarc: the Monograph*, MIT Press.

# Chapter 58

VIOLA

# BILL VIOLA

## THE VISIONARY LANDSCAPE OF PERCEPTION

### The Landscape is the Imagination

Our landscape and our imagination seem to represent opposites. I think of the difference between soft and hard, the mental and the physical, a thought and a rock. But I also think of the equality of these two things, the transformation of one into the other. For example, a thought can move a rock. A mountain can inspire a thought.

I think of infinities and limits. The imagination is infinite; the landscape is limited. As William Blake said, "Everything to be believed is an image of truth." Yet today satellites have mapped the entire surface of the earth, the entire landscape, down to a resolution of 30 feet or less.

The landscape is infinite and the imagination limited. I see an endless plain under a blue sky while I think of all the places on earth that cannot be touched in a single life time. Yet try as I might, I cannot image the moment of my death.

The unknown territory is an important traditional aspect of our environment and a vital part of the structure of our minds. The unknown place on the other side of the mountain, across the sea, around the corner . . . unknown because the senses do not penetrate.

I think of lying in bed as a child, staring at the dim ceiling, gripped in terror trying to imagine what they could possibly mean when they said, "the universe is infinite and goes on forever." I realized then that there is a limit to my mind's reach.

Then I try to capture all of the thoughts I have had since then. All of the directions my work has taken me, and the endless stream of idea possibilities that lie before me. I sit down to write this, and I am aware long periods of time, geographical features become story points in a mental landscape.

The object of the fascination that foreigners have with American culture is also a source of its problems. The human presence of the newly arrived Europeans on this continent is not enough established to develop a story. People are floating on top of the land, like boats on an opaque sea. The deepest past of America is first of "the other," a separate race of dispossessed or disposed people; second, and finally, it is solely geological, the bare earth of The Grand Canyon, Monument Valley, etc. The distorted idea that the natural landscape is dead ("inanimate matter") comes from living on land without a story.

## Images tell Lies

Perception is the way we contact the world, it is the language of being, yet the senses have traditionally been considered the source of illusion.

An old expression from sound recording technology is "fidelity," fidelity of a recording. We talk about high fidelity, low fidelity. The real question is, of course, fidelity to what: to the object, the hard reality, or to the image, the soft reality?

Traditionally in television, fidelity has been to vision, to the visual image and not to reality, and rarely to the retinal image in the eyeball, even though the camera can be considered a crude and very rough model of the eye. The human visual image is binocular, it includes overlapping areas, double images, indistinct edges, and only a very small part of the center, called the fovea, shows focus in rich detail. Of course, human software, the mind, integrates this with information from the other senses and smoothes out these problems.

Artificial images do not portray reality accurately. They aspire to the image and not to the object, to visual perception and not to the experiential mind field. They do not, for example, show all sides of an object that we know from our experience to exist. The camera only sees three faces of a cube, for example, yet our hands can tell us that the other three simultaneously exist. The "realistic" way of showing all of the sides of the cube as an object in the visual image, specifically in the medium of painting, died out in Europe at the end of the Middle Ages, and was finally eliminated with the advent of vanishing-point perspective. After that, the "photo-realist" tradition, if we can call it that, developed from the Renaissance onwards. The back side of the object disappeared. Of course, the reason why artificial images succeed is that they rely heavily on the viewer's prior knowledge that, for example, objects do have all their sides. They involve the viewer's knowledge base in their functioning.

Human beings, therefore, have always been an integral part of any technology of images. Perception is the input channel to the mind, and with new technologies, the call is first to the body, then the mind will follow. Therefore we talk about "user-friendly," the ease of human interface, comfort of use, the accuracy of human perception. To increase concentration and involvement, movies use the black room, soft seats and a large screen to fully occupy the sensory field. Wilhelm Reich, the Austrian psychologist who was imprisoned in America because his work was too accurate and unsettling for the establishment, realized that in fragmented industrialized societies, the body was the neglected key. To reach the mind, his therapy focused on healing the body through touch. "When I put my hands on the body," he said, "I put my hands on the unconscious."

## The Earth is the Ultimate High Definition System

High definition denotes higher resolution. It is the next step in a long series of steps. So, let's take it to the ultimate: what is maximum resolution? First we must realize that reality itself has no resolution. Resolution is only a property of images. It is a property of who or what is doing the looking, not of what is being seen.

Reality itself is infinitely resolvable. Therefore ultimate resolution is a function of scale. Magnify reality and you move through planes of meaning: first, the familiar world; then the macro, or the ant's eye view; then the microscopic; the molecular; the atomic; etc. This is the physical approach. It has a long history in Western culture. In some ways, the history of science can be viewed as the journeying through increasingly refined scales of reality; as knowledge increases, so does space.

The limits of the physical approach are apparent as we move through the last remnants of the machine age. Hollis Frampton, the great American avant-garde filmmaker, called film "the last machine." He said it was "as close to software as the machine age can get." In the software age, we transform scale into information, into language. We move into a huge close-up of a human hair, and as we approach the images of molecules in action, we encounter a strand of DNA—the shape of a code, the form of information and a new depth becomes possible.

In the software age we are beginning to model ourselves on information processing and not on machine construction. Limitations become merely local boundaries defined by lack of adequate translations and transformations. And just as the presence of human beings in a specific place over long periods of time creates a story, the electronic image landscape is beginning to create a layering of mental archeology. This is the world we are learning to inhabit as images become our tools.

## Hardware equals Software

One of the original sources of all philosophy is the paradox of the hard and the soft: the body and the soul; the outer physical world and the world of thoughts and images within. This is one of the great mysteries of life, and the good thing about mysteries in the classic sense is that they don't have to be solved, only experienced. The great mystics of history bathed in the mystery. Their goal was to translate experiences, not images or descriptions. The original function of the statue of Buddha was simply as an image to aid in meditation. It was only later that, in some cultures, it became an object of divinity to be venerated and worshipped.

Technology, particularly imaging technology, exists on the border between the worlds. An unplugged TV set is not television. The time is past when we can discuss software apart from hardware. This is irresponsible and impractical. We are looking at a total living system. Software and hardware have always been related, ever since the days our monkey ancestors picked up the first tool and began to model nature. All hardware springs from a thought, a desire, or a need. The chair: to sit elevated in comfort. The telegraph: to speak over distances. All comes from the mind interacting with nature. Another example: the American urban landscape of today is a landscape formed in the shape of money. The desire to make money creates its form.

Suzuki Shunryu Roshi, the Zen master who founded the San Francisco Zen Center, said this about painting: "When you pick up the brush, you already know the results of your painting, or else you could not paint."

## The Future of Technology is the Future of What is Real

With each new step in the evolution of technology, we take a step closer to our ideal of higher and higher quality, which actually means creating things that look more and more like nature itself. Signal-to-noise ratio in sound is a technical term referring to the measure of the strength, and therefore the purity, of the signal as it exists over the chaotic noise of a disorganized background. We can also speak of the "signal-to-noise ratio of life." How close can we come to the true nature of things? The implied goal of many of our efforts, including technological development, is the eradication of signal-to-noise ratio, which in the end is the ultimate transparent state where there is no perceived difference between the simulation and the reality, between ourselves and the other. We think of two lovers locked in a single ecstatic embrace. We think of futuristic descriptions of direct stimulation to the brain to evoke experiences and memories. We think of experiments with drugs—LSD as a kind of movie to be taken internally. With advanced research on the brain it is possible that inner images can be accessed, but pure, transparent experience will probably remain an unattainable, implied goal, the measure for the connoisseur and the impetus for further refinement.

As human beings we require limits and boundaries to function. Our nervous system is one of difference registration. Boundaries create friction, and therefore create energy. Limits exist as challenges to provoke the means to transcend them and to propel us forward, with more limits coming into view as we arrive there—much like the mirage that continuously recedes on the road before us in the summer. Technology does constantly provoke us to ask what is real. Is television real? Some people say no, yet it has more effect on people today than the natural landscape does.

When asked what is real, most people turn inwards, to their individual experience. They think about hitting their head on a rock, an image of the face of their mother, or losing their job, or whatever. They do not necessarily think of themselves standing there at the moment the question was asked. At that moment, of course, all these things are memories, mental images. Memory is the residing place of life experience, the collection that reveals and/or fabricates order and meaning. What is real, therefore, is what is psychologically meaningful. At one time in the past, the mythic and symbolic were real. Today, physical science has influenced us to believe that the objects of the physical world are real. Yet, we surround ourselves with electronic images and transmitted information. Hollis Frampton called the movement in moving images "the movement of human consciousness itself. The images carry on our mental lives for us," he said, "darkly, whether we want them to or not." We already are, and always have been, in an imaginary landscape of perception.

Transcript of the original version presented in August, 1989, as part of a panel discussion at the 2nd Video Television Festival at Spiral Hall, Tokyo, and first published in *Delicate Technology*, eds. Video Gallery SCAN (Fujiko Nakaya) and I&S (Tokyo: Video Television Festival Organizing Committee, SCAN, 1989), 129–48. Also published as "Perception, Technology, Imagination, and the Landscape," in *Enclitic 11*. no. 3 (July 1992), 57–60, and as "Perception, technologie, imagination et paysage," in *Trafic 3* (Summer 1992), 77–82.

■ ■ ■

## Source

Viola, B. (1995) 'The Visionary Landscape of Perception', *Reasons for Knocking at an Empty House,* MIT Press: 219–225.

## Bill Viola (1951–)

Viola is one of the century's most long-standing and successful video artists, having been instrumental in establishing video as a key form of contemporary art. He has been experimenting with the form for over 40 years, creating video-tapes, sound environments, and works for television. In 2010 he created a video background to Wagner's opera *Tristan und Isolde*, a collaboration with the American director Peter Sellars, which has been seen internationally.

Much of Viola's work focuses on universal themes such as birth, death and the unfolding of consciousness, which often have roots in Eastern and Western philosophies, as well as the traditions of Zen Buddhism, Islamic Sufism and Christian mysticism. His early video-tapes, such as *Chott el Djerid (A Portrait in Light and Heat)* from 1979, explore our perceptions of the effect of light on human movement, or *The Reflecting Pool*, which plays with the effect of light on water over seven minutes. Other major works include *Going Forth by Day*, a five-part projected digital 'fresco' influenced by his interest in Italian Renaissance art, and *The Passions*, an examination of humans in states of high emotion. It is difficult to connect Viola with other twentieth-century art movements, as he has been instrumental in establishing video as a key art form in itself, but he was Nam June Paik's assistant for a short time and has connections with Bruce Nauman and also to Vito Acconci. There are other artists who would claim to have been influenced by his success. These would include the UK artist Sam Taylor-Wood and the German Mariele Neudecker.

Viola's work is heavily influenced by his interest in other religions, in European painting, and in the ways in which humans react to extreme situations. He works with his current interests and is not concerned with how the world views his obsessions. He works with his partner Kira Perov, who produces and documents all his work. Often he seems to imply that we should look at Renaissance European art for inspiration, as if we can explain our own emotional reactions by association with great Italian painters. His series *The Passions* was shown on high-definition plasma screens, and consisted of actors instructed to go through an 'arc of intensity' of the emotional range, so that we watch in slow motion their faces change from happiness to fear.

The essay included here comes from a collection of his writings and speeches, in which he explores the differences between perception, artificial images, and reality – making connections with mediaeval art and contemporary technology.

## Compare this article with writings by the following authors in this reader

**Lepage** – a director using technology
**Kandinsky** – an explorative visual artist
**Stein** – a writer concerned with perception

## Further Reading

Townsend, C. (2004) *The Art of Bill Viola*, London: Thames and Hudson.
Viola, B. (2002) *Going Forth by Day*, New York: Guggenheim Museum Publications.
http://www.billviola.com

# Chapter 59

## Robert Wilson

### INTERVIEW

*You've just returned from Paris where you produced* Great Day in the Morning, *an evening of Negro spirituals, with the celebrated American soprano Jessye Norman. In the summer of 1984, Norman will also be appearing in your staging of* Civil Wars. *How did this ongoing collaboration come about?*

About five years ago I was performing in Paris and Jessye was there singing at the same time. She's a big, big star in France, much bigger than she is in America. Various people had told me that I would like what she was doing so I went to one of her performances and I was overwhelmed by her – by the way she walked on stage, the way she stood and, of course, the way she sang. With the least amount of effort she can fill an enormous hall. That's Jessye's genius. She can sing the quietest, softest sound with her back to the audience and that sound will touch the back wall of the theater. So I was overwhelmed and I went backstage and stood in line and said, 'Hello, my name is Bob Wilson. You're absolutely fantastic and I would love to work with you.' She didn't know who I was and asked, 'What is it that you do?' 'Well, I'm a theatre director and artist. I make works for the theater.' 'Well,' she said, 'Thank you very much' and that was it. Then about eight months later I was in Texas visiting my family and I read in a Dallas paper that she was appearing at Tanglewood. I was coming back to New York anyway so I decided to go straight to Tanglewood and hear her sing. Again, I was overwhelmed. I went backstage and stood in a long line and finally when my turn came, she turned and said, 'Oh, Hello, Mr

Wilson, it's nice to see you again.' She has a phenomenal memory. Anyway, we had lunch the next day and I told her about a new piece that I was going to do in Berlin (*Death, Destruction and Detroit*). I made some drawings for her and tried to explain how I work. Then I told her that when I do the piece I would like her to come and see it. And she did come. Soon after that I began to make sketches and work on an idea for her. This was about three years ago. I showed her a diagram and said, 'Here's a possible structure for a two act work for you. What do you think the music should be? Should we find a composer to write for you?' And she said, 'Well, I've been thinking of doing something with Negro spirituals, the songs of the slaves, and I think these would be appropriate settings.' And the idea interested me because it didn't have anything to do with slavery necessarily, it wouldn't have to be an illustration of the music — you know, a black person in a field of cotton. So Jessye and I began talking and thinking about what songs to use and how they should be fitted together. We began a collaboration. Over the last two years we'd get together from time to time and rehearse and gradually we found what the piece was about. It was a very close collaboration. I really think I work best when I can build and create a work with someone.

*How would you characterize the relationship between the songs and your own visual presentation?*

I just picked settings that I thought were appropriate in some way for this music as a group of pictures or tableaux but which didn't necessarily illustrate the music. And everything had to be in scale to Jessye. There were certain moods in the landscapes that helped in deciding what songs to use but the songs are not meant to illustrate the background. The background is like a picture book that makes sense on its own. In *Great Day*, the visual is as important as what we hear. I think it helps us hear and the singing helps us see. I think what I disliked about opera when I first went was that I couldn't hear I was so visually distracted. I heard best when I shut my eyes. It's very difficult to see and hear at the same time and mostly we do one or the other. What I try to do in all my work is make a balance between what you hear and what you see, so that perhaps you can do both at the same time.

*These days your productions are usually greeted with instantaneous acclaim, but* Great Day *created something of a furor at its première in Paris. In fact, you were vigorously booed by a large faction of the audience at the end of the performance. I imagine the presence of Jessye Norman might have attracted a somewhat different audience than usually attends your productions, perhaps one unprepared for the kind of work you do.*

I think it's an audience that tends to go to concerts, recitals and opera, not necessarily my audience. She had sung many times at that theater and so a lot of people came expecting the kind of thing they had heard in the past. They also didn't understand what spirituals are. These songs are religious in nature, they're all from the Bible which was the only book the slaves had to read. They're not songs of anger; they're songs of nobility and dignity, the songs of an oppressed race. The problems resulted from a misunderstanding – audiences not knowing what the spirituals are, not knowing how the music came about or the way it was sung or simply the way it *was*, which was to some extent the way we presented it. They were frustrated and confused. The staging and designs responded to the religious nature of the music and the way the songs were sung. They were sung as a way of life – you heard singing as you woke up in the morning and dressed, you sang as you went through the day, it was the way you closed the day. Jessye said she always remembered hearing her grandmother sing all day long. Her mother too. The slaves grew up singing as part of life. It was not something they did for entertainment, it was a way of life. It was natural, like breathing, There was song all day long.

*And that's actually the form of* Great Day. *It's a kind of progression through the day.*

Right, that's it. It's a great day and a woman begins the morning singing. It starts early in the morning with the sunrise and it ends with the morning again. Singing is heard through the course of the day. I show various things that people would do every day. You see someone contemplating and someone walking in a forest.

You see someone waking up in bed and someone sleeping in the middle of the night. I made this room with a huge window.

It's not a specific room or even a window necessarily. It could be 1840 or 2040.

*Perhaps you could describe the scene on the lake, which drew both praise from critics and scornful laughter from some members of the audience. It seems to embody the spiritual nature of the work and the meditative qualities you were seeking to capture.*

There's a dock out in the lake and it's midnight.

There are stars in the sky and the moonlight is reflecting on the water. Jessye walks out in a blue robe and sings a song she wrote herself, a song based on a slave poem that's sung a cappella. There's a simple white chair at the end of the dock. She walks over to it and begins to sing 'Sometimes I Feel Like a Motherless Child.' A little golden light falls down on her as she sits in the white chair improvising the song. She's written a part for a cello and as it's played a grey Canadian goose moves across the sky, its wings slowly flapping. But she doesn't see it, her focus is turned inward. She has two or three very simple gestures that are counted and carefully lit. After sitting there for ten minutes or so, humming and singing, she stands up and begins to walk off. Just before she gets to the edge of the stage she kneels down and takes a handful of water from the lake and washes her face. And she begins to sing again. Then she turns and walks offstage in profile, humming the same music. And that's how we did these songs. We didn't present them like gospel numbers, adding tambourines and banjos and making an entertainment – all that came later. And so when Jessye was humming a song for ten minutes or sitting in silence the audience became very restless. But it would have been very inappropriate to present this music any other way and that was completely misunderstood – though not by the serious writers of the French press who did understand for the most part. I must say that I was surprised by the incredible reaction at the end, the bursts of boos and bravos. Some of the press wrote that it was an occasion similar to the première of *The Rite of Spring*, which had its first performance in the same theater over sixty years before. After that, there was no way of ever getting away from the idea of a controversy because audiences came expecting a controversial event and they acted controversial.

*Great Day in the Morning was to have been presented at the Brooklyn Academy of Music this winter but a few months ago performances were postponed. Was Great Day withdrawn so you could do some more work on it, as some have suggested, or was it once again a matter of financing?*

Financing and time. There wasn't enough time to mount it property. The work is in a finished state though I do intend to make a few changes. It will be performed in the future, possibly at Covent Garden and La Scala. It may also go to Africa and Moscow.

*During the past year you also produced* The Golden Windows *at the Munich Kammerspiele, a new work featuring one of your own texts.*

Yes. My text. I also designed, directed and lit it. It's a smaller scale work. I built a little house.

It's early evening. There's a door that opens – light streams from the doorway. Then midnight.

The house is in the center. Then the early morning.

The house is now at the left side of the stage. Those three perspectives.

*The title of the work and perhaps a few of its images were suggested by a story in a now forgotten book of homiletic fables by the American writer Laura E. Richards (1903). What was the attraction of this obscure story book?*

It was a fairy tale I heard as a child. I just remembered the story. Actually I had written the play before I thought of the title. The title didn't have anything to do with the play necessarily, but then it became part of it.

In the story a little boy gazes at a house on a distant hill which seems to have windows of gold and diamonds. One day he travels to the neighboring hill only to find a common farmhouse with ordinary glass windows. At the end of the story another house with golden windows appears to him in the distance. It is his own house, transfigured by the light of the setting sun. While *The Golden Windows* isn't based on this story, or even directly related to it, the two works do share the image of a house on a hill – a house whose appearance changes according to the time of day it is viewed – and most importantly, a sense of the transforming power of light.

Light plays an integral role in the work. It's like an actor. Mainly, though, I just liked the title.

*The play was performed in German and you worked with actors of the Kammerspiele.*

Yes. I used members of their repertory company. Brilliant, brilliant actors. I think it's the most difficult thing for actors of the Schaubühne or the Kammerspiele to perform my texts because they don't tell a story. That's what all their training is aimed at – telling a story, interpreting a text, psychological theater. And if you do that with my works the audience gets confused. You have to be able to say the text in a way that one can think about many sorts of things. If you say it in such a way that you must pay attention to every word you'll go crazy because one thought doesn't follow another thought logically. One thought can set off many thoughts. You have to sort of float with the situation.

*Do you think this work will ever be seen in America?*

There's a possibility that *The Golden Windows* could come to the United States in the summer or autumn of 1985. That will be the first time I have any time to stage it because I'm scheduled to do other things.

*American audiences have not seen a major Wilson work since* Einstein on the Beach *was presented here in 1976. Money is invariably given as the reason so few of your productions reach this country. Is it solely a matter of financing or are other factors involved?*

Financing has a lot to do with it. The other problem is where do you put it. Where do you put a work like *The Golden Windows*? In Munich I'm at the Kammerspiele, a municipal theater where I'm seen by a subscription audience. I have a poster from the Kammerspiele. Look at their season – they have plays by Chekhov, Shakespeare, they have *Medea*, a Sean O'Casey play, Goethe's *Tasso* and they have my work. Where in this city would you find a program like that?

*The resident theaters in this country might conceivably be a place where your work could be seen. Have you approached them?*

They haven't approached me, you can put it that way. Yes, I have gone to them on occasion but I don't have time to now. I have too many other things to do.

*What about the Metropolitan Opera? There was discussion at one point about an operatic version of* Death, Destruction and Detroit.

Well, we had talked about it, I guess. I'm not a popular person at the Met.

*You've also reached a stage in your career where you no longer have to accept compromise. You're in demand at subsidized European state theaters and festivals, organizations far better equipped to meet your exacting standards. Theater in this country usually means compromising in terms of just getting a play on.*

Entirely true. The Met is a very well-organized house and the labor is probably the best in the world for working with time. Still, they don't light a show the way I do. They don't rehearse the way I rehearse. There's not the same attention placed on detail. Lighting is an important part of my work. I usually spend years on my drawings and days setting light cues. Over here they light a show in eight hours. It's very hard to do the kind of work I do in structures in this country, it really needs a festival structure. And again there's the cost. *Civil Wars* in Los Angeles will be two and a half million dollars for three performances and that doesn't even include artists' fees. It's insane. Budgets, unions. *Einstein on the Beach* at the Metropolitan Opera cost $90,000 per performance. Just to run a show that was already created.

*The technical demands of your works also present certain difficulties. A Robert Wilson play can no longer be staged just anywhere.*

My work is unique, it means big houses. I work best in a large scale.

*You don't plan to produce your own shows in this country as you sometimes did in the past?*

I can't, though really in some way I do. Contracts with houses and unions. It's a whole profession. As a producer I'm not knowledgeable.

*In the past you've spoken with some bitterness of this country's lack of support for your work. Now that you're so busy creating works for the leading theaters and opera houses of Europe is this still such a concern with you?*

It's . . . a frustration. I don't want to be an expatriot but that's the way it is – I'm leaving this January and I don't come back to America until the very end of 1984.

*In a recent interview you announced your intention to do more interpretive work in the coming years.* Great Day in the Morning, *the first piece you've created to existing texts, represents a step in that direction. What was behind this decision?*

The creation of new works is what I do best but I also think it's important to do other things, and so I want to interpret other people's work. I'm doing a new opera with Gavin Bryars, an English composer, which is based on Euripides' *Medea*. It will be performed at the opera house in Lyon and then will come to the Paris Opera.

*What attracted you to this classic text?*

I don't know. I just read the play and was fascinated by it. I liked the architecture of the story. It was very different from my work and yet similar in some ways.

*Your* Medea *began life as a play with music. It's now a full-scale opera. What was the reason for this transformation?*

I'd just rather hear words sung than spoken, I think. I'll also be doing another version of *Medea* in Lyon, a baroque opera by Charpentier which has never been performed. Then I'm doing *Four Saints in Three Acts*, the Gertrude Stein-Virgil Thomson opera, in Stuttgart in May of 1985. I also plan to do *Parsifal* in 1986 or 87, then a *King Lear*, yes to Shakespeare's text, and maybe later I'll do some contemporary works.

*From time to time your work is described as a modern equivalent of Wagner's* Gesamtkunstwerk. *Now you are planning to produce several of the Wagnerian music dramas. I would be interested in knowing when you first encountered Wagner's music and at what point you contemplated staging his operas?*

The Wagner family came to Spoletto when I did *A Letter for Queen Victoria* in 1974 and they said, 'Oh, Mr Wilson, it's so beautiful. You're the perfect one to do Wagner.' Well, at that time I barely knew who Wagner was. So I said, 'Thank you very much. I'm flattered.' They asked me if I would be interested in coming to Bayreuth to direct something and I answered, 'Well, possibly, but do you ever do new works because I'm really interested in creating *new* works.' Gian Carlo Menotti was sitting next to me and he started kicking me under the table. 'No, no, we don't do new operas, Mr Wilson. We only do Wagner.' 'Well,' I said, 'I'm really not interested just now.' Then they asked me a couple of years later and I actually went to the festival. Finally they came when I did *Edison* – Wolfgang Wagner and his wife – and they said, 'We're going to do a new *Parsifal* and we want to talk to you about that,' and I said I was very interested in doing it. They said, 'Well, Mr Levine has already been contracted to conduct it. Could you work with him?' And I said, 'Yes.'

*After so many years as a German (even a family) institution, Bayreuth has begun seeking outside talent. There was a French team (Chéreau and Boulez) for the centennial* Ring. *This summer's cycle will be essentially an English production (Hall, Solti and designer William Dudley). And you and Levine would have logically consituted an American team.*

But Levine refused to work with me and he had already been contracted. It's sad. It was the hundredth anniversary. I mean, I don't particularly like Levine though there are some things he does conduct quite well, still I agreed to work with him because the best place to do *Parsifal* is, of course, Bayreuth.

*Later you were commissioned to create a* Parsifal *for the State Opera in Kassel, West Germany. Although this production was eventually canceled, I know you devoted a considerable amount of time to the project. I'd be interested in hearing how you set about approaching this monumental work, which would seem an ideal vehicle for you, resonating as it does so many of the themes and concerns of your own work.*

Well, everyone always said *Parsifal* would be the work to do so I started to listen to the music and I hired Annette Michelson, a writer and scholar, to work with me for a number of months on a concept. I looked at various productions and found out what other people had done with the opera. There's a beautiful one that Appia designed and the one Wieland Wagner did in the fifties was really great, beautifully proportioned. I tried to find what Wagner was attempting to do musically and also what he was trying to say with the text. I'll only do one *Parsifal* in my life and I want this to be one of the great ones. So I thought about the text and the music and the most complicated problem to solve was how to present a work that's very religious – it's very close to what I just did with Jessye – with a sincere religious attitude. It never seemed right to me to have this fake church service with these knights standing around singing and passing this holy grail. It was somehow sacrilegious, everything the work was supposed not to be. When I listen to the music here it's a religious experience but when I go to the theater and see this temple-church-whatever and these klutzy knights walking around with this cup, it's ridiculous, it's disturbing and it's all wrong. So that's one problem to solve. Then there's the idea that Parsifal is the innocent fool. How is that portrayed? Christopher Knowles would have been the perfect actor for me but someone like Manfred Jung playing this innocent fool is no good – in one sense, in another sense I guess it's o.k. You know when Levine does *Parsifal* at the Met there's a time in the third act when I feel I'm going to scream if he doesn't stop or he doesn't go faster. It's interminable. Yet it can be done in such a way that you say to yourself, 'I can listen to this for the rest of my life.' That's what's so fascinating about *Parsifal*. It can be unbearably long or it can be . . . forever. Here, I can show you the designs. They're all finished.

There's no house curtain. Instead there's a curtain of light.

Then a wall of water with the beams of light coming vertically across.

Eventually a lake appears at the back and that's the prelude.

The whole piece is in blue. Gurnemanz appears here at the downstage edge of the lake.

Just before Parsifal enters I have this enormous white swan, the swan that he's just shot, falling very slowly into the lake.

For the transformation scene – 'Time becomes space here' – I have a great disk of light that moves on stage from the side and an iceberg floating upstage.

Eventually the disk of light settles in the center of the lake. Parsifal stands downstage watching with his back to the audience the way the audience watches it.

I don't have the knights or any of that. Amfortas is carried out in his litter and he goes into the iceberg and takes out an Egyptian box. Inside is a clear glass chalice which is shaped like an X.

He holds it up and then he disappears. At the end, Gurnemanz comes into the ring of light and asks Parsifal, 'What have you seen?' And there's just the light, the whiteness. The idea is to make this mysterious temple of light. It's as if one were to see this big ring of light floating out here in the middle of the Hudson. It's all about light. And that's the first act. The second act starts the same way with the vertical beams of light crossing the water. We're still at the lake but now it's night and a metal tower rises out of the water.

It's like a fairy tale. That's where Chéreau missed the boat for me. His *Ring* is beautiful looking, gorgeous, but it's so serious and heavy. And it's fantastic to have an opera with giants and a dragon, it's stories for children. Klingsor appears in a window in the tower and he's a bad guy almost the way Ivan the Terrible is in the movie. Kundry is next to him – and I want to do it with Jessye – and her hair falls out of the tower. After their scene; the doors close and the tower sinks beneath the waves. Then we go underwater for the flower garden scene.

There are ferns and painted flowers that open. They're all flat with lights inside them, only the rocks are dimensional. The flower garden is all in color. It's like Chinese flowers that open in the water. At the end of the act Klingsor throws his spear at Parsifal. Here it's a rod of light. The scene is all back painted and at the moment Parsifal picks up the glowing rod, we turn on all the lights from behind and everything appears in cold black and white like a skeleton. Parsifal takes the rod of light and draws the outline of the chalice in light, and that's the end of the second act. The third act begins the same way as the first except that I've put the singers on the other side of the stage. For springtime (the Good Friday scene), I've created an enormous tulip that's lowered into the lake, like the big swan you saw in the first act.

I also bring all the chorus onstage for one brief moment when they're trying to convince Amfortas to perform the grail ceremony. We have him lying in his litter and they rush on and form a huge wall of bodies downstage.

The ring of light comes back on. It's now a black disk, which slowly falls into the lake, turning white when Parsifal stands on it. He takes the chalice from the Egyptian box in the iceberg and holds it up. The iceberg disappears.

At the end he leaves the stage. No one is on stage. Fire comes out of the ring of light and stars appear in the sky.

*In a sense what you've done is create your own mysteries within Wagner's larger ones. Your scenario also seems to have purged the opera of what many feel is mock Christianity. What interests me even more is how you will approach the work's complex psychological characterizations. How will you deal with Wagner's characters and the acting requirements of the piece?*

I can only tell you that it won't be psychological acting. It will be the opposite of what Chéreau did with the *Ring*. I never understood why they called that naturalistic acting. It's the most artificial, unnatural way of behaving on stage that I've ever seen in my life. But they all said that Chéreau has reinvented naturalistic acting. It's just too much for me. I'm not interested in that kind of thing.

*While your* Parsifal *will be produced at some future date, it's regrettable you were denied the chance to stage the Bayreuth centennial production. The occasion demanded some kind of great event — either a radical re-evaluation of the work or a personal commentary by a major contemporary artist, or at least a fresh sensibility. Certainly it provided an unparalleled opportunity in terms of visibility and critical attention. All things considered you probably would have been an ideal person for the job.*

I would have been the ideal person, yeah.

*Götz Friederich was eventually chosen to direct the centennial production, I believe at a relatively late date.*

You know why? Because Friederich can come in and do it in two days. I saw a new production of *Tristan* he did two years ago in Stuttgart. It was the third *Tristan* he had done that year. I was there the night before the last general rehearsal and he still hadn't decided where the singers were going to be. It never *was* decided. In the second act he never even told them where to go. Now, how on this earth do you do that? They had one big vulgar spot that followed the singers wherever they went, and of course, they went where they normally go anyway. It's ridiculous. So that's why it went to Friederich. It's perfect for Levine and the way he thinks and the way they run a house and the way they make art. And did you hear anything about the performances? No one even *mentioned* the *Parsifal* last summer. No one talked about it. The hundredth anniversary!

*It's been rumored that you will be staging* Tristan *at Bayreuth some time in the future, possibly with Jessye Norman as Isolde.*

Well, I would like to do it. I was asked. La Scala also asked me to do the *Parsifal* and I will if I get the rehearsal time I need. I would like Abbado to conduct, if he will work with me.

*You're one of the few American directors who works regularly with a dramaturg, a fixture of the German state theater system. Was the concept of a dramaturg new to you when you went to Berlin in 1979 to stage* Death, Destruction and Detroit *for the Schaubühne?*

That's right. I always had various people around when I was working before — advisors, people who did research — but I never really had the concept of a dramaturg in mind. When they first gave me one in Berlin I said, 'This is ridiculous.' I walk in and there's a staff of twenty people. What are they all going to do? 'A dramaturg?' I said, 'I wrote the play! How is he going to tell me what I'm doing with this crazy American language and all?' But they were very, very helpful – I learned so much about what I was doing and about the possibilities of what could be done. I've since learned to work very closely with dramaturgs and now I think it's almost essential to have one because I'm not scholarly, I don't have a strong background in history or a lot of formal or classical education and, anyway, it's very helpful to have someone like that to talk to. In Germany they've also translated my texts so they have to be writers as well as scholars because my texts are difficult to translate – there's slang and puns and things not immediately translatable. At the Schaubühne I worked with Peter Krumme who was excellent.

*Was he involved with the day to day rehearsals?*

Yes, he was there all the time and was directly involved with the actors and their interpretations. We worked as a team. When I produced *The Golden Windows* in Munich, again a fantasy thing with the kind of crazy texts I do, I worked very closely with Michael Wachsmann. He's brilliant but he doesn't say very much. 'Maybe this word should be over there' or 'Take that out' or 'Maybe there should be a slight hesitation in the middle of this word.' I work with what they tell me, with what they feel is correct. It's very much a collaboration. I really like working with a dramaturg and I think they're underestimated – in terms of my work anyway.

*While you've spent most of the last few years in Europe creating new works, you recently performed in Japan and will be returning there in the near future to produce several segments of* Civil Wars. *I'd think the Japanese would be an ideal audience, especially since the stylization, formality and durational qualities of their own theater forms logically prepare them for the imaginative demands of your work.*

That's what everyone has said and I was very nervous about it. I did the prologue to the fourth act of *Deafman Glance*, which is a murder scene, with a beautiful Japanese actress (Chizuko Sugiura). It was actually one of the first things I ever made for the theater. They were a wonderful audience and it was very well received. There was a scholar who came and wrote a piece saying that the work was timeless but it happened in this century. In some ways the play is very modern but he saw that it was timeless, it could have happened any time. And that's the Japanese, they live with such an awareness of tradition and the past. They're very contemporary, very modern but they're still building houses with bamboo and paper.

*You've made a number of video works in the last couple of years, some of which have been seen in this country. Are you planning to devote more time to media projects in the future?*

I think T.V. is the future. To be very honest with you I don't watch it because it doesn't interest me, but at the same time I'm fascinated by the possibilities of the medium and am already planning more works with T.V. I went to see Martha Graham's company when I was rehearsing an opera in Washington some time ago and I noticed that a work she had created in 1946 was listed in the program as having been copyrighted in 1977. I was told that she filmed it in 1977 and that established the copyright. That's what I want to do with my works. People are asking about *Einstein* in particular, and I will do it again some place and film it.

*Your works tend to play to a select, somewhat narrow audience made up of fans, theater people, writers, artists and art patrons. You've spoken in the past of wanting to attract new audiences to your work.*

Right.

*Are you still actively seeking a larger audience?*

Absolutely. I think that's what I'm trying to do with *Civil Wars*. It's on the scale of larger popular theater. That's how I intended it. It's an event, a large popular event. It's meant to be the way rock concerts are. I was in Rome a few weeks ago and Syberberg's film of *Parsifal*, which is four and a half hours long, was shown before three thousand people in a large open air space. It was fantastic. It was a big event. There was something exciting about being there, just like at a rock concert. I saw this *Napoleon* film at Radio City Music Hall and it was very exciting. It was in Japan when I was there. Everywhere it's been, it's been something special. It's an event and I think that's great. When I first went to hear a rock concert about fifteen years ago I thought, 'Gee, this is really the great opera of our time.' I don't think that when I go to the Metropolitan Opera. Maybe I do if I go to see Patrice Chéreau's *Lulu* at the Paris Opera. That's a great cultural event, but I don't go expecting such an experience at the Met. I mean, who's going to fly from Paris to see something at the Met? Chéreau just did *Peer Gynt* in Paris and people came from all over Europe. People went to Berlin for Peter Stein's *Oresteia*. That's an event. People come from all over Europe to see *The Golden Windows* in Munich. Who comes to Broadway to see *Sweeney Todd*? Who goes to see another John Dexter production at the Metropolitan Opera? Nobody! Nobody is interested. That's what's so *dull* about this city. No one comes here to see anything. People come from New Jersey to see Broadway musicals. It's all for a suburban audience.

*What about dance and avant garde theater?*

Well, if I want to see the avant garde of America I'll go to Europe. You can't see it here. Richard Foreman is working at the Paris Opera. I just saw his new piece at the Festival of Autumn. I go to Europe to see that kind of thing, not America. Maybe people will go to the Village to see Joe Papp's work if there's something special about it but Joe presents his work for an audience that is very select, very narrow. He calls it a public theater, a popular theater, but I don't think it's that at all.

*Do you think you can attract a popular audience as such to* The Civil Wars?

I hope so. I hope we get it done.

■  ■  ■

## Source

Wilson, R. (1983) 'Robert Wilson: Current Projects. Interview with Laurence Shyer', *Theater*, Summer/Fall: 84–91.

## Robert Wilson (1944–)

One of the most important examples in our time of the director as total scenographer. He is an artist who uses the stage as a three-dimensional and aural palette, working with sound, gesture, movement, light and time, to produce theatre pieces, which are often epic and concerned with the symbols and poetics of our century. The titles of some of these – *The Life and Times of Joseph Stalin* (1973), *Einstein on the Beach* (1976), *Death, Destruction, and Detroit* (1979), and *CIVIL warS* (1984) – show his interest in deconstructing twentieth-century myths and reconstituting them as elements in a total theatre piece – a 'Gesamtkunstwerk' in the Wagnerian sense. He has with major choreographers such as Lucinda Childs, and composer/performers such as Philip Glass, Gavin Bryars and Lou Reed, all of whose work helps to create a sense of material, which is constantly reinterpreting our preoccupations and ourselves. Wilson's work is often long, visually simple, and full of contrasts and contradictions that force the spectator to attend. His techniques owe much to modern technology – the freeze-frame, slow motion, playback – and his interest in the relationship between the mental and the physical has led him to examine the effects of dislocation on our perceptions of the world. Much of his later work has tended towards the interpretation and usage of classic texts or operas on the one hand, and towards installation work on the other.

In this interview Wilson's mode of thinking and perceiving is exposed by the way in which he speaks, carefully choosing words as he carefully chooses images for his work, currently moving through a phase of approaching classic texts from European literature.

## Compare this interview with writings by the following authors in this reader

**Anderson, Appia, Craig and Schlemmer** – other visual approaches to theatre
**Bausch** – performances that juxtapose the unexpected
**Brecht** – theatrical contrasts
**Cunningham** – American antecedents
**Foreman** – a contemporary American writer/director
**Kantor** – another approach to non-linear theatre
**LeCompte** – similar deconstructive concerns
**Lepage** – a parallel scope
**Meyerhold** – a much earlier view of total theatre
**Müller** – one of his major collaborators
**Piscator** – an earlier view of visual staging

## Further reading

Brecht, S. (1979) *The Theatre of Visions: Robert Wilson*, Frankfurt am Main: Suhrkamp.

Donker, J. (1985) *The President of Paradise*, Amsterdam: International Theatre Bookshop.

Holmberg, A. (1997) *The Theatre of Robert Wilson*, Cambridge: CUP.

Safir, M.A. (ed.) (2011) *Robert Wilson from Within*, Paris: The Arts Arena.

Shevstova, M. (2007) *Robert Wilson*, London: Routledge.

Shyer, L. (1989) *Robert Wilson and his Collaborators*, New York: Theater Communications Group.

Williams, D. and Bradby, D. (1988) *Directors Theatre*, London: Macmillan.

http://www.robertwilson.com

# A Chronology of Texts

# Index